POET & PEASANT
and
THROUGH PEASANT EYES

The threads of connection between Primitive Christianity and the world are to be sought not in the high regions of culture and power but in the lower levels of the common life of the people.
                                    Adolf Deissmann, 1922

POET & PEASANT
and
THROUGH PEASANT EYES

A Literary-Cultural Approach
to the Parables of Luke

by
Kenneth E. Bailey

Combined Edition
Two Volumes in One

William B. Eerdmans Publishing Company
Grand Rapids, Michigan

Poet & Peasant
Copyright © 1976 by William B. Eerdmans Publishing Company

Reprinted, May 1990

Through Peasant Eyes
Copyright © 1980 by Wm. B. Eerdmans Publishing Company
255 Jefferson Ave. S.E., Grand Rapids, Michigan 49503

This combined edition printed 1983

Library of Congress Cataloging in Publication Data

Bailey, Kenneth E.
  Poet and peasant; and, Through peasant eyes.

  Includes bibliographies and indexes.
  1. Jesus Christ—Parables. 2. Bible. N.T. Luke—
Criticism, interpretation, etc. I. Title.
BT375.2.B23 1983   226 .406   83-5581
ISBN 0-8028-1947-8

POET & PEASANT

To my parents, Dr. Ewing and Annette Bailey, who spent their lives humbly in the service of God in Kentucky, Egypt, and Ethiopia. They lived and labored among the very Middle Eastern peasants whose insights were a starting point for this study. Without my parents' life of dedication as a constant example and inspiration I would never have gone to the Middle East and this study would never have been written. To them this work is gratefully and affectionately dedicated.

ACKNOWLEDGMENTS

The poet and peasant may be able to labor without a library, but not the exegete. The present writer wishes to pay special tribute to Miss Lucille Hager and Mrs. William Danker, formerly of Concordia Seminary library, St. Louis, Missouri, for their many extra efforts in acquiring relatively rare resources; to Father L. J. Daly and Dr. C. J. Ermatinger of the Knights of Columbus Vatican Film Library at the Pope Pius XII Library of the St. Louis University, for making available the inestimable treasures of the Vatican Library; and to the directors of the British Museum, London, for allowing access to the Arabic manuscript holdings.

Beyond the written resources, this study relies heavily on twenty years of discussion of the culture that informs the text of the parables, with countless friends all across the Middle East from farmer, mayor, and pastor to professor, merchant, and doctor. To these countless hundreds no words of thanks are adequate to express the debt owed.

To my students and colleagues at the Near East School of Theology, Beirut, Lebanon, a special word of thanks must be expressed for their constant stimulation and encouragement. Most of all I wish to express my appreciation to Rev. Hovannes Aharonian, President, who was kind enough to release me from teaching duties that this study might be written; to Dr. Paul Löffler, whose counsel and encouragement convinced me to make the study; and to Dr. William Holladay, whose work in Old Testament poetry first opened my eyes to new possibilities in the New Testament.

No word of thanks is adequate to express the debt owed to the faculty of Concordia Seminary, St. Louis, Missouri, among whom and for whom this study was originally written in 1972. Whatever merit the work may have is due to a significant degree to the tireless efforts of Dr. Martin Scharlemann, my advisor.

Above all, I must express formally my gratitude to my dear wife Ethel, who has sustained me through to the dawn, and to my children Sara and David, who have been "fatherless" for too long.

CONTENTS

ABBREVIATIONS

Arndt *St. Luke*	William F. Arndt, *The Gospel According to St. Luke* (St. Louis: Concordia, 1956).
ATR	*Anglican Theological Review*
Bauer-A., G. *Lexicon*	W. Bauer, *A Greek-English Lexicon of the New Testament and Other Early Christian Literature,* trans. and adapted by W. F. Arndt and F. W. Gingrich (Chicago: University of Chicago Press, 1957).
Bengel *Gnomon*	Johann A. Bengel, *Gnomon of the New Testament,* trans. C. T. Lewis and M. R. Vincent; 2 vols. (New York: Sheldon, 1963 [1742]).
Bishop *Jesus*	E. F. F. Bishop, *Jesus of Palestine* (London: Lutterworth, 1955).
BJRL	*Bulletin of the John Rylands Library*
Black *Aramaic Approach*	Matthew Black, *An Aramaic Approach to the Gospels and Acts,* 3rd ed. (Oxford: Clarendon, 1967).
Bornkamm *Jesus*	G. Bornkamm, *Jesus of Nazareth,* trans. Irene and Fraser McLuskey from the 3rd German ed. (New York: Harper, 1960).
Bruce *Synoptic Gospels*	A. B. Bruce, *The Synoptic Gospels. The Expositor's Greek Testament,* Vol. I (New York: Doran; Grand Rapids: Eerdmans, n.d.).
Bruce *Parabolic*	A. B. Bruce, *The Parabolic Teaching of Christ,* 3rd rev. ed. (New York: A. C. Armstrong, 1890).
Bultmann *Tradition*	Rudolf Bultmann, *The History of the Synoptic Tradition,* trans. from the 2nd German ed. by John Marsh (New York: Harper, 1968).
Burney *Poetry*	C. F. Burney, *The Poetry of Our Lord* (Oxford: Clarendon, 1925).

Cadoux
Parables

A. T. Cadoux, *The Parables of Jesus* (London: James Clarke, n.d.).

Caird
Luke

G. B. Caird, *The Gospel of St. Luke* (Baltimore: Penguin, 1963).

CBQ

The Catholic Biblical Quarterly

Creed
St. Luke

J. M. Creed, *The Gospel According to St. Luke* (London: St. Martin, 1930; New York: Macmillan, 1965).

Crossan,
In Parables

J. D. Crossan, *In Parables* (New York: Harper, 1973).

Daube
"Inheritance"

David Daube, "Inheritance in Two Lukan Pericopes," *Zeitschrift der Savigny-Stiftung für Rechtsgeschichte, Romanistische Abteilung* 72 (1955), 326–344.

Derrett
"Prodigal Son"

J. D. M. Derrett, "Law in the New Testament: The Parable of the Prodigal Son," *NTS* 14 (1967), 56–74.

Derrett
"Steward"

J. D. M. Derrett, "Fresh Light on St. Luke XVI. 1. The Parable of the Unjust Steward," *NTS* 7 (1961), 198–219.

Dodd
Parables

C. H. Dodd, *The Parables of the Kingdom,* rev. ed. (London: Nisbet, 1961).

ExpT

The Expository Times

Feldman
Similes

A. Feldman, *The Parables and Similes of the Rabbis,* 2nd ed. (Cambridge: University Press, 1927).

Fitzmyer
"Manager"

J. A. Fitzmyer, "The Story of the Dishonest Manager (Lk. 16: 1–13)," *Theological Studies* 25 (1964), 23–42.

Fletcher
"Riddle"

D. R. Fletcher, "The Riddle of the Unjust Steward. Is Irony the Key?" *JBL* 82 (1963), 15–30.

Gächter
"Oriental"

P. Gächter, "The Parable of the Dishonest Steward after Oriental Conceptions," *CBQ* 12 (1950), 121–131.

Giblin
"Luke 15"

Charles H. Giblin, "Structural and Theological Considerations on Luke 15," *CBQ* 24 (1962), 15–31.

Godet
St. Luke

F. Godet, *A Commentary on the Gospel of St. Luke,* trans. from the 2nd French ed. by E. W. Shalders and M. D. Cusin (New York: Funk & Wagnalls, 1887).

Goebel
Parables

Siegfried Goebel, *The Parables of Jesus,* trans. Professor Banks (Edinburgh: T. & T. Clark, 1883).

Horowitz
Jewish Law

George Horowitz, *The Spirit of Jewish Law* (New York: Central Book, 1953).

HUCA

Hebrew Union College Annual

JBL — *The Journal of Biblical Literature*

Jeremias *Jerusalem* — Joachim Jeremias, *Jerusalem in the Time of Jesus,* trans. F. H. and C. H. Cave; 3rd ed. (Philadelphia: Fortress, 1969).

Jeremias *Parables* — Joachim Jeremias, *The Parables of Jesus,* rev. ed.; trans. from the 6th German ed. by S. H. Hooke (London: SCM, 1963).

Jeremias *Theology* — Joachim Jeremias, *Theology of the New Testament* (New York: Scribner, 1971).

Jones *Art* — G. V. Jones, *The Art and Truth of the Parables: A Study in Their Literary Form and Modern Interpretation* (London: SPCK, 1964).

JSS — *Journal of Semitic Studies*

JTS — *Journal of Theological Studies*

Jülicher *Gleichnisreden* — Adolf Jülicher, *Die Gleichnisreden Jesu,* 2 vols. (Tübingen: J. C. B. Mohr, 1910).

Kelley *Significance* — Robert Kelley, "The Significance of the Parable of the Prodigal Son for Three Major Issues in Current Synoptic Study" (unpublished Ph.D. thesis, Princeton University, 1971).

Leaney *St. Luke* — A. R. C. Leaney, *A Commentary on the Gospel according to St. Luke. Black's New Testament Commentaries;* 2nd ed. (London: A. & C. Black, 1966).

Levison *Local Setting* — N. Levison, *The Parables: Their Background and Local Setting* (Edinburgh: T. & T. Clark, 1926).

Linnemann *Parables* — E. Linnemann, *Jesus of the Parables,* trans. John Sturdy (New York: Harper, 1966).

Lund *Chiasmus* — N. W. Lund, *Chiasmus in the New Testament* (Chapel Hill: University of North Carolina Press, 1942).

Manson *Sayings* — T. W. Manson, *The Sayings of Jesus* (London: SCM, 1937).

Manson *Teaching* — T. W. Manson, *The Teaching of Jesus,* 2nd ed. (Cambridge: University Press, 1935).

Miesner *Chiasm and Paul* — D. R. Miesner, "Chiasm and the Composition and Message of Paul's Missionary Sermons" (unpublished Th.D. Thesis, Concordia Seminary in Exile, 306 North Grand, St. Louis, Missouri, 1974).

Miller *Luke* — Donald G. Miller, *The Gospel According to Luke* (Richmond: John Knox, 1959).

Montefiore *Rabbinic* — C. J. G. Montefiore, *Rabbinic Literature and Gospel Teaching* (London: Macmillan, 1930).

NTS   *New Testament Studies*

Oesterley   William O. E. Oesterley, *The Gospel Parables in the Light of Their*
Jewish   *Jewish Background* (London: SPCK, 1936).
Background

Plummer   A. Plummer, *The Gospel According to St. Luke. International*
St. Luke   *Critical Commentary*, ed. C. A. Briggs *et al.*, Vol. XXVII (New
York: Scribner, 1906).

Rengstorf   K. H. Rengstorf, *Die Re-Investitur des Verlorenen Sohnes in der*
Re-Investitur   *Gleichniserzählung Jesu Luke 15:11–32* (Cologne: Westdeutscher
Verlag, 1957).

Rihbany   A. M. Rihbany, *The Syrian Christ* (Boston: Houghton Mifflin,
Syrian   1916).

Sa'īd   Ibrāhīm Sa'īd, *Sharḥ Bishārat Lūqā* (Beirut: Near East Council
Lūqā   of Churches, 1935, 1970).

Scharlemann   Martin H. Scharlemann, *Proclaiming the Parables* (St. Louis:
Parables   Concordia, 1963).

B. T. D. Smith   B. T. D. Smith, *The Parables of the Synoptic Gospels* (Cambridge:
Parables   University Press, 1937).

C. W. F. Smith   C. W. F. Smith, *The Jesus of the Parables* (Philadelphia: West-
Parables   minster, 1948).

Str.-B.   P. Billerbeck and H. Strack, *Kommentar zum Neuen Testament*
aus Talmud und Midrasch, 6 vols.; 2nd ed. (Munich: C. H. Beck,
1924, 1956).

Stuhlmueller   Carroll Stuhlmueller, "The Gospel According to Luke," *The*
Luke   *Jerome Biblical Commentary*, ed. Raymond E. Brown, Joseph A.
Fitzmyer, and Roland E. Murphy (Englewood Cliffs: Prentice-
Hall, 1971), Vol. II, pp. 115–164.

TDNT   *Theological Dictionary of the New Testament*, ed. G. Kittel and G.
Friedrich; trans. and ed. G. W. Bromiley; 9 vols. (Grand Rapids:
Eerdmans, 1964–1974).

Thomson   W. M. Thomson, *The Land and the Book,* 2 vols. (New York:
The Land   Harper, 1871).

Trench   R. C. Trench, *Notes on the Parables of Our Lord* (New York:
Notes   Harper/Revell, n.d.).

Via   D. O. Via, *The Parables: Their Literary and Existential Dimension*
Parables   (Philadelphia: Fortress, 1967).

ZNW   *Zeitschrift für die neutestamentliche Wissenschaft und die Kunde*
der älteren Kirche

Part One
INTRODUCTION

Chapter 1

THE PROBLEM AND THE TASK

THE UNFINISHED WORK

William Thomson, famous nineteenth-century missionary, traveler, and author, described twenty-five years of surface study of Palestine as it relates to the Bible in his two-volume work, *The Land and the Book*. When he comes to describe Jerusalem he makes this remarkable statement:

> Do not set out . . . resolved to make *discoveries*. There is not a foot of ground that has not been already scrutinized by a thousand eyes as keen as yours, and the old adage, "If *true* not *new*, if *new* not *true*," may be applied to Jerusalem and her monuments with more propriety than to any other place on earth.[1]

Many in our day doubtless feel the same way about the parables of Jesus. Surely after centuries of study and reflection there is nothing fundamentally new in these stories. But even as there was far more to be discovered about the city of Jerusalem than Thomson ever dreamed, even so there is a great deal yet to be precisely understood in the deceptively simple parables of Jesus.

In spite of the wide attention given to the parables in past and in recent scholarship, two aspects of parabolic interpretation still need serious attention. These aspects are the cultural milieu and the literary structure of the parables.

The culture reflected in the Dominical parables is that of first-century Palestine.[2] While the externals of the Palestinian scene relevant to the parables have been analyzed with precision, the internal aspects of personal relationship and attitude have been imprecisely discerned. A more precise delineation of the Oriental culture that informs the text of four major Lucan parables is the first task of this study. The second aspect is that of literary structure, a facet of the parables that has probably had less attention than any other. The theology of the four

---

[1]Thomson, *The Land*, II, 468 (emphasis his). The author gathered his material during a trip through Palestine in 1857.
[2]Bultmann, *Tradition*, 166.

parables selected will then be set forth in the light of this reappraisal of the underlying culture and our analysis of their structure.

These two tools, an understanding of the cultural setting and an analysis of literary form, are here applied to four major Lucan parables against the background of contemporary critical discussions of the material. Before proceeding to a discussion of these two tools, we shall examine briefly three contemporary approaches to the parables.

MAJOR TRENDS IN RECENT PARABOLIC INTERPRETATION

The major interpretive method followed by the Church throughout the centuries was the allegorical method. A full review of this method and its history has been set forth elsewhere and need not detain us.[3] The modern period was initiated by Adolf Jülicher, who demonstrated conclusively the inadequacies of the allegorical method but offered no satisfactory alternative.[4] Bugge and Fiebig along with Strack and Billerbeck opened to scholarship the Jewish background of the parables.[5] This brings us to an examination of the three major approaches of the current scene. The first of these is that of C. H. Dodd and Joachim Jeremias.

(1) The Historical-Eschatological: Dodd and Jeremias

With Dodd another of the presuppositions of Jülicher was seriously challenged. His famous expression "realized eschatology" became the starting point for a reappraisal of the parables in his influential book, *The Parables of the Kingdom* (1935, rev. 1961). In this volume Dodd was able to point out that no one would have crucified an itinerant preacher who went around encouraging people with general moral principles. Hunter, endorsing Dodd, writes, "Would men have crucified a Galilean Tusitala who told picturesque stories to enforce prudential platitudes? Of course they would not!"[6] Dodd saw the context of the parables to be Jesus' preaching of the kingdom that was being realized in and through his ministry. At the same time, Dodd was interested in examining the parables on two

---

[3]A. M. Hunter, "The Interpreter and the Parables," *Interpretation*, 14 (1960), 77–81; Jülicher, *Gleichnisreden*, I, 203–322; Kelley, *Significance*, 4–19.

[4]A thoughtful analysis of Jülicher is provided by Via, *Parables*, 2–22. The four major weaknesses of Jülicher's position are: a rejection of all allegorical elements; the acceptance of Aristotle's categories as a model for understanding the parables; the reduction of the parables to general moral principles; and the strict insistence on only one point of comparison for each parable.

[5]C. A. Bugge, *Die Haupt-Parabeln Jesu* (Giessen: J. Ricker, 1903) (for a view of Bugge cf. Jones, *Art*, 20); Paul Fiebig, *Altjüdische Gleichnisse und die Gleichnisse Jesu* (Tübingen: J. C. B. Mohr, 1904); *idem, Die Gleichnisreden Jesu im Lichte der rabbinischen Gleichnisse des neutestamentlichen Zeitalters* (Tübingen: J. C. B. Mohr, 1912); *Str.-B.*, I–IV.

[6]Hunter, "The Interpreter," 83.

levels: that of the ministry of Jesus and that of the early Church. Dodd understood that the Church reused the parables and at times shifted their emphases. In the Gospels we have the parables in their church setting. Dodd set out to discover the original setting of the parables in the ministry of Jesus.[7]

In his famous volume *The Parables of Jesus* (trans. 1958, rev. 1963), Jeremias pays tribute to Dodd and understands his own work as a continuation of what Dodd has done. Jeremias worked out and applied to the parables a set of ten methodological tools. With these he attempted to distinguish between the situation in the life of the early Church and the situation in the life of Jesus.[9] He criticized Dodd for concentrating exclusively on the eschatological kingdom and chose as his own emphasis the conflict aspect of the parables as reflected in the ministry of Jesus. He understood many of them to have been spoken originally in vindication of the gospel.[10]

Jeremias, more than any modern scholar, uses all of the responsibly gathered information regarding the Palestinian background of the parables. He quotes from ancient rabbinic sources as well as from the remarks of the shepherd boy who first found the Dead Sea Scrolls in 1947. Journals of travelers, observations of contemporary Western residents in Palestine and the like are all carefully screened for valuable hints toward the recovery of the original intent of the parables.[11] Combining a concern for the meaning of the parables in the life of Jesus with a study of their Palestinian background, Jeremias has given us the twentieth century's most influential work on the parables.

(2) Jones: Parables as Art

Contemporary with Jeremias' search for the original meaning of the parables in the ministry of Jesus is the work of G. V. Jones, *The Art and Truth of the Parables* (1964). His study of the parables as art forms is a significant new venture in parabolic interpretation.

Jones is one of the voices calling for some type of wider application of the parables beyond what is possible with the ''severely historical'' approach. Much

---

[7]Dodd's position has been criticized by many as being ''severely historical.'' In the preface to the 1961 edition he responds to that criticism and says, ''To any reader who may feel (as I know some have felt) that my severely historical treatment of the parables robs them of universal and contemporary interest, I can only repeat what I have said on pp. 146–7. By all means draw from them any ''lesson'' they may seem to suggest, provided it is not incongruous with what we may learn of their original intention. . . . The Gospels do not offer us in the first place tales to point a moral. They interpret life to us, by initiating us into a situation in which, as Christians believe, the eternal was uniquely manifested in time, a situation which is both historical and contemporary in the deepest possible sense'' (Dodd, *Parables*, 8).

[8]Jeremias, *Parables*, 21.

[9]*Ibid.*, 113f.

[10]*Ibid.*, 21.

[11]For a more detailed review of Dodd and Jeremias cf. Kelley, *Significance*, 30–43; Jones, *Art*, 26; Scharlemann, *Parables*, 24; Via, *Dimension*, 21–24.

of Jones' book is a review of previous work on the parables. He examines the form-critical contribution, the Hebrew tradition, the discussion of symbolism and allegory. His conclusion on the last is that we must not work with rigid presuppositions that artificially restrict interpretation.[12] Jones' own views are set forth in chapters 5 and 6, entitled "The Art of Parable and the Parable as Art"[13] and "Towards a Wider Interpretation."[14] His main point is that the parables are fashioned out of the raw material of human life by a creative imagination. As a work of art a parable is not just a propositional statement "about how one should behave or how God acts,"[15] but is "independent of time."[16] The parable sets forth the truth about God and man "regardless of the passage of time or the changing environment."[17] Thus the parable achieves for Jones an "independent and 'typical' existence."[18] The broader application he calls for is possible, he believes, without allegorization. He summarizes his position by saying,

> On the whole, however, the allegorical equation is not required; a wider application of the parable is obtainable without it if what is indicated is a pattern of human behaviour, a paradigm of existence, or a picturesque account of God's relations with man. This method of extended interpretation can be described as "existential" (though not in the philosophical technical sense) because the parables concerned provide a statement about or a criticism of life dealing with concrete conditions of existence at any time.[19]

Thus Jones feels that the problem of "what it meant" *versus* "what it means" can be solved by seeing the parables as works of art with their own independent timeless existence. Yet he insists this is not true of all parables. He divides the parables into three classes. Some, he argues, are so historically bound that they have no application beyond first-century Palestine. Others have a didactic content which has *some* application beyond the original situation. The third group he calls "parables capable of more general application." The last half of his book is an exposition of the Prodigal Son as an illustration of this third type.

Thus in summary, Jones sees some of the parables as works of art having an independent timeless significance. The artistic nature of these parables allows for an application beyond the historical situation.

(3) Linnemann and Via: The Existential Perspective

The most recent thrust in parabolic interpretation is the existential. Eta Linnemann and Dan O. Via represent this view.

---

[12]Jones, *Art*, 109.
[13]*Ibid.*, 110–132.
[14]*Ibid.*, 135–166.
[15]*Ibid.*, 122.
[16]*Ibid.*, 123.
[17]*Ibid.*
[18]*Ibid.*, 125.
[19]*Ibid.*, 163.

In a recent book, *Jesus of the Parables* (trans. 1966), Linnemann has provided a discussion of the nature of parables and an exposition of eleven parables most suited to her point of view. Her approach is a combination of the presuppositions and methodologies of Jeremias, with his interest in the historical, and the existential hermeneutical approach to the parables of Ernst Fuchs.[20] What Linnemann proposes cannot be fully understood without seeing her as a part of a philosophical movement that goes back at least to Schleiermacher and moves through Dilthey, Bultmann, and the later Heidegger to Fuchs. For Linnemann, Fuchs is the most important of these thinkers. His hermeneutical principles have been fully expounded and need not detain us here.[21]

In the first section of her work Linnemann sets forth her basic principles of interpretation. She begins by distinguishing between similitude, parable, illustration, and allegory.[22] She quotes Bultmann's well-known laws for parabolic analysis[23] and then briefly examines introductory formulas. She affirms that the parables of Jesus are parables of conflict, meant to win agreement from his opposition. In this connection she writes,

> It is not enough to consider what ideas the narrator has connected with the parable; it must also be observed what ideas, images, and evaluations were at work in the hearers of the parable, in what the opposition between the narrator and his listeners consisted, and how accordingly his words must have acted on them.[24]

Here she stands with Jeremias.

In the tradition of Jülicher she affirms that there can be only one point of comparison.[25] The parable itself, she insists, is all the narrator says to his original listeners.[26]

Her debt to Fuchs is evident in her discussion of understanding, which, she says, is "guided by the way reality 'enters into language.' "[27] Again borrowing from Fuchs, Linnemann describes a parable as a "language event." She writes,

> A successful parable is an event that decisively alters the situation. It creates a new possibility that did not exist before, the possibility that the man addressed

---

[20]In her Foreword, Linnemann pays tribute to Bultmann, Jeremias, and Fuchs (*Parables*, xiii). Fuchs wrote the introduction to her book and was adviser for the work itself, which was her thesis. The influence of both Fuchs and Jeremias is everywhere evident.

[21]Richard N. Soulen, "Biblical Hermeneutics and Parable Interpretation in the Writings of Ernst Fuchs" (unpublished Ph.D. thesis, Boston University, 1964), p. 28; Paul J. Achtemeier, *An Introduction to the New Hermeneutic* (Philadelphia: Westminster, 1969).

[22]Linnemann, *Parables*, 2–8; Jeremias prefers to recognize that the Hebrew *Mashal* covered a wide range of overlapping categories; cf. Jeremias, *Parables*, 20.

[23]Bultmann, *Tradition*, 188–192.

[24]Linnemann, *Parables*, 22f.

[25]*Ibid.*, 23. Remarkably she affirms this without evidence or argumentation. In so doing she ignores the debate on this point which has continued since Jülicher.

[26]*Ibid.*, 24. Thereby, in her view, all the applications in the parables are later additions.

[27]*Ibid.*

can come to an understanding with the man addressing him across the opposition that exists between them.[28]

She then goes on to explain that the "language event" character of the parable not only creates a new possibility for understanding, but also forces the listener to a decision. Even if the listener refuses the new possibility of understanding, he still makes a decision. His choice is to reject the new understanding. This rejection then becomes opposition.[29] Thus Linnemann builds firmly on the work of Fuchs and yet, at the same time, goes beyond him.

Linnemann's unique advance on the existentialist interpretation of Fuchs is her understanding of "interlocking." According to her, the parable makes a "concession" to the opposition by representing their point of view in the parable. The claim of the narrator is also represented. In the parable the two points of view "interlock" and in this interlocking there is created the possibility of a new understanding between the two sides. In telling a parable, the narrator is claiming that one thing represents another. Linnemann writes,

> This "claiming one thing as another" together with the "concession" produces the phenomenon of *interlocking*. In the parable the verdict of the narrator on the situation in question "interlocks" with that of the listener. Both evaluations of the situation go into the parable.[30]

At this point her line of reasoning makes a perplexing shift. She first asserts that the "new possibility" created by the parable is a new understanding between the original narrator and the listener. She then affirms that the listener comes to a new understanding of *himself* which is also defined as a "change of existence" and as a "new life." The last emphasis is easily traceable to her adviser Fuchs; but it is not clear how she has made the shift from the one to the other, or in what way they are related.

She concludes her discussion of the "language event" with an affirmation that we can participate in the same event created by the first telling of the parable through the medium of proclamation.[31] Here she shows her indebtedness to Bultmann.

In summary, she affirms the necessity of the historical approach and combines it with a Fuchsian-Bultmannian concept of parable as "language event" in which we can participate through preaching.

The second recent voice in this school is Dan O. Via. In *The Parables* (1967), Via discusses both Jones and Linnemann, pointing out deficiencies in

---

[28]*Ibid.*, 30. In this connection she explains the risk involved. The narrator risks everything "on the power of language" (*ibid.*, 32).

[29]This understanding of parables hangs on their having been addressed to opponents. She affirms that practically all the parables were so addressed.

[30]*Ibid.*, 27; emphasis hers.

[31]All through her discussion she affirms the need for a sound historical base for the parables. Much of her exegesis is a wrestling with the historical question. Thus her debt to Jeremias is also clear.

both.[32] If Jeremias was interested in the historical and Linnemann in the historical-existential, then Via is concerned with the existential-aesthetic. Thus he shares Jones' concern for the aesthetic and he overlaps with Linnemann's application of existentialism. His case is well stated, and he debates with the existential philosophers and theologians on the one side and with a wide range of literary critics on the other side. No brief review can do him justice.

The first half of his work is devoted to a discussion of methodology. He is determined to move away from the "severely historical," which in his view fails to do justice to the existential and to the aesthetic. He feels that the historical work has been done, and that he can rely with confidence on Dodd, Jeremias, T. W. Manson, and others.

In his first chapter, Via discusses parable and allegory. He rejects the "one-point" approach as "artificially restrictive."[33] The one-point approach destroyed the basic unity of the parable by isolating a single element and relating it directly to the referent. Yet the allegorization of the past is also rejected. In allegory the meanings of the different elements in the parable are determined by referents *outside* the parable, not by elements *within* the parable. Yet, according to Via, parables can have allegorical elements in them without becoming allegories. He writes, "The allegorist does not begin with an image which suggests a meaning, but he begins with an idea or meaning and looks for an image to represent it."[34]

The historical approach comes under criticism because we cannot be sure what the original situation was, and because such an approach "ignores the basic human element in the parables."[35] Furthermore, the historical approach, Via feels, leaves the parable with nothing to say to the present and it ignores its aesthetic nature as a work of art.

In his second chapter Via is concerned with the problem of theological language. He affirms that the historical is important because "our efforts at translation are not to be mere sounding boards for our previously held ideas."[36] The artist writes better than he knows, and the purpose of parables is to provide a better understanding of existence.[37] The well-known existentialist categories of the necessity of knowing that existence can be gained or lost, the language-event, self-understanding, authenticity, verification analysis, functional analysis, the verification principle, inauthenticity, preunderstanding, ontic and ontological are all discussed against a background of the works of Fuchs, Dilthey, Bultmann, and

---

[32]Via, *Parables*, 23. A noteworthy recent study in some ways close to Via is J. D. Crossan, *In Parables* (1973).

[33]Via, *Parables*, 3.

[34]*Ibid.*, 6.

[35]*Ibid.*, 22.

[36]*Ibid.*, 28.

[37]*Ibid.*, 39.

Linnemann.[38] He defines the goal of interpretation as translating the text into new terms so that "the language of the text might become an event."[39] In this section Via stands squarely in the existentialist tradition of Ernst Fuchs. Exposition is hermeneutics, and its goal is a new self-understanding on the part of the listener.

Via's third chapter is on parables, aesthetics, and literary criticism. He argues that the parables are genuine works of art and that a failure to deal with this fact has led to the one-point theory of interpretation. He writes,

> From the aesthetic standpoint, to isolate one element in a literary work for special consideration breaks the unity of the work and obscures the meaning of that element by removing it from the context which provides its meaning.[40]

Yet at the same time a work of art in general and a parable in particular does not just point inward but also outward. It has meaning within itself and also beyond itself. This Via explains by borrowing an illustration from Murray Krieger, a modern literary critic. Via writes,

> If the work [of art] operates properly, it is related to the world sequentially as window, mirror, and window. First it is a set of windows through which we see the familiar world referentially. Then the windows become mirrors reflecting inwardly on each other. In this set of reflecting mirrors the familiar and the hitherto unperceived are organized in a new pattern of connections so that in this pattern there is an implicit or preconceptual existential understanding. Finally the mirrors become windows again, giving us a new vision of the world. Thus the work, being at once word and world, leads both somewhere else and terminally to itself. But even as window the second time the work still offers a pre-conceptual understanding, and the latter is conceptualized only in criticism.[41]

Thus Via makes room for the internal unity of the different elements that have meaning only in relation to each other and at the same time allows for a conceptualization of those elements. Later he summarizes his own argument by saying, "In this chapter it has been argued that a work of literary art means [i.e., has meaning] both in and through itself but that the inner, non-referential meaning is dominant."[42]

Again and again he returns to a discussion of the damage done to the parables by the one-point exegetical approach which destroys this "centripetally organized unity of form and content...."[43] As an alternative he suggests that in the case of Jesus' parables, "... Interpretation should not isolate one point but

---

[38]For a full review of these aspects of Via's work cf. Kelley, *Significance*, 92–120.

[39]Via, *Parables*, 52.

[40]*Ibid.*, 76.

[41]*Ibid.*, 84.

[42]*Ibid.*, 86.

[43]*Ibid.*, 88. At the same time he assumes that the severely historical method necessarily goes hand in hand with the one-point approach that does this destructive work. *Ibid.*, 89.

should call attention to the total configuration, to the nature of the interconnections, and to the understanding implicitly contained therein."[44]

His own literary tools, which he wishes to use on the parables, come from the categories familiar to literary criticism. They are narrative, fiction, plot, encounter, dialogue, the protagonist's power of action, symbolism, the tragic, and the comic.

In the second half of the book he illustrates his method by interpreting a series of "tragic" and a series of "comic" parables. His remarks are divided into "historical-literary criticism," "literary-existential analysis," and "existential-theological interpretation." His main interest seems to be "literary-existential analysis."

REACTION AND ASSESSMENT: A REMAINING TASK

Having concentrated on five major voices that are still with us in the sixties and seventies, we can summarize their main emphases diagrammatically as follows:

Dodd, Jeremias = historical

Jones   = (historical)   aesthetic

Linnemann   = historical - existential

Via   = (historical)- existential - aesthetic

Dodd and Jeremias are interested in the historical, which they demonstrate to include the eschatological. Jones concentrates on the aesthetic, assuming that the historical work has already been done. He asserts a timelessness for the aesthetically constructed parable. Linnemann takes the historical seriously and works at it. To this she adds the existential. Via assumes the historical and says he is building on Dodd and Jeremias. He is grateful to Jones for initiating the discussion on the aesthetic but is critical of him for not developing it. He is grateful to Linnemann for taking the existential seriously and criticizes her for leaving out the aesthetic.

On the sweep of parabolic exegesis in this century Kelley provides a thoughtful summary. He writes,

> Each major emphasis has brought a corrective to the situation that was inherited and then has had to be corrected itself. We have no reason to believe that the pattern will be any different in the case of the existentialist approach to the parable and its latest devotee, Via. Jülicher liberated the parables from extravagant allegorization but misunderstood their nature as parables of Jesus. Historical exegesis rescued us from interpreting the parables as mere illustrations of general moral principles when it placed them in the framework of

---

[44]*Ibid.,* 93.

Jesus' ministry critically reconstructed and eschatologically described. Such rigorous historical methodology in turn has its own built-in hazard, namely, that of pre-occupation with parables as concrete and functional instruments for instruction and disputation in first century circumstances to an extent that they might have little to say to the current twentieth century situation. Via, yielding to the contemporary pressure for relevance, seeks to remedy any such deficiency by taking the parables as aesthetic objects whose enduring subject matter and translatable content is none other than an understanding of existence, in faith and unfaith, authentically and inauthentically. Our reaction to his approach is that while he may have brought parables into the present and made them eventful thereby to many moderns, he has done so at the price of considerable disservice to them both as parables and as parables of Jesus.[45]

In the above diagram it can be seen that a historical-aesthetic approach to the parables has not been made. The only two scholars who have asked the aesthetic question (Jones and Via) are the ones who show the least interest in the historical setting. Those who have wrestled seriously with the historical (Dodd, Jeremias, and Linnemann) have not been concerned with the aesthetic. A brief critique of each of these approaches will make clear the extent to which the historical has not been brought together with the aesthetic.

Jeremias and Dodd, with their influential works, have laid the foundation of the twentieth-century recovery of the historical-eschatological setting of the parables. Their only difficulty is that at times the raw material for a precise delineation of the culture that informs the text was not available to them. Furthermore, they provide no format for an aesthetic appreciation of the parables as art forms. This lack has at times led them to judge as miscellaneous secondary collections made by the Church, units of material that are better understood as primary unified pericopes with their own integrity. Nevertheless, anyone who struggles to understand the parables in their original setting owes these two men a debt that is beyond description.

Of the four approaches in the above diagram, Jones seems the most concerned to break out of the original historical setting. Jones has a good point. When one stands in front of Michelangelo's statue of Moses, the impression is not that of sixteenth-century Italy, but of "the angry man of God." There *is* an element of timelessness to a great work of art that helps it break out of the historical setting in which it was created. Yet in the case of the parables, if the historical is not taken seriously, they become like floating balloons, ready to follow the prevailing winds.

The difficulty with the existentialist approach generally is put succinctly by Kelley, who writes,

The danger we see in this sort of orientation is that it yields a picture of Jesus not as a wandering Jewish rabbi who instructs disciples, replies to opponents, and stimulates crowds, but rather of an existentialist theologian, wearing a

---

[45]Kelley, *Significance*, 127f.; emphasis his.

Bultmannian or Heideggerian face, who by parabolic speech dramatizes ontological possibilities for hearers.[46]

If the existentialist approach helps to illuminate aspects of the parables for a certain segment of modern man, then this approach should be discussed and evaluated in those terms. To superimpose categories involved in "what it means" back into "what it meant" is, in a sense, a new form of allegorization.

Linnemann has given some very profound insights into the nature of the way some of the larger parables of conflict must have functioned originally. In the case of the parable of the Prodigal Son, there *is* "interlocking" in the parable. The parable authentically represents the position of the Pharisees. They considered sinners to be as unrighteous as pig herders working for gentiles. Their view then "interlocks" with the view of Jesus as represented in the words and actions of the Father. A new possibility of relationship between Jesus and his opponents is opened up by the telling of the parable.

Her theory breaks down, however, when we discuss a parable directed to the disciples. All such parables she quietly ignores. Her confidence that we can participate in that event through a re-creation of it in preaching is also only a partial understanding of how the hermeneutical problem can be solved. Can we really participate in the language event of the parable in the same way that a first-century Pharisee did who stood in opposition to a Galilean rabbi?[47]

We have already questioned the appropriateness of Via's existentialist categories for a study of first-century Palestinian parables. Leaving this question aside, it must be affirmed that Via has issued a timely call for an appreciation of the parables as art forms. However, in analyzing the parables he used the categories of Western literature. Kelley observes this as he writes,

> Too hastily . . . Via hurries over the material related to parables as an Eastern form in order to determine how they stand up to scrutiny under Western standards. The latter literary tradition may be more meaningful to us in the contemporary setting but the earlier associations with a Palestinian background are of no less importance, particularly where the parables of Jesus are under discussion.[48]

Rather than looking, as Via has done, for "comic," "tragic," "the protagonist's power of action," and "plot," Eastern literature must be examined using its own literary art forms. Then when the question is asked, "What are the primary literary art forms in Eastern literature?" the almost exclusive answer is, "Stories and poems." Thus, if we would investigate the parables aesthetically, we

---

[46]*Ibid.*, 132.
[47]Linnemann only touches on this problem in passing. It is her intent to concentrate on "what it meant" and leave the hermeneutical problem outside the scope of her study. This is also our intention. However, it is our conviction that each parable has a "theological cluster" that is a part of "what it meant." This cluster we feel is translatable through preaching with the aid of the impact of the artistic elements of the parable. (Cf. pp. 37f.)
[48]Kelley, *Significance*, 130, n. 2.

must examine them to see if Eastern poetical forms occur in the text, and if the stories have a distinct literary form.

Finally, Via has been much more concerned to relate the aesthetic to the existential, rather than to the historical. Hence, not only have the aesthetical aspects of the parables not been examined in the light of their own literary forms, but in addition no attempt has been made to combine such an aesthetic analysis with a serious study of the historical setting of the parables in first-century Palestine. [49]

It is our conviction that the historical must be reexamined in the light of additional evidence from the cultural milieu of the parables. In addition the aesthetic must be viewed in the light of Oriental literary forms. This twin task is the subject of the present study.

With this in mind, we turn to a discussion of an adequate methodology.

---

[49]An excellent series of three articles on the parables in modern interpretation is provided by J. D. Kingsbury, ''Ernst Fuch's Existentialist Interpretation of the Parables,'' *Lutheran Quarterly,* 22 (1970), 380–395; *idem,* ''Major Trends in Parabolic Interpretation,'' *Concordia Theological Monthly* 42 (1971), 579–596; *idem,* ''The Parables of Jesus in Current Research,'' *Dialog* 11 (1972), 101–107.

Chapter 2

METHODOLOGY (1): THE CULTURAL PROBLEM

THE BASIC PROBLEM: CULTURAL FOREIGNNESS

The parables confront the exegete with what can be called the cultural problem. When studying the apostle Paul, one is dealing with theology expressed in conceptual language. But in the case of parables, their theology is expressed in stories about particular people who lived in a given cultural setting at a specific time in history. To understand the theology of parables, therefore, we must recapture the culture that informs the text. The culture of the synoptic parables is that of first-century Palestine.[1] Palestinian Christians saw their own culture reflected in the parables and could thereby understand the teller/author's intent directly. But when the cultural base of the Church ceased to be Palestinian the parables inevitably became stories about foreigners. This "foreignness" of the culture that informs the parables we have called *the cultural problem*.

The purpose of this chapter is to set forth a methodology that will be as adequate as possible for solving this cultural problem. We will try to demonstrate that such a methodology involves (1) discussing the cultural aspects of the parables with Middle Easterners, (2) examining pertinent ancient literature, and (3) consulting the Oriental versions of the Gospels. Furthermore, once we have established as precisely as possible the culture that informs the text of the parables, there remains the question of how the interpreter is to arrive at the *point* of the parable and whether that point is simple or multiple. We will attempt to show that each parable has a "cluster" of theological motifs that together press the listener to make a single response.

---

[1]Bultmann, *Tradition*, 166.

A REVIEW OF TYPES OF SOLUTIONS TO THE CULTURAL PROBLEM

This cultural problem has been given a number of answers. Through the centuries the Church, faced with this issue, has allegorized, indigenized, universalized, existentialized, and, on occasion, given up in despair. These solutions must be examined briefly in turn.

Origen's answer was to allegorize the details of the parables and thus deny culture any role in interpretation. We are all grateful to Jülicher[2] for having discredited this exegetical method which allows the introduction of nearly anything into virtually any parable.

A second solution, used almost unconsciously, is to "indigenize" the cultural elements of the parables. In this case, the exegete assumes that first-century people thought much like himself. What does it mean for a man to knock on his neighbor's door at midnight in the first century? It is only reasonable to assume, runs the argument, that it would mean roughly the same thing as knocking on a neighbor's door today. Sooner or later, the exegete will say, "It is only reasonable to assert . . . ," to which we must ask, "Reasonable to whom?" Or he says, "It is only natural to affirm . . . ," to which we must ask, "Natural for whom?" Does the commentator mean natural for the Americans, the British, or the Germans? Once identified, the fallacy of indigenization is readily recognizable.

Plummer, for example, notes that the father in the story of the Prodigal Son turns and addresses the servants immediately after hearing his son's confession. Plummer affirms that of course this order must have been given after the two had returned to the house because no servant would run out and down the road.[3] He is apparently thinking of a nineteenth-century British butler, and does not realize that a Middle Eastern listener would naturally assume the servants had followed the father down the road. Unconsciously Plummer has read his own cultural pattern back into the parable. Far more often the exegete overlooks significant elements in a parable because they are not important to the exegete's own world.

A third method is to "universalize" the cultural elements. In this case the exegete assumes that all men are basically alike. After all, all men understand fathers, sons, and neighbors. All men experience death, separation, and suffering. In all cultures, goes the argument, the basic human relationships displayed in the parables are similar, and so a study of Palestinian culture is not really so important after all. To a certain extent this is, of course, true. There is a humanity that all men share, and there are common problems that all men try to solve. But patterns for expressing those problems or even discussing them are quite different. To "universalize" in practice becomes to "indigenize." The one who says, "All men think alike," really means, "All men think like me."

---

[2]Jülicher, *Gleichnisreden*, I, *passim*.
[3]Plummer, *St. Luke*, 375.

A fourth method is to existentialize. This, in reality, shifts the discussion from exegesis to hermeneutics. The hermeneutical question is, of course, very important, but the historical question of "what it meant" must be answered prior to a hermeneutical concern for "what it means." One cannot even intelligently discuss participation in a "language event" until it is clear *what* language event is proposed. Without the historical question, the language event becomes a creation of the exegete.

A fifth alternative is to despair. There are two aspects to this reaction. There is the question of the time gap. We are twenty centuries away from the peasant world of Palestine in the days of Jesus. Then there is the question of distance. We live in the West and Jesus and his audience were Easterners. The Western exegete must move "over" and "back." Bultmann has admitted frankly that it is impossible to recover what the parable of the Unjust Steward originally meant.[4] In the sixteenth century Tomas de Vio Cajetan held the same position.[5] The information is too scanty, so the argument goes; the path back too narrow. The original meaning of the parables in their Palestinian setting is irrecoverably lost, we are told.

It is our view that none of these five alternatives is either appropriate or necessary. Our conclusion is that the Oriental culture that informs the text of the parables can be recovered in a rather systematic fashion. This enterprise of recovering that culture we will call "Oriental exegesis."

ORIENTAL EXEGESIS: A PROPOSAL

In this section we will begin with a definition, and then proceed to examine the archaic nature of the life style of Middle Eastern peasantry. Past attempts at gaining insights from Middle Eastern peasantry will be examined, and, finally, our own experience of working with Middle Eastern people will be set forth with a description of the necessary controls.

A Definition of "Oriental Exegesis"

The culture that informs the text of the Gospel parables can be delineated in a relatively precise manner by bringing together three tools. The culture of contemporary conservative peasants must be examined to see what the parables mean in their setting. Oriental versions need to be studied to see how Oriental churchmen through the centuries have translated the text. Ancient literature pertinent to the parables must be read *with* the insights gained from these other two sources, not in isolation from them. The text must be examined against the background of

---

[4]Bultmann, *Tradition,* 199.
[5]Apparently from his *Evang. cum commen . . . Thomae de Vio Caietani in quattuor Evang. et Apostol. . . . Commentarii,* etc. (1530). Quoted by Trench, *Notes,* 324.

information gleaned from these three sources. These three tools need to be used *along with* and not in isolation from the other skills of modern scholarship.

Thus "Oriental exegesis" is a method of studying a culturally conditioned text. The method is to use the standard critical tools of Western scholarship in combination with cultural insights gained from ancient literature, contemporary peasants, and Oriental versions.

We must now examine in some detail how each of these three tools is to be used. The first of these is ancient literature.

Ancient Literature: Its Importance and the Exegete's Problem in Assessing It

Modern scholarship has been engaged for well over a century in trying to rediscover the cultural context of the Bible. Ancient literature has been examined with precision and sensitivity for clues regarding the culture that informs the text of the parables. It is difficult to exaggerate the importance of this literature. The problem is that cultural attitudes in any literature are assumed and only rarely, if ever, explained. To examine ancient Middle Eastern literature in order to discover the cultural assumptions of a given scene is like looking for raw diamonds in a gravel pit when one has never seen a raw diamond. It is like an amateur examining an archeologist's bulk. The observer must know what he is looking for before he can see anything, even if there is a great deal to be seen.[6] Ben Sirach reports that a nobleman is known by his walk.[7] He is referring to the slow, dignified pace of the Middle Eastern patriarch, which is a sign of the patriarch's stature in the community. This fact, noted by Ben Sirach, is one of the crucial keys to the parable of the Prodigal Son. It is a key that lies available; yet heretofore it has remained unnoticed and unused.

In summary, the culture that informs the text of the parables is often illuminated by ancient literature. Somehow, the exegete must discover what he is looking for before he can search meaningfully in that ancient literature. The answer is partially found in our second tool, which will now be examined.

The Contemporary Middle Eastern Peasant and His Oral Tradition as a Tool for Recovering the Culture of the Parables

In this section we will observe the archaic nature of the life of Middle Eastern peasantry, review past attempts at gleaning insights from this peasantry, and outline the unfinished task as well as its method and controls.

---

[6]Some Johannine editor was aware of this principle when he added the phrase "The Jews do not use vessels in common with the Samaritans," in John 4:9. The editor knew his reader had a cultural problem. Our problem is the same, only much more profound.
[7]Sir. 19:30.

The Archaic Nature of His Life Style

In the south of Egypt, in the mountains of Lebanon, and in the isolated communities of upper Syria and Iraq, there are peasant communities which have lived in remarkable isolation from the rest of the world. It is not only their isolation that has enabled them to preserve ancient ways of life, however, but also that they regard changelessness as being of highest value. This principle is of great antiquity and is not unknown in the Bible. All the wisdom literature of the ancient East, including the wisdom literature of the Bible, affirmed the supreme value of changelessness. Only in the static was there meaning. This was also asserted by ancient Egyptian religion, which taught that at creation God launched Egyptian society in its totality.[8] To preserve meaning was to preserve the status quo. This identity of value and changelessness has maintained itself in Middle Eastern peasant society all through the centuries. Thus today, the finest compliment for a gentleman in the village is "Ḥāfiẓ al-taqālīd" (preserver of the customs).

In his famous anthropological study of the Middle Eastern peasant, Father Henry Ayrout has this to say:

> The fellaheen have changed their masters, their religions, their language and their crops, but not their manner of life. . . . Violent and repeated shocks have swept away whole peoples, as can be seen today from the ruins of North Africa or Chaldea. . . . But the fellaheen have held firm and stood their ground. . . . They are as impervious and enduring as the granite of their temples, and as slow to develop. . . . This is not merely an impression. We can see the fellah using the same implements—the plough, the shadûf, the saqia . . . the same methods of treating the body . . . many of the same marriage and funeral customs. Through the pages of Herodotus, Diodorus Siculus, Strabo, Maqrîzi, Vansleb, Père Sicard and Volney we can recognise the same fellah. No revolution, no evolution.[9]

Many villages are not connected to the outside world by any road. Access is on foot or by donkey. There is a town crier and a village weaver. Doors of streets are closed at night. A colloquial Arabic is spoken, which is sprinkled with Greek, Aramaic, Syriac, and even Akkadian words. Young girls make Astarte-type fertility figurines good enough to fool all but the professional archeologists.

Not only is the life of such peasants remarkably archaic but their intellectual life is in the form of poems and stories preserved from the past. Men gather nightly in the village for what is called "ḥaflat samar" (social gathering for samar), which is cognate with the Hebrew shamar, "to preserve." They are gathering to preserve the intellectual life of their community by the recitation of

[8]Henri Frankfort, Ancient Egyptian Religion (New York: Harper, 1961), 49.

[9]Henry Habib-Ayrout, The Fellaheen, trans. Hilary Wayment (Cairo: R. Schindler, 1945), 19f. M. S. Seale, after a lifetime in the Middle East, writes, "before the great transformations of modern times, the 'unchanging East' really was unchanging." Cf. Morris S. Seale, The Desert Bible, Nomadic Tribal Culture and Old Testament Interpretation (London: Weidenfeld and Nicolson, 1974), 21.

poems and the retelling of stories. When a village patriarch begins, "marrah ayyām al-sulṭān" (once in the days of the sultan), or "marrah ayyām al-Rūm" (once in the days of the Byzantines), or more generally, "marrah zamān" (once long ago), he becomes to a certain extent like an Englishman telling a story from the days of King Arthur's court. As such a patriarch relates some narrative out of the distant past he enters a world that *may* be culturally somewhat different from his own. Yet that ancient world, with its traditional attitudes and archaic life style, is known and preserved in these stories. Thus village life has a double layer of cultural mores. There is the culture of the peasant himself and that of the traditional oral literature he recites. Through careful and patient contact with these two layers of culture, one is able to penetrate to and understand archaic forms of culture to a remarkable degree.

The next obvious question is, Has this task not already been done? Has not the work of gleaning insights for parabolic understanding from contemporary Middle Eastern peasants not already been accomplished? It is our conviction that it has been done partially and at times imprecisely, as a review of attempts at examining this peasantry will reveal.

Past Attempts at Gleaning Insights from Middle Eastern Peasantry

In this section we will review three past types of efforts at gaining biblical insight from contemporary peasants. Jeremias has written:

> As one who was privileged to live in Palestine for some years, I can testify from my own experience how much new light has been thrown ... upon the gospels ... [by] the study of both ancient and modern Palestine. ...[10]

Jeremias has used to its fullest every scrap of responsibly gathered information from contemporary conservative Middle Eastern peasants. The difficulty is that much of the data has been gathered casually and not always precisely. The materials fall into three categories. These we have labeled (1) the view from the saddle, (2) the view from the study window, and (3) the view from the single village.

First, there is *the view from the saddle*. In the nineteenth century the Reverend W. Thomson, missionary to Syria, spent a number of years on horseback riding through Bible lands.[11] From roughly 1850 through the First World War, a virtual flood of literature was written by pilgrims, travelers, and temporary residents of Palestine. Theirs was a view from the saddle; they saw Palestine "riding through." Much was observed of significance and value. Topography, weather, the agricultural year, the way people built their houses, the way they

---

[10]Joachim Jeremias, *The Problem of the Historical Jesus,* trans. N. Perrin (Philadelphia: Fortress, 1964), 17.

[11]Cf. p. 1, n. 1. Occasionally Thomson did make cultural observations; when he did so they are excellent. His major interest was the identification of geographic sites.

farmed the ground, and so forth, were noted; and our knowledge of the Bible was enriched.

The problem of the literature of this period is that most of it was written by people who stayed in the Middle East for relatively brief periods of time. Thomson spoke Arabic fluently and spent twenty-five years in the area. By contrast, the majority of Western authors were there only for short periods, and had little knowledge of Arabic and brief exposure to Middle Eastern ways. They wrote books or articles on their return to the West that on occasion influenced the direction of parabolic interpretation to a significant degree.[12] The people who were long-term residents in the Middle East were, generally speaking, not scholars. Quite naturally they wrote devotional literature, which tended to bypass the kinds of questions scientific scholarship asks. The scholars among them like Thomson were primarily interested in the identification of biblical sites.

After the view from the saddle comes *the view from the study window*, where the author settled down in the Palestinian scene and examined much of the same material but with greater precision. The outstanding work of Dalman will probably never be surpassed. Everything that could be measured, diagrammed, photographed, or charted, he recorded. His seven volumes (1928–1942) preserve the externals of Palestinian life in a precise and admirable way.[13] However, Dalman remained the Western professor looking on from the outside. His view was "from the study window." For parabolic interpretation we need to know more than the external appearance of agricultural tools. We rather need to know the inner workings of the society of people that uses them. At the same time, E. F. F. Bishop, an Anglican missionary and Arabic scholar, was resident in Jerusalem, meeting weekly with his Western friends to discuss what the entire Palestinian scene meant to the Bible. His three books[14] have many valuable insights, mixed with much quaint reminiscence. Bishop partially moved out of his study. By his own admission much of his material came out of a discussion group that "was essentially missionary."[15] Yet Bishop had hundreds of Arab friends with whom he was in conversation; and he used Arabic versions of the Gospels for exegesis, although he never identifies which versions. However, since he was an Arabic scholar with no specialization in New Testament, his material does not engage with contemporary scholarship.

A third contribution can be called *the view from the single village*. Here we turn to two men, Abraham Rihbany[16] and N. Levison.[17] Rihbany was a Christian

---

[12]In the exegetical section we will examine in detail the case of Margaret Gibson and her influence on the contemporary understanding of the parable of the Unjust Steward.

[13]G. Dalman, *Arbeit und Sitte in Palästina* (Gütersloh: Bertelsmann, 1928–1942), 7 vols.; *Sacred Sites and Ways*, trans. P. P. Levertoff (London; SPCK, 1935).

[14]Bishop, *Jesus; idem, Apostles of Palestine* (London: Lutterworth, 1958); *idem, Prophets of Palestine* (London: Lutterworth, 1962).

[15]Bishop, *Jesus*, 20.

[16]Rihbany, *Syrian*.

[17]Levison, *Local Setting*.

Syrian peasant who emigrated to America before the First World War and became a pastor. He came from a very conservative peasant world and realized that the world of his youth was significantly different from that of the West. He wrote, "Whenever I open my Bible, it reads like a letter from home."[18] Levison was an Oriental Jew who grew up in Palestine in the nineteenth century. He became a Christian, emigrated to England, and became a clergyman there. His book, *The Parables: Their Background and Local Setting* (1926), is introduced with these words:

> My qualifications for supplying the local coloring are based upon my great privilege of having been brought up in Galilee, within sight of Nazareth and the surrounding country. . . . When I say that, up to the time I was sent to school in Jerusalem, . . . I had not seen a vehicle of any description, and that the Old Testament narratives were as intelligible as the recently written accounts of yesterday's events, it may indicate how primitive and free from change our life in Safad was.[19]

The work of both Rihbany and Levison is of great value. A difficulty with both these books is that they are for the most part not scholarly but devotional. Many of the questions, therefore, which scholarship raises are not answered. But more than this, methodologically speaking neither pastor looked beyond the recollections of his own village. It never occurred to Levison that Safad might not reflect universal attitudes across Middle Eastern peasantry. Levison apparently had not read Rihbany. We do not know from reading Levison and Rihbany whether or not their recollections can be substantiated from Syrian, Lebanese, and Egyptian villages. In spite of this drawback, the work of these two men is important because they are Middle Easterners describing their own culture, not Westerners observing them from the outside. The information they give is usually valuable. Yet it is piecemeal and partial.

The Unfinished Task: Its Method and Its Controls

In the last twenty years I have tried to glean insights from the view from the saddle, the view from the study, and the view from the individual village, with a view to working out a methodology that may help to delineate more precisely the Oriental culture that informs the text. I prefer to call this *the view from the mastaba*, the *mastaba* being the mud-brick or stone bench outside the peasant's house on which he sits and talks with his friends by the hour.

As a part of a village literacy team for five years, I was privileged to live in Oriental villages for long periods of time. Naturally, the villages themselves were among the most isolated and primitive, because they were the villages where the highest rates of illiteracy were to be found. Living in the village, I was able to become a part of the scenery and could interact with the village people not as a guest or stranger, researcher or scholar, but as an ordinary resident. With no

---

[18]Quoted in Bishop, *Jesus*, 8.
[19]Levison, *Local Setting*, x.

camera or notebook, I could watch people interacting with each other. Over a period of years, I gradually came to the realization that a new layer of perception is available when we ask a fresh set of questions of the biblical text.

The crucial questions are those of *attitude, relationship, response,* and *value judgment.* What is the *attitude* of a sleeping neighbor to a call for help in the night? What is the *relationship* between a landowner and his renters? What is the expected *response* from a father when his son requests his inheritance? What *value judgment* do the renters make regarding the steward when he suggests the reduction of rents?

I discovered that the Oriental storyteller has a "grand piano" on which he plays. The piano is built of the attitudes, relationships, responses, and value judgments that are known and stylized in Middle Eastern peasant society. Everybody knows how everybody is expected to act in any given situation. The storyteller interrupts the established pattern of behavior to introduce his irony, his surprises, his humor, and his climaxes. If we are not attuned to those same attitudes, relationships, responses, and value judgments, we do not hear the music of the piano. With the parables, the music of this "piano" contains significant aspects of the theology that called the story itself into being.

In addition to residence in the individual village, for twenty years I have proclaimed the gospel and administered the sacraments to village congregations all across Egypt and Lebanon. This has put me in touch with a wide range of village people and village pastors. What is more important, this ministry has assured a relationship of intimacy and trust that has made possible the asking of cultural questions related to the parables. Thus, I have been privileged to observe what the parables mean when seen through peasant eyes.

The primary method of gaining insight has been to engage individuals and groups in extended discussion on the meanings of the parables. The conversation usually began, "Now, if this had happened in your village in the days of your grandfather, what would it have meant?" In time I have worked out the following methodological controls:

1. The resource person must have spent at least the first twenty years of his life in a conservative, basically illiterate, isolated peasant community.

2. The primary method of collecting the information must be oral conversation in Arabic. In a "word culture" such as we have in the Middle East, nearly everything that matters takes place orally. Oriental thought is most appropriately expressed in an Oriental language.

3. The primary resource person with whom I talk must be a person whom I have known as a friend for at least five years. This guards against receiving the stylized answers of the Easterner responding to the foreigner.

4. The resource person with whom I talk must know enough about the biblical witness to understand the questions put to him.

Gradually I have been able to develop a team of about twenty-five primary resource people from Iran to the Sudan with whom I have been in conversation around key questions regarding the culture that informs the text of the parables.[20] The majority of these twenty-five are Arab pastors who themselves have wrestled with the text. The insights gained from one resource person have been shared with as wide a Middle Eastern audience as possible, to assure that they ring true with a wide spectrum of Middle Eastern people. This has been done in the course of lecturing to Middle Eastern church groups, in extended discussions with Middle Eastern seminary students and pastors, as well as through a weekly Arabic radio broadcast. During my years on the faculty of the Near East School of Theology, Beirut, Lebanon, I have been privileged to work with colleagues from Syria, Lebanon, Germany, Holland, France, England, Ireland, and America. Insights have been refined and corrected through numerous discussions with these colleagues. There has been an occasional opportunity to consult with visiting Eastern and Western scholars.

The insights gained in some cases confirm what we already know. Other known insights are refined, still others rejected, and some new raw material has been uncovered to aid in parabolic understanding.

Our third tool is the Syriac and Arabic versions of the Gospels. This additional avenue of insight into the parables will now be examined.

The Significance of the Oriental Versions for Exegesis

Oriental versions have been used for purposes of textual criticism but rarely for exegesis. It is now readily recognized that translation is inevitably interpretation. For example, anyone who translates the parable of the Unjust Steward into Arabic or Syriac must decide what word he is going to use for οἰκονόμος. There is no word in either language with the same range of ambiguity found in the Greek word. The translator *must* decide whether in his opinion the οἰκονόμος is an estate manager or a moneylender. He has to make this exegetical decision in order to translate. The decision is crucial because the entire direction of one's understanding of the parable turns on the answer given to this initial question. The translator of an Arabic or Syriac version gives his answer to this exegetical question as he translates. A second- or third-century Syriac translator will inevitably reflect in his translation his understanding of the culture that informs the text. The crucial point is that he lived in an ancient Eastern world that surely had a culture nearly identical to the culture of the parables themselves. Thus, when asking the *cultural* question, especially the older Oriental versions offer crucial raw data for exegesis.

For this study we have selected a series of eighteen Arabic and Syriac versions. The selection has been made on the basis of three factors: time, geography, and type. In regard to time, the texts selected stretch from the second to the twentieth centuries. Early versions have been given preference, but medieval and modern translations by Eastern scholars have not been ignored. The geographic origin of each text, as far as is known, has been considered in the selection. Egypt,

---

[20]A brief description of these friends and consultants is given in Appendix B.

Mount Sinai, Lebanon, Syria, Iraq, and Edessa are all represented. By "type" we refer to the fact that "church translations" have been balanced with versions produced by known Arabic and Syriac scholars, such as Hibat Allah Abu al-Faḍl Ibn al-'Assāl, the great exegete of Cairo in the thirteenth century, and the eleventh-century prince of Arab exegetes Abu al-Faraj 'Abd Allah Ibn al-Ṭayyib of Baghdad. Appendix A lists the versions selected and gives a brief description of each. Space does not permit the inclusion of all the evidence gleaned from these versions. Over a thousand texts in Arabic and Syriac were read with care, and where they are significant for an understanding of the culture of the parables here discussed this will appear in the notes.

In summary, the proposed method is to discuss the culturally oriented questions that arise from the text with as wide a sampling of carefully selected Middle Eastern Christians as possible. Major Arabic and Syriac versions will be examined minutely to see how Oriental churchmen have understood the text. With insights from these two sources in mind, pertinent ancient literature will be examined for further comparison. These three sources will be applied to the text along with the standard tools of contemporary scholarship.

The lingering question remains and will always remain: How can we be sure the Middle Eastern peasant has not changed his culture and attitudes across the intervening centuries? In answer to this, it must be said emphatically that the insight gained from the contemporary peasant must *always* be rejected if we have a more ancient or in any way more authentic alternative. If we do not have such an alternative, then the options are either to accept the cultural world view of the medieval Middle Eastern peasant (compared with ancient versions and literature), or to fall back on one of the rejected alternatives set forth above.[21] Any commentator who moves through any parable inevitably makes a series of culturally influenced judgments; the question is not, Shall we interpret, making cultural judgments as we go along, or shall we not? Rather it is, *Whose* culture shall we allow to inform the text for us?[22]

A final methodological concern is to establish an exegetical stance in respect to Jülicher's insistence that each parable has only one point. This question will now be examined.

DISCERNING THE THEOLOGICAL CLUSTER

In this section we shall attempt to show that a parable has three basic elements. First, the parable has one or more points of contact (referents) within the real world

---

[21]Above, pp. 28–29.

[22]At times I feel like a visitor who approaches a woodcarver at his bench. The carver is working away with a slightly dull chisel. The visitor pulls out a sharper chisel from his pocket and suggests, "Sir, I think this might be a better tool for the piece of work you are doing." The carpenter does not miss a stroke or look up but replies, "On what basis (tap, tap) do you think it is legitimate (tap, tap) to introduce (tap, tap) the use of chisels (tap, tap)?"

of the listener, which can be called "symbols." The second element in a parable is the "response" that the original listener is pressed to make to the original telling of the story. The third element is a combination of theological motifs in the parable that together pressed the original listener to make that response. This combination we choose to call the "theological cluster." Thus, one or more symbols with corresponding referents in the life of the listener impel him to make a single response which has in view a cluster of theological motifs.

Initially it must be said that any attempt to state in propositional terms a tightly constructed interlocking system of interpretative principles, which can be applied uniformly to all the parables of Jesus, is doomed to failure. The parables are artistically told stories that break the boundaries of all rationalistic systems.[23] The best that can be done is to outline a stance vis-à-vis the parables that will free them to challenge the reader to respond in terms of repentance, faith, and discipleship.

Any attempt to outline such a stance from which to view the parables must begin with Jülicher's struggle with the allegorical method. Allegory treated the parables as cryptograms that must be decoded. This evaluation of the parables Jülicher demonstrated to be utterly false.[24] He was anxious to establish and strictly maintain the unity of each parable. Each parable, therefore, could have only one point of comparison, one tertium comparationis, which Jülicher decided was some general ethical principle.

The direction of the argument is clear. Each parable has unity. That unity requires a single point of comparison; this in turn means that it carries a single significant thought. This line of reasoning must be carefully examined.

What then is meant by a point of comparison? At this juncture the discussion is greatly complicated by a confusion in terminology. Linnemann writes,

> Parables are meant to be forms of argument. It is for this reason that they have only one point of comparison. One can hardly argue several things at once. For this reason we must carefully distinguish between what a parable is arguing and what it assumes. As soon as we draw from a parable a number of different significant ideas, we can be sure that we are missing the meaning that the parable had for its first narrator.[25]

---

[23]We have accepted Jeremias' judgment where he writes, "A distinction was drawn between metaphor, simile, parable, similitude, allegory, illustration, and so forth—a fruitless labour in the end, since the Hebrew mašal and the Aramaic mathla embraced all these categories and many more without distinction. This word may mean in the common speech of post-biblical Judaism, without resorting to a formal classification, figurative forms of speech of every kind: parable, similitude, allegory, fable, proverb, apocalyptic revelation, riddle, symbol, pseudonym, fictitious person, example, theme, argument, apology, refutation, jest" (Jeremias, Parables, 20). Manson writes, "A parable is a literary creation in narrative form designed either to portray a type of character for warning or example or to embody a principle of God's governance of the world and men. It may partake of both natures" (Teaching, 65).

[24]Jülicher, Gleichnisreden, I, 118–148.

[25]Linnemann, Parables, 23.

From this quotation it is clear that "point of comparison" for Linnemann means "significant idea." Cadoux calls this point of comparison a "point of contact" and understands it quite differently. He writes,

> Allegory, being merely representative, touches that which it represents at many points, while the parable's essential function is to evoke a judgment in one field and secure its application in another; it does not therefore follow that there is only one point of contact between the story of the parable and the other field to which we carry the judgment evoked by the story. Indeed, it is comparatively seldom that it is so. The judgment elicited by the story is generally a judgment upon a more or less complex situation, and there is always a certain contact between the people and things of this situation and those of the situation to which the judgment is carried. In Nathan's parable there is obviously a certain connection between the rich man and David, the poor man and Uriah, the ewe-lamb and Bathsheba. And further than this, so long as the story of the parable is not unnaturally shaped into similarity with the features of the field to which it is applied, so long as the points of similarity grow naturally from the story, they may be multiplied with advantage, for then they assist the passage of judgment from the one field to the other.[26]

Cadoux is talking about the *referents* in the life of the listener that correspond to the different symbols in the parable.

On the surface, these two authors sound somewhat contradictory. One calls for a single point of contact, the other for many. Actually, they are discussing different aspects of the parable. For Linnemann the parable is a form of argumentation. She says, "One can hardly argue several things at once." For Cadoux the parable evokes a single judgment. To do so it may need a number of points of contact with reality outside the parable. Thus it *may* be possible to combine Cadoux and Linnemann by saying that a parable usually has a number of symbols which contribute to a single argument.

There is also a divergence between these two authors. Where Cadoux says that a parable is intended to "evoke a judgment," Linnemann holds that a parable is a "form of argument." Linnemann seems to be concentrating on the author of the parable, whom she understands to be arguing a point. Her concept calls for logic, intellectualization, and conceptualization. The debater wants to make his point and convince you intellectually that he is right. Cadoux's phrase, "evoke a judgment," focuses on a more kerygmatic note of an interaction between the author of the parable and the hearer who is expected to respond. Cadoux's focus on judgment seems more appropriate to the nature of parables; yet we prefer the word "response." The purpose of a parable perhaps is best understood as intending to "evoke a response" from the listener.

Furthermore, Cadoux's observation that a parable may have a number of points of similarity between the world of the parable and the real world of the listener is well taken. Once the interpreter has shaken himself loose from the stance

---

[26]Cadoux, *Parables*, 50f.

that sees the parable as a secret cryptogram, with a code that must be broken, then more than one symbol in the parable pointing to more than one referent in the life of the listener can be admitted with no danger to the unity of the parable. Nathan's parable[27] has three symbols which aid the teller in pressing David to make a single decision. These three symbols have corresponding referents from the real situation that called forth the telling of the parable. Their identification is obvious. However, the interpreter must not treat such identifications as the beginning of a road along which he is expected to travel and then proceed to find referents for all the elements in the parable. The exegete must look for referents only for the elements that the original listeners would have identified. These symbolic elements must contribute to the unity of the parable found in the single response the listener is challenged to make.[28]

Before proceeding we must examine and define "response" as used in this discussion of parables. Dodd writes, "The way to an interpretation of a parable lies through a judgment on the imagined situation, and not through the decoding of the various elements in the story."[29] Thus Dodd, like Cadoux, sees a parable as calling for a "judgment" on the part of the listener. This we prefer to define as a "response." What then is this response? In answer to this question Manson's definition of "parable" is helpful. He says,

> A parable is a picture in words of some piece of human experience, actual or imagined. As such it is a work of art. Further, this picture portrays either an ethical type for our admiration or reprobation, or some principle of the rule of God in the world, or it does both things at once. . . . In actual working, then, every true parable is a call to a better life and a deeper trust in God, which things are but the Godward and manward sides of a true religion, the obverse and reverse of the one medal.[30]

In our understanding of the matter, the response the listener to a parable is called upon to make covers both aspects of a parable as defined by Manson. Depending on the nature of the parable, the response of the listener may be a decision to act in a particular way or to accept a new understanding of the nature of God's way with men in the world. This latter type of response will most likely also lead the listener to act in a particular way toward his fellow man. Some parables, as Manson has indicated, involve both. Thus the line between "a new understanding of the 'rule of God in the world' " and a "decision to act in a particular fashion" is usually blurred. Manson says a parable issues "a call to a better life and a deeper trust in God." The listener's response involves hearing one or both of these calls depend-

---

[27]It is possible to make a distinction between a parable and an example story. But it is clear that the Hebrew *Mashal* and Aramaic *Mathla* covered both types of stories.

[28]Recent studies have argued that parables do have allegorical elements in them. Matthew Black, "The Parables as Allegory," *BJRL* 42 (1960), 273–287; Raymond E. Brown, "Parable and Allegory Reconsidered," *Novum Testamentum* 5 (1962), 36–45. Symbolism is probably more accurate than allegory.

[29]Dodd, *Parables*, 21.

[30]Manson, *Teaching*, 80f.

ing on the parable. This brings us to the third aspect of the parable, namely, the theological cluster.

The response invoked by the telling of the parable is informed by, or composed of, a cluster of theological themes that can be analyzed and discussed separately. Sometimes the theological themes are implied directly in what is said in the parable, sometimes they are presupposed. David hears Nathan's parable and makes the single response, "I am a sinner." At the same time, the awareness that he and Uriah are brothers under one covenant is a part of that response; so is the awareness of the holiness of God, who expects righteousness from his anointed king.[31] These different theological themes *together,* through the artistry of the parable, press the king to make his single response. The unity of the parable is to be found in that single response.

The three aspects of the parable are now clear. The parable may have a number of symbols with corresponding referents in the life of the listener. The parable calls for a single response that is usually informed by a cluster of theological themes.

With the awareness that diagrams tend to oversimplify, these three aspects of each parable may be diagrammed as follows:

I. The telling of the parable

II. The listener's response

III. Reflection on the ground and content of that response

A story is told from life that has one or more referents in reality which press the listener to make a single response which is informed by a cluster of inter-related theological themes.

Thus, the Pharisee, listening to the telling of the parable of the Prodigal Son, is pressed by a multiplicity of referents to make a single response to be reconciled to his "family" (which included the father and the brother). At the same time it is possible to discern a cluster of theological motifs that inform this single response.[32] In this vein, Hunter says,

---

[31] Any ancient king who assumed himself to be above the laws of his kingdom, and therefore not bound by them, would not have come to David's conclusion in similar circumstances.

[32] C. W. F. Smith writes, "It will be observed that many of the details are so apt that, once the central point is grasped, many applications may be made and deductions drawn" (*Parables*, 113; cf. also Cadoux, 50f.). Jones states, "To insist that there shall be one point and one point only, and that a

> ... In the parable there is one chief point of likeness between the story and the meaning, and the details simply help to make the story realistic and so serve the central thrust of the parable—like the feathers which wing the arrow.[33]

While it is not clear what Hunter intends with the word "meaning," his illustration is worth considering. An arrow is a single unit. But it is composed of shaft, head, and feathers. The three elements combine to form an effective missile for the bow. The feathers are not to be dismissed as an unnecessary secondary decoration. All three are essential to the nature and effectiveness of an arrow.

Thus the call for a single response does not necessarily mean a single significant idea. In a parable we find a group of interlocking themes—the "theological cluster." Different aspects of a given parable symbolize different yet *interrelated* theological themes. These combine to press for a single response.

Dodd insists that the details of a parable do not have independent significance.[34] To this we can agree. Yet the details have dependent significance, that is, they have meaning in a dependent relation to the other elements in the parable.

To approach it from another angle, Manson has written of the parables:

> ... Illustrations will not be parables in the sense that the parables of the New Testament are parables. They [illustrations] are merely the embellishment of something else, namely the chain of logical reasoning; they are the sugar-coating on the theological pill. The true parable, on the other hand, is not an illustration to help one through a theological discussion; it is rather a mode of religious experience. It belongs to the same order of things as altar and sacrifice, prayer, the prophetic vision, and the like. It is a *datum* for theology, not a by-product. It is a way in which religious faith is attained and, so far as it can be, transmitted from one person to another. It is not a crutch for limping intellects, but a spur to religious insight: its object is not to provide simple theological instruction, but to produce living religious faith.[35]

If we can accept Manson's definition of a parable as *datum* for theology, the question must be raised, Are single theological themes in the New Testament ever discussed in isolation? They may be on relatively rare occasions. Certainly such isolation is not the rule. A certain type of philosophically oriented mind is able with some effort to isolate a single theme and discuss it in depth. But in the New Testament it is much more common to find theological themes discussed in clusters. Who is to say that John 3:16 discusses only "love" or "the world" or "believing" or "perishing" or "eternal life"? This does not mean that there is no unity in this verse, but it does signify that the unity is found in a theological cluster of concepts.

In the case of the parable of the Sower, the listener is called to "hear the word of the kingdom and bear fruit." This decision to hear and bear fruit is based

---

parable shall be understood only as a whole, and not in relation to its part (which is supposed to turn it into an allegory), is pure dogmatism" (*Art*, 140).

[33]A. M. Hunter, *Interpreting the Parables* (London: SCM, 1964), 10.

[34]Dodd, *Parables*, 18.

[35]Manson, *Teaching*, 73.

on and informed by a cluster of theological motifs. Among these are:

1. The kingdom is like a seed growing slowly; it is not an apocalyptic revolutionary disruption.

2. The parable speaks of grace. The sower sows liberally even in potentially unfruitful ground.

3. Fruit-bearing is an essential mark of the kingdom.

4. The parable offers the listener hope. There is assurance of a harvest in spite of difficulties.

These theological motifs are to be understood only in tension with each other within the unity of the parable,[36] which is centered in the *call to hear the word of the kingdom and bear fruit*. Such an understanding does not allow for identifying the thorns with the Jewish leaders, and the good soil with the Church. A cluster of motifs forms the ground and content of a single response.

In summary, a parable is not an illustration but is a mode of theological speech used to evoke a response. The parable may have a number of referents in the life of the listener to whom it is addressed. The listener is challenged by the telling of the parable to respond. This response is informed by a cluster of theological motifs.

SUMMARY AND CONCLUSIONS

Knowledge of the culture that informs the text of Gospel parables is crucial to a full understanding of them. The impact of such cultural elements has, in the past, been discerned only partially. Significant elements of the cultural setting of the synoptic parables can be delineated more precisely through discussion with contemporary peasants, through minute examination of Oriental versions of the Gospels, and by a careful study of pertinent ancient literature. These three tools must be used in addition to the standard critical tools of scholarship. The present study seeks to combine the use of these four tools, conjoining them with an analysis of various literary structures used in parables. To this matter of literary structure we now turn.

---

[36]Via argues that the one-point approach is "artificially restrictive." Of this approach he writes, "Important elements in the parable may be overlooked and the meaning of the parable attenuated" (*Parables*, 3). Jones affirms that exemplary stories "can be invoked to illustrate several things" (*Art*, 118); cf. also Manson, *Teaching*, 80; Jeremias, *Parables*, 131; M. Dibelius, *From Tradition to Gospel*, trans. B. L. Woolf (New York: Scribner, 1935), 249, 253.

Chapter 3

METHODOLOGY (2): FOUR TYPES OF LITERARY STRUCTURES IN THE NEW TESTAMENT AND THEIR SIGNIFICANCE FOR THE INTERPRETATION OF PARABLES

In a recent address to the Society of Biblical Literature James Muilenburg called for a move beyond form criticism to "rhetorical criticism." He said that his primary interest was:

> ... in exhibiting the structural patterns that are employed for the fashioning of a literary unit, whether in poetry or in prose, and in discerning the many and various devices by which the predictions are formulated and ordered into a unified whole. Such an enterprise I should describe as rhetoric and the methodology as rhetorical criticism.[1]

The intentions of this chapter are in harmony with Muilenburg's interests. Since the above address the entire topic of literary analysis in biblical and non-biblical literature among linguists and biblical scholars has mushroomed enormously to the extent that even the subject of "literary structures (rhetorical criticism) in the New Testament" is a full study in itself (cf. Bibliography, section F). Here we are interested in this field as it affects the interpretation of the parables. We will attempt to (1) review briefly the history of interest in literary structures in biblical literature, (2) define our terms, (3) outline four types of literary structures in biblical literature, and finally (4) conclude some working principles for the passages under consideration.

---

[1]James Muilenburg, "Form Criticism and Beyond," *LBJ* 88 (1969), 8. Martin Kessler in a recent article has emphasized the new mood among a growing number of biblical scholars who insist on the artistic integrity of a literary product. This "new criticism" has been called in Germany *Werkinterpretation,* and it is "exemplified by . . . the insistence on the formal integrity of the literary piece, the *Kunstwerk.*" Cf. Martin Kessler, "New Directions in Biblical Exegesis," *Scottish Journal of Theology* 24 (1971), 320. This chapter and indeed the entire study can be seen as being in line with this new attempt to appreciate the finished literary product, the *Kunstwerk.* Morris S. Seale in a significant recent book, *The Desert Bible, Nomadic Tribal Culture and Old Testament Interpretation* (London: Weidenfeld and Nicolson, 1974), speaks of the text of the Bible and of his refusal "to carve it up, to catalogue it or to otherwise 'atomize' it" (p. 2). Furthermore this chapter is written with an awareness of the work of Leach, Levi-Strauss, Barthes, Beauchamp and other structuralists. We are not concerned here with structuralism or semiology as ideologies but with *literary* structure as outlined by Muilenburg above.

A REVIEW OF PAST SCHOLARSHIP ON THE QUESTION OF LITERARY STRUCTURES

In the eighteenth century, J. A. Bengel made brief reference to the presence of *chiasmus* in a number of passages in the New Testament.[2] His illustrations were within the proper definition of *chiasmus*, that of two lines of poetry with the second line reversing the order of the first, and thus creating an ABBA pattern.

In the early nineteenth century John Jebb wrote about certain biblical passages:

> There are stanzas so constructed that, whatever be the number of lines, the first line shall be parallel with the last; the second with the penultimate; and so throughout, in an order that looks inward, or, to borrow a military phrase, from flanks to centre. This may be called introverted parallelism.[3]

Thomas Boys of the same period looked for literary structures in the Psalms.[4] John Forbes in 1854 advanced the work of Jebb.[5] Late in the nineteenth century, William Milligan of Scotland observed structure in some passages in the Apocalypse.[6] E. W. Bullinger in the same period overworked his schemes so irresponsibly as to discredit more than to advance an interest in literary structures in biblical literature.[7] In 1925 C. F. Burney's monograph, *The Poetry of Our Lord*, was published, and it remains a major reference work in the field.[8] Burney concentrated on parallelism, accentual rhythm, and rhyme. At times he left out sections of a verse to achieve his rhythm. He can also be faulted on other specifics. Yet his work remains basic to all further discussion.

In the thirties, the subject of literary analysis in the New Testament was touched on briefly by Bultmann, Manson, Goguel, Streeter, and Taylor.[9] Of this group Manson wrote regarding the synoptic material attributed to Jesus,

---

[2]Bengel, *Gnomon*, *passim*.

[3]John Jebb, *Sacred Literature* (London: n.p., 1820), 53.

[4]Thomas Boys, *Key to the Book of Psalms* (London: n.p., 1825).

[5]John Forbes, *The Symmetrical Structure of Scripture* (Edinburgh: T. & T. Clark, 1854).

[6]William Milligan, *Discussions on the Apocalypse* (London: n.p., 1893), *passim*.

[7]E. W. Bullinger, *Figures of Speech used in the Bible* (London: Eyre and Spottiswoode, 1898); *idem*, *Key to the Psalms* (London: Eyre and Spottiswoode, 1890); *The Companion Bible* (Oxford: University Press, 1948 [1913]).

[8]Burney, *Poetry*. During the same period Cladder, Schmidt, and Loisy tried to demonstrate that the New Testament is Greek poetry and should be divided into *stichoi*. Their views were almost universally rejected by later scholarship. Cf. Hermann J. Cladder, *Zur Literaturgeschichte der Evangelien* in *Unsere Evangelien. Akademische Vorträge* (Freiburg: Herder, 1919), I; Alfred F. Loisy, *L'Evangile selon Luc* (Paris: Nourry, 1924); P. Schmidt, *Der Strophische Ausbau des Gesamttextes der Evangelien* (1921). An excellent review of the work of these men is found in Lucetta M. Mowry, "Poetry in the Synoptic Gospels and Revelation, a Study of Methods and Materials" (unpublished Ph.D. thesis, Yale University, 1946), 4. Mowry lists the Schmidt volume in her bibliography. I have not been able to locate the book or any reference to it outside of her thesis.

[9]Bultmann, *History*, 70; T. W. Manson, *Teaching*, 50–56; Maurice Goguel, *The Life of Jesus*, trans. Olive Wyon (New York: Macmillan, 1945), 296–303; B. H. Streeter, "Poems of Jesus," *The Hibbert Journal* 32 (1933/34), 9–16; V. Taylor, *Formation of the Gospel Tradition* (London: Macmillan, 1935), 88–100.

A still greater extension of the phenomenon of parallelism, and one which has not so far as I am aware been noticed as such, is to be found in the words of Jesus. Here the parallelism covers not single clauses containing each one simple idea, but still larger aggregates each of which contains many clauses.[10]

Manson concludes his discussion by saying, "Perhaps we should regard this strophic parallelism as the most distinctive characteristic of his poetry and his special contribution to the forms of poetry in general."[11]

In the forties, three authors are worthy of brief note. Olmstead, an Aramaic scholar and historian, tried to provide an English translation of the Dominical sayings, keeping in mind the Aramaic he assumed to lie behind them. He was not specifically interested in literary form, but printed lines in poetic format when he determined that the saying had poetic structure.[12]

Mowry's Yale thesis seems to be the only dissertation ever written in this country on the topic of New Testament poetry.[13] She rather arbitrarily accepts the category of accentual rhythm as essential for determining what shall be called poetry. She concludes that there are twenty poetical sayings in the synoptic Gospels. These she divides into three categories: the gnome of the wise man, the oracle of the prophet, and the psalm.[14] Mowry feels that she has determined the absolute minimum for synoptic poetry. Yet, granting her methodological principle that a couplet must have accentual rhythm to be poetry, two of her twenty pieces of poetry must be struck and her "absolute minimum" reduced to eighteen. In two cases she has indicated a stress for the verb "to be" in the present tense.[15] At the same time she insists that "retrovertability" into Aramaic is a necessary quality for a couplet to be called Dominical poetry.[16] Nonetheless, in spite of her undefended arbitrary selection of meter as determinative of what sections of the New Testament are poetry, and her putting stresses on nonexisting words, her work is useful. In a number of synoptic passages she does substantiate both parallelism and rhythmic meter.

The third author of the forties is N. W. Lund,[17] whose 428-page book produced varied reviews. McGinley was quite favorable and felt that Lund had demonstrated his point "beyond cavil."[18] H. J. Cadbury of Harvard was critical yet positive. In his opinion, Lund had rather badly overworked some of his

---

[10]Manson, *Teaching*, 54.

[11]*Ibid.*, 56. This last statement no longer stands, as a result of the discovery of the same "strophic parallelism" in the Old Testament and in Qumran, as we shall see.

[12]A. T. Olmstead, *Jesus in the Light of History* (New York: Scribner, 1942), *passim*.

[13]A DIATREX computer printout at University Microfilms, Ann Arbor, Michigan, in January, 1972, produced *no* references.

[14]Mowry, *op. cit.*, 144–235. She finds seventeen illustrations of the first category, two of the second, and one of the third.

[15]*Ibid.*, 144, 156.

[16]*Ibid.*, 133.

[17]Lund, *Chiasmus*.

[18]Laurence J. McGinley, review of Lund, *Chiasmus*, in *Theological Studies* 13 (1942), 452–54.

material but "some of the evidence is inescapable."[19] T. W. Manson has the longest review, in which he also is positive, yet sharply critical. He concludes by saying, "While it must be said that Mr. Lund has overdriven his thesis in many directions, it must still be admitted that he has a thesis. There are clear cases of the kind of arrangement he describes."[20]

Jeremias has an extended essay on chiasm.[21] Regarding it, Miesner observes,

> Jeremias (p. 152) praised Lund's work in the Old Testament as "eine Reihe guter und überzeugender Belege für Chiasmus am A T." Yet, elsewhere (p. 145) he strangely described Lund's work of over 25 years as "völlig unbrauchbar."[22]

Having worked with Lund's book for a number of years, I find T. W. Manson and H. J. Cadbury the most accurate and useful evaluations. Lund has certainly pushed his scheme too far. As Cadbury has rightly suggested, each piece of evidence must be examined on its own merits and neither rejected nor accepted *a priori*. There is no doubt that Lund broke some significant new ground in the analysis of literary structures.

For over twenty years little was done. Then in 1965 John Bligh reopened the discussion with a book on Galatians[23] in which he organizes the entire book of Galatians into interlocking structured literary forms. Now in the seventies many scholars in different fields are taking literary analysis seriously.[24]

Thus there has been a small but relatively steady stream of scholars who have worked in this area variously called chiasm or literary analysis or New Testament poetry or rhetorical criticism. Much is yet to be done. Before we can proceed to our own analysis a few terms must be defined.

A DEFINITION OF TERMS

In the absence of uniformity of vocabulary, we will define our own terms. The categories of synonymous, antithetical, and synthetic parallelisms are established and will be used on occasion. Then when parallel lines follow each other in an AA' BB' CC' DD' pattern they will be called *standard parallelism*. This form of parallelism is common to the Old Testament and is well known in the Psalms and

---

[19]H. J. Cadbury, review of Lund, *Chiasmus,* in *Journal of Religion* 23 (1943), 62f.

[20]Manson, review of Lund, *Chiasmus,* in *JTS* 45 (1944), 85.

[21]Joachim Jeremias, "Chiasmus in den Paulusbriefen," *ZNW* 49 (1958), 145–156.

[22]Miesner, *Chiasm and Paul,* 42, n. 73.

[23]John Bligh, *Galatians in Greek, A Structural Analysis of St. Paul's Epistle to the Galatians* (Detroit: University of Detroit Press, 1966).

[24]Bibliography section F. Also Miesner's bibliography, *Chiasm and Paul,* 360–65. Matthew Black's important work, *Aramaic Approach,* concentrates on two-line parallelism, alliteration, assonance, and paronomasia. He does not discuss the question of literary structure.

the Prophets.[25] It is found also in the New Testament. A clear example is in Luke 21:23–24, which is as follows:

> A   Alas for those who are with child
> A′   and for those who give suck in those days
>
> B   For great distress shall be upon the earth
> B′   and wrath upon this people
>
> C   They will fall by the edge of the sword
> C′   and be led captive among all nations.

When parallel lines are in an A B C–A′ B′ C′ pattern they will be called *step parallelism*. A clear example of this type which falls within this study is Luke 11:9–10, as follows:

> A   Ask, and it will be given you
> B   Seek, and you will find
> C   Knock, and it will be opened to you.
>
> A′   For every one who asks receives
> B′   And he who seeks finds
> C′   And to him who knocks it will be opened.

When the parallel lines are inverted in an A B C D–D′ C′ B′ A′ structure the pattern will be called *inverted parallelism*. This pattern can be seen clearly in Amos 5:4b–6a:

> 1   *Seek-me and-live*
> 2   and do-not-seek *Bethel*
> 3   and-*Gilgal* do-not-enter
> 4   and to-*Beer-sheba* do-not-cross-over.
> 3′   because *Gilgal* an exile shall-be exiled
> 2′   and-*Bethel* shall-come to-nothing
> 1′   *Seek Yahweh and-live.*[26]

As this field of study expands there is the need for increasing precision in vocabulary. Often the word *chiasm* is used loosely to refer to all types of literary structures, particularly those with some inversion of themes. This word properly refers to two lines where the themes are reversed in the second, such as Mark 2:27:

---

[25]It must be noted emphatically that this brief discussion is incomplete. Any well-written piece of literature has a series of interlocking correspondences that together form the artistry of the piece. We are presupposing the literary tradition of the Old Testament. The trained eye will note other patterns of correspondence that we do not discuss. We observe all through this chapter the literary pattern that appears to us to be dominant. The criterion for that dominance is the strength of the correspondences.

[26]The words connected with dashes indicate that the words so connected represent one word in the original Hebrew. In each case we shall present the structured material on the page in the above forms to aid the eye in identifying the lines that are parallel.

This particular stanza has the main point at the beginning and the end, not the middle. In the New Testament we have observed the climax more often in the center. Yet each pericope must be examined on its own ground.

```
        A                    B
The sabbath was made for man,
        B            A
not man for the sabbath.
```

If one were to draw a line connecting the A's and the B's the lines would form an X, which is the Greek letter *Chi,* hence *chiasmus.* This is often shortened to *chiasm.* We shall preserve this precise technical term for simple A B B A patterns of various types.

Extended inversions are used in so many different ways that some term is needed to cover all of them. We prefer to speak of the *Inversion Principle.* The wide application of its use will become evident as we proceed. It is possible to try to make subtle distinctions between "poetry," "heightened prose," "rhetorical prose," "nonpoetic parallelism," and the like. Obviously, "poetry" is what a given people using the word in a certain culture understand as poetry. The structures we intend to examine can be called *patterned semantic relationships.* They are at least this. Some of the material we shall examine has long been identified as poetry, some not. The material to be analyzed can be understood to fall into four basic *types,* some of which are clearly prose, others are perhaps better understood as poetry. It is to these four types that we now turn.

FOUR TYPES OF LITERARY STRUCTURES IN THE NEW TESTAMENT

Briefly stated these four are as follows:

a. Longer or shorter sections of prose that use the inversion principle for an outline.

b. Poetic sections that use a variety of parallelistic devices in a variety of forms (we have identified seven).

c. Sections that have a tight parallelism in the center but are encased with one or more sets of matching sections of prose.

d. The parables in Luke usually follow a *Parabolic Ballad* form that is distinct from the above.

Part of the complexity of this subject is because the above four are not used in isolation from one another. An author may mix his literary types and may well have done so unconsciously. Here we can only attempt a preliminary analysis with the full knowledge that much is yet to be done before these types and forms are fully understood in the New Testament. To the first of these types we now turn.

TYPE A–Prose Sections That Use Inversion as an Overall Outline

This type is perhaps the most common, and the most universal.[27] But not only in

---

[27]Miesner has fully documented the use of literary structure in classical Greek and Latin literature. Cf.

the ancient world was the inversion principle at work. Two young men today carry out the following conversation:

> *The Dialog*
>
> A   Are you coming to the party?
> B   Can I bring a friend?
> A   Boy or girl?
> B   What difference does it make?
> A   It is a matter of balance.
> B   Girl.
> A   O.K.
> B   I'll be there.[28]

> *The Dialog with*
> *the Inversion Showing*
>
> A   Are you coming to the party?
>   B   Can I bring a friend?
>   C   Boy or girl?
>   D   What difference does it make?
>   D′   It is a matter of balance.
>   C′   Girl.
>   B′   O.K.
> A′   I'll be there.

Unknown to either young man, they asked four questions and then answered them in an inverted fashion. The literary structure of the discourse is A B C D—D′ C′ B′ A′. A fascinating number of such illustrations have come to my attention and demonstrate that the use of the inversion principle is relatively universal and often subconscious. Thus as we find these in biblical literature the question must always be asked whether the inversion is deliberate. The question is of some significance. When a biblical author is using the inversion principle deliberately he often places the climax in the center. Usually he reinforces this climax by relating it specifically to the beginning and end of the structure. Usually there is a "point of turning" just past the center of the structure. The second half is not redundant. Rather it introduces some crucial new element that resolves or completes the first half. When the inversion principle is used with conscious precision most, if not all, of these elements appear and are crucial for a proper interpretation of the passage. In the little conversation given above, speaker A wants to know if his friend is

---

Chiasm and Paul, 60–69. Worthy of special note are George E. Duckworth, *Structural Patterns and Proportions in Vergil's Aeneid: A Study in Mathematical Composition* (Ann Arbor: University of Michigan Press, 1962); R. B. Steele, "Chiasmus in the Epistles of Cicero, Seneca, Pliny and Fronto," *Studies in Honor of Basil L. Gildersleeve* (Baltimore: Johns Hopkins Press, 1902), 339–352; C. H. Whitman, *Homer and the Heroic Tradition* (Cambridge, Mass.: Harvard University Press, 1958). [28]E. A. Schegloff, "Notes on a Conversational Practice," *Studies in Social Interaction*, ed. D. Sudnow (New York: The Free Press, 1972), 78f.

coming, thus the beginning and the end are crucial for him. But speaker B is trying to communicate, "If I can bring my girlfriend, I'll come." The center of the structure is secondary for both speakers. However, in cases we shall examine, the specific features listed above will be seen prominently. What then of biblical literature?

In Daniel we can observe a clear case of our Type A—a prose inversion. The major features that repeat are as follows:

Daniel 3:13–30

The king in anger commands that SMA[29] be brought in

Serve my God or you will be punished
Who is the God who will deliver you

The God we serve will deliver us from the king
We will not serve or worship the golden image

The fire is heated seven times

The king orders SMA bound and cast into the fire
SMA are bound and cast into the fire

the king asks about three men bound in the fire

the king sees four men loose in the fire
one like a son of man

The king orders SMA to come out
SMA come out

The fire did not touch them

The God of SMA delivered his servants from the king
They did not serve or worship any God except God

Speak against the God of SMA and you will be punished
There is no other god who can deliver in this way

The king promotes SMA in Babylon.

The use of the inversion principle is clear. The material seems to be straightforward prose. The climax is obviously the center.[30]

Barbara Thiering has observed this use of the inversion principle in the *Hodayoth* of Qumran. A clear example is in 9:29b–36b. Its structure is:

---

[29]SMA is an abbreviation for Shadrach, Meshak, and Abednego. It may be significant that there are precisely twelve full repetitions of the three names.

[30]The inversion principle has been found by Stephen Bertram to have been used in the construction of the entire book of Ruth. Cf. Stephen Bertram, "Symmetrical Design in the Book of Ruth," *JBL* 84 (1965), 165–68. A significant number of other OT passages using the inversion principle have been brought to my attention; some of the studies are as yet unpublished. In Tertullian the inversion principle has been discovered to cover entire books. Cf. R. D. Sider, "On Symmetrical Composition in Tertullian," *JTS* 24 (1973), 403–423.

Because thou hast known me from my father
and from the womb (   )[31]
(   ) my mother thou hast dealt kindly with me
from the breasts of the one conceiving me are thy mercies
and from the lap of the one rearing me (   )

And from my youth thou hast illuminated me
with the wisdom of thy judgments

and with certain truth thou hast upheld me
and with thy holy spirit thou hast delighted me
and (   ) till this day
and the rebuke of thy righteousness with (   )
and thy guiding peace delivers my soul
and with my steps the abundance of forgiveness
and infinite mercy with thy judgments of me

and until I am old
thou takest care of me

for my father knew me not
and my mother to thee abandoned me
for thou art a father to all the sons of thy youth
and thou rejoicest in them as the one who conceives loves her babe
and as a foster father in the lap thou carest for all thy creatures.[32]

In this translation we have followed Thiering's format. However, the first and the last stanzas are in almost perfectly balanced step parallelism. The first has:

my father
the womb
my mother
the one conceiving
the lap.

The last has:

my father
my mother
a father
the one conceiving
the lap.

Moving to the New Testament, a clear case of Type A is Luke 18:18–30:

1   A certain ruler asked him,
"Good teacher, what having done I shall inherit *eternal life*?"   ETERNAL LIFE

2   And Jesus said to him,
"Why do you call me good?
No one is good but one, even God.

---

[31]These blank spaces are meant to indicate lacunas in the text.
[32]Barbara Thiering, "The Poetic Forms of the Hodayoth," *JSS* 8 (1963), 191; my translation.

You know the commandments:

Do not commit adultery	7	(loyalty to family)
Do not kill	6	
Do not steal	8	(property)
Do not bear false witness	9	
Honor your father and mother."	5	(loyalty to parents)

THE
OLD OBEDIENCE
—fulfilled

And he said,
"All these I have observed from my youth."

3 And hearing Jesus said to him,
 "One thing you still lack.
 Sell everything you have
 and distribute to the poor
 and you will have treasure in heaven
 and come and follow me."

THE NEW OBEDIENCE
—demanded (the ruler)

 4 And hearing this
  he became deeply grieved
  for he was very rich.

NEW OBEDIENCE
—too hard

  5 And seeing him Jesus said,
   "How hard it is
    for those who have possessions
     to *enter the kingdom of God.*
   It is easier for a camel to go through a needle's eye
    than for a rich man
     to *enter the kingdom of God.*"

ENTER THE
KINGDOM

 4' And those who heard said,
  "And who is able to be saved?"
  But he said, "What is impossible with men
   is possible with God."

NEW OBEDIENCE
—too hard
—possible only
 with God

 3' And Peter said,
  "Lo, we have *left everything we possess*
   and *followed you.*"

THE NEW OBEDIENCE
—fulfilled (disciples)

2' And he said to them,
 "Truly I say to you
 there is no one who has left

house	(property)
or wife	(loyalty to family)
or brothers	(loyalty to family)
or parents	(loyalty to parents)
or children	(loyalty to family)

 for the sake of the kingdom

NEW OBEDIENCE
—fulfilled (any man)

1' who will not receive much more in this time
 and in the age to come—*eternal life.*"

ETERNAL LIFE

Here the material is clearly organized by use of the inversion principle. The question of eternal life occurs in stanza 1 and is repeated in stanza 1'. In stanza 2 five of the Ten Commandments have been selected but are rearranged so as to have "loyalty to family" at the top of the list and "loyalty to parents" at the bottom with the question of "property" in the center. In 2' there is also a list of five items all of which discuss the three topics singled out for attention by a special arrangement in stanza 2. The two demands required of the ruler in 3 are met by the disciples in 3'. Both the ruler (4) and the bystanders (4') find this too demanding. The parable (utilizing step parallelism) occurs in the climactic center. Obviously "inherit eternal life" (1 and 1') is identical to "enter the kingdom of God" (5). Thus a short parable is placed in the center of what we have preferred to call a "theological mosaic" constructed around the inversion principle.

In Galatians 3:5–14 the following use of the inversion principle is observable:

Galatians 3:5–14

A   Therefore he who supplies *the Spirit to you* and works miracles among you,
is it by works of the law or *by hearing with faith?*
Thus Abraham *"believed God,* and it was reckoned to him as *righteousness."*

B   So you see that *it is men of faith* who are the *sons of Abraham.*
And the Scripture, forseeing that God would *justify the gentiles* by faith
preached the gospel beforehand to *Abraham.*
In thee shall *all the gentiles be blessed.*
So then, those *who are men of faith* are *blessed with Abraham* who had faith.

C   For all who rely on works of the law are under a *curse*
for it is written, *"Cursed* be everyone who does not abide
by all the things written in the book of the law, and do them."

D   For it is evident that no man is justified before God
by *the law*

E   because, *"He who through faith is righteous shall live."*

D'   And *the law* does not rest on faith
but "He who does them shall live by them."

C'   Christ redeemed us from the *curse* of the law
having become a *curse* for us
for it is written, *"Cursed* is every one who hangs on a tree."

B'   That to the *gentiles*
the *blessing of Abraham*
might come in Jesus Christ

A'   that the *promise of the Spirit*[33]
we might receive through faith.

The parallels in the above inversion are as follows:

---

[33]This structure is slightly revised from John Bligh, *Galatians in Greek,* 34. Bligh has found the inversion principle all through the book of Galatians. As with Lund, each piece of evidence must be examined on its own merits.

```
A    Spirit, faith, righteousness
  B    Gentiles, blessing of Abraham
    C    Curse
      D    Law
        E    Righteousness by faith
      D'   Law
    C'   Curse (Christ)
  B'   Gentiles, blessing of Abraham (Christ)
A'   Spirit, faith, promise.
```

All the parallels are strong and unmistakable. The climax is in the center. The center is related theologically to the beginning and the end. This is particularly clear when the two quotes in A and E are compared. The second half introduces Christ, who is the significant missing element in the first half. Unit B is internally inverted, again with the center (Abraham) repeated at the outside.

Turning to one of the later books of the New Testament, the same Form A can be found in 2 Peter 3:8–18. The structure is as follows:

2 Peter 3:8–18

1   *Do not let this one fact escape you, beloved*
     that with *the Lord one day* is as a *thousand* years
     and a *thousand years* as *one day.*

  2   He is not slow, *the Lord* of *the promise,* as some *count* slowness
       but he is *forbearing* toward you.

    3   He is not wishing that any should perish
         but that all should reach repentance.

      4   The *Day of the Lord* will come like a thief.
           Then *the heavens will pass away with a loud noise*
           and *the elements will be dissolved with fire*
           and *the earth and the works that are upon it* will be burned up.

        5   Since all these things are thus to be dissolved
             what sort of persons ought you to be in lives of holiness and
             godliness

      4'   waiting for the hastening, the coming of the *Day of God*
           because of which the heavens will be kindled and dissolved
           and *the elements will melt with fire*
           and a new heaven and *a new earth we await according to his promise*
           in which righteousness dwells.

    3'   Therefore beloved, since you wait for these things
         be zealous to be found by him without spot or blemish and in peace.

  2'   And the *forbearance* of *our Lord*
       count it as *salvation.*

(So also our beloved brother Paul wrote to you according to the wisdom given him, speaking of this as he does in all his letters. There are some things in them hard to understand which the ignorant and unstable twist to their own destruction as they do the other scriptures.)[34]

1'   You therefore *beloved, knowing* this beforehand
       beware lest you be carried away with the error of lawless men and lose your
            own stability
       and *grow in the grace and knowledge of Our Lord and Savior Jesus Christ*
       to him be the glory both now and *to the day of eternity*. Amen.

The structure climaxes again in the center, where the reader is told (in the 1st line) that what has been described will be dissolved and that thus (the 2nd line) he should live in holiness and godliness. This admonition to a godly life recurs in 3' and at the end of the structure in 1'. The addition of ethical specifics is the new feature of the second half.

The question as to whether these structures are conscious or unconscious has not been resolved. In the case of Luke 18, where the order of the laws selected from the Decalog has been rearranged for discernible purposes and divergent material brought together to create the "theological mosaic," it seems clear that the use of the inversion principle was conscious and deliberate. In the Galatians passage, the selection of passages from the Old Testament and their arrangement in a special order also makes the inversion almost certainly deliberate. The Second Peter structure and the example from Daniel are more open to the possibility of being unconscious uses of inversion.

TYPE B—Seven Poetical[35] Forms Using a Variety of Parallelistic Combinations

Before we illustrate the different forms of parallelistic structures, for clarity's sake we will first define the forms to be discussed. The seven fall into three categories: forms with one stanza;[36] forms with two stanzas; forms with three or more stanzas. The forms will be labeled and defined as follows:

With one stanza:

Form I: Parallelisms formed into a single stanza that inverts single words or brief phrases.

Form II: Parallelisms formed into a single stanza that inverts clauses, full sentences, or double lines.

Form III: Parallelisms formed into a single stanza by the use of step parallelism.

---

[34]This long comment about Paul, perhaps a later gloss, has little to do with the rest of the passage and could just as easily have appeared almost anywhere in the entire book of Second Peter.

[35]We are using the word "poetry" here rather loosely. When the parallelism between matching lines is as precise as that found in the poetic sections of the Old Testament or that found in the *Hodayoth* of Qumran, we choose to call it poetry. It may well be "parallelistic prose" and could be called "artistic prose," among other things. By the word "poetry" in this section we intend to indicate a multiplicity of correspondences and a precision in those correspondences not found in the other types.

[36]By "stanza" we intend a series of correspondences that together complete an idea or balance out a known literary form.

With two stanzas:

Form IV: A poem with two stanzas in which the second stanza is a parallel repetition of the first.

Form V: A poem with two stanzas in which the second stanza begins with the theme appearing at the center of the first stanza.

With three stanzas:

Form VI: Parallelisms formed into three stanzas in which the third stanza is parallel in some way to the first and the center is extended to a stanza by itself.

Form VII: A parallelistic structure of three or more stanzas in which a number of the above types are combined.

Examples of each of these forms will now be examined.[37]

Form I (A Single Stanza that Inverts Single Words or Brief Phrases)

Examples of Form I are as follows:

Amos 5:24

> Let-roll-down
>> like-waters
>>> justice
>>> and righteousness
>> like-a-stream
> ever-flowing.

Amos 5:7

> The-one-who-turns
>> to wormwood
>>> justice
>>> and righteousness
>> to-the-earth
> casts-down.

---

[37]The supreme significance of poetry for an oral-tradition community is discussed by Nicholson, who quotes Ibn Rashiq's comment on the poet: "A poet was a defense to the honor of them all, a weapon to ward off insult from their good name, a means of perpetuating their glorious deeds and of establishing their fame forever." Cf. R. A. Nicholson, *A Literary History of the Arabs* (Cambridge: University Press, 1962), xxii. It is well known that every period of the literary history of the Bible was significantly represented by poetry. This extends into the intertestamental period with the Qumran literature. Kraft writes of the importance of the Qumran Thanksgiving Psalms "for an understanding of what New Testament writers regarded as poetry." Cf. C. F. Kraft, "Poetic Structure of the Qumran Thanksgiving Psalms," *Biblical Research* 2 (1957), 16. Seale, *The Desert Bible,* describes graphically what poetry means to an oral-tradition community; cf. pp. 18–23.

An illustration of the inversion of phrases is Amos 5:14–15a.

```
1   Seek-good
  2   and-not-evil
    3   that you-may-live
      4   and-he-will-be Yahweh
      4'  God-of Hosts
    3'  with-you as-you-said
  2'  hate evil
1'  and-love-good.
```

The theme of "Good" is placed at the outside and "God" at the center.

Note also Isaiah 60:1–3.

```
    1   Arise
      2   shine
        3   because it-has-come your-light
          4   and-the-glory
            5   of-Yahweh
              6   upon-you has-risen
                7   for-behold darkness shall-cover the-earth
                7'  and-thick darkness the-people
              6'  and-upon you shall-arise
            5'  Yahweh
          4'  and-his-glory upon-you shall-be seen
        3'  and-they-shall-come the-gentiles to-your-light
      2'  and-kings to-the-brightness
    1'  of-your-rising.[38]
```

Each of the seven semantic units is repeated in the second half of the poem in inverted order. The focus in the center of the structure is "darkness" (7 and 7'). This is encased in an envelope of "resurrection" (6 and 6'). The theme of resurrection is repeated for special emphasis on the outside.

A mixing of words and clauses is seen in 9:9b–10b of the *Hodayoth*, which has the following structure:

```
For I-know thy-truth
  And I-choose
    A-judgment-of-me
    And in-scourging-of-me
  I-delight
For I-hope in-thy-grace.[39]
```

This same mixing is demonstrated by Paul in Romans 10:8–10.

```
1   This is the word of faith which we preach
  2   "If you confess
```

[38]Cf. Lund, *Chiasmus*, 44.

[39]Thiering, *JSS* 8, 204; my translation. She provides a series of illustrations of this form.

```
   3   with your mouth
     4   'Jesus is Lord'
        5   and believe
           6   in your heart
              7   'God raised him from the dead'
              7'  you will be saved''
           6'  for with the heart
        5'  one believes
     4'  unto righteousness
   3'  and with the mouth
 2'  confesses
1'  unto salvation.
```

The theme of salvation appears in 7' and 1'.

The well-known opening to John's Gospel is a Form I and appears as follows:

```
 1   In the beginning
   2   was
     3   the word
        4   and the word
           5   was
              6   with God
              6'  and God
           5'  was
        4'  the word.
     3'  This one
   2'  was
 1'  in the beginning with God.⁴⁰
```

The last line summarizes the beginning and the middle.

---

[40] N. W. Lund, "The Influence of Chiasmus upon the Structure of the Gospels," *ATR* 13 (1931), 42:

As we indicated above (cf. n. 25) we have space here only to point out what appears to be the dominant literary structure. Yet it is significant to observe in this simple stanza two literary structures at work together reinforcing one another. The same stanza can be seen as follows:

```
 1   In the beginning
   2   was
     3   the word
     3'  and the word
   2'  was
 1'  with God
 1   and God
   2   was
     3   the word.
     3'  This one
   2'  was
 1'  in the beginning with God.
```

Form II (One Stanza with Full Clauses, Sentences, or Double Lines)

This is perhaps the most important of all these parallelistic forms. Below are five representative examples:

Amos 9:1–4

A   Strike the-capitals until the-doorjambs shake
     breaking-them on-the-heads-of all-of-them

   B   and-the-remainder with-the-*sword*
       I-will-slay

     C   shall-not-*flee-away* among-them the-one-who-flees
        and-shall-not-escape among-them an-escaper

       D   if-they-dig *to-Sheol*
          from-there my-hand shall-take-them

         E   and-if they-*climb-up to-the-heavens*
            from-there I-will-bring-them-down

         E'   and-if they-*hide on-the-peak-of Carmel*
            from-there I-will-search-them-out to-take-them

       D'   and-if they-hide from-before my-eye *in-the-bottom-of the-sea*
         from-there I-shall-command the-serpent and-it-shall-bite-them

     C'   and-if-they-*go into-captivity*
       before-the-face-of their-enemies

   B'   from-there I-shall-command *the-sword*
       and-it-shall-slay-them

A'   and-I-have-set my-eyes on-them
     for-evil and-not for-good.[41]

The semantic parallels are as follows:

God brings judgment
   the *sword*
     no escape *away*
       no escape *down*
         no escape *up*
         no escape *up*
       no escape *down*
     no escape *away*
   the *sword*
God brings judgment

This same use of two structures on the same lines reinforcing each other we will observe below in much greater complexity in Acts 2:23–36; cf. pp. 80–82.

[41]Revised from Lund, *Chiasmus*, 86f.

In this poetic structure there seems to be no turning point at center, yet the center is still the climax. There is no escape, *not even in heaven*.

Psalm 89:28–37

My mercy will I *keep* for him *forevermore* and my covenant shall stand fast with him.	KEPT FOREVERMORE
His seed also will I make to *endure* forever and *his throne* as the days of heaven.	HIS SEED, THRONE, ENDURE
If *his children* forsake my law and walk not in my judgments	DAVID'S CHILDREN
if they *break my statutes* and keep not my commandments	THEY BREAK—STATUTES
then will I visit their transgression *with the rod* and their iniquity *with stripes*.	JUDGMENT
Yet my mercy will I not utterly take from him not prove false in my truth.	MERCY
My covenant will I not break not after the thing that is gone out of my lips.	I BREAK NOT—COVENANT
Once I have sworn by my holiness *unto David* will I not lie.	DAVID
His seed shall endure forever and *his throne as the sun before me*.	HIS SEED, THRONE, ENDURE
It shall be established forevermore as the moon and the witness in the sky standeth fast.[42]	ESTABLISHED FOREVERMORE

The climax of judgment and mercy is powerfully reinforced by the inversion. Mercy also opens the poem. The point of turning occurs as usual just past center with the word "Yet."

The same form but with seven units occurs in Matthew 13:13–18 as follows:

Therefore I speak to them in parables,

1   because seeing *they see not*
and hearing *they hear not,* nor understand.

2   And *it is fulfilled to them*
the *prophecy* of Isaiah which says,

3   "Hearing *you shall hear*
and shall *not understand*

4   and seeing *you shall see*
and shall *not perceive*.

5   For this people's *heart* is become dull

---

[42]Cf. John Forbes, *The Symmetrical Structure of Scripture* (Edinburgh: T. & T. Clark, 1854), 40.

6   and the *ears* are dull of hearing

    7   and their *eyes* they have closed
    7′   lest they should perceive with the *eyes*

6′   and hear with the *ear*

  5′   and understand with the *heart*, and should turn again
      and I should heal them.''

  4′   But blessed are *your eyes*
      for they see

3′   and *your ears*
    for *they hear*.

2′   For truly *I say unto you*
    that many *prophets* and righteous men

1′   desired to see what *you see*, and *did not see*
    and to hear what *you hear*, and *did not hear*.[43]

A striking example of the use of inverted parallelism is in John 5:24–29:

Truly, truly I say to you,

He who *hears my word and believes* him who sent me
   he has *eternal life*   LIFE
he does not come to *judgment*
   but he has *passed from death to life*.   JUDGMENT

   Truly, truly I say to you
     the *hour is coming* and now is
       when *the dead will hear the voice of the Son of God*
       and *those who hear will live*.

      For as the Father has *life* in himself
        so he has granted the son also to have *life* in himself   LIFE
       and has given him authority *to execute judgment*   JUDGMENT
        because he is the Son of man.

   Do not marvel at this
     for *the hour is coming*
       when all *those in the tombs will hear his voice*
       and *they will come forth*

those who *have done good*
  to the *resurrection of life*   LIFE
those who have *done evil*
  to the *resurrection of judgment*.[44]   JUDGMENT

---

[43]Revised from Lund, *Chiasmus*, 233f. The author seems to have begun with the text from Isaiah. This text already had the Heart—Ears—Eyes = Eyes—Ears—Heart inversion in it. The new author adds 4′ and 3′ to balance the remaining sections of the OT quote and then extends the stanza to seven by adding 1 and 2 to the beginning and matching it with 2′ and 1′ at the end.

[44]This five-stanza poem was first noted by John Forbes, *Symmetrical Structure*, 69. Quite independently the identical structure was discovered by Lucy Brown, my former student at the Near East School of Theology, Beirut, Lebanon. A remarkable aspect of this particular structure is that the first

One of the most remarkable poetic structures in all of the New Testament is Ephesians 2:11–22. Jews and Gentiles in the flesh form the first two stanzas. Jews and Gentiles in the spirit form the last two. The center three stanzas have a threefold repetition of the "two becoming one." The structure is as follows:

Therefore remember

1	that then you *the Gentiles in the flesh* the ones *called uncircumcised*	GENTILES (IN THE FLESH)
2	by those *called circumcised* which is *made in the flesh by hands*	JEWS (IN THE FLESH)

    3   that you were once *separated from Christ*
           alienated from the citizenship of Israel
           strangers to the covenants of promise

      4   having *no hope*
           and *without God in the world.*

        5   But now in Christ Jesus *you who were once afar off*
              have been brought near in the blood of Christ.

          6   For *he is our peace*
                who *has made the two one*
                and *has destroyed the dividing wall of hostility in his body*

            7   abolishing the law of commandments and ordinances
                  that *of the two he might create* in himself *one new man*

          6'   *so making peace*
                reconciling the two in one body to God through the cross
                bringing the hostility to an end in it.

        5'   And he came and preached peace *to you who were far off*
             and peace *to those who were near*

      4'   for through him we both have *access*
           in one spirit to the Father.

    3'   *So then you are no longer strangers and sojourners*
        but *you are fellow citizens with the saints*
        and *members of the household of God*

2'	built upon the foundation *of the Apostles and Prophets* (Jesus Christ himself being the chief cornerstone in whom the whole structure is joined together) and growing into a holy temple *in the Lord*	JEWS (IN THE LORD)
1'	into which *you are* also built for *a dwelling place of God in the spirit.*	GENTILES (IN THE SPIRIT)

Stanza 3 matches 3' with inverted parallelism,[45] the rest are step parallelisms. One additional comment in 2' brings this hymn into line with 1 Corinthians 3:11.

---

two stanzas are *realized eschatology*. The judgment has *passed* and the hour is *now* for the dead to hear the voice. In the last two stanzas we have a balancing *futuristic eschatology.*

[45]This set of six lines could be read as three separate units and not as one unit. We have kept the above

Form III (One Stanza Using Step Parallelism Rather Than Inverted Parallelism)

A clear example of this is Isaiah 55:10–11, which is structured as follows:

A   For as-it-comes-down the-rain and-the-snow from-the-heavens
  B   and-there returns-not but-waters the-earth
    C   causing-it-to-give-birth and-causing-it-to-sprout
      D   and-giving seed to-the-sower and-bread to-the-eater

A′   So shall-be my-word which goes-forth from-my-mouth
  B′   it shall-not-return to-me empty
    C′   for it-shall-accomplish that-which I-requested
      D′   and-succeed in-that for-which I-sent-it.

A New Testament example is Luke 6:20–26:

1   *Blessed* are the poor
   for yours is the kingdom of God

  2   *Blessed* are those now hungry
    for you shall be satisfied

    3   *Blessed* are those that weep now
     for you shall laugh

      4   *Blessed* are you when men hate you
(and when they exclude you and revile you, and cast out your name as evil, on account of the Son of man. Rejoice in that day, and leap for joy, for your reward is great in heaven)[46]
      for so their fathers did to the prophets.

1′   But *woe* to you that are rich
   for you have received your consolation

  2′   *Woe* to you that are full now
    for you shall hunger

    3′   *Woe* to you that laugh now
     for you shall mourn

      4′   *Woe* to you when all men speak well of you
      for so their fathers did to the false prophets.

---

form because the author all through this literary piece seems to be working with two- and three-line units.

[46]The long expansion in unit 4 is not artless. There are seven phrases. Three negatives are followed by a reference to the Son of man, which is then balanced by three positive phrases. Thus a single couplet has been expanded to form a stanza in itself. Freedman has noticed the same phenomenon in some OT parallelisms. Cf. David N. Freedman, Prolegomenon to G. B. Gray, *The Forms of Hebrew Poetry* (New York: Ktav, 1972 [1915]), XXXVI. Freedman writes, "It is as though the poet deliberately split a bicolon or couplet, and inserted a variety of materials between the opening and closing halves of that unit to form a stanza."

Form IV (Two Stanzas, the Second Parallel to the First)

This form is much rarer, especially in the New Testament. Two examples will suffice to illustrate its presence.

Acts 4:8–12

I   *Text*   *unifying themes*

A   Rulers of the people   (You rulers)
     and elders of Israel

   B   if we are being examined today   (A man—whole)
          concerning a good deed to a cripple

   B′   by what means
           this man has been saved   (How saved?)

A′   be it known to you all
       and to all the people of Israel   (All the people—know)

II

A   by the name of Jesus Christ of Nazareth whom you crucified
      whom God raised from the dead(By name of Jesus—you killed, God raised)

   B   by him this man is standing before you—whole.(By Jesus—a man whole)

      C   This is "the stone which was rejected (by you) builders(You rejected)
            which has become the head of the corner"   (Exaltation)

   B′   and there is not in anyone else—salvation   (Only by Jesus—salvation)

A′   for there is no other name under heaven given among men
       by which we must be saved.   (By name of Jesus—we must be saved)

Major relationships between stanzas

I   A   You rulers
        B   A man whole
        B′   Salvation
      A′   *All* the people

II   A   You crucified
         B   A man whole
         B′   Salvation
       A′   *We* must be saved

The second passage chosen to illustrate Form IV, Acts 2:23–26, is much more sophisticated. It is actually a "counterpoint form." The material matches in a 1–10, 10–1 pattern as well as 1–5 5–1, 1–5 5–1. We will observe the overall 1–10 first:

A   *This one* (Jesus) . . . *you crucified and killed*

   B   but *God raised him up,* having loosed the pangs of death
          (because it was not possible for him to be held by it).

C   David says, "I saw the Lord always before me, for he is at my right hand. . . ."

MEN, BROTHERS, IT IS NECESSARY TO SPEAK TO YOU BOLDLY

D   that the patriarch David died and was buried
(and his tomb is with us to this day).

E   *Being therefore a prophet, and knowing*

F   *that God had sworn with an oath to him*

G   that he would set one of his descendants upon his throne

H   *he foresaw and spoke*

I   of the *resurrection of the Christ*

J   that *he was not abandoned to Hades*

J'   *nor did his flesh see corruption.*

I'   *This Jesus God raised up*

H'   of that *we are all witnesses.*

G'   Being therefore exalted at the right hand of God

F'   *having received from the Father the promise of the Holy Spirit*

E'   *he has poured out this which you see and hear.*

D'   For David did not ascend into the heavens

C'   but he himself says, "The Lord said to my Lord, Sit at my right hand. . . ."

ASSUREDLY THEREFORE LET ALL THE HOUSE OF ISRAEL KNOW

B'   that *God has made him Lord and Christ*

A'   *this Jesus whom you crucified.*

Lines A and A' are on the theme of *crucifixion*. Lines B and B' combine on *resurrection*. Lines C and C' are quotations from David. Both mention *my right hand*. In both halves of the structure, immediately after the quotation from David, there is a vocative address directed to the audience. Each address is composed of three semantic units. In the second these are reversed. This can be seen as follows:

MEN, BROTHERS＼   IT IS NECESSARY TO SPEAK   ＿▸BOLDLY TO YOU

ASSUREDLY THEREFORE ◂＿＿   LET THEM KNOW   ＿▸ALL THE HOUSE OF ISRAEL

Or, to state it in another way, the first vocative address is put in different words, reversed, and placed in the corresponding position in the second half of the structure.[47] Lines D and D' refer to the fact that David did not ascend but died and was buried. E and E' are semantically somewhat weaker or perhaps just more subtle. Line E refers to the prophet who knew. Line E' tells the listeners that they *see and hear,* that is, that they also *know.* In line F, God makes a promise. In line F', he fulfills a promise. G and G' discuss *enthronement.* H and H' speak of

---

[47]This vocative address ties the hymn to a specific historical setting. Without it the hymn could be put into any context where an apostle was addressing Jews. Because this pair of vocatives are not a part of the discussion we have chosen not to give them identifying letters.

witness, the prophetic and the apostolic. I and I' return to the theme of the
resurrection. J and J' are on the *death* of Christ.

This hymn has a series of expansions. The first is the apparent interpolation
of "delivered up according to the definite plan and foreknowledge of God by the
hands of lawless men," which appears in line A. Most of this interpolation occurs
in the speech in Acts 4:28. Line B is expanded with "because it was not possible
for him to be held by it," and line D is expanded with "and his tomb is with us to
this day." Both of these last appear to be explanations of the text. They could be
antiphonal responses. Yet they sound more homiletical than liturgical. The two
quotations from David have expanded far beyond the balancing phrase, "my right
hand." The first one is clearly a later expansion in that part of it appears in the
poem itself in lines J and J'. In all, there are five expansions of the original poem.[48]

At the same time the same lines form two matching stanzas. This can be
seen as follows:

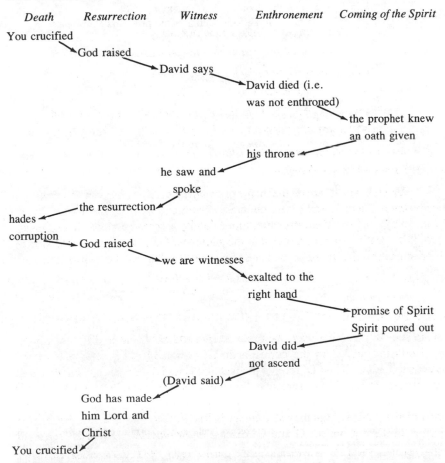

[48]These would seem to indicate that the material is much earlier than the date of the composition of the
book of Acts. It would also indicate that the poem had had wide use and that the final editor of the

Form V (Two Stanzas with the Center of the First Forming the Outside of the Second)

A clear case of this type is Luke 4:16–20:

A 1   And Jesus returned in the power of the Spirit to Galilee.
  And a report went forth through the whole neighborhood concerning him
   and he taught *in their synagogues*
  Being praised by all.
 And he came to Nazareth, where he had been brought up.

B 1   And he entered (as his custom was on the Sabbath) *into the synagogue*
 2 and he stood up to read
 3 and there was given to him the book of the prophet Isaiah.
  4 And opening the book, he found the place where it was written,

    5 "*The Spirit of the Lord* is upon me, because he has anointed me
    6 *to preach* the good news to the poor.
     7 He has *sent me* to proclaim to the prisoners *freedom*
      8 and to *the blind recovery of sight*
     7' to *send forth* the oppressed ones in *freedom*
    6' to *proclaim*
    5' *the acceptable year of the Lord.*"

   4' And having closed the book
  3' after giving it back to the attendant,
  2' he sat down
 1' and the eyes of all *in the synagogue* were fixed on him.

The ideas that repeat are:

He returned—to Galilee
 the whole neighborhood
  in their synagogues
 praised by all
he came—to Nazareth

into the synagogue
 he stood up
  was given to him the book
   opening the book

    the Lord
     to preach
      he has sent me—freedom
       to the blind—*sight*
      to send forth—freedom

---

material either does not recognize the poetic structure (and thus does not restore the poem to its original form) or for some reason chooses not to restore it, or he himself is the author of the expansions. It is difficult to attribute a poem as stylistically perfect as this one to the same hand that expands it and thus destroys that original balance. Answering all these questions is beyond the scope of this study.

to proclaim
the Lord

closed the book
giving it back
he sat down
the *eyes* of all *in the synagogue* were on him

"In the synagogue" is the center of stanza 1, and this same theme becomes the beginning and the end of the second stanza. This is the distinctive feature of Form V. Also we observe that the second stanza climaxes on the theme of "opening the eyes," and at the very end of the same stanza the *eyes* are on him.

Form VI (Three Stanzas with the Third Stanza Repetitive of the First

This form will occur twice in the material discussed in the exegetical section. Here we intend only to illustrate that this form is used widely in New Testament Literature. We have selected three examples.

Luke 11:29–32

This generation is evil, seeking a sign
but no sign shall be given to it except the sign of *Jonah*.
For as Jonah became a sign to the *Ninevites*
so will the Son of man be to this generation.

The queen of the south will arise at the judgment
with the men of this generation and judge them.
For she came (from the ends of the earth) to hear the wisdom of *Solomon*
and behold something greater than *Solomon* is here.

The men of *Nineveh* will arise at the judgment
with this generation and judge it.
For they repented at the preaching of *Jonah*
and behold something greater than Jonah is here.

The stanzas are clearly A–B–A with Jonah–Solomon–Jonah.

Romans 11:17–24

I   But if some of the branches were broken off
and you being a wild olive shoot
were grafted in their place
to share the richness of the olive tree
do not boast over the branches

(if you boast, remember it is not you that support the
root, but the root that supports you).

II   Then you say, The branches were broken off
so that I might be grafted in.

True, through unbelief they were broken off
you through faith stand fast.

 So do not become proud
 but fear.

For if God the natural branches did not spare
neither you will be spared.

Note then the kindness and the severity of God
toward the fallen severity, on you the kindness of God

  (provided you continue in his kindness
  otherwise you too will be cut off).

And even they, if they do not persist in unbelief
will be grafted in

III for God is able to graft them in again.
 For if you have been cut from what is by nature a wild olive
  and grafted, contrary to nature
   into a cultivated olive tree
    how much more these natural branches will be grafted
    into their own olive tree.

The outer units are also inverted. They relate to each other as follows:

I Branches—broken off	III they—grafted in
wild olive	wild olive
grafted in	grafted in
olive tree	cultivated olive
branches (broken off)	natural branches—grafted in

The step parallelism is presumably the primary form because the last line of stanza III is reflected in the center of stanza II, not the center line of stanza III. This structure has two bracketed comments. The first is a comment on the question of boasting; the second is a hortatory repetition of the threat of being cut off.

 John 16:20–22

 Truly, truly, I say to you

I You will weep and lament
  but the world will rejoice.

 You will be sorrowful
  but your sorrow will turn into joy.

  II *When* a woman is in travail
   she has *sorrow*
    because her hour has come

  but *when* she is delivered of the child
   she no longer remembers her *anguish*
    for joy that *a child is born* into the world.

III   So you have sorrow now
　　　　but I will see you again

　　　and your hearts will rejoice
　　　　and no one will take your joy from you.

The "Joy and Sorrow" theme dominates the first and third stanzas, while the second stanza breaks into step parallelism with an illustration that informs both the first and the last. This three-stanza Form VI often occurs in this simple form in the Gospels.

Form VII (Complex Combinations of the Above)

These structures are the most complex and the most controversial. None occurs in the parabolic material under discussion in this study. They can be observed in the work of Bligh, Lund, and Miesner.[49]

In conclusion we have observed seven forms in biblical literature that exhibit precise parallelism in their structure. The Old Testament material has long been called poetry. It is our view that much of the New Testament material which has the same forms also deserves this designation.

TYPE C—Sections That Have a Tight Parallelism in the Center But Are Encased Within One or More Sets of Prose Envelopes

A simple example of this type is Acts 5:1–6, whose structure is as follows:

> But a man named Ananias with his wife Sapphira sold a piece of property, and with his wife's knowledge he kept back some of the proceeds, and brought only a part and laid it at the apostles' feet. But Peter said,
>
> A　　"Ananias, why has Satan filled your heart
> 　　　　to lie to the Holy Spirit?
> 　　　　　　　(and to keep back a part of the proceeds of the land?)[50]
>
> 　　B　　While it remained unsold
> 　　　　　did it not remain your own?
>
> 　　B　　And after it was sold
> 　　　　　was it not under your authority?
>
> A　　Why have you contrived this deed in your heart?
> 　　　You have not lied to men but to God."
>
> When Ananias heard these words, he fell down and died. And great fear came upon all who heard of it. The young men rose and wrapped him up and carried him out and buried him.

---

[49]Bligh, *Galatians, passim;* Lund, *Chiasmus,* 242–286; Miesner, *Chiasm and Paul,* 97–272. Miesner's work is worthy of special attention.

[50]The correspondences between lines in this center section are extremely tight. For this reason this explanatory aside is bracketed. It has no parallels, and is redundant.

The four couplets are encased within sections of prose. In the example of Luke 18 given above, the central parable of six lines was encased within four sets of prose envelopes. The famous 1 Corinthians 13 has at its beginning and end a discussion of gifts for the church. The four couplets of parallelism quoted above from Luke 21 also fit into this category, as does Acts 26:2–29, where ten couplets of standard parallelism are encased within six matching sets of prose envelopes, and Romans 10:9–10, which is encased in three envelopes.

TYPE D—The Parabolic Ballad[51]

The sayings of Jesus often employ a series of three-line stanzas. An example of this is in Luke 6:32–36:

1   And if you *love* those who love you
    what credit is that to you?
      For even sinners love those who love them.

2   And if you do *good* to those who do good to you
    what credit is that to you?
      For even sinners do the same.

3   And if you *lend* to those from whom you hope to receive
    what credit is that to you?
      Even sinners lend to sinners, to receive as much again.

4   But *love* your enemies
    do *good*
      and *lend* expecting nothing in return
        (and your reward will be great).

The last stanza is a three-line recapitulation of the first three.

An editor close to Matthew with his interest in rewards seems to have gone through Luke, and we find editorial comments on the question of rewards sprinkled through the structured sections of Luke again and again.

Sometimes the parables in Luke fall into step parallelism, at other times inverted parallelism is used. More often they are structured along the lines of three-line stanzas. These stanzas may or may not be inverted. Each stanza introduces a new scene or a significant shift of action. A clear example of this parabolic ballad is found in Luke 10:30–35:

A man was descending from Jerusalem to Jericho:

1   and he fell among *robbers*   COME
    and they stripped him and beat him   DO
      and departed leaving him half dead.   GO

    2   Now by chance a certain *priest* was going down that road   COME

---

[51]John Dominic Crossan in a recent major article ("Parable as Religious and Poetic Experience," *Journal of Religion* 53 [1973], 330–358) has described the parables of Jesus as "poetic metaphors"; cf. pp. 349f. Our "parabolic ballad" can be seen as further evidence for Crossan's thesis.

	and when he saw him	DO
	he passed by on the other side.	GO
3	Likewise a *Levite* when he came to the place	COME
	and saw him	DO
	he passed by on the other side.	GO
4	And a certain Samaritan, traveling, came to him	COME
	and when he saw him	DO
	he had compassion on him.	DO
3'	He went to him	COME
	and bound up his wounds	DO
	and he poured on oil and wine.	DO
2'	Then he put him on his own beast	DO
	and led him to the inn	DO
	and took care of him.	DO
1'	The next day he took out two denarii	DO
	and gave them to the manager saying, "Take care of him	DO
	and whatever more you spend I will repay on my return."	DO

In this case the stanzas are inverted.[52] The priest was of sufficient rank to be known to have been riding, and could have taken the man to the inn. The Levite, being of a lesser rank, might not have been riding, but he could at least have rendered first aid. The Samaritan in the second half reverses the actions of the first three stanzas. It is of particular interest to note the comparison between the first and last stanza:

THE ROBBERS (1)
1. took his money
2. beat him
3. left him half dead (and will not return)

THE SAMARITAN (1')
1. spent his own money
2. cared for him
3. left him cared for and promised to return.

Some of the lines are redundant and apparently included in the story only to fill out the literary form. Note particularly the last line of stanza 2', "and took care of him."[53]

---

[52]Crossan has also observed the use of inversion in this parable. Cf. *In Parables,* 62. However, he has not observed the precise nature of the Samaritan's actions in compensating for all who came before him. The suggestion that the priest was riding an animal may be too speculative. If this is rejected we would have simple 1–2,2–3–2',2'–1'. That is, the Samaritan carries out two distinct acts. He *renders first aid* and *transports* the man to the inn. These two actions can be read as matching the two religious leaders who should have rendered aid (without the inversion of 2–3–3'–2'). Either way the parabolic ballad form is intact.

[53]Here in Luke 10:25–37 not only is the parable very carefully structured but the dialog between Jesus and the lawyer has the following form:

This parabolic ballad structure (Type D) will occur in a number of the parables under discussion in this study.

SUMMARY AND CONCLUSIONS

We have observed in the New Testament and elsewhere four types of literary structures. One of them (Type B) uses carefully balanced parallelisms and is found in seven different forms. The fourth (Type D) is a ballad type more suitable for storytelling. When the author is using a literary structure the discovery of that structure is found to be crucial for exegesis for several reasons. The structure may:

1. identify the climactic center;

2. show how the author is relating the center to the outside;

3. make clear the turning point of the passage and alert the reader to look for a significant shift of emphasis in the second half;

4. provide a crucial key to understanding by enabling the reader to see what words, phrases, or sentences are matched with what other words, phrases, or sentences in the structure;

5. demonstrate where newer material has been fitted into an older piece of literature;

Round One

Lawyer–Question 1   *"What* must *I do* to inherit *eternal life?"*

    Jesus–Question 2   "What about the law?"

    Lawyer–Answer 2   "Love God and your neighbor."

Jesus–Answer 1   *"Do this* and *live."*

Round Two

Lawyer–Question 1   "Who is my neighbor?"

    Jesus–The parable of the Good Samaritan

        Question 2   "Which of these three became a neighbor?"

    Lawyer–Answer 2   "The one who showed mercy on him."

Jesus–Answer 1   "Do and keep on doing this."

Again this takes us beyond the topic of this chapter. This is a dialog structure that we have not discussed. We note it only because it is a further illustration of the use of the inversion principle. A full interpretation of the parable in its Lucan setting must take into account the structure not only of the parable itself but of the dialog. Crossan (*In Parables,* 61) has observed the general form but has not noted the inversion at work within it.

6. mark off the literary unit itself with clarity (the beginning and the end are usually distinct and thus the unit is identified);

7. provide crucial evidence for textual problems.

8. The parabolic ballad literary type opens new doors for understanding the parables, and a range of New Testament problems related to them.[54]

---

[54]Miesner succinctly identifies the function of chiasm as fourfold, "Memory, beauty, meaning and textual considerations" (Miesner, *Chiasm and Paul*, 44).

Part Two

AN ANALYSIS
OF FOUR PARABLES
AND TWO POEMS IN THE
TRAVEL NARRATIVE
OF LUKE

Chapter 4

THE LITERARY OUTLINE
OF THE TRAVEL NARRATIVE
(JERUSALEM DOCUMENT): LUKE 9:51–19:48

All the biblical passages selected for this study fall in the so-called Lucan Travel Narrative. The Narrative itself has a very precise literary outline that aids significantly in determining the divisions between units of the tradition and in identifying the main subject of each unit. For these reasons the structure of the Travel Narrative must be examined.

In this section we will attempt to demonstrate that 90 percent of the material in the Travel Narrative of Luke has a carefully constructed inverted outline. Some short pieces of tradition do not fit the structure and seem to have been included, usually between sections, on the basis of word association.[1]

Stagg speaks for many scholars when he says of the Travel Narrative, "it is most difficult if not impossible to outline."[2] Evans finds it "completely amorphous."[3] Yet Goulder discovered what he believed to be a "chiastic structure."[4] Our proposal is a revision and extension of Goulder's suggestion. Goulder tried to work all of the material into his structure. Some of it, we are convinced, does not

---

[1]It must be understood that this is intended to be a brief presentation of the literary structure of the Travel Narrative. A full debate with other views on the structure would be a lengthy study in itself. For a discussion and review of recent scholarship on the Travel Narrative, cf. J. H. Davies, "The Purpose of the Central Section of Luke's Gospel," *Studia Evangelica*, II(=*Texte und Untersuchungen*, Band 87), ed. F. L. Cross (Berlin: Akademie-Verlag, 1963), 164–69; Bo Reicke, "Instruction and Discussion in the Travel Narrative," *Studia Evangelica*, I(=*Texte und Untersuchungen*, Band 73), ed. Kurt Aland *et al.* (Berlin: Akademie-Verlag, 1959), 206–216; W. C. Robinson, Jr., "The Theological Context for Interpreting Luke's Travel Narrative (9:51ff.)," *JBL* 79 (1960), 20–31; Frank Stagg, "The Journey Toward Jerusalem in Luke's Gospel," *Review and Expositor* 64 (1967), 499–512; J. Schneider, "Zur Analyse des lukanischen Reiseberichtes," *Synoptische Studien. Alfred Wikenhauser zum siebzigsten Geburtstag* (Munich: Zink, 1953), 207–229; Hans Conzelmann, *The Theology of St. Luke*, trans. Geoffrey Buswell (New York: Harper, 1961), 60–73; G. Ogg, "The Central Section of the Gospel According to St. Luke," *NTS* 18 (1971), 39–53.

[2]Stagg, *loc. cit.*, 499.

[3]C. F. Evans, "The Central Section of St. Luke's Gospel," *Studies in the Gospels. Essays in Memory of R. H. Lightfoot*, ed. D. E. Nineham (Oxford: Blackwell, 1957), 40.

[4]M. D. Goulder, "The Chiastic Structure of the Lucan Journey," *Studia Evangelica*, II, 195–202.

fit. He identified six idea units. Our proposal is ten "sections" that follow a precise inverted outline. This outline is as follows:

THE STRUCTURE OF THE JERUSALEM DOCUMENT (Luke 9:51–19:48)

THE TEN DOUBLE SECTIONS (++ extra material inserted into the sections) { EXTRA MATERIAL INSERTED BETWEEN SECTIONS

1. *JERUSALEM: ESCHATOLOGICAL EVENTS 9:51–56*
   (a) Day—"the days were fulfilled" 51
   (b) Death—"for him to be delivered up" 51
   (c) Fulfilment—"he sent messengers before his face" (Mal. 3:1)
   (d) Judgment—the call for fire to destroy the village (Mal. 3:5 ??)
   (e) Salvation—"the Son of man came not to destroy but to save" 55b[5]

2. *FOLLOW ME 9:57–10:12*
   (a) People come to Jesus 9:57–62
   (b) Jesus sends out the seventy 10:1–20 (++ woes on Chorazin and Bethsaida 10:13–15)

{ HIDDEN FROM THE WISE 21
ONLY THE SON KNOWS THE FATHER 22
BLESSED ARE YOUR EARS 23–24

3. *WHAT SHALL I DO TO INHERIT ETERNAL LIFE? 10:25–41*
   (a) Dialog on the law 25–28
   (b) Love the neighbor—the Good Samaritan 29–37
   (c) Love the Lord—the story of Mary and Martha 38–42

4. *PRAYER 11:1–13*
   (a) The right content for prayer—the Lord's prayer 1–4
   (b) Assurance in prayer—the friend at midnight 5–8
        —a poem on a father's gifts 9–13

5. *SIGNS AND THE PRESENT KINGDOM 11:14–32*
   (a) A sign of the kingdom—the dumb speak 14
   (b) Signs and the kingdom 14–26 (++ blessed is he who keeps the word 27–28)
   (c) Signs and the Son of man (Jonah and Solomon) 29–32

{LIGHT, DARKNESS AND THE EYE 33–36

6. *CONFLICT WITH THE PHARISEES: MONEY 11:37–12:34*
   (a) Conflict with the Pharisees, money—seven woes 11:37–54
        (++ seven misc. sayings 12:1–12)
   (b) Money—the rich fool 12:13–21
   (c) Do not be anxious—treasure in heaven 22–34

7. *THE KINGDOM IS NOT YET AND IS NOW 12:35–59*
   (a) The kingdom is not yet—"be like men waiting" 35–48
   (b) The kingdom is now—fire upon the earth 49–53
        —interpret the present time 54–56
        —the judgment is near 57–59

---

[5]Cf. J. M. Ross, "The Rejected Words in Luke 9:54–56," *ExpT* 89 (1973), 85–88. With Ross we suggest a restoration of these words.

8. *THE CALL OF THE KINGDOM TO ISRAEL 13:1–9*
    (a) Repent or perish—Pilate and the Galileans 1–5
    (b) Produce or perish—the unfruitful fig tree 6–9

9. *THE NATURE OF THE KINGDOM 13:10–20*
    (a) Love and not law—the healing on the Sabbath—a woman 10–14
    　　　　　　　　　—what about your ox or ass? no reply 15–17
    (b) Humility—the kingdom is like mustard and leaven 18–20

10. *JERUSALEM: ESCHATOLOGICAL EVENTS 13:22–35*
    (f) Salvation—"will those who are saved be few . . . enter by the narrow door"
    (e) Judgment—"depart from me . . . you . . . thrust out of the kingdom"
    (d) Vision—"you will *see* Abraham and the prophets in the kingdom"
    (c) Fulfilment—the ingathering of the messianic banquet of the kingdom (Mal.
    　　　　　　　1:11)
    (b) Death—"Herod wants to kill you"
    (a) Day—"today, tomorrow, and the third day—I am made perfect"
    (a) Day—"today, tomorrow, and the coming day—I go"
    (b) Death—"the prophet must not die away from Jerusalem"
    (c) Fulfilment—a failure of the messianic ingathering—"I would have gathered
    　　　　　　　you under my *wings* (Mal. 4:2?) and you would not"
    (d) Judgment—a *lament* over Jerusalem "Jerusalem . . . killer . . . your house
    　　　　　　　forsaken
    (e) Vision—"you will *not see me* until you say 'blessed is he who comes in the
    　　　　　　　name of the Lord' "
    (f) ——————??

9' *THE NATURE OF THE KINGDOM 14:1–11*
    (a) Love and not law—a healing on the Sabbath—a man 1–4
    　　　　　　　　　—what about your ass or ox? no reply 5–6
    (b) Humility—"he who humbles himself will be exalted" 7–11

8' *THE CALL OF THE KINGDOM TO ISRAEL AND TO THE OUTCASTS 14:12–15:32*
    (a) The great banquet 14:12–24
    　　　　—the cost of discipleship 25–35
    (b) The lost sheep and lost coin 15:1–10
    (c) The two lost sons 15:11–32

7' *THE KINGDOM IS NOT YET AND IS NOW 16:1–8, 16*
    (a) The kingdom is not yet
    　　　——————??? (19:12–26)
    (b) The kingdom is now—the unjust steward 16:1–8
    　　　　　　　　—everyone is pressed by the kingdom 16:16

$$\left\{\begin{array}{l}\text{THE LAW IS STILL VALID 17}\\ \text{DIVORCE 18}\end{array}\right.$$

6' *CONFLICT WITH THE PHARISEES: MONEY 16:9–31*
    (a) Money—God or Mammon 9–13[6]
    (b) Conflict with the Pharisees, money 14–15[6]
    (c) Lazarus—the need for treasure in heaven 19–31

——————————

[6]For a discussion of the shift of 16:9–15 see below, pp. 116f.

$$\left.\begin{array}{r} \text{OFFENSES } 17{:}1{-}2 \\ \text{FORGIVENESS } 3{-}4 \\ \text{FAITH } 5{-}6 \\ \text{DUTY } 7{-}10 \end{array}\right\}$$

5' SIGNS AND THE COMING KINGDOM 17:11–37

  (a) A sign of the kingdom—lepers cleansed 11–19

  (b) Signs and the kingdom of God 20–21

  (c) Signs and the Son of man (Noah and Lot) 22–37

4' PRAYER 18:1–14

  (b) Assurance and steadfastness in prayer—the Unjust Judge 1–8

  (a) The right attitude in prayer—the Publican and the Pharisee 9–14

$$\{\text{CHILDREN AND ETERNAL LIFE } 15{-}17$$

3' WHAT SHALL I DO TO INHERIT ETERNAL LIFE? 18:18–30

  (a) Dialog on the law 18–21

  (b) Love for neighbor—"Give to the poor" 22–28

  (c) Love for the Lord—"We have left our homes and followed you" 28–30

$$\{\text{PREDICTION OF THE PASSION } 31{-}34$$

2' FOLLOW ME 18:35–19:9

  (a) People come to Jesus—the blind man 35–43

  (b) Jesus goes out—the call to Zacchaeus 19:1–9

1' JERUSALEM: ESCHATOLOGICAL EVENTS 19:10, 28–48

  (f) Salvation—"The Son of man has come to seek and to save the lost"

$$\{\text{THE KINGDOM OF GOD IS NOT YET } 19{:}11{-}21$$

  (e) Vision—seeing the mighty works they said, "Blessed is He who comes in the name of the Lord"

  (d) Judgment—a *lament* over Jerusalem—"They will not leave one stone upon another"

  (c) Fulfilment—cleansing of the temple—the purification of the Sons of Levi (Mal. 3:2–4)

  (b) Death—Jerusalem leaders seek to kill him

  (a) Day ——————— ???

  ("Destroy this temple and after *three days* I will raise it up again." Cf. John 2:19, where this reference to "three days" is attached to the cleansing of the temple. This tradition itself occurs in Mark 14:58; 15:29.)

The shorter units of material that are apparently not a part of the original collection are marked. Many of these seem to have been placed in their present position because of word association with units already in the structure. Some add a special theological emphasis (cf. 16:17 as a corrective to 16:16).

Obviously there is no "traveling" done at all and the title "Travel Narrative" is a misnomer. Furthermore, many are confused as to where the "Travel Narrative" ends. The above outline makes it clear that 9:51–19:48 is the full sweep of the document. We prefer to call it the "Jerusalem Document."

The semantic correspondences between the units are very strong and need no comment.[7] The double ten inversion occurs both in Acts 2:23–36 and Ephesians 1:3–14. The repetition of Jerusalem on the outside and at the center gives it a prominence that is unmistakable. Death and the eschatological day are the climax of the document. There is also a suggestion of a shift at the center. In the second half of the structure the theme of humility is emphasized. This theme is formally introduced in a discussion of humility (14:7–11), which ends with the statement, "For every one who exalts himself will be humbled, and he who humbles himself will be exalted." The theme of humility is then seen in:

The Cost of Discipleship	14:25–33
The Lost Son	15:11–32
The Unjust Steward	16:1–8a
(who considers begging and digging)	
Dives and Lazarus	16:19–31
The Servant Coming in from the Field	17:7–10
The Publican and Pharisee	18:9–14
Zacchaeus	19:1–10

This theme is not necessarily dominant in each of these pericopes. It seems rather to be more prominent in the units of the lower half of the structure than in the upper half. This theme may have helped determine which of two matching units was placed in the second half and which was introduced in the upper half. The point of turning of such a structure is usually the unit just past the center. This holds true here as well. The lament over Jerusalem, reference to the death of the prophet, and the hint of the triumphal entry all occur in the second half of section 10. The shift to a special emphasis on humility we have mentioned. Another significant shift can be seen in section 8' with its call to the outcasts added to the call to Israel.

The structure raises a number of questions that are beyond the scope of this study. It is our view that a pre-Lucan Jewish-Christian theologian arranged the material into the ten-unit pattern. The arrangement itself is the result of considerable theological reflection. The climax on death and the eschatological day in Jerusalem is not an accident. Luke himself claims that he used written sources. Is it not possible that this was one of them? Luke, we conjecture, had this document available to him. He did some cautious editing, moved in some new material, and shifted two pericopes out of their original position. He then incorporated the edited document into his Gospel.

For our purposes the document with its outline is significant for delineating blocks of material and determining their main themes as understood by the

---

[7]Miesner has discovered a significant parallel to the Jerusalem Document in Acts 12:25–21:16 (cf. *Chiasm and Paul*, 273–290). The special importance of Miesner's discovery is of course that it occurs in a second volume written by Luke. At the same time the OT also has examples of large blocks of material arranged in an inverted pattern. Cf. Stephen Bertram, "Symmetrical Design in the Book of Ruth," *JBL* 84 (1965), 165–68; Edwin M. Good, "The Composition of Hosea," *Svensk Exegetisk Årsbok*, 31 (1966), 21–63.

theologian/editor of the document. Of particular interest for this study are sections 6, 7, and 8. They appear in the structure as follows:

6. *CONFLICT WITH THE PHARISEES: MONEY 11:37–12:34*
     (a) Conflict with the Pharisees, money—seven woes 11:37–54)
         (++seven misc. sayings 12:1–12)
     (b) Money—the rich fool 12:13–21
     (c) Do not be anxious—treasure in heaven 22–34

7.- *THE KINGDOM IS NOT YET AND IS NOW 12:35–59*
     (a) The kingdom is not yet—"be like men waiting" 35–48
     (b) The kingdom is now—fire upon the earth 49–56
            —interpret the present time 54–56
            —the judgment is near 57–59

8. *THE CALL OF THE KINGDOM TO ISRAEL 13:1–9*
     (a) Repent or perish—Pilate and the Galileans 1–5
     (b) Produce or perish—the unfruitful fig tree 6–9

8' *THE CALL OF THE KINGDOM TO ISRAEL AND TO THE OUTCASTS 14:12–15:32*
     (a) The great banquet 14:12–24
        —the cost of discipleship 25–35
     (b) The lost sheep and lost coin 15:1–10
     (c) The two lost sons 15:11–32

7' *THE KINGDOM IS NOT YET AND IS NOW 16:1–8, 16*
     (a) The kingdom is not yet
     —————————??? (19:12–26)
     (b) The kingdom is now—the unjust steward 16:1–8
        —everyone is pressed by the kingdom 16:16

                       {THE LAW IS STILL VALID 17
                       {   DIVORCE 18

6' *CONFLICT WITH THE PHARISEES: MONEY 16:9–31*
     (a) Money—God or Mammon 9–13[8]
     (b) Conflict with the Pharisees, money 14–15[8]
     (c) Lazarus—the need for treasure in heaven 19–31

All three sections have eschatological overtones but each has a different emphasis. Sections 6 and 6' discuss money, death, and the life to come. The parable of the Rich Fool in section 6 and the parable of Lazarus and the Rich Man in 6' are clearly on this topic. Then the dicussion of mammon in 16:9–13 also clearly discusses this subject. In 6' the Pharisees are linked to the discussion of money (see 16:14–15).

The eschatological warnings of sections 7 and 7' are concerned with the coming of the kingdom, not with death. Thus the overall structure of the Jerusalem

---

[8]For a defense of the shift of 16:9–15 from its present position in the text to the place seen in the above outline see below, pp. 116f.

Document requires a break between 16:1–8 and 16:9–13. This will be discussed in detail as part of the exegesis of these verses.

The eschatology of sections 8 and 8′ is related to the call of the kingdom, not death. Thus sections 7 and 7′ are closer to 8 and 8′ respectively than to 6 and 6′. This, then, means that the parable of the Unjust Steward is closer to the parable of the Prodigal Son which precedes it than to the section on Mammon which follows it. This also will be discussed in detail as part of the exegesis.

In summary, it can be stated that the Jerusalem Document does have a structure. This structure is neither historical nor exclusively theological but rather literary. By comparison with the corresponding sections, divisions between blocks of material can be made with greater precision. Dominant themes in different sections also show up more clearly. The literary structure provides new evidence toward solving a wide spectrum of synoptic problems which lie beyond the scope of this study.

Since Luke 16:1–13 illustrates in one passage the various aspects of culture and literary structure that this study attempts to set forth, this passage will be dealt with first. Luke 11:5–13 is structurally similar to 16:1–13 and will thus be studied second. The fifteenth chapter of Luke will then be considered last.

Chapter 5

EXEGESIS OF LUKE 16:1-13

THE UNJUST STEWARD (LUKE 16:1-8)

In the first part of this chapter we intend to show that the parable of the Unjust Steward is an eschatological warning to sinners. In the parable a dishonest steward discovers that his master expects obedience and judges those who fail him. The steward also discovers extraordinary mercy. He decides to risk everything on the unqualified mercy of his master. He knows that if he fails, he goes to jail; if he succeeds, he is saved. His plan was the right one and he is praised for it. The entire parable is cast in the form of a "Parabolic Ballad" (Form D). The theological cluster includes insight into the nature of God, into the crises that the kingdom brings to the sinner, and into the only hope for man's salvation.

Many commentators affirm that this parable is the most difficult of all the synoptic parables. As we have observed, the problems are so complex that both Tomas de Vio Cajetan (1469–1534) and Rudolf Bultmann declared them insoluble.[1] The multiplicity and complexity of the problems of this parable are succinctly stated by C. C. Torrey, who writes,

> This passage [Luke 16:8f.] brings before us a new Jesus, one who seems inclined to compromise with evil. He approves a program of canny self-interest, recommending to his disciples a standard of life which is generally recognized as inferior: "I say to you, gain friends by means of money." This is not the worst of it; he bases the teaching on the story of a shrewd scoundrel who feathered his own nest at the expense of the man who had trusted him; and then appears to say to his disciples, "Let this be your model!"[2]

The seeming incongruity of a story that praises a scoundrel has been an embarrassment to the Church at least since Julian the Apostate used the parable to assert the inferiority of the Christian faith and its founder.[3] Our need for a more

---

[1]See above, p. 29.
[2]Charles C. Torrey, *Our Translated Gospels* (New York: Harper, 1936), 59.
[3]Scharlemann, *Parables*, 81.

precise understanding of the culture that informs the text is perhaps greater in this parable than in any other. The text is in excellent condition with only a few minor variants, some of which we will note as we move through the parable.[4]

The disciples are the primary audience. In verse 1 they are addressed specifically, but the Pharisees are assumed by Luke to be included among the listeners, for in verse 14 they, too, heard "all these things."

The word "parable" is not mentioned in verse 1, but neither is it included in the parable of Lazarus except as a variant. Apparently Luke assumes that the word "parable" given in 15:3 is to cover the parables of chapter 16 as well.[5]

Three initial questions must be discussed at some length before proceeding to the parable itself. They are,

1. Is the master assumed to be an honorable man, or is he a partner-in-crime with his steward?

2. Has the steward obliged the renters to sign bills for amounts greater than the actual debts? Is his reduction of the debts merely a surrender of his dishonest "cut"?

3. Is the steward an estate manager dealing with land rentals or is he an authorized agent for a moneylender?

The interpretation of the entire parable hinges on the answers given to these three questions. We will examine each of them in turn.

Everything indicates that the master is an upright man. In the immediately preceding parable of the Prodigal Son, the father is clearly a noble man; and the sons, by contrast, are ignoble. In the parable of Lazarus the rich man is ignoble, but Lazarus is judged worthy of eternal life. One naturally assumes the same character contrast in the parable of the Unjust Steward. Furthermore, the steward is clearly labeled "unjust," yet no breath of criticism is leveled at the master. If the master were ignoble, he would have acted in a very different manner. The steward is dismissed, but not scolded, punished, or jailed.

Some scholars follow a line of argument that forces them to assert a partner-in-crime status for the master. Oesterley writes, "The lord commends the dishonesty of his steward and may, therefore, not unreasonably be regarded as belonging to the same category."[6] Derrett implies a criticism of the character of the master when he concludes that the master is pleased to acquire an unearned reputation for piety by approving the actions of his steward.[7] At the end of the

---

[4]The authenticity of the parable is almost beyond question. D. R. Fletcher writes, ". . . It hardly seems plausible that an apocryphal parable involving such obvious difficulties of interpretation should have been incorporated by the early Christian community into its traditions of the parables of Jesus." Fletcher, "Riddle," 15.

[5]The Old Syriac, the Arabic Diatessaron, the Peshitta, and Ibn al-Ṭayyib add the word "parable" to this verse in their translations. Thus these translators clearly understood this text as a parable.

[6]Oesterley, *Jewish Background,* 197. Cf. also Caird, *Luke.* Caird writes of the master, "He was, in fact, no less a son of this world than his steward" (p. 187).

[7]Derrett, "Steward," 216f. Cf. also Via, *Parables,* 159. Via suggests a "scheming businessman" for the master; cf. Arndt, *St. Luke,* 375. In contrast, Smith writes, "There is nothing in the parable to

parable the master is deceived. Were he ignoble, we would expect from him a stream of anger directed toward the steward. This does not happen. Any line of argumentation that places the person and character of the master in a bad light will need substantial support.

The second question deals with the action of the steward. There is a strong current in modern scholarship that affirms that the steward has inflated the bills to enrich himself. In the crisis of his dismissal, he subtracts his "cut" from the bills. This opinion can be traced to Margaret Gibson. In 1902 Gibson, an Arabic and Syriac scholar at Cambridge, wrote a letter in comment on this parable to the *Expository Times*. She said,

> ... I know that at the present time, wherever Orientals are left to their own methods, uncontrolled by any protectorate of Europeans, the plan is to farm out taxes or property of any description. The steward would therefore demand from the cultivators much more than he would pay to the overlord, perhaps even double, and pocket the difference himself.[8]

Gibson shows the attitude of an imperialistic age in assuming the cultural superiority of Europeans. This assumption by itself is enough to render suspect her judgments on the "natives." Furthermore, Gibson was a resident of Cambridge and came to the Middle East only as traveler, scholar, and pilgrim. In spite of this, her almost casual suggestion was picked up and endorsed by a rather amazing list of scholars.[9] It is our view that Gibson has made a basic mistake in her evaluation of Middle Eastern customs. In light of the influence her remark has had, it must be examined with some care.

Gibson may be giving an accurate description of land renting practices in the Turkish Empire at the turn of the century. She suggests that this pattern is an appropriate frame of reference for this parable. Her exact meaning is not clear. Does she intend to say, "Middle Eastern landowners are not smart enough to keep their stewards from cheating; European control is more intelligent and can provide this safeguard"? This is obviously false, and we can assume that this is not what

---

prepare us to take an unfavorable view of the employer's character" (B. T. D. Smith, *Parables*, 109). Derrett in a more recent article (" 'Take thy bond . . . and write fifty' (Luke XVI.6). The Nature of the Bond," *JTS* 23 [1972], 438–440) discusses the nature of the bond in the parable, but again requires that the master be a partner-in-crime with his steward. His data are from the Greek world and thus do not apply.

[8]Margaret Gibson, "On the Parable of the Unjust Steward," *ExpT* 14 (1902/1903), 334. Scharlemann, *Parables*, 88, has noted that this suggestion was first made by M. Evers in "Das Gleichniss vom ungerechter Haushalter" (1901). Hermann Marx, in a revision of Evers' work published in 1908 (*Die Gleichnisse Jesu* [Berlin: Reuther & Reichard, 1908], 83), refers to this suggestion of Evers and calls it "eine höchst originelle Auffassung." Evers seems to have made his "original interpretation" independent of any insight into the culture of the area.

[9]W. D. Miller, "The Unjust Steward," *ExpT* 15 (1903/1904), 332–34; E. Hampten-Cook, "The Unjust Steward, I.," *ExpT* 16 (1904/1905), 44; Gächter, "Oriental," 121–131; C. B. Firth, "The Parable of the Unrighteous Steward (Luke xvi.1–9)," *ExpT* 63 (1951/1952), 93–95; Derrett, "Steward," 198–219; Fitzmyer, "Manager," 23–42; Stuhlmueller, *Luke*, 149.

she intends. Rather she seems to be saying, "Middle Eastern landowners agree with their agents on a fixed amount which they expect to receive from land rentals. The owners then allow their agents to inflate the bills beyond this amount to whatever the traffic will bear, even up to 50 percent." No doubt wealthy Turks owning land in Arab provinces during the last days of Imperial Turkey did function in this manner. Yet such an assumption has at least the following implications:

1. The master is dishonest.

2. He is willing to allow his steward's profits to be almost as great as his own.

3. He does not care if the leading citizens of the local community are badly cheated. Thus he has no social relationship to them.

4. The steward does cheat the debtors mercilessly on a regular basis.

5. The steward has been given tacit permission to cheat the debtors as much as he wants. He will be closely watched. If he is caught cheating the master he will be dealt with in a ruthless fashion.

6. The steward is hated bitterly by all the renters. Restoration to their good graces would be almost impossible under any conditions. Proverbially speaking, if they ever get him down they will beat him to death.

None of these assumptions fits the parable under consideration.

Gibson is correct in assuming that the renters paid something to the steward. Officially the steward received a fee from the renters. Derrett argues convincingly that the steward is a legal "agent" for the master and so acted under the Mishnaic regulations governing such agents.[10] The Mishna mentions specifically a fee to be paid by the renter to the agent who draws up the rent contracts.[11] In addition to this (judging from modern village customs), the steward will likely receive a little something "under the table" from most, if not all, of his master's renters. A token amount is considered legitimate and honorable. At feast time, harvest time, and at other important social occasions, he will likely expect some gratuity from his master's renters.[12] He is criticized only if his demands are unreasonable.

None of this appears in the accounts. What is recorded on the bills is known to the master. This is clearly evident in the Mishnaic passage cited above, which says of agents, "They may not write contracts of share-tenancies or fixed-rate tenancies except with the knowledge (and agreement) of both parties, and the tenant must pay the fee."[13] What is written on the bills is public information discussed openly in the community.

Furthermore, if the steward tries to inflate the bills, the debtors will be fully aware of what is happening. They can appeal to the master unless he is a

---

[10]Derrett, "Steward," 201–204.

[11]Mishna *Baba Bathra* x.4.

[12]The amazing flow of expensive gifts between company executives at Christmas time is a Western equivalent to the same practice.

[13]*Baba Bathra* x.4.

partner-in-crime. If the steward has been cheating the debtors to the extent of 20 to 50 percent of their bills, he will be bitterly hated by them. Once he falls from power he will have to leave the community. No further deception, even if it is to their economic advantage, will lead those debtors to welcome him into their homes.

For years I have been discussing this point with consultants from the Middle East and beyond to India. The village cultural pattern is everywhere the same. A dishonest steward has many ways to cheat. Every time he buys or sells anything he will make a "cut." But all his extra profits are "off the record." What is written on the debtors' bills he must deliver to the master.[14]

The Turkish landowner in the Middle East is vividly remembered as corrupt, ruthless, and indifferent to any suffering he or his steward might cause his renters. This total scene, however, is quite different from the one that confronts us in the parable. At the very beginning, someone cares enough about the welfare of the master to report the actions of the dishonest steward. The master is clearly a part of the community. The wealthy, distant, foreign, ruthless landowner is unknown in the synoptic parables.[15]

Finally, according to Jewish law, if an agent buys for less or sells for more than the price specified by the principal, the extra profits belong to the principal, not to the agent.[16] Thus, it must be concluded that Gibson's dated, superficial

---

[14]Part of the confusion in this regard arises because the Middle Eastern moneylender *does* ask the debtor to sign for more than he receives. The purpose of this subterfuge is to avoid the laws against exorbitant interest rates. The question of land rentals *vs.* money lending will be discussed below. The details of the parable point to the former. Making the steward into a moneylender creates new problems and inadequately solves old ones.

From antiquity comes an illustration of this money-lending practice. Josephus records how Herod Agrippa about 33–34 A.D., when nearly bankrupt, borrowed money from a banker. Josephus writes that the banker, called Protos, "complained that Agrippa had defrauded him of some money, and forced Marsyas Herod's agent to draw up a bond for 20,000 Attic Drachmas but to accept 2,500 less." Josephus *Antiquities* xviii.6.3. Translation from *Josephus*, ed. Louis H. Feldman, Vol. IX in the *Loeb Classical Library* (Cambridge: Harvard University Press, 1965), 103.

In his translation Whiston gives a note saying, "Spanheim observes that we have here an instance of the Attic quantity of use-money, which was the eighth part of the original sum of 12%, for such is the proportion of 2,500 to 20,000." Cf. *The Works of Flavius Josephus*, trans. W. Whiston (London: Ward, Lock, n.d.), 455, n.1. Spanheim turns out to be Ezekiel Spanheim, a late 17th-century author and expert on both Greek coins and Josephus. (E. Spanheimii. Fl. Josephi . . . Opera Omnia . . . accedunt nunc primus notae . . . ineditae in universa Fl. Josephi opera . . . 1726.) This is an example of writing a larger figure than the debt owed. However, this illustration does not apply to the parable. Greek commercial law underlies the illustration. Furthermore, the money is borrowed directly from the banker Protos and not from someone he represents. Also, Herod already owed the sum of 2,500 Drachmas, so Protos is collecting previous debts. Finally, the percentages in the parable are not consistent and much higher.

[15]Luke 12:42–48 is a case in point. There the master is absent but on returning is very upset when he finds that his steward has been mistreating those under him.

[16]Horowitz, *Jewish Law*, 552. In this particular case, Horowitz is quoting from the *Mishnah Torah of Maimonides* and thus the legislation is late and may not apply. Yet it does demonstrate the working assumption that the principal knows the financial rates used by his agent.

surmise leads in the wrong direction. Her suggestion is inappropriate to the cultural elements in the parable.

The third question is that of the profession of the steward and the nature of the debts owed. There are two aspects to this question. First, is the steward a legal "agent" and, if so, is he paid or does he have to fend for himself financially? Second, is he an estate manager dealing with land rentals or a moneylender supervising cash? Under this question we will argue that the steward is a legal "agent" and most likely a *shaluah* (or *shaliah*). He is paid. The rich man is a landowner, and thus the steward is an estate manager. The debtors are *hakirīn* who have rented land for which they must pay fixed amounts of produce. We will deal with the question of "agency" first.

Regarding "agency," Horowitz gives a convenient summary of Mishnaic legislation.[17] He points out that there were three kinds of "agents." These were:

1. A general agent (*shaluah*) who labored either gratuitously or for a fee.

2. A sarsor, a broker or middle man who was always a paid agent.

3. A mursheh, who was an attorney appointed by written instruction to recover property or a debt and authorized to bring suit.[18]

The general agent was "one sent." Often the task for which he was sent was a personal family affair like the arranging of a marriage.[19] In such a case it is easy to understand why the agent might not be paid. He would most likely be a member of the family or a friend of social status equal to the principal. To pay him in such special circumstances would be an insult. On the other hand, Horowitz makes quite clear that the agent was usually paid.[20]

We do not have enough information in the story to determine with finality which of the three alternatives is most appropriate to the steward of the parable, yet the *shaluah* is by far the most probable. In any case, Horowitz' discussion makes it quite clear that all three types of agents were usually paid. The *shaluah* could work gratuitously, but this would be an exception.

---

[17]Horowitz, *Jewish Law*, 538–568.

[18]*Ibid.*, 539.

[19]b.Tal. *Massektoth Ketanneth* 186; Horowitz, *Jewish Law*, 544.

[20]Horowitz assumes that the agent (*shaluah*) is paid and notes the exception to this general assumption when he says, " 'Shaluah' is also used in a narrower sense of a gratuitous agent, one who renders services as a favor" (*Jewish Law*, 539). The same point is confirmed later in the discussion where Horowitz writes, "But when he was entitled to a fee or commission, it sometimes became a question whether he had fully performed" (*ibid.*, 541). Referring to all three types of agents in general, Horowitz says, "The agent is entitled to repayment of the ordinary, regular and customary expenses which he incurred on behalf of the principal . . . and to payment of his hire, fee or commission if it was an employment for hire" (*ibid.*, 549). This evidence is overlooked by Gächter, who states flatly, "He [the master] did not pay the steward for his services, for the steward was supposed to be in a position to gain his livelihood from those who were under him. He hired out the different portions of the master's property to cultivators. They had to pay revenues from which one part would go to the master, one part to the steward" (Gächter, "Oriental," 127). This theory of the unpaid steward who has to live by his wits is unsupported by evidence from any quarter.

In regard to the profession of the steward we must begin with the Greek word itself. T. W. Manson lists three alternatives for the word οἰκονόμος:

1. an overseer or head-servant responsible for the welfare and discipline of the rest of the household staff (Luke 12:42);

2. a bailiff or estate-manager;

3. a civic official like a city treasurer (Romans 16:23).[21]

Manson favors the second, estate manager.

All the Syriac versions for "steward" read *rab bayto,* which means "manager of the house." This is somewhat ambiguous but leaves no room for "money-lending agent." All but two of the Arabic versions have *wakīl* (estate manager).[22] Otto Michel traces the word through the LXX to the Hebrew *'asher 'al habbayit.*[23] In rabbinic literature the οἰκονόμος becomes a kind of chief slave who supervises the household "and even the whole property of his master."[24] The chief slave is called a *ben bayit.* In Luke 16, however, the steward is not sold, but dismissed. Michel suggests for Luke 16:1 "housekeeper," "estate manager," or "accountant,"[25] and suggests the Aramaic *gizbar,* which agrees with Ibn al-Ṭayyib's eleventh-century Arabic version and is still within the range of words referring to a landed estate and its manager. Thus the Greek word itself, along with its Hebrew, Aramaic, Syriac, and Arabic equivalents, points to "estate manager."

Again the Mishna provides significant information, in this case in the laws governing land rentals. There were three types of renters. These were,

1. a tenant on shares (aris or kablan) who paid a percentage of his crop to the owner;

2. a tenant who paid a fixed portion of the crop to be grown (hoker);

3. a tenant (soker) who paid rent in money.[26]

The second type fits exactly the conditions of the story. The Blackman edition of the Mishna spells out the situation in a note where a *ḥakīr* is defined as the tenant "who agrees to pay a certain quantity of produce irrespective of the yield."[27] Derrett argues at some length that the debtors cannot be renters because "the vital point is that under any such agreement the obligee *owes* nothing at all until the time for payment."[28] Derrett fails totally to see that the steward is not *collecting* the

---

[21]Manson, *Sayings,* 291.

[22]The two exceptions are the Diatessaron, which gives *qahramān* meaning "butler," "steward," or "household manager," and Ibn al-Ṭayyib, who translates "storehouse keeper." Thus in the Middle East the story has almost always been understood specifically to refer to an agricultural scene with a manager and *never* as a money-lending tale.

[23]Otto Michel, *TDNT,* V, 149–153.

[24]*Ibid.,* p. 149.

[25]*Ibid.*

[26]Cf. Horowitz, *Jewish Law,* 334; Mishna *Baba Metzia* ix.1–10.

[27]*Mishnayoth, Order Nezikin,* ed. Philip Blackman (London: Mishna Press, 1954), 223, n.2.

[28]Derrett, "Steward," 213; emphasis his.

amounts. The amounts are not *due* until harvest, but they are indeed *owing* from the day the agreement is signed. Even after the bills are changed there is no attempt to collect even the reduced amounts. In regard to Derrett's argument, we are obliged to state that he has not used Horowitz and the Mishna widely enough, and has misunderstood the very agricultural scene he is rejecting.

Having dismissed the possibility of the debtors being land renters, Derrett works out a very elaborate scheme arguing that cash debts were liquidated and reinstated in agricultural produce in order to avoid the laws of usury.[29] This is, of course, possible, but if we assume the debtors to be *ḥakirīn* there is no need to postulate such a complicated scheme of which the parable itself gives no hint.

When we ask, How do we know that the debts are usurious? Derrett answers, "Their very large amounts show that something suspicious was afoot."[30] That will hardly do as an assumption for what becomes the foundation of the entire argument.[31] Derrett also asserts that if the master were a landowner and his debtors tenants, "Jesus would have said so."[32] We would argue in the opposite direction. In an agricultural setting, with the laws and customs surrounding the *ḥakīr* well known, it would be redundant to tell peasant listeners that a rich man was a landowner and that his debtors were land renters. In the parable of the Prodigal Son, the father is a landowner. This is clear from the details. Yet this fact is not stated; it is implicit. By contrast, if the master were a banker, *then* the audience would need to be told.

The crucial weakness in the "moneylender" theory is that it of necessity implicates the master in dishonest dealings. Fitzmyer uses the "money rental" category. When he comes to the question of the master's integrity, he tries to protect the master by saying, "The master may well have been ignorant of the original transactions."[33] Granted the master does not know how much the steward is getting indirectly, but he knows *exactly* the amounts charged for rental of the large tracts of land in his estate. Even if he is a moneylender, he knows exactly where his money is, and what is due him. It is hard to imagine any type of banking anywhere in the world in any period where this would not be the case. Fitzmyer is trying to avoid making the master a partner-in-crime with the unrighteous steward. If usury is recorded in the bills, the master necessarily becomes such a partner.[34]

---

[29]*Ibid.*, 244.

[30]*Ibid.*

[31]Quite to the contrary the Oriental storyteller delights in the use of large amounts. Jesus is no exception; cf. Matt. 18:23–35.

[32]*Ibid.*

[33]Fitzmyer, "Manager," 36.

[34]Manson bypasses the entire landowner *vs.* moneylender debate by suggesting that the debtors are "buyers." He writes, "Both debtors would seem to be persons who have purchased goods from the estate and have not yet paid for them" (Manson, *Sayings*, 291). This view must be rejected in that any estate selling its oil and wheat to merchants would naturally be paid in cash, not kind. There would be no point in selling a hundred jars of oil for a hundred jars of oil. This solution creates more problems than it solves. An excellent review of the relevant data on the word steward can be read in W. L. Hendricks, "Stewardship in the New Testament," *Southwestern Journal of Theology* 13 (1971), 25–33.

An additional significant source of information on this culturally oriented question is the Arabic commentary on Luke by Dr. Ibrāhīm Saʿīd of Cairo.[35] Commenting on Luke 16:2, Saʿīd writes,

> Thus the owner requested his manager to present to him the contracts signed by the farmers and countersigned by the manager, in order to show how much was owing to the owner by each partner from the produce of his fields.[36]

Saʿīd clearly assumed that the debtors were renters and that the setting was that of an estate with land rented out to farmers.

As in the case of Luke 15, the community must be considered to be one of the *dramatis personae*.[37] The Middle Eastern peasant always thinks and acts as part of his community, not as an individual isolated from it. The general public is first mentioned in verse 1, where we are told, "Charges were brought to him." We are not told who brought these charges. Even if these were only fellow servants, clearly a wider circle of people was involved than just the master, the steward, and the debtors.

One of the more suspect cultural value judgments made almost unconsciously by many exegetes is the assumption that an Oriental master does not want to be bothered and gives little attention to his estate and almost no supervision to his manager. This is simply not true. Life has always been precarious in the East. Anyone who manages to become rich anywhere in the world naturally keeps a close watch on his source of wealth. The master in this story is specifically mentioned as such a type in that he cares enough about preserving his wealth to fire a wasteful steward.

In summary, clearly the most probable cultural setting for the parable is that of a landed estate with a manager who had authority to carry out the business of the estate. The debtors were most likely renters. *hakirīn,* who had agreed to pay a fixed amount of produce for the yearly rent. The steward was no doubt making extras "under the table," but these amounts were not reflected in the signed bills. He was a salaried official who, in addition, was paid a specific fee by the renter for each contract. The master was a man of noble character respected in the community who cared enough about his own wealth to fire a wasteful manager. With these relatively clear answers to our three initial questions we can proceed to the text itself.

---

[35]Dr. Saʿīd, who died in 1971 in his late 70s, was the Helmut Thielicke of the Arab world. His Arabic language was compared to that of Kahlil Gibran, the Lebanese poet. His long ministry engaged him in seminary teaching, preaching, and writing. Born about 1890, he spent his childhood and young manhood in the isolation of a tiny village in the south of Egypt. His many books include full commentaries on Luke and John. Saʿīd was a personal friend of Emil Brunner and other scholars, but publishing only in Arabic he has remained unknown outside the Arab world. As an Arabic-speaking scholar, he was competent in English, Greek, Hebrew, and French. He was only casually aware of form criticism and does not discuss it. However limited his commentaries may be in some respects, regarding the question of the Oriental culture that informs the text of the parables, his work must be taken seriously. We will take note of Saʿīd's work all through the exegesis.

[36]Saʿīd, *Lūqā,* 407. Here, as throughout, the translation of his work is my own.

[37]Cf. Derrett, "Steward," 217, and Bruce, *Synoptic Gospels,* 584. (Cf. below, pp. 167f.)

Luke 16:1–8 is carefully structured along the lines of a parabolic ballad (Type D). The structure is as follows:

A   There was a rich man who had a steward   RICH MAN—STEWARD
     and charges were brought to him   STEWARD—A RASCAL
     that he was wasting his goods.

  B   And he called him and *said* to him, "What is this I hear
       about you?   WHAT DOING?
          Turn in the account of your stewardship   FIRED AS STEWARD
          for you can no longer be steward."   OUT OF WORK

  B   And the steward *said* to himself, "What shall I do   DO WHAT?
       because my master is taking the stewardship
       away from me?   FIRED AS STEWARD
          I am not strong enough to farm and ashamed to beg.   OUT OF WORK

     C   "I know what I will do   DO THIS
          so that when I am put out of the stewardship   FIRED AS STEWARD
          they may receive me into their own houses."   NEW JOB

  B'   So summoning his master's debtors one by one   DO—ACT LIKE A
       he *said* to the first, "How much do you owe my master?"   STEWARD
       And he said, "A hundred measures of oil."   WIN FAVOR
          And he said to him, "Take your bill and sit down quickly and write fifty."

  B'   Then he *said* to another, "And how much do you owe?" DO—ACT LIKE A
       And he said, "A hundred measures of wheat."   STEWARD
          And he said to him, "Take your bill and write eighty."   WIN FAVOR

A'   Then the master commended the dishonest steward
     for his wisdom   RICH MAN--STEWARD
     because the sons of this age are wiser   STEWARD A WISE RASCAL
     than the sons of light in their own generation.

We observe seven stanzas of three lines each with one extra explanatory line in the fifth stanza. As is very often true of the Lucan parabolic form, a significant number of the stanzas begin with direct speech. The words in capitals to the right of the structure indicate something of the parallelism. In the briefest way the seven stanzas may be characterized as follows:

    Rich man, steward
        problem
        problem
          idea
        solution
        solution
    rich man, steward.

In the case of the good Samaritan there are three visitors on the road. The vineyard owner sends three times to his vineyard (Luke 20:9–16). For the great banquet there are three types of people invited (Luke 14:15–24). The nobleman who goes to the far country receives reports from three servants (Luke 19:11–27). But here there are only two illustrations of debt reductions. The reason is obvious once the ballad structure of seven stanzas is identified. Two stanzas set up the problem. The climax is in the center with the announcement of a new plan. B' and B' solve the problem created in B and B and in A' we are back to the rich man and his unfaithful steward. With this structure in mind we will proceed through the text.

The steward is summoned and addressed with the first question: (literally translated) "What this I hear about you" (with no verb to be). The word order is Semitic, idiomatic, and forceful. All of our Oriental versions maintain this identical word order. The Syriac has a present participle, "What is this that I am hearing?" which is in keeping with the Greek syntax. The implication is, of course, "I have been hearing for a long time, and I am still hearing a steady stream of things about you." It is the stock formula that a master almost always uses in such a context. The servant does not know how much the master knows and may be frightened into divulging information the master does not have. The steward, intelligent man that he is, remains silent. He has been asked a specific question by his master. His silence cannot be dismissed as insignificant.

The master then breaks the silence with the ultimatum, $\dot{\alpha}\pi\dot{\sigma}\delta\sigma\varsigma\ \tau\dot{\sigma}\nu\ \lambda\dot{\sigma}\gamma\sigma\nu$ $\tau\tilde{\eta}\varsigma\ \sigma\dot{\iota}\kappa\sigma\nu\sigma\mu\dot{\iota}\alpha\varsigma\ \sigma\sigma\upsilon$. Two important questions must be answered at this point. First, Is the steward fired now or later? And second, Is the steward asked to "surrender the account books" or "get the accounts in order"?

The first question is problematic. When dealing with the debtors, the steward acts as if he is not yet fired. In verse 3 he says, "My master *is taking* the stewardship away from me." He then talks about the time "*when* I am put out of the stewardship."[38] At the same time, the present tense of the verb (i.e. "You *are* no longer able") indicates that he is fired on the spot. Manson writes, "The master takes immediate action. He orders the steward to hand over his accounts, and dismisses him from his post."[39]

In the conservative village today a steward is always fired on the spot. The owner is afraid of exactly the kind of thing that happens in this parable. If the rascal has time, he will embezzle more. The Oriental versions, without exception, make this point clear. The Old Syriac reads, "never again," and a number of the Arabic versions make the same point.[40] Furthermore, the Mishna stipulates the conditions that govern dismissal of an agent. Horowitz writes,

> The appointment and powers of the agent may be revoked at any time with or without good cause, and whatever the agent does after revocation is not

---

[38]These time references may explain why the Byzantine text changed the present tense $\delta\acute{\upsilon}\nu\eta$ to the future $\delta\upsilon\nu\acute{\eta}\sigma\eta$. The Byzantine reading is certainly in error. The present tense $\delta\acute{\upsilon}\nu\eta$ is attested by p^{75} B ℵ D Θ al.

[39]Manson, *Sayings*, 291.

[40]Ibn al-Ṭayyib has "from now on"; the new Jesuit "after today"; the Diatessaron "now it is not possible." The rest of the Arabic versions have *ba'd*, which in this context also means "from now on."

binding on the principal. *It takes effect,* however, only from the time that it is brought home to the agent or the person with whom he is dealing.[41]

In the case of this steward he *is* notified. Thus legally his authority as an agent is immediately cancelled. At the same time, more generally speaking, his dismissal is in progress, and he still has some room to maneuver until he turns in the account books and leaves the building, because word of his dismissal is not out. To summarize, we observe that from the text, the Mishna, the Oriental versions, and from modern practice it is clear that the steward is fired on the spot and his authority is terminated immediately. Regarding the question of the account books, the meaning of the word ἀπόδος is clear and can be translated "surrender" or "turn in." In the modern village, a steward in such circumstances is always asked to surrender the books, never to balance the accounts. The master knows that the steward has the skill to falsify the accounts and thus they are not examined for evidence of his guilt or innocence. Gächter argues convincingly that ἀπόδος τὸν λόγον τῆς οἰκονομίας cannot mean "give an account of your stewardship" because, used in that sense, λόγος has no article.[42] Saʿīd, quoted above, understands the accounts to be written documents.[43] Thus with Gächter, Saʿīd, and Scharlemann, it can be argued that the phrase means "surrender the account books."

The listener/reader of the parable expects the steward to be silent after the first question. But after the steward is told, "You're fired; turn in the books!" the listener/reader expects a classic debate in which the steward loudly and insistently protests his innocence. There are many standard ploys he can use to try to defend himself and blame everybody else, including the master himself.[44] But, to the amazement of all, the steward is again silent. His speech, a soliloquy, is given on his way to get the accounts. He walks out having offered no defense. This silence is supremely significant in the Oriental context. The man is indirectly affirming by his silence at least the following:

1. I am guilty.

2. The master knows the truth; he knows I am guilty.

3. This master expects obedience; disobedience brings judgment.

4. I cannot get my job back by offering a series of excuses.

L. M. Friedel wrote, "Had the steward anything to say in self-defense, he would say it now, but he confesses his guilt in the briefest form possible by saying

---

[41]Horowitz, *Jewish Law,* 542; emphasis mine.

[42]Gächter, "Oriental," 127. Cf. Matt. 12.36, Acts 19.40, Rom. 15.12, Heb. 13.17; 1 Pet. 4.5. Scharlemann notes that *logos* is the official record or account kept by the manager for his master (Scharlemann, *Parables,* 84).

[43]Saʿīd, *Lūqā,* 407.

[44]Adam knew some of these; cf. Gen. 3:8–12.

nothing.''[45] The steward does not reflect on how he can get his job back. All his energy is focused toward the future.

At the same time, the steward discovers at this point something else about his master that is supremely significant. He is fired but not jailed. The Mishna makes quite clear that an agent was expected to pay for any loss of goods for which he was responsible. The steward can be tried and jailed. Rather, *he is not even scolded*. The master, under the circumstances, has been unusually merciful toward him.[46] Thus, in one scene, this servant has experienced two aspects of his master's nature. He is a master who expects obedience and acts in judgment on the disobedient servant. He is also a master who shows unusual mercy and generosity even to a dishonest steward. The thoughtful listener/reader of the parable would not miss either of these facts.

Stanza three opens with the steward wrestling with his crisis, trying to find a solution. Remarkably, he considers digging. An educated man in authority is not expected to consider manual labor. We expect him to reject this as a possibility because it is beneath his dignity. Surprisingly, his only reason is his physical weakness. He also rejects begging. This, likewise, is to his credit in a society that accepts begging as a legitimate, although despised, profession.[47]

His problem is not just his next meal. Ben Sirach makes clear that the status of the perpetual guest is intolerable.[48] That he wants and needs another job is evidenced by his considering digging and begging. But since he has been dismissed for wasting his master's property, who would hire him? He needs to create a situation that will change this devastating public image. In stanza four (the climax) a plan is born. The listener/reader is not told what the plan is; rather, as in all good drama, he watches it unfold.

It is our understanding of the parable that the steward's plan is to risk everything on the quality of mercy he has already experienced from his master. If he fails, he will certainly go to jail. If he succeeds, he will be a hero in the community. Following the details of the story closely, we will try to demonstrate that this is the plan that popped into his scheming mind with the introductory dramatic aorist ἔγνων.

The key to his situation is that no one yet knows he is fired. They will find out soon enough and so he has to act quickly. Friedel writes, ''For he realizes that if there is any escape from digging or begging it must be prepared now, before he hands over the account book, before he is definitely out of office.''[49] First he

---

[45]L. M. Friedel, ''The Parable of the Unjust Steward,'' *CBQ* 3 (1941), 338.

[46]The agent was liable for the loss of money or goods entrusted to him if he could not prove that they had been stolen; cf. Horowitz, *Jewish Law,* 552f. Horowitz also indicates that ''his responsibility was broadly that of a bailee'' (*ibid.,* 552), and at times the bailee was responsible even in the case of theft (*ibid.,* 518–526). In Matt. 8:23–35 servants are jailed for debts; how much more can a servant expect to be jailed for money irresponsibly wasted?

[47]Sir. 40:28–30.

[48]Sir. 29:21–28.

[49]Friedel, *loc. cit.,* 339.

"summons" the debtors. Only if he were still in authority would he have the right to send out lesser servants and "summon" these relatively rich and thereby important men to come and see him (their wealth is evident from the large rents owed). The assumption of such a summoning would naturally be that the steward has some important message to relay to them from the master. As it turns out, this is exactly what the steward wants them to assume. It is not harvest time. The amounts of the bills are set and outstanding but not yet due. All the details are significant. He calls the debtors in one by one because he does not want them talking to one another and asking too many questions. He is in too much of a hurry for titles. The debtors are not greeted with even "Friend" or "Sir." To the first he says specifically, "Write quickly."[50] To the second he says almost rudely, "And you."[51] He must finish before the master finds out what he is doing. This fact is crucial to the story. As we have seen, the steward was legally powerless from the moment he was notified of his dismissal. If the debtors have any way of knowing that there is any deception involved they will not cooperate. If a lesser servant enters the room and announces that the steward is fired the scheme fails. The renters may entertain suspicions (the community knows him; cf. 16:1), but as long as they have no knowledge they can and will cooperate. If they *know* or *could have known* and *then* cooperate they will be breaking faith with the master in a very serious way, and the master will no longer rent land to them. This is one of the more significant cultural factors that is ignored by nearly all commentators. The relationship between the owner of the land and his renters is a significant personal and economic relationship. In his summary of social relationships evidenced in the parables of the rabbis, Rabbi Feldman comments on the relationship between the owner of the land and his renters. He writes, "Personal relations were often friendly—sometimes quite intimate."[52] In these parables the typical evil renter is a man who cares nothing for the interests of the landowner.[53] Thus the point is made that a relationship of mutual concern was expected. In the parable of the Unjust Steward there is no criticism of the renters. They are assumed to be upright citizens of the local community. As with the master, a partner-in-crime status for the debtors must not be imported into the parable.

---

[50]This "write quickly" in the text is almost universally ignored by the commentators. We understand it to be a crucial key to a proper understanding of what is going on. He must finish before the master finds out what he is doing, but also before the renters themselves find out that it is all dishonest.

[51]This phrase, "And you," in addressing a relatively wealthy renter, is jarring to Oriental ears. The Oriental versions give the reader a slight shock with this phrase.

[52]Feldman, *Similes*, 239.

[53]Feldman gives an illustration where a renter portrayed as an unrighteous man says, "What care I for the owner of the garden?" (*ibid.*, 40). I find it hard to believe that this is unique to the Middle East. No farmer renting land anywhere in the world wants to anger the owner of the land and risk being denied the right to rent in the future. One could argue that they think there is safety in numbers. The master cannot expel *all* of them from the land lest he have no one to work it. But this, too, is inappropriate to the parable. The parallels in rabbinic similes make this clear. The relationship between renter and landowner is important as a *social* as well as a financial relationship. Furthermore, if the master is angered, he will find ways to take revenge even if he does not directly expel them.

Sa'īd significantly labels these debtors "partners."[54] Thus, from the haste of the steward and from modern and ancient custom, it is clear that the debtors assume the entire bill-changing event to be legitimate. First of all, the debtors are led to believe that the steward is still in authority. This assumption is unmistakably clear from the story itself. The steward says, "How much do you owe *my master*?" He directly asserts that he is still employed.[55] We have already noted that he *summons* them. Thus they arrive assuming that he is still in authority. The second assumption is that the master has authorized the bills and that the steward has talked him into it. This is the only assumption that fits the story. The steward asks the debtors to make the changes in their own handwriting. They accept. The amounts reach to 50 percent. We must assume that the debtors are confident that the master has approved.[56] If there is any doubt about this, as we have indicated, they will not cooperate. The risk is too great. Finally, the steward naturally takes credit for having arranged the reductions. He need say little or nothing. The bills are not due. These sudden reductions come, as it were, "out of the blue." The steward may quietly let it be known, "I talked the old gentleman into it." We can easily reconstruct the kind of small talk that would have taken place during the bill changing. After all, he, the steward, was in the fields day after day. He knew that the rain was bad, the sun hot, and the worms active. The steward thus achieves the position of a factory foreman who has arranged a generous Christmas bonus for all the workers. The bonus itself is from the owners. But the foreman is praised for having talked the owners into granting it. The last part of this assumption is also inescapable. The steward will not carry out a plan that does not reflect to his credit in a significant way. There would be no point in doing so.

In summary, then, the steward openly asserts that he is in authority. The debtors assume that the reductions are authorized; otherwise they would not cooperate.[57] The steward quietly lets the debtors know that he has arranged for the reductions. With these assumptions all the cultural elements fall easily into place.

---

[54]Sa'īd, *Lūqā,* 407.

[55]The steward's soliloquy in v. 3 has the same phrase. It is true that this idiom is his customary speech. However, in v. 5 he is speaking officially and so is, in fact, claiming a relationship.

[56]Derrett endorses this assumption and writes, "Without such a presumption no one would deal with a man through his steward" (Derrett, "Steward," 203). Derrett's point is not quite the same as ours. Derrett assumes that the agent must have had this kind of broad authority as an official part of his agency. Thus as long as his agency was not revoked he could make such reductions and, even if the master didn't like it, he would be bound to accept. But as we have seen the agency *was* revoked. Besides, the reductions are enormous and unprecedented, and even if the steward had the strict legal authority to make such reductions, the debtors could not cooperate if they knew that the master was not in prior agreement.

[57]Fletcher, "Riddle," 17, asks, "What kind of friends are these who are bought by such a device?" (that is, the device of cheating the master). Fletcher asks the right question; he gives the wrong answer. He concludes the key to the parable is irony, because obviously self-respecting debtors would not allow themselves to be bought by dishonest tricks. But as we have argued, from the debtors' point of view they are not being "bought" with dishonest tricks. They do not know there is any cheating involved. So far as they are concerned, all is aboveboard. Therefore they will cooperate, and only therefore does the steward come out as a hero.

The steward takes the bills from his drawer, cupboard, or file, observes the amount, and asks each debtor how much it is. The debtor affirms the amount written.[58] The steward then announces a reduction that, in each case, amounts to about 500 denarii.[59] That the values of the two reductions are roughly equivalent is another indication of his haste. It is much easier to subtract 500 denarii worth from each bill than to debate the fairness of a percentage with each debtor.[60]

In the case of the *ḥakirīn* the Mishna provides for reductions in the fixed rents.[61] If trees die, or blight spreads across a field, or a spring dries up, the owner is expected to make a reduction. Discussions of this kind always take place between renter and owner in the Middle East even if there is no legislation to provide for them. Usually the renter would have to request and argue for some reduction. Here a generous reduction is offered unsolicited.

Sa'īd makes the intriguing suggestion that, with the letter-symbol system of writing, the changes indicated would have been the simplest stroke of the pen. It would entail changing a ק to a ו and a ק to a ף.[62]

Stanzas three and four present the problem. Stanzas five and six reveal the solution. Stanza seven will now appear as a mirror of stanza one. The steward finishes his daring plan by gathering up the freshly changed accounts and delivering them to his master. The master looks at them and reflects on his alternatives. The master knows full well that in the local village there has already started a great round of celebration in praise of him, the master, as the most noble and most generous man that ever rented land in their district. He has two alternatives.

---

[58]The point of the questions is, ''Do you agree that the amount recorded on the bill in front of me is an accurate statement of the rent agreement?'' The steward is not asking for information. He has the written statement in front of him. He is establishing agreement. This important discussion between a steward and his master's renters is fascinating to observe. Often the renter is illiterate and the steward has to confirm the amount through reference to witnesses present at the time of the making of the agreement, to the time of day when it was made, the weather, contemporaneous events, a smell in the air, the place, and other such confirming particulars.

[59]Cf. Caird, *Luke,* 188. Caird writes, ''The liquid measure (*bath*) was approximately 8¾ gallons, and the dry measure (*cor*) was a little under 11 bushels. The value of 50 baths of oil and 20 cors of wheat would be the same—about 500 denarii.''

[60]The changes in the bills are in the handwriting of the debtors, not the steward. It could be argued that the steward orders the debtors to make the changes so that there will be nothing written in his handwriting. Thus he could claim innocence of the entire affair. But this is not likely. The bills are in his possession and what happens to them is his responsibility. More likely, requesting them to do the writing was standard practice. It assures that they have agreed to the bills as they now stand (and the steward has not tampered with them). This is apparently the point that Rabbi Simon ben Gamaliel (early second century) was worried about when he suggested the agent make out two copies of the bill. Cf. *Mishnayoth, Order Nezikin,* ed. Philip Blackman (London: Mishna Press, 1954), 223. But the renter was protected as long as he wrote the figures. This may be the reason why Simon ben Gamaliel's suggestion was rejected. Here the handwriting demonstrates that the debtors have been identified.

[61]Mishna *Baba Mitzia* ix.1, 6.

[62]Sa'īd, *Lūqā,* 408. There is also the possibility that a Greek translator of an Aramaic text of the parable may have confused the final ''F'' and the final ''N'' of his original. In the script of the times the two letters are very similar. Cf. E. L. Sukenik, *The Dead Sea Scrolls of the Hebrew University* (Jerusalem: The Hebrew University, 1954), folio 39, lines 14–17.

He can go back to the debtors and explain that it was all a mistake, that the steward had been dismissed, and thus his actions were null and void.[63] But if the master does this *now,* the villagers' joy will turn to anger, and he will be cursed for his stinginess.

Second, he can keep silent, accept the praise that is even now being showered on him, and allow the clever steward to ride high on the wave of popular enthusiasm. This master *is* a generous man. He did not jail the steward earlier. To be generous is a primary quality of a nobleman in the East. He reflects for a moment and then turns to the steward and says, "You are a very wise fellow."[64] One of the Old Testament definitions of "wisdom" is an instinct for self-preservation.[65] In a backhanded way the actions of the steward are a compliment to the master. The steward knew the master was generous and merciful. He risked everything on this aspect of his master's nature. He won. Because the master was indeed generous and merciful, he chose to pay the full price for his steward's salvation.

In the above discussion we have assumed that the "lord" of verse 8a is the master of the parable. This question must now be examined in detail.

The problem is as old as the Peshitta and has been debated all through the modern period. Obviously if the master of verse 8a is the rich man, then this phrase is the climax of the parable. If he is not, then the parable ends with verse 7. Manson notes:

> In view of the beginning of V. 9, "And I say unto you," there can be little doubt that Luke thought that "the lord" in V. 8 meant the steward's master; and this probably means that that was the way in which the words were taken by the compiler of the source on which he is here dependent.[66]

But then Manson proceeds to give the standard reason why many commentators find this Lucan understanding difficult to accept. The question is, How could a master who dismisses a steward for wasting his goods in verse 2 praise him in verse 8? Manson suggests that the only way the master in verse 8 could be the master of the story is if he heard about the steward's actions, stopped them, and "secured

---

[63]Mishna *Gittin* iv.1; Horowitz, *Jewish Law,* 542. This is against Derrett, who writes, "The debtors writing their new acknowledgements and destroying the old ones were safe." There is no evidence for his assumption that the old bills are destroyed. Derrett has overlooked the Mishnaic evidence that the agent, once notified of dismissal, was legally powerless and the principal not bound by his actions. Cf. Derrett, "Steward," 216; Gächter, "Oriental," 129.

[64]At the conclusion of his discussion Derrett notes: "That the steward's prudence was beneficial to the steward was evident; that it redounded to the master's reputation with the public was obvious. An ungracious repudiation was out of the question." Derrett, "Steward," 217. Here we are in basic agreement with Derrett. But for Derrett the issue is the master's "piety." We would insist that, rather, it is the master's generosity that is heralded in the community.

[65]See below, pp. 105f., for an extended discussion of this word.

[66]Manson, *Sayings,* 292.

himself against pecuniary loss.''[67] But if our line of interpretation above is sound, we have a quite adequate reason for praising the steward at the end of the parable.[68]

In agreement with Manson, Jeremias writes,

> The change of subject (καὶ ἐγὼ ὑμῖν λέγω) at the beginning of v. 9 seems to point decisively to the conclusion that the lord in the parable is intended. This may have been the meaning of the tradition as it lay before Luke, characteristic of whose style is the phrase ὑμῖν λέγω (with ὑμῖν preceding).[69]

Jeremias argues that Luke thought the κύριος of verse 8 was the master of the story but that Luke was mistaken. Jeremias then proceeds to present three arguments for identifying the κύριος with Jesus. They are:

1. The master of the story would not have praised a deceitful steward.

2. The absolute use of κύριος in Luke's gospel in some instances refers to God; elsewhere (except 12:37, 42b; 14:23) it always (18 times) refers to Jesus.

3. Luke 16:9 is like 18:8, where the comments of Jesus himself are clearly injected into the parable.[70]

The first of these arguments we have already discussed above. There is good reason for the master of the story to praise the dishonest steward.

Regarding the second, by ''the absolute use of κύριος'' Jeremias apparently means κύριος as a title without modifiers (excluding the vocative). His evidence, however, needs reexamination. The ''absolute use of κύριος,'' as Jeremias defines it, occurs in Luke twenty-one times. Eighteen times it means Jesus, and only three times someone else. But when we look at the parabolic material, the results are as follows:

meaning: The master of the story	meaning: Jesus
12:37	12:42
12:42b	18:6
14:23	

To this list we then add the disputed 16:8, the present passage. Jeremias' case seems to be that of numerical weight, that if there are eighteen cases of the absolute use of κύριος that refer to Jesus and only three that do not, then the probability is that 16:8 refers to Jesus. But within the parabolic material this weight vanishes. Furthermore, in the same section Jeremias has already noted that Luke is dealing with traditional material.[71] In such presumably non-Lucan traditional material one

---

[67]*Ibid.*

[68]An Oriental master is often pleased that a servant is clever enough to outwit him. This point was made to me by Dr. Hassan Askari of India.

[69]Jeremias, *Parables*, 45.

[70]*Ibid.*; Crossan (*In Parables*, 110f.) clips the parable as early as v. 7.

[71]Verse 7 has a historic present, which is rare in Luke. The words for the weights and measures are Hebrew words left untranslated. The story itself is culturally quite Oriental.

must be extremely cautious about drawing conclusions based on Lucan stylistic peculiarities.

Jeremias' third argument is disputed by Fitzmyer when he writes,

> ... Jeremias along with many others (J. M. Creed, E. Klostermann, W. Grundmann, K. H. Rengstorf, J. Schmid, etc.) understand "the master" in v. 8a as Jesus. In this they appeal to the sense of v. 8b, which almost certainly reflects a statement of Jesus and seems out of place in the mouth of the master of the parable. These writers also appeal to Lk 18:6, where an observation of *ho kyrios* is recorded, who cannot be anyone else but Jesus. And in 18:8 there follows a similar introduction of a saying by *legō hymin* (see 16:9).—However, the situation in chap. 16 is not the same as that in chap. 18. There is an earlier mention of *kyrios* in 16:3, 5, whereas there is nothing similar in Lk 18. Moreover, in Lk 12:42, although the first instance of the absolute use of *ho kyrios* refers to Jesus, the second one is generic and does not refer to Him at all. . . .[72]

The Oriental versions give unambiguous, yet divergent, answers. The Old Syriac has "the master." The Peshitta makes the word refer to Jesus by translating "our Lord/master." The word is the well-known "marana" of the end of Revelation.[73] The Harclean returns to "the master." Medieval Arabic versions follow the Peshitta, but all of the nineteenth- and twentieth-century translations return to "the master," meaning the lord of the parable. Fakhūrī, in the Būlusiyah version, makes it doubly explicit by translating "the master praised *his* steward" [emphasis mine]. Saʿīd also clearly identifies the master as the rich man of the parable.[74]

Finally, if the κύριος of verse 8 refers to Jesus, the parable is left without an ending. Fitzmyer observes, "Without v. 8a the parable has no real ending. From the beginning, the reaction of the master to the manager's conduct is expected; it is finally given in v. 8a."[75]

Fitzmyer is right. As an Oriental story, the parable builds to a climax awaiting the owner's response at the end of the parable. One of Bultmann's principles for the telling of a similitude is what he calls "the law of end stress."[76] Verse 8a when read as a part of the parable is an almost perfect example of this principle. It is almost universally conceded that Luke understood the master of verse 8 to be the rich man of verse 1. There seems to be no remaining argument to

---

[72]Fitzmyer, "Manager," 27f., n.8.

[73]This shift from the Old Syriac "the master" to the Peshitta "our Lord/master" may be the result of the "spilling" of unambiguous meaning from one verse to an ambiguous word or phrase in another. Verse 9 is a clear Dominical saying. This fact may have influenced the way the Peshitta translators read v. 8. We will note other examples of this same "spilling" effect later in the exegesis of other parables.

[74]Saʿīd, *Lūqā*, 409.

[75]Fitzmyer, "Manager," 27. Furthermore the literary structure of the parabolic ballad requires that the master be the master of the story. Stanza seven balances stanza one as we have noted. In stanza one the reader is introduced to a rich man and an unfaithful steward. In the balancing stanza, stanza seven, the form requires and the listener/reader expects a return to the rich man and his dishonest steward.

[76]Cf. Bultmann, *Tradition*, 191.

deter us from accepting Luke's judgment and reading verse 8a as the climax of the parable.[77]

Many earlier commentators worried over how Jesus could use a dishonest man as an example. But this need not delay us. The Middle Eastern peasant at the bottom of the economic ladder finds such a parable pure delight. Nothing pleases him more than a story in which some David kills a Goliath.

Yet there is an unusual feature to this story. The storyteller in the East always has a series of stories about the clever fellow who won out over the "Mister Big" of his community. The remarkable feature of this parable is that the steward is *criticized* as "unrighteous" and called a "son of darkness." The average Oriental storyteller would not feel any compulsion to add such a corrective to this type of story. Thus the Western listener/reader is surprised at the use of a dishonest man as a hero. The Eastern listener/reader is surprised that such a hero is criticized.

The parables of Jesus have a surprising list of unsavory characters. In addition to this steward are the unjust judge, the neighbor who does not want to be bothered in the night, and the man who pockets someone else's treasure by buying his field. As Smith notes,

> The parable of the Unjust Steward, whose conduct goes from bad to worse, is only the most outstanding example of a class of parables, the use of which appears to be a unique and striking feature of Christ's teaching.[78]

In three of the four cases listed above, Jesus is using the rabbinic principle of "from the light to the heavy," which means generally, "how much more." That is, if this widow got what she wanted from this kind of judge (18:1–9), how much more you and God? If this man got bread in the night from this neighbor (11:5–7), how much more you from God. If this dishonest steward solved his problem by relying on the mercy of his master to solve his crisis, how much more will God help you in your crisis when you trust his mercy.

Verse 8a, moreover, has two key words that must be examined: φρονίμως and ἐπαινέω. All the older Oriental versions translate φρονίμως with some form of *ḥokmah*, "wisdom." The universality of this translation in the Syriac is significant. Clearly, for the Eastern fathers, there was no particular problem in using the Semitic word *ḥokmah* in this context.[79] Wisdom in the Old Testament, in

---

[77] The ὅτι of v. 8 can be read as a *Hoti recitative*. Gächter understands it in this light and translates, "Whereupon the master praised his dishonest steward: 'He has acted wisely' " (Gächter, "Oriental," 130). The Old Syriac and the Peshitta have the maddeningly ambiguous *d*, but the rest of the Oriental versions, without exception, have a causative. However, direct speech is usually spoken *to* someone and with a *Hoti recitative* we would expect, "*You* have acted wisely." Either way, the interpretation is not affected. If accepted, this suggestion nonetheless reinforces our observation that the first lines of the stanzas of the parabolic ballad very often have direct speech.

[78] B. T. D. Smith, *Parables*, 109.

[79] Sa'īd's commentary prints the Van Dyke-Bustānī Arabic text at the top of the page. Thus Sa'īd has to deal with *ḥokmah* in the mouth of the master praising his steward. Sa'īd writes, "He [the rich man] praises him for his *ḥikma* [Arabic; = Heb. and Aram. *ḥokmah*] and does not praise him for his high character, as if he is amazed at his superior intelligence but not pleased at the crookedness of his heart. This is demonstrated in that the master does not return the steward to his position" (*Lūqā*, 409).

certain contexts, definitely carries the idea of cleverness. Fohrer writes, "חכם can be used for a nonmoral cleverness and skill deployed in self-preservation."[80] This quality of wisdom is found as early as the Exodus account where Pharaoh urges his people to act "wisely" and kill all the Israelite children (Exod. 1:10), and as late as the illustration of wisdom in self-preservation of the ants, badgers, locusts, and lizards in Proverbs (30:24–28). This aspect of wisdom fits exactly into what is said of the unjust steward. In the Septuagint both σοφία and φρόνησις translate ḥokmah. The second is less frequent and less theologically freighted. Philo emphasized the practical qualities of φρόνησις.[81]

It seems only reasonable to assume that the original Aramaic word in this story was ḥokmah. The meaning in this context was the "cleverness and skill deployed in self-preservation."[82] The Greek translator, intending this lesser quality of wisdom, avoided the use of σοφία and translated with φρονίμως.

In harmony with this, the eschatological overtones of the word must not be overlooked. Jeremias[83] endorses Preisker's definition of φρονίμως[84] as "having grasped the eschatological situation" and argues that this meaning is specifically intended in this verse. Fitzmyer approves of Jeremias' interpretation and adds,

> . . . The adverb is used precisely in this eschatological sense in the parable. The manager stands for the Christian confronted with the crises that the kingdom brings in the lives of men.[85]

In summary, the steward is praised for his wisdom, or ḥokmah. This means his skilfulness in self-preservation. He is sensitive to the hopelessness of his situation. He is aware of the one source of salvation, namely, the generosity of his master.

In discussing the parable of the Unjust Steward in the light of Qumran, Kosmala argues that the steward is not "the unrighteous steward" but rather the "steward of unrighteousness," and that this is eschatological language, referring primarily to the world that lies under the power of wickedness. He writes, "The expression οἰκονόμος τῆς ἀδικίας, therefore, describes a man who is completely bound up with this world in which ἀδικία is the ruling principle."[86] This would further indicate the eschatological thrust of the parable.

Turning to the second word (to praise) it is significant that the Old Syriac version reads shabaḥ (to praise), which is identical with the Hebrew shabaḥ. Yet, the Syriac word carries a fascinating additional meaning of "to keep in good

---

[80]G. Fohrer, *TDNT*, VII, 484.

[81]Philo *Quod Deus Imm* 35, quoted by R. C. Trench, *Synonyms of the New Testament* (9th ed., London: James Clarke, 1961), 263. Trench has a good discussion of the two words well documented from ancient sources; cf. also Trench, *Notes*, 333, n.b.

[82]Fohrer, *loc. cit.*

[83]Jeremias, *Parables*, 46.

[84]H. Preisker, "Lukas 16, 1–7," *Theologische Literaturzeitung* 74 (1949), 89.

[85]Fitzmyer, "Manager," 32, n. 21.

[86]Hans Kosmala, "The Parables of the Unjust Steward in the Light of Qumran," *Annual of the Swedish Theological Institute* 3 (1964), 115.

repute, to sustain the credit of.''[87] This meaning fits the steward's situation exactly. We can only speculate as to whether or not such a secondary meaning may have been a part of the original Aramaic of the parable in its Palestinian setting. The word in later Jewish Aramaic means only "to praise."

Of greater significance is the eschatological usage of the Greek word in the New Testament itself. Preisker writes, '' '$\epsilon\pi\alpha\iota\nu\sigma$' signifies the acceptance or approval of the righteous by God alone in the Last Judgment.''[88] The verb form appears in the New Testament only in Paul's First Epistle to the Corinthians and here in Luke.[89] Yet, the idea of a divine master offering approval in an eschatological setting is present in Matthew.[90] Thus the Greek word, on the level of the story itself, carries the meaning of simple approval of what the steward has done. At the same time, on a theological level this word provides additional evidence for interpreting the parable as being primarily concerned with eschatology.

A summary of the theological cluster of this parable can be briefly stated as follows: God (the master) is a God of judgment and mercy. Because of his evil, man (the steward) is caught in the crisis of the coming of the kingdom. Excuses will avail the steward nothing. Man's only option is to entrust *everything* to the unfailing mercy of his generous master who, he can be confident, will accept to pay the price for man's salvation. This clever rascal was wise enough to place his total trust in the quality of mercy experienced at the beginning of the story. That trust was vindicated. Disciples need the same kind of wisdom.[91]

This brings us to verse 8b. Here we will try to demonstrate that it is a part of the original telling of the parable. It provides the necessary corrective to the approval of the unjust steward. He is praised for his wisdom in knowing where his salvation lay, not for his dishonesty. Furthermore the literary form indicates that it

---

[87]R. P. Smith, *A Compendious Syriac Dictionary*, ed. J. P. Smith (Oxford: Clarendon, 1903), 556.

[88]Preisker, *TDNT*, II, 587.

[89]1 Cor. 11:2, 17, 22a, 22b.

[90]Matt. 25:21, 34.

[91]There is a wonderful story in the oral tradition of the Middle Eastern peasantry which tells of a condemned murderer during the days of the famous sultan Saladin. The killer was condemned to death and kept crying, "I want to see the Sultan." Finally he was taken into the presence of the great Sultan where he cried out, "O most gracious Sultan, my sins are great but the mercy of the Sultan is greater." He was released.

A modern version of the same story was related to me in 1965 by one of the leaders of the Arab section of Jerusalem, a man named Abū Alfons. In 1960, the wife of a condemned spy came to Abū Alfons for advice on how to free her husband. He told her to wait outside the palace for the king's motorcade to form and then throw herself in front of the king's car. He explicitly instructed the lady *not* to plead innocence, with the warning, "You know he is guilty and so does the king, To offer excuses is to destroy all hope. Throw yourself on the mercy of the king!" The lady carried out the instructions. The Jordanian monarch knows full well how a noble king is expected to act and the spy was released. The Western reader can imagine the result if a similar event took place in front of the White House or at Number Ten Downing Street. All of this is to point out that Jesus, in using this particular theme, was appealing to a well-known aspect of Middle Eastern cultural life that was important enough to survive in medieval story and in contemporary life.

is a part of the original parable. The three lines of the last stanza balance the three lines of the first stanza.

A number of contemporary arguments must be discussed. Jeremias argues that verse 8b is a part of the series of additional interpretations that stretches from verse 8b to verse 13.[92] Fitzmyer reflects much of contemporary thinking when he comments,

> . . . The saying preserved here represents an independent logion of Jesus which has been joined to the parable (either by Luke or his source). For it follows strangely on V. 8a, and indeed on the whole preceding parable.[93]

However, there is nothing strange about the presence of this comment at this place in the text. As we have observed, this comment makes it clear that the man is not being praised for his dishonesty.[94]

Jeremias and others argue that the parable was originally directed to the unconverted and then redirected to the Church at a later period.[95] This idea would give weight to the suggestion that 8b was added by the Church. However, the parable is more than an appeal to the listener/reader to act. It is also an appeal to insight and faith to understand a crucial aspect of the nature of the kingdom of God. Kosmala writes:

> The people to whom this parable is addressed cannot have been the "unconverted", they were rather people who were Jesus' followers and indeed belonged to the "converted", they were the "children of the light". The parable is introduced by the words: "He spoke to the disciples" (16:1), for what Jesus says in it is a plain criticism of the children of the light. . . .[96]

Thus the parable does not fit as a parable spoken only to the disciples, nor does it fit as a parable spoken only to outsiders. The Lucan setting is ambiguous, with disciples mentioned in verse 1 and Pharisees in verse 14. This ambiguity seems appropriate.

The subject of this pericope in the overall structure of the Jerusalem Document discussed above is the Coming of the Kingdom. In a parallel pericope in the upper half of the structure, Peter asks, "Lord, are you telling this parable for us or for all?" Thus the ambiguity surrounding the question of who is addressed in the parable is reflected in both 16:1–8 and 12:35–40.

It could be argued that verse 8b is not a part of the original parable but rather an addition attached to the parable by a Church nervous about a story that praises a dishonest steward. But as we have noted, the phraseology of 8b is distinctively Palestinian, and the Palestinian Church would have understood the parable and

---

[92]Jeremias, *Parables,* 108.

[93]Fitzmyer, "Manager," 28f.

[94]The Palestinian character of the comment has been fully documented elsewhere and need not detain us; *ibid.,* 28, n. 10; Jeremias, *Theology,* 169.

[95]Jeremias, *Parables,* 47.

[96]Kosmala, *loc. cit.,* 117f.

would not have been nervous about it. If 8b were Greek in vocabulary and inspiration this argument would be weighty. As it stands it does not follow. Thus, keeping in mind the literary structure and the other factors mentioned above, the greatest probability is that 8b is a part of the original parable.

Before we turn to verses 9–13 we must note the points of similarity between the parables of the Unjust Steward and the Prodigal Son. Many scholars have noted this connection.[97] A number of very specific points of relationship are to be noted.

1. Luke 16:1 does not tell us that a "parable" is about to be told. To get the word "parable" we have to return to 15:3. Thus Luke relates the two.[98]

2. In Luke 15 a son throws himself on the mercy of his father. In Luke 16 a servant throws himself on the mercy of his master.

3. The phrase δὲ καί in 16:1 is a favorite transitional device for Luke. It is used to show "that the parabolic discourse continues from the previous chapter."[99] The Old Syriac also uses a linking transitional phrase.[100]

4. Both the steward and the son betray a trust.[101]

5. Neither prodigal nor steward offers excuses.

6. The word "scattered" (διασκορπίζω) is applied to both. Furthermore, in the Syriac and Arabic versions, the word for the property wasted is in both stories identical.[102]

7. Both the steward and the prodigal experience extraordinary mercy from their superiors. The steward is not jailed for changing the bills; the prodigal is not punished for his having wasted the family's assets.

8. In both stories, there is a missing final scene. We do not know the final response of the older son or the final result of the steward's act.

Yet, at the same time, there is a shift to a new topic. One parable is on the topic of the gospel and the outcasts, the other is under the heading of the Coming of the Kingdom.[103] Luke 16:1–8 clearly has a number of ties to what precedes it. Later we will see that these connections are far closer than any links to what follows.

---

[97]Goulder clearly links the theology of the two parables, although he follows Derrett's interpretation and thus identifies repentance as the subject of both units (M. D. Goulder, "The Chiastic Structure of the Lucan Journey," *Studia Evangelica,* II [1963], 198). Manson wrote that the story of the Unjust Steward "may almost be regarded as an appendix to the parable of the Prodigal Son" (*Sayings,* 291). Derrett notes, "The parable [of the Unjust Steward] is a continuation of the theme started with the Lost Sheep and Prodigal Son, and not in antithesis to it" ("Steward," 199). J. A. Davidson says, "The background of the telling of the three parables in Lk. 15 seems to provide the clue to the meaning of the parable of the Unjust Steward" ("A 'Conjecture' about the Parable of the Unjust Steward (Luke xvi. 1–9," *ExpT* 66[1954], 31). Scharlemann writes, "This parable is a continuation of the theme started by the Lost Sheep and the Prodigal Son" (*Parables,* 83).

[98]Not too much can be made of this, in that the same can be said for the parable of Dives and Lazarus.

[99]Scharlemann, *Parables,* 83.

[100]The Old Syriac reads *tōb* (likewise, again).

[101]Cf. Scharlemann, *Parables,* 87.

[102]This is true of all but the literal Harclean.

[103]Cf. the discussion of the topical outline of the Jerusalem Document presented above in Chapter Four.

In this section, then, we have seen a parabolic ballad of an honorable master and his clever, dishonest estate manager. The manager is salaried, is probably an "agent," and deals with land renters who pay in kind. The steward is dismissed and admits his guilt by silence. He is not jailed and so discovers his master's mercy. He decides to risk everything on that mercy. Reductions are made in rents with the assumption of the master's approval. Praise flows from the local population to the master and to the steward. An ungracious repudiation by the master of such a "generous act" is out of the question. The steward is praised by the master of the story for his skill at self-preservation. Finally the parable returns to its starting point with a Dominical comment and provides unforgettable insight into the nature of God, the predicament of man, and the ground of salvation.

THE POEM ON MAMMON AND GOD (LUKE 16:9–13)

In this section we will attempt to demonstrate that Luke 16:9–13 is a carefully constructed poem with three stanzas on the single theme of mammon and God. The inversion principle is used in all three stanzas. Together they constitute a Form VI poem. The outer stanzas unite on the topic of mammon and God, and these relate to the climax of the entire poem which appears in the center, discussing mammon and the truth. The poem has been moved to this place in the text because it provides a corrective for the Greek reader, who may well misunderstand the parable. It is our view that Luke 16:9–13 has its own integrity and that it should be read and interpreted apart from the parable that precedes it. One of the important clues to making a sharp division between 16:1–8 and 16:9–13 is the introductory "And to you I say." Both here (16:1–13) and in Luke 11:5–13 there is a parable followed by a poem which has been confused with it. In the brief phrases that introduce each of the poems (cf. 16:9 and 11:9) we find the rare $\dot{\nu}\mu\hat{\iota}\nu$ $\lambda\acute{\epsilon}\gamma\omega$, with the verb after the pronoun.

    a.   Parable

    b. $\dot{\nu}\mu\hat{\iota}\nu$ $\lambda\acute{\epsilon}\gamma\omega$ + dominical poem on a related topic.[104]

The $\dot{\nu}\mu\hat{\iota}\nu$ $\lambda\acute{\epsilon}\gamma\omega$ can best be understood as evidence that an editor joined two units not originally occurring together.[105]

---

[104]Luke 12:22 may be a third example. There we have a parable followed by a poem, and some texts have the same "to you I say," again separating the parable and the poem.

[105]Aside from the cases discussed above, $\dot{\nu}\mu\hat{\iota}\nu$ $\lambda\acute{\epsilon}\gamma\omega$ is found in Luke only, in 6:27, where it again indicates a transition to a new subject. Jeremias observes that this unusual word order is characteristic of Luke's style (Parables, 45). In Luke there are 38 cases of $\lambda\acute{\epsilon}\gamma\omega$ $\dot{\nu}\mu\hat{\iota}\nu$ and only four of $\dot{\nu}\mu\hat{\iota}\nu$ $\lambda\acute{\epsilon}\gamma\omega$. $\dot{\nu}\mu\hat{\iota}\nu$ $\lambda\acute{\epsilon}\gamma\omega$ is unknown to Matthew. Mark uses it in 13:37 (but D reverses the word order). In John it is found in 13:33 and 16:4. Cf. also 1 Cor. 15:34; 15:51; 2 Cor. 8:10; 1 Thess. 4:15; 2 Thess. 2:5; Rev. 2:24. We can observe further that in a passage with non-Lucan, highly Semitic features such as a historic present and Aramaic words, it is striking to find a non-Semitic construction where the verb surrenders its normal position at the beginning of the sentence in such an idiomatic phrase. In Luke 6:27; 11:9; and 16:9 all our Oriental versions except the literal Harclean restore the verb to the front of the phrase.

Verses 9–13 must now be examined to determine their meaning and to see if they have a unified poetic structure. Many scholars feel that these verses consist of a series of three separate interpretations of the parable added by the early Church. These three interpretations we are told deeschatologize the parable and turn it into a hortatory injunction on how to handle money.[106] Jeremias writes, "In v. 9 we have an entirely different application of the parable from that which is given in v. 8a."[107]

Scholars from Jülicher to Jeremias have noted a break in thought starting with 16:9. In fact, the scene changes quite radically. The following major differences between the steward and the man with mammon can be noted:

1. In the parable there is a master, a steward, and a problem between them. In verse 9 there is no master, no steward, and thus no problem between them.

2. The steward is penniless; he considers begging and farm labor. In verse 9 the man with mammon presumably has a significant sum of mammon. He is offered advice on how to spend it.

3. The steward makes reductions for the relatively rich. In verse 9 the man with mammon is encouraged to give to the poor (presumably).

4. The steward is dealing with someone else's money. The man with mammon is dealing with his own money.

5. The steward is already in his crisis. He is dismissed. The man with mammon is encouraged to plan for the future. His crisis is in the indefinite future.

6. The steward's problem is his own sin, and his master's expectations. The man with mammon faces the problem of the insecurity of worldly goods.

7. The steward is dealing with debts not yet due. The man with mammon is offered advice about "cash in hand."

8. We will note below a relationship between verse 9 and verse 13. In verse 13 a *servant* is mentioned. The parable speaks of a *steward*.

9. The steward is unfaithful and unrighteous. The character of the man with mammon is not criticized.

Thus it is evident that a clear separation must be made between 16:1–8 and 16:9–13.[108]

Having established a clear break between 16:8 and 9 we now intend to demonstrate that verses 9–13 are a very carefully constructed poem with a unified theme. The three stanzas have the following overall structure:

---

[106]C. H. Dodd: "We can almost see here notes for the three separate sermons on the parable as text" (*Parables*, 26); cf. John Reumann, *Jesus in the Church's Gospels* (Philadelphia: Fortress, 1968), 194.

[107]Jeremias, *Parables*, 46; cf. also p. 30.

[108]Jeremias suggests that the original audience of v. 9 may have been tax farmers "and others classed as dishonest persons" (*Parables*, 46). But the importance of the crucial message of the entire poem for any group of listeners would lead one to conclude that the wide circle of sinners, disciples, and Pharisees indicated in Luke 15:1, 2; 16:1, 14 is more appropriate as the audience for such a poem.

Luke 16:9–13

I.   MAMMON AND GOD

I say
to you: A   for yourselves make
                     B   friends
                            C   from mammon the unrighteous
                            C′   so that when it fails
                     B′   they may receive
               A′   you into the eternal tents.

II.   MAMMON AND THE TRUTH

               D   The one faithful in little
                    also in much is faithful

                    E   and the one in little unfaithful
                         also in much unfaithful is.

If
therefore   F   in the unrighteous mammon
                       faithful you are not

                  F′   the TRUTH
                       who to you will entrust?

And
if   E′   in what is another's
                       faithful you are not

                  D′   the what-is-yours
                       who will give to you?

III.   MAMMON AND GOD

               G   No servant can serve two masters.
                     H   Either the one he hates
                            I   and the other he loves
                            I′   or the one he is devoted to
                     H′   and the other he despises.
               G′   You cannot serve God and mammon.

This poem is preserved with no extra phrases or pious expansions. It shows a powerful and subtle unity of thought and a simplicity founded on great complexity of poetic structure. Structure and content will be examined by stanzas, then the internal relationships between stanzas will be considered. Finally, external relationships to other blocks of nearby material will be studied.

Stanza I—Mammon and God

The inverted parallelism is evident. The lines move as follows:

     You

          They (friends)

> Mammon[109]
>
> Mammon (it)[110]
>
> They
>
> You

This stanza is an example of poetic structure type A.

In lines A and A′ the dominant semantic relationship is "you." There may also be a relationship between "make" and "eternal tents." The average person in any age assumes that property (mammon) is for the "making" of "earthly tents," that is, for securing earthly life. By placing lines A and A′ opposite each other, the poem says boldly that this is not the case.[111]

Jeremias has noted that the "friends" of line B may mean the angels, and that "they may receive" in line B′ is a circumlocution for "God." He writes, "The 'friends' are possibly the angels, i.e. God (a conjecture which is supported by v. 9b where the 3rd person pl. alludes to the angels as a circumlocution for God). . . ."[112]

The first stanza then is a Form I poetic structure with three semantic units. Each unit has strong relationships to the parallel unit.

Stanza II—Mammon and the Truth

Verses 10–12 form the second stanza. These also offer six idea units, as does the third stanza. In contrast to Stanza I this stanza has double lines. It is an example of Form II. A number of patterns of correspondence may be noted:

First, each of the six bicola can be seen as relating to each other in this fashion:

> D   faithful +
>
> E   unfaithful −

---

[109]Hauck observes that "mammon" most likely has its origin in the root '*mn*. It means generally, "that in which one trusts," and specifically, "property and anything of value" (F. Hauck, *TDNT*, IV, 388). Mammon is here called "unrighteous." Manson notes succinctly, "All money gets dirty at some stage in its history" (*Sayings*, 293). Ben Sirach has some significant things to say about how "a peg will stick in the joint between two stones, and sin will wedge itself between selling and buying" (Sir. 27:2). Fitzmyer defines the use of the word in this pericope as "The tendency wealth has to make men dishonest" ("Manager," 30, n. 15).

[110]The Byzantine text reads ἐκλίπητε, but both Western and Alexandrian texts have a singular referring to mammon. Both readings refer to death.

[111]The phrase "the eternal tents" is a throwback to the tabernacle. No suggestion of impermanence is meant. Ps. 61:5 reads, "I will dwell in thy tabernacle forever."

[112]Jeremias, *Parables*, 46, n. 85. However, Jeremias prefers the meaning "good works." Many other scholars have noted the possibility of "that they may receive you" meaning God or the angels. Trench, over a century ago, listed both "angels" (as in the parable of Lazarus) and "God" as possible alternatives (cf. *Notes*, 339). Manson notes, "In the Rabbinical writings it is a common way of avoiding the mention of the divine name to use the verb in the 3rd person plural, just as in this verse" (*Sayings*, 293). Cf. also Oesterley, *Jewish Background*, 200; Fletcher, "Riddle," 24; B. T. D. Smith, *Parables*, 112.

F   unfaithful −

F′   faithful +? (a wistful "faithful")

E′   unfaithful −

D′   faithful?? +? (a wistful "faithful")

Unit D speaks of faithfulness while D′ talks of a hoped-for faithfulness. E and E′ are on the theme of unfaithfulness. In the center mammon and the truth are contrasted.

Then the definite and indefinite pronouns form a striking eight-unit pattern:

D   the one (faithful in little)

     the one (faithful in much)

E   the one (unfaithful in little)

     the one (unfaithful in much)

F   you (with mammon unfaithful)

F′   you (entrusted with the truth?)

E′   you (unfaithful with another's)

D·   you (entrusted with yours?)

Furthermore, the first two bicola have an internal structure. The first of them (D) is chiastic. The second (E) has its two lines parallel to each other.

D   The one faithful in little

     also in much is faithful

E   and the one in little unfaithful

     also in much unfaithful is.

The poet is careful not to use the same poetic device twice in a row.

The center of the stanza has a play on words in Aramaic. The climax of this type of poetry is always the center. Thus, the center of this stanza is the heart of the entire poem. In this center, words rooted in 'mn are used in a remarkable way. Substituting the appropriate Aramaic words the verse reads,

if therefore in the unrighteous *mamon*

'*amen* you are not

the '*emunah*

who will *yeyminken*?[113]

---

[113]Hauck, *TDNT*, IV, 388. Hauck writes, "The original Aramaic of the saying in Luke 16:10f. would thus contain a pun, for πιστός, πιστεύσει, τό ἀληθινόν also belong to the stem אמן." In regard to the word ἀληθινόν, we are faced with a number of alternatives. However, all the more likely candidates have 'mn at their root. Bultmann opts for 'mt; cf. *TDNT*, I, 249.

To summarize, this second stanza is a highly artistic example of Form II. The climax in the center is clear and striking. The stanza is intact.

Stanza III—Mammon and God

The inverted parallelisms in these six lines are clear. They are: "Two Masters, Hate, Love—Love, Hate, Two Masters." The stanza alone is another example of Form II.

Relationships Between Stanzas I and III

Three specific relationships tie the two outer stanzas together. They are:

1. Each stanza has six idea units.

2. Both stanzas I and III are enclosed with "you."

   A   you

   A'   you

   G   servant (by implication, "you")

   G'   you

3. The strongest relationship between the two outer stanzas is the repetition of the "God and mammon" theme. They are treated differently, but nevertheless the two subjects are the same.

Relationships Between the Two Outer Stanzas and the Center Stanza

We have noted that "God and mammon" is the main point of the first and last stanzas. The center of such constructions has a particular prominence, and thus stanza I has "mammon" as its focus while stanza III centers on "love and devotion." The second stanza has a double center with "mammon" and "the truth." The centers of all three stanzas thus stand opposite to each other in the following fashion:

I	MAMMON ⌐
II	MAMMON ←
	THE TRUTH ⌐
III	LOVE AND DEVOTION ←

In summary, the internal unity of Luke 16:9–13 is strong and artistically satisfying. The three stanzas unite to form a single Form VI poem. The overall theme centers around God, mammon, and the truth. The two outer stanzas tell the reader that mammon is for building treasure in heaven and that you cannot serve both God and mammon.[114] The climax in the center stanza warns the listener that he may not be trusted with the truth unless he proves trustworthy with mammon.

What then is to be said about the origin of this poem? The following points can be made with some confidence:

1. The poem is a unit and must have been shaped into its present form by a single poet of remarkable skill.

2. The inverted parallelism used here was common to the writing prophets.

3. The presence of an Aramaic word and an Aramaic wordplay demonstrate that the material came from the earliest level of the tradition.

4. Because it is poetry, its preservation in an oral tradition for half a century is no more problematic than the preservation of the oracles of Amos.

5. Verse 9 is so obscure that, as Fletcher has said, "presumably nothing so obscure would have been introduced into the tradition and erroneously attributed to Jesus."[115]

6. Luke attributes the material to Jesus of Nazareth. There seems to be no remaining argument to keep us from accepting Luke's judgment.

One final question remains. If 16:9–13 is a separate subject related to but clearly distinct from the parable of the Unjust Steward, then why is it placed directly after the parable? We would suggest that Luke has moved it here for two reasons: first as a corrective for the non-Oriental reader; second because of the close word associations with the parable. But before examining these two reasons we must observe its suggested original place in the Jerusalem Document (travel narrative).

The first part of the discussion centers around the crucial verse 16. This verse reads, "The law and the prophets were until John: since then the good news of the kingdom of God is preached καὶ πᾶς εἰς αὐτὴν βιάζεται." This last phrase is often translated, "and everyone enters it violently," or, "everyone presses into it." This is to take the verb βιάζεται as a deponent thus having an active meaning. Schrenk admits, "Philologically possible is the pass.: 'Every man is pressed into.'" This passive reading he then dismisses as "artificial."[116] However, Hibat Allah Ibn al-'Assāl in his great critical edition of 1252 translates, "and everybody because of it is under pressure."[117] Ibn al-'Assāl has taken the verb as a

---

[114]Manson has rightly suggested: "The point of this saying [v. 9] is . . . that by disposing of worldly wealth in the proper way, one will have treasure in heaven. The true parallel to this verse is in such sayings as Mt. 6[19ff.]; Mk. 10[21]; Lk. 12[33f.]" (*Sayings*, 293). Luke 12:15 is one of the few places in Luke where possessions are discussed, although the word mammon is not used in the Greek nor in most of the Oriental versions. The Syriac versions use a different word. But the Arabic texts have the identical word, thus tying the passages even more closely together. Then in the narrative section in Luke 12:32–34, the theme of treasure in heaven is clearly very close theologically to Luke 16:9.

[115]Fletcher, "Riddle," 19.

[116]G. Schrenk, *TDNT*, I, 612.

[117]Cf. British Museum Oriental Ms. No. 3382 Folio 252. Ibn al-'Assāl was one of the greatest scholars of his century and this version of the Gospels was his greatest work. It is a critical edition that uses a

passive and read the εἰς as a causative. Significantly, one of the clear cases of the causative use of εἰς is in the Jerusalem Document at Luke 11:32.[118] Ibn al-'Assāl puts both of the traditional translations mentioned above in his apparatus; the first he traces to the Coptic, the second he finds in an Arabic version translated from the Greek. We have seen that Luke 16:1–8 is a warning to the listener that the kingdom has come and that he is in the crisis of decision regarding it. 16:16 as translated by Ibn al-'Assāl brings this verse theologically into line with the parable in a profound way. By contrast then the poem on Mammon, God, and the Life to Come is, theologically, related profoundly to the parable that follows (Lazarus and the Rich Man). In the text of Luke we now have the pericopes in the following order:

> *Eschatological warning*
> 16:1–8—the unjust steward
>
> *Money and the life to come: the Pharisees*
> 16:9–15
>
> *Eschatological warning*
> 16:16
>
> (Verse 17 seems to have been added by Jewish Christians close to Matthew who were nervous about the statement on the Law in verse 16. Verse 18 on divorce seems to have nothing to do with the context.)
>
> *Money, and the life to come*
> 16:19–31

It is our view that the original Jerusalem Document had the two discussions of *money and the life to come* together and the two *eschatological warnings* together. That is, Luke has moved Luke 16:9–15 ahead of 16:16. When 16:9–15 is moved back to its presumed original position the balance of the Jerusalem Document seen above is restored.[119]

We are then obliged to ask, Why did Luke move them? As we have suggested, his first reason was to provide a corrective for his Greek readers. The parable is an esoteric Oriental parable which Theophilus is bound to misunderstand. He, Theophilus, will no doubt think Jesus is encouraging dishonesty. Luke does his best as an editor. He moves a poem on faithfulness with money to a position immediately following the problematic parable,[120] thus hoping to protect Theophilus from a potentially serious misunderstanding.

That the poem on Mammon is theologically very close to the parable of Lazarus and the rich man has long been noted. Manson writes, "We may leave the

---

series of twenty-eight symbols to refer to variant readings and translations which he found in Greek, Coptic, and Syriac versions. He includes the full range of omissions, interpolations, and substitutions to which he makes reference in his apparatus. His translation of this verse first drew my attention to this possibility, which is grammatically legitimate on the basis of the Greek and makes profound sense in the context of the chapter.

[118]Bauer-A., G., *Lexicon*, 229.
[119]See above, pp. 116f.
[120]Cf. Creed, *St. Luke*, 205.

question open whether this verse [v. 9] would not stand more appropriately as the moral of the parable of Dives and Lazarus.''[121] If our theory is correct, then this poem on Mammon in fact originally introduced the parable of Lazarus to which it is theologically close.

Luke's second possible reason for moving verses 9–15 ahead is word association. It is well known that in the synoptic Gospels pericopes are often placed together because of word association.[122] Hiers has noted the very strong word association between verse 4 and verse 9.[123]

a. in order that whenever I shall be turned out   (v. 4)
    in order that whenever it fails   (v. 9)

b. they may receive me into the houses of them   (v. 4)
    they may receive you into the eternal tents   (v. 9)

However, word association does not necessarily indicate that the two units of material brought together have the same subject; nor does it suggest that the compiler necessarily intended them to be understood as being on the same subject.[124]

There are at least two good reasons, then, why the poem on Mammon is placed directly after the parable of the Unjust Steward, although divergent in subject from it.

To summarize, we have seen in this section that the parable of the Unjust Steward is a parabolic ballad followed by a three-stanza poem on Mammon. The parable in an unforgettable backhanded way illuminates, from a unique angle, the splendor of the grace of God in which alone the believer must trust. The poem on Mammon speaks of the relationship between faithfulness with money, God, and the truth. The poet wonders if any dishonest man can be trusted with God's truth. When the two passages are read as a single subject, both are put out of focus. All the evidence points to each unit having its own special message and style. Theories that suggest the second block of material to be a gradual collection of early Church comments on the parable prove to be inadequate to the structural and theological nature of the material. The poem is the work of a skilled Palestinian poet in the first century. There remains no reason to doubt that the author was Jesus of Nazareth.

---

[121]Manson, *Sayings,* 293; cf. Creed, *St. Luke,* 305.

[122]Cf. Luke 17:20–21, and 22–37 under the topic of "lo here, lo there"; Luke 11:14–23 and 24–26 under the topic of "demons"; Luke 11:27–28 and 29–32 under the topic of "hearing and repeating through preaching"; Luke 12:22–31 and 32–34 under the topic of "fear."

[123]Richard H. Hiers, "Friends by Unrighteous Mammon: The Eschatological Proletariat (Luke 16:9)," *Journal of the American Academy of Religion* 38 (1970), 30–36.

[124]Gächter, "Oriental," 131, n. 40, writes, "St. Luke may have received the parable with this catchword composition from tradition; this is more likely than that he himself created the somewhat incongruous sequence of the *logia* of Jesus." The literary structure of the Jerusalem Document offers more reasons for the order of the logia in it than Gächter has seen. But he did notice the use of "catchword composition."

6

EXEGESIS OF LUKE 11:5-13

THE FRIEND OF MIDNIGHT (LUKE 11:5-8)

The parable of the Friend at Midnight is a parabolic ballad with some of the features of the poetical Form IV. It has two stanzas of six units each, and each stanza inverts. In this section we intend to demonstrate that this parable opens with a question expecting an emphatic negative answer. The question can be paraphrased, Can you imagine having a guest and going to a neighbor to borrow bread and the neighbor offers ridiculous excuses about a locked door and sleeping children? The Middle Eastern listener responds, "No, I cannot imagine such a thing!" The parable climaxes around the question of the "sense of honor" or "blamelessness" of the man asleep, which leads him in the night to fulfil the host's request. "Importunity" is best understood as an inappropriate foreign element, which has "spilled" into the parable from the verses immediately following it. The cultural elements of the parable fall into place once the key word $\dot{\alpha}\nu\alpha\acute{\iota}\delta\epsilon\iota\alpha$ is properly understood. The parable teaches that God is a God of honor and that man can have complete assurance that his prayers will be heard. Finally, a poem on a different aspect of the subject of prayer (11:9–13) is placed after the parable. In this section we will examine the parable and in the next section comment on the poem that follows it.

The overall structure of the Jerusalem Document[1] places this passage in clear parallel to Luke 18:1–14. There, as in 11:1–13, originally separate units of the tradition have been assembled by the compiler. Bultmann rightly identifies three separate units, verses 1–4, 5–8 and 9–13.[2]

Our first task is an examination of the literary structure of the parable, which is as follows:

---

[1]See above, pp. 80ff.
[2]Bultmann, *Tradition,* 324. Thus in the case of this passage it is readily recognized that a parable is followed by a related yet distinct piece of the tradition which may have had no original relationship to it.

And he said to them,
    Can any one of you imagine having a friend and going to him at midnight

(WHAT WILL NOT HAPPEN)

A 1   and saying to him, "Friend, *lend me* three loaves   REQUEST (GIVE)
   2   for a friend of mine has arrived on a journey
                            REASON FOR REQUEST
    3   and I have nothing to set before him."   APPEAL TO DUTY
    3'   And will he answer from within, "Don't bother me.
                                  DUTY REFUSED
  2'   The door is now closed and my children are in bed with me.
                              REASON FOR REFUSAL
 1'   I cannot get up and *give* you anything"? REQUEST REFUSED (GIVE)

   I tell you   (WHAT WILL HAPPEN)

B 1   though he will not *give* him anything NOT ANSWER REQUEST (GIVE)
   2   having arisen   ARISING
    3   because of being his friend NOT FOR FRIENDSHIP'S SAKE
    3'   but because of his avoidance of shame
                              BUT FOR HONOR'S SAKE
  2'   he will get up   WILL ARISE
 1'   and *give* him whatever he wants.[3]   REQUEST GRANTED (GIVE)

    A number of features of the parable appear once the structure is seen. We observe that the outside lines of each stanza unite around the theme of *giving*. The center of each stanza climaxes on the topic of *honor*. To understand this more clearly the culture of the story must be examined with care. As in the case of two-stanza poems (Form IV) where the second stanza is patterned after the first, the climax of the entire literary piece is the center of the second stanza. This is especially clear here where we have translated the key word under discussion "avoidance of shame." The details of the text and its culture must now be examined with care.

    The parable of the Friend at Midnight begins with the familiar τίς ἐξ ὑμῶν. This characteristic phrase occurs three times in Q,[4] four times in Luke's special source,[5] and once in John.[6] This phrase, says Jeremias, "Does not seem to have any contemporary parallels."[7] Jeremias argues convincingly that the phrase "seeks to force the hearer to take up a definite standpoint."[8]

    An older view understood the interrogative of τίς ἐξ ὑμῶν to have been lost in the prolonged sentence.[9] Jeremias understands the question to run on

---

[3]As in all the literary structures in this study, the above reflects the Greek word order.
[4]Matt. 6:27 parallels Luke 12:25; Matt. 7:9 parallels Luke 11:11; Matt. 12:11 parallels Luke 14:5.
[5]Luke 11:5; 14:28; 15:4; 17:7.
[6]John 8:46.
[7]Jeremias, *Parables*, 103.
[8]*Ibid.*
[9]Plummer, *St. Luke*, 298; Arndt, *St. Luke*, 297.

through verse 7, and to expect an emphatic negative answer.[10] A careful examination of all the occurrences of this phrase in the New Testament sustains Jeremias' view.[11]

A number of the texts using this phrase would need some adjustment in the traditional translation to make them into questions expecting emphatic negative answers. But in each case such a shift makes lucid sense. Luke 14:5 would read:

> Can any one among you imagine a son falling in a well and he shall not immediately draw him up on the Sabbath day?

And Luke 15:4 would be translated:

> Can any one among you imagine having a hundred sheep and having lost one of them, not leaving the ninety-nine in the wilderness and going after the one that is lost?

Other texts with this phrase are already translated in a way that expects a negative answer; for example, Luke 17:7 (RSV):

> Will any one of you who has a servant plowing or keeping sheep, say to him when he has come in from the field, "Come at once and sit down at table"?

Understanding the phrase $\tau\acute{\iota}\varsigma\ \acute{\epsilon}\xi\ \acute{\upsilon}\mu\tilde{\omega}\nu$ in Luke 11:5 as expecting an emphatic negative answer is crucial to the interpretation of this parable. Jesus is asking, "Can you imagine going to a neighbor, asking for help to entertain a friend and getting this response?" The Oriental responsibility for his guest is legendary. The Oriental listener/reader cannot imagine silly excuses about a closed door and sleeping children when the adequate entertainment of a guest is the issue. To understand this, the presuppositions of the Oriental scene must be noted in some detail.

Contemporary exegetical literature is full of references to the need to travel by night because of the heat. This is true in the desert areas of Syria, Jordan, and Egypt. It is not customary in Palestine and Lebanon, where there is some elevation inland and a breeze from the sea along the coast.[12] Thus the arrival of the friend at midnight is unusual.

Rihbany may be responsible for the idea found in many modern works that three loaves are a meal for one person.[13] This is true of the very small Syrian loaves; it is not true of the bread eaten in the rest of the Middle East. One type of such bread is thin, flat, and nearly two feet across. Other kinds are round, raised,

---

[10]Jeremias, *Parables*, 103, 157.

[11]Jeremias has not examined the John 8:46 reference, which does not introduce a parable. Yet it also expects a negative answer. James 2:13–16 has the phrase also, and again it does not introduce a parable but yet expects a negative answer. 1 Pet. 4:15 is a statement, not a question.

[12]This is another example of confusing peasants and bedouins of the desert. In the summer it is customary for the bedouin to travel at night because of the intense heat. For the peasant, especially in Palestine, traveling at night would be exceptional.

[13]Rihbany, *Syrian*, 215.

but much larger than the Syrian variety. A guest is given one unbroken loaf, which is often more than he will eat. The host, as Rihbany rightly observes, "needed to put before his guest more than the exact number of loaves for one adult meal."[14]

Jeremias claims that the Palestinian peasant bakes every day and that "it is generally known in the village who has some bread left in the evening."[15] The Indian peasant bakes every day, but the Middle Eastern peasant does not. Our experience confirms Bishop, who writes,

> It looks too as if the house in question [the sleeper's house] had recently completed baking a batch of loaves—sometimes enough to last for a week or more at a stretch. . . . His [the host's] supplies were finished till the family's dough had been taken to the village oven [the next morning].[16]

Village women cooperate in bread baking, and it is known who has baked recently. There may be some bread left in the host's house, but he must offer the guest a complete unbroken loaf. To feed a guest with a partial loaf left from another meal would be an insult.

The host *must* serve his guest and the guest *must* eat. Rihbany writes, "He [the host] must set something before him, whether the wayfarer is really hungry or not."[17] More than this, the issue is not food as such, but rather food adequate for the occasion. Sa'īd writes, "He [the host] has the responsibility of the magnanimous Oriental host to prepare to offer the guest that which is beyond his ability to provide."[18]

The crucial element in this initial portion of the parable is that the guest is guest of the *community*, not just of the individual. This is reflected even in the complimentary language extended to the guest. He is told, "You have honored *our village*," and never, "You have honored *me*."[19] Thus the community is responsible for his entertainment. The guest must leave the village with a good feeling about the hospitality of the village as a community.[20] Again Rihbany writes, "Owing to the homogeneous character of the life in the East, borrowing has been developed there into a fine art."[21] In going to his neighbor, the host is asking the

---

[14]Rihbany, *Syrian*, 215. Sa'īd observes that one is for the guest, one for the host, and one for "the angel of the table," which he claims is a rabbinic custom. He gives no documentation. Sa'īd, *Lūqā*, 30.

[15]Jeremias, *Parables*, 157. Jeremias documents this last observation with a reference to A. M. Brower, *De Gelijkenessen* (Leiden: Brill, 1946), 211.

[16]Bishop, *Jesus*, 176. My own discussions with a wide range of Palestinians and Lebanese confirm Bishop against Jeremias.

[17]Rihbany, *Syrian*, 214.

[18]Sa'īd, *Lūqā*, 300.

[19]The guest is also told, "You have honored our house," but the reference to the larger community is dominant. The individual is never mentioned.

[20]This attitude is clearly reflected negatively in Luke 9:51–55. It is the community at large that has rejected them and John wants revenge on the community as a whole, not on a person or even a family.

[21]Rihbany, *Syrian*, 214f. While living in primitive Middle Eastern villages, we discovered to our amazement that this custom of rounding up from the neighbors something adequate for the guest extended even to us when we were the guests. We would accept an invitation to a meal clear across the village, and arrive to eat from our own dishes which the villagers had borrowed quietly from our cook.

sleeper to fulfil his duty to the guest of the village.[22] As long as the request is modest enough, refusal is unthinkable. In this case, the request is the humblest element of the entire meal, namely, the bread that will be dipped into the common dish.

Bread is not the meal. Bread is the knife, fork, and spoon with which the meal is eaten. The different items of the meal are in common dishes. Each person has a loaf of bread in front of him. He breaks off a bite-sized piece, dips it into the common dish, and puts the entire "sop" into his mouth. He then starts with a fresh piece of bread and repeats the process. The common dish is never defiled from the eater's mouth because he begins each bite with a fresh piece of bread. The bread must be flavored with something for the meal. In absolute desperation the bread is dipped into a dish of salt. Thus the Oriental phrase "eating bread and salt" means the eaters were in abject poverty and had nothing with which to flavor their bread except salt. The host of the parable asks for bread. Everybody knows that he also needs to borrow the meal itself that will be eaten with the bread. This becomes clear in the last line of the parable.

Sa'īd comments on the host's confidence that his request will be granted. This confidence, says Sa'īd, is based on three things:

1. He (the host) is a host and not a borrower. He is not asking for anything for himself.

2. He goes to one friend in order to honor a second friend.

3. He is asking for the food of bare subsistence.[23]

The host starts his rounds. He will gather up the greater portion of the meal from the various neighbors. He will also borrow the best tray, pitcher, cloth, and goblets that the neighborhood has to offer.[24] That he has a whole list of needs is seen at the end of the parable, where the sleeper gives him "whatever he needs."

The host has plenty of food. Olives are gathered at harvest time and preserved in salt for the year; also stored are grape-molasses and cheese (most of which is made when the cows are fresh). All of the family's food supplies are gathered and prepared on a yearly basis and stored in a raised loft at the end of the one-room peasant dwelling. When the host says, "I have nothing," he is speaking idiomatically and means, "I have nothing adequate to serve my guest so that the

---

[22]The structure of the stanza places this appeal to duty in the climactic center.

[23]Sa'īd, *Lūqā*, 300f. The word for "bare subsistence" is *al-kafāf*. It is a very strong word in Arabic and means that which is just enough to keep a man from starving. Sa'īd means the borrower is asking for the humblest item possible, the bread with which to eat.

When a host is being complimented on his meal he will try to turn the compliment by remarking, "This meal is nothing but bread and salt." He means, "Before you, my noble guests, the best I have to offer is only your ordinary fare, indeed, only as bread and salt. You deserve far better."

[24]If we reject allegory and assume an authentic detail in John 2:6, we would have there an illustration of jars gathered from the neighbors for the large gathering. The average family would have only one.

honor of our village will be upheld.''[25] Again the appeal to community duty is the main point.

With this background in mind, verse 7 becomes clear. Verses 5 through 7 are together the extended question that expects an emphatic negative answer. Jesus is saying, ''Can you imagine having a friend and going to him with the sacred request to help you entertain a guest, and then he offers silly excuses about sleeping children and a barred door?'' The Oriental listener/reader knows the communal responsibility for the guest and responds, ''No, we cannot imagine it.''[26]

A great deal has been made of the fact that the children are asleep and the door bolted. But these are weak considerations. The door bolt is not very heavy. Even if the children do stir, they will fall asleep again. The hypothetical excuses suggested are so unthinkable, they are humorous.[27]

A few scholars argue for some ambiguity regarding the subject of πορεύσεται. Jeremias understands verses 5–7 as follows:

> Can you imagine that, if one of you had a friend who came to you at midnight and said to you, ''My friend, lend me three loaves, because a friend has come to me on a journey, and I have nothing to set before him'', you would call out, etc.[28]

Thus Jeremias has understood φίλον as the antecedent to the verb πορεύσεται.[29] However, a nearly identical construction occurs in an unambiguous form in Luke 17:7. A comparison of the two texts is revealing. Luke 17:7 reads:

> Will any one of you—who has a servant—say—to him (the servant)

---

[25]Manson has caught some of this. He writes, ''The contents of the larder are inadequate to the claim of hospitality'' (*Sayings*, 267). Jeremias thinks the host intends to return the bread (*Parables*, 257). To return anything as insignificant as three loaves of bread would be an insult. It would be like an American housewife returning a borrowed tablespoon of sugar. On the other hand, the sleeper *will* get back what he has lent (which turns out to be much more than just bread, as v. 8 indicates). When the sleeper has a guest he will also make the rounds to provide a sumptuous meal and will most certainly stop at this neighbor's door. Jeremias concludes that the focus of the story is that ''God helps as unconditionally as the friend did'' (*Parables*, 105). This remark is puzzling in that in his major discussion of the parable (pp. 157–59) he does not refer to the ''unconditional'' nature of the transaction. Granted the sleeper does not ask for anything back and demands no payment. Nevertheless, it is clearly understood that the present host is available to return the favor in an emergency. This aspect of the cultural situation simply is not applicable theologically and no lesson is to be drawn from it.

[26]Cf. Jeremias, *Parables*, 158. The details of the hypothetical complaint are authentic. The sleeper is irritated. There is no title (cf. Manson, *Sayings*, 267). The peasant home in Palestine is one room with most of the room in a raised portion for the family. The children are asleep with the parents on this portion. The door is closed just prior to retiring (Rihbany, *Syrian*, 215f.). The reference to ἤδη here means ''for some time''; cf. Jeremias, *Parables*, 176.

[27]Rihbany knows the sleeper's answer is inadequate. He writes, ''The man within runs counter to the best Syrian traditions in his answer'' (*Syrian*, 215). Without the awareness of an alternative, Rihbany then tries to make sense out of the traditional understanding of the text.

[28]Jeremias, *Parables*, 158.

[29]Creed makes the same identification, which he admits makes for ''an awkward change of subject'' (*St. Luke*, 157).

τίς δὲ ἐξ ὑμῶν   δοῦλον ἔχων ἐρεῖ αὐτῷ

Luke 11:5 is roughly similar:

τίς ἐξ ὑμῶν   ἔξει φίλον πορεύσεται αὐτόν
(the friend)

Thus the antecedent of the verb "to go" is "you," not "friend." It is, thus, much more likely that the "friend" is the sleeper, and the listener to the parable is expected to identify with the host, not the sleeper.[30]

The significance of the passage hangs on the meaning of the key word ἀναίδεια in verse 8. In Christian usage the word came to have two meanings: "shamelessness" (a negative quality) and "persistence" (a positive quality). We will need to determine if the second meaning properly applies linguistically and theologically to the text.

In ancient Greek literature the word meant "shamelessness." From Archilochus in the seventh century B.C. through Plato, Sophocles, Herodotus, and Pindar in the fifth, to Demosthenes in the fourth, all references point to "shamelessness."[31]

In Epictetus (A.D. 50–130) there is a significant use which joins ἄπιστος with ἀναιδής. Epictetus is offering advice on the necessity of rejecting externals which destroy the purpose of life. His listener asks about what position he will hold in the city. Epictetus answers,

> Whatever position you can, if you maintain at the same time your fidelity (πιστόν) and sense of shame (αἰδήμονα). But if when you wish to be useful to the state, you shall lose these qualities, what profit could you be to it, if you were made shameless (ἀναιδής) and faithless (ἄπιστος)?[32]

Thus the word in early second-century usage was clearly a negative word which could be linked with ἄπιστος. There is no sense in Epictetus of "persistence."

Turning to the papyri, Moulton and Milligan give three examples. In one, a man proves himself ἀναιδής by levying contributions on the inhabitants. A second, from A.D. 49, refers to people who "shamelessly refuse to pay" (ἀναιδευόμενοι μὴ ἀποδῶναι). The third reads, "At the hands of the greedy (πλεονεκτικῶς) and shameless (ἀναιδῶς) the authorities have had enough."[33] Once again the quality referred to is strictly negative. Again there is no suggestion

---

[30] All our Oriental versions in an unambiguous fashion identify the listener with the host. In the parallel parable of the Unjust Judge, the listener is again identified with the petitioning widow, not the judge.

[31] This is true of the adjective and the abstract noun. Cf. Henry G. Liddell and Robert Scott, *A Greek-English Lexicon*, rev. H. S. Jones and R. McKenzie (Oxford: Clarendon, 1940), 105.

[32] Epictetus *Enchiridion* xxiv; for the Greek text cf. *Simplicii Commentarius in Epicteti Enchiridion*, ed. Iohannes Schweighaeuser (Lipsiae: in Libraria Weidmannia, 1800), 232; the English translation is slightly revised from *The Discourses of Epictetus*, trans. George Long (n.p.: A. L. Burt Company, n.d.), 432.

[33] J. H. Moulton and G. Milligan, *The Vocabulary of the Greek Testament* (Grand Rapids: Eerdmans, 1930), 33; my translation.

of "persistence."[34] Preisigke gives two illustrations of ἀναιδής, which he translates *schamlos* and *rücksichtslos*.[35]

From early Christian literature, Lampe gives ἀναιδεύομαι, which he translates "lack shame" and "behave shamelessly," and ἀναιδίζομαι, which he lists as "act with impudence."[36]

In the Greek of the canonical Old Testament the form ἀναιδής is associated with "impudence of face" or "sternness of face."[37] In the Aramaic portion of Daniel, the prophet, on hearing that the king has ordered the death of the wise men of Babylon, asks cautiously, "Why has the severe (harsh) decree come out from the face of the king (ἡ γνώμη ἡ ἀναιδής)?"[38] The Aramaic word is *ḥaṣaf*. The significance of this reference is that this same Aramaic word is the Syriac word for ἀναίδεια that appears in all the Syriac versions and has (or perhaps acquires?) the secondary meaning of "persistence." Clearly the Daniel text does not have any hint of this meaning.

The other unusual reference in the LXX is Jeremiah 8:5. The text talks of "perpetual apostasy" (*meshubah niṣṣaḥat*), which is translated in the LXX as ἀποστροφὴν ἀναιδῆ. Thus we have one clear reference to ἀναίδεια meaning "continual" or "perpetual," although it still occurs in a negative context. There is the possibility that the LXX translator is giving an interpretative translation and understands "perpetual apostasy" as "shameless apostasy." Yet the LXX reading of Jeremiah 8:5 can be accepted as a precedent for the later Christian usage. Ben Sirach has both the adjective and the abstract noun. In all cases the reference is negative and means "shameless."[39]

In summary, then, in the LXX ἀναίδεια is overwhelmingly negative and, with one possible exception, means "shameless" or "defiant, angry, harsh."

Moving to Josephus, the word exclusively means "shameless" or "impudent" as far as we have been able to trace. Marcus translates it "shamelessness."[40] Thackeray uses "impudent."[41] Again, the quality referred to is negative. With one exception, it has no reference to continuity or persistence.

The problem is that in the parable of the Friend at Midnight, the negative meaning of "shamelessness" is problematical. Is it "shameless" for the believer to take his requests to God in prayer? Surely not. To make sense out of the parable,

---

[34]In the second of these, "persistent" would make sense. However, Moulton and Milligan translate it "shameless."

[35]Friedrich Preisigke, *Wörterbuch der griechischen Papyrusurkunden* (Berlin: Selbstverlag der Erben, 1925), I, 88.

[36]G. W. H. Lampe, *A Patristic Greek Lexicon* (Oxford: Clarendon, 1961), 103.

[37]Prov. 25:23; 7:13; Deut. 28:50; Eccl. 8:1; Dan. 8:23. The Hebrew words are עַז עֹז זַעַם. The adverb occurs in Prov. 21:29. Dogs are described as ἀναιδεῖς τῇ ψυχῇ in Isa. 56:11.

[38]Dan. 2:15. So Theodotion. The LXX has πικρῶς.

[39]Cf. Sir. 23:6; 26:11; 40:30, for the adjective, and 25:23 for the abstract noun.

[40]*Josephus*, trans. and ed. R. Marcus and ed. A. Wikgren (Cambridge: Harvard University Press, 1963), 427 (*Ant.* xvii.119).

[41]*Josephus, the Life*, trans. H. St. J. Thackeray (London: William Heinemann, 1926), I, 131; also *Wars* i.224.

the Church apparently felt the necessity of taking a negative quality (shamelessness) and turning it somehow into a positive quality. The answer that finally achieved almost universal acceptance was "persistence." The victory of "persistence" over "shamelessness" was so complete by the twelfth century that Euthymius, a Greek monk, was able to define ἀναίδεια as τὴν ἐπιμονὴν τῆς αἰτήσεως.[42] It is not possible to ascertain precisely how and when this shift took place, but some of the lines of movement can be noted.

In the Latin the move involves a change of vocabulary. Improbitatem[43] gradually gives way to importunitatem,[44] which finally becomes dominant. In the Coptic versions two words appear, las and matlas. Both mean primarily "shamelessness," but both acquire the additional meaning of "persistence."[45] Did the Coptic, like the Greek, acquire this additional meaning primarily, if not exclusively, as a result of this text? Is the same true of the Syriac ḥaṣaf?

The Arabic versions unanimously give "persistence" as a translation.[46] Thus, in all the versions examined, the problem of the negative "shamelessness" which appears in the parable of the Friend at Midnight was solved by changing the meaning of ἀναίδεια to "persistence."

This solution to the problem is inadequate contextually, theologically, linguistically, and stylistically. Persistence in prayer is one of the dominant themes of the parable of the Unjust Judge. The woman is persistent. She finally gets an answer. However, unlike the widow of Luke 18, the host in Luke 11 (as traditionally interpreted) is given an answer immediately. The answer is, No! Presumably the "knocker" persists until the sleeper is forced to change his mind. The synoptic teaching about prayer is that the pious are to be persistent *until* an answer is given. But once they receive an answer, are they to cajole God to get him to change his mind if the answer displeases them? Or, rather, are they to respond with "Thy will be done"? Cadoux comments on the persistence that supposedly will influence God to change his mind and writes, "If such a parable were spoken today with such a meaning, it would be condemned as clumsy, misleading, dangerous and irreverent."[47] Sa'īd avoids the problem by saying, "The persistence is not to get God to deal compassionately with us, but rather to prepare us for

---

[42]Cf. Bruce, *Synoptic Gospels*, 548; no reference given.

[43]Old Latin d f i l q vg.

[44]BF c ff[22] r aur.

[45]The information on the Coptic versions has been kindly gathered for me by Professor Wahīb G. Kāmil of the Coptic Institute of Higher Studies in Cairo. He has checked the versions available to him and quotes from two Coptic-Arabic Dictionaries, *Qāmūs Qalādiyūs Labīb*, 251, and *Qāmūs Kirām*, 151.

[46]At the same time, in the eleventh century, Ibn al-Ṭayyib in his commentary tries with some difficulty to make sense out of "shamelessness." Cf. Paris Ar. 86, folio 131. The last case of its appearance to my knowledge is in the 1252 text of Ibn al-'Assāl, who lists it in the margin.

[47]Cadoux, *Parables*, 36. Cadoux has identified the problem. His solution is to divorce the parable totally from its Lucan context and from any relation to the parable of the Unjust Judge. He concludes that the point of the parable is ethical instruction. A man may be justified in straining one relationship for the sake of another (*ibid.*, 152). This kind of radical surgery, as we shall see, is unnecessary.

receiving his blessings.''[48] This may be good theology, but it is questionable exegesis. Yet Saʿīd does recognize the problem. Clearly, turning ἀναίδεια into "persistence" creates severe theological difficulties.

The story has *no* record of any persistence aside from this debatable word.[49] Traditionally we assume that he persists in his knocking. In fact, the borrower does not knock at all; he calls. To knock on a neighbor's door in the night would frighten the neighbor. A stranger knocks in the night; a friend calls. When he calls, his voice will be recognized and the neighbor will not be frightened. The poem that follows the parable (vv. 9–13) has in it a clear reference to persistence and to knocking. This poem is most likely the source of the shift from "shamelessness" to "persistence." The idea of persistence has probably "spilled over" from the following poem. The parable itself does not say he persisted in anything.

Finally, the idea of persistence does not fit the structure of this second stanza of the parable. The key to the problem is the identification of the antecedents of some of the prepositions and nouns. For clarity's sake we shall observe again the inversion of this second stanza, this time concentrating on the subject of each line.

			The subject of each line is:
I say to you,			
B 1	if he will not give to him		the sleeper
2	having arisen		the sleeper
3	because of being a friend of his		the sleeper
3′	but because of his (ἀναίδεια?)		?
2′	he will arise		the sleeper
1′	and will give him whatever he needs.[50]		the sleeper

It is clear that the entire stanza is talking about the sleeper and that line 3′ should also apply to him. Whatever the disputed word means it applies to the man in bed, not the host outside the door. Furthermore the matching line in the first stanza of the parable (A–3′) speaks of the sleeper's potential refusal of duty. Here we expect a discussion that relates to the same man and the same topic. Thus we have two problems in our traditional understanding of this line. We have a mistranslation of the key word ἀναίδεια and have applied it to the wrong man.

To summarize: theologically speaking, persistence after an answer is given is not consistent with the synoptic understanding of prayer. The story has no record of any repetition of the act of calling for help. The poetic structure requires that

---

[48]Saʿīd, *Lūqā*, 301.

[49]Some of the Latin fathers were apparently aware of this, because a number of the Latin texts add *et se illa persevera verit pulsans*. Cf. c ff2 i l vg^{el}. The Dutch Liege Harmony went one step further and reads, "He continues knocking and shouting" (quoted in Black, *Aramaic Approach*, 291). The Greek present imperative "stop bothering me" clearly implies that the action has begun, but it tells us nothing about how long the action has been in process.

[50]The inverted nature of the sentence was observed by Bengel, who wrote, "The arrangement of the words is studied δώσει, ἀναστάς, ἐγερθεὶς, δώσει: though he will not *give, rising up*, yet *being aroused he will give*" (Bengel, *Gnomon*, I, 446). Black, *Aramaic Approach*, 59, lists this verse as an illustration of asyndeton. Ἀναστάς is unnaturally placed after the opening phrase even though it precedes it in time. The resulting awkward construction is necessary for the literary balance.

ἀναίδεια be applied to the sleeper. The problem of "shamelessness" in a text about prayer has been recognized. The traditional solution has been to read "persistence" into verse 8. This solution is inadequate.

Modern scholarship has recognized that ἀναίδεια means basically "shamelessness." Four different solutions have been proposed for the problem created here by this meaning.

The first is to accept the translation of shamelessness and apply it to the host. A few scholars working with this solution assume that he is shameless in his initial coming at night.[51] Others combine "shameless" with "persistent." The host is shameless in coming at night, and shameless in persisting. They translate ἀναίδεια, then, as "shameless persistence."[52]

Also within the scope of this solution are those who soften "shamelessness" to "boldness" and thereby turn it into a positive quality. The shift is subtle but significant. They argue that we are to come boldly to God in prayer and that this in particular was an essential message for the timid Gentile Christians. Harris writes, "Such a teaching would have special relevance for Gentile Christians who did not have the heritage of Jewish piety."[53]

The difficulties of these solutions are severe. As we have seen, the word ἀναίδεια does not, through the first century, mean persistence, and there is no reference to any persistence in the story. The shift from a negative "shamelessness" to a positive "boldness" is imaginative but unsupported. (Why was παρρησία not used if this was the intent of the text?)

A second solution is offered by Levison, a Palestinian Hebrew Christian, who observes that ἀναιδής is related to 'zz, which includes the idea of "strengthening." He suggests that some form of 'zz is likely behind the Greek. Thus he concludes that the idea of "strengthening" is the point. Levison writes, "He [the sleeper] will not rise to give it [the bread] to him because he is his friend, but in order to strengthen, fortify, or encourage him."[54] Levison specifically denies that this parable has anything to do with the parable of the Unjust Judge.[55] He thus makes the sleeper out to be a noble-hearted man concerned for his friend in need. This evaluation of the character of the sleeper is extremely questionable. If he will not offer aid for friendship's sake, how is he to be made over into a nobleman? The parable hints at excuses he would like to use; but, as we shall see, he does not use them. The literary structure of the Jerusalem Document specifically relates the two parables of the Friend at Midnight and the Unjust Judge.[56] The

---

[51]Bengel, *Gnomon*, I, 446; N. Geldenhuys, *Commentary on the Gospel of Luke* (Grand Rapids: Eerdmans, 1951), 326.

[52]Cf. Jülicher, *Gleichnisreden*, II, 273; B. T. D. Smith, *Parables*, 147; Leaney, *St. Luke*, 187; and many others.

[53]O. G. Harris, "Prayer in Luke-Acts" (unpublished Ph.D. thesis, Vanderbilt University, 1966), 87f.

[54]N. Levison, "Importunity? A Study of Luke XI.8," *The Expositor*, Series 9, 3(1925), 460; also Levison, *Local Setting*, 78–84.

[55]Levison, "Importunity?" 459.

[56]See above, pp. 80f.

judge cares nothing for the woman and the sleeper cares nothing for the host. The sleeper does not like the host and will not help him for friendship's sake. Clearly we are dealing with a man of ignoble character. Levison clearly recognizes the problem of "persistence," but his solution must be judged inadequate.

A third solution is offered by Anton Fridrichsen. He writes,

> Contrary to all that customary explanation has made it mean, this word [ἀναίδεια] in this context can only be interpreted: he [the petitioned one] will fulfil the request because of his own shamelessness, namely, that which will be brought to light through his refusal. Thus he will help him, not because of friendship, but so that by any means he will not be judged specifically or generally to be an ἀνὴρ ἀναιδής.[57]

Fridrichsen accepts "shamelessness" as a negative quality. He applies it to the sleeper, not to the borrower. He recognizes the crucial fact of a community with its pressures and understands the text to mean that the sleeper does not have shamelessness, does not want it, and acts so as to avoid it. Yet this solution flounders on the αὐτοῦ. If the text reads "because of shamelessness" the sleeper did so-and-so, this would be an excellent solution. However, we are informed of "his shamelessness," which clearly describes a quality that the sleeper already has, not one he wants to avoid. Fridrichsen has dismissed the idea of "persistence" and has rightly seen that the quality in question applies to the sleeper. He is also aware of the presence of the community. Yet his solution is inadequate.

Jeremias does not reject "persistence" but accepts Fridrichsen's solution. Jeremias refers to Fridrichsen and writes, "for the sake of his (own) shamelessness, that is to say, that he may not lose face in the matter."[58] The difficulty here is that Jeremias has made a subtle, yet extremely significant shift from a negative quality to a positive quality. When he quotes Fridrichsen and says, "for the sake of his (own) shamelessness," we are dealing with a negative quality. When Jeremias adds his own comment, "that is to say, that he may not lose face in the matter," he has shifted to a positive quality of supreme importance in Oriental life. This shift may be subtly implied in Fridrichsen. Jeremias makes it explicit. If I understand these men correctly they are saying,

> Fridrichsen: He acts to avoid a quality of shamelessness which he does not have.

> Jeremias: He acts to preserve a quality of honor which he does have.

Granted, the two ideas are the opposite sides of the same coin; nevertheless, we are left in the dark how this shift is to be made. We are back to the same problem the fathers faced in the early centuries. How is the negative "shamelessness" to be changed into a positive quality appropriate to a parable teaching something about prayer? We are convinced that both Jeremias and Fridrichsen are wrestling with the

---

[57]A. Fridrichsen, "Exegetisches zum Neuen Testament," *Symbolae Osloensis* 13 (1934), 40; my translation.
[58]Jeremias, *Parables*, 158.

right issue, and that Jeremias has jumped to the right conclusion. We will now try to demonstrate that there is evidence for this "leap" to a positive quality such as Jeremias has made.

In any language "d" and "t" are very close linguistically, and this relates to one possible solution to our problem. The Westerner pronounces both of these letters by touching his tongue to the roof of his mouth just above the teeth. The Middle Easterner touches the tongue to the teeth themselves rather than the roof of the mouth. This brings the two sounds even closer together. In commenting on the dentals Wright says, "ד often interchanges with ת, as in the Hebrew radicals תור and דור, Arabic [tār] and [dār]."[59] He further comments,

> ד and ת undergo a slight modification in Hebrew and Aramaic, when immediately preceded by a vowel. In this position they receive a sound nearly approximating to th in that and think respectively.... I should remark that where ד and ת are retained in modern Syriac of Urumiah, their sound is hard, and very little difference is perceptible between them.[60]

The same conclusion is documented by O'Leary, who says:

> In Mandaean t frequently becomes d, and so very generally in Aramaic transcription from the Greek, but here it must be remembered that in medieval and modern Greek t is often sounded as d, thus ἀρτάβη = ארדבא....[61]

This confusion is evident in the New Testament from Luke 16:6, where some texts have βάτους[62] while others read βάδους.[63]

Is it not possible that this same confusion has occurred in Luke 11:8 and ἀναίδεια was originally ἀναίτιος? This would make the text read, "Because of his blamelessness he will arise and give to him what he wants." This is exactly the sense that Jeremias has suggested and provides a possible understanding of how the text could be read in this fashion. Negatively, unlike Luke 16:6, here in Luke 11:8 we have no manuscript evidence for such a change from d to t. Suggestions of this kind are easy to make and attractive, but must be accepted only with great caution.

There is also another alternative. The word ἀναίδεια etymologically is the word αἰδώς with an alpha privative. Αἰδώς has two meanings:

1. Sense of shame, sense of honor, self-respect
   (a positive quality)

2. Shame, scandal (a negative quality)

---

[59]W. Wright, *Lectures on the Comparative Grammar of the Semitic Languages* (2nd ed., Amsterdam: Philo Press, 1966), 53.

[60]*Ibid.,* pp. 53–55.

[61]De Lacy O'Leary, *Comparative Grammar of the Semitic Languages* (London: Kegan Paul, Trench, Trubner, 1923), 55.

[62]p⁷⁵ B Θ E F G H S V U Ω.

[63]p¹,²²,⁵² א B C L T Z Δ Ψ Origen.

In the Greek language ἀναίδεια negates the first, not the second. Thus we have:

αἰδώς   + alpha privative =   ἀναίδεια

meaning: a sense of shame   meaning: without a sense of shame
(a positive quality)   (a negative quality)

However, in Semitic languages, to my limited knowledge, there is no word that covers both "shame" and "sense of shame," the first negative and the second positive.

Shame is an extremely important quality in Eastern culture generally. Some areas of life are governed by law, but much of life is controlled by the "shame" (negative) that is avoided because of the individual's inner "sense of shame" (positive). The first is negative and is to be avoided at all costs; the second is positive and is to be encouraged. The importance of the concept of shame in the East is partially indicated in that there are special words for "shame" and other quite different words that mean "sense of shame."

Jeremias refers to one of the weighty Semitic words referring to "a sense of shame" (kissuf),[64] which he connects to this parable, perhaps rightly so if our line of reasoning can be substantiated. For an Aramaic-speaking person "shame" was, so far as we can tell, exclusively a negative word. What the translator of this story from Aramaic to Greek may have intended was:

αἰδώς   + alpha privative =   ἀναίδεια

Meaning: shame   meaning: avoidance of shame
(negative)   (positive)

In English we achieve this same shift with the word "blameless." Thus:

blame   + negation =   blameless
(negative)   (positive)

Thus, what our text may represent is a literal translation from the Aramaic.[65] The translator began with a negative, added an alpha privative, and had what was for him a positive quality (avoidance of shame). The kissuf suggested by Jeremias is precisely the "avoidance of shame" suggested above. This possibility fits admirably into the cultural pattern of the story. The sleeper knows the borrower must gather up the essentials for the banquet from the various neighbors.[66] If the sleeper refused the request of anything so humble as a loaf of bread the host would

---

[64]Jeremias, Parables, 158, n. 27.

[65]We are not here assuming an original Aramaic text or an Aramaic gospel, but merely that the material is Palestinian in culture, which in turn assumes Aramaic words and phrases at the heart of the material. Cf. Gustav Dalman, Jesus-Jeshua (New York: Ktav, 1971 [1929]). Moulton noted, "In Luke, the only NT writer except the author of Heb to show any conscious attention to Greek ideas of style, we find (1) rough Greek translations from Aramaic left mainly as they reached him, perhaps because their very roughness seemed too characteristic to be refined away." James H. Moulton, A Grammar of New Testament Greek, I, Prolegomena (Edinburgh: T. & T. Clark, 1906, 3rd ed. 1908), 18.

[66]This is against Jülicher, who argues that the host is obliged to continue knocking because there is nowhere else he can get help (Gleichnisreden, II, 273). On the contrary, the host can go to any home in the village except the houses of those with whom he may be currently feuding.

continue on his rounds cursing the stinginess of the sleeper, who would not get up even to fulfil this trifling request. The story would be all over the village by morning. The sleeper would be met with cries of "shame" everywhere he went. Because of his desire for "avoidance of shame" he will arise and grant *whatever* the borrower wants.

This usually neglected detail at the end of the parable provides fairly conclusive evidence against ascribing any "persistence" or "shamelessness" to the host. If the host was shameless in his request, or if he continued knocking or calling until the sleeper finally had to get up against his will and fulfil the request to get rid of the host, then certainly the sleeper would have granted the three loaves of bread and *no more*. If the request was granted in anger or irritation there would have been no giving him "whatever he wants." That the host received much more than the bread is evidence that the entire transaction was completed in a spirit of good will.

Although *kissuf* is a good prospect for the original Aramaic word in the story, *tam* and *naqi* must also be considered. These words then put us into the family of ἄμωμος, ἄμεμπτος, ἀμώμητος, and ἀναίτιος, which brings us to the same word suggested above. *Naqi* as an Aramaic abstract noun (*neqqiyuth*) means "respectability" or "dignity," which is an intriguing possibility.

The theological cluster of this parable includes two major items. The first deals with *the nature of God*. The parable said to the original listener/reader, "When you go to this kind of a neighbor everything is against you. It is night. He is asleep in bed. The door is locked. His children are asleep. He does not like you and *yet* you will receive even more than you ask. This is because your neighbor is a man of integrity and he will not violate that quality. The God to whom you pray also has an integrity that he will not violate; and beyond this, he loves you."[67]

The second theme in the theological cluster is *assurance for man*. Again we are in the range of *a minore ad maius*. If you are confident of having your needs met when you go to such a neighbor in the night, how much more can you rest assured when you take your requests to a loving Father?

In summary, the parable of the Friend at Midnight is seen to be an Oriental story of a man who knows his request in the night will be honored even by a neighbor who does not like him. The key to the parable is the definition of the word ἀναίδεια. This word took on the meaning of "persistence." It is here more appropriately translated "avoidance of shame," a positive quality. The literary structure of the entire parable makes clear that this quality is to be applied to the sleeper. Thus the parable tells of a sleeping neighbor who will indeed preserve his honor and grant the host's request and more. Even so, man before God has much more reason to rest assured that his requests will be granted.

---

[67]Our cultural presuppositions in the last half of the 20th century tend to make us uneasy about seeing "the preservation of honor" as a virtue that is appropriate to God. Given the importance of this concept in the Eastern value system, it would be surprising if Jesus did not use such a quality as a prime virtue for the Father. The center of each stanza climaxes on the question of honor.

THE PARABLE/POEM ON A FATHER'S GIFTS (LUKE 11:9–13)

We will try to demonstrate in this section that Luke 11:9–13 is a parable composed of three unforgettable comparisons. This parable is then encased in two stanzas of Form III poetry (step parallelism). It is a mixed parable/poem construction, yet the three stanzas together make up a three-stanza unit which approximates the poetic Form VI. The poem is most probably addressed to the opponents of the gospel, and affirms that a Heavenly Father gives good gifts to *all* his children.

Luke 11:9–13 is best understood as a separate pericope and not as originally a part of the parable of the Friend at Midnight.[68] At least four reasons lead to this conclusion:

1. Both in Luke 16:1–13 and here in 11:5–13 a parable is followed by a related pericope having a different literary style, and the two pericopes are connected with the peculiar Lucan phrase "and to you I say."

2. There are four special shifts in setting and emphasis between 11:5–8 and 11:9–13.

3. The parable has one literary form; verses 9–13 have a distinctively different form.

4. The poem is addressed to the disciples; the poem speaks to the opponents of the gospel.

These must be examined in turn.

We have already observed the very unusual phrase "and to you I say" (with the verb occurring last). This is again evidence of someone tying together two pericopes that were not originally one literary unit.

A second reason for separating the parable from the parable/poem is the shift of setting and emphasis between 11:5–8 and 11:9–13. Four specific shifts are clear. They are:

1. In the parable a neighbor deals with a neighbor; in the poem a father deals with his son.

2. In the parable there is no one asking for something good and receiving something bad. In the poem this is the burden of the imagery.

3. In the parable there is no reference to persistence. So far as we know the host asks only once. In the poem continued action is implied by the present tenses of the verbs.

4. In the parable the friend *calls* to his neighbor; in the poem *knocking* is introduced.

These specific shifts of imagery and emphasis make clear that the poem in 11:9–13

---

[68]This is recognized by many scholars: cf. Bultmann, *Tradition,* 324; Jeremias, *Parables,* 90; Jones, *Art,* 141, 149. Jones sees it as a new parable and calls it the parable of "the child asking for bread" (*ibid.*).

is a separate block of material. The style of 11:9–13 must now be examined in detail. We will attempt to demonstrate the following literary structure:

And to you I say

    1   *ask,* and it shall be *given* to you
        2   seek, and you shall find   2ND person
            3   knock, and it shall be opened to you.

    1'   For everyone who *asks* receives
        2'   and the one who seeks finds   3RD person
            3'   and to the knocker it shall be opened.

And will any one of you

    A   if the son *asks* the father for bread,
    A'   will he *give* him a stone?

    B   or a fish, instead of a fish
    B'   will he *give* him an eel (snake)?

    C   or if he *asks* an egg
    C'   will he *give* him a scorpion?

If therefore

    4   you being evil
        5   you know good gifts   2ND person
            6   to *give* to your children

    4'   how much more the Father
        5'   out of heaven Holy Spirit   3RD person
            6'   shall *give* to those *asking* him.

Burney has identified the first and the third stanzas as poetry.[69] We agree, but see them as the outer stanzas of a three-stanza poem.

The first stanza is a clear example of step parallelism. The pattern is: ask, seek, knock—ask, seek, knock.[70] The present tenses of the imperatives imply continued action and can be translated, "keep on asking, seeking, knocking." The emphasis on "everyone," which is reinforced in the Old Syriac, can be understood as an appeal to the outcasts; even they will receive if they ask. It could also be spoken in defense of the universality of the gospel. Jesus could be saying to the Pharisees, "Everyone who asks will receive, even sinners, not just the so-called righteous."[71]

---

[69]Burney, *Poetry,* 67, 82.

[70]In the Old Syriac the first three lines rhyme at the end and the second three at the beginning, with a repetition of "everyone" at the start of each line.

[71]Jeremias has assumed that the emphasis on "asking" springs from "the experience of the *beggar*" (*Parables,* 159; emphasis his). Rather, the background of this language is life in the East in general. Asking is a part of life on all levels of society. Jesus is using language from the daily interchange of social and economic life. In the Middle East, the beggar's profession is recognized as legitimately ordained of God but his position is nevertheless despised. Cf. Sir. 40:28–30; these words are overlooked by Jeremias, *loc. cit.,* n. 35.

The second stanza contains a textual problem. Both the Nestle-Aland and the Bible Society critical texts prefer two figures rather than the three.[72] Yet there is significant textual evidence from all the major families to include the bread-stone image in some form as part of the Lucan text.[73] Matthew 7:7–11 has the same poem that we are considering here. In the Matthean version the central stanza has only two figures, the stone-bread and the fish-serpent. If all three figures are included in the Lucan text for textual and poetic reasons, the Lucan version is left somewhat longer than the Matthean. This latter situation seems to be relatively frequent. In this study we observe the two other cases where a block of material common to Luke and Matthew is abbreviated in Matthew.[74]

T. W. Manson points out that the question of the original form of the poem must include a discussion of "Q." He writes,

> The three short (two-stress) lines in v. 10 answer to the three lines in v. 9; and the triple form is carried into the short parable which follows (vv. 11f.), although there is serious doubt about the text. . . . Many scholars regard it as an assimilation of the text of Lk. to that of Mt. But the question whether it stood in Lk. is distinct from the question whether it stood in Q; and, leaving the text of Lk. on one side, we have three points in the parable. The first is attested by Mt. (and Lk.?), the second by Mt. and Lk., the third by Lk. alone. The evidence for the place of the first point in Q is at least as good as that for the third; and the fact that the poem is in a triple form favors a three-fold parable.[75]

In another connection Manson also observes that we have to deal with "one of the favorite practices of the first Evangelist, abbreviation, which he carries out even at the expense of poetic form."[76]

When Manson refers to the triple form of the poem, he is talking only about verse 9. When we observe that verse 13 also has a triple form and that the poem on mammon in Luke 16:9–13 consists of three stanzas with a double three in each stanza, Manson's point is further strengthened. Thus it can be accepted that the stanza originally had three double images.[77]

One naturally suspects some kind of special relationship between the contrasting items suggested in each of the double lines. Sa'īd is again helpful. He writes,

> Bread, fish, and eggs are the ordinary food of a common man. . . . A round stone looks like a round loaf (Luke 4:3), and there is little outward difference

---

[72]*Novum Testamentum Graece*, ed. Eberhard Nestle and Kurt Aland (editio vicesima quinta, Stuttgart: Württembergische Bibelanstalt, 1964), 181; *The Greek New Testament*, ed. Kurt Aland *et al.* (2nd ed., Stuttgart: The United Bible Societies, 1968), 256.

[73]Alexandrian (א L), Caesarean (Θ), Western (D[gr] Sy[c]), Byzantine (A E F G H).

[74]Matt. 18:12–14 parallels Luke 15:3–10; Matt. 6:24 parallels Luke 16:9–13. If Luke is expanded to fit Matthew, why is Matthew not expanded with the egg-scorpion image to fit Luke?

[75]Manson, *Sayings*, 81.

[76]Manson, *Teaching*, 53.

[77]All our Oriental versions except Sy[s] have three double images. Again the Old Syriac has closer sound correspondences than the Greek. In this second stanza in each case the second line begins with "lmu" and ends with "leh."

between the snake of the sea which is a kind of fish and a snake of the land which is an ordinary snake . . . and the scorpion all folded up looks like an egg.[78]

Bishop quotes Masterman regarding the *Barbut* (*clarias macamcracanthus*), a type of fish in the Sea of Galilee that can reach five feet in length, crawl on land, and has the appearance of a snake. Bishop mentions that it is among the unclean fish.[79] It seems quite likely that this is the "snake" of the story. The fisherman would regularly catch both edible fish and the eel-like creatures which would be cast back into the sea as unclean and nonedible. If a son asked for a fish would his father give him a "snake" out of the sea?

In addition to the visual correspondence here suggested, there is also the possibility of some auditory correspondence. In the Old Syriac given above "fish" is *nuno* and snake is *ḥewyo*. Six of our oldest and finest Arabic versions have fish as *ḥūt* and snake as *ḥayyah*. This word for snake is common but *ḥūt* is a rare word for fish. It is fairly obvious that the common word *samak* has been rejected and *ḥūt* selected for its assonance with *ḥayyah* (snake).[80]

Thus there is good evidence that the second stanza had three double images in "Q" and perhaps in Luke. The three images are brief antithetical parallelisms. Each of the couplets has the same message. A son will unfailingly receive from his father and the gift will be good.

In the third stanza we are faced with a textual problem that fortunately does not affect the clear poetic structure.[81]

Arndt explains ὁ ἐξ οὐρανοῦ as being a contraction of ὁ ἐν οὐρανῷ ἐξ οὐρανοῦ.[82] Yet there is some good textual evidence for omitting the ὁ.[83] This reading, popular in the early versions, is also represented in the Arabic.[84] With this omission the text reads in many of the Syriac and the Arabic texts, "How much more the father from heaven gives holy spirit." This would in turn lead to a slight shift in the word placement in the last three lines of the final stanza. The following would be required:

4′ πόσῳ μᾶλλον ὁ πατὴρ

5′ ἐξ οὐρανοῦ δώσει πνεῦμα ἅγιον

[78]Saʿīd, *Lūqā*, 303.

[79]Bishop, *Jesus*, 83, quoting from E. W. G. Masterson, *Studies in Galilee* (Chicago: University of Chicago Press, 1909), 45; cf. also Jeremias, *Parables*, 226.

[80]The Arabic versions are of course late, but the translators must have either sensed a wordplay in the Syriac they were translating, or remembered a wordplay in local vocaublary. Vat. Borg.Ar. 95 is from an early Greek ms. and no. 71 of the same collection from the Old Syriac. Both make this wordplay. Ibn al-Ṭayyib translating from the Peshitta also has this correspondence.

[81]Matt. 7:11 has the gift as simply ἀγαθά. Luke has apparently changed this to πνεῦμα ἅγιον, or to ἀγαθὸν δόμα, or to δόματα ἀγαθά. The Matthean form is simpler and quite likely more primitive. The shift in Luke may be to provide a smooth transition into the discussion of Beelzebub. Cf. Cadoux, *Parables*, 76.

[82]Arndt, *St. Luke*, 298. Arndt offers no documentation for his suggestion.

[83]p75 ℵ L X Ψ itᵃ²,ᵈ,ᶠ vg syrᶜ,ᵖ copˢᵃ,ᵇᵒ arm geo.

[84]Both Ibn al-Ṭayyib and Ibn al-ʿAssāl have, "The father gives from heaven."

> 6′   τοῖς αἰτοῦσιν αὐτόν.

The second line is thus left excessively long. At the same time, line 5 places διδόναι after ἀγαθά, which allows for the following construction of that stanza:

> 4   εἰ οὖν ὑμεῖς πονηροὶ ὑπάρχοντες
>
> 5   οἴδατε δόματα ἀγαθὰ
>
> 6   διδόναι τοῖς τέκνοις ὑμῶν.[85]

Following this word order of lines 4, 5, and 6 we may cautiously speculate that an original Aramaic of lines 4′, 5′, and 6′ may also have had the verb "to give" at the head of the final line. This would require moving δώσει ahead two words in the final stanza. With the awareness of what Manson calls the "many rash acts" that have been committed *metri causa*,[86] making such a minor shift of word order leaves the six lines as follows:

> 4   εἰ οὖν ὑμεῖς πονηροὶ ὑπάρχοντες
>
> 5   οἴδατε δόματα ἀγαθὰ
>
> 6   διδόναι τοῖς τέκνοις ὑμῶν
>
> 4′   πόσῳ μᾶλλον ὁ πατὴρ
>
> 5′   ἐξ οὐρανοῦ πνεῦμα ἅγιον
>
> 6′   δώσει τοῖς αἰτοῦσιν αὐτόν.

Even without this slight shift of word order the balance of

> Giver
>
>   gift
>
>   receiver

is still intact for each stanza. The shift merely provides a more symmetrical semantic balance.

Thus the third stanza is also a carefully constructed example of step parallelism. The principle of *kal va homer,* common to the Dominical sayings, is again employed. The theme centers on the quality of the gifts. The one who asks of God can be assured of even better gifts than those a father gives his son.

A number of striking features tie the first and last stanzas together. The structure of ABC-A′B′C′ appears in both. There is also a clear case of *inclusio*.

---

[85]The earlier position in the sentence for the verb "to give" in lines 4′, 5′, and 6′ is preferred in Semitic word order, but the later position in lines 4, 5, and 6 maintained itself all through the Syriac versions only to lose it in the Arabic. This would indicate that with the Syriac versions this word order was maintained for some reason other than the normal order of the sentence. It is our suggestion that poetic balance is the reason. As the sense of the poetry was lost, the Semitic sentence structure gradually dominated and the Arabic word order is the result. The position of the verb in line 5′ remained unchanged in all our Oriental versions.

[86]Manson, *Teaching,* 53.

The verbs "ask" and "give" both occur in line 1 and most likely both were in line 6'. Both verbs either occur or are implied in each of the three illustrations in the center stanza. Thus, in a very artistic fashion these two verbs unite the entire poem. If "Holy Spirit" is an editorial change, the original poem may well have had the simpler "good things." In an original Aramaic this would give two stresses to each of the six lines in the third stanza to match the rhythm of the first stanza. But most striking of all, the first three lines of the first stanza are addressed to the second person. Each line is directed to "you." Then lines 1'2'3' are directed to the third person. The same shift from second to third person occurs in the third stanza. Lines 4, 5, and 6 are specifically addressed to "you." Then again the last half of the third stanza (lines 4'5'6') shifts to the third person.

The second stanza is naturally the climax. It combines in vivid imagery the major thrust of each stanza. These are as follows:

> Stanza I—*all* will receive.
>
> Stanza II—*all* will receive and the gift will be *good*.
>
> Stanza III—the gift will be *good*.

The images of this second stanza are simple and striking. They are constructed so that even if the listener remembers only one of them it is enough. He will have the two major emphases of the overall poem.

The question must now be raised: To whom was this material originally addressed? Was it spoken to the disciples, to the crowds, or to the opponents of the gospel? The problem focuses on the introductory phrase τίς ἐξ ὑμῶν. Jeremias argues that it "generally introduced sayings of Jesus addressed to opponents."[87] The texts themselves indicate a broader usage than Jeremias allows. The seven occurrences in the synoptic Gospels fall into the following categories:

1. Texts clearly addressed to the opponents of the gospel
     The ox falling into a pit on the Sabbath
          (Matt. 12:11 par. Luke 14:5)
     The Lost Sheep
          (Luke 15:5)

2. Texts that are clearly addressed to the disciples
     The discussion on unworthy servants[88]
          (Luke 17:7)
     Anxiety and the lilies of the field
          (Matt. 6:27 par. Luke 12:25)

---

[87]Jeremias, *Parables*, 145.

[88]It could be argued that Luke 17:7 supposes an economic level beyond the disciples of Jesus, but not so. In the East, families of remarkably modest means engage servants. Down through the lower middle class, servants are the accepted pattern. Anyone with enough money to own a boat would naturally have a servant. There is no evidence that the original followers of Jesus were entirely of the poorest of the poor. In any case, the Matt. 6:27 text is clearly intended for the disciples.

3.   A text addressed to the multitudes
The building of a tower[89]
(Luke 14:28)

Thus, in the case of Luke 11:5–8 and 11:9–13, the introductory phrase τίς ἐξ ὑμῶν does not automatically determine the setting for us.

We must then ask, Is it possible to determine the intended audience of this poem? In our view, the internal evidence of the texts themselves and the external structure of the Jerusalem Document both point to a setting of disciples for the parable and opponents of the gospel for the poem. The first has been discussed above; the second will now be examined.

In the case of the poem on a Father's Gifts, the internal evidence seems to point to a hostile audience. Jesus addresses the listeners as ὑμεῖς πονηροὶ ὑπάρχοντες, which is most likely addressed to the Pharisees.[90] In addition to the "you being evil" phrase, which is clearly addressed to opponents, the entire first stanza can perhaps best be understood as being addressed to these same opponents. "*Everyone* who asks, receives," can be in defense of sinners and publicans receiving. The admonition to ask, seek, and knock sounds very much as though Jesus is talking to those who have not yet done these things.[91]

The overall structure of the Jerusalem Document, as we have seen, connects Luke 11:1–13 with 18:1–14. In the latter passage the compiler of the material has indicated that the parable of the Unjust Judge was spoken to the disciples.[92]

---

[89]Jeremias' attempt to understand all these texts under the first heading is unconvincing (*Parables*, 103, 145). Arguing that τίς ἐξ ὑμῶν is addressed to the opponents of the gospel, Jeremias does not discuss how this can hold true for the parable of the Friend at Midnight, which he admits teaches that God is a God "who hearkens to the cry of the needy and comes to their help" (*Parables*, 159).

[90]Cf. Matt. 12:34. Jeremias argues that the polemical nature of lines 4–6' is obvious because of "the change from the second to the third person" (*Parables*, 144f.). His point is that only in addressing opponents would Jesus shift to the third person and thus avoid saying, "shall give to *you* who ask him." The difficulty is that Jeremias has not observed the poetic structure which balances the first and third stanzas. In the first stanza, as we have noted, this same shift takes place from second to third person. Yet there it is clear that the line addressed to the second person, "Ask and it shall be given to you," is balanced with the line addressed to the third person, "For everyone who asks, receives." Therefore, the shift from second to third person in lines 4–6' cannot be used to argue for "opponents of the gospel" as the original hearers.

[91]It must be granted that a precise delineation of audience cannot be made in the case of this poem. There is, in lines 1–3, the element of assurance that an answer will be given. This theme is most appropriate for the disciples, not the opponents of the gospel. The topic of assurance provides a smooth transition from the parable to the poem. In like manner, the theme of eschatology appeared both in the parable and in the poem in Luke 16 and provided a smooth transition from one to the other. Yet like the poem in Luke 16, this theme of assurance of an answer, which connects this poem in Luke 11 to the parable, is not the main thrust of the first stanza of the poem. The main point of the stanza is that *all* men shall receive. We have noted that the Old Syriac gave this "all" a threefold repetition. The Pharisees think that only *some* who call on the name of the Lord will be saved, but Jesus insists that "*everyone* who asks, receives." Again the parallel with the parable of the Publican and the Pharisee is helpful.

[92]The "theme" of Luke 18:1 goes back to 17:22. Furthermore, the introduction and the conclusion of the parable point to a disciple audience.

Then the parable of the Pharisee and the Tax Collector is clearly addressed to the opponents of the gospel.[93] Luke 11:1–13 may have been compiled with the same division in mind, that is, with the first half of the unit (11:1–8) addressed to the disciples and the second half (11:9–13) to a Pharisaic audience.[94]

Thus internal as well as external evidence points to a Pharisaic audience for the poem on a Father's Gifts. In conclusion and summary, the parable/poem on the Father's Gifts, which follows the parable of the Friend at Midnight, is stylistically divided into three stanzas with each stanza containing three double lines. As such it approximates a Form VI poetic structure. It is most probably addressed to the opponents of the gospel. The parable/poem dramatically states that a gracious father always grants good gifts (Holy Spirit) to *all* who seek him. The poem is stylistically and theologically distinct from the parable that precedes it. There is no reason to doubt that both have equal antiquity in the tradition, and have been brought together by a compiler of the Jerusalem Document with no intention that the second should be understood as a commentary on the first.[95] As in the case of Luke 16:9–13, a poem of this quality, with close semantic correspondences uniting the whole, must come from the mind of a single poet. It is theoretically possible that an anonymous poet in the Palestinian community has recast different strands of traditional material into a poem of his own creation. It is much more likely that the author is Jesus of Nazareth.

---

[93]The editor in Luke 18:9 states specifically that the parable is spoken to "some who trusted in themselves that they were righteous and despised others." Internally the parable substantiates the accuracy of this setting. The outcast publican's prayers are heard.

[94]Jeremias has observed the relationship between Luke 11:9–13 and the parable of the Pharisee and the Tax Collector in Luke 18. Of the former he writes, "The usual attack of the opponents of Jesus on his proclamation of the gospel to the despised may most naturally be suggested as its occasion. Publicans pray to God (Luke 18:13f.), and he listens to them—shocking! But Jesus replies: 'Your eyes are closed against the fatherly goodness of God. Consider how you behave towards your children. If, although you are evil you know how to give good gifts to your children, why are you unwilling to believe that God will give the gifts of the New Age to those who ask him?' " (*Parables*, 145).

[95]Jeremias understands Luke 11:9–13 as a group of logia "used by Luke as the application of the parable," and feels the point of the parable "has been distorted by this expansion" (*Parables*, 105). The distortion comes about (as in the case of Luke 16:9–13) when we read the poem as a conclusion to the parable. It seems clear that this was not the intent of the compiler himself even as he certainly did not intend the parable of the Pharisee and the Publican to be read as the conclusion to the parable of the Widow and the Judge.

Chapter 7

EXEGESIS OF LUKE 15[1]

THE LOST SHEEP AND THE LOST COIN (LUKE 15:4–10)

In this section we intend to demonstrate that Luke 15:4–10 is a single unit in the form of a double parable, and that each half of the double parable has a literary structure. The cultural elements will be reexamined with the literary structures in mind. We will first examine the Lucan setting and then proceed to the Lost Sheep and the Lost Coin.

The Lucan Setting (15:1–3)

Some modern scholars feel that the setting given to the Lost Coin, the Lost Sheep, and the Lost Sons is secondary and yet historically accurate.[2] Jeremias, on the other hand, argues that Luke 15:1–3 is a part of the Evangelist's source and not the product of his redactional efforts.[3] Jeremias also understands the introduction to be historically accurate, so that the *Sitz im Leben* of this set of parables is not the presentation of the gospel so much as the "defense and vindication of the gospel."[4] Jeremias' point is clearly affirmed in verses 2 and 3. Jesus is presented as defending his association with sinners. If it can be agreed that the setting is historically accurate, the question of its being primary or secondary is of little importance. The more important question is that of the cultural significance of table fellowship. This question must now be examined.

Table fellowship anywhere in the world is a relatively serious matter. This is especially true in the Middle East. In his most recent statement Jeremias says,

> To understand what Jesus was doing in eating with "sinners," it is important to realize that in the east, even today, to invite a man to a meal was an honour. It

---

[1]For a brief popular discussion of some of the material in this chapter cf. Kenneth Bailey, *The Cross and the Prodigal* (St. Louis: Concordia, 1973).
[2]Dodd, *Parables*, 193; Linnemann, *Parables*, 69.
[3]Jeremias, *Parables*, 100.
[4]*Ibid.*, 124.

was an offer of peace, trust, brotherhood and forgiveness; in short, sharing a table meant sharing life. . . . Thus Jesus' meals with the publicans and sinners . . . are an expression of the mission and message of Jesus (Mark 2:17), eschatological meals, anticipatory celebrations of the feast in the end-time (Matt. 8.11 par.), in which the community of the saints is already being represented (Mark 2.19). The inclusion of sinners in the community of salvation, achieved in table-fellowship, is the most meaningful expression of the message of the redeeming love of God.[5]

In the East today, as in the past, a nobleman may feed any number of lesser needy persons as a sign of his generosity, but he does *not* eat with them. However, when guests are "received" the one receiving the guests eats with them. The meal is a special sign of acceptance. The host affirms this by showering his guests with a long series of compliments to which the guests must respond. Jesus is set forth in the text as engaging in some such social relationship with publicans and sinners. Small wonder the Pharisees were upset.[6]

In addition to "eating with sinners" there is the possibility that Jesus was himself hosting sinners. The accusation, "This one receives sinners and eats with them," is closely parallel to Mark 2:15f. In this Marcan text Jesus is clearly the host for the meal. The same may be true in Luke 15:2. In Luke the verb δέχομαι often does imply hospitality.[7] The προσδέχομαι of 15:2 is synonymous with the simpler form.[8] If this is the intent of 15:2, it is very significant inasmuch as the guest is assumed in any Oriental banquet to be bringing honor to the house in which he is entertained. The order of the traditional rounds of compliments mentioned above makes this clear. The host begins by referring to the honor brought to his house by the guests. The guests can then respond either by invoking the honor of God on the noble host or by affirming that they, too, have received honor by being in the host's presence. Even if modern village banquet customs are judged too recent to be used as evidence for ancient banquets, it can certainly be affirmed that for Jesus to *host* sinners would have been a much more serious offense to the Pharisees than merely to eat with sinners informally or to accept their invitations, as in the case of Zacchaeus of Jericho.[9] Thus, as host or guest, it is little wonder that Jesus' table fellowship with sinners offended the cultural and theological sensitivities of the Pharisees. The importance of the issue for both Jesus and his opposition is reflected in the fulness of his defense recorded in Luke 15:4–32.

In summary, Luke 15:1–3 is seen as an authentic setting for the parables

---

[5]Jeremias, *Theology*, 115f.

[6]A rabbinic injunction stated, "The wise say, 'Let not a man associate with sinners even to bring them near to the Torah' " (*Mechilta* 57b on Exod. 18:1; quoted from Montefiore, *Rabbinic*, 355). Jeremias points out that for the Pharisee, entertaining the non-Pharisee was "if not entirely forbidden, at least protected by very scrupulous limitations" (*Jerusalem*, 267).

[7]Luke 9:5; 9:53; 10:8, 11; 16:4, 9; 22:17.

[8]W. Grundmann, *TDNT*, II, 57.

[9]Both acts are clearly an offense to the Pharisees, as reflected in the διεγόγγυζον of Luke 15:2 and 19:7. Yet to host sinners would most likely be the greater offense.

that follow. The issue is Jesus' welcome of sinners to table fellowship either as fellow guest or as host. This issue is of crucial importance for Jesus and for his opponents. The parables of 15:4–32 are a defense of Jesus' actions. To the first part of this defense we now turn.

The Parable of the Lost Sheep (15:4–7)

These verses are a parable cast into the Form VI poetic structure. Further research is required before it will be possible to determine whether this is poetry or merely parallelistic prose. For this study we will assume the latter, observing however that the three-stanza poetical form is used. In this section the structure of the parable will be examined and the pertinent cultural elements set forth. We will attempt to understand the theology of the parable in the light of these two aspects.

In the three-stanza form the first stanza is semantically related to the third, and the second stanza often uses a different poetic device from the outer two. The structure of the parable is as follows:

A   What man of *you,* having a hundred sheep

B   and having lost *one* (*ḥadh*) of them

C   does he not leave the *ninety-nine* in the wilderness

    1   and go after the *lost* one

        2   until he *finds* it, and having *found* it

            3   he places it upon his shoulders *rejoicing* (*ḥedhwa*)?

                4   And coming *to the home*
                    he calls *to the friends* and neighbors

            3'   saying to them, *rejoice* (*ḥedhwa*) with me

        2'   because I have *found* my sheep

    1'   which was *lost.*

A'   I say to *you* that thus there is more *joy* (*ḥedhwa*) in heaven

B'   over *one* (*ḥadh*) sinner
      who repents

C'   than over *ninety-nine* righteous persons
      who need no repentance.

The semantic correspondences between the parallel lines are as follows:

1   which man of you (a direct address to the audience)
2   one
3   ninety-nine

     A   the lost
       B   find
         C   joy
           D   restoration

```
         C'  joy
      B'  find
   A'  the lost
```

```
1'   I say to you (a direct address to the audience)
2'   one
3'   ninety-nine
```

Although to our knowledge this poetic structure has not been previously identified, the presence of literary structures generally in the parables has been noted. Jones refers to "thought-rhyme" or "kolometric harmony," and lists this parable as an example.[10] B. T. D. Smith discusses the tendency toward "schematization" and the love of "parallelism and of formulas" in the parables of Christ.[11] In a recent article Giblin approaches Luke 15 from the same perspective and notes:

> ... Closer attention to literary structure reveals wondrously the theological finality of a given work. Perhaps the interrelation of certain structural elements in a reasonably large and well-defined unit like Lk 15 will reveal to one who studies its compositional features as a *whole* a number of interesting and profitable theological insights.[12]

Giblin gives his own structural analysis of the Lost Sheep and the Lost Coin. He comments that the material has a "remarkable parallelism of structure."[13] Thus the literary structure given above is in line with hints stemming from other studies.

The structure itself is similar to Luke 11:9–13. Both have three stanzas. In both, the first stanza is reflected in a slightly different form in the third. In both, the outer two stanzas use step parallelism. There is a direct "to you" reference to introduce stanzas I and III in both poems. Three semantic units are prominent in the outer stanzas of both. Both use a poetic device in the center that is different from the outside. The climax of each is in the center.

At the same time there are some differences. In this parable on the Lost Sheep the outer stanzas are not doubled. The center has its semantic units inverted rather than in parallel.[14] Seven semantic units appear in the center rather than six. In spite of these variations, the overall structure of the parable identifies it structurally with Luke 16:9–13 and 11:9–13.

The semantic correspondences between *you, one,* and *ninety-nine* which link stanzas I and III need no further comment. In addition to the semantic correspondences, there is a striking play on words tying these stanzas together.

---

[10]Jones, *Art,* 73–75. The usual spelling is "colometric."

[11]B. T. D. Smith, *Parables,* 37.

[12]Giblin, "Luke 15," 18.

[13]*Ibid.,* 19. Giblin concentrates on parallelisms between the Lost Sheep and the Lost Coin. These certainly do exist. It is our view that the internal parallelisms are more precise and more important.

[14]A three-stanza structure with inverted parallelism in the center stanza was observed in Luke 16:9–13.

Matthew Black has noted a paronomasia in an underlying Aramaic of this parable between "one" (*ḥadh*) and "joy" (*ḥedhwa*).[15] This auditory correspondence runs through the entire poem and strengthens the unity of the three stanzas. *Ḥadh* occurs in the first stanza, *ḥedhwa* in the second, and both words in the third. Furthermore, the *ḥedhwa* (joy) is at the climactic center of the poem. Thus the two outer stanzas are linked by semantic and auditory correspondences.

This brings us to a consideration of the center stanza. The parables of Jesus are known for their naturalness and life-like qualities. Yet before and since Archimedes, anyone who finds anything cries out, "I have found it!" The natural thing for the shepherd of the parable to have said would be, "I have found my sheep." Instead we have a long, somewhat unnatural statement which is clearly constructed to provide the inversion of ideas that will fill out the parallelistic form and climax on "joy at restoration" in the center of the parable. This center must now be examined with care.

Matthew Black notes in his chapter on "Semitic Poetic Form"[16] a series of texts in the Old Syriac which have striking poetic correspondences between lines. He feels these Old Syriac readings "may well have preserved the true translation of the original Aramaic."[17] The center of this poem here in Luke 15:6 may be another illustration of Black's suggestion. In the Old Syriac this center reads,

> *wa'eto lebayteh*
>
> *waqro leroḥmaohi*

which gives close grammatical and auditory correspondences between the lines.[18] Furthermore, lines C′ and B′ have a double auditory rhyme in the Old Syriac.[19]

To summarize the structural elements in this section, the parable uses a Form VI structure. It has strong auditory as well as semantic correspondences. Both inverted and step parallelism are used. The climax, which is "joy in restoration," is highlighted by the parallelistic structure and by the word-rhyme between "one" and "joy." This brings us to a consideration of the cultural aspects of the parable.

---

[15]Black, *Aramaic Approach*, 184. Thus v.7 in Aramaic would include, "there is more '*ḥedhwa*' over '*ḥadh*'...." Black notes other poetic associations in the same passage that appear too faint to be convincing.

[16]*Ibid.*, 143–185.

[17]*Ibid.*, 159.

[18]The Greek text does not have καί at the beginning of the second line. The Old Syriac, the Peshitta, and most of the Arabic versions do have the copula. The additional word "the neighbors" in the Greek text interrupts the structure. Both p[75] of the Alexandrian family and Θ of the Caesarean omit it. It may have spilled in from the parable of the Lost Coin. Turner observes that occasionally the poetic structure of a passage "helps the textual critic"; cf. Nigel Turner, *Syntax*, Vol. III of James H. Moulton, *A Grammar of New Testament Greek* (Edinburgh: T. & T. Clark, 1963), 346.

[19]These are:

> *ḥedaw 'ammi*
> *deshekḥt 'erbi*

The telling of a parable about a shepherd in an address to Pharisees has a special problem. Moses was accepted as a shepherd. A Midrash on Exodus records a story of Moses searching out a lost kid and being told by God that he will lead Israel.[20] Kings were referred to by Ezekiel as shepherds (Ezra 34), and God himself was thought of as a shepherd (Ps. 23). Thus the figure of the shepherd was a noble symbol. By contrast, flesh-and-blood shepherds who in the first century wandered around after sheep were clearly 'am ha'areṣ and unclean. For the Pharisee, a "sinner" was either an immoral person who did not keep the law or a person engaged in one of the proscribed trades, among which was herding sheep.[21] Derrett observes the incongruity of despising shepherds in the flesh and approving of them in allegories. He writes,

> The shepherd was despised socially on account of his flocks' eating private property, whatever prestige the occupation of shepherd might have in the eyes of allegorists.[22]

It is difficult to know how the rabbis managed to revere the shepherd of the Old Testament and despise the shepherd who herded the neighbor's sheep. But this seems to have been the case.

If we accept that the parable was addressed to Pharisees (15:1–3), then the parable begins with a shock to their sensitivities. Any man who believed shepherds were unclean would naturally be offended if addressed as one. Yet Jesus begins, "Which one of you having a hundred sheep . . . does not he leave. . . ." Thus this beginning can be understood as an indirect and yet very powerful attack on the Pharisaic attitudes toward proscribed professions. To show deference to their feelings in this matter he would have had to begin the parable something like this: "Which man of you owning a hundred sheep, if he heard that the hired shepherd had lost one, would he not summon the shepherd and demand that the sheep be found under threat of fine?"[23] It can be seriously questioned whether any Pharisee would ever take up the task of a shepherd under any condition. Thus the decision to address Pharisees as shepherds is a culturally and theologically conditioned decision of some significance.[24]

---

[20]Midrash on Exodus, Shemoth Rabba iii.1, quoted by Oesterley, Jewish Background, 181.

[21]Jeremias, Parables, 132; Jerusalem, 304. Herdsmen appear twice on the rabbinic lists of proscribed trades. Jeremias notes, "most of the time they were dishonest and thieving; they led their herds on to other people's land . . . and pilfered the produce of the herd" (Jerusalem, 305, also 310f.).

[22]Derrett, "Prodigal Son," 66, n. 1.

[23]The modern Christian has a kindly attitude toward Rahab. But woe to any preacher who begins his sermon, "Now which one of you ladies, if she does so-and-so."

[24]In the East, the social status identified with particular professions is a very serious matter. Major Jarvis, the British governor of Sinai in the thirties, notes the sharp distinctions between classes. A camel driver was very careful not to be known as a fisherman, and if caught fishing would point out to the visitor that he was a camel driver, not a fisherman (C. S. Jarvis, Desert and Delta [London: John Murray, 1938], 217; idem, Three Deserts [London: John Murray, 1936], passim).

In an isolated Egyptian village of Der al-Barsha in 1958–59 I tried to introduce a brick machine into the village. The mud bricks are still made as in the days of Moses. A wall built of them lasts only a

Another cultural factor needs consideration. The text says, "Which one of you having a hundred sheep. . . ." Aramaic, like Syriac and Arabic, has no verb "to have" and thus the Greek ἔχων is translated in all our Oriental versions with *lah*.[25] My Palestinian, Syrian, and Lebanese shepherd friends all agree that anyone wealthy enough to own a hundred sheep will hire a shepherd, or let some less affluent member of the extended family take care of them. The average family may have five to fifteen animals. A number of families get together and hire a shepherd. The shepherd may own some of the animals and be from one of the families. Thus, in the case of a small herd of about forty animals, the shepherd leading them may be their sole owner.[26] In the case of a hundred sheep the shepherd is probably not their sole owner. The verb in question (ἔχω) in the New Testament can mean "hold in one's charge or keeping."[27] Thus, "have a hundred sheep" can mean "be responsible for a hundred sheep" and need not necessarily mean *own* a hundred sheep.

This does not mean that the shepherd in this parable is a "hireling." The extended family owns the sheep. The shepherd is not a "hireling" nor a "stranger."[28] He is a member of the extended family and naturally feels responsible before the entire family clan; any loss is a loss to all of them. This understanding of the culture clarifies the joy in the *community* reflected at the center of the parable. In short, the extended family loses if a sheep is lost; the whole clan rejoices if the lost is found. This element of "rejoicing" in the parable also needs examination.

The parable/poem, reinforced by its structure, tells the listener/reader that the shepherd rejoices twice: once when he finds the sheep (3), and a second time in community, back in the village (3'). The first occasion of rejoicing is remarkable. My shepherd friends in upper Galilee confirm Stuhlmueller's insight, "A lost sheep will lie down helplessly and refuse to budge. The shepherd is forced to carry it over a long distance."[29] Surprisingly, this shepherd *rejoices* in the burden of restoration still before him. This theme is prominent in this first parable and drops entirely out of sight in the second. It reappears in 15:11–32.[30] Sa'īd observes that the shepherd placed the sheep on his shoulders, "knowing that the hard work is yet before him."[31] This theme of the burden of restoration is important to note. The story does not end with the finding of the sheep. After the sheep is found it must be restored. It is the restoration with its implied burden and expressed joy that is the center of the second stanza and thus the climax of the entire poem.

---

few years and then cracks and falls. The brick machine produced bricks easily five times as strong. The young men in the village were without work and a ready market for the bricks was assured. The project was a complete failure, because brickmakers are of a lower class than farmers.

[25]There is a verb "to own" in all these languages. It is not used in any of these versions.

[26]This smaller herd would be the background of John 10:11.

[27]Bauer-A., G., *Lexicon*, 33b.

[28]Cf. John 10:11.

[29]Stuhlmueller, *Luke*, 148.

[30]Goebel, *Parables*, 198.

[31]Sa'īd, *Lūqā*, 294.

A minor, yet significant turn of phrase is the reference to the shepherd having himself lost the sheep. The listener/reader expects a passive, "if the sheep was lost," which would exonerate the shepherd from any blame.[32] Rather, the shepherd is clearly assumed negligent in his duty as a shepherd. He "loses" the sheep; the verb is an aorist active participle.

A further problem is posed by the phrase *"in the wilderness"* (Luke 15:4). The shepherd leaves the flock "in the wilderness." He then returns to "the house" with the lost sheep on his shoulders. The parable has few details, yet they are sufficient to allow a reconstruction. The roving tribesmen keep sheep in the open at night. Peasants, living on the edge of the pasture lands, bring the sheep to the courtyard of the family home at the end of each day. The reference to "the house" in the parable confirms that we are dealing with peasant shepherds. Levison writes,

> I have never seen in Syria, Palestine or Mesopotamia a flock attended by a single person. Two, and even three, shepherds are commonly employed. When one sheep is lost and the shepherd goes to seek it, the other shepherd takes the flock home. On arrival, the neighbors would at once notice the absence of the shepherd or they would be told of it, for apart from the possibility of the loss of the animal, it is often a question of the safety of the man. Should he encounter a wild beast, a single-handed shepherd, with only his stick and sling, is in a perilous predicament. The finding and bringing home of the lost sheep is, therefore, a matter of great thanksgiving in the community.[33]

The text, then, can mean "he left the flock while they were still in the wilderness." The point is that the shepherd counted the flock while they were still in the wilderness (not after they got back to the village), and after discovering that one was missing, he naturally departed from them "in the wilderness," leaving a second shepherd to guide the flock back to the village.[34] Thus the leaving of the

---

[32]Colloquial speech all across the Middle East is united in this regard. When any accident or misfortune is reported by the person involved, or by a third person, the passive is always used unless the speaker deliberately wants to blame the person in the story. Thus, the man who misses a train says, "The train went from me," rather than, "I missed the train." The student says, "The pencil went from me," not "I lost the pencil." The waiter says, "The dish fell," not "I dropped the dish." The parable of the Lost Sheep occurs in Matthew as well as Luke. The Matthean version reflects this expected pattern of speech and reads, "If one of them goes astray" (Matt. 18:13), which is the normal expression. The Lucan text *deliberately* blames the shepherd. This is striking and is quite likely original (see further below) inasmuch as Jesus is addressing the Pharisees, who are called on in the parable to identify themselves with the shepherd. If they do this, they see themselves as responsible for having lost the wandering sheep.

[33]Levison, *Local Setting*, 152f. Rihbany also discusses the shepherd and his helper (*Syrian*, 300). We recall that both these authors grew up in Middle Eastern villages.

[34]I am told by Palestinian shepherds that no man can care for a hundred sheep permanently by himself. He has no feed for the sheep. They must be led out each day. No man can count on perfect health 365 days a year (not to mention his family and community duties).

Bishop confirms that under no circumstances is a flock left unguarded in the wilderness (E. F. F. Bishop, "The Parable of the Lost or Wandering Sheep," *ATR* 44 [1962], 50). Thomson wrote of shepherds, "They never leave their helpless charge alone" (*The Land*, I, 299). The Oriental versions,

sheep in the wilderness need not be understood as an unauthentic element in the story. At the same time it must be observed that the ninety-nine *are* left hanging. We can assume all we like but we are not told of their return to the village. We know the lost sheep got home; we do not know what happened to the ninety-nine. We will return to this point later.

The shepherd rejoices in community. As we have noted above, this joy in community is quite likely due to two factors. First, the community rejoices in hearing that the shepherd is safe. Second, the herd is most likely owned by these same friends and neighbors. Bishop writes, ''There is the invitation to friends and neighbors in the village, who were concerned in what was likely a communal loss.''[35] The lost sheep is a community loss. The recovered sheep is an occasion for joy for all the neighbors. Even so, the sinner is lost from the community, and it is natural to expect communal joy at his recovery, not ''murmuring'' as in Luke 15:2.

Summarizing the significant cultural aspects of this parable, we have observed that Jesus makes a decision to oppose Pharisaic attitudes toward proscribed professions when he addresses them as shepherds. The shepherd in the story may not own all the sheep but still is not a hireling. Joy occurs twice in the parable. There is joy at finding the sheep, irrespective of the burden of restoration, and joy in community at the success of restoration. The shepherd is blamed for the loss of the sheep, and his leaving the sheep in the wilderness is not necessarily incongruous with Palestinian sheepherders' customs.

Before examining and summarizing the theological implications of the structural and the cultural factors discussed above, we must deal with the problem of the relationship between this version of the Lost Sheep and a similar parable that occurs in Matthew 18:12–24. The intent of this section is to demonstrate that the Lucan version is more original. The poetical and cultural elements of the parable already discussed will be the focal points of the discussion.

---

without exception, have no difficulty with the text as it stands. Had the text not fit the shepherd world as they knew it, they could very easily have moved the phrase ''in the wilderness'' ahead two words and left the verse to read, ''and leaving the ninety-nine, he went out in the wilderness.'' This alternative was not taken.

Bishop (*loc. cit.*) argues that the Semitic grammar underlying the Matthean account allows us to assume that the shepherd leaves the ninety-nine and *he* goes into the wilderness. He admits Luke cannot be read this way without some transposition. His understanding of the Matthean account is unconvincing. Bussby makes the intriguing suggestion that the Aramaic *turah* (mountain) has been confused during the oral tradition with *durah* (enclosure). Bussby quotes W. Wright as saying that the Aramaeans pronounced the ''d'' like the ''t,'' which could lead to the confusion; cf. F. Bussby, ''Did a Shepherd Leave Sheep Upon the Mountain or in the Desert?'' *ATR* 45 (1963), 93f. This is a reasonable proposal. My only difficulty with it is that, as indicated above, the Oriental versions have not sensed a problem. The Syriac could easily have changed the words back or shifted the word order if the Greek text had not fit the pastoral scene as they knew it.

[35]Bishop, *Jesus,* 166. The ms. Vat. Borg. 71 reads ''*They* called his friends and neighbors,'' indicating that the family and close friends rush out to bring the neighbors. This kind of interpretive comment reflects the communal nature of life that again and again informs the parables significantly. The shepherd is not an isolated individual but part of an extended family.

There is sharp disagreement among scholars over the question of which version of the Lost Sheep is more original, Luke's or Matthew's. Jeremias argues that the Matthean version is addressed to the Christian community, advising it to seek out the lost Christian apostates, while Luke's version is spoken in defense of Jesus' welcome of sinners and is directed against his opponents. Jeremias feels the Lucan situation is clearly more original.[36] Bultmann, on the other hand, is relatively confident that Luke's "fuller form" is secondary to the briefer Matthean version.[37]

Eta Linnemann follows Bultmann in her full discussion of the problem. She presents five major arguments in an attempt to prove the secondary nature of the Lucan version. These are:

1. Luke has "when he finds it," while Matthew gives "if he finds it." Linnemann feels that the "if" is more realistic and thus more original, and that by illuminating the uncertainty, the Church has allegorized the "good Shepherd" into the parable.

2. In Luke 15:5 the shepherd lays the sheep on his shoulders. This detail, she asserts, is a decorative expansion.

3. The shepherd cannot come back to the inhabited area, having left his unguarded herd alone in the wilderness. This detail in the Lucan version is seen as unauthentic.

4. To celebrate with the neighbors is unnatural for a shepherd.

5. The Lucan conclusion is "an allegorical exposition."[38]

These five arguments will be examined in turn.

With regard to the first, searching "until he finds it" does not exhibit an unnatural situation. The shepherd of Palestine has indeed to search "until he finds it" in the sense that he either has to bring back a live animal or bring back its remains as proof that he has not sold it.[39] Furthermore, on this point the Matthean version may actually be in harmony with the Lucan version. Matthew 18:13 has the particle ἐάν. Occasionally in the New Testament this particle is the equivalent of "when."[40] John 12:32, for example, reads, "and I, ἐάν I am lifted up." Here the meaning is clearly "when."[41] The Old Syriac also used a particle in Matthew 18:30 that can mean either "if" or "when," but means primarily "when." Burkitt

---

[36]Jeremias, *Parables*, 40. John's shepherd images are also addressed to opponents; cf. John 10:6, 19.

[37]Bultmann, *Tradition*, 171.

[38]Linnemann, *Parables*, 67–70.

[39]Cf. Amos 3:12. Because the sheep when frightened lies down and puts out a loud, incessant bleating, finding it is not considered impossible. The ground it travels in a day is not extensive and the assumption is that the sheep can be found if the shepherd is diligent. The sheep is too heavy for a wild animal to drag a great distance. Rihbany tells of an old shepherd of his acquaintance who never lost a sheep. He writes, "Whether the unfortunate sheep was yet alive or whether it had died, Yousef, as a good and faithful shepherd, always carried it back to the fold" (*Syrian*, 308).

[40]Bauer-A., G., *Lexicon*, 210.

[41]Cf. John 14:3; Heb. 3:7; 1 John 2:28.

translates the phrase, "and at what time he hath found it."[42] Thus searching "until he finds" the sheep is a fully authentic detail, and both the Matthean and Lucan versions can be understood to assume the shepherd searches until the sheep is found.

Linnemann has failed to notice that the Lucan version specifically blames the shepherd for the loss. The Matthean version, with its passive, leaves in doubt who is responsible. If, as Linnemann has argued, the Lucan version was allegorized to fit the church's image of the Good Shepherd, then this allegorizing was done in the most clumsy fashion possible.

Luke 15:5b reads, "He lays it on his shoulders, rejoicing." Linnemann understands this phrase to be a "decorative accretion." However, she has failed to see the structure of the parable that requires a repetition of the theme of "joy." This structure makes it clear that the phrase in question was not added after the composition of the parable.

At the same time, "joy at restoration" occurs at the center of the poem. "Restoration" alone is at the exact center and this is encased within a double reference to "joy."[43] Thus, *joy* is a part of the poem's climax. Furthermore, the theme of "joy," with its wordplay on "one," is clearly prominent in the entire poem-parable. Linnemann works with Jülicher's one-point-only approach to parables. Having decided that the single theme is that the one is more valuable than the ninety-nine, her hermeneutical principle does not allow her to see any theological significance in any of the other details of the parable. Thus, it is easy to dismiss as an accretion that which turns out to be a crucial part of the climax of the entire parable. The author is not just filling out a literary form when he repeats the theme of joy. The double repetition of "lost" may be for artistic and not theological reasons. But with "joy" appearing in the climax and also used in a wordplay that unites the poem, the double theme of joy is theologically significant as well as being artistically authentic. This significance will be examined briefly at the end of our discussion of the Lost Sheep. Thus, Linnemann's dismissal of Luke 15:5b as secondary to the original parable is seen to be destructive of the literary form and disruptive of the climax of the parable.

Linnemann states in her third argument that a Palestinian shepherd would not return "to the house" after finding his sheep. This position confuses the bedouin and the peasant. The bedouin lives in the wilderness and does not return to a village at night. The peasant-shepherd *does* return the sheep to his home in the village each evening.

The supposed "unnaturalness" of the shepherd's celebration with his

---

[42]F. C. Burkitt, *Evangelion da-Mepharreshe* (Cambridge: University Press, 1904), I, 103. The Peshitta changes to an unambiguous phrase that reads only "if." The Arabic versions use the particle *idha*, which also means both "if" and "when." The Syriac particle is *modi*. The Coptic Gospel of Thomas Logion 107 has the shepherd search "until he found it."

[43]In like manner, the Acts 2 poem examined above had the two related themes of cross and resurrection in the center. The cross was in the exact center and was encased within the closely related theme of resurrection.

friends is a cultural misjudgment of the scene. Village men gather almost nightly to discuss the events of the village, recite poetry, and tell stories from the oral tradition. It is fully as natural for the shepherd to call in his friends for a little celebration as it is for the woman in the parable of the Lost Coin.

Linnemann's final argument is that the Lucan conclusion is an "allegorical exposition." However, the final three lines of the parable-poem are required for the poetical structure, as we have noted, and contain the Aramaic wordplay on "one" and "joy."[44] The Matthean version has no discernible poetic structure and the Aramaic wordplay has disappeared. These features must be taken into consideration in any comparison between the two versions of the parable. In any case, a "hint of allegory" need not necessarily identify a text as secondary.[45] In fact, it may not be allegory at all, but rather symbolism. Thus, the so-called allegorical exposition in Luke 15:7 is required for the poetic structure and the Aramaic wordplay.

Finally, the question of the source of the Lucan version being in "Q" or "L" and the related problem of the reasons for the divergent account in Matthew lie beyond the scope of this study. We would only affirm in conclusion that the Lucan version as it now stands is authentically Palestinian linguistically, culturally, and stylistically. It can be understood as originating at the earliest point in the tradition, and most probably stemming from Jesus of Nazareth.

The Theological Cluster

This parable has a series of at least four themes that must be seen in relationship to each other. These themes together create the impact of this parable.[46] We would hesitate to give any one of these motifs priority over the others. Each is important and all four must be seen together, not in isolation from each other.

One clear emphasis is the *joy* of the shepherd.[47] Giblin sees that this is the main point of the twin parable. He writes, "The dynamic theme is the invitation to share in joy over the conversion of sinners."[48] Thus the joy is expressed in and shared with a community.

Closely related to this first theme is the *joy in the burden of restoration*. In this parable Jesus is defending his welcome of sinners. This welcome involves

---

[44]Jones writes, "It is absurd to state that Jesus did not 'clinch' his parables with an explanatory conclusion" (*Art*, 150). Linnemann, *Parables*, 67–70, presents no case to show that the elements in the conclusion are "allegory" and not "metaphor."

[45]Jones, *Art*, 135–166; Raymond Brown, "Parable and Allegory Reconsidered," *Novum Testamentum* 5 (1962), 36–45. The simplest solution may be that of Oesterley, who says, "We have here another instance of a parabolic theme being used for more than one purpose" (*Jewish Background*, 117).

[46]The allegorizers have their usual field day with this double parable. The lamp becomes the "Holy Spirit," the shepherd of course is the "Good Shepherd" (even though the parable specifically blames him for having lost his sheep), the wilderness is the Jewish nation, the house is the "Church," and no doubt someone has an identification for the broom. With Jülicher, this type of arbitrary introduction of foreign elements into the parable must be rejected.

[47]Cf. P. J. Bernadicou, "The Lucan Theology of Joy," *Science et Esprit* 25 (1973), 75–98.

[48]Giblin, "Luke 15," 22.

restoration to a community. The wandering sheep must be brought back to the fold now gathered in the village. This, for any shepherd, has a price. The search has its price but so does the act of restoration. In this theme of the burden of restoration there are clear Christological implications which point in the direction of the passion. The shepherd must carry on his shoulders the burden of the lost sheep, a detail that is specifically mentioned. Without the shouldering of this burden there is no restoration. This task the shepherd accepts with joy.

A third prominent theme is that of the *gracious love* which seeks the sinner. This theme is picked up by Manson as being primary for both the Lost Sheep and the Lost Coin. He writes,

> In both parables the point is the same: the endless trouble that men will take to recover lost property, and their deep satisfaction when they succeed. The inference is that the publicans and sinners really belong to God, despite all appearances to the contrary, and that God himself wants them back and will take trouble to win them back to Himself.... The characteristic feature of these two parables is not so much the joy over the repentant sinner as the Divine love that goes out to seek the sinner before he repents.[49]

One must be cautious in labeling this love "divine." The listening Pharisaic audience is encouraged to identify with the shepherd. Jesus seems to be saying, "The shepherd sought the lost. I seek the lost and so should you!" In the parable of the Lost Sons the Pharisaic audience is led to identify with the older son, not the father. Thus the father in that later parable more directly symbolizes divine love. Such divine love seems to be alluded to only indirectly in the parable of the Lost Sheep.

The last dominant theme is that of *repentance*. The parable raises two questions in relationship to repentance. The first is, "Who is expected to repent?" The second is, "What is the nature of this repentance?" The background to the first question is found in the rabbinic debate over the so-called "completely righteous." Some rabbis affirmed that there were indeed "completely righteous" persons whom God loved in a special way. Another opinion affirmed that God's greatest love was extended to repentant sinners. This debate is reflected in the Talmud, which reads,

> R. Hiyya b. Abba also said in R. Johanan's name: All the prophets prophesied only for repentant sinners; but as for the perfectly righteous (who had never sinned at all), "the eye hath not seen, O God, beside thee, what he hath prepared for him that waiteth for him."[50]

In this text Rabbi Abba is affirming that there are "the perfectly righteous." God loves them *more* than he does repentant sinners. The Talmud then offers the opinion of Rabbi Abbahu, who thinks "repentant sinners" are closer to God than these "perfectly righteous." He is in turn answered by an affirmation of the first

---

[49]Manson, *Sayings*, 283f.
[50]b. Tal. *Sanhedrin* 99a.

opinion, namely, that God prefers the "completely righteous."[51] The Talmud clearly gives Rabbis Abba and Johanan the last word.[52]

However, some centuries earlier, Ben Sirach wrote, "Do not revile a repentant sinner; remember that we all are guilty."[53] This text seems to deny the category of the "perfectly righteous." Such a denial is in keeping with Isaiah 53:6, where *all* sheep are reported to have gone astray. Jesus' view seems more in harmony with Isaiah and Ben Sirach than with the Talmud. In the synoptic Gospels the theme of "the perfectly righteous" is not apparent but the universal need for *all* to repent is affirmed.[54] Thus, in line with Ben Sirach and Isaiah 53:6, the reference in Luke 15:7 to "the ninety-nine righteous persons who need no repentance" is perhaps best understood as irony.[55] For Jesus all are lost sheep who need a shepherd to guide them. All men must repent. The literary structure obliges the listener to relate stanza I and stanza III. In stanza I the ninety-nine are left *in the wilderness*. The listener does not know if they are home or not. Jesus may be saying, "The angels cannot rejoice over the ninety-nine 'righteous' because they are not yet home." That is, the literary form reinforces the suggestion of irony. This brings us to the question of the nature and function of this repentance.

For first-century Judaism repentance was a way of bringing in the kingdom. In the preaching of Jesus repentance was a response to the kingdom already come. Bornkamm points out that for the rabbis repentance was a precondition for grace; it was a work by which a righteous man showed himself righteous. All this is clearly silenced in the parable of the Lost Sheep, where, as Bornkamm observes, "So little is repentance a human action preparing the way for grace, that it can be placed on the same level as being found."[56] The sheep does nothing to prompt the shepherd to begin his search except to become lost. In the parable the shepherd finds the sheep. Then, in the conclusion to the parable, there is reported joy over "one sinner who *repents*." Here "being found" is equated with "repentance."[57] Thus the parable of the Lost Sheep sets out a radically new understanding of the nature of repentance.

In summary, the parable of the Lost Sheep is a Palestinian parable constructed along the lines of a Form VI poem, with features that link it to other three-stanza poems in the synoptic Gospels. The cultural features are authentic and identify it as earlier than the Matthean version. Four theological themes interlock

---

[51]*Ibid*. "Repentant sinners" are בעלי תשובה. "Completely righteous" are צדיקי גמורה.

[52]Str.-B., II, 211f.

[53]Sir. 8:5.

[54]Cf. Luke 13:3.

[55]Miller, *Luke*, 120; Plummer, *St. Luke*, 369; Stuhlmueller, *Luke*, 148; Saʿīd, *Lūqā*, 403.

[56]Bornkamm, *Jesus*, 82.

[57]This new understanding of repentance is expanded in the parable of the Lost Sons, where an older son is also "found" but there is no repentance. Thus, there is more involved than just "being found." The one found must accept his lost condition and his need to be found and restored. One could argue that all this is implied in the parable of the Lost Sheep. In any case, it is clearly spelled out in the larger discussion in Luke 15:11–32.

in the parable. These are, joy in restoration to community, joy in the burden of that restoration, an unconditioned grace that seeks the lost, and a new understanding of repentance. Much of the same theology is reinforced by the second story, that of the Lost Coin, to which we now turn.

The Parable of the Lost Coin (15:8–10)

The Parable of the Lost Sheep and the Lost Coin may be viewed as a double parable. The Lost Coin has a literary structure that is simpler and less precise than that of the Lost Sheep. The cultural details are genuine. The theme of the burden of restoration is missing. This second half of the parable reinforces the themes indicated in the first half; yet there is some progression.

Once again we must analyze the structure of this part of the parable. The Lost Coin exhibits the following pattern:

Or what woman, having ten silver coins,[58]

    A   if she *loses* one coin

        B   does not light a lamp and sweep the house
           and seek diligently until she *finds* it, and *finding*

           C   she calls together her friends and neighbors
              saying, "*Rejoice with me*

        B'   for I have *found* the coin

    A'   which I had *lost*."

Even so, I tell you, there is *joy* before the angels of God over *one* sinner who repents.

The major semantic relationships are as follows:

Introduction—a woman[59] with ten coins

    A   one is *lost*

        B   search until she *finds*

           C   *joy* in community over restoration

        B'   because she has *found*

    A'   what was *lost*

Application—*joy* over *one* that repents.

---

[58]The parable of the Lost Coin is almost universally accepted as an original part of this twin parable. This rests on the similarity of the two images and on the ἤ which alone unites them. This ἤ represents the Aramaic *min*; cf. Jeremias, *Parables,* 141. He sees no reason to divide these even though the Lost Sheep was preserved independently (*ibid.,* 91). The Coptic Gospel of Thomas has another form of the Lost Sheep in Logion 107. For a good discussion of that Logion in relation to the synoptic accounts see J. B. Sheppard, "A Study of the Parables Common to the Synoptic Gospels and the Coptic Gospel of Thomas" (unpublished Ph.D. thesis, Emory University, Atlanta, 1965), 227–244.

[59]Jeremias calls her a "widow," but there is no evidence for this and the culture neither suggests nor demands it (*Parables,* 133).

The stylistic features in this parable show a number of similarities and some differences from the Lost Sheep. There is only one stanza. The entire structure is looser in construction, shorter and simpler. The introduction is shortened to "which woman," because to have said "which woman of you" to a group of Oriental men would have been an unpardonable insult. The basic inversion is the same in the two poems, but in this latter case the theme of joy is not doubled. The reason for this is obvious. In the case of the parable of the Lost Coin there is no burden of restoration. Once the coin is found it is automatically restored. Yet the theme of joy does appear in the center and the end and is thus again the climax of the poem/parable. The Aramaic play on words with "one" and "joy" (see above, p. 146) also occurs at the end.

Finally, in regard to the entire double parable, Luke 15:4–10 has a Form IV poetic outline. That is, it has two stanzas in which the second stanza is a repeat of the first, with the semantic units in the same order. This identification is not precise in that the parable of the Lost Sheep has three stanzas, as we have noted. Yet there is a general repetition of the structure, and the inversion at the center of each outline is identical to the other.

A number of cultural elements need to be noted. Rihbany makes the helpful observation that "the scarcity of money in the hands of the people makes the loss of a coin . . . a sad event."[60] Rihbany's point is that the peasant village is, to a large extent, self-supporting, making its own cloth and growing its own food. Cash is a rare commodity. Hence the lost coin is of far greater value in a peasant home than the day's labor it represents monetarily.

It has often been observed that the coin may be a part of the woman's jewelry or dowry.[61] However, a distinction must be made between the bedouin and the villager. Bedouin women wear their dowry in the form of coins hanging on their veils; village women do not. Sa'īd believes the coin is most likely part of a necklace. Village women do wear coins on necklaces. Obviously the beauty of the necklace as a whole is destroyed when one coin is lost. Again, the loss is more than the value of the single coin.[62]

The movement of peasant women in the village was and is extremely limited.[63] This woman clearly knew that the coin was in the house. She had not been out. Her diligence was prompted by the knowledge that it could be found if she would keep sweeping.[64]

---

[60]Rihbany, *Syrian*, 153.

[61]Bishop, *Jesus*, 191.

[62]Sa'īd, *Lūqā*, 394f.

[63]Jeremias, *Jerusalem*, "Appendix: The Social Position of Women," 359 376, esp 359–363. Jeremias notes that village women could go to the well but that "it was considered preferable for a woman, and especially an unmarried girl, in general, not to go out at all" (p. 360).

[64]The floor is most likely packed earth, not stone (Rihbany, *Syrian*, 154; against Jeremias, *Parables*, 135). Contrasting the shepherd as relatively rich and the woman as poor is strained (Jeremias, *loc. cit.*). They are both relatively poor.

In the cultural world of first-century Palestine, the very use of a woman in an illustration required a moral decision. Jesus is again rejecting Pharisaic attitudes toward groups of people in society. First it was the proscribed shepherds, now the inferior woman.[65]

Two aspects of the imagery in the parable of the Lost Sheep are intensified in the parable of the Lost Coin. First, the relative value of the thing lost is intensified. It is now one in ten, not one in a hundred; and, as we have noted, the coin may have had value beyond its monetary worth. Then second, the place of search for the lost is more narrowly confined. It is now the confines of a house, not the wide wilderness. Thus the assurance is intensified that the lost one *can* be found if the searcher is willing to put out sufficient effort.

In summary, we have noted that the structure is not as complex or as precise as Luke 11:9–13 and 16:9–13. The two parables form a single literary unit in which the second half reinforces the first half. The cultural elements are authentic and striking. Theologically the theme of "the burden of restoration" is missing, but joy, grace, and repentance are all present.

THE FATHER AND THE TWO LOST SONS (LUKE 15:11–32)

This parable has for centuries been called *"Evangelium in Evangelio."*[66] Nearly everyone who wrestles seriously with this pericope ends up with a sense of awe at its inexhaustible content. C. F. W. Smith writes,

> While Jesus was not a philosopher or a theologian (in the accepted sense), his parables alone provide material that neither the philosopher nor the theologian can exhaust. This is the mark of Jesus' supreme genius. We have a curious tendency, even in dealing with Jesus' humanity, to overlook his sheer intellectual stature.[67]

Here again structural and cultural elements may shed some new light on the nature of Jesus' creative genius.

This unit will be seen as a second double parable using the parabolic ballad type. The ballad form will be presented first; and then the different cultural aspects of the parable will be examined in the order in which they appear in the parable itself. Lastly, the parable will be seen to contain the themes of sin, repentance, grace, joy, and sonship.

Before proceeding to an examination of the ballad form of the parable, a word must be said about the imagery used. The parable is not an allegory. The

---

[65]The attitudes toward women in Ben Sirach and those described in Jeremias' "Appendix" noted above are roughly identical to what I have experienced among peasants today. In conservative areas, the speaker must apologize for using the word "woman" if the turn of conversation requires it.
[66]Arndt, *St. Luke,* 350.
[67]C. W. F. Smith, *Parables,* 19.

father is not God *incognito,* but an earthly father, as is conclusively demonstrated in verse 18. Yet he is a symbol of God. Jeremias writes, "The father is not God, but an earthly father; yet some of the expressions used are meant to reveal that in his love he is an image of God."[68] Jones says, "The parable about the prodigal son is not primarily about a spendthrift boy, but about the relations between God and the sinner and the self-righteous."[69] Giblin makes the useful distinction between strict identification and characterization.[70] His point is that to identify the older son as the Pharisee is to unduly narrow the intent of the parable. Jesus is describing a type of person; if we, or any part of his listening audience, fit the characterization, well and good.[71]

The Literary Structure of Luke 15:11–32

The previous verses (4–11) proved to be a double parable. Each half had a similar yet distinct structure. The same is true for verses 11–32. Here also we have a double parable and each half has its own structure. Again the two halves are similar yet different. As in all the parables, culture and literary structure must both be given due consideration for an adequate interpretation. The structure of the first half is as follows:

A   There was a man who had two sons

1   and the younger of them said to his father, "Father,   A SON IS LOST
give me the share of property that falls to me."
And he divided *his living* between them.

2   Not many days later the younger son sold all he had,   GOODS WASTED IN
journeyed into a far country   EXPENSIVE LIVING
and wasted *his property* in extravagant living.

3   And when he had spent everything   EVERYTHING LOST
a great famine arose in that country
and he began to be *in want.*

4   So he went and joined himself   THE GREAT SIN
to one of the citizens of that country   (FEEDING PIGS
and he sent him to his fields *to feed* pigs.   FOR GENTILES)

5   And he would gladly have eaten the pods   TOTAL
which the pigs ate   REJECTION
and no one gave him *anything.*

6   But when he came to himself he said,   A CHANGE
"How many of my father's servants have bread to spare OF MIND
but I perish here with *hunger.*

---

[68]Jeremias, *Parables,* 128.

[69]Jones, *Art,* 210.

[70]Giblin, "Luke 15," 18.

[71]Derrett understands the parable as another illustration of *kal va homer.* If an earthly father can act this way, then how much more God! (Derrett, "Prodigal Son," 72).

6'   "I will arise and go to my father and say to him,'Father, AN INITIAL
I have sinned against heaven and before you   REPENTANCE
and am no more worthy to be called your son; **make me a servant.**' "

5'   And he arose and came to his father.   TOTAL
And while he was at a great distance his father saw him ACCEPTANCE
and **had compassion** and ran and embraced him and kissed him.

4'   And the son said to the father, "Father,   THE GREAT
I have sinned against heaven and before you   REPENTANCE
and am **no more worthy** to be called your son."

3'   And the father said to the servants,   EVERYTHING GAINED
"Bring the best **robe** and put it on him   RESTORED TO SONSHIP
and put a **ring** on his hands and **shoes** on his feet.

2'   And bring the fatted calf and kill it   GOODS USED IN
and let us eat   JOYFUL CELEBRATION
and **make merry,**

1'   for this my son was dead and is alive,   A SON IS FOUND
he was lost and is found."
And they **began to make merry.**

When filled out with a bit more detail the parallels of the inversion are as follows:

1   A son is lost—"Give me my share"
2   Goods wasted in extravagant living
3   Everything lost—"he spent everything—he began to want"
4   The great sin—"feeding pigs for gentiles"
5   Total rejection—"no one gave him anything"
6   A change of mind—"he came to himself—I perish here"
6'   An initial repentance—"make me a servant (I will pay it back)"
5'   Total acceptance—"his father ran and kissed him"
4'   The great repentance—"I am no more worthy to be called your son"
3'   Everything gained—a robe, ring, and shoes (restoration to sonship)
2'   Goods used in joyful celebration
1'   A son is found—"My son was dead and is alive, was lost and is found."

The structure is a type D (parabolic ballad), which in this case has twelve stanzas that match each other using inverted parallelism. The second six reverse the first six, as we have observed. The first speech to the father is at the beginning. The second reversing the first comes in the middle. The end of the structure reverses the beginning. The center is again the point of turning as is expected in the use of the inversion principle. At the same time a series of lesser correspondences appear once the basic structure is seen. The last line of each of the first six stanzas (note the italics) has to do with his physical desires, losses, and needs. The second six stanzas in their final lines (note boldface type) deal progressively with the restoration to sonship and its ensuing joy. Remarkably this matchless ballad also has a type of counterpoint that we have observed in a significant number of literary structures in the New Testament. The same twelve stanzas with their inversion seen above also relate to one another thematically using step parallelism. This can be seen as follows:

> *The first six stanzas*
>   speech I
>   he leaves
>   in need but unrepentant
>   becomes a pig herder
>   eats nothing
>   is dying

> *The second six stanzas*
>   speech II
>   he returns
>   in need and truly repentant
>   becomes an honored son
>   feeds on fatted calf
>   is alive

In addition to the overall parallelisms there are a number of lesser correspondences worthy of note. Both 5' and 6' end with joy. The second line of stanzas 2, 3, and 4 mentions the *country*. A comparison of the second and third lines of 5 and 6 brings out that the pigs eat, his father's servants eat, but he is given nothing and is starving. In terms of the flow of the story the third line of 5 is redundant and out of place, but it functions significantly when the structure is once seen. With these semantic correspondences in mind the cultural elements must now be examined, some of which in turn will illuminate other parallelisms.

The Opening Stanza (15:11–12)

The opening stanza sets the stage for all that will follow. The prodigal is shown as wishing for his father's death in his request for his portion. The father demonstrates almost unbelievable love by granting the request. The older son's silence indicates a rejection of his responsibility to reconcile his brother to his father.

After affirming the presence of a father with two sons, the parable begins with the request of the younger, "Father, give me the share of property that falls to me."[72] For over fifteen years I have been asking people of all walks of life from Morocco to India and from Turkey to the Sudan about the implications of a son's request for his inheritance while the father is still living. The answer has almost always been emphatically the same. As I have noted elsewhere, the conversation runs as follows:

---

[72]Derrett ("Prodigal Son," 68) makes the observation that in Jewish history "Younger brothers are traditionally rebels. The older is worldly, niggardly, orthodox and hypocritical." All the patriarchs after Abraham were younger brothers, as were Abel, Jacob, Joseph, Gideon, David, and Judas Maccabaeus. Thus the younger brother–older brother characterization in this parable is in line with traditional types (cf. *ibid.*).

"Has anyone ever made such a request in your village?"

"Never!"

"Could anyone ever make such a request?"

"Impossible!"

"If anyone ever did, what would happen?"

"His father would beat him, of course!"

"Why?"

"This request means—he wants his father to die!"[73]

Levison writes, "There is no law or custom among the Jews or Arabs which entitles the son to a share of the father's wealth while the father is still alive."[74] Can it be confirmed from ancient literature that this son's request is an extraordinary insult to the father? In the following section we will try to demonstrate that this can be confirmed and that this cultural aspect of the parable sets the stage in a crucial way for all that follows.

In the Old Testament there are two customs worthy of note. The first is the oral will. Isaiah said to Hezekiah, "Command with respect to thy house, for thou shalt die" (2 Kings 20:1).[75] The context is clearly that of approaching death. The oral will was common all through the Old and New Testament period. It was always enacted under the shadow of imminent death and is thus irrelevant to the parable of the Prodigal Son, because in Luke 15:12 the father is assumed to be in good health.[76] The Old Testament also mentions giving a specific gift to someone in order to eliminate him from any rights in the inheritance. This seems to be the case in Genesis 25:6, where Abraham's sons by Keturah are given "gifts" and sent away "from his son Isaac." In the next verse Abraham dies. This disposition then is also some kind of final settlement at the end of his life. Daube notes,

> The whole arrangement in this case was due to the initiative, not of the sons to be emancipated—they were not as adventurous as the prodigal of the parable—but of Abraham, who wished to secure Isaac from possible rivals.[77]

---

[73]In the literally hundreds of times I have asked the question, "Do you know of anyone who has made such a request?" only twice did I receive a positive answer. In the first case Pastor Viken Galoustian of Iran, with a convert church of Oriental Jews, reported to me that one of his leading parishioners, in great anguish, reported to him, "My son wants me to die!" The concerned pastor discovered that the son had broached the question of the inheritance. Three months later the father, a Hebrew Christian (a physician), in previously good health, died. The mother said, "He died that night!" meaning that the night the son dared to ask for his inheritance the father "died." The shock to him was so great that life was over that night. In the second case a Syrian farmer's *older* son asked for his inheritance. In great anger his father drove him from the house. Cf. K. E. Bailey, *The Cross and the Prodigal* (St. Louis: Concordia, 1973), 31.

[74]Levison, *Local Setting,* 156.

[75]Cf. Deut. 21:16; Gen. 49:28–31; 2 Sam. 17:22; 1 Kings 2:1–9.

[76]Horowitz has a full discussion of wills, *Jewish Law,* 402–421.

[77]Daube, "Inheritance," 331.

Daube observes that Keturah's sons do not initiate the process, but he misses the cultural implications. Isaac and Keturah's sons wait respectfully for Abraham to make his own decision. There is no breath of a suggestion that Abraham is under any pressure. In all the Old Testament the prodigal's action is unknown.

Turning to the intertestamental period, there is the significant section in Ben Sirach where the sage argues in forceful terms against giving one's property to son, wife, brother, or friend during one's lifetime.[78] The day "life draws to a close" is the right time for such distribution.

Manson argues that people must have been guilty of passing on their property while in good health, otherwise Ben Sirach would not caution against it.[79] That such is not necessarily the case can be shown by an illustration. One can read in literature coming out of the American South in the late nineteenth century the strong admonition to distrust the "Yankees." Using Manson's line of argumentation we would have to affirm, "The Southerners during that period must have been prone to trust Yankees and thus there is this admonition against doing so." It is more likely, however, that Southerners of that period both did *not* trust Yankees and specifically warned each other not to do so. In like manner Ben Sirach's statement most likely reflects the accepted notion that passing on one's inheritance while in good health was unthinkable.[80]

In the Mishna the key passage, to which we shall return again and again, is *Baba Bathra* viii.7, which reads,

> If one assign in writing his property to his children, he must write, "from today and after [my] death." . . . If one assign in writing his estate to his son [to become his] after his death, the father cannot sell it since it is conveyed to his son, and the son cannot sell it because it is under the father's control. . . . The father may pluck up [produce] and feed it to whomsoever he pleases, but whatever he left plucked up belongs to his heirs.[81]

To the phrase "after [my] death" the editor appends this note: "This refers to a healthy person who desires to retain the right to benefit from his possessions (usufruct) during his lifetime." Jeremias and others have accepted this passage as being the best explanation of the legal situation behind the parable.[82] The Babylonian Talmud has a note giving an illustration of the kind of situation in which a man in good health might sign his estate over to his sons. The note explains the Mishna quoted above and reads,

---

[78]Sir. 33:20–24.

[79]Manson, *Sayings,* 287.

[80]Even if we grant that such a disposition may on occasion have taken place, there is the further crucial question as to who initiates the process. Ben Sirach assumes the father's initiative and says he should not do it. In the parable the son pressures his father, a possibility not even mentioned by Ben Sirach.

[81]*Order Nezikin,* Vol. IV in *Mishnayoth,* trans. and ed. Philip Blackman (London: Mishna Press, 1954), 212.

[82]Jeremias, *Parables,* 128.

I.e., a person in good health who desired, for example, to marry a second time, and wished to protect the sons that were born from his first marriage from the possible seizure of his estate by his second wife, in payment of her *kethubah*. [83]

Thus for special circumstances the Mishna provides for the willing over of one's inheritance before death, but there is no hint of any father having done so under pressure from a younger son.

Baba Mezia of the same Talmud reads, "Our Rabbis taught: Three cry and are not answered. Viz., he who has money and lends it without witnesses; he who acquires a master . . . ." The text then explains that among those who "cry out and are not answered" is "He who transfers his property to his children in his lifetime. . . ."[84] This quotation demonstrates that Ben Sirach's attitude was maintained unchanged at least until the writing of the Talmud. Derrett confirms that the major reason for a father's dividing his estate and signing it over to his sons during his lifetime was for the purpose of "determining what they would have after him and obviating disputes."[85] Derrett never suggests that a father did this under pressure from his sons.

Thus it can be documented that often the father before his death did "divide his living between them." But the startling fact is that, to my knowledge, in all of Middle Eastern literature (aside from this parable) from ancient times to the present, there is no case of any son, older or younger, asking for his inheritance from a father who is still in good health.

The prodigal's actions are all the more remarkable because his request is twofold. He requests the division of the inheritance. His request is granted. But this gives him ownership without the right to dispose of his share. The property is his but he cannot sell it. He wants more, so he pressures his father into granting him full disposition immediately. The Mishna quoted above provides for the legal settlement, but not for disposition by the sons during the father's lifetime. After signing over his possessions to his sons the father still has the right to live off the proceeds (the usufruct) as long as he is alive. Here the younger son gets, and thus is assumed to have demanded, disposition to which, even more explicitly, he had no right until the death of his father. The implication of "Father, I cannot wait for you to die" underlies both requests. It is even stronger in the second.

The misunderstanding of this crucial drama at the opening of the parable is of long standing. Jülicher thinks the boy is not at all impertinent, and that the title

---

[83]*The Babylonian Talmud, Seder Nezikin, Baba Bathra* II, trans. and ed. I. Epstein (London: Soncino, 1935), 573, n. 1.

[84]b. *Baba Mezia*, 75b.

[85]Derrett, "Prodigal Son," 59. This remains true in the East. It is standard procedure for the village father in Syria to settle his inheritance when he is old or anxious to "retire." He always reserves for himself what is called "ḥaqq al-manfaʿah," literally "the right of the profits" (usufruct). The purpose is exactly what Derrett reports, to prevent a quarrel after his death. Rihbany writes, "As a rule neither the law nor custom gives legal standing to a will. . . . As a general rule the father who does not divide his property legally between his sons before his death leaves to them a situation fraught with danger" (*Syrian*, 155f.).

"Father" in his initial request is as affectionate as the τέκνον in the mouth of the father at the end.[86] Linnemann quotes some of the biblical and rabbinic material that we have examined above, but fails to note that none of it shows a son requesting his inheritance from a healthy father.[87] She notes that there was a steady flow of Jews into the diaspora and assumes that this would be a normal event. This is not true. We have a similar situation in Lebanon today with nearly two million Lebanese living and working all over the world in their own "diaspora." But the young man with a living healthy father who goes off to make his fame and fortune does not request, receive, and sell his portion of the family estate before he goes! The most he can expect is his ticket and a little pocket money.[88]

Linnemann makes the amazing statement, "A farm was by the law of the time a family possession, and together with all that belonged to it passed to the eldest son."[89] She has taken this from J. Schmid,[90] who drew this remarkable conclusion from Leviticus 25:23, which reads, "The land shall not be sold in perpetuity." This passage refers to the time of the Jubilee and has nothing to do with inheritance. The request in Luke 12:13, "Teacher, bid my brother divide the inheritance with me," quickly demonstrates that estates were divided among sons.[91]

Not all scholars have failed to notice that the younger brother's request amounts to wishing his father's death. Bornkamm says of the prodigal that he "demands his own portion of his goods, and treats the father as if he were already dead."[92] Miller has written that it was the normal custom "for the heirs to receive their share at the death of the father (Hebrews 9:16–17)."[93] Via catches this implication in the second request; he writes, "Thus the prodigal's demand for the right of disposal was to treat his father as if he were dead."[94] Ancient literature and modern customs converge, and the request is seen as a profound break of relationship between the father and his son. The boy is indeed lost.

In light of the implications of the request, it is all the more remarkable that the father concurs. In the Middle Eastern milieu the father is expected to explode and discipline the boy for the cruel implications of his demand. It is difficult to imagine a more dramatic illustration of the quality of love, which grants freedom even to reject the lover, than that given in this opening scene. Derrett senses the

---

[86]Jülicher, *Gleichnisreden*, II, 338.

[87]Linnemann, *Parables*, 74f.

[88]This is not uniquely Middle Eastern. Many a young American farm boy in story and in fact leaves the farm to make his "fame and fortune." How many of them request, receive, and sell their portion of the family farm before they go?

[89]Linnemann, *Parables*, 74f.

[90]J. Schmid, *Das Evangelium Nach Lukas* (Gütersloh: Bertelsmann, 1934), 252.

[91]Cf. also Horowitz, *Jewish Law*, 378.

[92]Bornkamm, *Jesus*, 126.

[93]Miller, *Luke*, 120. Derrett, "Prodigal Son," 60f., makes a great deal of the fact that the son was expected to stay home and obey, and that his adventurous spirit is not admired. But he fails to appreciate the real nature of the assumption inherent in the request.

[94]Via, *Parables*, 169.

radical nature of the father's action, and argues in the light of Ben Sirach (Sir. 33:20–44) that no father would have granted such a request without making a tacit but certain reservation in his own favor. The father, says Derrett, "will by no means have prejudiced his own position."[95] He explains that the father must have made the "dismission" with the reservation that the son was still responsible for the father financially, if and when the father in his old age might need support. Derrett appreciates the radical nature of the situation. If the father does grant this request, he is jeopardizing his own "living." This, Derrett feels, no father would have done. We can grant to Derrett that no father known to the listener/reader would have concurred with the request without the kind of reservation Derrett suggests. However, the father in this story does grant possession *and* disposition. The son has ownership and the right to sell. If the father had made a reservation on the inheritance, he would not have granted the right of disposition. When the boy is allowed to sell his inheritance and emigrate, all reservations are rendered meaningless.

We get the same insight more directly from Saʿīd, who writes,

> The shepherd in his search for the sheep, and the woman in her search for the coin, do not do anything out of the ordinary beyond what anyone in their place would do. But the actions the father takes in the third story are unique, marvelous, divine actions *which have not been done by any father in the past.*[96]

Saʿīd himself was an Oriental patriarch of the old school, and sensed rightly that the actions of the father in this story are unique. The father is still an earthly father and is believable. At the same time, he demonstrates qualities of love beyond what is experienced and expected from any earthly father.[97]

Daube, Derrett, and Yaron are convinced that the inheritance is not distributed at this point, but rather that the father makes a "dismission" (*Abschichtung*) of a portion of his property which he gives to the younger son, who then loses all further claims to the inheritance.[98] The difficulty with this alternative is that it does not deal adequately with the phrase "and he divided to *them* his living," nor with the words of the father at the end of the story, "*All* that I have is yours." With Jeremias and Manson, the provision of "gift," whereby the property is assigned to the sons during the life of the father, seems to fit the context of the story more adequately.[99]

---

[95]Derrett, "Prodigal Son," 62.

[96]Saʿīd, *Lūqā,* 395f. (emphasis mine).

[97]W. H. Simcox writes, "The affectionate father in the parable trusts his sons more than the son of Sirach thought safe or wise" ("The Prodigal and His Brother," *The Expositor,* Series 3, 10 [1889, 126). The parable also shows the father's impartial love toward both sons. Both sons are assigned their portion. Luke 15:11 reads, "He divided to *them* his living." Giblin comments that v. 12 "reflects the father's impartial love for both sons as his sons" ("Luke 15," 29, n. 40).

[98]D. Daube, "Inheritance," 330; Derrett, "Prodigal Son," 60; Reuven Yaron, *Gifts in Contemplation of Death* (Oxford: Clarendon, 1960), 44.

[99]Jeremias, *Parables,* 128; Manson, *Sayings,* 287.

There is one final note in rabbinic legislation that is at times overlooked. In the case of a man in good health assigning his property to his sons as a "gift" with the reservation that they have the right of disposition only after his death, the "gift" was not valid unless it was a purely voluntary act free from all duress.[100] The father in this parable is specifically under duress. All he need do is admit this and the son gets nothing. Legally he must act as if he has decided on his own to give away his property and ignore that this is not the case. The remarkable nature of the love of this particular father becomes clearer and clearer the deeper one goes into the circumstances that may well have colored a first-century understanding of the story.

Daube makes another suggestion, which is picked up and turned into the major theme of a monograph by K. H. Rengstorf.[101] This suggestion has to do with the first-century Palestinian ceremony of the *qeṣaṣah*. The word literally means "a cutting off." The ceremony is described in *Ruth Rabba* vii.11 on 4:7, which reads,

> What is *keẓaẓah*? R. Jose b. Abin answered: If a man sold his field to a Gentile, his relatives used to bring barrels full of parched corn and nuts and break them open in the presence of children, and the children would gather them and proclaim, "So-and-so is cut off from his inheritance." If it was returned to him, they used to say, "So-and-so has returned to his inheritance." And likewise if a man married a woman who was not fitting for him, his relatives used to bring barrels full of parched corn and nuts and break them open in the presence of children, and the children would gather them and proclaim, "So-and-so is lost to his family." When he divorced her, they used to say, "So-and-so has returned to his family."[102]

Other rabbinic references to the same custom indicate that it was a jar or a pot that was broken.[103] Rengstorf asserts that the custom fell into disuse by the end of the first century, but that it was in force at the time of Jesus.[104] Rengstorf argues that this formal act of "cutting off" and then of restoration, which he calls "reinvestiture," is the specific background of the parable. His long argument is, however, unconvincing. The two acts that triggered the *qeṣaṣah* ceremony are given as selling land to a gentile and marrying an impure woman. Rengstorf himself states that the cause for this ceremony in the case of the prodigal son was that he took his property and wasted it in a foreign country.[105] However, the sale to gentiles, or more generally the loss of the property to gentiles, did not take place at the time of the son's leaving. When he left he had not violated either of the conditions that would have brought on the *qeṣaṣah*.[106] If the family had heard from

[100]Horowitz, *Jewish Law*, 374.

[101]Rengstorf, *Re-Investitur*.

[102]*Ruth*, trans. L. Rabinowitz, in *Midrash Rabbah*, ed. H. Freedman and M. Simon (London: Soncino, 1939), 87.

[103]Cf. p. *Kid*. i.5; p. *Ket*. 26d; p. *Kid*. 60c; p. *Ket*. ii.10.

[104]Rengstorf, *Re-Investitur*, 23.

[105]*Ibid.*, 71.

[106]That is, unless we assume he sold his share to gentiles when he left, which Rengstorf does not claim and the story does not suggest.

the prodigal while he was gone that he had lost everything to the gentiles and then carried out the *qeṣaṣah,* we would have to presuppose a great many details not given in the parable.[107] When the prodigal leaves he has had no dealings with the gentiles. Rengstorf's entire argument fails at this crucial point.

At the same time, the *qeṣaṣah* ceremony provides insight into the first-century Palestinian community important for an understanding of the culture of the parable. The fact of the *qeṣaṣah* ceremony is extremely significant as evidence of the solidarity of the extended family and the community. Family property lost to gentiles was a serious matter. An erring son who violated the community solidarity was dealt with in radical fashion. When the prodigal comes home, he has, in fact, lost his share of the family's property among gentiles. The village community will soon discover this. At that time, they may well break the jar in the street and cut him off. What he has done is a serious matter, not just toward his father but as regards the village and the entire extended family.[108] The son is breaking relationships not only with his father and brother but in a very radical way with the community at large.

The older son is mentioned twice in this opening scene. We are told in verse 11 that the father has two sons. In verse 12 we hear that the older son also receives his share of the inheritance. We expect him to respond in two ways. First he should loudly refuse to accept his share in protest against the implications of his brother's request. His silence strongly suggests that his relationship with his father is not what it should be. Then second, at this point the Oriental listener/reader also expects the older son to enter the story verbally and take up the traditional role of reconciler. Breaks in relationships are always healed through a third party among Middle Easterners.[109] The third party is selected on the basis of the closeness of the relationship to each side. In this case, the role of reconciler is thrust upon the older son by all the pressures of custom and community. His silence means refusal. The Talmud notes specifically that it was the sons who carried out the *qeṣaṣah* ceremony.[110] They were responsible for reconciliation as well as for the sign of its failure. If the older son hates his brother, he will still go through the motions of trying to reconcile for the sake of his father. This older son remains silent. Again his silence tells us of problems in his relationship to his father. Finally, as we have observed, the father "divided to *them* his living." Thus the older son also benefits from the transaction. He knows that the request is improper and is expected to refuse with loud assertions of unending loyalty to the father. Rather he accepts in silence. With the background in Old Testament literature which characterized

---

[107]Rengstorf's discussion of the shoes, the robe, and the ring, while presenting some good material and making a number of thoughtful observations, fails to assess adequately the culture of the Middle East. His arguments will be examined later.

[108]Daube notes, "Evidently, the younger son cut his personal ties with this kin as well as his proprietary ones" ("Inheritance," 329).

[109]U.S. Secretary of State Henry Kissinger in the winter of 1973/74 managed to achieve delicate disengagement settlements in the Middle East because he was willing to function in this classic Middle Eastern role.

[110]b. *Ket*. 28b.

older sons as "niggardly, orthodox and hypocritical"[111] it is easy to finish out the picture this parable sketches of this older son, a picture already visible in the opening verses.

In connection with this parable, Daube discusses the Old Testament technical term *yashabh yahadh* (to dwell together), which referred to the dwelling together of brothers on an estate after the death of the father. This state of affairs was considered the norm; as an institution it was idealized in Psalm 133:1.[112] (Thus Luke 12:13 is considered a deplorable request and indeed is so treated in the Lucan account.) Here the younger son, by selling his portion and leaving, refuses to attempt any future "dwelling together" with his brother. Yet, surely, both sons must be blamed for this failure. The ill will evidenced from the older brother's side at the end of the story is not "a root out of dry ground."

In the next stanza, after "not many days," the younger son turns his portion into cash.[113] The reason for the need for haste (not many days) is easy to reconstruct. It is not just his concern to "get on with it." Rather, as he goes from one prospective buyer to another, the intensity of the community hatred and disgust mounts. At every turn he is greeted with amazement, horror, and rejection. The Middle Eastern peasant's attachment to his land is as old as Naboth's relationship to his vineyard. The family estate is a significant part of the Middle Easterner's personal identity.[114] Although, as indicated above, the prodigal did nothing in the opening scene to call upon himself the *qeṣaṣah*, yet he certainly earned the intense displeasure of the entire community. Thus, even though in the Middle East the sale of property ordinarily drags on for months, the prodigal finished in a hurry and left.

To summarize this opening scene, the prodigal requests and receives possession and disposition of his portion of the inheritance. Both requests are unheard of in Eastern life and thought. Each means the son is in a hurry for his father to die. The father is expected to refuse and punish the prodigal. Instead, in an unprecedented act of love, the request is granted. The older son is expected to refuse his share and to fulfil the roll of reconciler. He fails on both counts. These failures indicate that his relationships to both his brother and his father are broken. Both sons fail even to try to live together in unity. The *qeṣaṣah* ceremony illustrates group attitudes toward members of the community who sell to gentiles.

Stanzas 2–6—In the Far Country (15:13b–17)

In this section the cultural aspects will be treated as they appear in the text. Here the prodigal gradually descends into his own hell. The six-stanza structure of the first half of the prodigal's story makes this clear.

---

[111]Derrett, "Prodigal Son," 68.
[112]Daube, "Inheritance," 327.
[113]Cf. Bauer-A., G., *Lexicon*, 789, *s.v.* συνάγω.
[114]The strongest evidence for this is that a million Palestinian refugees in the contemporary Middle Eastern scene do not want and will not accept resettlement elsewhere. The home village with its family inheritance is an integral part of their identity. The land does not belong to them; they belong to the land.

In the far country, the prodigal's money is soon gone. Foerster explains the phrase ζῶν ἀσώτως as follows:

> the dissipated life of the Prodigal without specifying the nature of this life . . . is simply depicted as carefree and spendthrift in contrast to the approaching dearth.[115]

This phrase does not tell us whether the money was wasted in moral or in immoral ways. By contrast, the Oriental versions are unambiguous. The Old Syriac decides the issue one way by an additional line which makes the text read, "He scattered his property in foods that are not fitting, because he was living wastefully with harlots." Starting with the Peshitta, this addition is removed and the text translated unambiguously in the other direction. A wide variety of words are used in the Arabic versions, but all of them (with one nineteenth-century exception) have terms meaning "expensive," "indolent," "luxurious," and "wasteful." These words all bring the Peshitta and the Arabic versions clearly in line with Foerster's definition. They do not label the prodigal as "immoral" but only as "wasteful." That the Greek text and the vast majority of the Oriental versions do not condemn the prodigal for immorality is significant, and provides a background for understanding properly the older son's remarks in verse 30, as we shall see.

Jeremias has traced a series of ten famines in and around Jerusalem, from 169 B.C. to A.D. 70 (excluding those resulting from war.)[116] Famine would have been a very powerful image for any first-century Palestinian audience. Furthermore, a lone Jew in a far country without money or friends would have been especially vulnerable in a great famine. The text seems to note this by adding an emphatic pronoun. Verse 14 reads, "*He* began to be in want."[117] He more than others was in need.[118]

The text then tells us graphically that he "glues" himself to a citizen of that country.[119] This lad is known in the community as having arrived with money and thus is expected to have some self-respect left. The polite way a Middle Easterner gets rid of unwanted "hangers-on" is to assign them a task he knows they will refuse. Anyone with food in a severe famine has a throng of petitioners at his door daily.[120] However, the pride of the prodigal is not yet completely broken and, to

---

[115]W. Foerster, *TDNT*, I, 507.

[116]Jeremias, *Jerusalem*, 140–44.

[117]The passage is full of Semitisms. Cf. Jack Sanders, "Tradition and Redaction in Luke XV, 11–32," *NTS* 15 (1969), 435. From the point of view of Semitic as well as Greek syntax, αὐτός is emphatic.

[118]The emphatic nature of the αὐτός in v. 14 is clear from v. 24, which has καὶ ἤρξαντο εὐφραίνεσθαι with no pronoun. In the Oriental versions the Syriac, the Peshitta, and the Harclean preserve the extra pronoun. Ibn al-'Assāl has "and *he also* began to be in want," thus making use of the emphatic nature of the pronoun but interpreting it to mean that the son as well as everybody else was in want. It can also mean he in particular, as an outsider, was in want. Cf. also Goebel, *Parables*, 202.

[119]Only someone who has lived in the East can fully appreciate this vocabulary. In the Middle East, the desperation of the indigent leads him to attach himself like glue to any potential benefactor. The Greek word is κολλάω.

[120]Arndt notes that "he forces himself on a citizen of the country. His services had not been requested" (*St. Luke*, 351).

the amazement of the listener/reader, the citizen's attempt to get rid of the younger son fails. He accepts the job of pig herder.

The "citizen" is most likely an "independent inhabitant with his own property."[121] The original Greek meaning of πολίτης as a political word, indicating a person of authority in the community, must be rejected.[122]

Linnemann feels that the "joining to a citizen" is a clear reference to the tax collectors and their going into the service of foreigners.[123] Jeremias reasons that the prodigal could not have observed the Sabbath, would be in association with unclean animals,[124] and thus was "practically forced to renounce the regular practice of his religion."[125]

The son is reported as "longing to fill his belly with the carob pods which the pigs ate." This sentence poses a number of problems. What were the pods? Did the prodigal eat them? If he did, why was he not filled? If he did not, why not? The carob pods are almost universally identified with the *ceratonia siliqua*.[126] The Harclean and the Old Syriac Sinaitic transliterate the Greek word, but the rest of the Oriental versions without exception use the word *kharnūb*. This same word in Aramaic rabbinic literature is an edible pod eaten by the poor. As a food it symbolized repentance. Rabbi Aha said, "Israel needs carob, (i.e. poverty) to be forced to repentance (i.e. only when Israel are reduced to such a state of poverty that they must eat carob do they repent of their evil ways)."[127] The difficulty is that *kharnūb* is eaten by and enjoyed by people of all ages all over the countryside of Palestine, Syria, and Lebanon. Rihbany writes regarding the carob pods,

> They are sold in almost every town in western Syria for food. Children are very fond of *kherrûb*. Some of the pods contain no small amount of sugar. In my boyhood days, a pocketful of *kherrûb*, which I procured for a penny, was to me rather a treat.[128]

Thus the *ceratonia siliqua* is edible and nourishing. There is a reference in rabbinic literature to a Rabbi Hanina ben Dosa who kept himself alive with carob pods.[129]

---

[121]H. Strathmann, *TDNT*, VI, 534.

[122]*Ibid*. The Oriental versions support this. The London-Paris Polyglots have "a man from the noblemen of the city," but the rest of the Arabic and Syriac versions read simply, "one of the sons of the city."

[123]Linnemann, *Parables*, 75f.

[124]M. *Ba. Kam.* viii.7, "no one may raise swine in any place"; "at the approach of the Messiah, pigs, the natural abode of devils, must hide themselves and pig keepers must fear for their safety" (Derrett, "Prodigal Son," 66). b. *Ba. Kam.* 82b tells of a pig sent up the walls of Jerusalem in a basket, which causes the earth to quake over a distance of four hundred pharasangs; and it is said, "Cursed be the man who would breed swine and cursed be the man who would teach his son Grecian wisdom."

[125]Jeremias, *Parables*, 129.

[126]Stuhlmueller, *Luke*, 148; Manson, *Sayings*, 288. It is also called "St. John's bread"; cf. Bauer-A., G., *Lexicon*, 430; *Str.-B.*, II, 241.

[127]Feldman, *Similes*, 124.

[128]Rihbany, *Syrian*, 158f. He admits there is a lot of pulp and little food value. *Kherrūb* is the colloquial word for *kharnūb*.

[129]*Str.-B.*, II, 214.

This renders unacceptable Jeremias' conclusion that the prodigal was too disgusted to eat the carob pods.[130] Linnemann's solution that he was *unable* to eat them implies that someone else was feeding the pigs and standing over the prodigal to see that he did not eat any of the pigs' feed. Her suggestion creates more problems than it solves.[131] Rihbany himself concludes that the text must mean simply that the prodigal was poor. But this solution is inadequate because of the verb ἐπ-εθύμει.

Jeremias has established linguistically that ἐπεθύμει with an infinitive in the Lucan source expresses an unfulfilled wish.[132] So the problem is that the text says the prodigal was unable to fill his stomach with κεράτιον. The word κεράτιον as we have noted is usually identified with *ceratonia siliqua*, which is commonly eaten every summer all across Lebanon and Syria. Everybody fills his stomach with *kharnūb*. Why was the prodigal not able to do so? The problem has not been recognized, because scholars have not realized that the *ceratonia siliqua* is eaten and enjoyed by all.

Clearly the identification of κεράτιον with *ceratonia siliqua* must be challenged. The latter contains enough sugar that molasses is made from it.[133] In a time of severe famine it is hard to imagine anything with significant human food value being fed to the pigs. The answer to this dilemma is found in that the Middle East has two kinds of *kharnūb*. This was observed nearly fifty years ago by Rendel Harris.[134] Harris translated from an Arabic dictionary entitled *al-Tāj* (the crown)[135] as follows:

> Carob: Abu Hanifa says: There is a wild and a Syrian variety of this shrub. The wild variety (called also thorny carob) has thorns and is used as firewood. It grows up to a cubit in height, has branches and bears berries light in weight and inflated, but these berries are harsh and are not eaten, *except in time of exigency*. The Syrian kind is sweet and eaten.[136]

Harris goes on to note an Old Syriac lexicon which also differentiates the two varieties. Lane, in his definitive Arabic dictionary, has this to say about the carob:

> There are two kinds, wild [*barrī*] and Syrian [*shāmī*]: . . . the former kind is thorny, . . . used as fuel, rising to the height of a cubit, with a fruit . . . black . . . and . . . disagreeable in taste, . . . not eaten except in cases of difficulty or distress; . . . the Syrian kind [is that to which the name of *Kharrūb* is now

---

[130]Jeremias, *Parables*, 129.

[131]Linnemann, *Parables*, 151, n. 11.

[132]Jeremias, *Parables*, 129, n. 75.

[133]Thomson, *The Land*, I, 22. Thomson also gives a picture of the tree and of the pod. The tree itself is large. Anyone picking pods for the pigs could certainly eat all he wanted in the process.

[134]Rendel Harris, "The Charobs of the Sea," *The Expositor*, Series 9, 2 (Oct. 1924), 301–304. The article is primarily a discussion of the obscure reference to "carobs of the sea" which appears in the Old Syriac. But at the end of the essay Harris offers a solution that seems most adequate to the problem. His suggestion was ignored most likely because few realized the fact of the problem.

[135]I have not been able to locate this dictionary. Harris gives the reference as Vol. I, 231.

[136]Harris, *loc. cit.*, 304; emphasis his.

commonly applied, the carob, or locust-tree; *ceratonia siliqua*; the fruit of which] is sweet, and is eaten. . . .[137]

This wild carob, not the *ceratonia siliqua*, fits the picture of the parable. The wild carob is more of a shrub, and pigs could grub for its berries. It *can* be eaten by humans, but is bitter and without nourishment. The prodigal could not fill his stomach with them. Regardless of how much he ate, he was not filled. The wild carob does not have enough nourishment to keep a man alive.[138] In summary, the parable depicts a pig herder trying desperately to get enough nourishment to keep alive from black, bitter berries which the pigs root from low shrubs. This shrub is not the *ceratonia siliqua* but is a wild carob that grows in the pasturelands of the Middle East.

"And no one gave him anything," is the concluding comment that fills in the picture. The verb is in the imperfect tense and thus may better be translated, "No one was giving to him." This can possibly mean that he tried his hand at begging and failed even at that.[139] It is probably better understood to mean, "No one was feeding him regularly." Obviously, he received something for feeding pigs; but in a time of famine, with the availability of a cheap labor force of the starving, his subsistence dole would have been very little. He specifically says, "I perish here with hunger." He is clearly not getting enough to stay alive. Presumably the pigs were eaten by the citizen. If and when the owner butchered, the herders (following Middle Eastern practice) would naturally be given the less desirable portions of the pig. It is easy to imagine a Jew of a noble family quite unable to eat such food even if he were starving. All the Syriac versions have a past tense of the verb "to be" followed by a present participle, reading specifically, "No one was giving him." This reinforces the possibility of our suggestion.[140] In any case, he was starving and needed to find some solution. This brings us to a consideration of the nature of his repentance in the far country.

There is rabbinic evidence that the phrase "he came to himself" in some sense means "he repented." In this section we will argue that this contemplated "repentance" in the far country is significantly different from his actual repentance before his father. Strack and Billerbeck argue that the phrase "he came to himself" means "he repented."[141] This simple conclusion needs careful examination.

Strack and Billerbeck identify חזר בו and הדר ביה as lying behind εἰς ἑαυτὸν δὲ ἐλθὼν in Luke 15:17a. In defense of their proposal it can be said that

---

[137]E. W. Lane, *An Arabic-English Lexicon*, Book I, Part 2 (New York: 1955 [1865]), 717a; brackets in 1955 ed. Most of the ellipses replace letter-references to Arabic sources.

[138]At the same time, the rabbi mentioned above *could* just manage to stay alive eating the sweet "Syrian carob."

[139]Jeremias' suggestion that he was stealing is unnecessary. Vat. Borg. Ar. 71 reads, "No one gave him alms," which understands specifically that he was begging, unsuccessfully.

[140]The Arabic versions have the verb "to be" in the past followed by a present tense, indicating also continuous action in the past.

[141]*Str.-B.*, II, 215.

ἔρχομαι at times does carry the idea of "come back, return," and the Semitic ב is closely related to Greek εἰς. Thus the Aramaic *hozer bo* does look linguistically very much like the "to himself he came" of verse 17.[142]

At the same time, a number of important factors weigh heavily against their proposal. First of all, the phrases Strack and Billerbeck have selected as lying behind the Greek do not necessarily represent the Greek of Luke 15:17a; and, furthermore, these phrases are relatively weak if thought of as referring to repentance. Strack and Billerbeck translate both rabbinic phrases "in sich gehen." Both expressions appear in a single passage in the Talmud.[143] The first phrase occurs early in the passage, which reads, אמר הקדוש ברוך הוא אם חוזר בו, which Strack and Billerbeck translate, "Gott sagt; Wenn der Gottlose in sich geht."[144] Goldschmidt translates the same phrase, "der Heilige, gebenedeiet er, sprach nämlich: wenn er umkehrt."[145] Thus there is some disagreement as to whether *hozer bo* should be translated "in sich geht." The same is true of the second phrase.[146] This in turn means that we cannot be quick to identify these Aramaic phrases as lying behind the Greek of Luke 15:17a.

The Aramaic word with its preposition *hozer bo* means "to turn around, return, retract, repent." Jastrow translates the imperative *hazor beka* as "come back (repent)." The perfect verb form, again with the preposition, is used of a woman who "reconsiders" her consent to marriage. She *hozrah beh*.[147] The second phrase, *hadar beyh*, means "to go around, come back, return." Jastrow defines it as a man who "went back on himself, changed his opinion."[148] Thus, as Aramaic phrases, these words have the distinctive meaning of "turning back" and can mean "reconsider" or "change an opinion" as well as, occasionally, "repent."[149] They can mean "repent" but they are relatively weak when used for "repentance."

A second consideration is that Luke 15:17a does not have μετανοέω. If the prodigal's prepared confession is a full repentance, why is this theological word not used?

Third, the rabbinical term for repentance is *tob*, the Aramaic equivalent of the Hebrew *shub*. Behm writes,

---

[142]Bauer-A., G., *Lexicon*, 310. The majority of the Arabic versions use *raja'a,* which is specifically "he came back."

[143]b. *Schab.* 104a.

[144]*Str.-B.,* II, 215.

[145]Lazarus Goldschmidt, *Der Babylonische Talmud* (Haag: Martinus Nijhoff, 1933), I, 592.

[146]The second phrase, הדר ביה, which also appears in b. *Schab.* 104a, is also translated "in sich geht" by Strack and Billerbeck and "er umkehrt" by Goldschmidt, *loc. cit.*

[147]M. Jastrow, *A Dictionary of the Targumim, the Talmud Babli and Jerushalmi, and the Midrashic Literature* (New York: Pardes, 1950), I, 446.

[148]*Ibid.,* I, 334.

[149]Significantly, *Ta'an.* 23b has "she prayed that they might repent," where the Aramaic is דליהדרו בתובתא, lit. "that they might return with repentance." Thus "repentance" is added to "return" indicating that *hadar* alone is not enough to mean "repent."

What the religious language of the OT expressed by שוב and the theological terminology of the Rabbis by עשה תשובה, תשובה or עבד תתובתא, תתובא the NT, like the Jewish Hellenistic writings, expresses by μετανοέω and μετάνοια.[150]

Thus the phrases suggested by Strack and Billerbeck are *not* used by the rabbis in their major discussions of repentance. In the key passages on repentance in the Mishna, the Talmud, the Midrashim, and the Shemone Esre, the words used are those listed above.[151]

Fourth, Syriac has the same theological term for repentance as the Aramaic (*tob*). This word is not used in the Syriac translations of Luke 15:17. They read, instead, "he came to his *nefesh*."[152] The word *nefesh* is an important term in Oriental thought. Its introduction in this text shifts the emphasis to a frame of reference distinctively different from that of "repentance." It is clear that the Oriental churches through the centuries have not understood this phrase as simply meaning "he repented."[153]

Fifth, in Luke 18:4 Codex Bezae has the identical words ἦλθεν εἰς ἑαυτὸν, which in that context clearly means something less than repentance. The judge feels no remorse—he merely wants to get rid of the woman who is giving him a headache, so he changes his mind.

In conclusion, we can admit that Strack and Billerbeck may have the right phrase underlying the Greek text. But even if this is the case, it is much weaker as a theological phrase than any expression using *shūb* or *tūb*. Some type of "return" or "repentance" is most probably indicated by verse 17, but only in a qualified sense.

The exact content of this repentance must now be examined in detail. Like the unjust steward in Luke 16, the prodigal does not offer excuses. He repents, but for what? Bornkamm has rightly identified the son's motive in the far country. He says, "For it is not his remorse for the sins he has committed, but to begin with, quite simply the realization that he has come to the end of his tether, which makes the son turn back."[154] Derrett, writing from a Jewish point of view, asks the significant question, "Many wonder how repentance preceded that return. Repen-

---

[150]J. Behm, *TDNT*, IV, 999.

[151]*Ibid.*, *s.v.* "μετανοέω," *passim*; Montefiore, *Rabbinic*, 390–422, "Appendix III on Repentance."

[152]The majority of the Arabic versions also include the word *nefesh* in their translation. The Polyglot reads, "he understood," and Ibn al-'Assāl has the very attractive "when his heart returned to him."

[153]Modern village colloquial speech in the Middle East has a very striking phrase that may be significant. When someone is so flustered as not to know where he is or what is happening around him, like a small child on hearing an unexpected automobile horn, they say, "He doesn't know where his *nefesh* has gone." The implication is that one's *nefesh* is something that can be separated from one and when this happens, confusion results. The Greek ἐξίστημι etymologically implies something of the same background.

[154]Bornkamm, *Jesus*, 126f. Jones also notes the shallow nature of the prodigal's motivation in the far country (*Art*, 182). Bruce writes, "his repentance has its source in hunger, and its motive is to get a bit of bread" (*Parabolic*, 285).

tance of what? Was he sincere? Was the father as foolish to readmit him as he was to give him the share initially?'' Derrett tacitly answers his own question with the further statement, ''This might well be the fundamental weakness of the parable.''[155] Derrett also observes that when the boy says, ''I have sinned against heaven and in your sight,'' he is confessing having failed to hold himself in readiness to take care of his father in his old age. The sin prompting his confession is a loss of money that had a moral responsibility attached to it, which, so far, he has refused to acknowledge.[156] The implication of this understanding of his sin is crucial. He thinks that if he had not lost the money, he would not have sinned. Thus the prodigal is motivated by hunger and he repents for having lost the money.

The further question of his relationships in the home community must be examined. His primary relationships are to his father, his brother, and to the village community.

The first and most important of these three is his relationship to his father. The key to understanding the prodigal's intentions in regard to his father is found in his face-saving plan. He will work as a hired servant (stanza 6'). The exact nature of the hired servant is generally overlooked in the literature. Oesterley identifies the three levels of servants on a first-century Jewish estate as follows:

1. *Bondsmen* (δοῦλοι), who as slaves were a part of the estate and indeed almost a part of the family.

2. *Slaves of a lower class* (παῖδες), who were subordinates of the bondsmen.

3. *Hired servants* (μίσθιοι).

Regarding this last class Oesterley writes,

The "hired servant" was an outsider, he did not belong to the estate, he had no personal interests in the affairs of his temporary master; he was merely a casual laborer to be employed when required. . . . His position was, therefore, precarious, . . . though, *unlike them, he was a free man.* . . .[157]

Oesterley states, however, that the "hired servant" though free was lower than the other two types of servants. This evaluation of his social status is contradicted by Jewish scholarship. Heinemann writes,

Work and the worker were held in high esteem in Tannaitic times. . . . It is a well-known fact, that most Tannaim were themselves artisans; a good many were even day labourers. No difference in social status appears to have existed between the dependent wage-earner and the more independent artisan (their

---

[155]Derrett, "Prodigal Son," 58. Derrett is right. From a Jewish understanding of repentance, as we shall note, the prodigal's motivation in the far country is suspect and needs some clear verification. The motivation is hunger. If he had been financially successful, he would not have considered returning home.

[156]*Ibid.,* 65. Derrett's point is that the prodigal has broken the fifth commandment. Bruce adds, "He will go home and he will make confession of his sin in well-premeditated form, suited at once to propitiate an injured father" (*Parabolic,* 287).

[157]Oesterley, *Jewish Background,* 186; emphasis mine.

legal status, too, was identical; both were called "hired workers"), nor was the worker considered socially inferior to his employer.[158]

Heinemann's work is well documented and can be considered authoritative. What he says is crucial to a proper understanding of what the prodigal is proposing as a solution to the problem of his future relationship to his father's house. As a "hired servant" he will be a free man with his own income living independently in the local village.[159] His social status will not be inferior to that of his father and his brother. He can maintain his pride and his independence. But there is more.

If the prodigal becomes a hired servant, he may be able to pay back what he has lost. In this connection Derrett writes,

> Working as a hired servant (sleeping off the premises) he could see to it that eventually with his wages, if not in other ways, he could give his father what, so long as the father lived, was only his due.[160]

With Derrett we can agree that the prodigal perhaps intended to work and thereby fulfil his moral responsibilities to the father. In losing the money he failed in these responsibilities. Now he will make up for what he has lost. In short, he will save himself. He wants no grace.[161]

There is possibly another aspect to what the prodigal plans to say to his father, which sheds light on the prodigal's understanding of their hoped-for future relationship. This dimension is clearly a part of the translation in the manuscript Vatican Borgianus Arabic 95, copied in 885. In that version, the word "make me" in the phrase "make me one of your hired servants" is translated iṣna'nī.[162] This can be translated, "Fashion out of me." The background of ποιέω clearly carries

---

[158]Joseph H. Heinemann, "The Status of the Labourers in Jewish Law and Society in the Tannaitic Period," *HUCA* 25 (1954), 265f. The period of the Tanna' im is reckoned from R. Hillel, which puts us clearly back into the first century. Cf. Horowitz, *Jewish Law*, xxxvii. Hillel himself, at least while a student, was a day laborer; cf. Jeremias, *Jerusalem*, 112f., 116.

[159]In the modern village the "hired servant" likewise lives in the village, not on the estate. A wealthy man may hire an artisan and bring him from some distant place with his helpers. In such an exceptional case the artisan and his assistants are housed temporarily on the estate. For example, a team of plasterers, famous in a given area, will be housed on the estate until the contractual work is finished.

[160]Derrett, "Prodigal Son," 65; Jülicher also identified the "hired servant" as a day laborer, a *Tagelöhner* (*Gleichnisreden*, II, 347). Cf. also Arndt, *St. Luke*, 351.

[161]The Palestinian Talmud has an interesting reference to the making of amends for misdeeds. It speaks of חזרת גמורה, a "true restoration" which involved חזירת ממון לא חזרת דברים. When mammon is involved then mammon must be returned, not just *debarim*. p. Tal. *Rosh Hash-Shaneh*, i.57c; quoted in Jastrow, *op. cit.*, I, 446f.

[162]Vat. Bor. Ar. 95 is an exceptionally important ms. It is translated from a Greek ms. of high quality and is carefully done. Luke has never been transcribed, to my knowledge. Matthew and Mark were published (cf. B. Levin, *Die griechish-arabische Evangelien-Übersetzung* [Uppsala: n.p., 1938]). The translator is faithful to his Greek original and at times even a bit too literal. Yet he leaves himself enough freedom to make his own exegetical understanding of the text felt. Having spent some time with this ms. I have the impression of a very perceptive exegetical insight appearing time and again in the selection of a key word or a turn of phrase. In Luke 15 he makes at least four culturally or theologically oriented exegetical decisions. This is the first of them.

this freight. Braun traces the word from its Old Testament roots as a term referring all through biblical literature to the creative activity of God. In the New Testament it is used "with reference to His helping and redeeming activity."[163] This may be a part of what the prodigal intends to say to his father. The son is commanding his father, which in itself is significant. The prodigal has a plan he feels is worthy of execution. He intends to order his father to carry it out. He may be implying, "Disregard the past; I'm sorry for what I have done. But I am not useless to you. I am still good raw material. Fashion out of me a workman."[164] Thus, in regard to the father the prodigal fully intends to confess his failure. That failure seems to be understood in terms of money lost. He has a plan that will give him independence from his father and provide an opportunity to compensate for his errors. With pride intact he intends to order his father to make him a hired servant. Stanza 6' balances 6 precisely. This brings us to a consideration of the prodigal's relationship to his brother.

If the prodigal works as a hired servant, he will not be eating his brother's bread. He knows full well that everything left in the estate is legally signed over to his brother. From the profits of the farm, the father has the right to feed whom he likes. But, if the Mishna can be applied, whatever is not consumed by the father and his friends is then added to the capital which the older brother will in time inherit.[165] Thus the older brother will most likely resent the prodigal's presence. Living at home would entail reconciliation to his brother, and apparently this is rejected. In any case, he works out an alternative that makes this kind of reconciliation unnecessary.

The prodigal's final problem is his relationship to the village. Any status in the village will initially be very difficult to achieve. He has failed in the far-off country. It is always difficult for any emigrant to return to his home village unless he has succeeded.[166] In the case of the prodigal, his return to the home village is greatly complicated by the manner of his leaving. He left having offended the entire community by taking and selling his inheritance while his father was still living. Now he has lost the money to the gentiles. Thus he can fully expect the extended family to cut him off with an enactment of the qeṣaṣah. His entry into the village will be humiliating and ruthless as the pent-up hostilities of the village are vented on him for having insulted his father, sold the land, and now lost it. For this problem he apparently has no solution. The village will simply have to be faced.

The prodigal's three primary relationships, as he sees them from the far country, can now be summarized. He plans to live in the village as a hired servant.

---

[163]H. Braun, *TDNT*, VI, 464.

[164]The verb is an aorist imperative implying the beginning of a new action. Cf. A. T. Robertson, *A Grammar of the Greek New Testament in the Light of Historical Research* (Nashville: Broadman, 1934), 851.

[165]Cf. Mishna *Baba Bathra* viii.7, "The father may pluck up (produce) and feed it to whomsoever he pleases, but whatever is left plucked up belongs to his heirs."

[166]My Lebanese friends tell me that the Lebanese emigrant never goes back to his village for any reason if he has failed economically in the diaspora.

With such a position his status will be secure. He can perhaps fulfil his responsibility to his father, and the problem of any relationship to his brother is eliminated. The village with its mockery will have to be faced. He will have to pay this bitter price in order to get home. He must go home because he is starving.

Having seen what the prodigal's planned confession meant in terms of his primary relationships, we may now examine this same confession in the light of rabbinic teaching on repentance. We shall attempt to show in this section that the planned confession is in harmony with rabbinic attitudes.

The rabbinic doctrine of repentance made use of Lamentations 5:21 and Malachi 3:7.[167] Lamentations reads, "Turn thou us unto thee, O Lord, and we shall be turned"; and the Malachi text gives, "Return unto me, and I will return unto you, saith the Lord." The confusion in the above Lamentations and Malachi texts over who must turn first, Israel or God, was resolved by the rabbis, who wrote, "A Bible verse says, 'Turn thou us and we shall be turned'; therefore God should begin. But another verse says, 'Turn unto me, and I will turn unto you.' So let us turn together simultaneously."[168] The Eighteen Benedictions also mention repentance where they read, "Cause us to return, O our Father, unto thy Law; draw us near, O our King, unto thy service, and bring us back in perfect repentance unto thy presence. Blessed art thou, O Lord, who delightest in repentance" (number five, *Teshubah*). This statement seems to indicate that man needs help from God for true repentance. At the same time, the worshiper who prays this benediction is already penitent and concerned to do what must be done to be sure of God's favor. He is afraid lest he not be able to do the work of repentance; and so God's help is invoked. The idea that repentance is a "work" which man does prior to God's acceptance of him is found all through rabbinic literature. Another midrash reads, "Three things can cancel evil decrees; namely, prayer, almsgiving and repentance."[169] And again,

> If Israel says, "We are poor, we have no offering to make," God replies, "I need only words." If they say, "We know nothing" [for by words the Midrash means the words of the Law], God says, "Then weep and pray before me, and I will accept your prayer."[170]

Thus for the rabbis repentance was primarily a work of man which assured him of God's favor.

Furthermore, the idea of reparations and of atonement became a part of the doctrine of repentance. A man was expected to make reparations before he could repent. This was why a shepherd could not fully repent; he did not know how many fields he had trespassed, therefore he could not make adequate reparations.[171] The

---

[167]Montefiore, *Rabbinic,* 390–422.

[168]Lam. R. on v. 21; Midrash Ps. 85:4.

[169]Midr. Ps. 18:3.

[170]Montefiore, *Rabbinic,* 404.

[171]*Ibid.,* 402. Montefiore feels that this injunction against the shepherds has to be taken with a grain of salt.

act of repentance was itself an atoning work. Reparations and atonement were made by the act of repentance. After the destruction of the temple the atoning aspect of repentance became dominant. According to Maimonides repentance replaced the sacrificial system. He wrote, "There is nothing left us but repentance which, however, atones for all transgressions."[172] In this connection, Montefiore writes,

> Fasting and prayer, repentance, and "good works," ritualism independent of sacrifice, and high doctrine transcending it, enable the people and their teachers to overcome the shock of the Temple's loss, and to fashion a religion superior to that of the priests.[173]

In this statement Montefiore lists repentance as one of the theological elements used by the rabbis to replace the entire sacrificial system, which ended with the destruction of Jerusalem.

In summary, it can be said that for the rabbis, repentance was a work that man did to earn God's favor. At times man needed God's help. God had to come part of the way as man came the rest of the way. The work of repentance had to be sincere and accompanied by reparations for the sin along with a determination to avoid all further sin. Repentance atoned for sin.

Applying this to the prodigal, we see him preparing to make the reparations that will demonstrate his sincerity. The confession itself can be understood as a partial work of atonement by which he begins to make up for what he has done. It is clear that Derrett, from his Jewish point of view, feels that, if this kind of plan had been carried out, the parable would have been more believable and would have avoided its "fundamental weakness."[174]

The Oriental farmer and landowner lives in his village, not in isolation out on his land. This has always been the case. The background of Isaiah 5:8 makes this clear. It reads,

> Woe to those who join house to house
>   and add field to field,
> until there is no more room,
>   and you are made to dwell alone
>   in the midst of the land.

Clearly the picture is that of buying field after field of the agricultural land and of joining house to house in the village where the homes are in tight proximity to each other. The threat is that if the wealthy continue their practice, they will finally buy out all the surrounding families, forcing them out of the village and off the land. The result will be that the wealthy will end up dwelling alone in the midst of the land, which is the worst possible fate for the gregarious Middle Eastern villager. Even into modern times, the larger houses of the older Oriental estates usually do

---

[172]*Ibid.*, 396.
[173]*Ibid.*, 394.
[174]Derrett, "Prodigal Son," 58.

not stand in grand isolation at the center of the cropland.[175] Thus we can confidently assume that the father lives in a village as part of the community.

Most likely the father expects his son to fail. He is assumed dead. If he makes it back, it will be as a beggar. The father also knows how the village (which certainly has told him he should not have granted the inheritance in the first place) will treat the boy on his arrival. The prodigal will be mocked by a crowd that will gather spontaneously as word flashes across the village telling of his return. Ben Sirach mentions four things that terrify him. Two of them are "slander by a whole town, the gathering of a mob."[176] The prodigal son returns to face both of Ben Sirach's terrors, the slander of a whole town and certainly the gathering of a mob. As soon as the prodigal reaches the edge of the village and is identified, a crowd will begin to gather. He will be subject to taunt songs and many other types of verbal and perhaps even physical abuse.

The father is fully aware of how his son will be treated, if and when he returns in humiliation to the village community he has rejected. What the father does in this homecoming scene can best be understood as a series of dramatic actions calculated to protect the boy from the hostility of the village and to restore him to fellowship within the community. These actions begin with the father running down the road.

An Oriental nobleman with flowing robes never runs anywhere. To do so is humiliating.[177] Ben Sirach confirms this attitude. He says, "A man's manner of walking tells you what he is."[178] Weatherhead writes, "It is so very undignified in Eastern eyes for an elderly man to run. Aristotle says, 'Great men never run in public.' "[179] The text says, "He had compassion." We would suggest that this "compassion" specifically includes awareness of the gauntlet the boy will have to

---

[175]Thomson gives a population listing for all the principal cities of Syria, Lebanon, and Palestine for the nineteenth century and adds, "I need scarcely remind you that the entire population is gathered into towns and villages" (The Land, I, 247). This is so universally evident from archeology as to need no documentation.

[176]Sir. 26:5f. The pressures of the community in the tightly knit Oriental village must be felt to be believed. Custom demands that a mother or sister or wife caught in any type of extramarital sex be killed by the men of the family. The execution is unfailing and immediate. Conversation in depth with the people involved is revealing. Question: "How can you do this? Do you not love your mother?" Answer: "O yes, very, very deeply." Question: "Then how can you bring yourself to do this?" Answer: "The talk of the people! You cannot bear the talk of the people! You must do it!"

[177]A pastor of my acquaintance was not accepted as the pastor of a particular church because, in the judgment of the elders, he walked down the street too fast. This custom is preserved even in a modern Middle Eastern metropolis by the Orthodox priest who, of course, still wears the long robes and is careful to walk at a slow, dignified pace.

[178]Sir. 19:30. It is not fully clear what Ben Sirach is referring to, but the most natural assumption is that he is discussing the slow, stately walk expected of men of position, age, and rank in that society.

[179]L. P. Weatherhead, In Quest of a Kingdom (London: Hodder and Stoughton, 1943), 90. Weatherhead does not document his quotation from Aristotle. Cf. also Jeremias, Parables, 130. Bengel wrote in the eighteenth century, "Parents ordinarily are not disposed to run and meet their children" (Gnomon, I, 474); cf. E. C. B. MacLaurin, "The Semitic Background of the use of 'En Splachnois'," Palestinian Exploration Quarterly 103 (1971), 42–45.

face as he makes his way through the village. The father then runs this gauntlet for him, assuming a humiliating posture in the process! Bruce has noted that such an action would "soon draw a crowd to the spot."[180]

The father makes the reconciliation public at the edge of the village. Thus his son enters the village under the protective care of the father's acceptance. The boy, having steeled his nerves for this gauntlet, now, to his utter amazement, sees his father run it for him. Rather than experiencing the ruthless hostility he deserves and anticipates, the son witnesses an unexpected, visible demonstration of love in humiliation. The father's acts replace speech. There are no words of acceptance and welcome. The love expressed is too profound for words. Only acts will do. Sa'īd writes,

> Christ reports for us the words of the son to his father, but does not give anything about a speech of the father to his son. For in reality,
> the father substitutes kisses for words
> and replaces assertion with expression
> and eyes speak for the tongue.[181]

Stanza 5 is a picture of total rejection. Here in stanza 5' is *total* acceptance. In this public visible demonstration of unexpected love the father is just as earnestly searching for his son as the shepherd and the woman searched for what they had lost.[182]

Quoting Bornhäuser, Linnemann asserts that the kiss on the cheek is a sign of equality and that the father's kiss prevents the son from kissing the hand or the feet of his father.[183] This latter part of the assertion is quite likely correct. The boy would have kissed his father's hand or perhaps even his feet but is prevented from doing so.[184]

The first part of Bornhäuser's assertion is in error. The father's kiss is not a sign of equality. An Oriental father is never his son's equal. Rather it is a sign of reconciliation and forgiveness. When a serious quarrel has taken place in the village and reconciliation is achieved, a part of the ceremony enacted as a sacrament of reconciliation is a public kiss by the leading men involved.[185] There is no assumption of "equality." One party may be of higher status and the other of

---

[180]Bruce, *Synoptic Gospels*, 582. Bruce is the only author I have found who has noted the inevitable presence of a quickly gathered crowd. Derrett thinks "small boys" would have brought word from a previous village. This is unlikely, but he notes correctly that an ever present crowd of young boys is an inevitable part of anything that happens in the village. Cf. Derrett, "Prodigal Son," 65.

[181]Sa'īd, *Lūqā*, 401. With his matchless command of the Arabic language Sa'īd here breaks into rhymed prose. Sa'īd then observes that the father is pouring out kisses on a dirty son, and says, "The father is not kissing the son's cleanliness, but his person (*nafsahu*)" (*ibid.*).

[182]Miller, *Luke*, 120f.

[183]Linnemann, *Parables*, 77. She is quoting K. Bornhäuser, *Studien zum Sondergut des Lukas* (Gütersloh: n.p., 1934), 114.

[184]Rihbany writes, "Upon coming home from a journey I always saluted my parents by kissing their hands, as a mark of loving submission" (*Syrian*, 337).

[185]Cf. Gen. 33:4. Esau is not saying, "You are my equal," but rather, "I forgive you."

lower. It would be unthinkable for any father publicly to assert that his son was his equal!

The word καταφιλέω can mean either "kiss tenderly" or "kiss again and again." The first meaning would be feminine and quite inappropriate. The second is in Middle Eastern custom fully masculine and culturally accurate.[186]

The son responds with only a *part* of his prepared speech. The listener/reader has already been told the entire speech and so knows what to expect. The offer of a solution, "Make me as one of your hired servants," is missing.[187] Commentators too numerous to note assume that the father interrupted him.[188] It is our understanding that this misses the crucial nature of what is happening here at a very critical part of the story. If the boy is interrupted, he can finish his speech later, after the father completes giving his orders to the servants. We *could* assume that his failure to do so indicates a self-interest which says, "This is better than I expected. Why not take all I can get? I'll keep silent and accept. If he will give me sonship, who cares about being a workman?"

Certainly this is not what the omission signifies. Given the prodigal's previous mind-set, sonship has certain distinct disadvantages. If he accepts sonship, he will have to live with his brother and be fed from his brother's property. He will again be under the total authority of his father. He will be denied the self-satisfaction of having "earned his own way." Accepting sonship requires a deliberate decision with broad ramifications. Clearly he has changed his mind. Via has understood the significance of this change. He writes, "Repentance finally turns out to be the capacity to forego pride and accept graciousness."[189]

Following this line of argument, we must ask, "Why did he change his mind?" and, more precisely, "What are the ramifications of his decision?" As we have seen, the prodigal comes home with a rabbinic understanding of repentance. He is shattered by his father's demonstration of love in humiliation. In his state of apprehension and fear he would naturally experience this unexpected deliverance as an utterly overwhelming event. Now he knows that he cannot offer any solution to their ongoing relationship. He sees that the point is not the lost money, but rather the broken relationship which he cannot heal. Now he understands that any new relationship must be a pure gift from his father. He can offer no solution. To

---

[186]Against Manson, *Sayings,* 288.

[187]Harmonizers tried to "improve" on the story by adding "make me as one of your hired servants" to this verse. The best textual evidence omits it. All our Oriental versions except the Harclean also omit the phrase. Ibn al-'Assāl does not even list the phrase in his apparatus.

[188]There is a strong exegetical tradition from at least the Reformation that translates the εἶπεν δέ of the beginning of v. 21 with "*but* he said," indicating a contrast. (Luther, King James, American Standard Version, Revised Standard Version, New English Bible, Jerusalem Bible.) The one modern exception is the New American Bible. The Oriental versions, however (with the exception of the Peshitta and the Harclean), imply continuity rather than contrast. With the Oriental versions, the father's actions are understood to be in continuity with the radically new attitude seen suddenly in the speech of the son.

[189]Via, *Parables,* 171.

assume that he can compensate his father with his labor is an insult. "I am unworthy" is now the only appropriate response.[190]

In his famous eleventh-century Arabic commentary on the Gospels, Ibn al-Ṭayyib gives some astute Oriental insights into this text. He writes,

> The text says, "Make me as one of your hired servants." This means those who have repented but who are not yet worthy of the position of sons because their repentance is not complete. The text says, "And he arose and came to his father." This means he was inclined toward God with repentance. . . . The text says, "He (the father) hurried and fell upon his bosom and kissed him," as a sign of the greatness of his mercy and compassion and that he does not hold his son's monstrous sins against him but welcomes him with joy. The text says, "He said to him, 'Father, I have sinned against heaven and before you and I am no longer worthy to be called your son,' " because you are good and I am evil. It says that he was determined, if he met his father, to say to him, "Make me one of your hired servants." But he did not say this. We say that he did not say it because of what he saw of his father's love.[191]

In this comment Ibn al-Ṭayyib affirms that the hired servant plan had something to do with an incomplete or partial repentance. The father's welcome is clearly an outpouring of grace. But of special note for our discussion is Ibn al-Ṭayyib's comment on the reason for the omission of the offer to become a hired servant. He says that the prodigal changed his mind "because of what he saw of his father's love." Love was demonstrated and became visible. This worked a change of mind. The son decided against offering to become a servant. The willingness to become a hired servant itself signified for Ibn al-Ṭayyib a partial repentance. Full repentance came as a result of a demonstration of love.

After the prodigal's repentance and confession (stanza 4') the father turns to address the servants (stanza 3'). The servants are there on the road with the crowd.[192] They are specifically told to *dress* the son as servants do a king. He is not told to go and bathe and change his clothes. This order to dress the prodigal assures

---

[190]Via has noted that the boy undergoes a very significant change at the edge of the village. He writes, "Only when the event of forgiveness occurred and shattered his own view of things did his understanding change. . . . Natural man's legalistic understanding of the divine-human relationship is shattered only by the unexpected event of forgiveness which comes to him from beyond himself (*Parables*, 174).

In the nineteenth century, Godet wrote, "There is a wide difference between the confession uttered by the prodigal son, ver. 21, and that which had been extracted from him by the extremity of his misery (ver. 18, 19). The latter was a cry of despair; but now this distress is over. It is therefore the cry of repentant love. The terms are the same: *I have sinned*; but how different is the accent. Luther felt it profoundly; the discovery of the difference between the repentance of fear and that of love was the true principle of the Reformation. He cannot come to the end; the very assurance of pardon prevents him from finishing and saying, *make me as . . .* according to his first purpose" (*St. Luke*, 378). With the exception of Via, Godet's point has been neglected. It is our contention that the cultural scene presents strong evidence that his insight is correct.

[191]*Sharḥ al-Injīl li-Ibn al-Ṭayyib*, Paris Arabic 86, folio 131; my translation.

[192]Arndt correctly observes, "The father calls out an order to the slaves, who may be imagined to have followed him as he went out to meet the beggarlike person approaching in the distance" (*St. Luke*, 352; against Plummer, *St. Luke*, 375).

proper respect from the servants, who naturally are eagerly awaiting some clue from the father to tell them how they should treat the son. If the father had indicated displeasure with so much as an indifferent shrug of the shoulder, the servants would have done nothing for him.

The best robe is most certainly the father's.[193] The Oriental listener/reader would immediately assume this. The "first" (i.e., best) robe would be the robe the father wore on feast days and other grand occasions.[194] The point is that, as the guests arrive at the banquet, and as people stream in to see him, to hear his story, and to congratulate him on his return, the father's robe will assure acceptance by the community. With this command the father assures reconciliation between his son and his servants. At the same time, the father assures the completion of the son's reconciliation to the community.[195]

Does the robe carry any eschatological significance? Quite likely. Jeremias argues at some length that it does. Isaiah 61 is given special attention in the teachings of Jesus. Verse 10 of that chapter reads, "For he has clothed me with the garments of salvation, he has covered me with the robe of righteousness."[196] Jeremias writes,

> It may be remembered that Jesus spoke of the Messianic Age as a new garment (Mark 2.21 par. . . .), and that he compared forgiveness with the best robe with which the father clothed the prodigal son (Luke 15.22); hence we cannot doubt that it is this comparison that underlies Matt. 22.11–13. God offers you the clean garment of forgiveness and imputed righteousness.[197]

The ring is quite likely a signet ring, which means that he is trusted in a remarkable way.[198] The shoes are the sign of his being a free man in the house, not a servant.[199] Derrett writes regarding the servants, "They put his sandals on as a sign that they accept him as their master—indeed no order could have expressed this more conclusively."[200]

---

[193]Plummer has rightly observed that it cannot be the son's robe without an αὐτοῦ (*St. Luke*, 376). Rengstorf argues at great length that his robe is an official ceremonial robe that was publicly stripped from the boy when he was cut off in a *qeṣaṣah* ceremony (*Re-Investitur*, 39). I find his discussion unconvincing. The story specifically states that the son "gathered together" (realized) *all* that he had. The fact of such a ceremonial robe is undemonstrated. The *qeṣaṣah* was most likely not invoked. Furthermore, the rabbinic references to the *qeṣaṣah* make no mention of any ceremonial robe.

[194]Cf. Esther 6:9, where wearing the king's robe is described as a special honor.

[195]This latter is already accomplished to a large degree by making the welcome public. Dressing him in the father's best robe confirms and seals what he has already done at the edge of the village.

[196]Cf. Matt. 5:3; 11:5; Luke 4:18; 7:33. Cf. L. C. Crockett, "The Old Testament in the Gospel of Luke with Emphasis on the Interpretation of Isaiah 61:1–2" (unpublished Ph.D. thesis, Brown University, Providence, R.I., 1966).

[197]Jeremias, *Parables*, 189.

[198]Cf. Derrett, "Prodigal Son," 66; 1 Macc. 6:15; Gen. 41:42; Esther 3:10; 8:2; Jeremias, *Parables*, 130; Rengstorf, *Re-Investitur*, 30.

[199]Jeremias, *Parables*, 130.

[200]Derrett, "Prodigal Son," 66. Rengstorf argues that putting on shoes is a sign of asserting ownership. In the Middle East, shoes and feet in any reference are degrading and insulting. Shoes are unclean. They are combined in common speech in all kinds of insults. Rengstorf interprets the removal of shoes at the

Lastly the father orders the killing of the fatted calf. The selection of a calf rather than a goat or a sheep means that most, if not all, the village will be present that evening. The entire animal will spoil in a few hours if not eaten. Jeremias thinks the banquet is only for the family and the servants.[201] This is certainly in error. To kill a calf and not invite the community would be an insult to the community and a waste for the family. Indeed, the main point of killing such a large animal is to be able to invite the entire community. As with the woman and the shepherd, the joy must be shared on all sides.

Rihbany discusses the covenantal nature of killing an animal for the sake of a guest. He writes,

> The ancient custom, whose echoes have not yet died out in the East, was that the host honored his guest most highly by killing a sheep at the threshold of the house, upon the guest's arrival, and inviting him to step over the blood into the house. This act formed the "blood covenant" between the guest and his host. It made them one. To us one of the most cordial and dignified expressions in inviting a guest, especially from a distant town, was, "If God ever favors us with a visit from you, we will kill a *zebihat!*"
>
> In his great rejoicing in the return of his son, the father of the prodigal is made to receive him as he would a most highly honored guest. "The fatted calf"—and not only a sheep—is killed as the *zebihat* of a new covenant between a loving father and his son, who "was dead and is alive again"; was lost, and is found.[202]

Middle Eastern peasants have preserved customs of this kind from antiquity. When a new house is built, a sheep is killed and its blood spread on "the lintel and the two doorposts" in a manner that sounds very much like Exodus 12:21–27. Without other evidence, however, I am uneasy about accepting Rihbany's conclusion. I have not found Rihbany's proposal to reflect a deep and widespread attitude. Yet, on the positive side, he does point up the extraordinary honor that is extended to the

---

burning bush as meaning, "I take off my shoes as a sign that God owns this ground." It is better understood as, "I take off my shoes because I do not want to defile *holy* ground with my unclean shoes." Rengstorf argues that a man takes off his shoes when going into a house rather than putting them on. This also is not quite true. He takes off his shoes to have his feet washed. But he does not then go around barefoot. If the floor is packed earth, it is too dirty; if it is stone it is too cold. A man takes off his shoes when he reclines on a couch, or sits cross-legged on it. In a number of the foot-washing scenes in the New Testament the people involved were reclining. Rengstorf also uses Ps. 60:8, "Upon Edom I cast my shoe," as evidence of asserting ownership. Rather it is a very strong insult. At Assiut College in Egypt in the early sixties a young American teacher, inexperienced in Oriental attitudes toward shoes, woke a sleeping student one morning by throwing a shoe across the room at him. A thousand students rioted that day in protest over the "insult." In a public speech the speaker apologizes before using the word "shoes" in deference to its being nearly a four-letter word. The only place in biblical literature where there is some relationship between shoes and ownership is Ruth 4:7. However, there the author has to explain the custom to the reader because already by his time it had died out. This section of Rengstorf's discussion is very weak. Cf. Rengstorf, *Re-Investitur*, 39.
[201]Jeremias, *Parables*, 130.
[202]Rihbany, *Syrian*, 160.

son by the slaughter of such a large animal. This size feast requires over a hundred people in attendance to eat the animal. A calf is slaughtered for the marriage of the eldest son, or the visit of the governor of the province, or some such occasion. The calf means at least a joy so great that it must be celebrated with the grandest banquet imaginable. The purpose of such a banquet includes a desire to reconcile the boy to the *whole* community.

The father's speech ends in stanza 1'. The prodigal still has the option of preferring the freedom of an independent status in the village, far from the complications of living with his brother. Perverted pride would lead him to insist that he is "too humble" for sonship. Rather, he accepts pure grace. Grace wins. His abbreviated confession is his last word. Via describes this acceptance as a move from irresponsibility to a new contextual freedom.[203] Now the father and his younger son can begin to make merry. Indeed a son is found.

The first half of the parable ends with the beginning of the celebration of the return. The story has now come full circle. The literary structure presented above can now be more fully understood. In the light of the underlying culture it is of particular interest to compare the son's first speech at the beginning and his second in the center. Each line has its match. This can be seen as follows:

> *Speech I*
> a.   Father
> b.   give me my share of property
> c.   (he divided his living.)

> *Speech II*
> a'. Father
> b'. I have sinned against heaven and you
> c'. I am no more worthy to be called your son.

Line a is an address. Line b means he wants his father to die. Line b' reflects this as he confesses the enormity of his sin. Line c tells us that he receives all that is his due and thereby cuts his relations with the family. Line c' admits this. In stanza 6 he admits he needs help—he is starving. His proposed self-help solution matches this in 6'. As is usual in such structures, the real point of turning occurs just past the center. In stanza 5' is the unbelievable visible demonstration of unexpected love in humiliation. A genuine repentance flows from that in 4' and the rest of the stanzas flow in sequence. Thus the literary structure reinforces the cultural elements in determining the movement of the story.

This homecoming scene presents the picture of a servant who plans to confess and compensate. The father then demonstrates unexpected love in humiliation. The servant is overwhelmed by grace and becomes a son. The scene provides a new understanding of repentance as acceptance of grace and the confession of unworthiness. The two rejoice together.

---

[203]Via, *Parables*, 166.

The Christological Implications of the Homecoming Scene

The apparent absence of any reference in this parable to the work of Christ is a problem that has been given four basic types of answers in modern times. These must be considered.

First, there were the nineteenth-century liberals who rejoiced that the true gospel has no atonement. The gospel in Harnack's view has to do "with the Father only and not with the Son."[204] This view fails to take into account the cultural background we have outlined above. It solves the problem by saying, "There is no problem."

A second approach is to claim that, after all, this parable is not a "complete compendium of theology." Those who take this approach say in effect, "The parable teaches that God loves sinners *while* they are still sinners. This is enough. We should not expect a full theological statement. The atonement is missing, never mind."[205] This answer dismisses the problem. Granted, the parable should not be thought of as a "complete compendium of theology." At the same time, the parable does depict how God reconciles men to himself.

A third position affirms that there are indirect, yet clear Christological references in the parable; never mind the atonement. Jeremias writes,

> Jesus . . . claims that in his actions the love of God to the repentant sinner is made effectual. Thus the parable, without making any kind of christological statement, reveals itself as a veiled assertion of authority: Jesus makes the claim for himself that he is acting in God's stead, that he is God's representative.[206]

Giblin says,

> Jesus's activity as man is the way in which God's mercy is seen and realized. Thus, in Lk 15 we seem to have a theologically analogous statement of the words in Jn 14.9, . . . "He who has observed me has observed the Father. . . ." . . . It is He [Jesus] to whom the character portrayal of the Father most immediately applies.[207]

This view offers thoughtful answers to the question of Christology generally but leaves unanswered this same question as it relates specifically to the atonement.

---

[204]Adolf von Harnack, *What Is Christianity?* trans. Thomas B. Saunders (New York: Harper, 1957 1900), 144. Harnack uses as his primary evidence the publican in the temple, the widow and her mite, and the lost son (*ibid.*, 143). For centuries Islam has used the parable of the Prodigal Son in anti-Christian polemic attempting to prove that Christian theology is at odds with the message of Jesus. They claim the parable of the Prodigal Son to be in perfect harmony with Muslim theology. Jülicher asked the question, "Kann denn ein Sünder sich von selber bekehren, und wird ihm vergeben ohne Christe Mittlerschaft, ohne seinen Opfertod?" He answers his question with a clear "Yes." Cf. *Gleichnisreden*, II, 364f. For Jülicher the atonement was merely "die Lieblingsdogmen der 'Biblizisten' " (*ibid.*, II, 334).

[205]Manson, *Sayings*, 286.

[206]Jeremias, *Parables*, 132; his emphasis. Cf. Via, *Parables*, 171f.

[207]Giblin, "Luke 15," 25. Giblin affirms that the point of the parable is "to explain the plan of salvation which goes beyond strict justice" (*ibid.*, 24).

A fourth view finds Christology and hints of the atonement in certain elements of the parable. Karl Barth attempts what he calls a "not allegorical but typological or *in concreto* Christological exposition. . . ."[208] He sees no simple identification of Jesus with the lost son. Instead, as he puts it,

> . . . We do not do justice to the story if we do not see and say that in the going out and coming in of the lost son in his relationship with the father we have a most illuminating parallel to the way trodden by Jesus Christ in the work of atonement, to His humiliation and exaltation.[209]

Giblin sees the same symbolism in Luke 15.[210] These identifications of Christological elements in the prodigal himself by Barth and Giblin seem strained. The prodigal is a symbol of the publicans and sinners.[211] It is a long jump from them to Jesus. Can Jesus and the publican be symbolized by the same prodigal?

Gollwitzer has seen Christological overtones in other aspects of the parable. He writes, "Jesus ist das Entgegenlaufen des Vaters heraus aus dem Hause. Jesus ist aber auch die Kraft der Erinnerung an die Vaterschaft Gottes."[212] Gollwitzer then concentrates on the second statement.[213] Of all those in this fourth category, Giblin is the most satisfying. He neither introduces some new type of allegorizing nor does he violate the cultural influences that inform the text. He writes,

> . . . His [Christ's] redemptive love is reflected in the activity of His public life, too, not just on Calvary (where Christ's sacrificial love was perfectly achieved and also where His act of satisfaction was completed). Redemptive love is the *creative* love which truly makes us God's people in spite of ourselves. . . . In the subtle portrayal of redemptive love in Luke 15, Jesus is the one in and through whom the heavenly joy is shown to men: the Father is thus seen in and through Jesus's contact ("mediation") with men. Jesus Himself is the efficacious sign of the reconciliation and new life (cf. Lk 15, 32 *ezēsen*) . . . .[214]

---

[208]Karl Barth, *Church Dogmatics*, trans. G. W. Bromiley (Edinburgh: T. & T. Clark, 1958), IV/2, 25.

[209]*Ibid.*, 23. This view is endorsed by Stuhlmueller, *Luke*, 148f.

[210]Giblin, "Luke 15," 30.

[211]The prodigal son himself, at least since Augustine and likely before, was identified with the gentiles. It is highly unlikely that this identification was intended by Jesus. The prodigal begins *at home*. He is not a stranger brought in from the outside. Ibn al-Ṭayyib mentions this identification of the prodigal with the gentiles and argues against it (Paris Arabic Ms. 86, folio 129).

[212]Helmut Gollwitzer, *Die Freude Gottes, Einführung in das Lukasevangelium* (Berlin-Dahlem: Burckhardthaus-Verlag, 1952), 176.

[213]However, regarding the prodigal's *Erinnerung* of his father, if we would look for some theological identification here, the Holy Spirit might be more appropriate. The "spirit" of the father stirs the boy to remember a better life in a better fellowship. Yet this also must be rejected. To move in this direction would be to try indeed to make the parable a complete compendium of theology. This temptation must be resisted. If we would look for theology that is perhaps more "overheard" than "heard," it must be clearly a part of the cultural setting in which the parable was first told. To fail to adopt this as a methodological principle is to surrender the parable again to some new form of irresponsible allegorization.

[214]Giblin, "Luke 15," 30.

In harmony with the cultural setting we have outlined above, we would propose an expansion of this fourth position.

For Palestinian listeners, initially the father would naturally be a symbol of God.[215] Then, as the story progresses, the father comes down out of the house and, in a dramatic act, demonstrates unexpected love publicly in humiliation.[216] The literary structure and the cultural milieu of the story identify this dramatic act as the turning point of the first half of the parable. Surely Jesus intended his listeners to see in this act a dramatic representation of his welcome of sinners. When the father leaves the house to come out to his son in love and humility, he demonstrates at least a part of the meaning of the incarnation and the atonement.[217]

It is instructive to reflect on what would have happened in the story if the father had not presented a visible demonstration of unexpected love. The result would obviously have been one more hired servant, but no son. As we shall see, the father already had a servant-type son in the house. He wanted something more; and this was the only way to get a son, given the fact of estrangement and the mind-set of the boy. The father's love was always deep and abiding. But the son did not understand it. If the father had waited in the house, he would have had another servant. If he goes out in a shattering, humiliating demonstration of that love, the boy will see and may understand. If he does, then the father will have a son. In conclusion, then, the atonement is at least "overheard" in the parable.

The Older Son (15:24–32)[218]

In this section the literary structure will be examined and then the cultural aspects of the story will be discussed. Finally the theological cluster will be analyzed. The burden of the argument will be to show that this second half of the parable is culturally and stylistically a repetition of the first half. The externals are different, but the essential nature of each of the two halves is the same. Furthermore, the father's response to each of his sons is essentially identical.

The older son appears on the scene in the fields. He is outside the house. His path to the banquet hall is step by step presented as parallel to the road just traveled by the prodigal. This path is illuminated by the literary structure, which will now be examined.

B   Now the elder son was in the fields

---

[215]Cf. Isa. 63:16, "Thou, O Lord, art our Father."

[216]We shall see that the father is obliged to do the same thing for the older son (Via, *Parables*, 171).

[217]This is an expansion of Gollwitzer's first statement, above, p. 189.

[218]The unity of 15:11–32 has been accepted by the majority of scholars in the past sixty years. In historical order these include: Jülicher, Manson, C. W. F. Smith, Daube, Jeremias, Bultmann, and Linnemann. The most recent challenge to the parable's unity is from Jack T. Sanders, "Tradition and Redaction in Luke XV, 11–32," *NTS* 15 (1969), 433–38. Sanders has been fully answered by Jeremias, "Tradition und Redaktion in Lukas 15," *ZNW* 42 (1971), 172–189. Cf. also Jeremias, *Parables*, 131. Thus Manson's judgment still stands: "There is, in fact, no good reason for supposing that the story is anything but a perfect unity" (*Sayings*, 285).

1   and as he came and drew near to the house
     he heard music and dancing   HE COMES
     and he called one of the boys and asked what this meant.

  2   And he said to him, "Your brother has come   YOUR BROTHER—SAFE
       and your father has killed the fatted calf   A FEAST
       because he received him with peace."

     3   But he was angry and refused to go in   A FATHER COMES
          so his father came out   TO RECONCILE
          and was entreating him.

          But he answered his father, "Lo these many years *I have served you*
          and I have never disobeyed your commandments COMPLAINT I
                                                          (HOW YOU TREAT ME)
          yet *you never gave me a kid* to make merry with my friends.

       4'   "But when *this son of yours* came   COMPLAINT II
             who has *devoured your living with harlots*   (HOW YOU TREAT HIM)
             you killed for him the fatted calf."

     3'   And he said to him, "Beloved son,   A FATHER TRIES
           you are always with me   TO RECONCILE
           and all that is mine is yours.

  2'   "It was fitting to make merry and be glad   YOUR BROTHER—SAFE
         for this your brother was dead and is alive,   A FEAST
         he was lost and is found."

     [And he came and entered the house   ????????[MISSING]
     and joined in the music and dancing
     and he began to make merry.

     And the two sons were reconciled to their father.]

     Again we are dealing with a parabolic ballad (Type D), which forms
three-line stanzas. The inversion principle is again used. The correspondences
between the matching stanzas are clear and strong. In the climactic center the two
complaints match line for line in step parallelism. In stanza 3 the father comes to
reconcile while in 3' we hear his reconciling speech. Stanza 2 is a report of the feast
and the banquet by a young boy; in 2' the father defends his inauguration of these
same events. The ending is missing—there is no stanza 1'. The significance of this
will become evident as we proceed. Here we can note that the structure of the
parabolic ballad makes clear that something is unfinished. In brackets we have
tried to reconstruct what might have been there if the second half of the parable had
ended joyfully like the first half. With the structure in mind we turn to the details of
the text.
     The older son draws near and hears συμφωνίας and dancing. The word
συμφωνία perhaps refers to a double pipe.[219] The ancient Oriental versions

_____
[219]George F. Moore, "συμφωνία—Not a Bagpipe," *JBL* 24 (1905), 166–175. Moore is answering
Barry, who in a previous issue tried to argue that it was a bagpipe. Moore is agreed that the word refers
to a musical instrument. He is uncertain exactly what instrument is implied but writes, "The name

universally include singing. In most cases this seems to have come from understanding συμφωνία as meaning "voices together." This verse has more variety in
translation in the Oriental versions than any verse examined for this study. The
following are all represented:

1. "The voice of singing and symphonia" (Old Syriac)

2. "The voice of much singing" (Peshitta, Diatessaron, Ibn al-Ṭayyib)

3. "The voice of singing and dancing" (Harclean)

4. "Voices singing together and boisterous clapping" (Vat. Borg. Ar. 71)

5. "Voices singing together" (Ibn al-ʿAssāl)

6. "Voices and dancing" (Vat. Borg. Ar. 95, Polyglots)

7. "Joining of voices and singing" (Propagandist)

8. "Singing and dancing" (Shidiac, Jesuit–1, Jesuit–2)

9. "The voice of musical instruments and dancing" (Van Dyke, ʿAbd al-
   Malik)[220]

It is clear that there is a loud, boisterous, joyous celebration in progress when the
older son approaches the house.

The question of why the older son was not notified immediately is handled
most adequately by Linnemann, who calls it a "stage-managed" effect. She
writes,

> The listener to a parable is quite content with such "stage-productions" as long
> as it passes only the bounds of probability and not of possibility. If the story as a
> whole seems credible, he will not be worried by small divergences from what
> is customary in real life.[221]

At the same time, there are good reasons for not notifying him. Doubtless the
father knows that the older brother will be upset and, if notified, may even try to
prevent the banquet. In any case, the parable has him appear when he does in order
to heighten the comparison between the two sons.

συμφωνία, in its etymological sense, would apply more properly to the double pipe" (*ibid.*, 172). Cf.
Phillips Barry, "On Luke xv. 25, συμφωνία: Bagpipe," *JBL* 23 (1904), 180–190.

[220]The very curious feature of all these is that in spite of the variety they all include "singing" (except
the two modern Protestant versions). Even the critically translated, scholarly "Jesuit-2" finished in
1970 includes singing. It is beyond the range of this study to try to sort out the textual maze that lies
behind these versions. It can be said that the heavy emphasis on "singing" means the Oriental churches
have understood the assembled guests to be boisterously involved in the celebration. The musical
instruments would be played by a select few (not necessarily professional). The dancing would be done
by men individually and again would be the activity of a few known to be skilled. The singing
(accompanied with loud rhythmic clapping, cf. Vat. Borg. Ar. 71) would engage a much wider circle.
The scene is not that of sedate guests entertained quietly by professionals, but of a loud party with
everyone involved. This, at least, is the picture the Oriental churches have seen. The guests are
"rejoicing together" (cf. 15:4, 7).

[221]Linnemann, *Parables*, 10.

The timing of the feast is significant. Jeremias writes, "After the feast comes music (loud singing and hand clapping) and dancing by the men."[222] However, this presupposes more order than is customary in the unstructured life of the Oriental village.[223] As soon as the father decides to butcher a calf and thus decides to invite most, if not all, of the village, all attention in the village is focused on the father's house. The calf is not roasted on a spit but cut into sections and baked in bread ovens. Obviously, most of it will have to be timed to be ready for the early evening, when the men return from the fields. When some of it is cooked, the music starts. This may be the pipes and/or a drum. The music signals to the village that there is something to eat. There is no formal, official "beginning." People come, sing, dance, drink wine (which will naturally flow on such an occasion), talk, eat, go out, come back, and so forth. Everything is in motion. The music does not start after the meal but before it. The meal cannot be over at the time when most of the men come in from the fields, which is naturally the time when the older brother also appears. The eating and drinking will last half the night. In summary, the sound of music means things are in progress, food is being served, guests have arrived. We can assume that many are in process of arrival at the hour of return from the fields.

True to his character, the older son is initially suspicious. A son with a normal relationship to his family would enter immediately, eager to join the joy, whatever its source. On hearing the beat of the music he knows immediately that it is a joyous occasion. Village rhythms are specific and known. The older son does not rush in as expected. He is unnaturally suspicious.

An explanation is demanded from a "young boy." The word can mean "son" or "servant" or "young boy." The traditional translation is "servant." Evidence from a number of directions points to "young boy" as preferable. The Syriac versions all have *ṭalyo*, which is primarily "young boy." Burkitt translates this phrase in the Old Syriac "He called one of the lads."[224] Ibn al-Ṭayyib, the Polyglots, and Vat. Borg. Ar. 71 translate with *al-fityān*, which clearly means "young boy."[225]

---

[222]Jeremias, *Parables*, 130.

[223]This is an important aspect of nearly everything that happens in the Oriental village. The Arabic proverb says, "Movement is blessing," which turns out to mean "confusion is blessing." The point is that life is dull in the village. When any event takes place it causes movement and results in confusion. The more confusion the more enthusiasm, the more enthusiasm the more *barakah* (blessing).

[224]Burkitt, *Evangelion da-Mepharreshe*, I, 353. The Peshitta is unambiguous, reading "young boys." This Syriac word has two plurals. The consonants are identical; the change is in the vowels. The word written *ṭulye'* means "young boys," but written *ṭalyo'* means "servants." The Peshitta uses the former and thus specifically reads "young boys." Cf. T. H. Robinson, *Paradigms and Exercises in Syriac Grammar* (Oxford: Clarendon, 1962), 48; R. P. Smith, *A Compendious Syriac Dictionary*, ed. J. P. Smith (Oxford: Clarendon, 1903), 174; C. Brockelmann, *Lexicon Syriacum* (2nd ed., Halle: Max Niemeyer, 1928), 276.

[225]'Abd Allah al-Bustānī defines this word clearly as "young boy." He admits only tentatively that it may carry the connotation of "servant." Cf. 'Abd Allah al-Bustānī, *Fākihat al-Bustān* (Beirut: American Press, 1930), 1055. With both the Syriac word and the early Arabic we are dealing with a

In addition to this evidence from the Oriental versions, two specific elements in the story dictate that it is a young boy and not a servant. First, the older son in the text calls to ἕνα τῶν παίδων. He calls to one out of a group. We are not dealing with an American farm. The entrance to the house is not through the kitchen. In the Oriental home the door from the street opens into a courtyard which provides access to the front part of the house. The older son meets the παῖς before he reaches the house.[226] In the Oriental village, when a large banquet is held, the adults attend but not the children. The young boys in particular congregate in great numbers outside the house, stir up great clouds of dust, sing and dance in tune to the music, join in the excitement of the feast. Although not officially present, they are an inevitable part of any village celebration. They are the first group the son would meet.

The second detail is more conclusive. The young boy calls the father "your father." No servant would talk this way. If he were a servant he would have to say, "My master has done thus and so." His vocabulary indicates rather conclusively that he is a young boy and not a servant.[227]

Arndt notes the imperfect in verse 26. That is, "he kept asking him," implying a series of questions.[228] The past continuous is significant because the older son must find out if his brother came back wealthy or poor. Later in the story, the older son in fact knows his brother lost everything. The listener/reader is left to assume he found out from this boy.

The older son reflects on the state of affairs and quickly decides not to enter the house. Custom requires his presence. At such a banquet the older son has a special semi-official responsibility. He is expected to move among the guests, offering compliments, making sure everyone has enough to eat, ordering the servants around and, in general, becoming a sort of major-domo of the feast. The custom is widespread all across the Arab world and on into Iran, where in the village the older son stands at the door barefoot to greet the guests. Part of the meaning of the custom is the symbolic nature of the gesture, by which the father says, "My older son is your servant."

To reinforce this symbolic meaning, many times the older son does not eat with the guests. This custom or attitude is significant for the parable. Even if we attribute this to a later development in village attitudes in the Middle East, clearly

---

word like "boy" in English. In certain specific contexts the word "boy" can mean a servant. When a British colonial official at dinner called "Boy," this is what he meant. Such a word ordinarily, however, does not in English, Syriac, or Arabic carry this meaning. The rest of the Arabic versions have *ghilmān*, which is also primarily a "young boy" but in certain contexts can mean "servant."

[226]The servants are all busy with the banquet *in* the house.

[227]In addition to this evidence, both δοῦλος and μίσθιος have already been used in the story. If the παῖς is a servant, why is not one of these words used? Moreover, the most important thing the servants have done in connection with the events of the day is to dress the prodigal. This the παῖς talking to the older son does not mention. For a "young boy" in the street the most important event is the feast, which the lad does mention in his response.

[228]Arndt, *St. Luke*, 352. Only three of our Oriental versions use a past continuous.

the sons of the host are a part of the family that is giving the banquet and honoring the special guest. If the older son enters the house, he is at least seen to join the family in honoring the prodigal. He himself affirms that a circle of guests is present when he says, ''You never gave me a kid that I might make merry with my friends.'' The obvious implication is, ''You are making merry with your friends and you have denied me the privilege of making merry with my friends.'' If he wants to fight with his father over the way his brother was received, he should first enter the house and fulfil his role as joint host. He is expected publicly to embrace and congratulate his brother, and to accept the compliments that will be showered on him from the guests who assume his joy at having his brother back. He is expected to show special honor to his brother as the honored guest. When all are gone, *then* he can complain that the boy should not be trusted and should not have been welcomed in this public fashion. Rather, the older son chooses to humiliate his father publicly by quarreling while the guests are present.

Middle Eastern customs and the Oriental high regard for the authority of the father make the older son's actions extremely insulting. Yet it is certainly an insult in any culture publicly to refuse to participate in a banquet hosted by the father and so to exhibit a serious quarrel in the family to public gaze.[229]

There is now a break in relationship between the older son and his father that is nearly as radical as the break between the father and the younger son at the beginning of the parable.[230] The story of Esther has a similar scene. King Ahasuerus summoned Queen Vashti to appear at a banquet. She refused. The king ''was enraged and his anger burned within him.''[231] Her refusal was a very serious matter. She was deposed.

Arab literature provides a very interesting illustration of the same theme of a son insulting his father at a banquet. The story is told of ʿĀmir ibn ʿĀmir Mā al-Samā surnamed Muzayqiyah, who sat on the throne of Maʾrib (the Yemen) in the third century. The agriculture of the kingdom of Maʾrib was sustained during this period by a great diversion dam called the Maʾrib dam. The king, so the story goes, discovered that the dam would break before the general public had any suspicions about its condition. Knowing that a general announcement would destroy all property values and anxious to sell his lands at a good price, he set up a clever ruse. He invited the chief men of the city to a splendid banquet and arranged for his older son to insult him with the guests present. When this charade was enacted the king vowed that he would have to kill his boy. The guests remonstrated, whereupon the king insisted that if he could not kill his son, then at least he would not stay in a city where he had been insulted publicly by his son

---

[229]The tenses of the verbs should not be given too much weight. The verse reads, ''He was angry (aorist) and was not willing (imperfect) to go in.'' His refusal to enter the house was clearly a continuous action, but so was his anger, as evidenced by his speech to his father.

[230]Derrett identifies the older son's actions as a clear violation of the Fifth Commandment (''Prodigal Son,'' 68).

[231]Esther 1:12.

before his guests. He proceeded to sell all his property at a good price and then announced the imminent break of the dam and led a pilgrimage of people away from the doomed valley.[232]

For our purposes this story is a magnificent illustration of how serious a matter it is when a son in the Middle East insults his father at a banquet. In the case of this story, such an insult is serious enough to provide a convincing reason for the king's sale of his property. Luke 15:28 must be seen in the light of such attitudes. The father butchers a calf. All the important people of the village will naturally attend. The anger and refusal to participate on the part of the older son are profoundly deep public insults against the father.

The listener/reader expects anger similar to that of King Ahasuerus to burn within the heart of the father. He is expected to ignore the boy and proceed with the banquet, or in some way punish him for public insolence, or at least demonstrate extreme displeasure. However, for the second time in one day, the father goes down and out of the house offering in public humiliation a demonstration of unexpected love. Bornkamm writes, "Here, too, the father comes out, no less anxious for the older one, and entreating him, just as he had the younger one."[233] The father comes out to entreat,[234] not to scold or to rebuke, as is expected. What will be the response? We are now at the climax of this second half of the parable (stanzas 4 and 4').

It is surely hard to find in the history of literature any man who so completely condemns himself with his own words as this older son. The younger son was stunned by the awareness of the price paid by the father to demonstrate unexpected love publicly. A significant shift in his total attitude resulted. The older son has invited harsh punishment for insolence. The father comes entreating. It is only reasonable to expect this demonstration of unexpected love to have a similar telling effect on the older son. Unfortunately this does not happen.

What, then, will his response be? Instead of a confession, there is a double complaint.[235] What specifically does the son say and what do his words imply? At the least the following can be noted:

1.   The older son addresses his father with no title. Titles are used all through the story in direct speech up to this point. The sudden absence of any title is significant.[236]

2.   The older son demonstrates the attitude and spirit of a slave, not a son. Literally he says, "I have *slaved* for you. . . ."

---

[232]Reynold A. Nicholson, *A Literary History of the Arabs* (Cambridge: University Press, 1962), 15f.

[233]Bornkamm, *Jesus,* 127f. As Plummer notes, ἐξελθών here is parallel to δραμών in v. 20 (*St. Luke,* 378). Linnemann says, "The same gesture of love is again repeated" (*Parables,* 79); cf. Manson, *Sayings,* 289; Jones, *Art,* 202. These sources all see love offered, but fail to appreciate its price.

[234]The imperfect is again used—παρεκάλει. The entreating was a process.

[235]If the older son's problem is the killing of the calf, as Derrett points out, the father is fully in his right in using the *usufruct* of the estate as he sees fit; cf. Mishna *Baba Bathra* viii.7.

[236]In the Johannine story of the woman at the well, the title dramatically disappears when the woman is surprised and irritated; cf. John 4:17. The steward in Luke 16 also fails in his haste to use any titles.

Sa'īd lists the principal characteristics of the older son. First on his list is "His failure to offer the esteem of a son to his father. . . . He has been living in the house with the spirit of a slave, not with the familiarity of a son."[237] The older son's entire perception is warped by this attitude. Giblin writes,

> The older son's complaint thus reflects his judgment that the feast was meant to show what the younger son was worth (as the kid he felt he himself should have received would have been given in payment of what his long-standing services were worth). In reality, the feast was an expression of the father's heartfelt joy.[238]

His attitude is clearly, "I have worked, where is mine?" He reflects the atmosphere of a labor dispute over wages.

3. He has just insulted his father publicly and yet is able to say, "I have never disobeyed your commandment."[239] Sa'īd again writes,

> This is the spirit of the Pharisees by which he (the older son) enters into the ranks of the "ninety-nine who need no repentance"; thus even if he has never disobeyed his father's commandments, yet he has with this action broken the commandment of love.[240]

Sa'īd elaborates on the meaning of the older son's action in a comparison between the two sons. He writes,

> The difference between him and his younger brother was that the younger brother was estranged and rebellious while absent from the house, but the older son was estranged and rebellious in his heart while he was in the house. The estrangement and rebellion of the younger son were evident in his surrender to his passions and in his request to leave his father's house. *The estrangement and rebellion of the older son were evident in his anger and his refusal to enter the house.*[241]

---

[237]Sa'īd, *Lūqā*, 403. Derrett writes, "The ex-prodigal was willing to be a servant, as the elder brother was content to be thought (v. 29)" ("Prodigal Son," 66).

[238]Giblin, "Luke 15," 28. Jones comments, "The older son's obedience has always been based on a misunderstanding" (*Art*, 171).

[239]There is definitely a crowd listening. The Oriental listener/reader gets the distinct feeling that the older son is playing to the gallery. The young boys in the street are all there. The music and dancing will automatically stop the moment the crowd is stunned by the father's act of unexpected love. All the guests wait and listen initially expecting the boy to be punished. What is said will be remembered and retold in the village for literally years.

[240]Sa'īd, *Lūqā*, 402.

[241]*Ibid.*, 403; emphasis mine. Sa'īd is, of course, writing for an Arab reader. There is thus naturally no explanation or elaboration or defense of these points. They are self-evident in Oriental culture. The key word *murtaddan* I have translated "estrangement and rebellion." This forceful word is the Islamic term for a Muslim who has apostatized and left the religion of Islam, and thus on Islamic terms betrayed his family, his country, and his religion. It is the most powerful word Sa'īd could have used in this context. Caird writes, "The elder contrived, without leaving home, to be as far away from his father as ever his brother was in the heathen pigsty" (*St. Luke*, 182).

4. The older son accuses his father of favoritism with the words, "To me you never gave a kid." This sentence is very egocentric. The preposition "to me" stands first in the word order.[242] The older son's complaint includes the contrast, "He gets a calf, I don't even get a goat." This can be read a number of different ways. Derrett thinks it is a false humility. The difficulty with this is that the mood of false humility does not fit the emotion of anger.[243] Assumptions of sarcasm must be rejected.[244] The phrase is better seen as an accusation of favoritism. The older son is saying, "You obviously love this worthless fellow more than you love me. You have given him a calf. I have yet to receive even a goat."[245] Sa'īd writes, "He (the older son) denies all the unmerited favor his father has extended to him. 'You never gave me a kid'; for whom then was the fatted calf?"[246] The accusation of favoritism is unfair.

5. The older son declares that he is not a part of the family. Again Sa'īd is helpful with his Oriental perspective on family relationships and his understanding of the meanings of the phrases used. He writes,

> He [the older son] shows disgust with his father's house. [He says] "that I might make merry with my friends." Thus he is no better than the prodigal son who took his portion and traveled into a far country. The difference between them is that the prodigal son was an "honorable sinner" in that he was perfectly open to his father. He told his father all that was in his heart. But the older brother was a "hypocritical saint" because he hid his feelings in his heart. He re-

---

[242]Goebel, *Parables*, 208. In the Oriental versions only the literal Harclean places the preposition first in the sentence. These versions demonstrate that placing the preposition first is unusual for a Semitic sentence. Goebel, reading it as a Greek sentence, also affirms it to be emphatic. Ibn al-'Assāl, the great medieval Coptic exegete, caught this emphasis in his translation, which reads, *lam tu'ṭini ana.* (The pronoun is suffixed to the verb and then repeated a second time for emphasis.)

[243]Derrett, "Prodigal Son," 70. Derrett writes, "This implies his own abstemiousness in comparison with the younger generally" (*ibid.*). The Mishna characterized the stubborn and rebellious son as one who gorges himself on beef (M. *San.* viii.2; b. *San.* 68–70). If this line of reasoning is followed we would see the older son asserting moral superiority over his brother and implicating his father in having provided the opportunity for the younger "rebellious" son to gorge himself on beef. This is perhaps a bit too complicated.

[244]Sarcasm is a non-Middle Eastern form of speech. There is no equivalent in Arabic; I have tried in vain to explain this particular form of speech to my Arab friends and have failed. Irony is known, but not sarcasm.

[245]This interpretation is supported by the Old Syriac, which adds the word *ḥadd* (you did not give me *one single* kid, etc.). The recent Jesuit translation includes this phrase, as well as the medieval text used for the printing of the Propagandist version. The nineteenth-century Jesuit and the modern Bulusiyya translations add, "And you, you never gave me," which again emphasizes the accusation of favoritism, although in a slightly different way.

[246]Sa'īd, *Lūqā*, 403. The older son is living off his father's usufruct. Every meal is a gift out of the father's bounty. In the last phrase Sa'īd means to say that the calf is killed for the entire family and the entire family gives the feast. The older son is full partner in the feast. He is expected to participate fully. He should be able to "make merry" fully at *this* feast. Linnemann concludes in error that there has been no feasting since the prodigal left. There is no hint of this in the story. The older son is complaining that he has not had a chance for a *special* party alone with his cronies. Linnemann, again in error, calls the "kid" a "lamb" (*Parables*, 79).

mained in the house all the while hating his father. He denies any relationship to his brother, and thereby denies any relationship to his father. He says, "This is your son" rather than saying "my brother." . . . With this statement the older son removed himself from the sacred family and passed judgment of "outcast" upon himself.[247]

Sa'īd states the case in strong yet appropriate language. The older son has removed himself from the fellowship of his family. This is all the more evident when we note that the older brother's friends do not include his brother nor his father nor the family's guests. Emotionally the older brother's community is somewhere else, and he says so.

6.   The older son announces his concept of "joy." For the older son, a good meal with his cronies is an appropriate occasion for joy. The recovery of a brother as from the dead is not.[248] He is not willing to rejoice at this banquet. Give him a goat and, apart from his family, he will rejoice. For the father the calf is a public symbol of the joy that is already present. The older son wants some good meat to create a different kind of "joy." The clear emphasis on joy all through Luke 15 makes these contrasting concepts all the more striking.

7.   The older brother attacks his younger brother. Derrett argues convincingly that the phrase "your living" (when we expect "his living") is really an attempt to say, "He doesn't love you. If he did, he would have preserved his portion to take care of you in your old age. See, he has devoured *your* living with *harlots*."[249] The more obvious insult is the reference to harlots. Sa'īd comments,

> The word "harlots" is not heard in the story itself. He [the older son] volunteers this exaggeration in order to label his brother with this polluted accusation.[250]

There is also the distinct possibility that the older son is attempting to demonstrate that his brother is a rebellious son. If the prodigal can be made to fit this category, then he must be killed, according to the law in Deuteronomy 21:18–21.[251] Thus in summary, the older son's speech is a brilliant picture drawn by contrasting two

---

[247]Sa'īd, *Lūqā*, 403f. Plummer observes that the older son "wants to have his father's property in order that he may enjoy himself *apart from him*" (*St. Luke*, 378; his emphasis).

[248]All through the exegetical tradition of the Oriental churches reflected in their versions there is a very interesting emphasis made in this verse. From Vat. Borg. Ar. 95 and some mss. of the Diatessaron (cf. A. S. Marmardji, *Diatessaron de Tatien* [Beyrouth: Imprimerie Catholique, 1935], 253, n. 291) through to the modern Jesuit version there is the addition of *bihi*, which makes the verse read, "That I might make merry *with it* with my friends." The point is emphasized that the older son's idea of joy is a full stomach.

[249]Derrett, "Prodigal Son," 65. Vat. Borg. Ar. 95 adds another interpretive touch emphasizing the same point. It reads, "Who has eaten your living, *all of it* with harlots," thus stressing the enormity of the younger son's disregard for his continuing moral responsibility to take care of his father in his old age.

[250]Sa'īd, *Lūqā*, 404.

[251]Suggested by Derrett, "Prodigal Son," 56, n. 2. Jeremias thinks αὐτός is here used contemptuously, "This son of yours" (*Parables*, 131). This must be rejected because the same word is used by the father in both v. 24 and v. 32, where obviously no contempt is implied.

stanzas (4 and 4′). We see a son whose attitudes and relationships are sadly perverted and whose only redeeming feature is that he carries out orders.[252]

How will the father respond after this attack on his integrity? As observed in the first half of this parable, when a literary structure inverts there is usually a crucial new feature just past the center, a point of turning, a place of special emphasis. We are not disappointed in this ballad. The father is expected to be furious. Rather there is an outpouring of love. If he orders the son to enter the house and fulfil his duty as a member of the family, the son will certainly obey. But what would be gained? He already has a servant in the person of this young man. He wants a "son." The father bypasses the omission of a title, the bitterness, the arrogance, the insult, the distortion of fact, and the unjust accusations. There is no judgment, no criticism, no rejection, but only an outpouring of love. In striking contrast to the older son, he begins with a title and an affectionate one at that. Rather than υἱός he now uses τέκνον.

This conciliatory word τέκνον is all the more remarkable in light of the agony of rejected love which the father must endure. The offer of unexpected love in a public humiliating act has not produced a humble confession as in the case of the prodigal but rather a calloused arrogance. Sa'īd says of the father's final speech,

> These words come out of a wounded, suffering heart, because the father longed to have his joy complete in that he would be greatly pleased to see his two sons together in his house. But the love that knows no weariness makes a most gracious announcement.[253]

The father's final speech (stanza 3′) is a verbal expression of the "entreating" mentioned in stanza 3.[254] The speech contains at least four major points.

1.   The father's words are an appeal for the son to rejoice in his brother's

---

[252]Amazingly, a small group of modern scholars find the older son's attitudes perfectly natural and reasonable, e.g., Linnemann, *Parables*, 79. Leaney writes, "The elder son's indignation is natural; it is false to the whole spirit of the story to represent him as a monster of hidden selfishness. His father does not rebuke him but reminds them that he is 'always with' him; the relation between them never needed mending (*St. Luke*, 219). Leaney's line of argumentation is clear. He assumes that if the older son had committed gross error he would have been sharply rebuked. But this is specifically not what happened to the prodigal. He did commit gross error. He was not rebuked. The second half of the story is a repeat performance of the first half. Linnemann and Leaney have missed the Oriental culture that is the background of Sa'īd's remarks above. Giblin observes Leaney's comment and affirms that "the elder son's reaction is 'natural'—at least in the sense that it places him with the majority of mankind under similar circumstances" ("Luke 15," 17f.). With Giblin we can agree; the natural man does not understand grace and the gospel any more than the older son did.

[253]Sa'īd is referring in this last sentence to the father's final speech (*Lūqā*, 404). Jer. 3:19b has no connection with the parable but echoes the same sentiment.

[254]The tenses of v. 28 may be significant. It reads, "He came out (aorist) and was entreating him (imperfect)." Manson understands from this that the father was entreating the son and his pleading was interrupted with the son's harsh complaint (*Sayings*, 298). This shift in tenses fits what is happening. However, we have noted places where similar changes of past tenses have not been significant or such an understanding of them appropriate; thus we must be cautious here also.

return. The Greek text is ambiguous. We are not told specifically who is supposed to rejoice. Is the intent "we" should rejoice, or "you" should rejoice? The text simply says, εὐφρανθῆναι δὲ καὶ χαρῆναι ἔδει. Most modern English translations inject their own exegetical understanding into the translation with the addition of "we," thus resolving the ambiguity.[255] The Arabic versions of the last six hundred years agree. However, the earlier versions either leave the text neutral like the Greek or render it "you."[256] The manuscript Vat. Borg. Ar. 95 is especially noteworthy. We observed above that this particular text identified the older son's joy as focused in a full stomach. In this version the debate over the nature of authentic joy is continued in its reading of verse 32, "It is necessary for you that you should rejoice and sing hallelujah (tahallal)." This tells the older son what the focus of his joy should be in contrast to what it is.

It is impossible to be dogmatic regarding the intent of the text. However, with Luther and most of the older Oriental versions, the texts seem to suggest "you" rather than "we." The proximity of "yours" in the preceding phrase and "your" in the following verse supports this translation. In any case, the issue is clear. Is the welcoming of a brother who has not made reparations and has not demonstrated his sincerity an appropriate occasion for great joy or not? Or is joy better found in a good meal with like-minded friends? Giblin writes,

> He should have spontaneously joined in the rejoicing as one who understood how his own father's heart went out (esplagchnisthē, v. 20) to the other son who was, after all, his own brother.[257]

The stories of the Sheep, the Coin, and the Prodigal all have the theme of joy as a climax in or near the center of the story and at the end. Here joy is dramatically missing in both places. We can hardly imagine the father seeking this son in joy. The end is missing. We are not told if the father experiences the joy of finding him. There is no stanza 1'. The story only speaks of a pleading for the joy that is absent.[258]

2.   The father assures the older son that his rights are fully protected even though pure grace has been extended to the prodigal. Manson writes, "The assurance 'all that is mine is thine' is no doubt meant to tell the elder brother that the return of the prodigal does not affect his rights in any degree."[259]

3.   The father subtly points out to his older son that a servant category is inappropriate for their relationship. The son has said, "I have served all these years and have not even received a kid." The father answers, "You are the heir. You own everything already. All that is mine is yours. How can I possibly give you more?" The older son's request is based on a misunderstanding. Giblin writes,

---

[255]So King James, New American Bible, New English Bible, Jerusalem Bible, and the J. B. Phillips translation. The Revised Standard Version maintains the ambiguity.

[256]Outstanding among those which translate the text "you must rejoice" are the Curetonian Old Syriac, the Diatessaron, Vat. Borg. Ar. 95, and Ibn al-'Assāl. Luther has "Du solltest aber fröhlich."

[257]Giblin, "Luke 15," 29.

[258]Giblin finds in this an illustration of inclusio (ibid., 22, n. 23).

[259]Manson, Sayings, 290.

He is told that all the father has is his—that is, he is advised that he is simply not in a position to be paid as though he were a hired man (*misthios*); much less is he expected to work as a slave (*doulos*).[260]

This should have been evident from the father's offer of love in coming out to the older son. No master humiliates himself publicly and leaves a banquet to go out to extend love to an insolent servant. Yet, his I-am-a-servant-where-is-my-pay speech comes *after* the demonstration of love.

At the same time, there is another unhappy aspect to the dialog. On the basis of the Mishnaic legislation discussed above[261] it is instructive to reflect on the direction the conversation is taking.

Older son: "You never gave me a kid."

Father: "All that I have is yours."

Older son: "Yes, but I don't have the right of disposition. I own everything but I still can't slaughter a goat and have a feast with my friends."

Father: "Oh, I see, you also want me gone."

The conversation does not reach this point, but the older son's mind is moving in this direction. He has owned everything since his brother left. He is irritated that he cannot dispose of it at will and host a banquet for his friends. This much he admits openly. From his perspective, starting with the problem he has posed, the obvious solution is *disposition,* which will be his right only after the father dies. His younger brother was granted disposition and had all the banquets he wanted. Why cannot the older son have the same privilege? So the story seems to have come full circle.

4.   The father's speech is neither an apology for the banquet nor a reproach directed against the older brother, but primarily a cry from the heart for an understanding of grace.[262] Very gently, the father reminds the older brother that this is *your* brother—but this hardly categorizes the speech as an attack.[263] On the other hand, I am uneasy with any connotations of the father's "apologizing," which an Oriental father never does to his sons, or even defending what he has done, as if it needed any defense. Rather his speech must be seen as an articulation of the compassionate appeal that has already been extended to the older son in the father's act of going out to him in the presence of the village.

As in the case of the younger son, again the father has no choice. If he punishes the son the answer will be, "Why are you punishing me? I have done nothing!" If he ignores him, the "servant" goes on demanding his own. The visible and verbal appeal of love offers the only hope to the father, who wants not

---

[260]Giblin, "Luke 15," 29.

[261]See pp. 163f.

[262]If the exegete translates "you should rejoice" he usually interprets the text as a reproach, "you ought to be glad; cease your anger." If he translates "we must rejoice" he sees the speech as a defense of joy, "We had to rejoice, don't blame us." Linnemann thinks both are really the same (*Parables,* 79).

[263]Against Sanders, *NTS* 15 (1969), 438.

servants but sons. The younger son was dead and is alive. The older son is likewise dead. Can he come to life?

It is certainly right not to make a one-to-one identification of the Pharisees with the older son and publicans with the younger son. Instead, Jesus is discussing two basic types of men. One is lawless without the law, and the other lawless within the law. Both rebel. Both break the father's heart. Both end up in a far country, one physically, the other spiritually. The same unexpected love is demonstrated in humiliation to each. For both this love is crucial if servants are to become sons.

This last half of the parable clarifies a potential misunderstanding of repentance that could be deduced from the first double parable. Repentance does not quite equal being found. The father goes out and finds both sons. One understands and accepts the status of being found. The other, so far as we know, does not, and remains lost.

The conclusion is missing. There is no stanza 1', as we have observed. Jones feels that this is one of the signs that the parable is truly great art.[264] The chapter begins with the question of eating. It ends with an open invitation for the complainers to join the banquet. Sa'īd writes,

> and it is to be regretted that "the curtain" dropped on this drama with the older son still outside!!! Did the father succeed in convincing him? Or did the older son remain outside to the end? The Pharisees had to give their answer to this question.[265]

The parable engrosses the sensitive listener/reader. Not only the scribes and Pharisees, but each man must decide what his response will be.

The Christological implications of this second section are the same as those of the first section. The father leaves the house in a visible demonstration of unexpected love offered in humiliation. The same implicit Christology "overheard" in the first half of the parable can be found here as well.

Recent scholarship has questioned the unity of the chapter as a whole.[266] Some elements unite the chapter. Both double parables discuss the lost and found, the joy that must be shared, and the subject of repentance. Other elements divide 15:4–10 from 11–32. Each half of the parable of the Lost Sheep and the Lost Coin has an introduction and a conclusion. Luke 15:11–32 lacks both. Furthermore, Luke 15:11–32 is not linked with what precedes by $\mathring{\eta}$, as in the case of the parable of the Lost Coin. The parable of the Prodigal Son begins with $\epsilon\mathring{\iota}\pi\epsilon\nu$ $\delta\acute{\epsilon}$, which parallels verse 3.[267]

---

[264]Jones, *Art*, 168.

[265]Sa'īd, *Lūqā*, 404.

[266]Giblin, "Luke 15," 20; Bultmann, *Tradition*, 328.

[267]Giblin argues that the father does not search for his son ("Luke 15," 20). He sees in this a further divergence between the two units. However, the father does go out in search, not only once but twice. The father does not go into the far country. The reason for this is now clear. Jesus wants to heighten the comparison between the two sons and point up the necessity of the father's going out to each of them in

In addition to these minor linguistic features, the most compelling reason to see these two units of material as redactionally combined is the shift of reference. In the first double parable, Jesus clearly wants the audience to identify with the shepherd and the woman. This is indicated by the question, "Which one of you?"[268] Then in the second double parable the audience is led to identify with the elder son, not the father. The missing conclusion is strong evidence for this. The audience is encouraged to see itself standing there in the person of the older son murmuring against the "sinner" seated at the banquet. The material is perhaps best understood as two units appropriately combined by the Lucan source,[269] or by Luke himself.[270] Each unit is a double parable. Jesus no doubt on many occasions faced Pharisaical complaints against his eating with sinners. Here parables spoken on two such occasions are combined.

Fuchs identifies the banquet at the end of the chapter as "the proleptic celebration of the kingdom of God."[271] To study the relationship between the banquet reported here and the messianic banquet of the end-time would be a study in itself and is beyond the scope of this work.[272] The suggestion is a good one and worthy of much reflection. If this could be substantiated there is little wonder the Pharisees were upset, because Judaism also identified the kingdom of God with a banquet, but for them no "sinners" would be honored guests at such a banquet.

A comparison between the literary structure of the first and the second half of this parable is noteworthy. The climactic center of each is a speech by a son. The first son (in stanzas 6 and 6') knows he is lost and in need. He knows where help can be found. The second son also gives a speech in the center of the literary form (stanzas 4 and 4') but it is a complaint. Unexpected love is demonstrated in response to these central stanzas in each case. The first son descends in stanzas 1–6 and then starts back up in 6'–1'. The older son also descends. In stanzas 1 and 2 he suspiciously inquires about the meaning of this joyous occasion. In 3 he is angry and insults his father. In 4 and 4' we hear two bitter complaints. There is then no return, no response to extended grace, no reversal of the chilling climax of the

---

turn. He achieves this with a unity of place (both meetings between father and son take place in the same approximate vicinity). There is a unity of time (both take place on the same day) and a unity of action (for both, the father must personally leave the house in a humiliating public demonstration of love).

[268]He cannot say, "Which woman of you," because even if there were some women in the audience, such a phrase would be an insult. He is content with "What woman. . . ."

[269]Manson, Sayings, 283.

[270]Bultmann, Tradition, 328.

[271]E. Fuchs, Das Urchristliche Sakramentsverständnis (Schriftenreihe der Kirchlich-Theologische Sozietät in Württemberg, 8 Bad Cannstatt, 1958), 24, 38, as quoted in Linnemann, Parables, 80; Jeremias, Theology, 115f. In reference to v. 2, Giblin writes, "The word prosdechomai is consistently associated in the N. T. with themes like the coming kingdom, redemption, parousia, envoys of and sharers in the 'good news' " ("Luke 15," 16).

[272]Another theme of significance that is beyond the scope of this study is the relationship of the theology of this chapter to the Pauline doctrine of Justification. Godet writes, "How from this parable St. Paul might have extracted the doctrine of Justification by Faith is easy to understand" (St. Luke, 381; cf. also Rengstorf, Re-Investitur, 69).

structure. The first structure is complete and resolves in joy. The second only reaches the father's speech, which is almost identical to each son (cf. A–1' and B–2'). Finally the last note of the parable offers a hint of *inclusio*. At the beginning a living father is wished dead. At the end, a "dead" son is found alive. The similarity of speeches, the similarity of the father's actions, the similarity of insults against the father all make clear that the two sons are presented in the story as being essentially the same. They differ only in their responses to unexpected love.

The Pharisee listening to the telling of the parable is pressed to see himself in the figure of the older son and make the judgment, "I am the man." The ground and content of such a judgment are found in a theological cluster that contains at least five primary themes. These are as follows:

1. Sin.

    The parable portrays two basic types of sinful man and illustrates the nature of their sin and its results.

2. Repentance.

    Two types of repentance are demonstrated. One is the repentance of a man who thinks he can save himself. The other is the repentance of a man who knows he cannot.

3. Grace.

    The parable illustrates the nature of God's freely offered love and tells of its cost. It is a love that seeks and suffers in order to save.

4. Joy.

    Joy is known in finding and in celebrating communally the restoration of the one lost.

5. Sonship.

    One son is restored from death and from servanthood. A second insists on remaining a servant.

None of these can be dealt with in isolation. Each is seen in dynamic tension with the others. Each theme can be reflected upon separately, but to deal with one is to touch on all.

Finally, let us try to summarize all of Luke 15:11–32. A father's younger son requests and receives possession and the right of disposal of his portion of the inheritance. Both the request and the granting of it are exceptional in Eastern life and thought. The prodigal is in a hurry for his father to die. The father is expected to refuse and punish the prodigal. Rather than punish his son, the father grants the request in an unprecedented act of love. The older son refuses to be a reconciler. Both sons fail to try to live together in unity.

The prodigal sells, and leaves, and loses all. He sees his sin as primarily the loss of the money and his ensuing inability to care for his father. Reduced to herding pigs for a gentile and eating bitter wild carob beans, he decides to go back to his village but not to his home. Planning to work as a servant and live in the village, he intends to save himself. He presumably—and with reason—is intensely apprehensive of his initial reception in the village.

On his return, the prodigal is overwhelmed by an unexpected visible demonstration of love in humiliation. He is shattered by the offer of grace, confesses unworthiness, and accepts restoration to sonship in genuine humility. Sin is now a broken relationship which he cannot restore. Repentance is now understood as acceptance of grace and confession of unworthiness. The community rejoices together. The visible demonstration of love in humiliation is seen to have clear overtones of the atoning work of Christ.

The older son then insults his father publicly and demonstrates himself to be as "lost" as his brother was in the far country. The father extends the same love in humiliation, but no confession and repentance result. Rather, the older son launches a bitter tirade against the father. The parable closes with a final appeal for reconciliation. Both sons are seen as rebels needing a visible demonstration of love to win them from servanthood to sonship. Cultural and stylistic considerations make this similarity between the two sons clear. The listening Pharisee is pressed to see himself in the older son and to respond by accepting reconciliation. The major themes of the parable are sin, repentance, grace, joy, and sonship. When studied in the light of the Oriental culture that informs the text, this parable is indeed the *Evangelium in Evangelio*.[273]

---

[273]Arndt, *St. Luke,* 350.

CONCLUSIONS

In summary, it can be said that a new methodology has helped to delineate more precisely the cultural elements that inform the parables. The awareness of these elements has uncovered a new set of questions which have led to a new dimension of perception in parabolic understanding. The discovery of literary types and poetic forms has led to a more accurate division of traditional material into pericopes and a new understanding of the original meaning of the material itself. The parabolic ballad form used in the parables has helped to clarify key elements in the parables studied. The concept of the theological cluster has been discerned, providing a method of perceiving the multiplicity in unity that is the theology of parables. Pericopes previously identified as secondary comments on parables are seen to have their own distinct form, integrity, and subject. A "spilling" phenomenon has been identified where meaning from one pericope has spilled into a second pericope placed beside it by an editor. The spilling has blurred translation and interpretation in both pericopes as the interpreter tries to understand them together. A literary outline has been discovered for Luke 9:51–19:48 which seems to identify the material as a pre-Lucan document.

It is the earnest desire of the present author that this study may provide a stimulus for further research into both culture and literary structure, that more of the dust of the ages might be wiped from the parables of Jesus, and that we might hear, ponder, and respond as did the first audience.

APPENDIX A

A BRIEF DESCRIPTION OF THE ORIENTAL VERSIONS USED IN THIS STUDY

The major Middle Eastern versions are in Syriac, Coptic, and Arabic. Due to my own linguistic limitations, the only Coptic versions used have been those translated into Arabic.

Aside from language, three principles have guided the selection of the texts, namely, time, geography, and type. In regard to time, texts have been selected that stretch from the second or third to the twentieth century. As much geographic spread as possible has been represented. In the matter of type, the texts fall into three categories. Some texts are "church translations." Their translators are unknown. These versions had wide circulation in known Oriental churches and thus reflect the exegetical understanding of those churches as a community. A second category we have called "individual versions." These are the work of known exegetes of some fame in the Oriental Christian world. The third category has been named "Eastern-Western versions." These translations are the work of Oriental churchmen laboring with Western scholars who were resident in the Middle East.

The Church Translations

THE OLD SYRIAC (C. 200)

The Old Syriac is preserved in two mss., the Sinaitic and the Curetonian. Each of these was printed in the nineteenth century.[1]

---

[1]For a full description of all the old Syriac manuscripts, cf. Arthur Vööbus, "The Syriac Versions," in *Early Versions of the New Testament. Papers of the Estonian Theological Society in Exile* (Stockholm: n.p., 1954), VI, 67–132. For a more recent discussion, cf. H. S. Pelser, "The Origin of the Ancient Syriac New Testament Texts— A Historical Study," in *De Fructu Oris Sui. Essays in Honour of Adrianus van Selms,* ed. I. H. Eybers *et al. Pretoria Oriental Series* 9 (Leiden: Brill, 1971), 152–163. Pelser is convinced that the Old Syriac and the Diatessaron both stem from an earlier text tradition. The texts used for this study were R. L. Bensly, J. Rendel Harris, and F. C. Burkitt, *The Four Gospels in*

THE PESHITTA (C. FIFTH CENTURY)

The origin of the Peshitta is shrouded in mystery. Burkitt's long-accepted theory that Rabulla was its author has been exploded by Vööbus.[2] The version became the Syriac vulgate. The antiquity of the version, its popularity, and its gradual emergence from many hands give it unique significance for our exegetical purposes as a church translation. We have used the American Bible Society edition[3] along with Vatican Syriac 269.

VATICAN BORGIANUS ARABIC 71

Vööbus argues convincingly that this version, made in the twelfth century, is translated from the Old Syriac, not the Greek.[4] It enjoyed wide circulation in the Melkite churches of the East,[5] and for this reason we have selected it as one of our "church versions."

THE COPTIC VULGATE (10TH CENTURY)

The oldest copy of this version is at the University of Beirut and is dated 1048. The translation itself was made in the tenth century.[6] This remarkable version was the dominant text for the Coptic Christians for nearly a thousand years. We have used Vatican Coptic 9.

THE PARIS AND LONDON POLYGLOTS (17TH CENTURY)

The Paris Polyglot New Testament was printed in two volumes in Paris in 1630 and 1633. The London Polyglot appeared in 1654–1658. These versions were the first printed Arabic Bibles, and are the Arabic versions quoted in the critical notes of the Kittel Old Testament and the Nestle-Aland New Testament. This Arabic text was reprinted separately in England in 1811. It is this edition that we have used for our study.[7]

Syriac Transcribed from the Sinaitic Palimpsest (Cambridge: University Press, 1894); F. Crawford Burkitt, *Evangelion da-Mepharreshe* (Cambridge: University Press, 1904), 2 vols.; Agnes S. Lewis, *The Old Syriac Gospels* (London: Williams and Norgate, 1910).

[2]Vööbus, *loc. cit.*, 90.

[3]*The New Testament in Syriac* (London: British and Foreign Bible Society, 1905–1920). The Gospels are a reprint of a critical edition of the Peshitta published in 1901 by G. H. Gwilliam (Oxford: Clarendon, 1901). Pelser argues that the Peshitta stems from the third century. Cf. Pelser, *loc. cit.*, 162.

[4]Vööbus, *loc. cit.*, 290; against Ignazio Guidi, "Le Traduzione degli Evangelii in Arabo e in Etiopico," *Reale Accademia dei Lincei* 275 (1888), 6.

[5]Vööbus, *loc. cit.*, 289.

[6]John A. Thompson, "The Origin and Nature of the Chief Printed Arabic Bibles," *The Bible Translator* 6 (January 1955), 10.

[7]*The Holy Bible Containing the Old and New Testaments, in the Arabic Language* (Newcastle-upon-Tyne: Printed by Sarah Hodgson, 1811).

PROPAGANDIST VERSION (17TH CENTURY)

This version was produced by the Roman Catholic Congregatio de Propaganda Fide in Rome. Work began in 1622 and was not completed for fifty years. Competent Syrian church fathers labored over the text, drawing from a wide range of current Eastern manuscripts.[8]

The Individual Versions

THE ARABIC DIATESSARON

The question just how much of the Arabic *Diatessaron* reflects the text of Tatian is not our concern here. The translation to Arabic was most likely done in the early eleventh century by the famous Abu al-Faraj 'Abd Allah Ibn al-Ṭayyib, in Baghdad. This prince of Arab exegetes Graf calls "Philosoph, Arzt, Mönch und Priester in einer Person."[9] Thus we have a version made by an able eleventh-century Arab Christian scholar. For this study we have used the critical edition of Marmardji.[10]

ABU AL-FARAJ 'ABD ALLAH IBN AL-ṬAYYIB (11TH CENTURY)

This same Iraqi scholar is one of the known translators of the Peshitta into Arabic.[11] We have used Vat. Syr. 269 copied in 1368. In a number of cases the Arabic provides an insight into how the Syriac sounded to the ear of the author.[12]

THE HARCLEAN SYRIAC (7TH CENTURY)

This version was probably translated by Thomas Harclean; it is preserved in a magnificent manuscript (Vat. Syr. 268) which may be the autograph.[13]

VATICAN BORGIANUS ARABIC 95 (8TH–9TH CENTURY)

This famous codex is at the head of a group of codices translated from the Greek. It has been argued that the translation is prior to the rise of Islam.[14] Matthew and Mark were described and transcribed by Levin.[15] To my knowledge,

---

[8]For a full description of this version, cf. Thompson, *loc. cit.,* 51–55. This version was reprinted as *Kitāb al-'Ahd al-Jadīd* (London: Charles Watson, 1833).

[9]Georg Graf, *Geschichte der Christlichen Arabischen Literatur. Studi e Testi* 133 (Rome: Citta del Vaticano Biblioteca Apostolica Vaticana, 1947), II, 160.

[10]A. S. Marmardji, *Diatessaron de Tatien* (Beirut: Catholic Press, 1935).

[11]Cf. Graf, *op. cit.,* I, 150.

[12]For further information on this version cf. Louis Cheikho, "Nusakh 'Arabiyah Qadīmah fi al-Sharq min al-Injīl al-Tāhir," *Al Machriq* 4 (1901), 97–109, reprinted in Jūsif Qūshaqjī, *Ta'rīb al-Anajīl wa-A'māl al-Rusul* (Beirut: Catholic Press, 1964), 148–155.

[13]Vööbus, *loc. cit.,* 376. For further information cf. *ibid.,* 118–121. With Vat. Syr. 268 we have used J. White, *Sacrorum evangeliorum versio syriaca philoxeniana* (Oxford: Clarendon, 1778).

[14]Vööbus, *loc. cit.,* 293. Vööbus notes that this position was put forward by Baumstark but rejected by Graf.

[15]Bernhard Levin, *Die Griechisch-Arabische Evangelien-Übersetzung Vat. Borg. ar. 95 und Ber. orient. oct. 1108* (Uppsala: Almquist & Wiksells, 1938).

Luke has never previously been studied. The manuscript of Luke is badly water stained, yet the archaic script is beautiful when clear. The date of the copy used is from the ninth century. Evidently the Mount Sinai monastery is its place of origin. My own judgment is that it is the work of a very perceptive exegetical mind.[16]

HIBAT ALLAH IBN AL-'ASSĀL (13TH CENTURY)

Hibat Allah was one of three famous brothers who lived and wrote in Cairo in the thirteenth century. He produced a *critical* version of the four Gospels with an elaborate system of symbols so that he could record the variants between the Coptic, Greek, and Syriac versions available to him.[17]

The Eastern-Western Versions

THE SHIDIAC VERSION (1851)

This minor version was done by Faris al-Shidiac with the help of Thomas Jerrett of Cambridge.[18]

VAN DYKE–BUSTĀNĪ (1860)[19]

This Protestant version is notable for its simplicity, accuracy, and beauty. It soon became the major Arabic Bible for the masses in the Middle East among Protestants and Orthodox. The story of its translation has been fully told by Thompson.[20]

JESUIT–1 (1878)[21]

Jesuits working in Lebanon produced this version in 1878. Again Eastern and Western scholars labored together. The style is more classical than other versions.[22]

BŪLUSIYAH–FAKHŪRĪ (1954)[23]

This version was the first new Arabic translation effort in the twentieth century. Father George Fakhūrī, a Lebanese monk of the Paulist order, is the sole source of this thoughtful version.

---

[16]For a full introduction cf. Levin, 1–69.

[17]For a full description of this critical system, cf. Duncan B. Macdonald, "The Gospels in Arabic," *The Hartford Seminary Record* 3 (April 1893), 163–176; note esp. pp. 169f.; for a brief review of the three brothers and their works, cf. A. J. B. Higgins, "Ibn al-'Assal," *JTS* 44 (1943), 73–75; D. B. Macdonald, "Ibn al-'Assal," *Encylopedia of Islam* (Leiden: Brill, 1927), II, 364. Macdonald by his own admission had only a brief span of time to look at the manuscript. He failed to discover the extent to which Ibn al-'Assāl gives *variant readings* in terms of the text and not just *variant translations* from versions of his time. Cf. British Museum Oriental Ms. 3382.

[18]*Kitāb al-'Ahd al-Jadīd Lerabbinā Jasū' al-Masīh* (London: SPCK, 1851).

[19]*Kitāb al-'Ahd al-Jadīd* (Beirut: American Press, 1860).

[20]Thompson, *loc. cit.*, 98–105.

[21]*Al-Kitāb al-Muqaddas al-'Ahd al-Jadīd* (Beirut: Jesuit Press, 1878).

[22]Cf. Thompson, *loc. cit.*, 146–49.

[23]*Al-Kitāb al-Muqaddas al-'Ahd al-Jadīd* (Harisa, Lebanon: Paulist Press, 1954).

JESUIT–2 (1969)

The second modern Jesuit version is the work of a French Jesuit, Father Hamawie of the Catholic Press in Beirut,[24] Ustaz Bustānī, a renowned Christian Arabic scholar, and Father Jūsif Qūshaqjī, a trained Syrian exegete of the Jesuit order.

'ABD AL-MALIK–THOMPSON (1973)

John A. Thompson and Butrus 'Abd al-Malik, under the sponsorship of the American Bible Society, have recently finished a new Protestant updating of the Van Dyke–Bustānī version.[25]

Dr. Thompson, a published Old Testament scholar, was for over twenty years professor of Old Testament in the Cairo Evangelical Seminary, Cairo, Egypt. Dr. 'Abd al-Malik was a professor of Oriental languages at the American University in Cairo.

---

[24]*Al-Kitāb al-Muqaddis al-'Ahd al-Jadīd* (Beirut: Catholic Press, 1969).
[25]*Kitāb al-'Ahd al-Jadīd* (Beirut: The Bible Societies in the Near East, 1973).

APPENDIX B

RESOURCE PERSONS

This is a selected, representative list of primary resource people who have, over a twenty-year period, helped the author understand the Middle Eastern culture that informs the parables of Jesus. A full list of resource people would run into the hundreds. My thanks go as well to all my Middle Eastern friends whose names do not appear here.

SUDAN

Wesley Stāsī

Rev. Stāsī is director of the literature program of the Sudan Evangelical Church, Kartoum.

Nathaniel Kur

Mr. Kur is a teacher of English and Religion. He is a member of the Dinka tribe from the South Sudan and a former student at the Near East School of Theology in Beirut, Lebanon. I am indebted to Mr. Kur and other African students who have helped me gain an insight into oral tradition from a people who have preserved centuries of the wisdom of their people exclusively in oral form. Mr. Kur's insights have provided points of contact with and contrast to Middle Eastern cultural points of view.

EGYPT

Adīb Qaldas

Rev. Qaldas is a pastor in the village of Dayr abu Hinnis. Pastor Qaldas' people live in isolation across the Nile River in a community at least 1600 years old. For over a year I was privileged to listen to Pastor Qaldas preach to his own people. Many points of cultural significance assumed by both preacher and congregation were a new point of departure for me.

Fahīm 'Azīz, Ph.D.

Dr. Fahīm was pastor of a small congregation in the south of Egypt for nearly twenty years. He now teaches New Testament at the Cairo Evangelical Seminary in Cairo. He combines a genuine Oriental background with exposure in depth to Western critical studies.

Ḥannā al-Khuḍārī, Ph.D.

Dr. Khuḍārī grew up in the simple village of al-Bayāḍīyyah in the south of Egypt. I was privileged to work with him in the villages of Dayr al-Barshā and al-'Izzīyah. Although his field is Systematic Theology, his own upbringing in simple peasant surroundings has equipped him admirably to help me ask the right questions of the parabolic text.

Ḥāris Quriṣah

For twenty-five years Rev. Ḥāris was pastor of village congregations in the south of Egypt. He is a master at exposition in the peasant home in the context of the traditional pastoral call. Listening to him teach and interact with village people has been a significant source of new insights.

Ibrāhīm Sa'īd, D.D.

Dr. Sa'īd's book on Luke is quoted all through the exegetical section of this study. I have benefited from his commentaries on Luke, John, Ephesians, and Revelation. Because of Dr. Sa'īd's Oriental perspective and keen mind, his books are a rare contribution to our subject.

Rifqī Matūshāliḥ

Rev. Rifqī is a pastor in the village of Dayr al-Barshā where my wife and I were resident for nearly two years. While we were living in the same house with pastor Rifqī, unnumbered conversations became opportunities for him to interpret to us what was happening around us. We could witness a given event in village life and understand the language spoken. Pastor Rifqī told us what both meant.

Ṣamū'īl Ḥabīb

Rev. Ḥabīb is director of the Coptic Evangelical Society for Social Services. With his keen research-oriented mind, Pastor Ṣamū'īl has been a crucial source of authentic and reliable information.

Shaykh Mus'ad

Elder Mus'ad is a patriarch of the village of Dayr al-Barshā. He is an Oriental patriarch with the stature, dignity, and wisdom of the classical sage, and is one of the most eminent Oriental wise men I have been privileged to know. His indirect contribution to this study is immeasurable.

The People of Dayr al-Barshā

In their midst I saw an isolated Oriental village live and move and have its being. After two years residence, contacts were maintained, and our perception and awareness of Oriental life were significantly deepened by this living community.

LEBANON, SYRIA, PALESTINE[1]

The People of 'Almā al-sha'b

This village lies on the southern border of Lebanon, and its people have

---

[1]The unity of culture across these three areas makes it appropriate to treat key resource people from these three countries as a group.

extended to me a warm welcome. Conversations with shepherds, farmers, merchants, and teachers have answered many questions.

Ibrāhīm Dāghir

Rev. Dāghir served as a pastor in churches in southern Lebanon for thirty-five years. Now in his seventies, he has taught me more of Lebanese-Syrian culture than any other single person. His own boyhood in an isolated village above Sidon, his long service on the slopes of Mount Hermon, and his lifetime reflection on the Scriptures have made him a mine of information on Oriental life and how it influences the meaning of the text.

Samū'īl Ḥannā

Mr. Ḥannā is a theological student from the village of 'Ayn al-Sha'rah. This village is situated on the eastern slopes of Mount Hermon, not far from the villages where Aramaic is still spoken. Since there are no roads to the village, life there has kept its ancient flavor. Samū'īl's opinions have been given due consideration.

Jabrā Ḥelū

As a guest in Pastor Ḥelū's home in the village of Minyāra, Lebanon, I was privileged to spend many long and pleasant evenings listening to the retelling of the oral tradition of the Helu family and the Syrian people.

Riyāḍ Jarjūr

Mr. Jarjūr of Syria is a student at the Near East School of Theology. Nuhād (below), Riyāḍ, and Samū'īl are only examples of the Syrian and Lebanese students from whom I have learned so much.

Nabīl Jabbūr

Mr. Jabbūr, of Syria, has taken it upon himself to ask the Oriental question and see what it means for the text.

Qayṣar Ma'lūf

Mr. Ma'lūf is a farmer and pastor in villages on the slopes of Mount Lebanon. As a guest in Mr. Ma'lūf's pulpit and home in Khirbit Qanafār, I was able to learn far more than I could teach.

Nuhād Ibrāhīm

Nuhād, a student at the Near East School of Theology, has carried his own research questions back to his village and family and has contributed significantly to the gradual growth of this study.

Butruṣ Talyā

Mr. Talyā, a former resident of al-Jazīrah, Syria, wandered for two years as a shepherd while living with his family in an all-Christian village in upper Syria. Thus, in his youth he was in contact with ancient cultural forms of community life. Himself a trained biblical scholar, Mr. Talyā's help has been significant.

IRAQ

As in the case of textual criticism, it is not the weight of numbers but other factors that determine the significance of a given witness. My only resource person in Iraq has been Mr. *Jūsif Mattā* of Mosul and Baghdad. Mr. Mattā is from a village of northern Iraq. He spent nine years in a Syriac Orthodox monastery in preparation for the priesthood, but then became a Protestant. His knowledge of Syriac and his long-term exposure to village and ecclesiastical life in northern Iraq make him a vital resource person for this study.

IRAN

Because of its distance and the fact that a cultural and linguistic line is crossed once one moves from Iraq to Iran, resource people have not been sought in Iran. However, the unique background and ministry of *Viken Galoustian* has made it imperative that his insights be allowed to contribute to our search for cultural factors in biblical literature. Rev. Galoustian was for many years the pastor of a unique congregation in Teheran composed of roughly half Muslim converts and half Jewish converts. The questions that arose out of his ministry and some of the answers he found to those questions have proven significant as one more piece in a cultural puzzle.

SELECT BIBLIOGRAPHY

A. GENERAL

Beare, F. W., "Concerning Jesus of Nazareth," *JBL* 87 (1968), 125–135.

———. *The Earliest Records of Jesus*. New York: Abingdon, 1962.

Bornkamm, Gunther. *Jesus of Nazareth*. Translated by Irene and Fraser McLuskey with James M. Robinson from the 3rd German edition. New York: Harper, 1960.

Bultmann, Rudolf. *The History of the Synoptic Tradition*. Translated from the German by John Marsh. Revised Edition. New York: Harper, 1963.

———. *Theology of the New Testament*. 2 vols. Translated from the German by Kendrick Grobel. London: SCM, 1955.

Conzelmann, Hans. *An Outline of the Theology of the New Testament*. Translated from the German by John Bowden. New York: Harper, 1969.

Daube, David. *The New Testament and Rabbinic Judaism*. London: University of London, 1956.

———. *Studies in Biblical Law*. Cambridge: University Press, 1947.

Derrett, J. Duncan M. *Law in the New Testament*. London: Darton, Longman and Todd, 1970.

Fuchs, Ernst, "Studies of the Historical Jesus," *Studies in Biblical Theology*, No. 42. Translated from the German by Andrew Scobie. London: SCM, 1964.

Jeremias, Joachim. *New Testament Theology*. New York: Scribner, 1971.

———. *The Problem of the Historical Jesus*. Translated from the German by Norman Perrin. Philadelphia: Fortress, 1964.

Jülicher, Adolf. *Itala Das Neue Testament in Altlateinischer überlieferung*, III. *Lucas Evangelium*. Berlin: de Gruyter, 1954.

Nicholson, R. A. *A Literary History of the Arabs*. Cambridge: University Press, 1962.

O'Leary, de Lacy E. *Comparative Grammar of the Semitic Languages*. London: Kegan Paul, Trench, Trubner, 1923.

Taylor, Vincent, *The Formation of the Gospel Tradition*. London: Macmillan, 1935.

Wright, William. *Lectures on the Comparative Grammar of the Semitic Languages*. 2nd edition. Amsterdam: Philo, 1966.

B. THE ORIENTAL VERSIONS

Bensly, Robert L., J. Rendel Harris, and F. Crawford Burkitt, editors. *The Four Gospels in Syriac Transcribed from the Sinaitic Palimpsest*. Cambridge: University Press, 1894.

Burkitt, F. C. *Evangelion da-Mepharreshe*. 2 vols. Cambridge: University Press, 1904.

Cureton, W. C. *Remains of a Very Ancient Recension of the Four Gospels in Syriac*. London: J. Murray, 1858.

Darlow, T. H., and H. F. Moule. *Polyglots and Languages Other Than English*. Vol. II in *Historical Catalogue of the Printed Editions of Holy Scripture in the Library of the British and Foreign Bible Society*. New York: Kraus Reprint, 1964.

Graf, Georg. *Geschichte der Christlichen Arabischen Literatur*. Vol. I. Vatican City: Biblioteca Apostolica Vaticana, 1944.

————. *Verzeichnis arabischer kirchlicher Termini*. Louvain: L. Durbecq, 1954.

Guidi, Ignazio, "Le traduzioni degli Evangelii in Arabo e in Etiopico," *Atti della Reale Accademia dei Lincei,* anno cclxxv [1888]. Pp. 5–37.

Guillaume, Alfred, "The Version of the Gospels Used in Medina circa A.D. 700," *Al-Andalus* 15 (1950), 289–296.

Higgins, A. J. B., "The Arabic Version of Tatian's Diatessaron," *JTS* 45 (1944), 187–199.

————, "Ibn al-'Assal," *JTS* 44 (1943), 73–75.

————, "The Persian and Arabic Gospel Harmonies," *Studia Evangelica,* I. Edited by Kurt Aland *et al*. Berlin: Akademie-Verlag, 1959. Pp. 793–810.

Hill, J. H. *The Earliest Life of Christ*. 2nd edition. Edinburgh: T. & T. Clark, 1910.

The Holy Bible containing the Old and New Testaments in the Arabic Language. Newcastle-upon-Tyne: Sarah Hodgson, 1811.

Hyatt, J. P., "Recent Contributions to the Study of the Ancient Versions of the New Testament,"*The Bible in Modern Scholarship*. Edited by J. P. Hyatt, Nashville: Abingdon, 1965. Pp. 357–369.

de Lagarde, Paul, editor. *Die Vier Evangelien arabisch*. Leipzig: F. A. Brockhaus, 1864.

Levin, Bernhard. *Die Griechisch-Arabische Evangelien-Übersetzung Vat.Borg. ar. 95 und Ber. orient oct. 1108*. Uppsala: Almquist & Wiksells, 1938.

Lewis, Agnes S., and Margaret D. Gibson. *The Palestinian Syriac Lectionary of the Gospels*. London: n.p., 1899.

Macdonald, Duncan B., "The Gospels in Arabic," *Hartford Seminary Record* 3 (April 1893), 163–176.

Metzger, Bruce M., "A Survey of Recent Research on the Ancient Versions of the New Testament," *NTS* 2 (1955/56), 1–16.

The New Testament in Syriac. London: British and Foreign Bible Society, 1905–1920, 1950.

Pelser, H. S., "The Origin of the Ancient Syriac New Testament Texts— A Historical Study," *De Fructu Oris Sui. Essays in Honour of Adrianus van Selms.* Edited by I. H. Eybers *et al. Pretoria Oriental Series* 9. Leiden: Brill, 1971. Pp. 152–163.

Pusey, P. E., and G. H. Gwilliam. *Teraevangelium Sanctum Iuxta Simplicem Syrorum Versionem ad fidem Codicum.* Oxford, Clarendon, 1901.

Qūshaqjī, Jūsif. *Ta'rīb al-Anajīl wa-A'māl al-Rusul.* Beirut: Catholic Press, 1964.

Vööbus, Arthur. *Early Versions of the New Testament. Papers of the Estonian Theological Society in Exile,* VI. Stockholm: n.p., 1954.

———. *Studies in the History of the Gospel Text in Syriac. Corpus Christianorum Orientalium Subsidia Tome III,* CXXVIII. Louvain: L. Durbecq, 1951.

White, J. *Sacrorum Evangeliorum Versio Syriaca Philoxeniana.* Oxford: n.p., 1778.

Wright, William. *A Short History of Syriac Literature.* Amsterdam: Philo, 1966 [1894].

C. THE MODERN MIDDLE EASTERN PEASANT CULTURE AND THE PARABLES

Bishop, E. F. F. *Apostles of Palestine.* London: Lutterworth, 1958.

———. *Jesus of Palestine.* London: Lutterworth, 1955.

———, "Local-Colour in Proto-Luke," *ExpT* 45 (1933/34), 151–56.

———. *Prophets of Palestine.* London: Lutterworth, 1962.

Dalman, G. H. *Arbeit und Sitte in Palästina.* 7 vols. Gütersloh: Bertelsmann, 1928–1942.

———. *Sacred Sites and Ways.* Translated from the German by Paul P. Levertoff. London: SPCK, 1935.

Grant, Elihu. *The Peasantry of Palestine: The Life, Manners and Customs of the Village.* Boston: Pilgrim Press, 1907.

Hanauer, James. *The Folklore of the Holy Land.* London: Duckworth, 1907.

Jeremias, Joachim. *Jerusalem in the Time of Jesus.* 3rd edition. Translated from the German by F. H. and C. H. Cave. Philadelphia: Fortress, 1969.

Levison, N. *The Parables: Their Background and Local Setting.* Edinburgh: T. & T. Clark, 1926.

Masterman, Ernest William Garney, *Studies in Galilee.* Chicago: University of Chicago Press, 1909.

Neil, James. *Everyday Life in the Holy Land.* London: SPCK, 1924.

Newton, F. E. *Fifty Years in Palestine.* London: Coldharbour Press, 1948.

Rihbany, A. M. *The Syrian Christ.* Boston: Houghton Mifflin, 1916.

Scherer, George H. *The Eastern Colour of the Bible*. London: National Sunday School Union, 1929.

Thomson, W. M. *The Land and the Book*. 2 vols. New York: Harper, 1871.

Wilson, Charles Thomas. *Peasant Life in the Holy Land*. London: John Murray, 1906.

D. THE ANCIENT JEWISH AND ARAMAIC BACKGROUND TO THE PARABLES

Billerbeck, P., and H. Strack. *Kommentar zum Neuen Testament aus Talmud und Midrasch*. 6 vols. 2nd edition. Munich: C. H. Beck, 1924.

Black, Matthew. *An Aramaic Approach to the Gospels and Acts*. 3rd edition. Oxford: Clarendon, 1967.

————, "The Recovery of the Language of Jesus," *NTS* 3 (1957), 305–313.

Crockett, L. C., "The Old Testament in the Gospel of Luke with Emphasis on the Interpretation of Isaiah 61:1–2." Unpublished Ph.D. Thesis, Brown University, Providence, R.I., 1966.

Dalman, Gustaf. *The Words of Jesus*. Translated from the German by D. M. Kay. Edinburgh: T. & T. Clark, 1902.

Dalman, G. H. *Jesus-Joshua; Studies in the Gospels*. Translated from the German by Paul P. Levertoff. New York: Macmillan, 1929.

Edersheim, Alfred. *The Life and Times of Jesus the Messiah*. 2 vols. 2nd edition. London: Longmans, Green, 1883.

————. *Sketches of Jewish Social Life in the Days of Christ*. New York: Hodder and Stoughton, n.d.

Epstein, I., editor. *The Babylonian Talmud*. 35 vols. London: Soncino, 1935–1960.

Falk, Z. W. *Hebrew Law in Biblical Times*. Jerusalem: Wahrmann Books, 1964.

Feldman, Asher. *The Parables and Similes of the Rabbis*. Cambridge: University Press, 1924, 2nd ed. 1927.

Fiebig, Paul W. J. *Altjüdische Gleichnisse und die Gleichnisse Jesu*. Tübingen: J. C. B. Mohr, 1904.

————. *Die Gleichnisreden Jesu im Lichte der rabbinischen Gleichnisse des neutestamentlichen Zeitalters*. Tübingen: J. C. B. Mohr, 1912.

Goldschmidt, Lazarus, editor. *Der Babylonische Talmud*. 11 vols. Haag: Martinus Nijhoff, 1933.

Heinemann, Joseph H., "The Status of the Laborer in Jewish Law and Society in the Tannaitic Period," *HUCA* 25 (1954), 263–325.

Horowitz, George. *The Spirit of Jewish Law*. New York: Central Book, 1953.

The Mishnah. Translated from the Hebrew by Herbert Danby with Introduction and Brief Explanatory Notes. 7 vols. London: Oxford, 1950.

Mishnayoth. 7 vols. Translated and edited by Philip Blackman. London: Mishna Press, 1954.

Montefiore, C. J. G. *Rabbinic Literature and Gospel Teaching*. London: Macmillan, 1930.

———. *The Synoptic Gospels*. 3 vols. 2nd edition. London: Macmillan, 1927.

Moore, George F. *Judaism in the First Centuries of the Christian Era, the Age of the Tannaim*. 2 vols. Cambridge: Harvard, 1927.

Oesterley, W. O. E. *The Gospel Parables in the Light of Their Jewish Background*. London: SPCK, 1936.

Seale, Morris S. *The Desert Bible. Nomadic Tribal Culture and Old Testament Interpretation*. London: Weidenfeld and Nicolson, 1974.

Smith, Morton, *Tannaitic Parallels to the Gospels*. Vol. VI of *JBL Monograph Series*. Philadelphia: Society of Biblical Literature, 1951.

Stewart, Roy A., "The Parable Form in the Old Testament and the Rabbinic Literature," *Evangelical Quarterly* 36 (1964), 133–147.

Torrey, Charles C. *Our Translated Gospels*. New York: Harper, 1936.

Yaron, R. *Gifts in Contemplation of Death in Jewish and Roman Law*. Oxford: Clarendon, 1960.

E. GENERAL STUDIES ON LUKE

Arndt, William F. *The Gospel According to St. Luke*. St. Louis: Concordia, 1956.

Bengel, Johann A. *Gnomon of the New Testament*. Translated from the Latin by C. T. Lewis and M. R. Vincent. 2 vols. New York: Sheldon, 1862 (1742).

Cadbury, Henry J. *The Making of Luke-Acts*. London: SPCK, 1958.

Caird, G. B. *The Gospel of St. Luke*. Baltimore: Penguin, 1963.

Conzelmann, Hans. *The Theology of St. Luke*. Translated from the German by Geoffrey Buswell. New York: Harper, 1961.

Creed, John Martin. *The Gospel According to St. Luke*. London: St. Martin, 1930; Macmillan, 1965.

Davies, J. H., "The Purpose of the Central Section of Luke's Gospel," *Studia Evangelica*, II. Edited by F. L. Cross. Berlin: Akademie-Verlag, 1963. Pp. 164–69.

Dillersberger, Josef. *The Gospel of Saint Luke*. Translated from the German. Westminster, Md.: Newman, 1958.

Ellis, E. Earle. *The Gospel of Luke*. London: Thomas Nelson, 1966.

Evans, C. F., "The Central Section of St. Luke's Gospel," *Studies in the Gospels Essays in Memory of R. H. Lightfoot*. Edited by D. E. Nineham. Oxford: Blackwell, 1957. Pp. 37–53.

Farmer, W. R., "Notes on a Literary and Form-Critical Analysis of Some of the Synoptic Materials Peculiar to Luke," *NTS* 8 (1962), 301–316.

Geldenhuys, Norval. *Commentary on the Gospel of Luke*. Grand Rapids: Eerdmans, 1951.

Gollwitzer, Helmut. *Die Freude Gottes, Einführung in das Lukasevangelium*. Berlin-Dahlem: Burckhardthaus-Verlag, 1952.

Goulder, M. D., "The Chiastic Structure of the Lucan Journey," *Studia Evangelica*, II. Edited by F. L. Cross. Berlin: Akademie-Verlag, 1963. Pp. 195–202.

Hull, William E., "A Structural Analysis of the Gospel of Luke," *Review and Expositor* 64 (1967), 421–25.

Lampe, G. W. H., "The Lucan Portrait of Christ," *NTS* 2 (1956), 160–195.

Leaney, Alfred R. C. *A Commentary on the Gospel According to St. Luke*. 2nd edition. Black's New Testament Commentaries. London: A. & C. Black, 1958.

Manson, William. *The Gospel of Luke. The Moffatt New Testament Commentary*, III. New York: Harper, n.d.

Miller, Donald G. *The Gospel According to Luke*. Richmond: John Knox, 1959.

Ogg, G., "The Central Section of the Gospel According to St. Luke," *NTS* 18 (1971), 39–53.

Plummer, Alfred. *The Gospel According to St. Luke. International Critical Commentary*, XXVII. Edited by C. A. Briggs *et al.* New York: Scribner, 1906.

Reicke, Bo, "Instruction and Discussion in the Travel Narrative," *Studia Evangelica*, I. Edited by Kurt Aland *et al.* Berlin: Akademie-Verlag, 1959. Pp. 206–216.

Rengstorf, Karl Heinrich. *Das Evangelium nach Lukas. Das Neue Testament Deutsch*, V. Edited by Paul Althaus and Johannes Behm. Neubearbeitete Auflage. Göttingen: Vandenhoeck & Ruprecht, 1949.

Robinson, W. C., Jr., "The Theological Context for Interpreting Luke's Travel Narrative (9.51 ff.)," *JBL* 79 (1960), 20–31.

Sa'īd, Ibrāhīm. *Sharḥ Bishārat Lūqā*. Beirut: Near East Council of Churches, 1970.

Schlatter, Adolf von. *Das Evangelium des Lukas. Aus seinen Quellen erklärt*. Stuttgart: Calwer Verlag, 1960.

Schneider, J., "Zur Analyse des Lukanischen Reiseberichtes," *Synoptische Studien. Alfred Wikenhauser zum siebzigsten Geburtstag*. Munich: K. Zink, 1953. Pp. 207–229.

Stagg, Frank, "The Journey Toward Jerusalem in Luke's Gospel," *Review and Expositor* 64 (1967), 499–512.

Talbert, Charles H., "The Redactional Critical Quest for Luke the Theologian," *Pittsburgh Perspective* 11 (1970), 171–222.

F. POETICAL AND LITERARY ANALYSIS

Albright, William F., "A Catalogue of Early Hebrew Lyric Poems (Psalm 63)," *HUCA* 23 (1950/51), 1–19.

————, "The Earliest Forms of Hebrew Verse," *Journal of the Palestine Oriental Society* 2 (1922), 69–86.

Bertram, Stephen, "Symmetrical Design in the Book of Ruth," *JBL* 84 (1965), 165–68.

Bligh, John. *Galatians in Greek, A Structural Analysis of St. Paul's Epistle to the Galatians*. Detroit: University of Detroit Press, 1966.

Boling, Robert G., " 'Synonymous' Parallelism in the Psalms," *JSS* 5 (1960), 221–255.

Brown, Raymond. *The Gospel According to John*. 2 vols. *The Anchor Bible*. New York: Doubleday, 1966. Cf. cxxxv–cxxxvii, 267, 597, 667, 728, 859, 911.

Burney, C. F. *The Poetry of Our Lord*. Oxford: Clarendon, 1925.

Cross, F. M., and D. N. Freedman, "Studies in Ancient Yahwistic Poetry." Unpublished Ph.D. Thesis, Johns Hopkins University, Baltimore, 1950.

Curtis, William H., "His Form and Method of Teaching," *Jesus Christ the Teacher*. London: Oxford, 1943. Cf. pp. 66–82.

Dewey, J., "The Literary Structure of the Controversy Stories in Mark 2:1–3:6," *JBL* 92 (1973), 394–401.

Dupont, L., *et al.*, "Recherche sur la structure de Jean 20," *Biblica* 54 (1973), 482–498.

Ehlen, A. J., "The Poetic Structure of a Hodayat from Qumran." Unpublished Ph.D. Thesis, Harvard Divinity School, Harvard University, Cambridge, Mass., 1970.

Fenton, J. C., "Inclusio and Chiasmus in Matthew," *Studia Evangelica*, I. Edited by Kurt Aland *et al*. Berlin: Akademie-Verlag, 1959. Pp. 174–79.

Fitzgerald, A., "Hebrew Poetry," *The Jerome Biblical Commentary*. Edited by R. E. Brown *et al*. Englewood Cliffs, N.J.: Prentice-Hall, 1968. Pp. 238–244.

Forbes, John. *The Symmetrical Structure of Scripture*. Edinburgh: T. & T. Clark, 1854.

Freedman, D. N., "Prolegomenon" to G. B. Gray, *The Forms of Hebrew Poetry*. New York: Ktav, 1972. Pp. vii–liii.

————, "Archaic Forms in Early Hebrew Poetry," *Zeitschrift für die alttestamentliche Wissenschaft* 72 (1960), 101–107.

Goulder, M. D., "The Chiastic Structure of the Lucan Journey," *Studia Evangelica*, 11. Edited by F. L. Cross. Berlin: Akademie-Verlag, 1963. Pp. 195–202.

Gray, G. B. *The Forms of Hebrew Poetry*. New York: Ktav, 1972 (1915).

Grobel, Kendrick, "A Chiastic Retribution Formula in Romans 2," *Zeit und Geschichte*. Dankesgabe an Rudolf Bultmann zum 80. Geburtstag. Herausgegeben von Erich Dinkler. Tübingen: J. C. B. Mohr, 1964. Pp. 255–261.

Holladay, W. L., "Chiasmus, the Key to Hosea 12:3–6," *Vetus Testamentum* 16 (1966), 53–64.

————, "The Recovery of Poetic Passages of Jeremiah," *JBL* 85 (1966), 401–435.

Jebb, John. *Sacred Literature*. London: n.p., 1820.

Jeremias, J., "Chiasmus in den Paulusbriefen," *Abba*. Göttingen: Vandenhoeck & Ruprecht, 1966. Pp. 276–289.

Kosmala, Hans, "Form and Structure in Ancient Hebrew Poetry (a New Approach)," *Vetus Testamentum* 14 (1964), 423–445; 16 (1966), 152–160.

Kraft, Charles F., "Poetic Structure of the Qumran Thanksgiving Psalms," *Biblical Research* 2 (1957), 1–18.

———. *The Strophic Structure of Hebrew Poetry*. Chicago: University of Chicago Press, 1938.

Leon-Dufour, Xavier, "Trois Chiasmus Johanniques," *NTS* 7 (1961), 249–255.

Lohfink, Norbert. *Das Hauptgebot: Eine Untersuchung literarischer Einleitungstragen zu Dtn 5–11*. Rome: Pontifical Biblical Institute, 1963.

Lohr, C. H., "Oral Techniques in Matthew's Gospel," *CBQ* 23 (1961), 403–435.

Louw, J. P., "Discourse Analysis and the Greek New Testament," *The Bible Translator* 24 (1973), 101–118.

Lund, N. W. *Chiasmus in the New Testament*. Chapel Hill: University of North Carolina Press, 1942.

Malatesta, E., "The Literary Structure of John 17," *Biblica* 52 (1971), 67–78, 190–214.

Manson, T. W., "Poetic Form," *The Teaching of Jesus*. 2nd edition. Cambridge: University Press, 1935. Pp. 50–56.

Miesner, D. R., "Chiasm and the Composition and Message of Paul's Missionary Sermons." Unpublished Th.D. Thesis, Concordia Seminary in Exile, 306 North Grand, St. Louis, 1974.

Mowry, Lucetta M., "Poetry in the Synoptic Gospels and Revelation, a Study of Methods and Materials." Unpublished Ph.D. Thesis, Yale University, New Haven, 1946.

Robinson, D. W. B., "The Literary Structure of Hebrews 1:1–4," *Australian Journal of Biblical Archeology* 2 (1972), 178–186.

Robinson, T. H. *The Poetry of the Old Testament*. London: Oxford, 1947.

Schnackenburg, R., "Strukturanalyse von John 17," *Biblische Zeitschrift* N.F. 17 (1973), 196–202.

Schnider, F., and W. Stenger, "Beobachtungen zur Struktur der Emmausperikope (Lu 24:13–35)," *Biblische Zeitschrift* N.F. 16 (1972), 94–114.

Schubert, Paul, "The Structure and Significance of Luke 24," *Neutestamentliche Studien für Rudolf Bultmann*. Edited by Walter Eltester. Berlin: A. Töpelmann, 1954. Pp. 163–184.

Sider, R. D., "On Symmetrical Composition in Tertullian," *JTS* N.S. 24 (1973), 405–423.

Streeter, B. H., "Poems of Jesus," *The Hibbert Journal* 32 (1933/34), 9–16.

Talbert, C. H., "Artistry and Theology. An Analysis of the Architecture of Jn. 1,19–5,48," *CBQ* 32 (1970), 341–366.

Taylor, Vincent, "Sayings and Parables," *The Formation of the Gospel Tradition*. London: Macmillan, 1935. Pp. 88–118.

Thiering, Barbara, "The Poetic Forms of the Hodayoth," *JSS* 8 (1963), 189–209.

Torrey, C. C., "Metric Forms and Details," *The Second Isaiah*. Edinburgh: T. & T. Clark, 1928. Pp. 151–172.

Wilder, Amos, "The Poem," *Early Christian Rhetoric*. Cambridge: Harvard, 1971. Pp. 89–117.

Vanhoye, Albert. *A Structured Translation of the Epistle to the Hebrews*. Translated from the Greek and the French by James Swetnam. Rome: Pontifical Biblical Institute, 1964.

G. PARABOLIC HERMENEUTICS

Achtemeier, Paul J. *An Introduction to the New Hermeneutic*. Philadelphia: Westminster, 1969.

Barr, Allan, "The Interpretation of the Parables," *ExpT* 53 (1941/42), 20–25.

Black, Matthew, "The Parables as Allegory," *BJRL* 42 (1960), 273–287.

Brown, Raymond E., "Parable and Allegory Reconsidered," *Novum Testamentum* 5 (1962), 36–45.

Dodd, C. H., "The Gospel Parables," *BJRL* 16 (1932), 396–412.

Eaton, David, "Professor Jülicher on the Parables of Jesus," *ExpT* 10 (1898/99), 539–543.

Fuchs, Ernst, "Proclamation and Speech-Event," *Theology Today* 19 (1962), 341–354.

Hunter, Archibald M., "The Interpretation of the Parables," *Teaching and Preaching the New Testament*. Philadelphia: Westminster, 1963. Pp. 51–58.

––––––, "The Interpreter and the Parables," *Interpretation* 14 (1960), 70–84, 167–185, 315–332, 440–454.

––––––. *Interpreting the Parables*. London: SCM, 1964.

Marty, Martin E., "The Purpose of the Parables According to Mk. 4:10–12." Unpublished Bachelor's Thesis, Concordia Seminary, St. Louis, 1952.

Manson, W., "The Purpose of the Parables: A Re-examination of St. Mark 4:10–12," *ExpT* 68 (1957), 132–35.

Perrin, Norman, "The Modern Interpretation of the Parables of Jesus and the Problem of Hermeneutics," *Interpretation* 25 (1971), 131–148.

Piper, Otto A., "The Understanding of the Synoptic Parables," *Evangelical Quarterly* 14 (1942), 42–53.

Smart, James D., "A Redefinition of Jesus' Use of the Parables," *ExpT* 47 (1935/36), 551–55.

Vincent, J. J., "The Parables of Jesus as Self-Revelation," *Studia Evangelica*, II. Edited by F. L. Cross. Berlin: Akademie-Verlag, 1959. Pp. 74–99.

H. GENERAL STUDIES ON PARABLES

Barry, Colman, "The Literary and Artistic Beauty of Christ's Parables," *CBQ* 10 (1948), 376–383.

Beardslee, William A., "The Wisdom Tradition and the Synoptic Gospels," *Journal of the American Academy of Religion* 35 (1967), 232–240.

Brown, R. E. *The Parables of the Gospels*. New York: Paulist Press Doctrinal Pamphlet, 1963.

————, "Parables of Jesus," *The New Catholic Encyclopedia*, X. Edited by The Catholic University of America. New York: McGraw-Hill, 1967. Pp. 984–88.

Bruce, Alexander Balmain. *The Parabolic Teaching of Christ*. 3rd revised edition. New York: A. C. Armstrong, 1890.

Bugge, C. A. *Die Haupt-Parabeln Jesu*. Giessen: J. Ricker, 1903.

Cadoux, A. T. *The Parables of Jesus: Their Art and Use*. London: James Clarke, n.d.

Cantinat, Jean, "The Parables of Mercy," *Contemporary New Testament Studies*. Edited by M. Rosalie Ryan. Collegeville, Minn: Liturgical Press, 1965. Pp. 213–228.

Crossan, John D. *In Parables*. New York: Harper, 1973.

Dodd, C. H. *The Parables of the Kingdom*. Revised edition. London: Nisbet, 1961.

Findlay, J. A. *Jesus and His Parables*. London: Epworth, 1951.

Fonck, Leopold. *The Parables of the Gospel*. Translated from the 3rd German edition by E. Leahy. New York & Cincinnati: Frederick Pustet, 1914.

Funk, Robert W., "The Parables: A Fragmentary Agenda," *Jesus and Man's Hope*, II. Edited by Donald G. Miller and Dikran Y. Hadidian. Pittsburgh: A Perspective Book, Pittsburgh Theological Seminary, 1971. Pp. 287–304.

Goebel, Siegfried. *The Parables of Jesus: a Methodological Exposition*. Translated from the German by Professor Banks. Edinburgh: T. & T. Clark, 1883.

Jeremias, Joachim. *The Parables of Jesus*. Revised edition. Translated from the 6th German edition by S. H. Hooke. London: SCM, 1963.

Jones, Geraint Vaughan. *The Art and Truth of the Parables: A Study in Their Literary Form and Modern Interpretation*. London: SPCK, 1964.

Jülicher, Adolf. *Die Gleichnisreden Jesu*. 2 vols. Tübingen: J. C. B. Mohr, 1910.

Ladd, George Eldon, "The Life-Setting of the Parables of the Kingdom," *Journal of Bible and Religion* 31 (1963), 193–99.

Linnemann, E. *Jesus of the Parables*. Translated from the German by John Sturdy. New York: Harper, 1966.

Lithgow, R. M. *The Parabolic Gospel*. Edinburgh: T. & T. Clark, 1914.

Manson, T. W. *The Sayings of Jesus*. London: SCM, 1937, 1961.

————. *The Teaching of Jesus*. 2nd edition. Cambridge: University Press, 1935.

Martin, Hugh. *The Parables of the Gospels and their Meaning for Today*. London: SCM, 1937.

Michaelis, W. *Die Gleichnisse Jesu*. Vol. XXXII of *Die urchristliche Botschaft*. Dritte Auflage. Hamburg: Furche Verlag, 1956.

Mullins, Terence Y., "Parables as Literary Forms in the New Testament," *The Lutheran Quarterly* 12 (1960), 235–241.

Navone, John, "The Lucan Banquet Community," *The Bible Today* (December 1970), 155–161.

Robinson, Willard H. *The Parables of Jesus: In Their Relation to His Ministry*. Chicago: University of Chicago Press, 1928.

Scharlemann, Martin H. *Proclaiming the Parables*. St. Louis: Concordia, 1963.

Smith, B. T. D. *The Parables of the Synoptic Gospels*. Cambridge: University Press, 1937

Smith, Charles W. F. *The Jesus of the Parables*. Philadephia: Westminster, 1948.

Stewart, R. A., "The Parable Form in the Old Testament and Rabbinic Literature," *Evangelical Quarterly* 36 (1964), 133–147.

Thielicke, Helmut. *The Waiting Father: Sermons on the Parables of Jesus*. Translated from the German by John W. Doberstein. New York: Harper, 1959.

Trench, Richard Chenevix. *Notes on the Parables of Our Lord*. New York: Harper/Revell, n.d.

Via, Dan Otto. *The Parables: Their Literary and Existential Dimension*. Philadelphia: Fortress, 1967.

Wilder, Amos. *Early Christian Rhetoric*. Cambridge: Harvard, 1971.

Wiles, M. F., "Early Exegesis of the Parables," *The Scottish Journal of Theology* 11 (1958), 287–301.

I. SPECIAL STUDIES RELATING TO SPECIFIC PARABLES

Arnott, William, "The Unjust Steward in a New Light," *ExpT* 24 (1913), 508–511.

Barry, Phillips, "On Luke xv. 25, συμφωνία: Bagpipe," *JBL* 23 (1904), 180–190.

Bishop, E. F. F., "The Parable of the Lost or Wandering Sheep," *ATR* 44 (1962), 44–57.

Bretscher, Paul G., "Brief Studies: The Parable of the Unjust Steward—a new approach to Luke 16:1–9," *Concordia Theological Monthly* 22 (October 1951), 756–762.

Bussby, F., "Did a Shepherd Leave Sheep Upon the Mountains or in the Desert?" *ATR* 45 (1963), 93f.

Danker, F. W., "Luke 16:16—An Opposition Logion," *JBL* 77 (1958), 231–243.

Davidson, J. A., "A 'Conjecture' About the Parable of the Unjust Steward (Luke xvi. 1–9)," *ExpT* 66 (1954/55), 31.

Daube, David, "Inheritance in Two Lukan Pericopes," *Zeitschrift der Savigny-Stiftung für Rechtsgeschichte, Romanistische Abteilung* 72 (1955), 326–344.

Derrett, J. D. M., "Fresh Light on St. Luke XVI. 1. The Parable of the Unjust Steward," *NTS* 7 (March 1961), 198–219.

———, "Law in the New Testament: The Parable of the Prodigal Son," *NTS* 14 (1967), 56–74.

Fitzmyer, J. A., "The Story of the Dishonest Manager (Lk. 16:1–13)," *Theological Studies* 25 (1964), 23–42.

Fletcher, D. R., "The Riddle of the Unjust Steward. Is Irony the Key?" *JBL* 82 (1963), 15–30.

Francis, F. J., "The Parable of the Unjust Steward," *ATR* 47 (1965), 103–105.

Fridrichsen, Anton, "Exegetisches zum Neuen Testament," *Symbolae Osloensis* 13 (1934), 38–41.

Friedel, Lawrence M., "The Parable of the Unjust Steward," *CBQ* 3 (1941), 337–348.

Gächter, P., "The Parable of the Dishonest Steward after Oriental Conceptions," *CBQ* 12 (1950), 121–131.

Giblin, Charles H., "Structural and Theological Considerations on Luke 15," *CBQ* 24 (1962), 15–31.

———, "Why Jesus Spoke in Parables— An Answer from Luke 15," *Chicago Studies* 7 (1968), 213–220.

Hiers, Richard H., "Friends by Unrighteous Mammon: The Eschatological Proletariat (Luke 16:9)," *Journal of the American Academy of Religion* 38 (1970), 30–36.

Kelley, Robert, "The Significance of the Parable of the Prodigal Son for Three Major Issues in Current Synoptic Study." Unpublished Ph.D. Thesis, Princeton University, Princeton, N.J., 1971.

Jeremias, Joachim, "Zum Gleichnis vom verlorenen Sohn," *Theologische Zeitschrift* 5 (1949), 228–231.

Kilpatrick, G. D., "φρόνιμος, σοφός and συνετός in Matthew and Luke," *JTS* 48 (1947), 63f.

Kosmala, Hans, "The Parable of the Unjust Steward in the Light of Qumran," *Annual of the Swedish Theological Institute* 3 (1964), 114–121.

Levison, N., "Importunity? A Study of Luke XI.8," *The Expositor,* Series 9, 3 (1925), 456–460.

Lunt, R. C., "Expounding the Parables: III. The Parable of the Unjust Steward (Luke 16:1–15)," *ExpT* 77 (1966), 132–36.

Marshall, I. H., "Luke xvi 8—Who Condemned the Unjust Steward?" *JTS* N.S. 19 (1968), 617–19.

Mitton, C. Leslie, "The Unjust Steward," *ExpT* 64 (1953), 307f.

Moore, F. J., "The Parable of the Unjust Steward," *ATR* 47 (1965), 103–105.

Moore, George F., "συμφωνία—Not a Bagpipe," *JBL* 24 (1905), 166–175.

Murphy, J. J., "Two Parables: The Prodigal Son (Luke xv. 11–32); The Labourers in the Vineyard (Matt. xix.27; xx.16)," *Expositor,* Series 3, 9 (1889), 290–303.

Paul, Geoffrey, "The Unjust Steward and the Interpretation of Luke 16:9," *Theology* 61 (1958), 189–193.

Preisker, Herbert, "Lukas 16:1–7," *Theologische Literaturzeitung* 74 (1949), 85–92.

Rengstorf, Karl H. *Die Re-Investitur des Verlorenen Sohnes in der Gleichniserzählung Jesu Luke 15:11–32.* Cologne: Westdeutscher Verlag, 1957.

Riggenbach, Eduard, "Zur Exegese und Textkritik zweier Gleichnisse Jesu," *Aus Schrift und Geschichte. Theologische Abhandlungen Adolf Schlatter zu seinem 70. Gebürtstage.* Stuttgart: Calwer, 1922. Pp. 17–34.

Sanders, Jack T., "Tradition and Redaction in Lk. XV, 11–32," *NTS* 15 (1969), 433–38.

Schniewind, Julius D., "Das Gleichnis vom verlorenen Sohn," *Die Freude der Busse.* Göttingen: Vandenhoeck & Ruprecht, 1960. Pp. 34–87.

Sheppard, J. B., "A Study of the Parables Common to the Synoptic Gospels and the Coptic Gospel of Thomas." Unpublished Ph.D. Thesis, Emory University, Atlanta, 1965.

Walls, A. F., "In the Presence of the Angels (Luke XV 10)," *Novum Testamentum* 3 (1959), 314–16.

Williams, F. E., "Is Almsgiving the point of the 'Unjust Steward'?" *JBL* 83 (1964), 293–97.

INDEX OF AUTHORS

INDEX OF REFERENCES

THROUGH PEASANT EYES

To Ethel Jean

CONTENTS

PREFACE

The song writer composes a song and it is finished. The sculptor chisels at his marble and one day the statue is completed. But the exegete's task is never finished. He can only pause to record, somewhat fearfully, his findings at a certain point in time, with the prayer that they will be of some use to others and that he has been faithful with what thus far has been given to him. This is very much our feeling as we bring this study to a close. Wiser and more learned scholars have trod this same ground before us, and others will follow after. The parables of Jesus do not unlock all of their secrets to anyone. We can only invite the reader to join us along the path we have been privileged to walk for twenty-five years with the hope that the reader will find the direction of the journey meaningful.

The footnote system used in this study has attempted to make sources easily identifiable for the reader and, at the same time, to save the printing costs. All books cited in the text are listed by author in the Bibliography. Where more than one source is quoted from a single author a key word from the title is given in the text. In the case of the Mishna we have listed the tractate with reference as well as the appropriate page in the Danby edition. For the Talmud we have done the same for the Soncino edition, edited by Epstein. The essays quoted from *The Jewish People in the First Century* (cited as *JPFC*) are listed together in the Bibliography. The same has been done for the *Theological Dictionary of the New Testament* (cited as *TDNT*). The great commentary of Ibn al-Ṭayyib was published in Arabic in Cairo in 1908. However, the edition was theologically edited, as the introduction affirms. Thus we have used both the printed text and the Paris Arabic Manuscript 86 as sources for this important work. The translations from the Arabic versions and studies are all the responsibility of the author. Because of their extent it has seemed redundant to add "(my translation)" to each quotation. Responsibility for the accuracy of the translations is solely my own.

The list of those to whom we are indebted is too long to record in full. Only a few from among the many can be mentioned. Special gratitude is sincerely offered to my Arab Christian friends of two decades, who stretch from the Sudan to Iraq, who have taught me far more than I have communicated to them. Mention must be made of the great scholars of the Arab Christian past, such as Ibn al-'Assāl, Ibn al-Salībī, and Ibn al-Ṭayyib. These and other Arab Christian scholars of the medieval period remain virtually unknown and our debt to them through their Bible translations and commentaries is boundless. We are grateful also to the British Museum, the National Library of Paris, and the Vatican Library for microfilms of their works.

A special word of thanks must be extended to the good people of St. Stephen's Presbyterian Church of Oklahoma City, who have graciously made funds available for the acquiring of the bulk of the resources for the research of this study. In addition, they provided challenging stimuli and warm encouragement on the occasion of the presentation to them, in lecture form, of most of this material. My colleagues and students at the Near East School of Theology here in Beirut have been a constant creative forum for parabolic study. No word of gratitude is adequate to express my debt to my dear wife, Ethel, who, in addition to her love, criticism, and encouragement, has corrected my abominable spelling and typing and has produced a clean and flawlessly typed manuscript. To her this book is affectionately dedicated.

Beirut, Lebanon
Fall, 1979

INTRODUCTION

In a recent review article Walter Brueggemann comments on what he calls the "crisis of categories" in biblical studies. Brueggemann thoughtfully observes,

> Anyone who tries to teach Scripture in a classroom today is aware of the impatience of students with scholarly methods that appear pedantic and seem concerned with peripheral questions and do not cut through to the decisive pay-offs of the material (Brueggemann, 432).

He expresses a concern for "the vitality and dynamic of the text" (*ibid.*). This study is an attempt to use scholarly methods but yet to reach "the pay-offs of the material." It is written from within the "hermeneutical circle," that is, from within the family of faith to the community of believers, with the earnest hope of recovering something of the "vitality and dynamic of the text" that is available when it is seen from a Middle Eastern cultural perspective. When this Middle Eastern world is taken seriously in terms of both form and content a great deal of new insight is available. The rediscovery of these insights is the purpose of this study. The community of faith within which I write is that of Middle Eastern Arab Christianity. I have lived, worked, and worshiped within this community for nearly thirty years. Although critical questions will not be avoided, it is not our intent to review and debate all recent Western scholarly opinions. Thus much of the documentation that is expected in a technical publication the reader will find missing. A more technical approach to the parables is already available (Bailey, *Poet*). My own debt to the works of others cannot be adequately expressed in words, yet our purpose here is to introduce into the discussion *new data* rather than review interpretive insights already known.

Most current scholarship on the parables concentrates on the redactional question of how a particular evangelist uses, shapes, or creates material in the service of his own theological interests to meet particular needs in the church of his day. In this study we will attempt to examine ten of the parables of Jesus as Palestinian stories set in the ministry of Jesus. It could be argued that the material is created or shaped significantly by the Palestinian community in their obedience to the resurrected Lord who continues to teach them through the Spirit. As Bultmann has affirmed, material emerging from the historical Jesus is culturally indistinguishable from any creation of the Palestinian community (Bultmann, *Jesus*, 12–14). Yet after years of life in a Middle Eastern, oral-tradition peasant community, we find no convincing reason to question the basic authenticity of the parables as parables of Jesus of Nazareth. The material *is* Palestinian. No doubt the material has been reused by the evangelists for their own theological purposes. But it is our view that this reuse does not significantly obscure the original intent of the material that can be determined when the underlying culture and the literary form are carefully examined. The redactional quest for the theology of the evangelists is a valid pursuit worthy of much effort, but it is not our concern here. Rather, the original Palestinian setting, along with the timeless theological content, is the goal of our inquiry. This study is written out of a deep conviction that the literary form and the underlying culture of the parables need more careful attention than they have had thus far in contemporary studies. It is hoped that what is presented will be understandable to the nonspecialist as well as being of some interest to the specialist.

Before proceeding to the task, a few definitions are required, along with some attention to methodology. Initially we must ask the knotty question, "Just what is a parable?"

WHAT IS A PARABLE?

A lengthy debate surrounds this question. One scholar will admit to over seventy parables in the synoptic Gospels, and the next limits them to thirty. Classifications such as parable, example-story, simile, etc., are well-known distinctions that have been used by interpreters to sort out types of parables. At the same time, Jeremias, the twentieth century's most influential interpreter of the parables, observed,

> This word (parable) may mean in the common speech of post-biblical Judaism, without resorting to a formal classification, figurative forms of speech of every kind: parable, similitude, allegory, fable, proverb, apocalyptic revelation, riddle, symbol, pseudonym, fictitious person, example, theme, argument, apology, refutation, jest (Jeremias, *Parables*, 20).

With this in mind we prefer to look at the way a parable *functions* in the text of the New Testament rather than concentrate on its *type*. When we do this it quickly becomes clear that parables are not illustrations. Manson has stated this most profoundly where he observes that "minds trained in Western modes of thought" are accustomed to theological arguments set forth in abstractions. Then to help "popularize these conclusions" they may be illustrated from ordinary life. But, says Manson,

> The true parable . . . is not an illustration to help one through a theological discussion; it is rather a mode of religious experience (Manson, *Teaching*, 73).

A part of what we understand Manson to be saying can perhaps best be seen by creating a comparison. In Luke 9:57–58 the text reads, "As they were going along the road a man said to him, 'I will follow you wherever you go.' " If Jesus had been a Westerner he might have responded something like this:

> Bold statements are easy to make but you have to consider seriously what it will cost you to follow me. It seems evident that so far you have yet to do so. I must say to you plainly that I can offer you no salary or security. If my point is not yet clear, perhaps an illustration will help. For example, I do not even have a bed of my own to sleep on.

But Jesus replies,

> Foxes have holes,
> and the birds of the air have nests;
> but the Son of man has nowhere to lay his head (Luke 9:58).

Rather than the abstract statement followed by a clarifying illustration we have a dramatic confrontation, briefly stated in unforgettable terms. A lofty affirmation about the person of Jesus permeates the parabolic answer. An impact is made on the listener/reader that calls for a response. Theological implications oblige the mind to move out from this compact center in a number of directions. The response of the original disciple is missing. The reader must now respond. All of this takes place at once in an intense dramatic confrontation. A parable has been spoken! To assume that we can capture all that happens in a parable in an abstract definition is to misunderstand its nature. Yet we must try.

The parables of Jesus are a concrete/dramatic form of theological language that presses the listener to respond. They reveal the nature of the kingdom of God and/or indicate how a child of the kingdom should act. With this definition in mind, we must ask next where parables are found.

PARABLES ARE WHERE YOU FIND THEM

There are at least six different types of formats in which the parables of Jesus function. It is crucial for their interpretation to see how they function in these different settings. These six are:

1. The parable in a theological dialogue.

2. The parable in a narrative event.

3. The parable in a miracle story.

4. The parable in a topical collection.

5. The parable in a poem.

6. The parable standing alone.

Each of these requires brief examination. The first is the parable in a theological dialogue. An example of this is the theological discussion between Jesus and the rich ruler in Luke 18:18-30. The climax of the discussion occurs, as we will observe, in the telling of the parable of the Camel and the Needle. The parable has a crucial function in forming the climax of the entire discussion and cannot be isolated from it.

The banquet at the house of Simon the Pharisee in Luke 7:36-50 is an example of a parable in a narrative event. The parable of the Creditor and the Two Debtors functions as a part of the narrative event. There is dialogue but the dramatic actions of the silent woman are the focus of the entire scene.

The miracle story of the healing of the woman with a spirit of infirmity in Luke 13:10-17 becomes a theological debate between the head of the synagogue and Jesus, and thus also overlaps with type one above. Yet it is in a miracle story and again the parable of the Ox and Ass functions as a crucial part of the whole.

In Luke 11:1-13 we have a topical collection on the subject of prayer. The parable of the Friend at Midnight (Luke 11:5-8) is a part of that collection. A careful distinction must be made in such a collection among the different units of tradition that are included in a collection. That is, because a number of sayings on one topic are grouped together, it is easy to fail to perceive where the paragraph breaks should come and thus misinterpret the material (cf. Bailey, *Poet,* 110f., 134f.).

Occasionally, as in Luke 11:9-13, we have a very carefully composed poem on prayer. Jesus gives three striking parables in the central stanza of the poem (*ibid.,* 134-141). Their function in that climax is the key to the understanding of the entire poem.

Finally, a parable at times stands alone. In Luke 17:1-10 we have three topics in rapid succession, each of which has some parabolic speech. There is the parable of the Millstone and the topic of judgment on the tempter. This is followed by the parable of the Grain of Mustard Seed and the apostles' request for faith. Then comes the dramatic parable of the Obedient Servant in vv. 7-10. These three stand relatively alone with no clear connection to what surrounds them and no specific context.

Thus in all but the last type the parable functions as a crucial part of a larger literary unit. It is the larger unit in each case that must be examined to determine what the parable is all about. With a working definition of what parables are in the New Testament and where they occur, we must then ask how they are to be interpreted.

THE INTERPRETATION OF PARABLES

The literature on this topic is extensive enough to lead the interpreter to despair. In this section we will not try to review that literature; rather we will set forth our own particular Middle Eastern cultural perspective and indicate our own methodology. A number of aspects of parabolic interpretation need some explanation. The first is the idea of looking at a parable as a play within a play.

(1)   The Play within the Play

In his famous drama *Hamlet,* Shakespeare uses the relatively rare phenomenon of a play within a play. In act 3, scene 2 Hamlet is desperate to "catch the conscience of the king." He (Hamlet) brings in a troop of players to reenact a story similar to the murder of his father that the present king has perpetrated. The spectator to this particular scene observes action on two levels. There is the little drama being enacted by the troop of players. Then there is the conflict between Hamlet and his uncle the king. Hamlet uses the actors and their drama to communicate with his uncle. As the troop of actors proceeds with its "play within a play," we, the audience, shift our attention from watching them to watching Hamlet and his uncle.

In the parables of Jesus we have a similar situation. The *play* is taking place between Jesus and his audience. Many times his theological enemies are his audience and thus sharp conflict is involved. The *parable* often occurs as "the play within the play." That is, in Hunter's apt phrase, the parables are "weapons of war in a great campaign against the powers of darkness which took Jesus to the cross" (Hunter, *Then,* 9). In some cases, like the scene in the house of Simon the Pharisee, we have the entire play (a long dramatic scene) and within that play the parable is told. In other cases the "play" is quite short, as in Luke 18:9 where it is reduced to a part of a verse. Sometimes it is missing entirely, as in Luke 17:7-10. Wherever possible we must try to ascertain the audience and try to understand the attitude of the original audience to the topic discussed by the parable. Some scholars see these settings for the parables as later additions that must be stripped away to discover the original message of the parable. Granted, these settings have certainly been shaped into their present form by the evangelist or his source. Yet is it not our responsibility to try to take these settings seriously and see if they are appropriate to an understanding of the original message of the parable? That is, they may well have been composed by Christians in the post-Easter Church. They are most certainly interpretations. But is it not possible that they are *correct* interpretations? Is it not possible also that some of these settings were transmitted in the tradition with the parables to which they are attached? This study is made with the assumption that these options are viable alternatives. Thus two levels of interest must be kept in focus: the theological debate between Jesus and his audience, and the use Jesus makes of parables in communicating to that audience in that debate. This brings us to consider another aspect of the relationship between Jesus and his audience, namely that of a storyteller and his listeners.

(2)   The Storyteller and His Listener

If you hear an Englishman tell a story about the days of King Arthur and his court, the teller and the listener throw an invisible mental switch. Everyone knows how the characters are expected to act in the world of the knights of the round table. In any story Sir Lancelot is expected to respect the ladies, obey the king, rescue the oppressed, and protect his own honor. The storyteller has an invisible "grand piano" on which he plays. The known pattern of life from the days of King Arthur is the "piano" on which the storyteller plays. The main points, climaxes, bits of humor, and irony are all heightened by "variations on a theme," that is, by changing, reinforcing, rejecting, intensifying, etc., the known pattern of attitude and behavior. Imagine then an Englishman telling the same story about Sir Lancelot to Alaskan Eskimos. Obviously the music of the "grand piano" will not be heard because the piano is in the minds of the English listeners who share a common culture and history with the storyteller. In the case of the parables of Jesus, *we are the Eskimos*. The people who were attuned to hear the depths of what was being said in a parable were the first-century peasants of Palestine. We in the West are separated from them by both time and distance. Two thousand years have passed, and we are culturally Westerners and not Middle Easterners. What then is to be done?

(3)   Recapturing the Middle Eastern Culture that Informs the Parables

To try to hear more precisely the music of the unseen "grand piano" is the major task of this study. The present writer has spent twenty-five years at this task already, and is fully aware of its dangers and complications. Briefly, the method we have evolved is to make use of four tools. The first is to discuss the cultural aspects of the parable with a wide circle of Middle Eastern friends whose roots are in isolated conservative village communities and try to find how the changeless Middle Eastern peasant sees things. The second is to examine carefully twenty-four translations of the New Testament in Syriac and Arabic to see how Christians in this part of the world have understood the text from the second to the twentieth centuries. The point here is that translation is *always* interpretation. The translator must decide what the text means before he can translate it. A parable passes through the translator's mind on its way to the new language. Through a careful reading of a series of such translations one is able to learn a great deal about how Middle Easterners themselves have understood a given text. The third is to look for parallels in literature as close to the New Testament as possible. Finally, the literary structure of the parable or parable passage must be examined with care.

Three of these tools are nonproblematic. Clearly one should understand the literary structure of a passage, examine literary parallels in other writings, and note translations made in the languages of the area. But the principle of "discussions with contemporary peasants" always raises the question, "How do you know that the peasants of the Middle East have not changed their culture over the centuries?" Obviously, if we can confirm in ancient literature a cultural pattern that we find surviving in the contemporary conservative Middle Eastern village, there is no problem. For example, we observe that the Middle Eastern gentleman in the village always walks down the street at a slow, pompous pace in order to preserve his honor. The father of the prodigal in Luke 15:20 *runs* down the street. For the village patriarch today to run down a village street would be humiliating and degrading. Was it the same for the village father in the time of Jesus, or has the pattern of life changed? In this case we are fortunate. Ben Sirach, a gentleman scholar in Jerusalem early in the second century B.C., tells us plainly that a "gentleman is known by his walk" (Sir. 18:20). Thus pre-New Testament literature confirms what we discover in isolated villages today in northern Syria and Iraq, in the highlands of Galilee, and in the south of Egypt. But if we do not find anything in the literature that surrounds the New Testament, what then? What if the above Sirach text had not been written? Could we then trust our contemporary insight? It is a basic presupposition of this study that there is no escape from the problem. We choose not to suspend interpretation in the fond hope that a new Dead Sea scroll will miraculously turn up answering our questions. To interpret the parable *at all* is to choose a path through a forest of alternatives, all of which are culturally conditioned. That is, if we had not found the Sirach text confirming the significance of the slow walk for a gentleman in the village, what then? We could then say, "Thus we cannot assume the father's run down the road to be significant!" But to do so is to *make* a cultural judgment. In this case the judgment is to decide that his run is not significant. We then fall back on our own subconsciously assumed Western culture as a base for interpretation. For the American, the people in a parable start acting like Americans, and for the French, they look like French, and for the German, they become Germans. When there is no alternative it seems better to start with the Middle Eastern cultural pattern with the full awareness that *if* we find more evidence our present assumptions may be confirmed, revised, or rejected. In the meantime, let us do our best. The question is not, Shall we make cultural judgments as we interpret or not? Rather, there is no escape from asking, Whose culture is to inform our interpretations? Ours or someone else's?

This situation can perhaps be clarified by one further illustration. The Westerner reads Luke 2:7, "She laid him in a manger," and assumes that Jesus was born in a stable because, of course, mangers are in stables. This judgment is a culturally conditioned decision whether the Westerner knows it or not (we put animals in stables). However, the Middle Eastern Palestinian farmer reads the same text and assumes that Jesus was born in a private home. In the Middle East the villager's home is one room with a lower level at one end where the family donkey and cow are brought at night. The family lives on the upper level. This raised terrace has mangers built into the floor at the end nearest the animals. So the Middle Eastern peasant reads the same text and decides that Jesus was born in a private home. I have seen homes here in the Middle East with mangers in the floor that were built in the eleventh century. This is my earliest evidence. We are then faced with three alternatives:

1. We can continue assuming our own Western culture and proceed with our traditional view that Jesus was born in a stable.

2. We can say, "We don't have any first-century evidence about where animals were kept and so where Jesus was born is lost to us. Without such early evidence we should not even venture a guess. Luke 2:7 must remain obscure."

3. We can tentatively agree, "We *know* that the peasant has not changed his ways from the eleventh century until now, and it is reasonable to assume that the centuries before were also culturally unchanging. The assumption of birth in a private home suits the text and everything we know about the gregarious nature of close-knit Middle Eastern society, thus there is no reason not to use the evidence we have, and affirm birth in a private home."

The question about where Jesus was born, in a stable or a private home, is not crucial (cf. Bailey, *Manger*). In the case of Luke 2:7, if we decide on the second alternative and suspend interpretation, not much is lost. But in the case of the parables a great deal is lost because the very heart of the teaching of Jesus appears in the parables. To suspend interpretation for lack of evidence is unthinkable. It is also totally unacceptable to continue reading our own culture subconsciously into the parables once we become aware of what we are doing. The third alternative then presents itself and becomes the methodological assumption that is applied in this study when, and only when, there is no other evidence available. In short, the parables are stories about people who lived in a particular time and place. We cannot interpret these stories without making culturally influenced decisions as we proceed. We will use *all* the *best* evidence at our disposal irrespective of its incompleteness. Finally, what kind of cultural questions are we intending to ask?

In our concern for understanding the culture that informs the parables we are interested in asking the *internal* question. We are not primarily interested in geography, dress, formal customs, weather, and the agricultural year. Rather we are interested in the way people feel, react, and respond. Specifically we are interested in asking five questions at crucial points in each parable in order to recapture the music of the storyteller's piano. These are the questions of *response, value judgment, relationship, expectation,* and *attitude.* How is a father expected to *respond* when his younger son asks for his inheritance while the father is still alive? What is the *relationship* between a master and his servant? What *value judgment* does the listening audience make when guests fail to attend a banquet? What is the *attitude* of Middle Easterners toward imperialistic rulers? What kind of hero does the audience *expect* in the parable of the Good Samaritan?

At times we ask these questions of the people themselves in the story. At other times we ask them of the listening audience. Both sets of questions are crucial.

Some may object that such questions are an attempt to psychoanalyze the characters in the parables and that such a process is illegitimate. Yet every listening audience in any culture has an entire complex of attitudes, value judgments, known responses, etc. (the "grand piano" mentioned above). This same fabric of parabolic communication also existed between Jesus and his first listeners. Indeed, it is in this communication network that meaning is to be found. It is precisely there that the theology of the parable is encased, and a failure to ask these questions is to subconsciously substitute non-Middle Eastern responses and, in the process, fail to understand the dynamic of the parable. It is analogous to looking at the placid surface of the water on a rocky shore and failing to put on a rubber mask to view the fascinating world of color and motion beneath the surface. Speculative mind-reading of the characters in the parables is not the point. Rather we seek out the basic Middle Eastern responses to the human situations reflected in the parables.

(4) Literary Structure

The investigation of literary structure in biblical literature has been called rhetorical criticism. It is a large and developing field that has been described and need not detain us (Bailey, *Poet*, 44–75). However, a few introductory remarks to this important discipline are essential.

We are attempting to discover the patterned repetitions of words and phrases and their significance for interpretation. The basic forms of these patterned repetitions are established in the Old Testament, to which we must turn for a few illustrations and definitions.

The poetical books of the Old Testament, along with most of the prophetic writings and many sections of other books, make extensive use of Hebrew parallelism. This literary device is built on the use of two lines that relate to one another in some special way. The second line may be synonymous with the first, in which case it is called "synonymous parallelism." When the second line is the opposite of the first the couplet is labeled "antithetical parallelism." The second line may also be the climax of the first, or an illustration of it, or complete it in some way that is more felt than understood. This parallelism is sometimes called "synthetic."

With this two-line parallelism as a tool the poets of the Old Testament developed three basic literary styles of relating these separate parts of the parallelism. We have called these *standard* parallelism, *inverted* parallelism, and *step* parallelism. All three of these literary devices occur in Isaiah 55:6–10. In this case the parallelism can be seen clearly even in an English translation such as the RSV. The author begins (in vv. 6 and 7) with three couplets of *standard* parallelism. In each case the theme stated in the first line is repeated in the second. They are as follows:

A   Seek the Lord while he may be found,
A   call upon him while he is near;

B   let the wicked forsake his way,
B   and the unrighteous man his thoughts;

C   let him return to the Lord, that he may have mercy on him,
C   and to our God, for he will abundantly pardon.

In verses 8 and 9 the author uses *inverted* parallelism, which can best be seen when printed as follows:

A   For *my thoughts* are not *your thoughts,*
  B   neither are *your ways my ways,* says the Lord.
    C   For as the heavens are higher than the earth,
  B   so are *my ways* higher than *your ways*
A   and *my thoughts* than *your thoughts.*

We are still dealing with pairs of lines but the author has arranged them in a different order (as can be easily seen by observing the italicizing). The theme of "my thoughts/your thoughts" occurs at the beginning and is repeated at the end. The theme of "my ways/your ways" occurs in the second and fourth lines. The illustration/parable of the heavens and the earth occurs in the center. Parallelism is still used, but in this case it is *inverted* parallelism.

In verses 10 and 11 Isaiah turns to *step* parallelism, which can best be seen when printed as follows:

A   For as the *rain* and the *snow come down from heaven,*
  B   and *return not* thither but water the earth,
    C   *making it bring forth* and *sprout,*
      D   *giving seed* to the sower and bread to the eater,

A   so shall my *word* be that *goes forth from my mouth;*
  B   it shall *not return* to me empty
    C   but *it shall accomplish that which I purpose,*
      D   and *prosper in the thing for which I sent it.*

The four lines of the second verse match the four lines of the first verse in an ABCD–ABCD pattern, making a step design, and thus this poetic device can be called *step* parallelism. The first line of each stanza speaks of something "going out." The second talks of it "not returning." The last two present the results.

These three stylistic devices can be used in various combinations, but the basic literary building blocks are the three types of parallelism outlined above. A great variety of patterns is often found in *inverted* parallelism (sometimes called chiasm). Thus this device needs special attention.

Isaiah 55:8–9, examined above, is a clear case of inverted parallelism. In this case we are dealing with couplets of poetry and the pairs of lines relate to one another in an inverted fashion. In biblical literature the inversion of themes at times goes far beyond simple parallelisms. Sets of couplets, paragraphs, chapters, and even an entire book can be understood as having been composed on the basis of a series of themes that are stated and then repeated in an inverted fashion (cf. Bertram, 165–68). Thus we are obliged to go beyond inverted parallelism and talk of the *inversion principle*. Already in the illustration of the three couplets of *standard* parallelism given above (Isa. 55:6–7) Isaiah has used the inversion principle. He begins in the first couplet with a call to seek the Lord. The second couplet tells the wicked what must be abandoned. In the third couplet we return to the theme of the first couplet. Often (although not in this case) the writer places his climax in the center before he begins to repeat. Then again, often the center is related to the beginning and the end in some specific fashion. Just past the center there may be a *point of turning* that makes the second half significantly different from the first half. Thus there were a number of ways the author could heighten his message by the use of inversion. When these rhetorical devices occur they are important for any passage of Scripture; but the question arises, What significance do they have for parables?

In three of the passages selected for this study the parable is embedded in a theological dialogue. In two of these (Luke 7:36–50; 18:18–30) the parable proper occurs in the exact center of the dialogue and the dialogue is structured with the use of the inversion principle. More often the parables fall into a series of short scenes or stanzas. Elsewhere we have described this as the *parabolic ballad* form (Bailey, *Poet,* 72f.). Whether or not this literary form was intentional we cannot conclusively demonstrate. The movement of the parable, however, is clearly structured around these scenes. Thus they must be observed and studied for a fuller understanding of the parable. Often these scenes relate to one another in a discernible pattern, as in the parable of the Good Samaritan. These internal patterns will also be seen to be significant for interpretation.

One final note of caution must be sounded. If one is willing to accept sufficiently subtle theological relationships one can find parallelisms almost anywhere. Theological themes in the New Testament are all interrelated somehow if you stretch them enough. Around the turn of this century a British fundamentalist, E. W. Bullinger, wrote *The Companion Bible,* in which he worked at literary structure in such an irresponsible fashion that he virtually discredited the discipline for a full generation. A cautious start was again made by T. W. Manson. We are following leads from his work in this study. In working with students in the area of literary structure now for a number of years I have discovered the natural tendency to jump to conclusions and to superimpose onto the text all kinds of relationships that are not there. In this study doubtless some of our analysis needs further refinement. We can only hope that some useful progress has been made.

A few principles that help instill caution are perhaps in place.

a. The ideas that repeat in matching lines are the most important ideas in the line and demonstrate themselves to be so in the overall poem. If only minor words match then the structure suggested is imaginary.

b. Structural forms fall into types. A series of similar types needs to be found in different places in the Old and New Testaments before the researcher can be confident that he has identified anything of significance (cf. Bailey, *Poet*, 44–76).

c. The Old Testament Hebrew poetic line and the syntax of Hebrew and Aramaic must always be in the background to help determine where the poetic line begins and ends. For example, "he gave him" is usually one word in Semitic languages and cannot be broken into two lines.

d. Often an older piece of literature has a few extra comments attached to it for a new reader. These extra comments stand out because they break the literary pattern. The presence of such additional phrases in some of the literary structures of the New Testament introduces a game that any number can play. Mark off enough phrases as extra comments and you can make almost any literary pattern out of any New Testament paragraph. The greatest caution must be exercised in identifying any word or phrase as a later editor's comment. The break in that pattern made by the extra comment needs to be unmistakable. There must be a clear and discernible reason that has led someone at some stage in the transmission of the material to add a brief comment.

e. No translation can be trusted. Earlier, more formal translations, like the RSV, can be used with profit by the nonspecialist. Many recent English translations have taken great liberties in rearranging the words and phrases into an appropriate order for the English language. A good start can be made with an RSV translation, but a knowledge of the original languages is essential for a precise study of the literary structure of a passage.

f. When there is a structure in the text the relationships between lines are bold and unmistakable. Subtlety is a deadly enemy.

g. If the matching blocks of material are relatively long there needs to be a *series* of matching elements. For example, if one finds in any Pauline letter a reference to the cross, he unwarily may continue reading until he comes to a second reference and then affirm a connection between the two. He may have skipped over a dozen themes in order to find one that he calls a parallel. Bullinger's work is flawed by this error on nearly every page. Take any four paragraphs in the New Testament and you can find *something* that matches and affirms an ABBA or an ABAB structure for the four paragraphs.

h. Inversions have been found unconsciously expressed in a variety of places such as letters, office memos, and casual conversations (Schegloff, 78–89). In this study we are looking for a deliberate repetition that has its roots in the Hebrew parallelism of the Old Testament. The interpreter needs to look for special features such as a central climax that relates to the beginning and the end; a point of turning just past the center; hints of double inversion (cf. Bailey, *Recovering*, 269, 290f.); redundancy introduced to complete the parallelism; and bold repetitions that seem to be clearly deliberate. When such features occur the interpreter can be fairly confident that he is dealing with a conscious literary construction that is significant for exegesis.

It has been said of the saxophone, "It is an instrument that is easy to play poorly." In this same vein, rhetorical criticism is a tool for New Testament studies that is easy to use poorly.

(5)   The Problem of the One and the Many

Through the long centuries of the life of the Church the dominant method of interpretation was the allegorical method, in which every little part of the parable was given some mystical meaning. Parabolic interpretation became so confused that it is no wonder the Latin proverb emerged stating *Theologia parabolica non est theologia argumentative,* and thus affirming that no doctrine could be based on any parable. With the allegorical method anyone could read almost anything into almost any parable. The break away from allegory started with the Reformation and was finalized by a German scholar, A. Jülicher, at the beginning of this century. Because of the irresponsible extravagances of the past a number of scholars moved to the other extreme and rejected *all* allegory, insisting that there is only *one* teaching in each parable. It is our view that parables have in them more than a single theme and that these themes can be understood without either destroying the unity of the parables or falling back into the allegorizations of the past. It is instructive to remember David and Nathan. Nathan tells a story to David about a rich man, a poor man, and a lamb (II Sam. 12:1–6). David had stolen another man's wife and had had her husband killed. Nathan's story to David has three symbols:

> The rich man symbolizes David.
>
> The poor man symbolizes Uriah.
>
> The lamb symbolizes Bathsheba.

Two separate aspects of this parable must be observed with care. The first is this set of symbols that David (the original listening audience) understood instinctively. These (mentioned above) are *symbols,* not allegorizations. A symbol *represents* something else, an allegory *is* something else and has no other existence. These three symbols function in the story and without them the parable is pointless. But having identified the three symbols that *the original audience* (David) instinctively identified, we are *not* free thereby to start making other symbolical identifications. That is, we could take the city, the flocks and herds, the cup, the traveler, and the morsel, and assign them meanings of one kind or another, and in the end make the parable mean whatever we might want. Yet there *are* symbols in the parable. Moule perceptively compares a parable to a modern political cartoon that the reader has to "understand" (Moule, 96f.). The modern political cartoon *has* symbols. The cartoonist makes symbolic identifications that he knows the majority of his readers will interpret correctly. Thus, like the modern cartoon, the Gospel parable also has symbols. *The symbols to look for are the ones the original teller puts in the story for the purpose of communicating with the original audience.* The storyteller, in the telling of the parable, skillfully uses these symbols to press the original listener to make a single decision/response. In the case of the above, David is pressed to understand "I am the man." It is in that single response that the unity of the parable is to be found.

This brings us to the second question of "What does it mean for me?" We are now some 3000 years away from David and his world. If the parable is told specifically to call to repentance an Oriental king who has committed a particular evil, what can such a story mean to us living in a very different world? The answer to this question is to be found in the theological cluster that is at the heart of every parable. The parable has a cluster of theological motifs that together press the original listener to make his single response/decision. Nathan is trying to get David to make *one* move, but a number of theological themes combine in the telling of the story to press David to make that move. What are some of them? We can suggest the following:

1. The king is under the law, not above it. It is God's law, not the king's. God is offended.

2. The law specifies special rights for the "stranger within the gates." Uriah is a Hittite. David has denied Uriah these rights.

3. Unlike Egypt and Babylon, the women of the kingdom are not for the king's choosing like grapes on a vine.

4. David has many wives, Uriah only one. Simple justice has been violated.

All of these together press David to make the *single* move that he does make. Thus, even though I am not an Oriental monarch who has stolen my neighbor's wife, there is theological content in the parable that leaps the centuries and profoundly applies to me and to all of us. Once we identify the original listener and perceive the single response expected of him, we can discover the cluster of themes that evoked that response. It is in that cluster of theological themes that we find the message for all people in any place at any time. The lesson of Nathan's parable for today is *far* more than "Do not steal your neighbor's wife." Primarily it answers the ageless question, "Is the leader of a nation above the law?" In this study we will try to identify the original listener and attempt to discover what Jesus was trying to get him to understand and do. Then, through an analysis of that initial response/decision, we will be able to see what the text says to us. We will attempt to discern the multiplicity of theological themes in a parable (where they exist) without destroying its unity and without allegorizing its details.

In summary, in order to understand the parables of Jesus and to discern their message for today, the interpreter needs to go through eight basic steps, which can be carried out to some degree by the nonspecialist, and be pursued in much greater detail by the specialist. These steps can be briefly stated as follows:

1. Determine the audience. Is Jesus talking to the scribes and Pharisees, to the crowds, or to his disciples?

2. Examine carefully the setting/interpretation provided by the evangelist or his source.

3. Identify the "play within a play" and look at the parable on these two levels.

4. Try to discern the cultural presuppositions of the story, keeping in mind that the people in them are Palestinian peasants.

5. See if the parable will break down into a series of scenes, and see if themes within the different scenes repeat in any discernible pattern.

6. Try to discern what symbols the original audience would have instinctively identified in the parable.

7. Determine what single decision/response the original audience is pressed to make in the original telling of the parable.

8. Discern the cluster of theological motifs that the parable affirms and/or presupposes, and determine what the parable is saying about these motifs.

In the following chapters we intend to apply the above method to ten of the parables in Luke with the earnest hope that what is written here will help the reader, if ever so slightly, to recover something of the impact of the parables in their original Palestinian setting, and that in so doing "the decisive pay-offs of the material," the "vitality and dynamic of the text," will speak afresh to us in our day.

Chapter 1

THE PARABLE OF THE TWO DEBTORS
(Luke 7:36-50)

This deceptively simple, yet artistically and theologically complex, parable/ dialogue has much to offer to the careful interpreter. Like the parable of the Camel and the Needle's Eye (Luke 18:18-30), this text has a short parable set in the middle of a tightly constructed theological dialogue. Culture and drama overlap to heighten and inform the theology. Thus the parable must be examined in the light of both of these factors. The overall structure of the seven scenes will be examined, and then the separate sections studied in detail. First, then, the structure:

The overall flow of the theological mosaic is as follows:

> Introduction (the Pharisee, Jesus, the woman)
>> The Outpouring of the Woman's Love (in action)
>>> A Dialogue (Simon judges wrongly)
>>>> A Parable
>>> A Dialogue (Simon judges rightly)
>> The Outpouring of the Woman's Love (in retrospect)
> Conclusion (the Pharisees, Jesus, the woman)

The full text of the seven stanzas is as follows:

1   One of the Pharisees asked him to eat with him,   INTRODUCTION:
    and he went into the Pharisee's house and reclined.
    And behold, there was a woman who was a sinner in the city.

2   And when she learned, "He is dining in the Pharisee's house!"
    bringing an alabaster flask of *perfume,*
            and *standing* behind him *at his feet,*   IN THE HOUSE
                weeping she began to *wet* his *feet* with her *tears.* OF THE PHARISEE:
                And she *wiped* them with the *hair of her head,*   A WOMAN ACTS!
            and *kissed* his *feet,*
    and *anointed* them with the *perfume.*

3   Now when the Pharisee who had invited him saw it, he said to himself,
        "If this were a prophet, he would have known   A DIALOGUE:
        who and what sort of woman this is who is touching him,
        for she is a sinner."   SIMON JUDGES
        And Jesus answered and said to him,   WRONGLY
        "Simon, I have something to say to you."
        And he answered, "Teacher! Speak up!"

4   And Jesus said,*
            "Two debtors there were   A PARABLE
                to a certain money lender.
                    The one owed fifty denarii
                    and the other five hundred.
                They not being able to pay,
                he freely forgave them both.

5   Which of them will love him the more?"   A DIALOGUE:
        Simon answered,   SIMON JUDGES
        "The one, I suppose, to whom he freely forgave the more." RIGHTLY
        And he said to him,
        "You have judged rightly."

6   Then turning to the woman he said to Simon,   IN THE HOUSE
    "Do you see this woman? I entered your house!   OF THE PHARISEE:
    You gave me no water for my feet,   A WOMAN ACTS!
    but she has wet my feet with her tears, and wiped them with her hair.
    You gave me no kiss,
    but from the time I came in she has not ceased to kiss my feet.
    You did not anoint my head with oil,
    but she has anointed my feet with perfume.
            In consequence I say to you,
    her sins, which are many, have been forgiven,
    therefore she loved much.
    But he who is forgiven little, loves little."
    And he said to her, "Your sins have been forgiven."   CONCLUSION:

7   Then those who were reclining with him began to say to themselves,
    "Who is this who also forgives sins?"   JESUS
    And he said to the woman, "Your faith has saved you, go in peace."

_____

(*These three words are found in the Old Syriac and many of the Arabic translations.)

The structural flow of the drama in seven scenes is clear, with the major themes repeating in the second half of the structure (with a significant difference from the first half in each case). The inversion principle is used in the repetition. The parable occurs in the climactic center. Each of these sections will need to be examined in turn.

INTRODUCTION (Scene 1)

One of the Pharisees asked him to eat with him,
and he went into the Pharisee's house and reclined.
And behold, there was a woman who was a sinner in the city.

In these first lines all three major characters are introduced. We are presented with the Pharisee (soon to be known by the name Simon); Jesus, who accepts the invitation; and a woman, "who was a sinner in the city." In Luke 15:1-2 a parallel introduction of the same basic three (Pharisees, Jesus, and sinners) appears. In Luke 15:11 the parable of the Prodigal Son begins simply, "A certain man had two sons." Again, all three characters are introduced at the beginning.

We are not told the specific occasion for this particular invitation. Jeremias is most helpful:

We may at all events infer that before the episode which the story related took place, Jesus has preached a sermon which had impressed them all, the host, the guests, and an uninvited guest, a woman (Jeremias, *Parables*, 126).

This suggestion fits all the details of the story and is the best working assumption on which to proceed. Jesus preaches. An invitation is offered to him and accepted. The scene is set at a banquet, which adds a special coloration to the drama. The Pharisee, unlike the covenanter at Qumran, did not eat his meals isolated with his community (as evidenced by this very meal). At the same time, as Neusner has pointed out, "All meals required ritual purity" (Neusner, 340). The point of special importance is that the Pharisee was in touch with non-Pharisees at mealtime, and

This fact makes the actual purity-rules and food-restrictions all the more important, for they alone set the Pharisee apart from the people among whom he constantly lived (*ibid.*).

Thus, isolation from impure food and people was especially crucial for the Pharisee when he sat down to eat. Jesus enters into this kind of a world when he accepts the invitation.

Furthermore, as Safrai observes in his description of religion in first-century Palestine, groups of interested people formed religious societies, *haberim*, and held common meals for religious study.

They featured in particular the study of the Torah, and sometimes continued late into the night when they warmed to their discussions, or when there was a lecture from their teacher or a visiting sage (Safrai, *JPFC*, II, 803f.).

This banquet may well have been such an occasion. Jesus, a "visiting sage," is invited to a meal with the local intellectuals. Spirited discussion on a theological theme of mutual interest is expected. Yet surely no one could have anticipated the dramatic surprises in store for them.

We are told cryptically that "He went in" and "reclined." When the synoptics speak of "reclining" for a meal indoors they mean a banquet (Jeremias, *Eucharistic*, 48f.). Other guests are specifically mentioned at the end of the scene, and we can assume a relatively formal occasion where the traditional roles of guest and host are expected to be acted out with precision by all concerned.

Some of the Middle Eastern cultural details assumed by the text are fully described by Tristram, an astute nineteenth-century traveler.

> ... entertainment is a public affair. The gateway of the court, and the door ... stand open. ... A long, low table, or more often merely the great wooden dishes, are placed along the center of the room, and low couches on either side, on which the guests, placed in order of their rank, recline, leaning on their left elbow, with their feet turned away from the table. Everyone on coming in takes off his sandals or slippers and leaves them at the door, socks or stockings being unknown. Servants stand behind the couches, and placing a wide, shallow basin on the ground, pour water over it on the feet of the guests. To omit this courtesy would be to imply that the visitor was one of very inferior rank. ... Behind the servants the loungers of the village crowd in, nor are they thought obtrusive in so doing (Tristram, 36–38).

Tristram's observations explain how the woman achieved access to the house and how she could stand behind Jesus at his feet. The present writer can confirm much of the above from personal experience.

This same general banquet setting has been documented by Safrai in his discussion of home and family in first-century Palestine.

> Following the custom prevailing among the Greeks, diners reclined on individual couches. ... These couches were used for festive banquets as well as for regular meals (Safrai, *JPFC*, II, 736).

Dalman makes the same observation and finds documentation in the Talmud (Dalman, *Words*, 281; P.T. *Berakhoth* 12b). Also, Ibn al-Ṭayyib, a famous Iraqi scholar of the eleventh century, writing an Arabic commentary on this text observes,

> And the phrase "at his feet" and the phrase "she was behind him" is because he was reclining with his legs stretched out and this, along with the fact that she was "standing behind him," brings her to a position at his feet (Ibn al-Ṭayyib, folio 89ᵛ).

Ibn al-Ṣalībī, another famous Middle Eastern commentator writing in Syriac in the twelfth century, notes the significance of her being at his feet.

> She stands behind him because she is ashamed to approach his face for he knows her sins, and because of the respect she shows to his person (Ibn al-Ṣalībī, 98).

Furthermore, the feet are always placed behind the one reclining because of the offensive, unclean nature of feet in Oriental society from time immemorial until the present. In the Old Testament the ultimate triumph for the victor and insult to the vanquished was to "make the enemy a footstool" (cf. Ps. 110:1). Bitterly hated Edom is told, "On Edom I cast my shoe" (Ps. 60:8; 108:9). Moses is obliged to take off his unclean shoes at the burning bush because of the holiness of the ground (Ex. 3:5). John the Baptist uses the illustration of the untying of the shoes to express his total unworthiness in the presence of Jesus (Luke 3:16). As the scene develops, this setting becomes crucial in relation to an uninvited guest, a woman.

Thus the exterior setting is clear. Jesus is known and the community has heard him. He is invited to a banquet for further discussion. At such scenes in the traditional Middle East, the doors are open and the uninvited are free to wander in. Jesus and the other guests are reclining on low couches for the meal. Yet in the dynamics of the scene something is missing.

As Tristram observed, the host failed to wash the feet of Jesus and this is freighted with meaning for the Middle Eastern world in general, and for this story in particular as it develops. But this is not all. Jesus has also received no kiss of greeting. Again Tristram is helpful. Writing in 1894 he says:

> Besides omitting the water for His feet, Simon had given Jesus no kiss. To receive a guest at the present day without kissing him on either cheek as he enters, is a marked sign of contempt, or at least a claim to a much higher social position (Tristram, 36–38).

He goes on to explain how once in the interior of Tunis he was entertained, and in the middle of the banquet his servant whispered in his ear not to trust the host because he had not kissed him on entering. Tristram observes that his servant's warning proved "most timely" (*ibid.*, 38). The formal greetings were clearly of crucial significance in first-century times. Windisch defines the verb "to greet" as "to embrace" and observes that it can mean the embrace of greeting as well as the erotic embrace of love (Windisch, *TDNT*, I, 497). Windisch also notes, "To offer rabbis the *aspasmos* (greeting) coveted by them was the impulse of all pious Jews" (*ibid.*, 498). Jesus is identified as a rabbi (teacher) in the story. Thus, from a Middle Eastern cultural perspective, the failings of the host are glaring omissions (against Marshall, 306, 311). The anointing with oil is also omitted but is most likely less of an offense to the guest, although anointing with oil was a common procedure (cf. Deut. 28:40; Ruth 3:3; Ps. 23:5; Jth. 16:8). Thus it is clear that the accepted rituals of welcoming the guest are not merely overlooked in the telling of the story but have been callously omitted by a judgmental host.

Even in less formalized Western society, there *are* traditional pleasantries observed at the entrance of guests into a home. These include generally:

1. Remarks of welcome at the opening of the door with an invitation to enter.
2. Taking the guests' coats and depositing them in a prepared place.
3. Extending an invitation to sit down.

If all of these were deliberately omitted in the case of a guest of honor at a banquet, the insult would be unmistakable. As Scherer, a longtime resident in the Middle East in the nineteenth century, observes, "(Simon) violated the common customs of hospitality" (Scherer, 105). The significance of these omissions and Jesus' response to them will become clear as we proceed.

The traditional translation of the initial phrase describing the woman is, "And behold, a woman of the city, who was a sinner...." Some early Arabic translations, including Hibat Allah Ibn al-'Assāl, read, "And a woman who was a sinner in the city...." This translation is grammatically legitimate. Through these Arabic translations we can see that this is the way many Middle Eastern Christian scholars understood the text in the first millennium of the Christian era. These Arabic translations present the woman as actively engaged as a "sinner" in the city. This emphasis reminds us of the two separate aspects of the phrase in question. We are given crucial information about her life-style—she was a sinner *plying her trade* in the city. This emphasis gives the story an extra cutting edge and is quite likely a part of the original intent of the text. At the same time, her community *is* identified. She is dwelling *in the city*. Simon (as we will observe) knows perfectly well who she is. She is a part of that community (although an outcast from its religious groupings). This identification of her community will also prove important for the tension of the scene as it develops.

IN THE HOUSE OF THE PHARISEE: A WOMAN ACTS!
(Scene 2)

And when she learned, "He is dining in the Pharisee's house!"
bringing an alabaster flask of *perfume,*
   and *standing* behind him *at his feet,*
      weeping she began to *wet* his *feet* with her *tears.*
      And she *wiped* them with the *hair of her head,*
   and *kissed* his *feet,*
and *anointed* them with the *perfume.*

The inverted parallelism of the three actions of the woman are clear. The woman does three things to the feet of Jesus. She washes, kisses, and anoints them. For each separate service two actions are involved. In logical sequence these can be seen as follows:

a. She brings the perfume   — then anoints his feet with it.
b. She stands at his feet   — then kisses his feet.
c. She wets his feet with her tears   — then wipes them with her hair.

The inverted arrangement of the lines in the text (a b c—c′ b′ a′) *could* be the natural flow of the story. However, a much simpler way to describe the action would be,

> She entered and, standing at his feet, she began to wet them
> with her tears, and to wipe them with her hair, and to
> kiss them and anoint them with perfume she had brought.

Rather, six specific actions are described and it would seem that the inverted parallelism is intentional. Furthermore, the order of the three actions (wash, kiss, anoint) is maintained at the end of the scene in Jesus' speech to Simon. In this latter case, the natural flow of events would be: (1) the kiss on entering the house; (2) the washing of the feet; (3) the anointing of the head with oil. Significantly, this normal order is reversed to match the order of the actions of the woman. The grammatical forms also indicate the deliberate nature of the inverted parallelism. In the first three lines the Greek text has three participles (bringing, standing, weeping). In the last three lines there are three past tenses (wiped, kissed, anointed). Ehlen has demonstrated that the parallelism of grammatical construction in the Hymn Scroll of the Dead Sea Scrolls is an important part of the parallel construction of the poetry of the hymns (Ehlen, 33–85). Finally, as we will note (cf. below on scene 6), Jesus' description of the woman's actions are also cast in poetic parallelisms. Thus it is not surprising to find parallelism used in the description of the initial set of actions here at the beginning of the scene. The point is of more than artistic interest. When a biblical author uses the inversion of parallel lines deliberately, he often places the climax in the center. This feature appears here also with the weeping and the letting down of the hair in the middle. To these details we now turn.

In an Oriental banquet, the door of the house is open and there is a great deal of coming and going, as we have observed. The RSV translates, "When she learned that he was sitting at table in the Pharisee's house... ," and thus indicates that the woman finds out about Jesus' location after he has entered the house. The past tense of the verb "to be" is not in the text and the "that" (Gk. *hoti*) can better be understood as introducing direct rather than indirect speech. The story itself (cf. v. 45) tells us that either she entered with Jesus or before him because her dramatic action began "from the time I came in." Thus the story seems to assume that she has heard from the community where he was to be entertained. Indeed she was told, "He is dining in the Pharisee's house!" Bearing gifts she proceeded with him or before him to that place of meeting.

Her gifts are an expression of devotion in a sacrament of thanksgiving. The anointing of his feet is clearly intentional, because she has come prepared. Her washing of his feet is not premeditated because she has nothing with which to dry them and is obliged to use her hair. When we accept the story's own affirmation that she is present at the time of his entrance, it is easy to reconstruct what has triggered her startling action. Jesus is accepted by the community around him as a rabbi. Simon addressed him (in the Greek text) as "Teacher," which is one of Luke's words for rabbi (Dalman, *Words*, 336). All guests are treated with great deference in the Middle East and always have been. We need only recall the hospitality Abraham extended to his three visitors (Gen. 18:1–8). Levison, himself a Palestinian Hebrew Christian, describes the scene and its meaning:

> The studied insolence of Simon to his Guest raises the question of why he had invited Jesus to his house. When a guest is invited to any one's house, he expects to be offered the ordinary amenities of hospitality. When the guest is a Rabbi, the duty of offering hospitality, in its very best manner, is well recognized. But Simon invited Jesus to his house, and proceeded to violate every rule of hospitality.... In the East when a person is invited to one's house it is usual to receive him with a kiss. In the case of a Rabbi, all the male members of the family wait at the entrance to the house and kiss his hands. In the house, the first thing that is attended to is the washing of the guest's feet. None of these civilities were offered to the Master... (Levison, 58f.).

This woman has heard Jesus proclaim the freely offered love of God for sinners. This good news of God's love for sinners, even those like her, has overwhelmed her and triggered in her a deep desire to offer a grateful response. Edersheim, another Hebrew Christian, fills in the details. He translates "ointment" as "perfume" and writes, "A flask with this perfume was worn by women around the neck and hung down below the breast." Such a flask was "used both to sweeten the breath and perfume the person" (Edersheim, *Life*, I, 566). It does not take much imagination to understand how important such a flask would be to a prostitute. Her intent is to pour it out on his *feet* (she does not need it any longer). For her to anoint his head would be unthinkable. Samuel the prophet can anoint Saul and David on the head (I Sam. 10:1; 16:13), but a sinful woman cannot anoint a rabbi on the head. To do so would be extremely presumptuous. With this deeply moving, profoundly meaningful gesture of gratitude in her mind, she witnesses the harsh insult that Jesus receives when he enters the house of Simon, as Simon deliberately omits the kiss of greeting and the footwashing. The insult to Jesus has to be intentional and electrifies the assembled guests. War has been declared and everyone waits to see Jesus' response. He is expected to offer a few tight-lipped remarks about not being welcome and withdraw. Rather, he absorbs the insult and the hostility behind it and does not withdraw. In a foreshadowing of things to come, "He opened not his mouth." As we observed, to omit even the footwashing is to imply "that the visitor was one of very inferior rank" (Tristram, 38). The woman is totally overcome. They have *not even extended to him the kiss of greeting*! Her devotion, gratitude, and anger mix. She forgets that she is in the presence of a circle of men hostile to her also. Yet *she* cannot greet him with a kiss; such an action would be hopelessly misunderstood. What is to be done? Ah, she can kiss his *feet*! Rushing boldly forward she then breaks down and literally washes his feet with her tears. Now what? She has no towel! Simon would not give her one if she asked for it. So she lets down her hair and with it wipes his feet. After smothering them with kisses (the verb means literally to kiss again and again), she pours out her precious perfume on the feet of the one who announced God's love for her, who is here being abused by this calloused company. She is offering her love *and* trying to compensate for the insult that Jesus has just received (against Marshall, 306). In the process she offers a tender gesture that can easily be misunderstood. *She has let down her hair,* an intimate gesture that a peasant woman is expected to enact only in the presence of her husband. The Talmud indicates that a woman can be divorced for letting down her hair in the presence of another man (cf. Tosefta *Sotah* 59; P.T. *Gittin* 9.50d; quoted in Jeremias, *Parables,* 126, n. 57). Conservative areas of the contemporary Islamic world forbid male hairdressers to work on women's hair for the same reasons.

Even more striking is the evidence from the Talmud in connection with regulations about the stoning of an immoral woman. The rabbis are worried about the woman stimulating unchaste thoughts in the minds of the officiating priests. The text reads,

> The priest seizes her garment, it does not matter if they are rent or torn open, until he uncovers her bosom and loosens her hair. R. Judah said: if her bosom was beautiful he did not expose it, and if her hair was comely, he did not loosen it (B.T. *Sanhedrin* 45a, Sonc., 294; cf. also *Sotah* 8a, Sonc., 34).

Clearly the rabbis considered uncovering the bosom and loosening the hair to be acts that fall in the same category. In a concern to protect the officiating priests from unchaste thoughts these two acts alone are mentioned. This then demonstrates the significance of an immoral peasant woman's act of letting down her hair in the presence of Middle Eastern men. Indeed, this talmudic text demonstrates clearly the sense of shock that must have electrified the room when the immoral woman in our text loosened her hair before Simon and his guests. The provocative nature of the gesture is clear, and is not lost on Simon, as we will see.

Two of the woman's actions, as we have observed, were spontaneous responses to what she saw happening before her. But she *did* come prepared to anoint his feet with perfume. Lamartine, a French traveler in 1821, passed through the Middle East with a large retinue and was greeted everywhere as a European prince. He records that in the village of Eden, in the mountains of Lebanon, he was anointed on the head with perfume on arrival (Lamartine, 371). But here the woman anoints Jesus' feet. For an explanation of this extraordinary action we turn again to the early Arabic commentators Ibn al-Tayyib (himself a physician to the caliph in Baghdad in the eleventh century), comments on this verse: "For it was the custom in the past that noblemen were anointed with ointment in the houses of kings and priests" (folio 89ᵛ). If this cultural note can be entertained it is most enlightening. For her to anoint his head would be extremely presumptuous, as we have noted. No—but she can, as a servant, anoint his feet and thereby show honor to his noble person. Thus, while Simon's gesture implies Jesus to be of inferior rank, the woman's action bestows on him the honor of a nobleman in the house of a king.

The kissing of the feet is not only compensation for what Simon has refused, but also a public gesture of great humility and abject devotion. Again Jeremias is helpful where he offers a talmudic illustration of a man accused of murder who kisses the feet of the lawyer who has gotten him acquitted and thus saved his life (Jeremias, *Parables,* 126, n. 55). Thus in summary, triggered by observing the hostility that Jesus receives from his host, this outcast woman bursts forth in a series of three dramatic gestures. Others are mocking the one to whom she is anxious to show the deepest devotion. With her tears she washes his feet and, in a strikingly intimate gesture, lets down her hair to wipe them. Unworthy to kiss even his hands, she repeatedly kisses his feet. A costly perfume ordinarily used to make her attractive (perhaps to her customers) is poured on Jesus' feet. She may also be extending to him the kind of tribute ordinarily shown only to a nobleman in the house of a king. The entire dramatic action is carried out without any language, and indeed, language is useless in the presence of such costly and tender expressions of devotion and gratitude. The drama then shifts automatically and naturally to the response of Simon, the host.

For Simon, the calculated snub of the young rabbi is not proceeding according to plan. His deliberate refusal to offer the expected hospitality triggered an unprecedented act of devotion. A sensitive man could only humbly apologize to the guest and thank the woman for having compensated for his rudeness. But such is not to be. The drama moves on.

A DIALOGUE: SIMON JUDGES WRONGLY (Scene 3)

Now when the Pharisee who had invited him saw it, he said to himself,
"If this were a prophet, he would have known
who and what sort of woman this is who is touching him,
for she is a sinner."

And Jesus answered and said to him,
"Simon, I have something to say to you."

And he answered, "Teacher! Speak up!"

In scene 1, the principal characters were introduced in the order of the Pharisee, Jesus, then the woman. The drama now reviews the three principal characters in the same order. The Pharisee is mentioned first, and he surfaces not as a humble man confessing his failures as a host, but rather as a spiritual critic of the validity of the young rabbi's prophetic claim and of the woman's spiritual state. The woman's moving drama of thankfulness has passed him by. All he sees is an immoral woman who has let down her hair and who is, by her touch, defiling one of the guests, a guest not perceptive enough to know it.

Again, the dramatic touch of the scene is evident. Simon is engaging in what Shakespeare would label an "aside." Indeed it is a soliloquy, and a very revealing one at that. From it we see something of his real intent in inviting Jesus to his house—namely, to test the claim that Jesus is a prophet. His language is contemptuous; he refers to Jesus as "this" (Plummer, 211). The key word is "touching." The Greek word means both "to touch" and "to light a fire." The word "to touch" in biblical language is used on occasion for sexual intercourse (Gen. 20:6; Prov. 6:29; I Cor. 7:1). Obviously this is not intended here, but Simon's use of this word in this context has clear sexual overtones. He is affirming that in his opinion it is all very improper and Jesus (if he were a prophet) would know who she was and would (of course) refuse this attention from *such* a woman. Clearly, Simon has completely misjudged what is happening before him. Jesus *does* know who the woman is (cf. v. 47). Her actions are not the defiling caresses of an impure woman, but the outpouring of love from a repentant woman. Simon does not rejoice at this evidence of her repentance and he feels no remorse as she compensates for *his* failures. Rather he registers only more hostility to his guest. In passing it is worth noting that Simon *also* knows who she is. Jesus' knowledge of her is more evidence that the story assumes some contact between them before this incident takes place. Simon knows her only as an immoral woman. This does not imply immorality on his part. In the Oriental village immoral women are known and identified by everyone in the community. But the entire scene demonstrates Simon's total indifference to her restoration.

Again Ibn al-Ṭayyib makes an astute observation. In commenting on why Jesus accepted the invitation in the first place he says, "He goes in the hope of his (Simon's) acceptance of her repentance" (Ibn al-Ṭayyib, folio 89ᵛ). Thus Ibn al-Ṭayyib also implies that Jesus has had some previous contact with her and that she is coming to show gratitude for the gift of forgiveness. In fact, Ibn al-Ṭayyib makes the quaint suggestion that this woman has talked to the woman of Samaria, whose story is recorded in John 4. Be that as it may, his suggestion here is very much to the point. Clearly the woman is making a dramatic turn in her entire life's orientation. The story leaves us no doubt regarding the authenticity of her repentance. Yet we are also told that she is a resident of that same city and it is clear that she is known to Simon. If Simon and his other religious friends do not accept the authenticity of her repentance, no restoration to community will take place. The Lost Sheep is brought back *to the fold*. The Prodigal Son is returned *to the family*. Zacchaeus is *"also* a son of Abraham" and can no longer be rejected as an outsider according to Jesus (Luke 19:9). So here, Simon must be led to see the authenticity of her repentance so that she will be restored to fellowship *in her community*. Whether or not Ibn al-Ṭayyib's point can be made for the opening scene of the passage is beside the point. It can be made here.

At this point Simon makes an affirmation crucial for the story as it develops and crucial for our understanding of it. He rejects the validity of her repentance. She is still "a sinner" (v. 39). The grim faces around the room make it clear that she (in spite of this moving demonstration of sincerity) is still rejected as a sinner. What is to be done? The purpose of the parable and the dialogue that follows can be understood as a deliberate attempt to break the stylized attitudes toward "sinners" and "righteous" dominant in that society and make it possible for this woman to be welcomed back into a loving, caring, accepting community.

The dialogue turns again to Jesus. A typical "righteous" teacher of religion in any age could be expected to reject the woman. Jesus accepts her expressions of love with the full knowledge that they are being misunderstood by Simon and his friends. As the dialogue moves to its climax in the brief parable Jesus says, "Simon, I have something to say to you." Plummer assumes that Jesus is asking permission to speak (Plummer, 211). This exact phrase in contemporary villages, however, is used all across the Middle East to introduce a blunt speech that the listener may not want to hear. This is precisely what develops in this scene and the idiom thus understood fits perfectly into the dialogue. Simon indirectly confesses his own failures as a host by addressing Jesus with the title of Rabbi/Teacher. If he is worthy of the title that Simon grants to him, then he is worthy of the honor due the title, but this honor Simon withholds from him. Jesus' carefully chosen words are a brief parable whose structure we may now examine.

A PARABLE (Scene 4)

And Jesus said,	
"Two debtors there were	THE DEBTORS
to a certain money lender.	THE MONEY LENDER
The one owed fifty denarii	ONE DEBTOR
and the other five hundred.	THE OTHER DEBTOR
They not being able to pay,	THE DEBTORS
he freely forgave them both."	THE MONEY LENDER

As we have noted, Luke 18:18–30 is also an extended dialogue with a brief parable in the very center. In both passages the parable itself is cast in a simple literary structure. Debtors and money lender appear in the first two lines and again (but with a difference) in the last two. The center sets out the distinction between the two that is crucial to the entire scene. The structure is so simple that it may well be unintentional. Yet it contributes to the overall artistry of the entire passage. The point is clear. The verb here translated "freely forgive" is the Pauline verb "to offer grace." The two debtors are leveled in their need and neither is able to pay. The same grace is extended to each. The difference between them is set forth in the center of the parable. But in their indebtedness (at the beginning), in their inability to pay, and in their need for grace (at the end of the parable), they stand together.

Here the density of the language and its dramatic impact is heightened by the use of wordplay. Wordplay is not unique to this passage. At the center of Luke 16:9–13 there is a skillfully constructed wordplay that appears when the passage is retrotranslated into the Aramaic of the first century (cf. Bailey, *Poet*, 112–14). The historical present here in v. 40 is further evidence of a pre-Lucan tradition (cf. Jeremias, *Eucharistic*, 150f.). Black has identified a similar play on words in this passage (Black, 181–83). The woman is a *sinner*; the parable is about *debtors* and *creditors*; and the concluding discussion turns on *sin* and *love*. Black lists the Aramaic of these words as follows:

Sinner woman	=	*Ḥayyabhta*
creditor	=	*mar ḥobha*
debtor	=	*bar ḥobha* or *ḥayyabh*
sin	=	*ḥobha*
to love	=	*ḥabbebh* or *'aḥebh*

In Aramaic the word *ḥobha* means both debt and sin. This can be seen in the two versions of the Lord's prayer (Matt. 6:12; Luke 11:4), and in the parable of Pilate and the Tower (Luke 13:2, 4; cf. below, 78f.). Jesus uses this wordplay both to compare and to contrast the sinful woman (*ḥayyabhta*) with her sin (*ḥobha*) and Simon who is socially in debt (*bar ḥobha*) and has failed to love (*ḥabbebh*). This comparison (they are both sinners) and contrast (one loves, the other does not) now becomes the focus of the continuing dialogue.

A DIALOGUE: SIMON JUDGES RIGHTLY (Scene 5)

"Which of them will love him the more?"

Simon answered,
"The one, I suppose, to whom he freely forgave the more."

And Jesus said to him,
"You have judged rightly."

With a modified form of the Socratic method, Simon is led to reason out for himself the conclusion to which Jesus would bring him. Simon is pressed with a question, and seeing that he is being trapped, he can only lamely try to escape with "I suppose. . . ." Marshall notes, "Simon realizes he is caught in a trap" (Marshall, 311). Although Simon totally misunderstood the human scene in front of him, the logic of the parable is inescapable. Love, in the parable, is a response to unmerited favor, indeed, a response to pure grace. Having established this principle from the parable Jesus proceeds to an application that refers back to the actions of the woman and shocks the guests (and the reader) with its boldness.

IN THE HOUSE OF THE PHARISEE: A WOMAN ACTS! (Scene 6)

Then turning to the woman he said to Simon,
"Do you see this woman? I entered your house!

You gave me no water for my feet,
but she has wet my feet with her tears, and wiped them with her hair.

You gave me no kiss,
but from the time I came in she has not ceased to kiss my feet.

You did not anoint my head with oil,
but she has anointed my feet with perfume.
            In consequence I say to you,
her sins, which are many, have been forgiven,
therefore she loved much.

But he who is forgiven little,
loves little."

And he said to her, "Your sins have been forgiven."

In the Gospel of Luke there is a series of pairs involving one man and one woman. In Luke 4:25–27 two heroes of faith are held up as illustrations of the types of people who respond in faith and receive the benefits of God's grace. One is a woman (the widow of Zarephath), the other a man (Naaman the Syrian). In Luke 13:10–17 a woman is healed on the Sabbath. Then in 14:1–6 the same happens with a man. In each case the conversation turns on the treatment of the family ox and ass. The literary structure of the Travel Narrative parallels these two stories (Bailey, *Poet*, 79–85). In Luke 11:5–8 a man under difficult circumstances has his prayers answered. In 18:1–5 a similar parable is told of a woman. These are also parallel in the outline of the material (*ibid.*). In Luke 15:3–10 two people diligently search for what they have lost. One is a man, the other a woman. In all of these cases all of the people involved are noble examples. But here a man and a woman are compared, and the *woman* is the noble character (in spite of what the men in the room think of her) while the man is the ignoble character (in spite of his high opinion of himself). In a Middle Eastern world, still dominated almost exclusively by men, such dramatic scenes were and are a profound statement about the worth of women in a man's society (cf. Bailey, *Women*, 56–73). The shock of praising a despised woman in male company is bad enough. Yet the sharp edge of the criticism can be fully understood only in the light of the cultural expectations of the scene.

The guest in any society is expected to show appreciation for the hospitality extended to him regardless of how meager it might be. In the Middle East these expectations of the guest are solidified into an unwritten law. The host is expected to downgrade the quality of his offerings as inadequate for the rank and nobility of the guest. Irrespective of what is set before him, the guest *must* say again and again that he is unworthy of the hospitality extended to him. Richard Burton, the well-known nineteenth-century traveler and Orientalist, writes the following in his record of his famous trip to Mecca:

Shame is a passion with Eastern nations. Your host would blush to point out to you the indecorum of your conduct; and the laws of hospitality oblige him to supply the every want of a guest, even though he be a *déténu* (Burton, I, 37).

The possibility of a *guest* pointing out the indecorum of the *host's* actions is so remote that Burton does not even mention it. Yet amazingly in this passage it happens. Quoting from early Jewish sources Edersheim documents for us the traditional expectations of a noble guest:

> A proper guest acknowledges all, and saith, "At what trouble my host has been, and all for my sake!" While an evil visitor remarks: "Bah! What trouble has he taken?" (Edersheim, *Social*, 49).

Nelson Glueck, the famous Middle Eastern archeologist, records a modern illustration of the ancient social interchange of guest and host. Glueck was entertained by an Arab family living in the ancient ruins of Pella on the east bank of the Jordan.

> We were met and entertained at lunch by Dhiab Suleiman, the *Mukhtar* ("headman") of the village. It mattered not that he was poorly clothed, his house small, his people poverty-stricken. . . . We were exchanging polite conversational amenities with a prince of Pella. We drank his coffee, which slaked our thirst. We dipped pieces of his fragrant, freshly baked bread into a dish of sour milk, and ate the eggs which he boiled and peeled for us. We exclaimed honestly over the goodness of it all. . . . We under no circumstances could have refused his hospitality or stoned him with disdain or pity for his slender provender. I have forgotten many splendid feasts, but I shall never forget the bread we broke with him. The invitation to his board was a royal summons, and we commoners had no choice but to obey (Glueck, 175f.).

Glueck's experience has been repeated by the present writer many hundreds of times all across the Middle East, from the Sudan to Syria, for over twenty years. To attack the quality of the hospitality offered, regardless of the circumstances, is unknown in fact or fiction, in personal experience or in traditional story. Yet in the biblical drama before us, such an unprecedented attack on the inferior quality of the begrudging hospitality does take place and is forthrightly expressed in uncompromising terms. After such an outburst the listening company is pressed to make a decision regarding the speaker. The terms of this decision will need to be examined at the conclusion of the final speeches in the drama, to which we now turn.

The form of the language used here has long been identified as patterned after the Hebrew parallelisms of the Old Testament (Jeremias, *Theology*, 16). Plummer writes, "The series of contrasts produces a parallelism akin to Hebrew poetry. . . ." (Plummer, 212). We have noted the use of parallelism in the first description of the woman's actions (in that case, inverted parallelism). Thus it is no surprise to the reader to find parallelism used in this matching description of the woman's deeds. The parallelisms are not merely of artistic significance but, as we will note, clarify a crucial, centuries-old mistranslation of the text.

In regard to the setting of the speech, it must be noted that Jesus, "turning to the woman . . . said to Simon." That is, the speech is addressed to Simon but is delivered facing the woman. It is thus delivered as a speech in praise of her kindness and worth. Were Jesus facing Simon we would imagine a tone of harsh accusations—You, who failed in all of these duties! But delivered facing the woman, it takes on a tone of gentleness and gratitude, expressed to a daring woman in desperate need of a kind word. The entire speech concludes with a climax addressed to her, in which she is reminded that her sins have been forgiven.

The introduction to the speech provides a setting for what follows. Jesus begins with a question, "Do you see this woman?" Simon has concentrated on collecting evidence for a negative judgment on Jesus. He is now asked to give his attention to the woman and her actions. Jesus begins the confrontation with, "I entered *your house*!" The clear line of argument is, "I came in under your roof. I became your guest. You were responsible to extend to me the traditional forms of hospitality, but you refused!" The details then state clearly, "This woman whom you despise magnificently compensated for your failure." The language is very precise. The text reads, "You gave me no water for my feet." Jesus does not say, "You failed to wash my feet." It would be presumptuous to assume that Simon should have taken the role of a servant. Rather, Jesus courteously speaks only of the water. Had Simon provided water Jesus could have washed his own feet. But Simon did not even give him water. By contrast, this woman *herself* washed his feet, not with water but with her tears, and wiped them with her crown and glory as a woman, her hair. Footwashing as a courtesy extended to guests was observed in the Middle East up until the nineteenth century (cf. Jowett, 79).

Jesus continues, "You gave me no kiss." Just what Simon was expected to kiss is not mentioned in humility and deference. In the case of the other two actions the part of the body involved is specifically mentioned. (She washed the *feet*. In the following illustration the *head* and the *feet* are mentioned.) But what should Simon have kissed? Equals kiss each other on the cheek. The student/ disciple kisses the rabbi's hands, the servant his master's hand, and the son his parents' hands. In the garden Judas certainly kissed Jesus on the hand (contrary to popular opinions). In the parable of the Prodigal Son, the prodigal is prevented from kissing his father's hand or foot by the father's unprecedented falling on his son's *neck* and kissing him. In this case, it is a sign of reconciliation, not equality, but it is also clearly done to prevent the son from kissing the father's hand or feet (cf. Bailey, *Poet,* 182). Simon has greeted Jesus as "Rabbi/ Teacher." Thus Simon should have kissed his hand. Yet with great sensitivity Jesus does not say this, but simply states that there was no kiss of greeting at all. By contrast, the woman has *covered* his *feet* with kisses. (As we observed above, feet and shoes are signs of degradation in Middle Eastern society; cf. Scherer, 78). Both contrasts are made. Simon, not one kiss; the woman, many. Simon failed to kiss even his head; the woman has carried out the supreme gesture of devotion by kissing his *feet*. (The kissing of the feet is rare but not unprecedented. In the Talmud Bar Hama kisses the feet of Rabbi Papi in gratitude for the latter's successful defense of the former's legal case; B.T. *Sanhedrin* 27b, Sonc., 163.)

The third action also has a double contrast. Olive oil was commonly used for anointing the head of a guest. Such oil was and is cheap and plentiful. It was one of the common products of the countryside in first-century Palestine and constituted one of its main exports (Applebaum, *JPFC*, II, 674). The head, being the crown of the person, is considered worthy of an anointing. By contrast the woman has anointed his *feet* (which no one anoints, even with olive oil) *and* has used an expensive *perfume*. Thus the woman's action in anointing his feet has a double impact on the listener/reader (cf. Tristram, 39). In three clear actions the woman has demonstrated her superiority to Simon. And Simon has this pointed out to him publicly in poetic speech that will be remembered.

After this scathing rebuke the cutting edge of the conclusion is introduced with the phrase, "For the sake of this I say to you." The intent is somewhat ambiguous. Of the possible options the best meaning seems to be, "In the light of this exposure of your many failures I say to you. . . ." Then comes the much debated final pair of couplets, which we translate,

> her sins, which are many, have been forgiven,
> therefore she loved much.
>
> But he who is forgiven little,
> loves little.

Jesus does not actually forgive her sins on the spot (he is misquoted by the hostile guests in the following verse). Rather he announces a forgiveness that has already taken place in the past. The Greek text uses a perfect passive, "her sins . . . have been forgiven." The passive is to avoid the use of the divine name (Jeremias, *Parables*, 127). The perfect tense indicates a present condition that results from a past action. Ibn al-Ṣalībī, the twelfth-century Syrian scholar, came to this same conclusion : "Her actions show that her sins had been forgiven her" (Ibn al-Ṣalībī, 98). Jesus announces what God has done and confirms that action to the woman.

Finally, then, comes the much discussed phrase, "therefore she loved much." For more than a millennium this was translated in the East and in the West, "for she loved much." This latter translation has stood in many versions through the centuries in spite of the fact that it directly contradicts what precedes and what follows in the text. The question is, what is first, forgiveness or an outpouring of love? When we look to the parable and to the concluding couplet of the series now under examination the following can be seen:

The Text	*The Relationship between Love and Forgiveness in the Text*
In the parable of the Two Debtors:	a. Forgiveness is first. b. Then a thankful response of love.
In the concluding couplet ("He who is forgiven little, loves little"):	a. Forgiveness is first. b. Then a thankful response of love.
In the traditional translation of verse 47 ("her sins . . . have been forgiven, *for* she loved much"):	a. An outpouring of love is *first*. b. Then comes forgiveness as a reward.

It is amazing that for many centuries this clashing contradiction has stood and continues to stand in unnumbered translations. If the text has any internal integrity at all, this translation must be in error. Fortunately, at last, major versions are beginning to correct the mistake. The Catholic Jerusalem Bible reads, "For this reason I tell you that her sins, her many sins, must have been forgiven her, or she would not have shown such great love." The New English Bible translates, "Her great love proves that her many sins have been forgiven." Sadly, the 1971 revision of the RSV New Testament maintains the ancient error and still has the woman earning her forgiveness by her actions (in direct contrast to the parable). The key to the corrected translations seen in the Jerusalem Bible and the New English Bible is found in the Greek particle *hoti*, which often means "for" (as in the RSV) but can have what the grammarians call a "consecutive use," which makes the *hoti* show result and can be translated "therefore." Here in verse 47 we have a clear case of such use (cf. Jeremias, *Parables,* 127; Robertson, 1001; Bauer, 593; Plummer, 213; Blass, § 456). This brings verse 47a into harmony with both the parable and the statements that follow it and restores an internal integrity to the text and its message. Indeed, Jesus is pointing out that this woman is not a defiling sinner, but a forgiven woman who knows the extent of her evil ways and something of the grace of God, freely given to her in forgiveness. This awareness has motivated her lavish outpouring of grateful love. Jesus concludes with an obvious reference to Simon that needs careful examination.

Referring to Simon, Jesus says, "He who is forgiven little, loves little." This can be read in two ways. We can assume Jesus is saying, "You, Simon, are a righteous man, and your sins are few and thus very little of God's grace is required to cover these 'debts.' Therefore you have loved little." Much more likely the intent is, "You, Simon, have many sins (some of them we have just recounted). You have little awareness of them and have not repented. Thus you have been forgiven little and, naturally, loved little." Jesus has just listed in graphic terms some of the failures (debts) of Simon, and they reflect far more than formal inadequacies as a gracious host. Rather they indicate deep levels of pride, arrogance, hard-heartedness, hostility, a judgmental spirit, slim understanding of what really defiles, a rejection of sinners, insensitivity, misunderstanding of the nature of God's forgiveness, and sexism. The most damaging criticism of all is the fact that Simon witnessed the woman's dramatic action and still labeled her as a "sinner" (v. 39). Thereby he has refused to accept her repentance and has determined to continue to reject her as a sinner. Ibn al-Ṭayyib has some very thoughtful reflections on this point.

> And the two debtors refer to two types of sinners. One is a great sinner like the woman and the other is a little sinner like the Pharisee. By the phrase "a little sinner," either he means sin in reality or he refers to his (Simon's) conceit at his own perfection. This conceit robs him of virtue and the awareness that the one who is forgiven more loves more. Indeed, he told him (Simon) this parable for the purpose of reproving the Pharisee for the feelings he has harbored against any contact with sinners and to demonstrate to him that this woman's love for him is greater than his love because of the overflowing of his grace to her (Ibn al-Ṭayyib, folio 90^r).

In the same passage he also writes,

> And his saying, "The one who is forgiven little, loves little," means that the one who has many sins experiences a profound repentance, followed by a sincere love for God. But the one who has few sins boasts of his uprightness and thinks he has little need of forgiveness, and he has very little love for God (Ibn al-Ṭayyib, folio 89^r).

Thus, with Ibn al-Ṭayyib, we understand the text to present to the reader a picture of two great sinners. One sins without the law, one within the law. The first (the woman) has accepted forgiveness for her many sins and responds with much love. The second (Simon) has no real awareness of the nature of the evil in his life. He sees himself with few spiritual debts and thus in little need of grace. Consequently, having received little grace, he shows little (if any) love. This same contrast can be seen in the parable of the Lost Sheep. Does Jesus really think that there are any "ninety-nine who need no repentance?" Or is he rather laughing at a Pharisaical mentality that makes such an assumption (cf. Bailey, *Poet*, 154f.)? The sons in the parable of the Prodigal Son (Luke 15:11–32) and the two men at prayer in the temple (Luke 18:9–14) offer similar contrasts. The rebuke to Simon is stunning. The great unrepentant sinner (whose presence defiles) is Simon, not the woman. The prophet has not only read the woman's heart, he has read Simon's heart. The judge (Simon) becomes the accused. The drama begins with Jesus under scrutiny. The tables turn and Simon is exposed. Finally, we must ask, what is affirmed about Jesus himself?

The drama's affirmations about the person of Jesus are significant. Simon has thought that Jesus might be a prophet, perhaps even "the prophet" foretold in Deuteronomy 18:15 (a famous early Greek text, the Vaticanus, gives this reading in Luke 7:39). The test in Simon's mind is the ability to know the inner nature of people. In the drama Jesus demonstrates full understanding of the inner nature of the woman *and* of Simon. But the drama goes far beyond the simple affirmation that Jesus is a prophet. Jesus surfaces as the unique agent of God through whom God announces forgiveness and to whom a grateful response of love is appropriately demonstrated. The woman is praised for showing love to *Jesus* in response to the forgiveness she has received. Simon is sharply criticized for failing to do the same. Such functional affirmations about the person of Jesus are calculated to evoke from the listener/reader a response of recognition, affirmation, and obedience, *or* accusations of blasphemy against the impostor who presumes to act as God's unique agent. The drama does not leave us in doubt regarding the assembled guests at the banquet.

CONCLUSION: THE PHARISEE, JESUS, AND THE WOMAN (Scene 7)

Then those who were reclining with him began to say to themselves,
"Who is this who also forgives sins?"
And he said to the woman, "Your faith has saved you, go in peace."

All three principal characters were introduced at the beginning of the scene. Now at the end a concluding glance returns to these same major characters. The other diners are not impressed. They did not speak "among themselves"; along with the Syriac and Arabic versions, we prefer to translate more literally "in themselves." Like Simon, they are a bit nervous about verbalizing their criticisms (having just witnessed the withering attack that Simon has endured). Yet their criticism is beside the point. He has not actually forgiven the woman's sins (although this is not beyond him; cf. Luke 5:17-26); he has only acted in God's stead in the announcing of forgiveness and in the receiving of gratitude. They are at least puzzled, and at most offended. Again with our Arabic and Syriac versions, we prefer to read "who is this who *also* forgives sins?" Along with other outrages he *also* forgives sins (Plummer, 214). Finally comes the concluding remark to the woman, "Your faith has saved you, go in peace." Her *faith* (not her works of love) has saved her.

When the biblical author uses the inversion principle he usually states his major theme in the center and then repeats this theme in some way at the end (Bailey, *Poet,* 50ff.). This feature occurs here. The theme of God's freely offered love, accepted as unearned grace, is the major point of the parable in the center of the literary unit. This theme recurs at the end in the clear affirmation that salvation is by faith. She is mercifully sent away from the presence of her despisers in the peace of reconciliation to a loving heavenly Father whose unique agent must continue to endure hostility in the proclamation of that reconciliation to sinners like herself and like Simon. The scene (like the parable of the Prodigal Son) closes unfinished. We are not told the response of Simon (even as we do not know the final response of the older son in Luke 15 or of the three disciples in 9:57-62). Will he reevaluate the nature of his own indebtedness, repent, and offer expressions of grateful love that have so far been glaringly missing? Or will his hostility and opposition harden? Then and now the reader/listener must complete the parable in his own response to God's unique agent of forgiveness and peace. The drama ends, the literary form resolves itself, and a look backward is required.

In each parable we will seek to identify the decision/response that the original listener/reader was pressed to make, and to determine the cluster of theological motifs that comprise the impact of the parable, motifs that can instruct believers in every age. As Marshall has said, "a number of different motifs are present in the story" (Marshall, 304).

First, the original listener. Simon is pressed to understand and confess,

I am a great sinner (as was this woman). This I have not realized. I have not repented, nor have I heard the offer of the grace of God as this woman has. I have been forgiven little and thus I have loved God's agent (Jesus) little. If Jesus really wants to avoid sinners He should avoid me, not this woman whom I have despised.

The theological cluster of motifs that comprise the impact of this parable include the following:

1. Forgiveness (salvation) is a freely offered, unearned gift of God. Salvation is by faith.

2. When accepted, this salvation by faith immediately triggers costly acts of love. These acts of love are expressions of thanks for grace received, not attempts to gain more.

3. Jesus is God's unique agent through whom forgiveness is announced and to whom a grateful response of love is appropriately expressed out of an awareness that through him the believer has been forgiven much. The question in scene 7 is not answered. Each reader must bring his own response.

4. The offer of forgiveness to sinners involves the agent of that forgiveness in a costly demonstration of unexpected love. Within this theme one can overhear something of the meaning of the passion.

5. There are two kinds of sin and two kinds of sinners, namely Simon and the woman. Simon sins within the law, and the woman outside the law. Sinners like the woman often know that they are sinners; sinners like Simon often do not. Thus repentance comes hardest for the "righteous."

6. In a man's world and at a banquet of men, a despised woman is set forth as a heroine of faith, repentance, and devotion. She is the champion in these regards over a man. The inherent worth of women and the fact that the ministry of Jesus is for women and men is powerfully affirmed in the drama.

7. In a confrontation with Jesus the options are faith or offense. There is no middle ground. For Simon, either Jesus is a rude young man who insults his host, fails to show gratitude for a meal prepared in his honor, and presumes to act in God's place, or he is in fact God's unique agent who mediates forgiveness and appropriately expects humble and costly devotion to his person.

8. Jesus accepts Simon's invitation without hesitation. He is known as the friend of sinners and this includes a concern for the "righteous" as well as the outcasts.

May this great dramatic scene provide the same catharsis for us that it has for countless millions throughout the history of its telling.

Chapter 2

THE FOX, THE FUNERAL, AND THE FURROW (Luke 9:57–62)

The Text:

> And as they were going along the road
> A a man said to him,
>   "I will *follow* you   FOLLOW
>   wherever you *go*."   GO
>   And Jesus said to him,   COST TOO HIGH?
>   "Foxes have holes,   (a parable)
>   and birds of the air have roosts.
>   But the Son of man has nowhere to lay his head."
>
> B To another he said,
>   "*Follow* me!"   FOLLOW
>   But he said, "Lord, let me *go* first   GO
>   to *bury* my father."   COST
>   But he said to him,
>   "Leave the dead to *bury* their own dead.   COST
>   But you *go*   GO
>   and *proclaim* the kingdom of God."   FOLLOW
>
> A' And another said,
>   "I will *follow* you, Lord,   FOLLOW
>   but first let me (*go* and) take leave of those at my home."   GO
>   And Jesus said,
>   "No one who puts his hand to the plow   COST TOO HIGH?
>   and looks back   (a parable)
>   is of any use in the kingdom of God."

The three brief dialogues in this passage are often overlooked in discussions of parables. Certainly they do not fit the pattern of a parable as an extended story. Yet here also Jesus communicates his views by means of concrete comparisons. Two proverbs/parables occur in the dialogues. Each deserves the title of *mashal*

22

as defined by first-century Palestinian usage. We choose to include this trilogy under the umbrella of the parabolic speech of Jesus. In our discussion of how to interpret parables (see the Introduction), Jesus' response to the first brash volunteer was noted as a classical illustration of his use of the parabolic method of communication. These three cameos need to be considered together because the literary structure of the three forms a single unit, and because of their similarity of subject matter. To the structure set forth above we now turn.

In a recent discussion of the literary structure of this passage Louw writes, "The semantics of proverbial discourse must be based on phrase structure analysis and not on the traditional exposition of the individual's words" (Louw, 107). This is perhaps too strong—both are needed. Louw's exposition is flawed by a failure to consider the culture that informs the text, but his discussion does draw attention to the presence of a literary structure in the text and is at points helpful. The analysis given above allows a number of interlocking features worthy of note to surface.

As is often the case in biblical literature, we are working with three stanzas (cf. Bailey, *Poet*, 69). As is typical with this three-stanza form, the first and the third stanzas are linked together in a number of special ways. In this case there are four clear points of comparison that establish such linkage. Initially, in the first and third stanzas (A and A'), the person involved is a volunteer. He *offers* to follow. By contrast, the person in the middle dialogue is a recruit. He is *called* by Jesus to follow. Second, in A and A', Jesus answers with parables whose imagery comes from the outdoor world. The first is from nature and the second from the farming practices of the Palestinian countryside. The dialogue (B) has no parable; in its place is a direct command. The imagery of the dialogue is from the customs of village society, not from nature. Third, in the case of A and A', there is only one statement by each party. The second dialogue has three speeches. Finally, the literary form of the first and last conversations is identical. The flow of ideas is Follow + Go + a parable. By contrast, the central stanza breaks into inverted parallelism with its themes of Follow − Go − Cost + Cost − Go − Follow/Proclaim. This identical structure of three stanzas with step parallelism tying the outside stanzas together and the central stanza breaking into inverted parallelism is found in Luke 15:4-7 (Bailey, *Poet*, 144f.).

In addition to the features that unite the first and third dialogues, a number of semantic links tie the second and third together. Each ends with a reference to the kingdom of God. Each of the people involved pleads that he is willing, "But first. . . ." Finally, some features tie all three dialogues together. Obviously, the themes of Follow + Go + Cost are the focal points in each dialogue. The first is willing to *follow* and *go* anywhere but has not considered the *cost*. The second is asked to *follow*. He wants to *go* home to his family (and is told to *go* and *proclaim* the kingdom). The *cost* of discipleship is put in the form of a command. The third wants to *follow* and, like the second, wants to *go* home first. (The Old Syriac version has the verb "go" in this text, and we suggest that it may be original. In any case, it is implied.) He, like the first, is challenged to consider the *cost*. At the same time, stanzas A and A' are not identical. There is progression. In the first, a man offers to follow unconditionally and is challenged to consider the cost. The last volunteer seems to have done so. He offers to follow but with a very specific condition. With all of these interlocking parallelisms in mind, we now turn to an examination of each dialogue in turn.

THE FIRST DIALOGUE

A   a man said to him,
  "I will *follow* you   FOLLOW
    wherever you *go.*"   GO
        And Jesus said to him,   COST TOO HIGH?
  "Foxes have holes,
  and birds of the air have roosts.
  But the Son of man has nowhere to lay his head."

This parable has no cultural riddles. Yet it may have two levels of meaning. The first level is clear. This first would-be disciple represents the *centripetal* force of mission. He is drawn *in* to join the community of disciples. No one recruits him. Yet his understanding of what is involved seems shallow. Sa'īd notes, "He does not understand that 'follow' means Gethsemane, and Golgotha, and the tomb" (Sa'īd, 258). The idea of following a rejected, suffering Son of man would come as a jarring shock to any first-century Jew. In Daniel, the Son of man is to have dominion, glory, and kingdom and, "all peoples, nations, and languages shall serve him" (Dan. 7:14). The reader of Luke has already been told, "The Son of man must suffer" (Luke 9:22). Here the volunteer is not given details but only a graphic picture of total rejection. The point is not only "You, too, may have to suffer privation, and have you considered this?" but also, "Whatever your motives, keep in mind that you are offering to follow a *rejected leader.*" "Roosts" is a better translation than "nests." The birds always have roosts, but build nests only at certain times of the year. The point is (partially) that even the animals and birds have *some* place to rest, but the Son of man has none.

Aside from this obvious level of meaning drawn from the nature of foxes and birds, a political symbolism may be involved. T. W. Manson points out that the "birds of the air" were an apocalyptic symbol in the intertestamental period referring to the gentile nations. The "fox" was a symbol for the Ammonites who, as Manson says, "were a people racially akin to but politically enemies of Israel" (Manson, *Sayings,* 72). In similar fashion, Herod's family (due to Herod's Idumean parentage) was racially mixed and was always seen by the Jewish population of first-century Palestine as foreign (Stern, *JPFC,* I, 261–277). Jesus calls Herod Antipas "that fox" (Luke 13:32). Manson writes,

Then the sense of the saying may be: everybody is at home in Israel's land except the true Israel. The birds of the air—the Roman overlords, the foxes—the Edomite interlopers, have made their position secure. The true Israel is disinherited by them: And if you cast your lot with me and mine you join the ranks of the dispossessed and you must be prepared to serve God under those conditions (Manson, *Sayings,* 72f.).

It is our view that the political overtones of the sayings of Jesus are often overlooked. Anyone who lives in the Middle East (where every religious breath has political overtones) is obliged to consider some rarely asked questions of the text. The extensive use of the parables with their somewhat veiled symbols; the cryptic phrase, "He who has ears to hear, let him hear"; the resisted pressure to make him into a king; the need to cross to the north on various occasions out of Galilee into non-Jewish provinces, and many other passages indicate that a political dimension was constantly a part of the world in which Jesus lived (cf. Manson, *Messiah*). Even so here. An oppressed people are seldom allowed to declare publicly that they are oppressed. They must talk of their oppression in symbols. The terrors of the Herodian era, with its torture and murder, were fresh in the minds of all. No one dared criticize Rome. The Romans and their Herodian supporters were the powerful of the land and their spies were everywhere. As Manson suggests, Jesus in a veiled fashion may well be saying: Look, if you want power and influence, go to the "birds" who "feather their nests" everywhere. Follow the "fox" who manages his own affairs with considerable cunning. For, in spite of your expectations, the Son of man stands powerless and alone. Are you serious in wanting to follow a *rejected* Son of man?

The Christological affirmation of the passage is clear. Jesus is the Son of man, but his ministry is a suffering rather than a triumphal fulfillment of that title.

We are not told the outcome. The volunteer does not answer. As in many of the parables of Jesus (cf. Luke 7:47; 14:24; 15:32) the parable is left suspended. We do not know whether the volunteer tightened his belt, "set his face steadfast," and stepped into line with the others, or whether, stunned at the price to be paid and at the shocking prospect of a rejected leader, he fell back from the side of the road and watched them pass. Clearly this volunteer mirrors those in every age who glibly offer to follow Jesus with no serious reflection on the price or the implications of following a suffering, rejected master. The reader is obliged to complete the conversation with his own response.

The second would-be disciple does not volunteer, but rather is recruited. Thus we have the *centrifugal* force of mission. Jesus directs three commands to the bystander. They are as follows:

THE SECOND DIALOGUE

B To another he said, "*Follow* me!"	FOLLOW
But he said, "Lord, let me *go* first	GO
to *bury* my father." But he said to him,	COST
"Leave the dead to *bury* their own dead.	
But you *go*	GO
and *proclaim* the kingdom of God."	FOLLOW

The use of inverted parallelism has been noted above. Furthermore, the Greek language is very precise in its verb structure. The type of imperative used here (aorist) indicates a command to start a new action. The person involved has not followed and is commanded to begin to do so. His response has often been misunderstood. Plummer thinks that either the father has just died or is about to expire (Plummer, 266; Marshall, 410–12). But such an interpretation is totally foreign to our Middle Eastern scene. Ibn al-Ṣalībī comments, " 'Let me go and bury' means: let me go and serve my father while he is alive and after he dies I will bury him and come" (Ibn al-Ṣalībī, I, 223). The same point is made by Saʿīd, our contemporary Arab commentator: "The second (disciple) is looking far into the future, for he postpones following Jesus to a time after the death of his father . . ." (Saʿīd, 258). In commenting on the recruit's specific request, "Let me . . . bury my father," Saʿīd writes,

> If his father had really died, why then was he not at that very moment keeping vigil over the body of his father? In reality he intends to defer the matter of following Jesus to a distant future when his father dies as an old man, who knows when. Little does he know that Jesus in a very short time will himself give up his spirit (Saʿīd, 259).

Saʿīd's point is well taken. We are told that the three conversations take place "on the road." If this recruit's father had indeed died, then what is he doing whiling away his time at the roadside? Actually Saʿīd's case is even stronger than his own cogent argument. The phrase "to bury one's father" is a traditional idiom that refers specifically to the duty of the son to remain at home and care for his parents until they are laid to rest respectfully. The present writer has heard this specific language used again and again among Middle Easterners discussing emigration. At some point in the conversation someone will ask, "Are you not going to bury your father first?" The speaker is usually addressing the would-be emigrant who is in his early thirties. The father under discussion usually is assumed to have some twenty years to live. The point is, "Are you not going to stay until you have fulfilled the traditional duty of taking care of your parents until their death, and then consider emigrating?" Other colloquialisms reflect the same cultural background. In the colloquial Syriac of isolated villages in Syria and Iraq, when a rebellious son tries to assert his independence from his father, the father's final stinging rebuke is, *kabit di qurtly* ("You want to bury me"). The point is, "You want me to hurry up and die so that my authority over you will be at an end and you will be on your own." Obviously the same cultural assumption seen above is at work here. Among the Lebanese, an older person can still offer to a younger person a compliment when, as an expression of endearment, the older person says in Arabic, *tuqburnī ja ibnī* ("You will bury me, my son"). The meaning is, "I think so much of you that I look on you as my own child and sincerely hope that you will be the one who will care for me in my old age and lay me with respect in my grave." Again, the assumption governing the idiomatic language is that the son has the duty to remain at home until the death of the parents. Then, and only then, can he consider other options. Here we are dealing with community expectations, which can be roughly translated into Western terms as peer pressures. The recruit on the side of the road is saying, "My community makes certain demands on me and the pull of these demands is very strong. Surely you do not expect me to violate the expectations of my community?" Yet this is precisely what Jesus requires. The proclaiming of the kingdom of God can only mean announcing the kingdom of God as a present reality. Jesus says the spiritually dead can take care of the traditional responsibilities of your local community, but as for *you,* go and proclaim the arrival of the kingdom (the word *you* is emphatic in the Greek text).

THE THIRD DIALOGUE

A'   And another said,
　　　　"I will *follow* you, Lord,   FOLLOW
　　　　　　but first let me (*go* and) take leave of those at my home."   GO
　　　　　　And Jesus said,
　　　　　　　"No one who puts his hand to the plow   COST TOO HIGH?
　　　　　　and looks back
　　　　　　is of any use in the kingdom of God."

Like the first volunteer, this would-be disciple brashly offers to follow the master. Like the recruit in the second dialogue, he has a precondition. This condition is often translated, "Let me first say farewell to those at my home." This request seems as legitimate as that of the recruit before it. Surely he will be allowed to go home and say good-bye! Elisha, when called to follow Elijah, asked for time to "kiss my father and my mother" (I Kings 19:20). His request was granted and he even took time to butcher and roast a pair of oxen. Is it not reasonable that this volunteer's request be granted? The answer can only come from a careful examination of his precise request.

The Greek word traditionally translated as "to say good-bye to" is *apotassō*. It can mean "say good-bye to" or "take leave of." It occurs four times in the rest of the New Testament in reference to taking leave. The RSV translation typifies the New Testament understanding of this verb. These four texts are as follows:

　　　　Mark 6:46   "After he had *taken leave of* them he went into the hills. . ."
　　　　Acts 18:18   "After this Paul . . . *took leave of* the brethren. . ."
　　　　　18:21   "But on *taking leave of* them. . ."
　　　　II Cor. 2:13   "I did not find my brother Titus there, so I *took leave of* them."

Only in Luke 9:60 do we find the same Greek verb translated as "say good-bye." The distinction between the two translations is important in Middle Eastern culture. The person who is *leaving* must request permission to leave from those who are *staying*. The people who *remain* behind can "say good-bye" to those *leaving*. This gentle formality is observed to the letter all over the Middle East on formal and informal occasions. The one who leaves requests permission to go. He asks, "With your permission?" Those who remain behind then respond, "May you go in safety," or "God go with you," or "May you go in peace" (cf. Rice, 74f.). Such responses are the granting of the permission requested. The RSV translations listed above properly observe this distinction in all four cases quoted. Jesus and Paul in each case are the ones leaving someone else. Thus they properly "take leave of" those who stay behind. On more formal occasions in the English-speaking world this idiom is not entirely lost. At a banquet the guest "takes leave of" the host. In spite of the fact that "take leave of" translates *all other* cases of *apotassō* in modern English versions, in this one case the real intent of the text has long been obscured by translating "say good-bye to." The point is that the volunteer is asking for the right to go home and *get permission* from "those at home" (i.e., his parents). Everyone listening to the dialogue knows that naturally his father will refuse to let the boy wander off on some questionable enterprise. Thus the volunteer's excuse is ready-made. Shedding crocodile tears he can loudly insist that he wants to go but his father will not permit him. The Old Syriac translation reflects this as it reads, "Let me first explain my case to those in my house." The early Syriac fathers knew perfectly well that this volunteer was not going to go home to plant one last fond kiss on his father's cheek and hear his mother's parting words of encouragement. Rather he was requesting permission to submit the question of following Jesus to their authority. Later Syriac translations did not maintain this insight.

In the Arabic versions two other distinct alternatives appear, each of them a legitimate translation of the Greek text. The Greek says literally, "greet the-ones in the house of-me." The Greek definite article (here translated "the-ones") can be masculine (meaning "the people") or neuter (meaning "the things"). Also, the verb *apotassō* is the verb *tassō* with a preposition attached to the front. The verb *tassō* by itself means "fix," "order," "determine," or "arrange for." The addition of prepositions to the beginnings of Greek words often changes their meaning. But sometimes it merely adds emphasis to the original root. *Apotassō does* mean "to take leave of" or "to say good-bye to." There is the possibility that *apotassō* in this text was intended to mean "arrange for." For nearly a thousand years some Arabic versions have translated it in this fashion. They read, "First let me *make arrangements* for those at home" (cf. Vatican Coptic 9; Vatican Arabic 610; The London-Paris Polyglot; Schawayr). If we read the definite article mentioned above as a neuter rather than a masculine, the text can be translated, "First let me arrange for my possessions at home." The Vatican Arabic 610 has this translation in its original. A corrector has changed "the things" to "the people." The difficulty with this understanding of the text is the somewhat shaky assumption that the root *tassō* ("to arrange for") is the intended meaning of the word rather than the better attested "to take leave of." Yet the Arabic versions mentioned above are evidence that some Arabic fathers saw the problem. The second volunteer is not going home to "say good-bye." Recognizing this they struggled with a translation that would make sense in their cultural world. Rather than these Arabic solutions, we prefer to return to the Old Syriac for a starting place.

The Old Syriac version noted above seems to point us in the right direction. The Greek *apotassō* does carry the meaning of "take leave of" and is usually so translated in every other text in the New Testament. We need only apply this translation to the present text with the cultural awareness that he is asking for permission to go. In that cultural scene he is clearly saying, "I will follow you, Lord, but of course the authority of my father is *higher* than your authority and I *must* have his permission before I venture out." Ibn al-Ṭayyib says simply, "The one who wants to greet his family has his heart tied to his family" (Ibn al-Ṭayyib, folio 97 ᵛ). In our Middle Eastern world, traditionally the authority of the father is supreme. It is little wonder that the father became a symbol for God. An engineer in his forties will make the traditional visit from a large metropolitan area to his father in the village to ask permission for foreign travel, or a change of job, or an important business venture. Even if the trip is ceremonial and the son is in reality running his own life, yet he will make the trip as a sign of respect. Rice correctly observes that the Middle Easterner in traditional society in the past would submit all details of his life to his parents.

> On rising, each day, a man offers his prayers, and then goes to his father and mother to kiss their hands and ask their blessing. When he begins a new business, he asks the favor of God on his enterprise and ends with a desire that his parents will approve of, and bless him, in this matter (Rice, 60).

The present author will never forget a class of Middle Eastern seminary students who literally turned white when this text was expounded with its clear affirmation that Jesus is claiming an authority higher than the authority of the second volunteer's father. It is difficult to communicate the stunning shock that comes to a Middle Eastern reader/listener when the reality of the demands of this text are made clear. This shock must have been all the more disturbing when claims were made by a young man (Jesus) in his early thirties in the first century. The only alternatives were acceptance and compliance or rejection and hostility. The form Jesus uses to make this kind of a startling affirmation must now be examined.

Jesus' response to the second volunteer is like his response to the first volunteer. Each of them is told a parable that falls into three lines. This latter parable is agricultural. Jeremias has provided an accurate and most helpful summary of a part of the agricultural background of this figure.

> The very light Palestinian plough is guided with one hand. This one hand, generally the left, must at the same time keep the plough upright, regulate its depth by pressure, and lift it over the rocks and stones in its path. The ploughman uses the other hand to drive the unruly oxen with a goad about two yards long, fitted with an iron spike. At the same time he must continually look between the hindquarters of the oxen, keeping the furrow in sight.

> This primitive kind of plough needs dexterity and concentrated attention. If the ploughman looks round, the new furrow becomes crooked. Thus, whoever wishes to follow Jesus must be resolved to break every link with the past, and fix his eye only on the coming Kingdom of God (Jeremias, *Parables*, 195).

Not only was the instrument difficult to maneuver, but also the process of plowing a field was far more exacting a task than is generally observed.

> Ploughing was careful and thorough; the first breaking of the stubble after the harvest took the form of furrows opened with broad bands between them to facilitate the absorption of the rains. In the ploughing after the first rain, closer furrows divided by ridges were opened for drainage; only at the third ploughing, before sowing, were the furrows close-set without intervening bands. The final working was to cover the seed . . . the implement was larger and heavier than the modern Arab plough, which it in general resembled (Applebaum, *JPFC*, II, 651f.).

Clearly plowing was a very precise operation with strips left initially for the absorption of water. At a later stage furrows were shaped for drainage. A third plowing prepared the soil, and a fourth covered the seed after planting. Obviously anyone wanting to fulfill such a responsibility needed to give undivided attention to what he was doing.

Thus the image is strong and clear. The tension illustrated is between loyalty to Jesus as the inaugurator of the kingdom of God and its all-consuming demands, and loyalty to the authority of the family. Both loyalties have high priority for any serious-minded Christian. When they are in conflict, that conflict is excruciatingly painful. This text is another of the "hard sayings" of which the Gospels are disturbingly full.

A part of the tension of the dialogue is the underlying assumption of the necessarily close relationship between a disciple and his teacher. In the Middle East such a relationship has always been deep and binding. The Talmud states that "A father and his son or a master and his disciple . . . are regarded as one individual" (B.T. *Erubin* 73a, Sonc., 510). Becoming the student/disciple of a sage is not a simple matter of "signing up for a course" for the purpose of acquiring information. Rather it is the cementing of a lifelong relationship to a person. With this as an understood starting point Jesus is here demanding that his authority (the demands of the kingdom) take precedence over *all* other relationships.

The person who cannot resolve the tension of conflicting loyalties and keeps turning back to look over his shoulder to see what the family is ordering is judged "useless" for the kingdom of God. In summary we observe that the symbol of plowing is aptly chosen (against Bultmann, *History*, 28). The distracted plowman might catch the plow on a rock, and perhaps break its wooden point, or he might unnecessarily tire the oxen pulling futilely against a plow caught on a rock. Or the plow point will cut back into the previously plowed furrows (and thereby destroy work already done), or cut aimlessly into the unplowed ground and make the next few furrows more difficult. Or he will ruin the field's drainage system, or damage its water absorption potential, or leave the newly planted seeds exposed to the birds, etc. Thus the plowman labors in harmony with work already done, with work yet to be accomplished, and in teamwork with his plow and his oxen. It is not too much to say that the past, present, and future are kept in a delicate harmony in the immediate task at hand. Thus a plowman distracted by a divided loyalty will not be able to maintain this harmony. He will be not only unproductive, but destructive in the context of his labors. Again the dialogue is open ended. Pressed with clear-cut, yet painful alternatives the second volunteer must decide. He volunteered with the apparent confidence that his loyalty to the kingdom would be accepted as secondary to his loyalty to his family. The parable of the plow wipes out his assumption. What will he do? We are not told. Indeed, as before, each listener/reader must respond.

In conclusion and summary it is appropriate to try to focus on what specific decision/response the original listener is pressed to make and what theological motifs comprise the impact of each dialogue.

THE FIRST DIALOGUE

The original listener/participant of the dialogue is pressed to consider something like the following:

> "This 'Son of man' is not the victorious figure you expect. He walks the way of sorrows. Are you willing to walk that way with him?"

The theological cluster of motifs includes at least the following:

1. Would-be disciples of Jesus at times fail to consider seriously the cost of discipleship.
2. Jesus is the Son of man. But he does not fulfill his ministry in power and acclaim but in rejection and humiliation.
3. Would-be disciples are not accepted until they have consciously decided to pay the price of following a rejected leader.
4. There is a centripetal force in mission. Some disciples are attracted into the company of the faithful.

THE SECOND DIALOGUE

The recruit in the second dialogue is challenged with something like the following:

> "Loyalty to Jesus and the kingdom he inaugurates is more important than loyalty to the cultural norms of your society."

The theological cluster has at least the following themes:

1. Jesus accepts *no* authority higher than his own.

2. The cultural demands of the community are not acceptable excuses for failure in discipleship (irrespective of how long-standing and sacred those demands are).

3. The "follow me" of Jesus is defined by the command, "Participate in and proclaim the kingdom of God." Thus Jesus is the unique agent of God through whom obedience to the kingdom of God is expressed.

4. There is a centrifugal force in mission. This person is a recruit, not a volunteer. Jesus reaches out to call him.

THE THIRD DIALOGUE

Jesus challenged this volunteer with the intent of the following:

"My authority is absolute. The authority of even your own family (if it conflicts with my authority) is merely a distraction to be avoided if you would be of any use to me/the kingdom."

The theological cluster of the third dialogue involves the following motifs:

1. The call of the kingdom of God must take precedence over all other loyalties.

2. The disciple with divided loyalties is a disruptive force in the work of the kingdom and is thus unfit for participation in it.

3. To follow Jesus is not defined as feeling the glow of an inner light, or perceiving an intellectual insight, but is compared to the taking up of a strenuous, creative, consuming task like putting one's hand to a plow and joining a team of oxen.

4. Service in the kingdom of God is synonymous with following Jesus. Thus Jesus is the unique agent of God through whom loyalty to God is expressed. That is, to serve/follow Jesus is to serve/follow God.

Thus an examination of the literary structure and the underlying cultural assumptions helps unlock at least a part of the meaning of these carefully constructed dialogues for the original participants and listeners and for the reader/listener of today.

Chapter 3

THE GOOD SAMARITAN
"What must I do to inherit eternal life?"
(Luke 10:25-37)

Derrett describes this parable as "a highly scientific piece of instruction clothed in a deceptively popular style" (Derrett, 227). This description is verified when the parable is seen as a part of a theological discussion.

In Luke 7:36-50 we observed a parable as a part of a wider theological dialogue. In a parallel passage in Luke 18:18-30 we will study a similar case where the parable of the Camel and the Needle is the center of a much larger theological drama. Here also the parable is a part of a theological dialogue. No doubt the dialogue has been given its present balanced form by Luke or his source. It has been argued that the original thrust of the parable has been obscured by the reuse of material for a different purpose (Linnemann, 51-58). At the same time leading scholars have affirmed the basic unity and authenticity of the entire passage (cf. Jeremias, *Parables,* 202f.; Manson, *Sayings,* 259f.; Marshall, 440f.). Our study of the parable assumes this basic unity and authenticity.

The setting makes considerable difference in the interpretation of this particular parable. In Luke 7:36-50 and 18:18-30 the shortness of the parable and the length of the dialogue lead naturally to a consideration of the parable as a part of the dialogue. By contrast, the parable of the Good Samaritan is fairly long and the dialogue surrounding it relatively short. Thus there is a natural tendency for the reader to ignore the dialogue. When we do so the parable becomes only an ethical exhortation to reach out to those in need. Indeed, the average Christian across the centuries has understood the parable almost exclusively in this way. In this study we will try to discern the structure and content of the dialogue and look at the parable as a part of that dialogue.

The dialogue between Jesus and the lawyer is made up of eight speeches that fall into two precise rounds of debate. In each round there are two questions and two answers. The formal structure of each scene is identical. Shortened to the main themes the full dialogue is as follows:

Round one: A lawyer stood up to put him to the test and said,

(1) Lawyer: (Question 1) "What must I *do* to inherit eternal *life?*"

(2) Jesus: (Question 2) "What about the law?"

(3) Lawyer: (Answer to 2) "Love God and your neighbor."

(4) Jesus: (Answer to 1) "*Do* this and *live.*"

Round Two: He (the lawyer), desiring to *justify himself,* said,

(5) Lawyer: (Question 3) "Who is my neighbor?"

(6) Jesus: (Question 4) "A certain man went down from Jerusalem. . ." "Which of these three became a neighbor?"

(7) Lawyer: (Answer to 4) "The one who showed mercy on him."

(8) Jesus: (Answer to 3) "*Go* and continue *doing* likewise."

           (Bailey, *Poet,* 73f., n. 52).

A number of important features tie the two dialogues together. (1) In each case there are two questions and two answers. (2) In each the lawyer asks the first question, but rather than answer his question Jesus poses a second. (3) In each round the lawyer then answers this second question. (4) Each round closes with Jesus' answer to the initial question (cf. Crossan, 61). (5) The first dialogue focuses on the question of *doing* something to inherit eternal life. On examination, so does the second. Desiring to "justify himself" he asks for a definition of his neighbor. Clearly he is still asking what he must do to gain eternal life. (6) Each round is introduced with an analysis of the motives of the lawyer. In the first we are told that he wants to test Jesus. In the second we find that he wants to justify himself. (7) Each round ends with instructions on what to *do.* Thus a long series of interlocking themes makes clear that the two rounds of dialogue are parallel halves of the same discussion. This interrelatedness of themes will become clearer as we examine the text in detail.

ROUND ONE:

This dialogue uses the inversion principle. The first and last speeches are on the subject of *do* and *live,* the inner two on the topic of the *law.* The conversation thus ends where it started.

The full text with its inversions is as follows:

And behold, a lawyer stood up to put him to the test, saying,

(1) Lawyer: (Question 1) "Teacher, what shall I *do* to inherit eternal *life?"*

  (2) Jesus: (Question 2) He said to him, "What is written in the law?
                                   How do you read?"

  (3) Lawyer: (Answer to 2) And he answered,
                    "You shall love the Lord your God
                    with all your heart, and with all your soul,
                    and with all your strength, and with all your mind;
                    and your neighbor as yourself."

(4) Jesus: (Answer to 1) And he said to him,
                    "You have answered right; *do* this, and you will *live."*

Speech 1:

> And behold, a lawyer stood up to put him to the test, saying,
> "Teacher, what shall I *do* to inherit eternal *life?"*

Ibrāhīm Saʿīd astutely observes that there is a basic contradiction in the actions of the lawyer.

> The text says, "He stood up." This is a social courtesy and a greeting of respect. Then we read, "to test him." This is an inner deception coming from a corrupt heart (Saʿīd, 276).

Saʿīd's judgment is a bit harsh but nevertheless valid. In the Middle East the student has always stood to address his teacher out of courtesy. Here the lawyer not only stands to address Jesus, but also gives him the title of "Teacher," which is Luke's word for rabbi (Dalman, *Words*, 336). The use of this title is an affirmation that Jesus is at least an equal (Linnemann, 51). After these acts of deference the lawyer tries to "test him." The subject for the test is that of inheriting eternal life.

On the surface the question is pointless. What can anyone *do* to inherit anything? Only legal heirs inherit. Yet the wording has some precedent. In the Old Testament the idea of inheritance was primarily applied to Israel's privilege of inheriting the land of promise. This inheritance is understood as a gift of God. Israel does nothing to either deserve or earn it. Foerster, describing the word *inheritance* in the Old Testament, writes, "Israel did not conquer the land by its own achievements... but... God's free disposition gave Israel the land as its share" (Foerster, *TDNT*, III, 760). In the same discussion Foerster writes, "Israel possesses its land only by divine ordination" (*ibid.*, 774). After the Old Testament period the phrase "inherit the earth/land" is applied to the salvation which God extends to His people (cf. Dalman, *Words*, 126). "To possess the land" in Isaiah 60:21 is interpreted by the rabbis to mean participation in the salvation of the age to come (B.T. *Sanhedrin* 11; cf. Dalman, *Words*, 126). The inheritance becomes eternal life, and the way to achieve it is to keep the law.

No less than the famous Rabbi Hillel, an older contemporary of Jesus, said, "who has gained for himself words of Torah has gained for himself the life of the world to come" (Mishna *Pirke Aboth* 2:8; cf. Charles II, 696). An anonymous rabbinical saying reads, "Great is Torah, for it gives to them that practice it life in this world and in the world to come" (Mishna *Pirke Aboth* 6:7; cf. Charles, II, 712). In a book of Psalms, probably written by Pharisees about 50 B.C. and called The Psalms of Solomon, we are given even more details. Psalm 14:1-2 claims that God is faithful

> To them that walk in the righteousness of *His commandments,*
> In the law which he commanded us that *we might live.*
> The pious of the Lord shall live by it forever (Charles, II, 645; emphasis mine).

The same Psalm (14:9-10) ends,

> Therefore their [sinners'] *inheritance* is Sheol and darkness and destruction . . .
> but the pious of the Lord *shall inherit life* in gladness.

Thus sinners inherit Sheol, while the righteous, by keeping the law, inherit life eternal. Another early noncanonical book, called Slavonic Enoch, also treats the topic of eternal life as an inheritance. In chapter 9 Enoch is taken to Eden and told:

> This place (Eden), O Enoch, is prepared for the righteous, who endure all manner of offense from those that exasperate their souls, who avert their eyes from iniquity, and make righteous judgments, and give bread to the hungering, and cover the naked with clothing, and raise up the fallen, and help injured orphans, and who walk without fault before the face of the Lord, and serve him alone, and for them is prepared this place for *eternal inheritance* (emphasis mine; cf. Charles, II, 434f.).

Quite likely the audience and perhaps the lawyer expected from Jesus some kind of listing like the above as an explanation of the requirements of the law. It would then be possible to debate the fine points of what should and what should not be on the list. Jesus thus has two obvious alternatives. He can take the Old Testament approach and insist that the "inheritance of Israel" is a gift and that man can do nothing to inherit it. Such a stance would quite likely have sparked a sterile debate. Or he can go along with rabbinic opinion and concentrate on the law. Jesus chooses the latter.

Regarding the law, Ibn al-Ṭayyib suggests another possible aspect of the background of the text. He affirms that the lawyers were most likely uneasy about Jesus' attitude toward the law. Indeed, at least some leading rabbis (as we have just noted) affirmed that eternal life was achieved through keeping the law. But they were hearing disturbing noises from this young rabbi. Did he or did he not believe that the inheritance of Israel was available through a keeping of the law? Ibn al-Ṭayyib proposes that the "test" was to discover an answer to this question (Ibn al-Ṭayyib, folios 100–104). If Ibn al-Ṭayyib's suggestion is at all correct there is all the more reason for Jesus to reply by turning to the law. But rather than offer his own views, he skillfully solicits the questioner's opinion.

Speech 2:

He said to him,
"What is written in the law? How do you read?"

The phrase, "How do you read?" can mean, "May I hear your authorities with exposition?" (Derrett, 224). If this is correct the lawyer offers exposition by selection and order but without authorities. Jeremias argues that it means "How do you *recite* (in worship)?" (cf. Jeremias, *Theology,* 187). This would explain why the lawyer turns to the creed. Elements of each explanation may be involved.

Speech 3:

And he answered, "You shall love the Lord your God
with all your heart, and with all your soul,
and with all your strength, and with all your mind;
and your neighbor as yourself."

In Matthew and Mark this combination of Deuteronomy 6:5 (love God) and Leviticus 19:18 (love the neighbor) is attributed to Jesus. Derrett observes two occurrences of this combination in The Testaments of the Twelve Patriarchs and comments that there "may well be evidence that such a combination was commonplace in some quarters in Jesus' time" (Derrett, 225). If so, it is clear that Jesus *endorsed* this opinion and made it his own. Thus the lawyer may be doing the same thing that Jesus has just done. That is, Jesus knows any lawyer will affirm "keep the law" as an answer to this question on eternal life. So Jesus draws the lawyer out on the topic of the law. The lawyer in turn may know that Jesus has originated or affirmed this combination of love for God and neighbor as the essence of the law. Thus the lawyer quotes Jesus' own position in order to get it into the discussion so that the lawyer might "test" Jesus' loyalty to the law, as Ibn al-Ṭayyib has suggested.

Whatever the origin of the combination of these two texts and whatever the motive for its appearance in the dialogue, it is pure genius as a summary of duty to God and people. One of its most remarkable features is the fact that love for God (found in Deuteronomy) is listed first even though Deuteronomy is chronologically *after* Leviticus in the Old Testament (Derrett, 223). It is through a love of *God* that the believer is to approach people. This then has profound implications for the how, why, and who of the love for the neighbor.

We note also that the quotation is expanded from the Old Testament text to include "with all your mind." In Matthew 22:37 this phrase appears in the mouth of Jesus as a substitute for the phrase "with all your strength." In Mark 12:33 it comes after "with all your heart." Indeed, the "heart" for the ancient Hebrew was (among other things) the center of the intellect (he kept the law "in his heart," Ps. 119:11). Thus the phrase "with all your mind" can be seen as an expansive translation in the Greek Gospel of the meaning of the original Hebrew text (Derrett, 224, n. 5, offers another explanation).

Speech 4:

And he said to him,
"You have answered right; *do* this, and you will *live*."

A number of observations can be made here. (1) Barth observes that "Jesus praises him for his good knowledge and faithful recitation" (Barth, 417). Indeed, the man has the right theology, but the question is, Is he willing to act on it? His intellectual stance is excellent; his performance is still in question. (2) As in the case of Simon in 7:43, Jesus evokes the right answer from the lawyer himself. He does not tell him what to do, rather the lawyer tells himself. (3) The lawyer has asked about eternal life. Jesus widens the discussion to *all* of life. The Greek text has a future, "you shall live." This most certainly means the immediate future (i.e., do this and you will come alive). It could mean the future after death (do this and you will live in the next life). However, here in the Middle East, Syriac and Arabic translators have consistently agreed on the former. The Old Syriac version turns the verb into a present and reads literally, "do this and you are living." The Peshitta and Harclean Syriac (along with the Arabic versions) construct the grammar somewhat differently but also indicate a present result of a present action; do this *now* and *now* you will live. Finally, the text is a quotation from Joseph in Genesis 42:18. Joseph is talking about the near future when his younger brother is brought to him. (In the parallel discussion of the same topic in Luke 18 below we will observe this same shift from an exclusive interest in the life to come to an inclusion of the present.) (4) The verb "do" is a present imperative meaning "keep on doing." The lawyer requested definition of a specific limited requirement—"what *having done* I will inherit. . . ." The answer is given in a command for an open-ended life-style that requires unlimited and unqualified love for God and people.

Clearly the very law which the lawyer quotes sets a standard that *no one* can fully reach. In the parallel discussion on the same question in Luke 18:18–30 a standard is set that everyone listening judges impossible. They ask, "Who then can be saved?" The answer is given, "What is impossible with men is possible with God" (18:26–27). The same theological posture is seen here. By his answer, Jesus simply says, "You want to *do* something to inherit eternal life? Very well, just *continually* love God and your neighbor with the totality of all that you are." There is *no* line drawn. No list of how much is expected, such as we noted in Slavonic Enoch, is offered. Rather, the requirements are left limitless and, as Summers observes,

THE GOOD SAMARITAN 39

Jesus and Paul agree with their Jewish contemporaries that complete obedience to the law of God was the way to be right with God. They found that way ineffective in experience however, because of man's inability to give complete obedience to the law (Summers, 125).

The first round of the debate closes. But the lawyer has not yet given up the hope that he can earn his own entrance into eternal life. The law has been quoted. Now he needs some commentary, some *midrash*. The God whom he must love is known. But who is "this neighbor" whom he must love as himself? He needs some definition, perhaps a list. If the list is not too long he may be able to fulfill its demands. Thus he initiates the second round of the debate.

ROUND II

Speech 5:

He, desiring to *justify himself*, said,
"Who is my neighbor?"

This hope for self-justification is not a case of "excusing himself for asking Jesus, although he knows what Jesus thinks" (Jeremias, *Parables*, 202; Marshall, 447). Rather he simply hopes yet to *do* something and gain eternal life; hence the question. Karl Barth observes,

The lawyer does not know that only by mercy can he live and inherit eternal life. He does not want to live by mercy. He does not even know what it is. He actually lives by something quite different from mercy, by his own intention and ability to present himself as a righteous man before God (Barth, 417).

This same observation was drawn by Ibn al-Ṭayyib, who understood the question to mean that the lawyer wanted "to see himself as fully righteous" (Ibn al-Ṭayyib, folio 101ʳ). Ibn al-Ṭayyib continues,

The question put to the Christ, "Who is my neighbor," is asked in order that he will answer, "Your relative and your friend." The lawyer will then answer, "I have fully loved these." Then Jesus will praise him and say to him, "You have truly fulfilled the law." The lawyer will then depart, basking before the people, in the praise of his good works, and enjoying a newly won honor and confidence based on that praise (Ibn al-Ṭayyib, folio 101ᵛ).

It is pointless to press too far into the mind of the lawyer. Yet Ibn al-Ṭayyib's suggestions have some merit. In the parallel discussion with the ruler in chapter 18 the conversation does turn in this direction. There the law is recited. The ruler claims to have fulfilled it and probably expects praise for his noble efforts. There, as here, the questioner must be surprised by the unexpected turn of the conversation.

In harmony with Ibn al-Ṭayyib's suggestion we observe that the text of

Leviticus identifies the neighbor as being one's brother and "the sons of your own people" (Lev. 19:17–18). The rabbis understood this to include all Jews. They were divided over the proselyte and were sure that it did *not* include gentiles (Jeremias, *Parables*, 202). Jeremias notes a rabbinical saying "that heretics, informers, and renegades 'should be pushed (into the ditch) and not pulled out'" (*ibid.*, 202f.). John Lightfoot quotes a *midrash* on Ruth, chapter four:

> The gentiles, amongst whom and us there is no war, and so those that are keepers of sheep amongst the Israelites, and the like, we are not to contrive their death; but if they be in any danger of death, we are not bound to deliver them; e.g., if any of them fall into the sea you shall not need to take them out: for it is said, "Thou shalt not rise up against the blood of thy neighbor"; but such a one is not thy neighbor (Lightfoot, 107).

Thus the lawyer asked his question in a world that held a variety of views on just who the neighbor really was. Indeed, as Safrai observes, "The oral law was not fully uniform" (Safrai, *JPFC*, II, 794). There was a lively debate on points of interpretation.

The literary form is that of a seven-scene parabolic ballad and is as follows:

1	A man was going down from Jerusalem to Jericho	
	and he fell among *robbers*.	COME
	And they stripped him and beat him	DO
	and departed, leaving him half dead.	GO
2	Now by coincidence a certain *priest* was going down that road,	COME
	and when he saw him,	DO
	he passed by on the other side.	GO
3	Likewise also a *Levite* came to the place,	COME
	and when he saw him,	DO
	he passed by on the other side.	GO
4	And a certain *Samaritan*, traveling, came to him,	COME
	and when he saw him,	DO
	he had compassion on him.	DO
5	He went to him,	DO
	and bound up his wounds,	
	pouring on oil and wine.	
6	Then he put him on his own riding animal	DO
	and led him (it) to the inn,	
	and took care of him.	
7	The next day he took out and gave two denarii to the manager	DO
	and said, "Take care of him, and whatever more you spend	
	I, on my return, *I* will repay you."	

Jesus' immortal reply to the lawyer's query is here seen as a part of the continuing theological dialogue with the lawyer. It is an introduction to a second question. As in the first round, Jesus wants to solicit from the questioner his own answer. The parable is told to make this possible.

Yet on a deeper level, as T. W. Manson has astutely observed, "The question is unanswerable, and ought not to be asked. For love does not begin by defining its objects: it discovers them" (Manson, *Sayings,* 261). The unanswerable question remains unanswered; rather it is transformed in the response that Jesus makes. Initially the structure must be examined. This particular form we have called the "parabolic ballad" because of the balladlike stanzas into which the story falls (cf. Bailey, *Poet,* 72). The action shifts dramatically from scene to scene. The first three are dominated by the robbers, the priest, and the Levite. In each case the action can be characterized by the verbs *come, do,* and *go.* Each of them comes, does something, and leaves. The pattern is broken by the Samaritan who, contrary to all expectation, does not leave. From then on, each line describes an action (seven in all) on the part of the Samaritan in service to the wounded man. The list is long because the lone Samaritan must make up for the actions of everyone else. He compensates for their failures in an inverse order, hence the inverted parallelism, some of which has already been noted by Crossan (Crossan, 62). The Levite (scene 3) could at least have rendered first aid. This is the Samaritan's first cluster of actions (scene 5). The priest (scene 2) was certainly riding and could have taken the man to safety. The Samaritan does this as well (scene 6). The robbers (scene 1) take his money and leave him half dead with no intention of returning. The Samaritan (scene 7) *pays* from his own pocket, and leaves him provided for with a promise to return and pay more if necessary. The climax occurs in the center with the unexpected compassion of the Samaritan. The three-line form of each scene may be artificial. What is clear is that the parable is a drama in seven scenes. Each of these scenes needs careful attention.

Scene 1: The Robbers

A man was going down from Jerusalem to Jericho and he fell among *robbers*.   COME
And they stripped him and beat him   DO
and departed, leaving him half dead.   GO

The seventeen-mile descending road through the desert from Jerusalem to Jericho has been dangerous all through history. Pompey had to wipe out "strongholds of brigands" near Jericho (Strabo, *Geogr.* xvi.2.41; noted in Plummer, 286). Ibn al-Ṭayyib observes that there were many thieves on the Jericho-Jerusalem road (Ibn al-Ṭayyib, folio 102ʳ). The crusaders built a small fort at the halfway mark to protect pilgrims; thus robbers in the area must have been a serious threat. William Thomson has a dramatic description of a group of pilgrims traveling over the same road in 1857 with a large armed guard. One traveler fell behind and was "attacked, robbed and stripped naked" (Thomson, II, 445). Thus this road has always provided a perfect setting for this kind of drama.

The story intentionally leaves the man undescribed (Marshall, 447). Yet a Jewish audience would naturally assume that the traveler is a Jew. He is beaten, stripped, and left "half dead." The beating probably means he struggled with his attackers. In 1821 a British traveler, J. S. Buckingham, journeyed through Palestine. Near Capernaum he met a party that had been attacked by robbers. Two of their group had resisted and were beaten so badly that they had to be left behind (Buckingham, 475; cf. also Jeremias, *Parables*, 203). The rabbis identified stages for death. The "half dead" of the text is the equivalent for a rabbinic category of "next to death," which meant at the point of death. The next stage was called "one just expiring" (Lightfoot, 108). Clearly the man is unconscious and thus cannot identify himself. Nor can his identity be ascertained by any onlooker.

The wounded traveler's condition is not a curious incidental. He is unconscious and stripped. These details are skillfully constructed to create the tension that is at the heart of the drama. Our Middle Eastern world was and is made up of various ethnic-religious communities. The traveler is able to identify strangers in two ways. He can talk to the unknown man on the road and identify him from his speech, or, even before that, he can identify him by his manner of dress. In the first century the various ethnic-religious communities within Palestine used an amazing number of languages and dialects. In Hebrew alone there was classical Hebrew, late Biblical Hebrew, and Mishnaic Hebrew. But in addition to Hebrew, one could find settled communities in Palestine that used Aramaic, Greek, Southwest Ashdodian, Samaritan, Phoenician, Arabic, Nabatean, and Latin (cf. Rabin, *JPFC*, II, 1001–1037). The country had many settled communities of pagans (cf. Flusser, *JPFC*, II, 1065–1100). No one traveling a major highway in Palestine could be sure that the stranger he might meet would be a fellow Jew. A few quick questions and his language and/or dialect would identify him. But what if he was unconscious beside the road? In such a case one would need to take a quick glance at the stranger's clothes. In Marissa in Palestine wall drawings of distinctive Hellenistic garb have been recently discovered. These appear in early gallery tombs of a Sidonian community living there in Palestine (Foerster, *JPFC*, II, 973). These tomb paintings demonstrate conclusively that Jewish and non-Jewish costumes could be distinguished by sight in Palestine in the first century. The various ethnic communities of Dura-Europos, with their distinctive styles of clothing, are depicted in frescoes of the second-third century. This pattern remained unchanged, and even separate villages of Palestine and Lebanon had their distinctive traditional dress. Lamartine, traveling through Palestine in 1832, records observing a large group of Arabs at a distance and casually notes that they were from Nablous, "whose costume the tribe displayed" (Lamartine, 389). In the first century, at least, Greek and Jew each had their distinctive dress. But what if the man beside the road was stripped? He was thereby reduced to a mere human being in need. He belonged to no man's ethnic or religious community! It is such a person that the robbers leave wounded beside the road. Who will turn aside to render aid?

Scene 2: The Priest

Now by coincidence a certain *priest* was going down that road,	COME
and when he saw him,	DO
he passed by on the other side.	GO

The priest is most certainly riding. We deduce this from the fact that the priests were among the upper classes of their society. In this connection Stern observes, "Towards the close of the Second Temple period, the priesthood constituted the prestigious and élite class in Jewish society" (Stern, *JPFC*, II, 582). Elsewhere he refers to them as being in the "upper classes" (*ibid.*, 561, 582). In the Middle East no one with any status in the community takes seventeen-mile hikes through the desert. The poor walk. Everyone else in general, and the upper classes in particular, always ride. This is the natural assumption of the parable. The same kind of assumption prevails in the American scene when a farmer says, "I am going to town." If the destination is seventeen miles away you *know* he will be driving. He does not mention his car. There is no need to do so. Indeed, when the Samaritan appears, he too is riding but this fact is not mentioned. His riding animal happens to function in the story and so is mentioned but only after the Samaritan has ridden onto the scene. Furthermore, without this assumption the story loses a great deal of its thrust. If the priest had been walking, what could he have done besides offer first aid and sit, hoping that someone might come by with a riding animal who could *really* help him? The parable turns on the presupposition that what the Samaritan *did,* at least the priest *could* have done. If this is not true we would be obliged to conclude, "Of course the Samaritan should help the man; he is the only one who really can." Rather the parable assumes an equal potential for service, at least on the part of the priest and the Samaritan. Finally, the Samaritan might be a poor man, yet his animal is assumed. How much more the priest. Indeed, the upper-class status of the priest assures an image of a well-mounted aristocrat. Thus the parable in its original setting gives us a picture of a priest riding by, seeing the wounded man (presumably at some distance), and then steering his mount to the far side of the road and continuing on his way.

In trying to reconstruct the world in which this priest lives and thinks it is instructive to turn to Sirach 12:1-7:

> If you do a good turn, know for whom you are doing it,
> and your good deeds will not go to waste.
> Do good to a devout man, and you will receive a reward,
> if not from him, then certainly from the Most High. . . .
> Give to a devout man,
> *do not go to the help of a sinner,*

Do good to a humble man,
   give nothing to a godless one.
Refuse him bread, do not give him any,
   it might make him stronger than you are;
then you would be repaid evil twice over
   for all the good you had done him.
For the Most High himself detests sinners,
   and will repay the wicked with a vengeance.
Give to the good man,
   and *do not go to the help of a sinner* (emphasis mine).

Thus, help offered to sinners may be labor against God Himself who detests sinners. Furthermore, sinners' hands should not be strengthened. Clearly Ben Sirach cautions against helping *any* stranger. The priest may have been influenced by such ideas current in his time. More likely, he is the prisoner of his own legal/theological system. The priest's problem, writes Derrett, is "a balancing of commandments" (Derrett, 212). The rabbis taught,

> Whence do we know that if a man sees his fellow drowning, mauled by beasts, or attacked by robbers, he is bound to save him! From the verse, thou shalt not stand by the blood of thy neighbor (B.T. *Sanhedrin* 73a, Sonc., 495).

But the priest did not actually see it happen. Furthermore, how can he be sure the wounded man is a neighbor? When confronted with a mute, stripped body he is paralyzed. With speech impossible and distinctive dress missing, the observer cannot identify him. But not only is there the possibility that the wounded man is a non-Jew, but also he might be dead; if so, contact with him would defile the priest. The priest collects, distributes, and eats tithes. If he defiles himself he can do none of these things, and his family and servants will suffer the consequences with him.

A tithe of the tithe, called a "wave offering," was given by Levites to priests for consumption by the priest and his household. They could be eaten only in a state of ritual purity (Safrai, *JPFC*, II, 819). Also, while under the ban on defilement he could not officiate at any service and could not wear his phylacteries (*ibid.*, 799). Furthermore, the written law listed five sources of defilement. Contact with a corpse was at the top of the list. The oral law added four more. Contact with a non-Jew was the first of this additional list (*ibid.*, 829). Thus this poor priest was in critical danger of contracting ritual impurity in its most severe form from the point of view of both the written and the oral law.

Contracting ritual purity was a very serious matter. Safrai writes,

> the rules of purity were . . . always considered an end in themselves, not just a means to an end. They were held to be the best way of avoiding sin and attaining the heights of sanctity as all texts affirm, from Philo to the tannaitic period (*ibid.*, 832).

Thus the priest is struggling with trying to be a good man. He seeks to avoid sin and attain sanctity. An additional part of his struggle is related to the fact that he is (like the wounded man) traveling *down* from Jerusalem to Jericho. Large numbers of priests served in the temple for two-week periods and lived in Jericho. Any priest leaving Jerusalem on his way to Jericho would naturally be assumed to have fulfilled his period of service and be on his way home (Safrai, *JPFC*, 870). We are told that "Ritual purification ordinarily took place in the Temple" (*ibid.*, 877). Furthermore, the twice daily sacrifice in the temple was carried out by priests, Levites, and Jewish laymen called the "delegation of Israel." During the service a gong was struck at the time of the offering up of the incense. At the sound of this gong the chief of the delegation of Israel made all the unclean stand at the Eastern gate in front of the altar. Some commentators affirm that these people were unclean priests who were obliged to stand there "to shame them for their remission in contracting uncleanness" (Danby, 587, n. 12; cf. Mishna *Tamid* 4, 6). It is easy to imagine the burning humiliation that the priest would feel if he contracted ritual impurity. Having probably just completed his two weeks as a *leader* of worship in the temple, is he now to return in humiliation and stand at the Eastern gate with the unclean? Furthermore, in addition to the humiliation involved, the process of restoring ritual purity was time consuming and costly. It required finding, buying, and reducing a red heifer to ashes, and the ritual took a full week. Thus it is easy to understand the priest's predicament as he suddenly comes upon an unconscious man beside the road.

More specifically, he cannot approach closer than four cubits to a dead man without being defiled, and he will have to overstep that boundary just to ascertain the condition of the wounded man. Then, if he *is* dead, the priest will have to rend his garments. This action "conflicted with an obligation not to destroy valuable things" (Derrett, 213). Derrett thinks that wives, servants, and colleagues would have applauded his neglect of the wounded man and that the Pharisees would have found him justified in stopping and yet "entitled to pass by" (*ibid.*, 215). Finally, the commandment not to defile was unconditional, while the commandment to love the neighbor was conditional. Therefore the priest had a legal right to pass by (*ibid.*, 213). In commenting on the Jewish background of this parable Oesterley writes,

> The whole reason of the growth and development of the Oral Law was the need of providing for the ever-increasing new cases which the experiences of life brought to the fore. The *system*, therefore, was to blame; so that the priest and the Levite are looked upon as victims of an evil, or at least an inadequate, system (emphasis his; Oesterley, 163).

The priest was the victim of a rule book ethical/theological system. Life for him was a codified system of "do's and don'ts." This mentality persists in many forms in our day and continues to claim to offer the security of having quick answers to all of life's problems and questions. The answers assure the devotee that he is in the right and seem adequate until we face an unconscious man on the side of the road. When we do, we discover that subtly *the* agenda has become, "Maintain status within the supporting community," rather than, "Reach out in freedom to the one in need beside the road." This dynamic seems to have overtaken the priest and he passes by on the other side.

Scene 3: The Levite

Likewise also a *Levite* came to the place,   COME
and when he saw him,   DO
he passed by on the other side.   GO

Both Levite and priest fall into the Come-Do-Go action pattern established by the robbers. This action pattern classifies the priest and the Levite with the robbers. The priest and the Levite contribute to the wounded man's sufferings by their neglect. The word "likewise" indicates that the Levite is also descending and thus following the priest.

The Levite almost certainly knows there is a priest ahead of him. Derrett thinks that the Samaritan also knew the others had passed the wounded man. He reasons that the Samaritan would have been bound to see the others on the road regardless of which way he was traveling, "in view of the nature of the man's injuries and the contours of the road which make a long lapse of time and prolonged absence from view unlikely" (Derrett, 217). The traces of the old Roman road are still visible and the present writer has personally walked almost its entire length. Derrett's statement about the contours of the road is true. One is able to see the road ahead for a considerable distance most of the way. Furthermore, having traveled Middle Eastern desert roads by camel, by donkey, and on foot for twenty years, I know that the traveler is *extremely* interested in who else is on the road. His life may depend upon it. A question put to a bystander at the edge of the last village just before the desert begins; a brief exchange with a traveler coming the other way; fresh tracks on the soft earth at the edge of the road where men and animals prefer to walk; a glimpse in the clear desert air of a robed figure ahead; all of these are potential sources of knowledge for the Levite traveler. As I have determined by investigation, Middle Eastern peasants assume that the Levite does know there is a priest ahead of him on the road. For them the *story* assumes it. It is perhaps truer to the story to assume the Levite's knowledge of the priest on the road ahead of him than to assume his ignorance. This detail is significant for the fabric of the drama. Our reasoning is as follows. The Levite is not bound by as many regulations as the priest. Derrett observes, "a Levite might, had he wished, have allowed himself more latitude than would a priest" (*ibid.*, 211). Jeremias writes, "the Levite was only required to observe ritual cleanliness in the course of his cultic activities" (Jeremias, *Parables*, 203). Thus he *could* render aid, and if the man were dead or died on his hands, the repercussions for him would not be as serious.

In contrast to the priest, the Levite approaches the man. This is reflected in his actions. The priest, traveling, saw and passed by. But the Levite *came to the place*, then saw and passed by. Plummer writes, "The Levite came up to him quite close, saw and passed on" (Plummer, 287). The Levite does "come to the place" (even if *genomenos* is omitted). Thus the Levite may have crossed the defilement line of four cubits and satisfied his curiosity with a closer look. He then decided against offering aid and passed by. Fear of defilement cannot be his strongest motive. Fear of the robbers may be. More likely it is the example of the higher ranking priest that deters him. Not only can he say, "If the priest on ahead did nothing, why should I, a mere Levite, trouble myself," but,

> the Levite in his turn may have thought with himself, that it could not be incumbent on him to undertake a perilous office, from which the priest had just shrunk; duty it could not be, else that other would never have omitted it. For him to thrust himself upon it now would be a kind of affront to his superior, an implicit charging of him with inhumanity and hardness of heart (Trench, 314).

More than charging him with "hardness of heart" by stopping, the Levite would be criticizing the priest's interpretation of the law! When the professional reads the data one way, is the poor layman to call his judgment into question?

The Levite, like the priest, cannot find out whether or not the wounded man is a neighbor. This may be why he approaches him. Perhaps he can talk? Failing to find out, he then continues on. Whatever his reasons the result is the same; in spite of his religious profession, nothing in his total orientation leads him to help the wounded man.

The Levite is of a lower social class than the priest and may well be walking. In any case, he could have rendered minimal medical aid even if he had had no way to take the man to safety. If he was walking we can imagine him saying to himself, "I cannot carry the man to safety and am I to sit here all night and risk attack from these same robbers?" In any case, he fades from the scene following the priest.

Scene 4: The Samaritan

And a certain *Samaritan*, traveling, came to him,	COME
and when he saw him,	DO
he had compassion on him.	DO

As in 14:18–20 and 20:10–14 we are dealing with a progression of three characters. After the appearance of the priest and the Levite the audience expects a Jewish layman (Jeremias, *Parables*, 204). Not only is priest-Levite-layman a natural sequence, but, as we have observed, these same three classes of people officiated at the temple. Even as delegations of priests and Levites went up to Jerusalem and returned after their specified two weeks, so also the "delegation of Israel" went up to serve with them. After their terms of service one would naturally expect all three to be on the road returning home. The listener notes the first and the second and anticipates the third. The sequence is interrupted, however. Much to the shock and amazement of the audience, the third man along the road is one of the hated Samaritans. Heretics and schismatics are usually despised more than unbelievers. The centuries of animosity between the Jews and the Samaritans are reflected in the wisdom of Ben Sirach (50:25-26), *ca.* 200 B.C.

> There are two nations that my soul detests,
>   the third is not a nation at all:
> the inhabitants of Mount Seir, and the Philistines,
>   and the stupid people living at Shechem.

So the Samaritans are classed with the Philistines and Edomites. The Mishna declares, "He that eats the bread of the Samaritans is like to one that eats the flesh of swine" (Mishna *Shebiith* 8:10, Danby, 49). At the time of Jesus the bitterness between Jews and Samaritans was intensified by the Samaritans having defiled the temple during a passover just a few years earlier by scattering human bones in the temple court (cf. Josephus, *Antiquities*, 18:30). Oesterley observes,

> The Samaritans were publicly cursed in the synagogues; and a petition was daily offered up praying God that the Samaritans might not be partakers of eternal life (Oesterley, 162).

Jesus could have told a story about a noble Jew helping a hated Samaritan. Such a story could have been more easily absorbed emotionally by the audience. Rather, we have the hated Samaritan as the hero. The present writer can only confess that in twenty years he has not had the courage to tell a story to the Palestinians about a noble Israeli, nor a story about the noble Turk to the Armenians. Only one who has lived as a part of a community with a bitterly hated traditional enemy can understand fully the courage of Jesus in making the despised Samaritan appear as morally superior to the religious leadership of the audience. Thus Jesus speaks to one of the audience's deepest hatreds and painfully exposes it.

The Greek word "compassion" (*splanchnizomai*) has at its root the word "innards" (*splanchnon*). It is a very strong word in both Greek and Semitic imagery (cf. Bailey, *Cross,* 55f.). Indeed, the Samaritan has a deep "gut level reaction" to the wounded man. The Old Syriac version reflects the intensity of this word by translating, "He was compassionate to him and showed mercy," using two strong verbs. The Samaritan is not a gentile. He is bound by the same Torah that also tells him that his neighbor is his countryman and kinsman. He is traveling in *Judea* and it is less likely for him than for the priest and the Levite that the anonymous wounded man is a neighbor. In spite of this, *he* is the one who acts.

The text has a clear progression as we move through the scenes. The priest only goes *down the road*. The Levite comes *to the place*. The Samaritan comes *to the man*. As Derrett has observed, he too risks contamination, which if incurred extends to his animals and wares (Derrett, 217). With at least one animal and quite likely more (as we will note), and perhaps some goods, he is a prime target for the same robbers who just might respect a priest or a Levite as a "man of religion" but will have no hesitation in attacking a hated Samaritan.

The Samaritan has one advantage. As an outsider he will *not* be influenced as a Jewish layman might be by the actions of the priest and the Levite. We do not know which way the Samaritan is going. If he is going uphill he has just passed the priest and the Levite and is thus keenly aware of their actions. If he too is traveling downhill he, like the Levite, most likely knows who is ahead of him. Thus, somewhat like the Levite, he can say, "This unconscious man is probably a Jew and these Jews have abandoned him to die. Why should I get involved?" As we will note, if he does involve himself he will risk retaliation from the family and friends of the very Jew he is aiding. In spite of all these considerations he feels deep compassion for the wounded man and that compassion is immediately translated into concrete actions.

Scene 5: First Aid

He went to him,
and bound up his wounds,
pouring on oil and wine.

The center of the parable displays the unexpected appearance of the compassionate Samaritan. The rest of the action is the expression of that compassion. In this scene the Samaritan offers the first aid that the Levite failed to offer.

As in many of the parables, the language is deceptively simple. The Samaritan must first clean and soften the wounds with oil, then disinfect them with wine, and finally bind them up. However, this is not the order of the phrases in the text. The binding up of the wounds is mentioned first. Granted, the Greek syntax makes the actions simultaneous. But the Syriac and Arabic versions without exception give us two past tenses—he bound up and he poured. These translations make the peculiar order of the actions even more striking. Is it not possible to see the binding of the wounds deliberately mentioned first to heighten the impact of the theological overtones of the act? As Derrett has noted, the binding up of wounds is "imagery used of God as He acts to save the people" (*ibid.*, 220). God says to Jeremiah, "I will restore health to you, and your wounds I will heal" (Jer. 30:17). In the first ten verses of Hosea 6 there are no less than twelve phrases echoed here:

he has torn
he will bind us up
he will revive us
he will raise us up
that we may live before him
he will come to us
your love is like . . . the dew that goes early away
I desire steadfast love and not sacrifice
they transgressed the covenant
robbers lie in wait for a man
priests . . . commit villainy
in the house of Israel I have seen a horrible thing

God's first healing act is to bind up Ephraim's wounds. Indeed these phrases together could make a fitting prologue to the parable. Each phrase can apply to some part of the drama as it unfolds. Specifically in this text Ephraim is torn and left and finally cries out for help. We are then told that Yahweh

> will bind us up
> will revive us
> will raise us up
> will come to us.

All four phrases equally apply to the Samaritan who also first "bound up his wounds." The symbolism is clear and strong. God is the one who saves and chooses His agents as He wills. Similarly here God's sovereignty acts to save, and the agent is amazingly a Samaritan, a rejected outsider. As we will observe, the imagery can be understood to have Christological implications.

Furthermore, the oil and wine were not only standard first-aid remedies. They were also "sacrificial elements in the temple worship" (Derrett, 220). Likewise, the verb "pour" is from the language of worship. There were libations in connection with the sacrifices. Yet for centuries the call had been sounded for going beyond ritual in an effort to respond adequately to what God had done for them. Hosea (6:6) and Micah (6:7–8) called for steadfast love and not sacrifice. We have this same move, from the language of the sacrificial service to a discussion of actions of self-giving love, in Pauline writings, where he talks of his own life as a libation poured out "upon the sacrificial offering of your faith" (Phil. 2:17). Paul also calls for the Roman Christians to offer their own lives as a "living sacrifice" (Rom. 12:1). Thus for the prophets the language of the sacrificial altar evokes a concern for self-giving love. For Paul such language overlaps with such a call. The Jewish priest and Levite were the religious professionals who knew the precise rituals of the prescribed liturgy. In worship they officiated at the sacrifices and libations. They poured out the oil and the wine on the high altar before God. Here in the parable this same freighted language is applied to the Samaritan just after the priest and Levite have failed miserably in their ability to make the "living sacrifice." It is the hated Samaritan who pours out the libation on the altar of this man's wounds. As Derrett observes, "To show what is the *ḥesed* (steadfast love) which God demands one cannot be more apt than to show oil and wine employed to heal an injured man" (Derrett, 220). The Samaritan's total response to the man's needs (including this simple libation) is a profound expression of the steadfast love for which the prophets were calling. It is the *Samaritan* who pours out the true offering acceptable to God.

Yet, if and when the man regains consciousness, the Samaritan may be insulted for his kindness, because "Oil and wine are forbidden objects if they emanate from a Samaritan" (*ibid.,* 220). Not only have they come from an unclean Samaritan but the tithe has not been paid on them and by accepting them the wounded man incurs an obligation to pay tithes for them. He has recently been robbed and obviously has no way to pay even his hotel bill. As Derrett succinctly points out, the Pharisees would have been pleased if the wounded man had shouted, " 'Begone, Cuthean, I will have none of your oil or your wine!' " (Derrett, 221).

Scene 6: Transport to the Inn

Then he put him on his own riding animal
and led him (it) to the inn,
and took care of him.

As we have noted, these are acts of mercy that the mounted priest failed to carry out. The peculiar phrase here translated "his own riding animal" is not the ordinary genitive construction. The phrase most likely indicates that he had other animals, perhaps with merchandise. This animal is his own mount (cf. Jeremias, *Parables*, 204; Bishop, 172; Derrett, 217). The Old Syriac makes the riding animal into a donkey, which well may be the original behind the Greek text. We are not exactly sure about the Samaritan's next act. The Greek text can be read, "He *brought him* to the inn," or "He *led it* (the donkey) to the inn." The verb can mean either *bring* or *lead* and the pronoun can be masculine (he, the man) or neuter (it, the animal). Middle Eastern donkeys can easily carry two people, and if we assume the first, the Samaritan is riding with the wounded man. If we assume the second, he is acting out the form of a servant and leading the animal to the inn. The social distinctions between riders and leaders of riding animals is crucial in Middle Eastern society. Much to his surprise and humiliation, Haman (who expects to be the rider) finds himself leading the horse on which his enemy Mordecai is riding (Est. 6:7-11). These same social attitudes remain unchanged through the centuries. The famous Swiss traveler of the early nineteenth century, Louis Burckhardt, once shocked his Middle Eastern traveling companions by allowing his servant to ride his camel while he, Burckhardt, walked (Sim, 254). On numerous occasions I have tried to convince a young man leading the donkey on which I was riding to ride with me. The person involved always refused because to ride with me would be (from his point of view) presumptuous. So we may have here a case of a middle-class merchant with a number of animals and some goods who takes upon himself the form of a servant and *leads* the donkey to the inn.

His willingness to go to the inn and remain there overnight administering to the needs of the wounded man is a further act of self-giving love. Mosaic legislation established cities of refuge for people under the threat of death from blood vengeance retaliation. This legislation provided an escape valve for a custom it could not eradicate. The concept of retaliation, deeply reflected in the Old Testament, is still with us. Modern law in many Middle Eastern countries also makes certain allowances for blood vengeance killings. Thomson admits that originally he thought of the subject as "a curious question of ancient history." Then in villages of upper Galilee he saw it as a continuing part of life.

But as in the Jewish community in the time of Moses, so here, the custom of blood-revenge is too deeply rooted to be under the control of these feudal lords of the land; indeed, they themselves and their families are bound by it in its sternest demands. It is plain that Moses, clothed with all the influence and power of an inspired law-giver, could not eradicate this dreadful custom, and was merely commissioned to mitigate its horrors by establishing cities of refuge, under certain humane regulations, which are fully detailed in Numbers xxxv, and in Deuteronomy xix . . . the law of retaliation remains in all its vigor, and is executed with energy by the . . . tribes around (Thomson, I, 447).

Thus this phenomenon was a problem for Old Testament society and continued in full force through the nineteenth century. Thomson goes on to explain that this retaliation is made against any member of an attacker's extended family or his associates when *any* bodily injury is sustained. The actual assailant is sought if he is available; if not, anyone related to him in the remotest way may suffer. Thomson explains,

It is one of the cruel features of the *lex talionis,* that if the real murderer cannot be reached, the avengers of blood have a right to kill any other members of the family, then any relation, no matter how remote, and finally any member of this confederation. . . . Several of my intimate acquaintances have literally been cut to pieces by the infuriated avengers of blood and in some instances these poor victims had no possible implication with the clan involved (Thomson, I, 448).

What we are dealing with is an irrational response, not a reasoned action. We have no evidence of any inn in the middle of the desert. The natural assumption of the story is that the Samaritan took the man downhill to Jericho. Ibn al-Ṭayyib makes this assumption (folio 104ʳ; also Dalman, *Sacred,* 245; Ibn al-Ṣalībī, II, 121). In any case the inn is either in a community or in touch with one. The Samaritan, by allowing himself to be identified, runs a grave risk of having the family of the wounded man seek *him* out to take vengeance upon him. After all, who else is there? The group mind of Middle Eastern peasant society makes a totally illogical judgment at this point. The stranger who involves himself in an accident is often considered partially, if not totally, responsible for the accident. After all, why did he stop? Irrational minds seeking a focus for their retaliation do not make rational judgments, especially when the person involved is from a hated minority community. Much of what we are arguing for requires no special Middle Eastern cultural attitude but is rather a common human response. An American cultural equivalent would be a Plains Indian in 1875 walking into Dodge City with a scalped cowboy on his horse, checking into a room over the local saloon, and staying the night to take care of him. Any Indian so brave would be fortunate to get out of the city alive *even* if he had saved the cowboy's life. So with the Samaritan in the parable, his act of kindness will make *no* difference. Caution would lead him to leave the wounded man at the door of the inn and disappear. The man may still be unconscious, in which case the Samaritan would be completely protected. Or the Samaritan could remain anonymous to the wounded man. But when he stays at the inn through the night to take care of the man, and promises to return, anonymity is not possible.

The courage of the Samaritan is demonstrated first when he stops in the desert (for the thieves are still in the area). But his real bravery is seen in this final act of compassion at the inn. The point is not his courage but rather the price he is willing to pay to complete his act of compassion. This price he continues to pay in the final scene.

Scene 7: The Final Payment

> The next day he took out and gave two denarii to the manager
> and said, "Take care of him, and whatever more you spend,
> I, on my return, *I* will repay you."

So the story has come full circle. The inversion of themes in the stanzas of this parabolic ballad makes clear the reasons for this final scene. The parable as a story could just as easily have ended when the wounded man was brought to safety. But no, having made up for the failures first of the Levite, then of the priest, finally he compensates even for the robbers. Specifically the Samaritan's reversal of the actions of the robbers can be seen as follows:

The Robbers	*The Samaritan*
Rob him	Pays for him
Leave him dying	Leaves him taken care of
Abandon him	Promises to return

This comparison reveals the magnificent construction of the parable. The more natural place to take the wounded man would have been to the house of some relative or friend, if not his own home. But the parable is constructed to make this last scene possible. Obviously the Samaritan could not pay his family or friends, and there would be no point in his returning had the drama ended in the wounded man's village.

However, the actions of this scene are not just filler. They are true to first-century life. The wounded man has no money. If he cannot pay the bill when he leaves he will be arrested for debt (Derrett, 218). Innkeepers in the first century had a *very* unsavory reputation. The Mishna warns,

> Cattle may not be left in the inns of the gentiles since they are suspected of bestiality; nor may a woman remain alone with them since they are suspected of lewdness; nor may a man remain alone with them since they are suspected of shedding blood (Mishna *Abodah Zarah* 2:1, Danby, 438).

Jewish inns did not fare any better in popular opinions, for in Targum Jonathan the word "prostitute" is regularly translated "woman who keeps an inn" (cf.

Josh. 2:1; Judg. 16:1; I Kings 3:16). Thus the wounded man cannot anticipate a noble quality of life at an inn. From the parables of Jesus himself we know that people were imprisoned for bad debts (Matt. 18:23–35). Obviously the wounded man has nothing left. Thus if the Samaritan does not pledge to pay his final bill, whatever it comes to, the wounded man (on recovery) will not be able to leave. Derrett notes, "The Samaritan enabled him to 'get out of town'" (Derrett, 218). Derrett also observes that a Jew dealing with a Jew could have gotten his money back. But, "Our Samaritan had no hope of enforcing reimbursement" (*ibid.*, 219). The Samaritan is an unknown stranger. Yet, in spite of the cost in time, effort, money, and personal danger, he freely demonstrates unexpected love to the one in need. Is not this a dramatic demonstration of the kind of love God offers through His unique agent in the Gospel?

The exegesis of the early centuries consistently identified the Good Samaritan with Jesus himself. Indeed, in John 8:48, the Jews throw a taunt at him with the words, "Are we not right in saying that you are a Samaritan and have a demon?" But of far greater consequence is the costly demonstration of unexpected love that we see in the actions of the Samaritan. He appears suddenly and unexpectedly from the outside and acts to save. The traditional leaders of the community fail, yet God's agent arrives to "bind up the wounds" of the sufferer. As Barth has written,

> The good Samaritan . . . is not far from the lawyer. The primitive exegesis of the text was fundamentally right. He stands before him incarnate, although hidden under the form of one whom the lawyer believed he should hate, as the Jews hated the Samaritans (Barth, 419).

We have already observed functional Christology in 7:36–50. In this passage the overtones of Christology are in the parable itself, not in the narrative framework provided by the evangelist or his source. Is it not possible here to touch something of Jesus' own understanding of his own ministry as God's unique agent who comes as a suffering servant to save?

How then does this parable function in the dialogue between Jesus and the lawyers? The full text of this second round of the dialogue is as follows:

ROUND TWO:

He, desiring to justify himself, asked,

(5) Lawyer: (Question 3) "Who is my neighbor?"

  (6) Jesus: (after the telling of the parable asked Question 4)
"Which of these three do you think became a neighbor to the man who fell among the robbers?"

   (7) Lawyer: (Answer to 4) He answered,
"The one who showed mercy on him."

  (8) Jesus: (Answer to 3) And Jesus said to him,
"Go and you, *you do* likewise."

In the center of these four speeches we see Jesus reshaping the lawyer's question. He will not give the lawyer a list. He refuses to tell the lawyer who is and who is not his neighbor. Rather, the real question becomes, "To whom must you *become* a neighbor?" This question is then answered. The last statement is not a general admonition to good works but rather an answer to the lawyer's question about self-justification. The first round of questions and answers ended with a command to *do* something. This round ends in the same manner. The lawyer, in the opening question of this round, wants to know how many people he has to love to achieve righteousness by his own efforts. The word "you" is emphatic in the final statement. Jesus says to him, "Here is the standard that *you* must meet." Derrett understands from the parable that "unless we show love to all humanity . . . we cannot claim . . . to have obtained entrance to the Messianic age" (Derrett, 227). Hunter explains the same phrase as meaning, "This is what neighbor-love means, my friend, and if you want eternal life, this is the kind of action God requires of you" (Hunter, *Interpreting,* 73). Both authors are right. The only difficulty is—who is able to do these things? Who can meet this standard? We can almost hear the crowds say under their breath (as they do in 18:26), "Who then can be saved?" Here each half of the dialogue moves in this direction. Thus each round of dialogue ends with the same conclusion. What can I *do* to inherit eternal life? What can I *do* to justify myself? The only conclusion he can come to is, "These things are beyond me. Clearly I cannot justify myself, but all things are possible with God" (cf. Luke 18:27).

Finally then, seeing the parable in its dialogue setting, what is the lawyer to conclude and what theological motifs comprise the theological cluster of the passage? We would suggest the following:

The lawyer is pressed to understand:

I must *become* a neighbor to anyone in need. To fulfil the law means that I must reach out in costly compassion to all people, even to my enemies. The standard remains even though I can never fully achieve it. I cannot justify myself and earn eternal life.

The following theological motifs are contained in the overall scene:

1. The parable makes clear that any attempt at self-justification is doomed to failure. The standard is too high. Eternal life cannot be earned.
2. Yet the parable holds up an ethical standard to strive after, even though it cannot be fully achieved. Like the command to "be perfect" it remains a standard even though in its fullest expression it is impossibly high.
3. A code book approach to ethics is inadequate. As Derrett writes, "When the Pharisaic system can have such defects it needs serious re-examination" (Derrett, 222).
4. The Samaritan, a hated outsider, demonstrates compassionate love. Thus the parable is a sharp attack on communal and racial prejudices.
5. For Jesus, love is something you feel *and* do.
6. The parable gives us a dynamic concept of the neighbor. The question, "Who

is my neighbor?'' is reshaped into ''To whom must I become a neighbor?''
The answer then is—everyone in need, even an enemy!

7. God's sovereignty is not bound by the official leadership of the community of
   the faithful. When that leadership fails, God is still free to choose new agents,
   as He did with Amos, for the expression of His salvation.

8. Two types of sin and two types of sinners appear in the parable. The robbers
   hurt the man by violence. The priest and Levite hurt him by neglect. The story
   implies the guilt of all three. The failed opportunity to do good becomes an
   evil.

9. The passage makes a statement about salvation. Salvation comes to the
   wounded man in the form of a costly demonstration of unexpected love. In the
   process it seems to make a statement about the Savior. We cautiously suggest
   that Jesus, the rejected outsider, has cast himself in the role of the Samaritan,
   who appears dramatically on the scene to bind up the wounds of the suffering
   as the unique agent of God's costly demonstration of unexpected love.

May the theology and the ethical demands of this time-honored passage
inform and impower us afresh today.

Chapter 4

THE RICH FOOL
(Luke 12:13-21)

The Text:

One of the multitude said to him,
    "Rabbi, bid my brother divide the inheritance with me."
But he said to him,
    "Man, who made me a judge or divider over you?"
And he said to them,   GENERAL PRINCIPLE
    "Take heed, and beware of every kind of insatiable desire.
    For life for a person does not consist in the surpluses of his possessions."

1   And he told this parable, saying,
       "There was a certain rich man   GOODS GIVEN
       whose land brought forth plenty.

2   And he discussed with himself saying,
       'What shall I do,   PROBLEM
       for I have no place to store my crops?'

3   And he said, 'I will do this:
       I will pull down my barns and build larger barns;
       and I will store all my grain and my goods.   PLAN (PRESENT)

4   And I will say to my soul, "Soul!
       You have ample goods laid up for many years.   PLAN (FUTURE)
       Relax, eat, drink, and enjoy yourself"'

5   But God said to him, 'Fool!
       This night your soul is required of you,   GOODS LEFT
       and what you have prepared, whose will these things be?'

So is he who treasures up for himself,   GENERAL PRINCIPLE
and is not gathering riches for God."

As in the case of the Good Samaritan, we intend to take the dialogue setting of this parable seriously and see where it leads us. Here also the parable is long and the dialogue short. Yet again the setting colors the thrust of the parable as it now appears in the text. The rhetorical form of the passage will be examined and then the particulars of the text will be discussed in the light of that form. The literary form (see above) must first be examined.

The overall literary form of the passage is simple and clear. It begins with a single exchange between Jesus and an anonymous petitioner that takes the form of a demand and a response. There is one wisdom saying before the parable and a second after its close. The parable falls naturally into five stanzas. The first tells of goods given and the fifth closes the parable with these same goods left behind. In the center of the parable the rich man makes three speeches. It is clear that the first and second speeches are intended to be separate, because the second is introduced by the otherwise redundant words, "And he said." Also, one senses some time lapse between the rich man's enunciation of his problem and the announcement of his intended solution. The rich man's second and third speeches are spoken together, yet there is a shift of emphasis that divides the speech into two halves. He begins with the present, in which he will build his barns and store his crops. Then in the years to come he will enjoy the "good life." Looking, then, at these three statements, in the first (stanza 2) he outlines the problem. In the second (stanza 3), he decides on a solution. In the third (stanza 4), he reflects on his future in the light of that solution. In stanza 5, God speaks. The center is a crucial turning point, for the rich man in that speech decides what he will do to solve his problem. We have this same feature in the parable of the Unjust Steward (Luke 16:1–8). In that parable there are seven stanzas, but again the center has a soliloquy in which the principal character suddenly decides on a solution to the problem set forth in the opening stanzas (cf. Bailey, *Poet*, 95f.). This very climax in the third stanza is related to the beginning and the end of the parable. In this case the inner relationship is slight and likely unconscious, yet it is there. In the first stanza goods are *given*. In the central stanza they are *stored*. In the last stanza these same goods are *left*. Furthermore, the beginning and the end talk of God's gifts. That is, in the first stanza God gives plenty. In the fifth (as we will note below), the man's soul is discovered to be on loan from God. With this literary structure in mind we will proceed to an examination of the text.

THE INITIAL DIALOGUE

One of the multitude said to him,
"Rabbi, bid my brother divide the inheritance with me."
But he said to him,
"Man, who made me a judge or divider over you?"

As we have already seen in 10:25, the Greek word "teacher" in Luke can be traced to the Hebrew "rabbi" (cf. above, 35). The rabbi was expected to be knowledgeable regarding the law and ready to give a legal ruling. Jesus' understanding of his ministry, however, does not include passing judgment on legal cases. There was precedent for this. We are told that some sages "withdrew from public affairs and even thanked the Almighty for not knowing how to administer justice" (Safrai, *JPFC*, II, 963). Ibn al-Ṣalībī offers the intriguing suggestion that the brother involved was already a disciple and was thus under Jesus' authority. The greedy petitioner then wanted Jesus to tell the brother/ disciple to forsake everything by giving it (naturally) to the brother/petitioner (Ibn al-Ṣalībī, II, 132). Such details are in harmony with the story but are imaginative and unfounded.

Yet more can be substantiated. This petitioner is not asking for arbitration, but rather ordering the judge to carry out his wishes. He has already decided what he wants and he tries to *use* Jesus. To say, "Rabbi, my brother and I are quarrelling over our inheritance; will you mediate?" is one thing. To order Jesus to implement his plan is something else. It is little wonder that Jesus' response has a tinge of gruffness in it, as we will observe.

The specific background of such a request is well-known. The father dies and leaves the inheritance as a unit to his sons. Psalm 133:1 reflects on how pleasant it is when the sons manage to cooperate harmoniously in such a situation. Daube observes that "to dwell together" is a technical term in the Old Testament. It is an assumed standard. Thus when Abraham finds it necessary to break with his kinsman Lot, "it is regarded as a sad necessity which calls for justification" (Daube, 327; cf. Gen. 13:5-7). In the New Testament the same assumptions are operative. Luke 16:9 (par. Matt. 6:24) presents the dilemma of a servant in a household where the father dies and the servant suddenly has two masters.

In our text, one brother wants help in pressuring the other brother into finalizing a division between them. The rabbis stated that if one heir wanted a division of the inheritance it should be granted. (Roman law required agreement on the part of both parties; cf. Daube, 328.) Thus the petitioner seems to be saying, "Everybody knows the opinions of the rabbis. I am right, my brother is wrong. You, Rabbi Jesus, *you* tell him so!" The "inheritance" in such a context is most naturally understood to be property. Indeed, we are here dealing with the Middle East's most sensitive problem, both then and now, namely a cry for justice over the division of land.

The question of justice for those who cry out seeking it is an important concern of many biblical writers from Amos onward. Luke himself has more material from the tradition on the question of justice for the poor and downtrodden than any other evangelist. Early in Luke Mary expresses joy at the exaltation of those of low degree (Luke 1:52). A number of the parables offer hope for the poor (cf. The Great Banquet; Lazarus and the Rich Man). Luke 4:17, along with many other references, may be cited. Yet here we see the topic of justice dealt with in a unique way. Thus it is of special importance to examine carefully the "cry for justice" that is voiced here.

This particular cry can perhaps be characterized as a "naked cry for justice." A demanding voice says, "Give me my rights." We are left to assume that this petitioner is unwilling to consider his problem from any perspective other than his own. Lesslie Newbigin states the problem eloquently:

> If we acknowledge the God of the Bible, we are committed to struggle for justice in society. Justice means giving to each his due. Our problem (as seen in the light of the gospel) is that each of us overestimates what is due to him as compared with what is due to his neighbor. . . . If I do not acknowledge a justice which judges the justice for which I fight, I am an agent, not of justice, but of lawless tyranny (Newbigin, 124f.).

Newbigin describes precisely the position of the petitioner. He has decided what *his* rights are. He only wants assistance in pressuring his brother into granting those rights.

The naked cry for justice is voiced also in Shakespeare's tragedy, *Romeo and Juliet*. Tybalt kills Mercutio. Romeo then kills Tybalt, who is a relative to the Capulets (Juliet's family). With the bodies of the two dead men in full view, the crowd gathers and, with them, the prince. Lady Capulet speaks for her family and angrily demands the death of Romeo as the murderer of Tybalt. She says, "I beg justice, which thou, prince, must give!" (act 3, scene 1). Each family is "only demanding its rights." At the end of the play the same people are again gathered in the presence of the prince, only now there are two other bodies on the stage, those of Romeo and Juliet. The prince says,

> "Where be these enemies? Capulet! Montague!
> See, what a scourge is laid upon your hate,
> That heaven finds means to kill your joys with love!
> And I, for winking at your discords too,
> Have lost a brace of kinsmen:
>   All are punish'd" (act 5, scene 3).

To grant to each party their own understanding of their "rights" can lead to tragedy. A new perspective is needed. In Shakespeare's play, even the priest makes no attempt to introduce a new perspective to the two families or pronounce a word of judgment on their hates. Indeed, it takes a special brand of courage to tell antagonists that their naked cry for justice is not enough, that they must begin with a new understanding of themselves.

This rare courage is seen not only in this passage but also in Luke 13:1–3, where nationalists report an atrocity story to Jesus. As one who has been many times in precisely this same position, the present writer knows that the telling of such a story *demands* a sympathetic response from the listener. Jesus' answer requires great courage, as we will observe. We see this same kind of response here in Luke 12:13. In each text there is a strong plea for justice from a self-confident, powerless petitioner. In each case the answer is, "Look to yourself first!"

Jesus' answer to the demand of the petitioner "has the tone of disapproval" (Meyer, II, 416). This is supported by modern and medieval colloquial Arabic speech where *ja ragul* ("O man!") usually introduces a complaint against the one addressed, as is clearly the case here. This same connotation is documented by Muir, who mentions a case of its use in the caliph's court in Baghdad in A.D. 749. Ibn Hobeira, a member of the court, addressed Abu Jafar, the caliph's brother, as "O man!" This was taken as an insult and Abu Jafar immediately apologized for it "as a slip of the tongue" (Muir, 438, n. 1). Furthermore, Moses (unsolicited) sought to be a judge and was rebuffed (Ex. 2:14a). Jesus (solicited) refuses to be a judge and rebuffs the petitioner. Yet both begin with a broken relationship between two antagonists and try, in their separate ways, to achieve reconciliation. Together the two words "judge and divider" give the sense of Jesus' complaint. There is obviously a broken relationship between this man and his brother. The man wants the broken relationship finalized by total separation. But Jesus insists that he has not come as a "divider." The obvious alternative is "reconciler." He wants to reconcile people to one another, not finalize divisions between them. This brief dialogue is in full harmony with everything we know about Jesus, and it recurs in the Gospel of Thomas (logion 72). Its authenticity has been affirmed by leading Jewish and Christian scholars (Daube, 326–29; Manson, *Sayings,* 271). If this be true, then it was originally remembered in Aramaic and later translated into Greek. It is well-known that skilled translators can use the nuances of the receptor language to highlight a particular emphasis of the original. An illustration of this is Arberry's translation of the Koran, where a great deal of beauty and wordplay comes across to the English reader. Something of the same phenomena can perhaps be seen twice in this passage. The first is in this dialogue. The translator has selected a rare word, used only in this text in all of Biblical Greek, for the word "divider." In Greek it is *meristēs*. Drop the *r* and move the *i* and the word becomes *mesitēs*, which means "reconciler." Jesus has not come as a *meristēs* (divider) but rather as a *mesitēs* (reconciler). The form of this dialogue in the Gospel of Thomas is significant in this regard:

> (A man said) to him: Speak to my brothers that they divide my father's possessions with me. He said to him: O man, who made me a divider? He turned to his disciples (and) said to them: I am not a divider, am I? (Aland, 526).

In this version of the dialogue even greater emphasis is placed on the rejection of his role as a divider. The obvious answer to his question is, "No, you are rather a reconciler." But reconciliation will require the petitioner to gain a new perspective of himself. Miller writes,

> Jesus was not showing indifference to the claims of legal justice, but was insisting that there is a greater gain than getting an inheritance and a greater loss than losing it (Miller, 110).

The question is addressed in the plural, "Who made me a judge or divider over you (plural)?" Some of our Arabic versions use the dual "over the two of you." Others maintain the plural. Is Jesus addressing the crowd or only the two brothers? It is impossible to determine with precision, but the plural seems more appropriate. Jesus seems to be refusing to play a role of divider for all. After the somewhat hostile question comes the first of the two wisdom sayings that encase the parable.

FIRST WISDOM SAYING

And he said to them,
"Take heed, and beware of every kind of insatiable desire.
For life for a person does not consist in the surpluses of his possessions."

The first sentence is usually translated in reference to covetousness. The original language carries with it the overtones of insatiable desires that make the warning even stronger. The clear implication is that the petitioner will not have his problem solved if his brother *does* grant him his portion of the inheritance. Sa'īd observes, "Jesus becomes a judge *over* them, not *between* them. He judges the motives of their hearts, not their pocket books" (Sa'īd, 339). The word "life" in Greek is *zōē,* which, in contrast to *bia,* has to do with a special quality of life and not merely physical life.

The second sentence is awkward. Literally the two sentences read,

Take heed and beware of every kind of insatiable desire
    because not *out of the surpluses* to anyone
the life of him it is
    out of his possessions.

There is a repetition of the reference to possessions/surpluses. Bruce notes this and understands it to be "two ways of saying the same thing, the second a kind of afterthought" (Bruce, *Synoptic*, 557). Marshall concurs with C. F. D. Moule that two expressions may have been combined (Marshall, 522f.). However, if we are dealing with a parallel repetition of ideas in a rhetorical form, then it is not an afterthought but a necessary repetition for the completion of the form. We grant with Bruce that "The expression here is peculiar" (Bruce, *Synoptic,* 557), but the meaning is clear. People are infected with insatiable desires of many kinds. One of them is to acquire more possessions. They seek an enriching quality of life in these possessions in the fond hope that if they can only get enough material things these things will produce the abundant life. T. W. Manson writes,

It is true that a certain minimum of material goods is necessary for life; but it is not true that greater abundance of goods means greater abundance of life (*Sayings,* 271).

Jesus' cryptic answer warns the reader in two ways. First, with these presuppositions the desire for material things will prove insatiable. Second, the dreams of
the abundant life will never be achieved through such an accumulation of
surpluses.

The insatiable desire for a higher standard of living is widespread in the
modern world. The fond hope that LIFE will be the product of more consumption
is also very much with us. With the natural resources of the world dwindling and
the pressure for more possessions intensifying, some wrestling with the message
of this text would seem to be imperative if we are to survive. Again we note a
plural, "he said to *them*." The text is meant for all readers/listeners, not just the
two brothers. This wisdom saying introduces the parable itself.

STANZA ONE—GOODS GIVEN

And he told this parable, saying,
  "There was a certain rich man
  whose land brought forth plenty."

As in the case of many of the parables, this story has a literary background. Psalm 49 discusses the problem of wealth and its meaninglessness in the
face of death. According to Ben Sirach,

A man grows rich by his sharpness and grabbing,
  and here is the regard he receives for it;
he says, "I have found rest,
  and now I can enjoy my goods";
but he does not know how long this will last;
  he will have to leave his goods for others and die (Sir. 11:19-20).

Thus Jesus is dealing with a theme already well-known in the literature of the
audience (cf. also Eccl. 2:1-11; Job 31:24-28). What is important is what he
does with it. Here Jesus expands Ben Sirach's very short story into a drama. A
number of distinctive features appear in the process. (1) Rather than one speech
we have four, with two speakers. (2) God himself is heard at the end of Jesus'
parable. (3) The two accounts begin with different assumptions. Ben Sirach's
little story is directed to the wealthy who *acquire* their possessions (by sharpness
and grabbing). In contrast, Jesus' parable discusses wealth that is a *gift* from
God, not wealth acquired by human effort. That is, Ben Sirach's man reflects on
"What do I do with my earnings?" Jesus' man must ask, "What do I do with
what I have not earned?" That he does not perceive the question in this fashion is
part of what the parable is all about. (4) Jesus' version introduces the idea of
"loan." The man discovers his soul to be on loan. Was his wealth also on loan?
Ben Sirach's story carries none of these subtle overtones. (5) The life-style of
Ben Sirach's character is exposed (he is sharp and grabbing), but nothing evolves

from it. Jesus' story subtly and yet powerfully exposes both the life-style of the rich man and the resulting isolation that it creates. (6) Jesus' account is clearly focusing on surpluses. His man is already rich when the parable opens. He is then given additional wealth. Ben Sirach's man grows rich in the parable. These unique features will be further illuminated as we proceed.

Focusing on this first stanza we see a man who is already rich. We are not told how he got his riches, and the method of acquiring them is not criticized as it was in Sirach. This man has more than enough. On top of this, with no extra effort on his part, he is given the gift of a bumper crop. He did not earn it and he does not need it. His problem is what to do with unearned surpluses. With this problem in mind we turn to stanza two.

STANZA TWO—THE PROBLEM

And he discussed with himself saying,
"What shall I do,
for I have no place to store my crops?"

The text gives us a continuous past, "he was debating with himself." The subject was a matter of considerable concern and the debate lasted some time. There was no thought of "I really do not need any of this, I am already wealthy!" Nor is there any thought of "This extra wealth is a gift for which I can take no credit. God has given the increase." Rather, the bumper crops are simply referred to as "my crops" and the only question that concerns him is how to preserve them for himself. Ambrose aptly observes that the rich man *has* storage available in the mouths of the needy (cf. Trench, 337). Augustine talks about a man who stores grain on a damp floor and needs to move it upstairs lest it spoil; thus treasure to be kept must be stored in heaven, not on earth (Trench, 338). Ecclesiastes (5:10) observes,

He who loves money
   will not be satisfied with money;
nor he who loves wealth
   with gain; this also is vanity.

For us the text relates to the very important modern questions of excess profits in a capitalistic society and surplus value theories in Marxism. According to Paul, the Christian should work for two reasons. The first is so that he will not be a burden on others (II Thess. 2:7–12). The second is "so that he may be able to give to those in need" (Eph. 4:28). To explore the meaning of all of this for a Christian in a capitalistic society would go well beyond the intent and scope of this study. We would only observe in passing that this parable, with its presuppositions, speaks clearly to crucial questions of our own day.

Furthermore, the man is "dialoguing with himself." One of the striking features of the traditional Middle Easterner is his gregarious nature. Life is lived in tightly knit communities. The leading men of the village still "sit at the gate" and spend literally years talking to one another. The slightest transaction is worthy of hours of discussion. The present writer has engaged with the notables in such discussions in the gate and knows that often there seems to be a subtle pressure *not* to introduce the information that will settle the question under discussion. The reasoning seems to be—we have a wonderful discussion going, do not close it! In any case, the elder in such a community makes up his mind *in community*. He decides what he will do after hours of discussion with his friends. He does his thinking in a crowd. The text does not read, "he said to himself," as we have with the unjust steward (16:3) and the unjust judge (18:4). Rather, this man dialogues with himself. He obviously has no one else with whom to talk. He trusts no one and has no friends or cronies with whom he can exchange ideas. When he needs a dialogue he can talk only to himself. Thus we begin to get Jesus' picture of the kind of prison that wealth can build. He has the money to buy a vacuum and live in it. Life in this vacuum creates its own realities, and out of this warped perspective we hear him announce his solution.

STANZA THREE—PLAN (PRESENT)

And he said, "I will do this:
I will pull down my barns and build larger barns;
and I will store all my grain and my goods."

Plummer (324) has noted the chiasmus in this line:

I will tear down
   of me the barns
   and greater ones
I will build up.

The language of "tear down" and "build up" is classical prophetic language that refers to the call and ministry of the prophet (Jer. 1:10). It speaks of courageous acts in the name of God that call for suffering in their fulfillment. Here this noble language is sadly cheapened by this self-indulgent rich man who is determined that he alone will consume God's gifts. These gifts (for him, surplus wealth) have suddenly become "my grain and my goods." The list of *my* crops, *my* barns, *my* goods, and finally *my* soul, has often been noted. It was in the barns that the tithes and offerings were set aside. The priests and Levites came to the barns to collect them (Safrai, *JPFC,* II, 820). Our rich man has other things on his mind, as we see from his concluding speech.

STANZA FOUR—PLAN (FUTURE)

And I will say to my soul, "Soul!
You have ample goods laid up for many years.
Relax, eat, drink, and enjoy yourself."

This speech is not sad, rather it is pitiful. This wealthy, self-confident man has arrived, he has made it. All that he has longed for has now been realized. He needs an audience for his arrival speech. Who is available? Family? Friends? Servants and their families? Village elders? Fellow landowners? Who will "rejoice with me?" The father in the parable of the Prodigal Son has a community ready at any moment to join him in a festival of joy (Luke 15:22–24). The shepherd and the woman call in their friends and neighbors to rejoice over the found sheep and coin (15:6, 9). The gregarious Middle Easterner always has a community around him. But this man? He can only address himself. His only audience is his own *nefesh*.

To claim that he should be, talking to his body rather than his soul is a misunderstanding of the text. The word "soul" (*psuchē*) is the Greek translation of the Hebrew *nefesh*, which means the whole person. *Nefesh* reappears in the Syriac versions of this text, and the cognate Arabic word *nafs* is used almost exclusively in the Arabic translations. Thus the point is not that he is addressing his body as opposed to his soul. The issue is his mentality. He thinks that the total needs of the total person can be met by material surpluses well preserved for the owner's exclusive use.

The word we have translated "enjoy yourself" is a colorful word. Again the translator has managed to add a wordplay to the text by a careful selection of vocabulary. The rare word used in this passage for "to bring forth plenty" is *euphoreō*. The Greeks added the letters *eu* to the beginnings of words to intensify them. Something good becomes very good by this addition. Thus *angelleō* is to bring news: *euangelleō* is to bring good news, and in the New Testament becomes the word for proclaiming the gospel. *Phoreō* means to bear fruit; so *euphoreō* (v. 16) means to bear fruit in abundance. Then here in verse 19, the word we have translated "enjoy yourself" is *euphrainō*. The noun form of this same word is *euphrōn*, which is the state of self-enjoyment. The root of these two words is *phrōn*, which comes into English in our word dia*phragm*. The *phrōn* is the diaphragm. As Bertram observes, the diaphragm was "early regarded as the seat of intellectual and spiritual activity. The diaphragm determines the nature and strength of the breath and hence also the human spirit and its emotions" (Bertram, *TDNT*, IX, 220). So anyone with *euphrōn* possessed an added measure of the good life and all that it holds. This *euphrōn* " is often used for purely secular joy, and sometimes for the joy of the festive meal" (Bultmann, *TDNT*, II, 774). But at the same time it could also cover "the facts and processes of the intellectual or spiritual life" (*ibid.*, 772). Thus this rich man has a formula, which is:

euphoreō	*euphrainō*
(bring forth many things)	(enjoy all aspects of the good life)

It is not by accident that the speech to the *nefesh/psuchē* (the whole person) ends with a vision of *euphrōn*. We would suggest that the above is a deliberate play on words. Into this tidy equation comes the thundering voice of God.

STANZA FIVE—GOODS LEFT

But God said to him, "Fool! (*aphrōn*)
This night your soul is required of you,
and what you have prepared, whose will these things be?"

The New Testament has four words for "fool." These are:

anoētos — mindless
asophos — without wisdom
mōros — fool (cf. the English word moron)
aphrōn — fool/stupid

Plummer (554) identifies the last two as "much stronger" than the first two. Luke uses the first (6:11; 24:25) and certainly knew all four. In this text he has chosen *aphrōn*. The *a* prefix negates the word, as in the English "moral" and "amoral." So here, this rich man, who thinks that his *euphoreō* (many things) will produce *euphrōn* (the good life), is in reality *aphrōn* (without mind, spirit, and emotions). His formula for the good life is sheer stupidity.

The verb "is required" in Greek is a word that is commonly used for the return of a loan. His soul was on loan and now the owner (God) wants the loan returned. At the beginning of the parable we noted that his goods were a gift. Now it is clear that his life was also not his own.

The parable assumes a time lapse between stanzas four and five. The voice of God thunders at him (presumably) after he has "prepared" his maximum security storage bins. Thus, after his arrival, he is confronted with the stark reality of the world he has created with his wealth. As Manson succinctly observes,

> The sting of the words lies, however, not in the announcement that that man must die, but in the following question, which shows clearly the real poverty of his life. He is lonely and friendless in the midst of his wealth (Manson, *Sayings*, 272).

The listener/reader already knows this. Now we see that it takes the voice of God Himself to penetrate the rich man's self-created isolation and confront him with a chilling vision of himself. There is no accusing question, such as, "What have you done for others?" or "Why have you failed to help those in need?" or "Why are there no family and friends close to you who would be the natural recipients of your wealth?" He has no doubt developed impenetrable armor for just such an attack. Rather, God thunders: look at what you have done to yourself! You plan alone, build alone, indulge alone, and now you will die alone!

The story does not tell us that the rich fool does not have any family. Everyone has some family—even Howard Hughes. Rather, the rich fool does not know who will win the power struggle after he dies. He does not know who will finally gain control over all of his carefully secured wealth. Muir gives an

account of the last days of the fabulous Harun al-Rashid, the most illustrious and
wealthy caliph of history:

> Traveling slowly over the mountain range into Persia, Harun one day called
> his physician aside, and, alone under the shelter of a tree, unfolding a silken
> kerchief that girded his loins, disclosed the fatal disease he laboured under.
> "But have a care," he said, "that thou keep it secret; for my sons" (and he
> named them all and their guardians) "are watching the hour of my decease,
> as thou mayest see by the shuffling steed they will now mount me on, adding
> thus to mine infirmity." There is something touching in these plaintive words
> of the great monarch, now alone in the world, and bereft of the support even
> of those who were bound to rally round him in his hour of weakness (Muir,
> 481).

The same kind of a picture is painted by Browning in his poem "The Bishop
Orders His Tomb at Saint Praxed's Church." Indeed history and literature give
ample examples of the truth of what the voice of God announces to this stupid,
wealthy man.

What is his response? We are not told. This parable is also open-ended.
That a parable at times has aspects of a riddle becomes evident. Where does this
man's mind turn? What is the content of his next dialogue with himself? Is it, I
have rejected the living community of family and friends around me! Or, I am
mistaken; wealth does not bring genuine security! Or, why did I not help others
when I could? Or is the reader/listener expected to overhear the discussion of
Psalm 49:10 (LXX 48:11):

> the fool/stupid and the mindless alike must perish
> and leave their wealth to others.

If this is the case, Psalm 49 discusses the rich man's inability to *ransom* himself
with his wealth which he leaves behind. Is this the direction the listener's mind
is to go? Is this parable a commentary on Luke 9:23-24? The parable does not
finally give up its secrets. The rich man's silence leaves each reader/listener to
answer out of his own soul. The passage concludes with a second wisdom
saying, which must now be examined.

SECOND WISDOM SAYING

> So is he who treasures up for himself,
> and is not gathering riches for God.

For centuries we have had a theologically influenced translation in this
wisdom saying. The text gives us two *active* participles, "treasuring up" and
"gathering riches." Two centuries ago Bengel argued against our suggested
translation. He rightly points out that "for himself" (*heautō*) is not precisely
paralleled in the text with the construction *theō* (for God); rather the text has *eis
theon* (literally "into God"). He observes,

nothing can be added or diminished from the perfection of God (whether a man seeks His glory or not in laying out his wealth). He is rich *toward God*, who uses and enjoys his riches in the way that God would have him (Bengel, II, 109).

Bengel correctly points out the differences. The difficulty is that Bengel, like others, is obliged to turn the active participle "is enriching" into a passive "is rich," as he has done above. The two active participles are precisely parallel. Perhaps the original language does preserve some reluctance toward making "for himself" and "for God" precisely parallel because God needs nothing; indeed, the cattle on a thousand hills are His (Ps. 50:10). Yet the parallelism is there. The Arabic and Syriac versions are divided. Some translate with an active "is enriching" and others with a passive "is rich." The thirteenth-century version of Ibn al-'Assāl has "is rich" in the text and "is enriching" in the margin (folio 236ᵛ). When we ask these Oriental versions, Enriching with what? the answer is again ambiguous. We have "with God," or "in the way of God," or "in the things that are for God," or finally, "for God." The first can only mean "seeking to become rich in the reality of God Himself." The second and third are expansions of the first. The fourth is the translation we propose. As we have noted, the Greek has *eis theon* (literally "into God"). The preposition *eis* ("into") is on occasion used for the dative of advantage and translated "for" (cf. Bauer, 229). A clear case of this is in Luke 9:13 where the disciples are worried about feeding the five thousand and suggest that they must "go and buy food for (*eis*) all these people." Then *eis* is used to "denote reference to a person or thing" (*ibid.*). Luke 14:35 has this use of *eis* where the salt is referred to as "fit neither *for* (*eis*) the land nor *for* (*eis*) the dunghill." With these uses of *eis* in Luke just before and just after our text there is no syntactical reason for not understanding our text in the same fashion. Furthermore, when we translate "gathering riches *for* God" we need not be understood as trying to add to the perfection of God. All through Scripture God receives the *gifts* of the believers. So here the rich fool is characterized as one who is spending his energies trying to enrich himself rather than laboring in the service of God so as to offer *gifts* to God. Ibn al-Ṭayyib hints at this understanding of the text:

> He (Jesus) intends from this picture some one who stores up worldly treasure and does not achieve riches in divine things (Ibn al-Ṭayyib, folio 112ᵛ).

Ibn al-Ṭayyib does not indicate that the "divine things" are gifts for God, but he does have two actives for the verbs, "stores up" and "achieve riches." Thus he indicates that in each case the text is talking about an action in which the believer must engage.

Understood in this fashion we have the perfect complement to Luke 12:33 (par. Matt. 6:20), where the treasure in heaven is clearly "for yourselves." When standing alone such a text can lead to an otherworldly egocentricity, a way to take it with you. Put your money in the bank on the other side and you will be able to keep it for yourself! But if our proposal is plausible, this text is a corrective to that understanding. The "treasure in heaven" is indeed "for your-selves" (Luke 12:33). But in some profound sense it is also a gift to God, it is "for God" (Luke 12:21). Thus the general principle here stated at the end of the parable significantly complements the general principle at the beginning. The surpluses of material things (the first general principle) are to be spent in offering gifts to God (the second general principle). The gifts from God are to be returned to Him. Furthermore, the very energy directed to enriching the self with material things is misdirected. Such energy finally destroys the self that exerts it. Rather, the believer is directed to spend himself in "enriching God."

Finally, what is the response of the brother(s) and the crowd? Again there is silence. The rich man is silent in the parable, and so is the audience listening to its telling. Thus the listener/reader is pressed to finalize the tension of the text on two levels; that of the rich man, and that of the petitioner. What is he pressed to conclude? We would suggest the following:

The petitioner from the crowd is pressed to affirm,

> The real problem is not the division of inheritance, but a will to serve self rather than to serve God (by serving others, including the brother).

The theological motifs that inform the parable in its setting include the following:

1. A naked cry for justice, unqualified by any self-criticism, is not heeded by Jesus.

2. In a case of a broken personal relationship Jesus refuses to answer a cry for justice when the answer contributes to a finalizing of brokenness of that relationship. He did not come as a divider.

3. Jesus' parables often reflect a profound concern for justice for the poor. For him justice includes a concern for needs and not simply earnings (cf. Matt. 20:1–16). But here a self-centered cry for justice is understood by Jesus as a symptom of a sickness. He refuses to answer the cry but rather addresses himself to the healing of the sickness that produced the cry.

4. Material possessions are gifts from God. God does grant unearned surpluses of material things. Each life is on loan. The rich man in the parable assumed to own both ("my goods" and "my soul"). The parable presents him as mis-taken in both cases.

5. The person who thinks security and the good life are to be found in material things is stupid.

6. The abundant life is to be found in "treasuring up for God" rather than for self.

7. James talks of the rich man who will "fade away in the midst of his life-style (1:11). Jesus gives a parabolic picture of precisely this same phenomenon. This fool's wealth destroyed his capacity to maintain any abiding human relationships. He has no one with whom to share his soul, and worst of all, he does not even know he has a problem.

In our continuing concern to discover the pay-offs of the material, it is perhaps appropriate to reflect again on the parabolic answer to the petitioner's demand. The voice from the crowd calls out for justice in the division of the inheritance (probably held in land). Jesus' answer is to ask for a new perspective on the problem itself. He does not investigate who is right and who is wrong and then throw his weight on the side of justice (however right such an action may be in many circumstances). Rather he introduces a new perspective, indeed a theological perspective, from which to view the problem, and then leaves the problem itself unanswered. As we have indicated, the cry for justice over the division of land is the Middle East's most sensitive problem. In the following prose-poem the present writer has tried to apply the methodology used by Jesus in this passage. Today two voices cry out in the Middle East for a just division of the "inheritance." What answer can Christians give? Like this parable in Luke 12, the intent of the following is to suggest a different perspective from which an answer could perhaps emerge.

RESURRECTION
(Ode on a Burning Tank: The Holy Lands, October 1973)

I am a voice,
   the voice of spilt blood
      crying from the land.

The life is in the blood
   and for years my life flowed in the veins of a young man.
      My voice was heard through his voice,
         and my life was his life.

Then our volcano erupted
and for a series of numbing days
   all human voices were silenced
      amid the roar of the heavy guns,
      the harsh clank of tank tracks,
      the bone-jarring shudder of sonic booms,
         as gladiators with million-dollar swords
         killed each other high in the sky.

Then suddenly—suddenly
   there was the swish of a rocket launcher—
   a dirty yellow flash—
   all hell roared.
The clanking of the great tracks stopped.
   My young man staggered screaming from his inferno,
   his body twitched and flopped in the sand

And I was spilt into the earth—
   into the holy earth
      of the Holy Land.

The battle moved on.
   The wounded vehicles burned,

scorched,
and cooled.
The "meat wagons" carried the bodies away as
the chill of the desert night
settled on ridge and dune,
And I stiffened and blackened in the sand.

And then—and then
As the timeless silence
of the now scarred desert returned,
there—there congealed in the land,
in the land of prophet, priest and king—
I heard a voice—
a voice from deep in the land,
a voice from an ageless age,
a voice from other blood
once shed violently in the land.

The voice told me this ancient story;
precious blood intoned this ancient tale.

"A certain man had two sons.
One was rich and the other was poor.
The rich son had no children
while the poor son was blessed with many sons
and many daughters.

In time the father fell ill.
He was sure he would not live through the week
so on Saturday he called his sons to his side
and gave each of them half of the land of their inheritance.
Then he died.

Before sundown the sons buried their father with respect
as custom requires.

That night the rich son could not sleep.
He said to himself,
'What my father did was *not just*.
I am rich, my brother is poor.
I have bread enough and to spare,
while my brother's children eat one day
and trust God for the next.
I must move the landmark which our father has set in the middle of the land
so that my brother will have the greater share.
Ah—but he must not see me.
If he sees me he will be shamed.
I must arise early in the morning before it is dawn and move the landmark!'
With this he fell asleep
and his sleep was secure and peaceful.

Meanwhile, the poor brother could not sleep.
As he lay restless on his bed he said to himself,

'What my father did was *not just*.
Here I am surrounded by the joy of many sons
      and many daughters,
while my brother daily faces the shame
 of having no sons to carry on his name
  and no daughters to comfort him in his old age.
He should have the land of our fathers.
 Perhaps this will in part compensate him
 for his indescribable poverty.
Ah—but if I give it to him he will be shamed.
I must awake early in the morning before it is dawn
 and move the landmark which our father has set!'
With this he went to sleep
 and his sleep was secure and peaceful.

On the first day of the week—
 very early in the morning,
 a long time before it was day,
the two brothers met at the ancient landmarker.
 They fell with tears into each other's arms.
 And on that spot was built the city of Jerusalem.''

           —by Kenneth E. Bailey

Chapter 5

PILATE, THE TOWER, AND THE FIG TREE
(Luke 13:1-9)

In these verses we are dealing with two units of tradition (vv. 1-5, 6-9). Each unit discusses politics and repentance, and thus it is appropriate to examine them together. The second is labeled a parable. In the first, Jesus makes his point with the use of two concrete comparisons and thus the material falls under the category of parabolic speech. We do not have intellectualizing abstractions, but rather the theology is tied to two specific illustrations of people who were suddenly killed, the first by Pilate, and the second by a falling tower. Thus each unit of tradition can be seen as a type of parable.

Elsewhere we have called this material "The Call of the Kingdom to Israel" (Bailey, *Poet,* 81). This is then balanced in the Lucan Travel Narrative with a block of material that can be labeled "The Call of the Kingdom to Israel and to the Outcasts" (14:12-15:32; Bailey, *Poet,* 81).

Of the two units in this text the first is more general and addresses itself to the people. The second, as we will discover, is directed to the leadership of the nation. In each unit the literary structure will be examined and then the text studied in detail.

PILATE AND THE TOWER (Luke 13:1-5)

This passage opens with the following statement:

> And some came at that very time who told him of the Galileans whose blood Pilate had mingled with their sacrifices.

In the West we have traditionally translated the opening phrase of this verse as, "There were some *present* at that very time who. . . ." But Eastern fathers in the

74

Syriac and Arabic tradition, almost without exception, have legitimately read the verb *pareimi* as "come" rather than "be present." Thus they translate, "And some came at that time who. . . ." This understanding of the text indicates a break between passages and does not tie this unit of tradition to what precedes it. Plummer prefers this latter reading (Plummer, 337).

So atrocity storytellers suddenly appear and report to Jesus the incident of "the Galileans whose blood Pilate had mingled with their sacrifices." We are not told the intent of the storytellers. However, this intent is relatively clear to anyone who lives, or has lived, in a world of violent political conflicts. C. H. Dodd speaks of first-century Judaism's concern to maintain its identity:

> This aim, moreover, was being pursued in a situation in which resentment of pagan domination, and national sensitiveness, were mounting towards the fatal climax of A.D. 66. We have to allow for something approaching a war-mentality among large sections of the Jewish people—and we know how that can affect one's judgment. It was not clear to those who kept watch upon him that Jesus really cared for the national cause. When he was told about Pilate's slaughter of Galileans in the temple, he responded, not with indignant denunciation of Roman brutality, but with a warning to his own people to "repent" (Dodd, *More*, 96).

Josephus records a number of massacres during this period (*Antiquities* 7:45–62; 18:60–62; 20:113–17), but not this one. Plummer tries to make an historical identification (Plummer, 338). Marshall suggests that we are dealing with an historical event, "not attested from secular sources" (Marshall, 553). Marshall is more convincing than Plummer, yet neither solution is required. Civil and national violence spawns incredible rumors. One real massacre is enough to create stories about ten others. The present writer has recently completed eighteen months of agonizing with the Lebanese people in their civil war of 1975–76. The war was sparked by a massacre of twenty-eight in a bus on the outskirts of Beirut. From that time on, endless stories of massacres (some fact and some fiction) were rampant all across the land. Such stories serve a function in a community at war. The teller and the listener together are emotionally stirred to a point of rage that can then motivate them to heroism in retaliation. But woe be to the listener who dares ask, "Have you checked your sources?" Or who says, "Do not forget our hands are not clean either." All such talk is considered disloyal and the one who dares express such sentiments can expect a verbal, if not physical, attack. The brief report in the text has all the characteristics of such a violence-inspired rumor. Pilate's soldiers could have been so insensitive to Jewish religious practices as to attack worshipers in the very act of offering a sacrifice. But such an incident would hardly have escaped Josephus, who was not slow to criticize Pilate. Some minor attack on zealots in the city of Jerusalem could easily have been blown up into the report we have in the text. The expected response is, "How long, O Lord! Destroy the house of the evil Romans! Hear the cries of thy people!" A modernization of this same incident would be to go up into a Christian village in the Lebanese mountains and announce, "They came into the church with their machine guns and gunned down the faithful *in the very act of participating in the Holy Eucharist! The blood* of the worshipers *was mingled with the holy wine on the altar! NOW WHAT DO YOU THINK OF THAT*?!'' The listener *must* answer with sympathy and denunciation. In the case of Jesus, if his commitment to nationalistic goals is suspect (as Dodd suggests), then the report may well be intended to measure his loyalty to the national cause. If he does not want to voice an "indignant denunciation of Roman brutality" (Dodd, *More*, 96), then it is safest for them to walk away with Amos' admonition to silence as an operating principle (Amos 5:13). The voicing of such a denunciation would also be problematic.

Ibn al-Ṣalībī thinks that the reporters are trying to spring a trap:

> This event gave some of them an opportunity to tempt our Lord. They sent (the report) to him to see what he would answer. For if he said, "This killing is a clear case of injustice and oppression," they would then defame him before the Roman governor, claiming that he was overstepping the law and that his teachings violated that same Roman Law. But the Glorified One responded to their promptings with a call to repentance and compared this fearful event with the fall of a tower in Siloam (Ibn al-Ṣalībī, II, 139).

Ibn al-Ṣalībī's thoughtful suggestion is quite likely a part of the motivation of the questioners. They have made a political statement. If Jesus responds with a supportive reply, that answer could be used against him. But Jesus' answer demonstrates the same quality of courage seen in Jeremiah's announcements of judgment in a world of political uncertainty (Jer. 26). Jesus' response is neither denunciation of Rome, nor silence. To the form and content of that response we now turn. The literary form is as follows:

And he answered them,

1   "Do you think that those Galileans
        worse sinners they were
            than *all* the other Galileans because they suffered thus?

2   I tell you, No!
            But unless you repent
                you will *all* likewise perish.

3   Or those eighteen upon whom the tower fell (in Siloam and killed them).
        Do you think worse debtors they were
            than *all* the others who dwelt in Jerusalem?

4   I tell you, No!
            But unless you repent
                you will *all* likewise perish.''

There are two verses with a common refrain that together comprise four stanzas. Each verse is an illustration of violent death. The first is by the hated imperial ruler. The second is assumed by the text to be an act of God. The theme of ''all'' closes each stanza and ties the four together. The first line of the third stanza may have an editorial note with some extra information. If the fall of the tower on eighteen people was a noteworthy event that had caught the popular mind at the time of the telling (which seems to be the case because Jesus assumes the audience knows the incident), then the extra information about place and result would not be necessary for the original audience. As the sayings of Jesus are collected, recorded, and circulated, some extra details need to be added. The present author has identified a significant number of such footnotes with extra information that seem to have been attached to earlier compositions (Bailey, *Poet,* 67). In this case the point is insignificant theologically. Furthermore, we are not arguing that the material is any type of poetry with a specified line length; rather it is parallelistic prose with unspecified line length. Yet, if the bracketed information is an editor's note, the lines are in closer proximity to each other. We will observe below the same four-stanza structure in the parable of the Unjust Judge (Luke 18:1–8).

In regard to content, a number of points need to be made.

1. Jesus' answer *seems* to assume that the informers are trying to provoke a discussion on the relationship between sin and suffering. As we have noted above, the intent of the informers is not stated. Rather than read the account backward and supply the missing motive from the answer we would rather read the account forward from the original political statement and understand the response as a complete surprise. An atrocity story is told. Jesus is expected to respond with a denunciation of the Roman overlords. He does not. Rather, he opens the question of sin and suffering *and* concludes with a call for *them* to repent! Political enthusiasts struggling for their concept of justice do not ordinarily take kindly to such a call! The brief reference to the question of the relationship between sin and suffering is a bridge to the conclusion that focuses on repentance.

2. On the topic of sin and suffering, the text gives a double renunciation of a one-to-one relationship between them similar to the account of the man born blind in John 9:1–3. The popular attitude is there stated. The man is born blind. The disciples assume someone has sinned—either the man or his parents. Jesus denies both. In Luke 5:19 Jesus addresses the paralyzed man on the bed and announces the forgiveness of his sins. Jesus seems there also to be speaking to this same mentality. We can assume that the paralyzed man has been told that he is paralyzed because he is a sinner. Thus healing for him cannot be accomplished until he is assured of the forgiveness of his sins. In reference to our text, Edersheim makes the intriguing suggestion that the eighteen killed by the falling tower may have been working on Pilate's aqueduct. Pilate had taken money from the temple treasury for the building of the aqueduct, much to the horror of the local population. Thus if some masonry had fallen on such workmen, the entire countryside would naturally have assumed that this was a judgment from God for collaboration in such a project (Edersheim, *Life,* 222). The suggestion is all the more intriguing because it relates the two illustrations to Pilate. Some such

background may well have been the context of the falling stonework. Yet speculation is pointless. The text clearly affirms that in both cases (in the opinion of Jesus) the suffering of those involved cannot be traced to their sins.

3. The movement of the two illustrations is significant. The informants in effect ask, "What about the suffering of these national heroes struck down by our enemy?" Jesus answers, "What about the suffering of those whom God strikes down in the falling of a tower?" (There is no category of fate or chance in biblical literature. The biblical understanding of the sovereignty of God precludes it.) Thus Jesus refuses to discuss the suffering of the politically oppressed without broadening the discussion to include other types of sufferers. Those who suffer political oppression often quickly assume that their suffering is the only kind that matters, and a crass indifference may then develop to the suffering of others around them, particularly if it is of a nonpolitical nature. The incisive thrust of Jesus' response does not allow for such a narrowing of the discussion, irrespective of the grim nature of the political oppression presented.

4. In the first stanza we read of "sinners" and in the third of "debtors." The same shift with the identical words can be found in the two versions of the Lord's Prayer. Matthew gives us, "Forgive us our *debts* as we forgive..." (Matt. 6:12), and in Luke the same prayer is recorded, "Forgive us our *sins* as we forgive..." (Luke 11:4). Marshall observes that the presence of these two words in parallel texts demonstrates the Semitic background of the story (Marshall, 554). Simply stated, the first (debts) are the believer's unfulfilled duties in discipleship and obedience; the second (sins) are the overt evil acts that the believer commits. It has long been noted that the Aramaic word *ḥōbā'*, which occurs in both texts in the Old Syriac, carries both meanings. If we can assume an Aramaic background to this text (as we surely can with the Lord's Prayer), then quite likely here also the original would have had *ḥōbā'* in both texts. A sensitive translator into Greek may have known the two-sided nature of the word, and, finding no equivalent in Greek, he gave us half of the content of *ḥōbā'* in the first stanza and the other half in the second. Irrespective of this suggestion, we do have this two-sided nature of evil expressed in the words for sin that are parallel in these verses. The evil of which the political enthusiasts are urged to repent is described first as "sins" (v. 2) and then as "debts" (v. 4).

5. The stunning climax of the twice-repeated refrain is the call for the listeners themselves to repent, lest they also perish. This unexpected thrust gives us an illustration of the courage of Jesus, an understanding of a part of the reason why he was rejected by his community, and a profound insight into a part of his response to the oppressed struggling for justice. When Jeremiah opposed the political climate of his day he was protected by influential friends and his life was spared (Jer. 26:24). So far as we know, Jesus did not have powerful friends who could or would protect him. Nicodemus' one feeble attempt illustrates the point (John 7:50). In studying Luke 13:1–5 with Middle Eastern classes, the present writer has often had students marvel that Jesus was not physically attacked on the spot. This call for repentance is thrown in the face of nationalistic enthusiasts

who stand in opposition to Roman oppression. Those who fight for a just cause often assume that the struggle for the cause makes them righteous. It does not. The more intense the struggle for justice the more the oppressed tend to assume their own righteousness. This assumption of righteousness at times expresses itself as an arrogance that refuses any criticism. The subconscious rationale seems to be, "Our cause is righteous, thus we are righteous. Furthermore, after all that we have suffered, how *dare* you inflict any more wounds on us by your criticism." Attitudes of this type have on occasion surfaced on both sides of the barbed wire in the Middle East in the past thirty years. Only the strong and the brave can dare to endure the wrath of such oppressed and turn the attention away from criticism of the hated enemy to painful self-criticism with the warning, "Unless you repent, you will *all* likewise perish." In the synagogue in Nazareth there is a similar refusal on the part of Jesus to identify with the nationalism of his day. There he chooses two foreigners (one a woman) as illustrations of the kinds of people who through faith will receive the benefits of the now present kingdom of God. There the listening audience is so upset that they try to kill him. Here in Luke 13 we have no record of the audience reaction but can assume similar hostility. Anyone who would recast Jesus as a political revolutionary must not fail to take seriously the confrontation here in Luke 13.

This same call for repentance can be seen on its deepest level as a profound concern for the welfare of those whose outrage he refuses to reinforce. Jesus' speech should not be read simply as a rejection of the nationalistic struggle, nor as a concern for things "spiritual" rather than political. Rather he seems to be saying at least, "You want me to condemn evil in Pilate. I am not talking to Pilate. He is not here. I am talking to you. Evil forces are at work in your movement that will destroy you, Pilate or no Pilate. *You* must repent or *all* of you will be destroyed by those forces." Among those who struggle for justice there develops the attitude, "We are the angels and they are the devils." Blessed is the movement that is willing to listen to a courageous voice quietly insisting, "There are devils among us and angels among them. *We* must repent." He does not tell them to submit to Pilate. He is not acquiescing to Roman oppression. Rather he bravely demonstrates a deep concern for the people in front of him who will destroy themselves and all around them if they do not repent.

Finally, what is the precise response Jesus is hoping to evoke from the nationalists who bring him the atrocity story? At least this: "We ask him to look at evil in Pilate. He wants us to see evil in our own hearts. We must repent. If we do not, that evil will destroy us."

What then comprises the cluster of theological motifs found in this Dominical response to the atrocity story? We can identify at least the following:

1. Sin is defined both by evil acts and duties left unperformed.
2. There is no one-to-one relationship between sin and suffering. Easy theological judgments about the reasons for natural and political disasters must be rejected.

3. Any intense political movement must look deep within its own soul to repent of its own evil, lest it destroy itself and the very people it seeks to serve.

4. The compassion of Jesus reaches out to all who suffer, not only to those who are politically oppressed.

THE BARREN FIG TREE (Luke 13:6-9)

A clear identification of listeners is made in Luke 12:54. We have noted a slight shift of audience in 13:1, which reads, "And some came at that time who told him. . . ." Then 13:10 gives another clear break in setting with the move to a scene in the synagogue. Thus the text assumes a continuity between 13:1-5 and 13:6-9. The parable in verses 6-9 is comprised of five stanzas. The literary structure is as follows:

1	A man had a *fig tree planted* in his vineyard.	PLANT
	And he came seeking fruit on it	SEEK FRUIT
	and he found none.	NO FRUIT
2	And he said to the vinedresser,	MASTER SPEAKS
	"Behold! These three years	THREE YEARS
	I have come seeking fruit on this fig tree	SEEK FRUIT
	and I find none.	NO FRUIT
3	*Dig it out!*	DIG OUT
	Why should it exhaust the ground?"	SAVE THE GROUND
4	But he answering said to him,	VINEDRESSER SPEAKS
	"Master! Forgive it this year also	ONE YEAR
	until I dig around it	HELP FRUIT-BEARING
	and spread on manure.	HELP FRUIT-BEARING
5	And if it bears fruit in the future—	FIND FRUIT?
	And if not,	NO FRUIT
	dig it out."	DIG OUT

The overall structure of the parable is clear and only slightly modified from patterns we have observed in other parables. The "plant, seek fruit, no fruit" themes of stanza one are balanced by "find fruit, no fruit, dig out" in the last stanza. Thus the parable begins with a planting and ends with a threatened digging up of what was planted. Stanzas two and four are parallel and match each other almost line for line. Stanza two could roughly be called "the problem" and stanza four, "the hoped-for solution." As is usually the case when the inversion principle is used, the climax occurs in the center and is then mirrored thematically in some way at the end. This literary device is used here in that the motif "dig it out" occurs in the middle and again at the end. The critical point of turning occurs, as is usual in such structures, just past the center. At that point the voice of mercy pleads for additional grace. The literary structure is simple, balanced, and artistically satisfying. Each stanza will be examined in turn.

Stanza One

A man had a *fig tree planted* in his vineyard.	PLANT
And he came seeking fruit on it	SEEK FRUIT
and he found none.	NO FRUIT

In Joel 1:7 the close association of the fig and the vine is seen where the prophet says of the locust horde,

> It has laid waste my vines,
> and splintered my fig trees.

And again in 1:12,

> The vine withers,
> the fig tree languishes.

Thus, finding a fig tree in a vineyard is not unusual. In Isaiah 5:1–7 we have the classical Old Testament parable of the vineyard. There the symbols are identified. The owner of the vineyard is the Lord of hosts, and the vineyard itself is the house of Israel (Isa. 5:7). We can assume that the same symbolic identification would have immediately been made in this parable by Jesus' audience. There is then a crucial divergence of symbols. Isaiah discusses all the vines in the vineyard collectively. Jesus' parable concentrates on one plant in the vineyard that is a fig tree, not a grape vine. This selection may be in order to draw attention to the fact that he is discussing one particular tree and not the vineyard as a whole (in contrast to Isaiah). Also it may be because the fig in Palestine bears fruit ten months of the year so that at almost any time the owner can find fruit on it. In any case, the vine and the fig are closely related all through the Old Testament and together are a symbol of peace. For in time of peace each man will sit under his own vine and his own fig tree (Mic. 4:4; Zech. 3:10). Then, finally, the fig *in its first fruit* is Hosea's symbol of a pure, innocent, responsive people.

> Like grapes in the wilderness,
>   I found Israel.
> Like the first fruit on the fig tree
>   in its first season,
>   I saw your fathers (9:10).

Also, in 9:16 failure to bear fruit is used as a symbol for the idolatrous days in which Hosea lived. Thus Jesus could have had a variety of reasons for choosing a fig tree rather than a vine for this particular parable.

Whenever there is a clear literary background for a parable it becomes crucial to see what Jesus does as he reworks well-known material. In this case, the basic symbolism is unmistakable because it is already identified in the prototype in Isaiah 5:7, as we have noted. We find no reason to reject this same symbolism in the present parable. Thus the owner is again God and the vineyard (not the tree) is ''the house of Israel.'' The New Testament parable of the vineyard (20:9–16) has some of this same background. In the New Testament the text is specifically interpreted by the evangelist as spoken against the scribes and the chief priests. Luke 20:9 reads, "The scribes and the chief priests . . . perceived that he had told this parable against *them*." Thus the evangelists understood that parable to be against the *leadership* of the nation, not the nation itself. In Isaiah's parable the *vineyard* (the nation) is deliberately torn down by the owner (Isa. 5:5-6). By contrast, in the present parable of the Barren Fig Tree, the master is concerned for the fruitfulness of the vineyard and thus asks some very serious questions about a particular tree (the fig). It is unfruitful and is thus bleeding strength from the vineyard itself by its continuing presence. The master acts to *preserve* the health of the vineyard, not to destroy it. Thus in harmony with the clear symbolism of Luke 20:9-16 and Isaiah 5:1-7 we would see the problem discussed in this parable to be the crisis of fruitless leadership within the nation, not judgment on the nation of Israel itself (against Montefiore, *Gospels*, II, 965).

The text also preserves an authentic note of traditional culture. The landowner of the past did not get his hands dirty. Even so in this story. The vineyard owner does not himself plant a fig, but rather has it planted. The point is theologically insignificant but gives a stamp of authenticity to the parable as a story that fits Middle Eastern culture.

Thus, in a simple and straightforward manner, the problem is stated in the opening stanza.

Stanza Two

And he said to the vinedresser,	MASTER SPEAKS
"Behold! These three years	THREE YEARS
I have come seeking fruit on this fig tree	SEEK FRUIT
and I find none."	NO FRUIT

The owner and the vinedresser cooperated in the planting in the first stanza. Now they cooperate in the evaluation of the problem.

The common understanding of the time sequence is that the tree would have three years in which to grow. Then for three years the fruit was considered forbidden, according to Leviticus 19:23. The fruit of the fourth year (that is, the seventh year of the tree's life) was considered clean and was offered to the Lord (Lev. 19:24). The details in this brief parable are scanty, but the probable intent is that the master is seeking this seventh-year fruit specified in Leviticus 19:23 as an offering to the Lord. Indeed, he has been seeking it for three years. The master would not "come *seeking*" the unpurified fruit of years four to six of the tree's life. Thus for three years he sought the first fruits and has been disappointed three times. Now nine years have passed since the planting of the tree. The situation seems hopeless. If our identification of the symbolism of the parable is correct this stanza is saying that quite enough time has passed for the current leadership of the nation to produce the fruits expected of it (probably the fruits of repentance; cf. Luke 3:8). The master has waited patiently, long beyond the expected time of fruit-bearing. His conclusion is set out in stanza three.

Stanza Three

"Dig it out!	DIG OUT
Why should it exhaust the ground?"*	SAVE GROUND

Not only does the disappointing tree fail to produce fruit and take up space that could be used for other useful plants, but it drains strength out of the ground, thereby exhausting it. In his concern for good soil in the good vineyard the master orders the fig tree to be dug out.

Here an authentic note in the story appears. In the West, woodsmen cut down trees. In the Middle East, the tree is *"dug out."* The tree, with its stump and some of its root cluster, falls as one block and is removed. This agricultural practice is reflected in the text of Luke 3:9, where John says, "Even now the ax is laid to the *root* of the trees" (not the trunk). So the verb in 13:7 (*katargeō*) literally means "dig out," not "cut down." Thus the Palestinian agricultural scene, accurately reflected in the text, gives a vivid picture of a radical elimination of this unfruitful tree. The unfruitful leadership of the nation is to be rooted out. At this point in the parable a dramatic shift takes place.

Stanza Four

But he answering said to him,	VINEDRESSER SPEAKS
"Master! Forgive it this year also	ONE YEAR
until I dig around it	HELP FRUIT-BEARING
and spread on manure."	HELP FRUIT-BEARING

In biblical literature, when the stanzas relate to each other in an inverted fashion, there is often a crucial shift just past the center of the literary structure (Bailey, *Poet*, 48, 50f., 53, 61f., 72–74). This important feature, as we have noted, occurs in this parable. The speech of the master outlines the problem and is carefully matched by the speech of the vinedresser, who suggests a hoped-for solution. The prototypical parable in Isaiah 5 has *no* offer of grace. There the parable moves from the disappointment of the vineyard owner when a good crop is not forthcoming to *immediate* judgment. The owner announces that he will "remove its hedge . . . break down its wall . . . make it a waste . . . and command the clouds that they rain no rain upon it" (Isa. 5:5–6). The judgment is harsh, enacted by the owner himself and carried out at once. Some such final scene was surely expected for Jesus' version of this classical parable. The point of turning in this text is twofold. The fig tree is offered a period of grace and special attention is planned for it: the vinedresser will dig around it and add manure. Thus, when compared with the Song of the Vineyard in Isaiah, this parable has a striking emphasis on mercy that is usually overlooked in the light of the motif of judgment.

Another point of literary comparison is the story of Ahikar in the Pseudepigrapha (8:35, Charles, II, 775). The part of the story in question may be a later addition (Marshall, 555), yet it is of interest. In the story, Ahikar has a wayward adopted son who promises to reform. Ahikar tells the boy that he is like a palm tree beside a river that cast its fruit into the river. The owner decided to cut it down. The tree complained, offering to produce carobs if given one more year. The owner skeptically replied, "Thou hast not been industrious in what is thine own, and how wilt thou be industrious in what is not thine own?" (*ibid.*). Here the tree itself does the pleading, and more important we are given a negative answer. The reader is left with a strong negative impression—nothing can really be done—the situation is hopeless. Not so with the parable of Jesus. In Jesus' parable the fig tree is to be given one last chance. Again the theme of mercy is prominent.

The parable has two distinctive colloquialisms. The first is grammatical and the second cultural. The parable is told in the past tense. Suddenly in verse 8 there is an historical present, rare in Luke. That is, the text suddenly shifts to the present tense and reads, "Answering he says (*sic*) to him. . . ." This shift adds a colloquial vividness to the telling of the story and suggests that Luke is using traditional material (Marshall, 555). Then in Luke 20:19 both the people and the leaders understand that the parable of the vineyard is told against the scribes and chief priests. If our assumption is correct that this parable is also told against the religious leadership and that this would have been immediately sensed by the listening audience, then we have here a somewhat humorous peasant turn of phrase. The word "manure" (*koprion*) occurs only here in the New Testament. It is not the kind of language that is ordinarily used in religious illustrations. The vinedresser could have offered to spread on fresh earth, or water the tree each day, or even prune it back. If the fig tree represents the scribes and the chief priests, and the parable talks of the need to cast on some manure, then we have a clear case of what the comedians call "insult humor." What they need is a little manure spread around them. The original audience no doubt found the imagery humorous. Mild irreverence for people in positions of power is usually appreciated by a popular audience. With such details the sparkle and vitality of the parable appears along with its unmistakable cutting edge.

Christian allegorizers have had a field day with this parable all through the centuries. The "three years" have become everything from "law, prophets, and gospel" to the three years of the ministry of Jesus. In such cases the allegorization is misleading but harmless. But in this stanza the vinedresser has often been identified with Jesus, who is then seen arguing with God the Father. Such an identification could hardly have been imagined by the original audience nor intended by Jesus. The Christian allegorizer begins with his theology of the Trinity and from that makes the above identification. But when he does so, God the Father is seen as harsh and judgmental, and Jesus appears as gracious and loving. Thus a split is caused in the Trinity. For centuries Islam has characterized Christian theology as tritheistic; when such interpretations surface, unmistakable cracks appear in the concept of the unity of God to the extent that the Islamic accusation has some validity. If we return to the parabolic prototype in Isaiah 5, the owner is the farmer who both plants the vineyard and then tears it down when it produces wild grapes. Here two people debate the fate of the vineyard among themselves. It is far more appropriate to understand the debate as between mercy and judgment. Manson observes,

> The conversation between the owner of the vineyard and his workmen is reminiscent of Rabbinical passages in which the attributes of God debate, the attribute of justice with the attribute of mercy. If God dealt with Israel by strict justice, Israel would perish. But he does not. He gives another chance. And if it is madness to fly in the face of His justice, it is desperate wickedness to flout His mercy (Manson, *Sayings,* 275).

We disagree with Manson's identification of the fig tree with Israel, but agree with his understanding of the debate between justice and mercy. Judgment requires that the tree be dug out for the stated reasons. Mercy pleads for more grace and a second chance. The same tension is reflected all through the Old Testament and is intensely focused in prophets like Hosea, who can thunder harsh oracles of judgment in one verse and in the next say,

> How can I give you up, O Ephraim! . . .
> My heart recoils within me,
>   my compassion grows warm and tender (Hos. 11:8-9).

In this parable mercy and judgment are given voices. They are personified dramatically by the owner and the vinedresser who struggle *together* over the unfruitful vine. The tension itself is deep within the heart of God.

The theology of the Song of the Vineyard in Isaiah 5 is powerfully reinforced by the use of wordplay. The last part of verse 7 reads,

> and he looked for *mishpaṭ* (justice)
>   and behold, *mishpaḥ* (bloodshed)
> for *ṣedhaqah* (righteousness)
>   but behold, *ṣeʿaqah* (a cry).

In Jesus' dialogue of the vineyard there is quite likely a similar use of wordplay. This wordplay surfaces in the Old Syriac version of the parable. Given that Syriac and Aramaic are dialects of the same language, this wordplay may well have been present in the original Aramaic of the parable itself. It is as follows:

> dig it out   = *fsūqīh*
> forgive it/let it alone = *shbūqīh*

So the vinedresser pleads not *fsūqīh* (dig it out) but rather *shbūqīh* (forgive it). Thus the thrust of the main point of each voice (grace and judgment) is perhaps reinforced and made unforgettable by a skillfully constructed wordplay.

Stanza Five

> "And if it bears fruit in the future—   FIND FRUIT?
>   and if not,   NO FRUIT
> dig it out."   DIG OUT

The Greek phrase *eis to mellon* is often translated "next year." But the identical construction in I Timothy 6:19 is translated "for the future." The word *mellon* is commonly used for the future (Bauer, 502), which may be a better translation in this text. The voice of grace and mercy is talking. The vinedresser is pleading for grace (give it more time) and mercy (forgive it). These elements are strengthened if a specific time for the "execution" is not stated. The time of the future judgment is left unspecified.

In the second half of the verse, the "then" of the if-then construction (the apodosis) is missing. The RSV and many other translations supply the missing words "well and good," which are implied but not stated. The construction is classical (Marshall, 556) but the reason for it may be literary. In stanza four the vinedresser suggests two horticultural acts in an attempt to revive the fruitless tree. He will "dig around it" and "spread on manure." From a literary point of view, this gives the fourth stanza four lines to match the four lines of stanza two. The same concern for balanced stanzas may be at work in stanza five. The apodosis may have been omitted so that stanza five would have only three lines to match stanza one with its three semantic units. In any case, the meaning is clear; after the "acts of redemption" are completed and sufficient time for renewal is given, the fig tree must respond. If it does not, judgment will be the only option left. The health of the vineyard is too important and the master's expectation of fruit too strong to leave an unproductive tree indefinitely occupying good ground and sapping its strength.

Even so, the salvation offered has a special quality to it. It comes exclusively from the outside. The voice of mercy pleads for forgiveness yet one more time. Then redemptive *acts* that may lead to renewal (the production of fruit) are proposed. The word ordinarily translated "let it alone" (v. 8) is the New Testament word for "forgiveness," and there is no misunderstanding about what Jesus is discussing. Forgiveness can be offered yet again, but that will mean *nothing* unless some help for the tree comes from the outside. Renewal cannot come from within the resources of the tree itself. It cannot gather the strength it needs from its own roots. The *vinedresser* must act to save the tree and at the same time the tree must respond to those acts or they are of no avail. In this simple agricultural picture can we not overhear the great themes of God's own mighty redemptive acts?

Here, as in previous parables, we do not know what happens. This story is also open-ended. Does the owner grant the reprieve? Does the tree respond? We are not told. The action freezes like a TV spot and the reader/listener must respond.

In conclusion, then, what specific response is sought from the original audience by the telling of the parable? We suggest that the original audience is pressed to understand:

> The present spiritual leadership of the nation is fruitless. Judgment threatens. God in His mercy will act to redeem. If there is no response, judgment will be the only alternative. His love for the community of faith is too deep for it to be otherwise.

The cluster of theological motifs present in the parable include the following:

1. The spiritual leaders of the household of faith are planted in "God's vineyard" and are expected to produce fruit for Him.

2. When that leadership is fruitless it not only fails in its own obedience but also sterilizes the community around it. God cares for the community and will not tolerate this situation indefinitely.

3. Mercy is extended to unfruitful leadership in the form of forgiveness and renewing grace.

4. Only in the grace of God, freely offered to the fruitless leaders, is renewal possible. God acts to forgive and renew. These acts come from beyond the leaders, who cannot renew themselves.

5. God's offer of mercy must evoke a response from within or renewal will not take place and judgment will be inevitable.

Thus the two units of tradition are closely related. The first deals with the suffering of the community that results from the Roman leaders. The people are called on to repent. The second deals with the barrenness in the community that results from the failures of the national leaders, who need forgiveness and grace. Thus in the first (13:1–5) the people must repent. In the second (13:6–9) the leaders need forgiveness. In each, politics and repentance (forgiveness) are related in ways that instruct the faithful in every age.

Chapter 6

THE GREAT BANQUET
(Luke 14:15-24)

Luke 14 and 15 have in them some of the greatest passages in all of Scripture. Here the unqualified offer of grace to sinners is set forth in all of its majesty. Often the theological masterpiece of the parable of the Prodigal Son is allowed to overshadow that of the Great Banquet, which deserves equal attention. We will examine in turn the literary background, setting, structure, and culture of the parable. The interpretation will attempt to take all of these into consideration.

In Luke this parable is told at a banquet where the people recline. Our Arabic translations, following the Greek text, give us "reclined" rather than the RSV "sat at table." What is the precise setting? Jeremias has pointed out that with the exceptions of Luke 24:30 and Mark 16:14 the word "recline" in the Gospels always means either a meal out-of-doors or a banquet of some kind (Jeremias, *Eucharistic*, 48f.). Here we have a banquet. But was there a table? In the Old Testament the presence of a table for a meal seems to assume wealth or rank (cf. II Sam. 9:7; I Kings 13:20). The same can be said for the New Testament. There are many references to meals and eating but a physical table is mentioned only four times. It occurs in the story of the Canaanite woman who humbly suggests that the dogs can eat crumbs from the master's table (cf. Matt. 15:27 and parallels). The rich man in the story of Lazarus has a table (Luke 16:21). There is a table in the upper room (Luke 22:21) and in the eschatological messianic banquet hall (Luke 22:30). Granted, the meals held out-of-doors at which Jesus and the disciples "reclined" were not eaten on tables. Yet it is perhaps best to assume (as we did in Luke 7:36) that here also the guests are reclining on couches around a low table. The parable tells of a "great banquet" where property owners are the chosen guests. The setting is the house of a ruler (14:1) who is most certainly wealthy enough to be in the class of people who recline on couches around tables and not on the floor in peasant style. Thus, "reclined around tables" would perhaps best represent the scene. We must visualize relatively wealthy people reclining in Greco-Roman style at a formal banquet.

The parable itself is introduced by a pious outburst from a fellow diner (14:15) who says, "Blessed is he who shall eat bread in the kingdom of God!" With this statement we are clearly in the world of Palestinian speech and culture. "To eat bread" is a classical Middle Eastern idiom meaning "to eat a meal." It has long been identified as a Hebraism (Plummer, 360). T. W. Manson regards this introductory statement as "probably too good to be invented" (*Sayings*, 129). Thus, the guest reclining with Jesus introduces the subject of *eating* in the kingdom. Here as elsewhere the banquet is a symbol for salvation (Marshall, 587). This salvation culminates at the end of history with a final great banquet. That last great banquet is commonly referred to as the messianic banquet of the end times. So important is this latter theme as a background for an understanding of the parable that it must be examined briefly.

The idea of the sacred meal with God is deeply embedded in the Old Testament. In Psalm 23:5 we are told that God Himself spreads a banquet for the one who trusts in Him. Even more informative for our passage is Isaiah 25:6-9. This passage is most likely poetry that uses very old poetic forms (as confirmed to me by William Holladay of Andover-Newton Theological School in private correspondence). Our translation of the text is as follows:

Text (Isaiah 25:6-9)	*Major Themes*

6 And He will make, Yahweh of Hosts,
    for *all* the peoples on this mountain
a fat banquet, a wine banquet,
    a banquet of juicy marrow, of good wine.
	MAKE—A BANQUET
	ALL PEOPLES

7 And He will swallow on this mountain
    the face of the covering,
the covering over *all* the peoples,
    and the veil spread over *all* the nations.
	SWALLOW—VEIL
	ALL PEOPLES/NATIONS

8 He will swallow up death forever.
    And the Lord Yahweh will wipe away tears
        from off *all* faces.
And the reproach of His people
    He will take away from upon *all* the earth,
        for Yahweh has spoken.
	SWALLOW—DEATH
	ALL FACES
	
	TAKE AWAY—REPROACH
	ALL THE EARTH

9 It will be said on that day,
 	
    "Lo, this is our *God*;
      we have *waited* for Him
        that he might *save* us.
 	
    This is *Yahweh*;
      we have *waited* for Him;
        let us be glad and rejoice in His *salvation*."
	GOD
	WAIT
	SAVE
	
	GOD
	WAIT
	SAVE

In this remarkable text a number of important themes are brought together. Salvation is described in terms of a great banquet, which shall be for *all* the peoples/nations. The gentiles will participate after God has swallowed up death and their veil. The people swallow the banquet, God swallows up death and the covering. The veil is not removed, rather it is destroyed. Ordinarily the nations who come to the Lord must come bringing gifts (cf. Isa. 18:7; 60:4-7; Ps. 96:8). Here the banquet is pure grace—the participants from the nations bring nothing. The food offered is rich fare of the kind that is the food of kings. Verse 9 is often seen as a separate piece of tradition. Yet it *is* attached here by the editor and thus the waiting for the God who comes to save is emphasized. There is also the striking occurrence of five cases of *"all"* in verses 6-8.

This banquet theme was developed in the intertestamental period and understood to be related to the coming of the Messiah (cf. Jeremias, *Eucharistic*, 233f.), but somehow the idea that the gentiles would be invited to attend was muted. The Aramaic version of the passage, the Targum, paraphrases verse 6 as follows:

> Yahweh of Hosts will make for all the peoples in this mountain a meal; and though they suppose it is an honour, it will be a shame for them, and great plagues, plagues from which they will be unable to escape, plagues whereby they will come to their end (quoted by Gray, I, 429f.).

Clearly the vision of Isaiah is here lost. In I Enoch 62:1-16 the "kings and the mighty and the exalted and those who rule the earth" (obviously the gentiles) will fall down before the Son of man, who will drive them out from his presence. He will "deliver them to the angels for punishment" (v. 11); "they shall be a spectacle for the righteous" (v. 12); and "his sword is drunk with their blood" (v. 12). After this destruction of sinners the righteous and the elect shall eat with the Son of man forever and ever (v. 14, Charles, II, 227f.). Then, in the Qumran community, the great banquet was specifically connected with the coming of the Messiah. This is described in a short work called "The Messianic Rule" (1QSa 2:11-22). In this remarkable passage we read of how, in the last days, the Messiah will gather with the whole congregation to eat bread and drink wine. The wise, the intelligent, and the perfect men will gather with Him. These will all be assembled by rank. Verse 2:11 reads,

> And then (the Mess)iah of Israel shall (come),
> and the chiefs of the (clans of Israel) shall sit before him,
> (each) in the order of his dignity
> according to (his place) in their camps and marches (Vermes, 121).

The specifics of these ranks are carefully spelled out. First are the judges and officers; then come the chiefs of thousands, fifties, and tens; finally there are the Levites. No one is allowed in who is "smitten in his flesh, or paralyzed in his feet or hands, or lame, or blind, or deaf, or dumb, or smitten in his flesh with a visible blemish" (*ibid.*, 120). All gentiles are obviously excluded and, along with them, all imperfect Jews. Thus, Isaiah's open-ended vision has been blurred if not eliminated. For him the great day was coming when the veil of the gentiles would be destroyed and they would sit down with God's people. Enoch has the gentiles excluded, and the Qumran community in addition rejects all Jewish unrighteous along with those with any physical blemish. The pious guest in Luke 14:15 certainly assumes something of this background. Regarding the opinions of Jesus, the reader of Luke's Gospel already has an indication of his views on this topic from reading Luke 13:29, which is also an important part of the background of the parable before us. This verse is set in a structure which can be seen as follows:

Luke 13:28-34

The Ingathering for the Banquet

There will be weeping and chattering of teeth
when you see Abraham and Isaac and Jacob
and all the prophets in the kingdom of God, .
and you yourselves thrown out.

And they *will come* from East and West
and from North and South
and *sit at table* in the kingdom of God.

And behold, some are last who will be first,
and some are first who will be last.

   The Death of Jesus

   At that very hour some Pharisees came and said to him,
   "Leave and go away from here,
   for Herod wants *to kill you.*"

    The Great Day

    And he said to them, "Go tell that fox,

    'Behold I cast out demons and perfect cures
      today and tomorrow,
         and the *third day* I am made perfect.

    The Great Day

    Nevertheless it is necessary for me
      today and tomorrow
        and the *following/coming day* to go on my way.

   The Death of Jesus

   For it is not acceptable that a prophet die away from Jerusalem.'
   Jerusalem, Jerusalem, *killing* the prophets
   and *stoning* those who are sent to you.

The Ingathering

How often would I have *gathered* your children
as a hen *gathers* her brood under her wings,
and you would not" (cf. Bailey, *Poet*, 81).

The passage opens with the messianic banquet.

Three interlocking themes are stated and then repeated in an inverse fashion. In the preceding verses (13:23–28) we are told that in the final fulfillment of all things, some who think they are accepted will plead specifically, "We ate and drank in your presence" (13:26). That is, they will claim to have participated in table fellowship with him. But no, "I do not know you," comes the answer. Abraham, Isaac, and Jacob and all the prophets will be there, but these bystanders will be rejected. Then comes the double repetition of the threefold theme of the *ingathering* for the great banquet, a reference to the *death* of Jesus, and the *third* day (see above, p. 91).

The materials are clearly edited into this present form by Luke or his source. Each of the major themes is stated and then repeated in a reverse fashion. Significantly some of the motifs in Isaiah 25 reappear. There *will be* an ingathering. The faithful will come from all four corners of the compass. A dramatic reversal of positions is anticipated, for the last will be first, and some who are first will be last. Jerusalem is presented as the place where Jesus most earnestly desired to gather the faithful for the banquet, but they have refused. Here the ingathering for the messianic banquet is discussed, along with the twice-repeated theme of the death of Jesus, and a reference to his being made perfect on "the third day." These latter two themes are not repeated in our parable and so lie outside of the scope of this study, but are of importance for an understanding of the theology of the Travel Narrative as a whole, and for a full understanding of the messianic banquet in Luke, as well as Luke's theology of the cross. For our purposes we note specifically that Jesus anticipates a great eschatological banquet. Jerusalem's children are invited and they refuse. Some who expect to be there are turned away. The guests will come in from the four points of the compass.

To summarize the literary background of our parable we can see the great banquet of God described in inclusive terms in Isaiah 25. The Targum of the same passage reverses its terms. Enoch sees the gentiles excluded. The Qumran community turns the scene into an ordered banquet where only the worthy can attend and they by rank. In Luke 13 we read of a great ingathering and banquet with the patriarchs. Some have refused an earnest invitation. Many who expect to be there will be rejected. The guests come from the four corners of the earth. Lucan composition relates the "third day" and the death of Jesus to the banquet. With this Old Testament, intertestamental, and New Testament background in mind, we can proceed to the text.

The pious banqueter invokes a blessing on those who will be accepted on that great day. The expected response is something like, "O Lord, may we be among the righteous and be counted without blemish, worthy to sit with the men of renown on that great day." Rather than a traditional pious invocation, Jesus responds with a parable, whose literary form is as follows (cf. p. 93).

The parable begins with a reference to the banquet itself and those originally invited. We have a clear case of *inclusio* in that these same themes, with the same language, recur at the end. After the introduction the dramatic action

And he said to him,
"A man once gave a great banquet,   GREAT BANQUET
and he invited many.   MANY INVITED

1   And he sent his servant at the hour of the banquet to say, 'Come!
                                                           DO THIS
        Because all is now ready!'   BECAUSE OF THIS
        But they all alike began to make excuses.   EXCUSES

2   The first said to him, 'I have bought a field,   I DID THIS
        and I must go out and see it.   I MUST DO THIS
        I pray you have me excused.'   EXCUSE ME

3   And another said, 'I have bought five yoke of oxen,   I DID THIS
        and I go to test them.   I MUST DO THIS
        I pray you have me excused.'   EXCUSE ME

4   And another said, 'I have married a bride,   I DID THIS
        and therefore—   THUS I MUST
        I cannot come.'   NOT COME

5   So the servant came and reported this to his master.
     Then the householder in anger said to his servant, 'Go out
        quickly,   MASTER—GO
        into the streets and lanes of the city.   TO STREETS
        Bring in the poor, maimed, blind, and lame.'   FILL UP

6   And the servant said, 'Sir,   SERVANT
        what you commanded has been done,   I WENT
        and still there is room.'   NOT FULL

7   And the master said to the servant, 'Go out,   MASTER—GO
        into the highways and hedges,   TO HIGHWAYS
        and compel to enter, that my house may be filled.' FILL UP

For I tell you (pl.),
none of those men who were invited   THOSE INVITED
shall taste my banquet."   MY BANQUET

divides into seven speeches. We could even call the parable "The Banquet of the
Seven Speeches." These seven fall naturally into seven stanzas (almost seven
scenes) with certain key ideas repeating in the first four and then other key ideas
repeating in the last three. The master gives three speeches. Each of them begins
with a command related to the gathering of the guests. There are two invitations
to the original guests at the beginning of the parable, and two invitations to
outsiders (although to different people) at the end. The parable needs to be
examined one stanza at a time. To this examination we now turn.

INTRODUCTION

And he said to him,
"A man once gave a great banquet,   GREAT BANQUET
and he invited many."   MANY INVITED

STANZA ONE—A BANQUET PREPARED

"And he sent his servant at the hour of the banquet to say, 'Come!

Because all is now ready!'	DO THIS
But they all alike began to make excuses."	BECAUSE OF THIS
	EXCUSE ME

A great banquet is naturally hosted by a great man. The guests would be his peers and associates. This first invitation is serious and, as we will observe below, acceptance of it is a firm commitment. In the first stanza of the parable there is introduced a sequence of three ideas that will be repeated four times in a row. This sequence we have tried to indicate with the words at the right of the text. They are: DO THIS, BECAUSE OF THIS, and EXCUSE ME. The repetition of these three ideas will prove significant as we proceed. Then also, we notice two invitations.

A rabbinic commentary on Lamentations refers to the people of Jerusalem and notes that none of them would attend a banquet unless he was invited twice (*Midrash Rabbah Lam.* 4:2, Sonc., 216). This has often been taken as a background of the double invitation of the parable under discussion. However, the editors of the above text observe that the double invitation is "to make sure that the first invitation had not been sent to him in mistake." As the next paragraph illustrates, "such an error may have a tragic sequel" (*ibid.*, n. 5). In the text of the Midrash there follows a long story of a Jerusalemite who gives a dinner and sends out an invitation to a friend. By accident the invitation is delivered to an enemy and tragedy results. The entire context is irrelevant to the parable under discussion. Rather the double invitation is in perfect harmony with traditional Middle Eastern custom, which still persists in conservative areas. A village host must provide meat for a banquet. The meat will be killed and cooked on the basis of the number of guests. A host sends out his invitations and receives acceptance. He then decides on the killing/butchering of a chicken or two (for 2–4 guests), or a duck (for 5–8), or a kid (10–15 acceptances), or a sheep (if there are 15–35 people), or a calf (35–75). That is, the decision regarding the kind of meat and the amount is made mostly on the basis of the number of accepted invitations. Once the countdown starts it cannot be stopped. The appropriate animal is killed and must be eaten that night. The guests who accept the invitation are duty-bound to appear. The host completes his preparations. Then at the "hour of the banquet" a servant is sent out with the traditional message, "Come, all is now ready," meaning the meat is cooked and we are ready for you. Ibrāhīm Saʿīd has caught this in his comment on this verse:

> This is according to the accepted custom of noble men in the East who extend an invitation sometime before the banquet and then repeat the invitation by means of a messenger at the hour of the banquet (Saʿīd, 382).

Thomson confirms Saʿīd:

> If a sheikh, bey, or emeer invites, he always sends a servant to call you at the proper time. This servant often repeats the very formula mentioned in Luke

xiv. 17: Tefŭddŭlŭ, al 'asha hâder—Come, for the supper is ready (Thomson, I, 178).

Furthermore, Thomson finds the parable, "in all its details, in close conformity to the customs of this country" (*ibid.*, 179). The Greek text supports this cultural background. The present imperative "Come!" means literally "continue coming." The guests have begun their action by accepting the invitation. They continue it by responding to the messenger. Indeed, beginning with Esther (6:14) down through the first century, this double invitation can be documented in both Jewish and Roman works (Marshall, 587f.). Thus, the two invitations are in full harmony with the customs of the times. The initial acceptance obliges the guest to respond to the summons at the "hour of the banquet."

The language already triggers in the listeners' ears the rumblings of great events. "The *hour* of the banquet" approaches and the freighted message goes out, "Come! All is ready!" The theological intent is unmistakable. The hour of the messianic banquet has arrived. All is prepared, invitations are out; let those already invited attend the feast and enjoy the fellowship and nourishment of the long anticipated repast. But no! Here the parable takes a totally unexpected turn.

The text literally says, "They all from one began to make excuses." The phrase "from one" may be identified as an Aramaism meaning "all at once" (Creed, 191). This is supported by the reading from the Old Syriac version. Or it may be a Greek phrase meaning "unanimously" (Marshall, 588). We can catch the surprise registered in the idiom. There is also insult. Surely a last minute refusal to attend a great banquet is bad taste in any culture. In the Middle East it is considered a rude affront to the host. Thomson is again helpful: "It is true now, as then, that to refuse is a high insult to the maker of the feast" (Thomson, I, 178; cf. also Marshall, 588). Everything was flowing smoothly, the invitations were accepted, the animal butchered, the meat cooked, the guests summoned— and all at once—excuses! This brings us to the second stanza.

STANZA TWO—THE REAL ESTATE EXPERT

"The first said to him, 'I have bought a field,   I DID THIS
　　and I must go out and see it.   THUS I MUST DO THIS
　　I pray you have me excused.'"   EXCUSE ME

We observe the same repetition of themes: I did this (line one), thus I must do this (line two), therefore excuse me (line three). The statement is a bold-faced lie and everyone knows it. No one buys a field in the Middle East without knowing every square foot of it like the palm of his hand. The springs, wells, stone walls, trees, paths, and anticipated rainfall are all well-known long before a discussion of the purchase is even begun. Indeed, these items must be known, for in the past they were carefully included in the contract. Regarding the buying of land Thomson writes,

> It is not enough that you purchase a well-known lot; the contract must mention everything that belongs to it, and certify that fountains or wells in it, trees upon it, etc., are sold with the field. . . . Thus Abraham bought this field *and* the cave that was therein, *and* all the trees that were in the field, *and* that were in all the borders round about, were made sure (Thomson, II, 383; emphasis his).

The purchaser will also know the human history of the field. He will be able to tell you who has owned it for generations and to recite the profits of that field for an amazing number of past years. The few plots of agricultural land are so crucial to life that in Arab Palestine these plots had proper names (Lees, 213f.). The same overall situation has been noted in first-century Palestine. Applebaum observes the poverty of the Jewish farmer in New Testament times. He comments on

> the great skill and grit of the hard-working Jewish cultivator in wresting production from a minimal plot of ground. But over-population reduced the Jewish peasant unit of cultivation and endangered the cultivator's margin of livelihood (Applebaum, *JPFC*, II, 691).

Thus, in a world of increasing population, limited land space, and the growth of a landless tenantry, the host of the banquet is to believe that a field has been suddenly bought sight unseen.

A Western equivalent to this excuse would be the case of a suburbanite who cancels a dinner engagement by saying, "I have just bought a new house over the phone and I must go and have a look at it and at the neighborhood." The excuse is obviously paper thin and *no one* will believe it.

Again Ibrāhīm Saʿīd is helpful when he says, "What is the point of looking at the field after he has finished the purchase procedures?" (Saʿīd, 382). Saʿīd, writing in Arabic for Middle Eastern readers, assumes that the reader knows that the process of buying a field is long and complicated and often stretches over a number of years.

Derrett suggests a series of legal justifications for the guests' excuses. The land may be depreciating in value and the buyer may want (after examination) to retract the sale. He may need a written conveyance to acquire the property. He may need to assert his title by physically taking possession. Or finally, there may be religious questions regarding cultivation that relate to the keeping of the law (Derrett, 137). However, banquets were held *in the late afternoon* (Jeremias, *Eucharistic*, 44f.). In Luke 17:8 the dinner is clearly after the day's labors are over! Why, we must ask, is the "real estate expert" suddenly busy with these details? What was the dear man doing all morning? Derrett himself translates the excuse, "I am obliged to go out (of town) to view it" (Derrett, 137). So, are we to believe that he is preparing for out-of-town travel shortly before dark? If these complicated legal requirements were taking up his time, why did he accept the invitation to the banquet? After the meat was cooked and the banquet spread, at the end of the working day does he suddenly discover a long list of pressing business details? Black points out that the word *anankēn* carries the idea of "statutory custom" or "pressure" (Black, 225f., 228). Marshall interprets this to mean a "legal obligation" (Marshall, 589). This also is possible. However, in the timeless East one day is *always* as good as another. What is wrong with the following morning for these legal obligations, if there were such? The field will still be there in the morning. Real estate does not walk away. The buyer *did* accept to attend the banquet, and Marshall recognizes that "refusal to respond to the invitation at this point is an act of great discourtesy" (Marshall, 588). We find compelling reasons to see this refusal as a clear case of that same "great discourtesy."

Finally, if the man *wants* the host to believe him he can say, "I have been negotiating for a field for months and the owner has suddenly insisted that we settle tonight." Such an excuse would save the honor of the host and preserve the relationship between guest and host. But this is not his purpose. He is intentionally insulting the host by offering an obviously false excuse. (We noted that the banquet scene in Luke 7:36–50 also began with an intentional insult.) In addition to the possible legal aspects of the term, when the guest says, "I *must* go and see it," he is affirming that this field is of greater importance to him than his relationship to the host. In the Middle Eastern world where personal relationships are of supreme importance this equation strikes with special force. The speaker only partially covers this break in relationship by his courteous request for permission to be absent. (In passing, we observe that the close identity of the master and his servant is apparent in these first two speeches. He is talking to the servant and addresses the master.) The third stanza maintains the established pattern.

STANZA THREE—THE PLOWING EXPERT

> "And another said, 'I have bought five yoke of oxen   I DID THIS
>   and I go to test them.   I MUST DO THIS
>   I pray you have me excused.'"   EXCUSE ME

The three main ideas (noted on the right) are repeated now a third time. Again the excuse is ludicrous. Teams of oxen are sold in the Middle Eastern village in two ways. In some places the team is taken to the market place. At the edge of the market there will be a small field where prospective buyers may test the oxen. If they cannot pull together they are of course worthless as a team. In the smaller villages the farmer owning a pair for sale announces to his friends that he has a team available and that he will be plowing with them on a given day. Word spreads quickly in an oral tradition community. Prospective buyers make their way to the seller's field to watch the animals working and, of course, to drive them back and forth across the field to be assured of their strength and evenness of pull. All of this obviously takes place before the buyer even begins to negotiate a price. Again the excuse offered here is a transparent fabrication.

If we can reuse our modern surburbanite as a cultural parallel, in this case he calls his wife and says, "I cannot make it home tonight for dinner because I have just signed a check for five used cars, which I bought over the phone, and I am on my way down to the used car lot to find out their age and model, and see if they will start." On hearing this, even the most devoted wife will worry about her husband's sanity.

Jesus highlights his point by mentioning five *pairs* of oxen and specifically states that the agent is going to *test* them. As in the case of the real estate expert, the transparent nature of the excuse is unmistakable. Again Saʿīd, our Arab Christian commentator who grew up in a small Middle Eastern village, catches this point. He writes, "This excuse is not reasonable, because the testing of oxen takes place *before* they are bought, not after" (Saʿīd, 383). The point is not to "look them over" but to "*test* them" (as Saʿīd observes), and to see if they will perform as yoked oxen or not. The Greek word *dokimazō* has this clear intent. There is a subtle shift between the first excuse and the second. The first guest had not yet begun to go. He was pleading his case as he said, "I must go out and see it." This second guest says literally, "I am going to test them." He does not state an intention but announces an action in process. Fields are land, and land is holy. But oxen are animals, and animals are unclean. The second guest is saying to the host, "These animals are more important to me than my relationship to you." In spite of the rudeness of his excuse, he is still civil and requests to be excused. The same cannot be said about the third guest, whose speech must now be examined.

STANZA FOUR—THE PASSIONATE BRIDEGROOM

"And another said, 'I have married a bride,	I DID THIS
and therefore—	THUS I MUST—
I cannot come.' "	I CANNOT COME

Patterned speech sets up expectations and those expectations focus special attention on any change in the pattern. In this stanza we have the fourth repetition of the themes, I did this (line one), thus I must do this (line two), excuse me (line three). Only in this case the completion of line two is left to the imagination and line three is brief and rude. The third guest speaks with a simple past tense, "I married a bride." (The *gunē* can be a bride. Cf. Bauer, 167.) So did a lot of the rest of us. We can, however, give him the benefit of the doubt and assume that he means the recent past, "I have just married a bride." However, the wedding was not that day. Had there been a wedding in the village the host would not have scheduled his great banquet. No village can stand two grand occasions at once. All the guests would be at the wedding, and the competition would be pointless. But even if the recent past is indicated, his speech is still crude. Middle Eastern society maintains formal restraint in talking about women.

In Arabic the words *ḥarīm* (women), *ḥaram* (sacred), and *ḥarām* (forbidden) are from the same root. In a formal setting the men do not discuss their women. In the nineteenth century Thomson documented the fact that a man away from home, if he had only daughters at home, would address his letter to the son he hoped yet to father, because to address a letter to a woman would be improper. He talks of the extreme reluctance in the past of Middle Eastern men "to speak of the females of their families" (Thomson, I, 175f.). In intertestamental times Ben Sirach wrote in praise of a long list of famous people—and they are all men (Sir. 44–50). But more than that, the main meal of the day was in the middle of the afternoon (Jeremias, *Eucharistic,* 44f.). Thus this guest is saying, "Yesterday I said I would come, but this afternoon I am busy with a woman, who is more important to me than your banquet." Surely such an excuse would be rude in any society, and it is intensely rude in the Middle Eastern world and totally unprecedented. Some commentators have noted that a newly married man was exempted from military duty for a year (Deut. 20:7; 24:5; cf. Plummer, 361f.), and assume that this text is behind the excuse. Such is not the case. Deuteronomy is talking about a year's military service away from home. Our passionate guest has accepted the invitation. There is no war; he is not called to leave the village. The time away from home will be at most a few hours, and he will be back in his wife's arms late that same night. Finally, he does not even ask to be excused. The entire response is guaranteed to infuriate the most patient of hosts, East or West (Thomson, I, 179). What then does all of this mean?

The listeners to the parable could easily identify the theological movement of the story. The messianic banquet has been announced. Indeed, the "hour of the banquet" has come. Those invited (the leaders of the Jewish community) are told, "All is now ready." Thus in the person of Jesus the kingdom of God in some sense is at hand. Those who seek to "eat bread in the kingdom of God" initially must seek to eat bread with him (cf. Manson, *Sayings,* 129). Yet suddenly there is a stream of excuses. They complain that he eats with and welcomes sinners and does not keep the Sabbath in a strict fashion. Deeper reasons for his rejection may be that he does not fulfill their theological and nationalistic expectations of the Messiah. The parable says that as they reject Jesus (with these unacceptable excuses) they are rejecting the great banquet of salvation promised by God in Isaiah, that is, in some sense, even now set for them through the presence of Jesus in their midst. But not only do they reject the host, they also prefer other things. Manson writes,

> God gives the Kingdom; but the accepting of God's gift means the rejection of many other things. The Kingdom of God offers the greatest gifts, but it demands exclusive loyalty and whole-hearted devotion. The great feast is a feast and not a distribution of free rations. Those who wish to enjoy it must come in. They cannot have portions sent out for them to enjoy, while they busy themselves with other things (*ibid.,* 130f.).

With these theological implications in mind, we return to the text.

STANZA FIVE—THE OUTCASTS' INVITATION

"So the servant came and reported this to his master.
Then the householder in anger said to his servant, 'Go out
    quickly,   MASTER—GO
      into the streets and lanes of the city.   TO STREETS
        Bring in the poor, maimed, blind, and lame.' "   FILL UP

The host's anger is natural—he has been publicly insulted. But his response is grace, not vengeance. He turns to invite the outcasts of the village.
These poor, maimed, blind, and lame are *from the city*. They are a part of the
community, although ostracized from community life. Clearly these categories
symbolize the outcasts of Israel that were attracted to and welcomed by Jesus (cf.
ibid., 130).

We noted above that the Qumran community anticipated a rejection from
the messianic banquet of everyone who was "smitten in his flesh . . . or lame, or
blind" (cf. above, 90). For centuries commentators have observed that the poor
are not invited to banquets, the maimed do not get married, the blind do not go
out to examine fields, and the lame do not test oxen. The word "poor" in biblical
literature often has theological overtones meaning "humble and pious" (cf. Isa.
66:2; Matt. 5:3). Whether or not such meanings are intended here we cannot
determine, but it is clear that there is a radical reversal. The original guests
(assumed to be worthy peers of the host) refuse to respond to the good news that
the banquet is ready. They are confident that the banquet cannot proceed without
them and that the entire event will thus become a humiliating defeat for the host.
But not so—unworthy guests are invited. The host is not indebted socially to the
poor, maimed, blind, and lame, and they will not be able to respond in kind. His
offer is what we have described elsewhere as an "unexpected visible demonstration of love in humiliation" (Bailey, *Poet,* 182). The dramatic, visible nature of
the demonstration is clear. It is unexpected and breaks in upon the new group of
undeserving guests as a stunning surprise. The host may anticipate suffering,
since the original guests will be infuriated that their attempt to abort the banquet
has failed, and they will taunt the host as one who is unable to put together a
banquet without "bringing in this riffraff" (cf. Luke 15:2, "This man receives
sinners and eats with them"). Again, as in the case of the parable of the Prodigal
Son, this unexpected visible demonstration of love in suffering theologically
foreshadows the cross and demonstrates in dramatic form a part of its meaning.
The offer to the "outcasts of Israel" is an offer of costly grace. This offer, the
parable assumes, is accepted. The last two stanzas round out the final scene.

STANZA SIX—STILL ROOM

"And the servant said, 'Sir,   SERVANT
    what you commanded has been done,   I WENT
      and still there is room.' "   NOT FULL

STANZA SEVEN—THE OUTSIDERS

"And the master said to the servant, 'Go out,	MASTER—GO
into the highways and hedges,	TO HIGHWAYS
and compel to enter, that my house may be filled.' "	FILL UP

As we noted, the unworthy guests were *from the city* and thus a part of the community. Now, however, the servant is sent out into "the highways and hedges" to bring in people from beyond the town. The "highways" indicate the well-traveled roads. But much of the inter-village traffic moves on narrow paths built along the stone walls or hedges that line such paths. Marshall understands the "hedges" to be fences "along which beggars might rest for protection" (Marshall, 590). Beggars are found in villages and cities where large concentrations of people live. Furthermore there is no hint that this last group of guests are themselves outcasts from their society. They are from beyond the host's community and that is all we know about them. There is a general agreement among contemporary scholars that this latter invitation symbolically represents an outreach to the gentiles, and that Luke understands it in this fashion (Manson, *Sayings*, 130). However, some contend that such an outreach to the gentiles was not envisioned by Jesus and that this invitation to those outside the community is an expansion of the parable by the early Church "in a situation demanding missionary activity" (Jeremias, *Parables*, 64). To this question we now briefly turn.

Hunter has written,

> We are entitled to regard this mission to "the highways and the hedges" in Luke 14:23 as a secondary feature only if we can show that Jesus never envisaged a Gentile mission (Hunter, *Interpreting*, 57).

We would rather accept the burden of proof and ask if there is any material in Luke regarding the gentile mission that can most reasonably be traced to Jesus of Nazareth. The quest for an answer can certainly start with the parable under discussion. We have noted that Isaiah 25:6–9 is a crucial text for a clear understanding of this parable. There the inclusion of the gentiles in the great banquet of God is boldly set forth. One would then expect to find a similar inclusion of the gentiles in Jesus' banquet parable. When it occurs (given the Isaiah background) it is easier and more natural to assume it to be a part of the original parable than to argue for it as a later addition. Furthermore, in the parable the servant *does not* go out after the outsiders (gentiles) along the highways and by the hedges. The command is given but not carried out. It remains an *unfulfilled future task* as the parable closes. The order to invite the outcasts *within* the community *is* carried out in the parable. This parallels Jesus' own ministry in that he *did* carry out a ministry of inviting the outcasts of Israel into his fellowship. He *did not* carry out any major outreach to the gentiles. Indeed, the twelve were sent only to the lost within Israel (Matt. 10:5). Thus the details of the parable as it now stands precisely fit Jesus' own historical ministry. But is there other evidence in Luke or elsewhere of Jesus' interest in the gentiles?

Luke's interest in the gentiles is unmistakable (cf. Martin, 375f.). Simeon declares Jesus to be a "light for revelation to the Gentiles" (2:32). The genealogy is traced to Adam (Luke 3:38) and not to Abraham (Matt. 1:2). The quotation from Isaiah 40:3–5 in Luke 3:6 includes the phrase, "And *all flesh* shall see the salvation of God"; and the commission to the disciples at the end of Luke specifically mentions the gentiles (24:47). Our question thus becomes, Is there a direction set by Jesus himself that is then reflected on, enlarged, and fulfilled by the Church, or is all concern for the gentiles traceable only to the post-Easter situation?

The ministry of Jesus is clearly focused on "the lost sheep of the house of Israel" (Matt. 15:23). Johannes Blauw has argued that the resurrection is a great turning. There the centripetal force of mission (let the gentiles *come in* if they like, but do not *go out* to them) becomes a centrifugal force and the Church goes out to the gentiles with a message for all people (Blauw, 83f.).

Jeremias affirms the same position when he writes, "Jesus expressly rejected the idea that he was also sent to the Gentiles; his mission was confined to the lost sheep of the Israelite community" (Jeremias, *Promise*, 26). Jeremias also sees the message of the Old Testament as being always "centripetal; the Gentiles will not be evangelized where they dwell; but will be summoned to the holy Mount by the divine epiphany" (*ibid.*, 60). Jesus, he argues, understands only that the gentiles will be summoned in the final hour before the last judgment. Yet Blauw admits there are hints of the centrifugal force of mission in the Old Testament. Isaiah 42:4 reads,

> He will not fail or be discouraged
> till he has established justice in the earth;
> and the coastlands wait for his law.

This passage is among the famous Servant Songs of Isaiah, and clearly the servant in some sense is seen as going out to "establish justice in the earth." Then in Isaiah 49:6 (in another of the Servant Songs) the centrifugal force is more boldly stated. We read,

A And now the *Lord says,*		LORD SAYS
who formed me from the womb *to be his servant,*		MY SERVANT
B to *bring Jacob back* to him,	JACOB—BROUGHT BACK
and that *Israel* might *be gathered* to him,	ISRAEL—GATHERED
C for I am *honored* in the eyes of the Lord,		HONORED
and my *God* has become *my strength.*		MADE STRONG
A' *He says:*		LORD SAYS
It is too light a thing that *you should be my servant*		MY SERVANT
B' to *raise up* the tribes of *Jacob*	JACOB—RAISED UP
and to *restore* the survivors of *Israel;*	ISRAEL—RESTORED
C' I will give you as a *light to the nations,*	LIGHT TO NATIONS
that *my salvation* may reach to the *end of the earth.* "	SALV.
		TO ENDS OF EARTH

We have already observed the use of step parallelism in Isaiah (cf. above, xviii). Here, through the use of repeating couplets, the unique role of the servant is highlighted. In the first series the servant is formed from the womb (A) to restore Jacob/Israel (B) and is especially honored by God who has become his strength (C). This series of ideas is relatively traditional. But the second series contains a dramatic surprise. For we discover that it is too light a thing to be the servant of God (A') just for the restoration of Jacob/Israel (B'). Thus he is given as a light for the salvation of the nations (C'). The clear progression of the text clarifies the twofold role of the servant. He *is* formed/sent for the ''lost sheep of the house of Israel.'' But this is not enough for the greatness of the servant. He is strengthened and honored (C) so that he becomes the light of salvation to the ends of the earth (C'). Clearly there is a centrifugal force of mission set forth in the text. Thus we can say (with Blauw) that in the Old Testament the centrifugal force of mission is rare, yet it is present in the Servant Songs of Isaiah, which are prominent in the New Testament.

Are there hints, or even clear indications, of this centrifugal force of mission in the pre-Easter teachings of Jesus? We believe that there are. The central passage is the famous inauguration scene in the synagogue at Nazareth where Jesus announces and begins his ministry (Luke 4:14–30). The text quoted from the Old Testament is again from Isaiah (61:1–2), but this time it is an edited, composite quote that falls into seven idea units. These are as follows:

1	The *Spirit of the Lord* is upon me	SPIRIT OF THE LORD
2	for He has anointed me to *preach* to the poor.	PREACH
3	He has *sent me* to proclaim to the captives—*freedom*,	SEND OUT—FREEDOM
4	and recovering of *sight to the blind*;	SIGHT
3'	to *send out* the oppressed—in *freedom*,	SEND OUT—FREEDOM
2'	and to *proclaim*	PROCLAIM
1'	the acceptable *year of the Lord*.	YEAR OF THE LORD

As it now stands in Luke, this text differs from Isaiah 61:1–2 at four major points. As Lund has observed (Lund, 236–38), all four of these changes were necessary to create the present literary form of seven lines with three pairs and a climax in the center. We would add to Lund's observation the fact that the editing is not only for literary, but more significantly, for theological reasons. These four changes are as follows. First, the phrase ''to bind up the brokenhearted'' is removed from line 3. With this removal the line is of manageable length and begins with the word ''send'' and ends with the word ''freedom.'' Second, a full line is brought in from Isaiah 58:6 and stands in the present structure as line 3'. It also begins with the word ''send'' and ends with the word ''freedom.'' It has obviously been selected, at least partially, because it balances line 3 at the beginning and at the end. Third, the key word ''to proclaim'' (*kērussō*) in line 2' has replaced Isaiah's word, which means ''to say'' or ''to call.'' This is because the parallel line (2) has the verb "to preach" (*euangelizō*). In these two verbs we have the two great New Testament words for the proclamation of the gospel. After editing they stand in the text balancing one another. Finally, the last part of Isaiah 61:2, with its references to judgment on the gentiles, is omitted. Thus line 1' comes into balance with line 1. After editing, the inverted parallelism is completed. Of special interest for our purposes are the three central lines. In such inverted parallelisms the climax usually occurs in the center of the structure and thus this center deserves special attention. Here we note the following:

> 3   He has *sent me*—to proclaim to the captives—*freedom,*
>
> 4   and recovery of sight to the blind;
>
> 3'   to *send out* the oppressed—in *freedom,*

Line 3', as we have noted, was brought in from Isaiah 58:6 and placed in this text in order to balance line 3; and line 3 itself had the phrase "to bind up the brokenhearted" removed in order to make it of manageable length. Thus more editing has taken place on these two lines (3 and 3') than anywhere else in the composite quotation, and they occur in the center of the seven lines. The reason for this special care and placement is evident when the rest of the discussion in the synagogue is examined.

In Luke 4:25-27 Jesus draws on two remarkable heroes of faith from the Old Testament. Both are non-Jews. The first is the woman from Zarephath of Sidon. The second is Naaman from Syria. The text clearly has two stanzas with four lines in each stanza. The two stanzas relate to each other in step parallelism such as we noted above in Isaiah 49:5-6 and in 55:10-11. This step parallelism is as follows:

> 1   *There were many widows in Israel*
>
> 2   in the *days* of *Elijah,*
>
>   (when the heavens were shut for three years and six months
>   and there came a great famine over all the land)
>
> 3   and *Elijah* was sent to *none* of them
>
> 4   *except* to *Zarephath of Sidon,* to *a woman,* a widow.
>
> 1'   *And there were many lepers in Israel*
>
> 2'   in the *time* of the prophet *Elisha,*
>
> 3'   and *none* of them was *cleansed*
>
> 4'   *except Naaman, the Syrian.*

Each of the two stanzas has the same four themes. These are (1) many in Israel, (2) the prophet, (3) none was helped, and (4) except so-and-so. This sequence of ideas is carefully followed in each stanza. For our subject it is important to observe the second line of the first stanza. That line has some extra historical information that any synagogue audience would already know. However, Theophilus (for whom Luke was writing; cf. 1:3) would most likely not know the details of the life of Elijah and would therefore need this information. Without it the illustration is worthless. Any Greek reader will wonder just what the woman's problem was. In the second stanza, no additional information is necessary. Even if the reader knows nothing about Naaman the Syrian, it is obvious that a leper is cleansed. Thus the precise literary form of the original eight lines, with their repetitive step parallelism, makes it clear that the extra information in line 2 is added after the composition of the original eight lines. Consequently we are dealing with two literary layers. Someone has written the original matching eight lines and then at a later period someone else has added new information for non-Jewish readers. The parallelism of the original eight lines is as precise as Isaiah 49:5-6 and 55:10-11 and warrants the title of poetry. We would submit that the most natural assumption for the material is that the original poem is quoted from Jesus of Nazareth and that the additional historical information is added by Luke for his gentile readers. It is of course possible that the earliest Palestinian church has written the eight lines and Luke is expanding its construction. We are not affirming proof, but only trying to ascertain probability. These two striking illustrations in this type of a poetical form could easily maintain themselves intact for centuries if need be, in a Middle Eastern peasant society (as evidenced by the oracles of Amos, the pre-Islamic Arabic poetry, and many other cases). We would submit that there is no *historical* reason to deny that Jesus of Nazareth is the author of the original eight lines.

Then, in turn, these two illustrations stand in the text as a *midrash,* an interpretation of the heart of the Isaiah quote noted above. In the center of that quote in line 3 the prophet *is sent* to someone to proclaim freedom. In the matching line 3' the prophet *sends out* someone else in freedom. This precise shift also occurs in the two stanzas that we have just examined. Elijah is *sent* to the woman and Elisha *sends* Naaman *out* to his freedom. Putting these side by side we observe,

> He has *sent me*—to proclaim—freedom (like Elijah who was *sent* to the woman of Zarephath)
> To *send out* the oppressed—in freedom (like Elisha who *sent* Naaman *out* in freedom)

The first of these is a case of a *centrifugal* force of mission (Elijah goes *out* of Israel and helps the woman of Zarephath); the second is the more common *centripetal* force of mission (Elisha ministers to Naaman who is attracted *in* and comes to him in Israel). To whom then is this material traceable? Is it strictly a Lucan composition or can it be, in some sense, attributed to Jesus of Nazareth? The question must be asked regarding both form and content.

In regard to the composite Isaiah quotation, we observe that it was considered perfectly legitimate for a reader in the synagogue to skip from passage to passage in his reading, particularly if he was reading from the prophets. He was not supposed to skip too far, say from the end of a book to its beginning, and should not skip from book to book. But skipping *was* ruled legitimate, and the extent of the discussion in the Mishna (*Megillah* 4:4) and in the Talmud (B.T. *Megillah* 24a) makes it clear that it was a relatively frequent practice. Furthermore, Paul often gives us composite quotes and assumes their legitimacy (cf. I Cor. 2:9). They can be found in the Gospels as well (Mark 1:2–3). Thus Jesus could well have carefully thought out his theme and prepared ahead of time his composite text from Isaiah 58 and 61. At the same time, the Greek words for "to preach good news" *(euangelizō)* and "to proclaim" *(kērussō)* look as if they have been edited to match in Greek because these are the two great New Testament words for the proclamation of the gospel. Also the word "freedom" *(aphesis)*, which comes at the end of lines 3 and 3', is the same word in the Greek Old Testament in each text. But the Hebrew Old Testament has different words, although with identical meanings. That is, lines 3 and 3' match in Hebrew, but match even better in Greek. Thus it would appear that the text in its present form may have been influenced to some extent by the Septuagint (the Greek Old Testament), and thus by the early Church. In the light of this, we would affirm that the composite Isaiah text, as it now appears in Luke, represents major themes from Isaiah selected by Jesus in his discussion in the synagogue. The present literary structure of these texts may reflect early Church editing.

Then (as we have argued), the eight-line *midrash* (excluding its later historical addition) is most probably traceable to Jesus of Nazareth and reflects a centrifugal force of mission that he endorsed but did not fulfill, except in rare incidents. Jesus composes the eight-line *midrash*. Luke adds an explanatory comment. This centrifugal force of mission permeates and informs the entire passage. We have observed that the harsh criticism of the gentiles in Isaiah 61:2 is omitted. The very illustrations selected in the *midrash* set forth two gentiles as heroes of faith to be imitated. Why are two non-Jews made the heroes of faith rather than Abraham on Mount Moriah, or Moses at the Red Sea, or Jeremiah going out to buy a field? Is not the very wrath of the worshipers in the synagogue most likely partially related to this focus on the gentiles? Jeremias himself argues convincingly that verse 22 can best be understood to mean "they all bore witness against him . . . they were astonished that he spoke of the mercy of God" (Jeremias, *Promise,* 44f.). They expect him to continue reading in Isaiah 61:2b, "and the day of vengeance of our God." Rather than talking about the "foreigners" who shall "be your plowmen and vinedressers" (Isa. 61:5), two gentiles are held up as illustrations of the kind of faith that the kingdom demands. The audience is understandably furious. Thus in this crucial passage there is clear reference to the centrifugal force of mission, the going out even to the gentiles. The entire text *does* reflect Lucan and early Church theological interests, but these interests we see as traceable in the text to Jesus himself, and beyond him to Isaiah 49:5–6.

Two further passages need to be examined briefly. The first is the parable of the lamp. In Luke 11:33 the lamp is put on a stand "that *those who enter* may see the light." Here we are back to the centripetal force of mission. Only those who come *in* will see the light. The same is reflected in Matthew 5:15 where the lamp is put on a stand to "give light to all *in the house.*" Again the focus is on the centripetal force of mission. Only those "in the house" will see the light. Yet significantly, the preceding verse reads, "You are the light of the world. A city set on a hill cannot be hid." We expect to read, "You are the light of Israel," but not so. In a fashion reminiscent of Isaiah 49:6 the light on the hill is to shine out to *all the world.* Again, as in Luke 4:16–30, the centripetal and the centrifugal forces of mission are set side by side. The city on the hill sends light *out* to *all the world,* and the lamp is seen only by those who are *in the house.* Finally, in the case of the Greek/Canaanite woman of Tyre and Sidon (Matt. 15:21–30; Mark 7:24–30), we have a clear statement of the exclusive nature of the ministry of Jesus. He says to the woman that he was sent "only to the lost sheep of the house of Israel" (Matt. 15:24). The discussion then turns on to the symbols of food and the children's bread. Jeremias affirms that

> the key to the meaning of Jesus' words to the woman who sought his help lies in the fact that she understood that Jesus was speaking of the Messianic banquet. Her "great faith" (Matt. 15:28) consisted in her recognition, as shown by her words about the crumbs that the little dogs might venture to eat, that Jesus was the giver of the Bread of Life (Jeremias, *Parables,* 118, n. 14; *Eucharistic,* 234; *Promise,* 29f.).

If we accept Jeremias' argument, we have in this text a case of a gentile woman who sees in Jesus the bringer of salvation. Thus, in the very story where he specifically states that he has come *only* for Israel, we see him reach out to minister to a gentile woman who sees him as "the giver of the Bread of Life." (In Isaiah 49:5–6 we saw the same juxtaposition of restorer of Israel + light of salvation for the nations.) Unless we make a prior theological judgment that Jesus *could not* have had an interest in the gentiles, we have here a case of just such an interest. Is not this text simply saying "to the Jew first and also the Greek" (Rom. 1:16)? In the light of the texts discussed above, is it not possible to see the ministry and teachings of Jesus directed primarily to the Jewish nation, but with clear pointers in the direction of something beyond Israel which fulfills the great Servant Song in Isaiah 49:5–6? Elijah was sent *out.* The light from the city on the hill goes *out.* The Greek woman of Sidon *is* fed by the bread of life and she meets Jesus on non-Jewish land. It is in the light of these texts that the concluding verses of the parable of the Great Banquet must be examined. T. W. Manson succinctly remarks, "the whole parable [of the Great Banquet] might be regarded as a *midrash* on Isa. 49:6" (*Sayings,* 130).

When Luke 14:23–24 is considered in the light of the above, it becomes possible to see the two concluding stanzas as a part of the original parable. Not only is the suggestion of an invitation to the gentiles theologically harmonious with other things that Jesus has done and taught, but the very literary form of the parable should suggest that the last two speeches complete the series of seven. Furthermore, at the beginning of the feast there were two invitations to the original guests; thus it is not surprising that at the end of the parable there are two invitations to unexpected guests (granted, in one case they are the same people and in the other they are not). An argument against the originality of the second invitation is that it is missing in Matthew. However, if the two accounts of the parable are examined, it is clear that the Matthean version has had considerable editing. A long series of expansions colors almost every verse. If Matthew has taken the liberty to *add* this much material following his own interests, can it not be argued that he has also deleted other details for the same reason? The two invitations to the original guests in the *beginning* of the Lucan version are shortened to one invitation in Matthew. It would seem that in like fashion the two invitations to outsiders at the *end* are also reduced to one. What then does this final invitation mean?

In stanza six the servant tells the master that after the outcasts of Israel are brought in there is still room in the banquet hall. In stanza seven the invitation goes out to the gentiles. The key word here is "compel." The Spanish inquisition and other tragic subversions of the gospel have been perpetrated by the organized church using this text as support. Nothing could be further from its original intent. In the Middle East the unexpected invitation must be refused. The refusal is all the more required if the guest is of lower social rank than the host. (The unexpected guest may be half starving and in real need of the offered food, but still he senses a deep cultural pressure to refuse.) In Luke 24:28–29 we have, culturally speaking, a similar scene. This time Jesus receives the unexpected invitation. As a courteous Oriental he "made as though he would go further." The two men, again in true Middle Eastern fashion, "compel him" to stay. He is not forced against his will. Rather, they know he *must* refuse for the first fifteen minutes of discussion as a matter of honor. In order to convince him that they really *do* want him to stay, and that they really *do* have food, they gently drag him into the house. They compel him to stay. Even so in the parable, we have a classical case of an unexpected invitation from someone of a higher rank. A stranger from outside the city is suddenly invited to a great banquet. He is not a relative or even a citizen of the host's city. The offer is generous and delightful but (thinks the stranger) *he cannot possibly mean it*. After some discussion the servant will finally have to take the startled guest by the arm and gently pull him along. There is no other way to convince him that he is really invited to the great banquet, irrespective of his being a foreigner. Grace is *unbelievable*! How could it be true, asks the outsider. For me? What have I ever done for him? I cannot pay it back? The host is not serious! It is a most pleasant prospect, but considering who I am, he cannot mean it! The host knows that this kind of shock and unbelief will face the servant/messenger at every turn, so he instructs the same to overcome reserve and unbelief by the only method possible—with a smile grab them by the arm and pull them in. Demonstrate to them that the invitation is genuine! Compel them to come in (cf. *ibid.*).

Finally, the motive for this extra invitation is "that my house may be filled.'' The purpose of this final remark seems to be a concern to demonstrate that it is possible for the banquet to be *full* without the original guests. The occasion can be a grand success even in their absence. The noble host wants the new guests to feel total acceptance. They must not look around and say, ''See how many seats are vacant. What a shame! Poor man, he is rejected by the important people and has only the few of us at his banquet.'' No! His house must be full! This brings our consideration of the seven speeches to a close. The concluding remark must now be examined.

CONCLUSION

"For I tell you (plural),
none of those men who were invited   THOSE INVITED
shall taste my banquet."   MY BANQUET

There is some ambiguity in the text and considerable discussion among the commentators regarding this final sentence. Is it a part of the parable itself and thereby is the householder speaking (Derrett, 141; Marshall, 590f.)? Or is it a concluding remark of Jesus to his audience reclining with him at the banquet (Jeremias, *Parables*, 171–180)? With the awareness that it is possible to read the phrase either way, the text seems most probably a remark of Jesus to his audience. In Luke 15:7, at the conclusion of the parable of the Lost Sheep, we have a similar construction with a concluding Dominical comment. Luke 15:10 has the same formula (cf. also Luke 18:6 and 18:14). We have argued elsewhere that Luke 16:8 is not a similar construction. There the master of 16:8 is better understood as the master of the parable (cf. Bailey, *Poet*, 102f.). But in this text the shift to a plural ''I tell you'' is significant. The master talks in the singular to a single servant all through the parable and, indeed, does so in the concluding speech in stanza seven. Derrett argues that the host would often send portions of a banquet to his leading friends, who were ''unavoidably absent'' (Derrett, 141). But such, we have argued, is not the case. In the parable they deliberately absented themselves with flimsy excuses and the host was *angry*. How could he be angry at the unavoidably absent? Rather they are deliberately absent and obviously he is not going to send special portions out to the guests who have just offended him to the point of anger. For the host to report such a decision as the climax of the parable would be redundant. But as a statement of Jesus to the audience it becomes profoundly meaningful. He states symbolically that those who would like to ''eat bread in the kingdom of God'' (14:15) had better hurry and accept *his* invitation to table fellowship, because they *will not* be able to participate at a distance. Thus the sudden shift to a plural seems to indicate that the parable is over and that Jesus is addressing his audience.

Yet just below the surface the two possibilities fuse. The original guests who refuse the host will certainly (by their own choice) not participate in the great banquet. Furthermore the guests reclining with Jesus are in grave danger of excluding themselves from the banquet of salvation already spread by the inaugurator of the kingdom. If the understanding of the text presented above can be sustained, the banquet is openly called "my banquet." Thus Jesus identifies himself with the host. The banquet is his banquet. He extends the original invitation to the guests. He pleads with them to attend and records that their self-exclusion is final. Again T. W. Manson's reflections are worth noting:

> Jesus does not here teach either a mechanically operating predestination, which determines from all eternity who shall or shall not be brought into the Kingdom. Neither does He proclaim that man's entry into the Kingdom is purely his own affair. The two essential points in His teaching are that no man can enter the Kingdom without the invitation of God, and that no man can remain outside it but by his own deliberate choice. Man cannot save himself; but he can damn himself. . . . He (Jesus) sees the deepest tragedy of human life, not in the many wrong and foolish things that men do, or the many good and wise things that they fail to accomplish, but in their rejection of God's greatest gift (Sayings, 130).

This then brings us to an examination of the symbols that the original listening audience would instinctively have identified. In the light of these we will try to determine the single response that Jesus was trying to evoke from the listeners and, finally, attempt to discern the theological cluster of the parable. First, then, the symbols.

What precisely would the original audience have instinctively identified? At least the following can be affirmed with some confidence:

the banquet = the messianic banquet that ushers in the new age

the original guests = the leaders of Israel who are rightfully the first to be invited

the lame and poor of the city = the outcasts within the house of Israel

the guests from the highways and the hedges = the gentiles

To this we must add the person of Jesus himself. To try to identify God as the host in distinction to the servant, who becomes Jesus or John the Baptist or both, is to press the symbols beyond what could have originally been instinctively perceived by the original audience. Granted, many commentators through the centuries of the life of the Church have identified the person of Jesus with the host or with the servant; and in Qumran it *was* the Messiah who summoned the faithful to the messianic banquet. But the story has a close identification between the servant and his master that is typical of the Oriental world generally. The former is considered a mirror of the latter. We have already noted that the original guests address the servant as the master and ask directly to be excused. Indeed, all through the parable the servant is his master's voice. So the referent for this combined symbol is God acting through His unique agent, Jesus. Thus Jesus is able to affirm the banquet as "my banquet." At the same time, he is the unique agent of God, through whom God is acting in the inauguration of the messianic banquet of the age of salvation and in the invitations to the different types of guests. How then are these symbols used by Jesus for pressing the original audience to a concrete response?

The original audience could hardly have missed the thrust of the parable. Jesus is saying to them,

> God's Messiah is here. He is inviting you to the messianic banquet of the day of salvation. The banquet is now ready. Do not refuse! For if you do (with your ridiculous excuses) others will fill your places from among the outcasts of Israel, and (in the future) an invitation will go out to the gentiles. The banquet will proceed without you. It will not be cancelled or postponed. The eschatological age has dawned. Respond to the invitation or opt out of participation in God's salvation.

Like the parable of the Prodigal Son, this parable is told in defense of the gospel to the outcasts. In Luke 15:2 the Pharisaic complaint is specifically that Jesus *eats* with tax collectors and sinners. Table fellowship with Jesus *is* participation in the messianic banquet in anticipation of the completion of all things in the end time. What then are the theological themes found in this parable?

A rich cluster of theological motifs combine to give the parable unique power. Among these are:

1. Jesus is God's unique agent calling for participation in the messianic banquet of salvation.

2. The messianic banquet promised by Isaiah (Isa. 25:6-9) is inaugurated in the table fellowship of Jesus (realized eschatology). But the parable is left open-ended. All the guests are not assembled. The parable breaks off with the house not yet full. Thus there is an unfulfilled future anticipated by the parable (futuristic eschatology). The full vision of the messianic banquet is yet in the future, when the faithful will sit down in the kingdom with Abraham, Isaac, and Jacob (Luke 13:28-29). Thus the messianic banquet of the end times is both now and not yet.

3. The excuses people offer for refusal to respond to the invitation to join in the banquet are stupid and insulting. The original guests have their counterpart in every age.

4. The invitation to table fellowship at the banquet is extended to the unworthy who can in no way compensate the host for his grace. These outcasts may be from within or from without the community.

5. Grace is unbelievable. This is so true that some special pleading is required for many of the undeserving to be convinced that the invitation is genuine.

6. There is a centrifugal force of mission taught in the parable. The servant, with his invitation, is told to go out beyond the city. If God's salvation is to reach to the ends of the earth (Isa. 49:6) someone must take the message out and present it with all the winsomeness possible (Luke 14:23).

7. There is a self-imposed concept of judgment. Those who by their own choice reject the invitation thereby shut themselves off from fellowship with the host and his guests.

8. There is a warning addressed to the presumptuous in the believing community. God can get along without them. If they fail to respond to His invitation, He will proceed with outsiders.

9. Time runs out on the invitation. As Charles Smith has said, "Places are not kept open indefinitely at the Messianic table and those who assume . . . that there will always be room for them are likely to receive a rude shock" (C. Smith, 125).

10. The guests must be invited. No one "storms the party." Attendance is by invitation only. Yet the guests must respond and come in. There is no participation at a distance.

Containing as it does this rich series of tightly packed theological motifs, it is little wonder that this parable was given a prominent place along with the other parables spoken in defense of the gospel to the outcasts. Indeed, it speaks powerfully in any age.

The question of the believing communities' continuing table fellowship with Jesus is a question that is beyond the scope of a study of the parable itself. The parable, as we have observed, is not finished. Surely a part of the meaning of the communion service is the concept of continuing table fellowship with the now risen Lord in anticipation of the completion of the banquet of the end times. This parable profoundly relates to that understanding. Those who ate and drank with him during his earthly ministry were engaged in a proleptic celebration of the messianic banquet of the end times. This parable offers at least a part of the theological rationale for that celebration. Is not the communion service then an extension of this same celebration? Depending on our various traditions different answers can be given to this question. Yet surely all Christian theological traditions must deal with what is set forth so brilliantly in this banquet of the seven speeches.

One final consideration that is also beyond the scope of the study of the parable itself, but worthy of note in passing, is to observe the different ways Matthew and Luke deal with the problem of presumption. In Luke there is a series of parables that proclaims the concept of God's free offer of grace. These include (in order) the Great Banquet, the Lost Sheep, the Lost Coin, the Prodigal Son, and (as we understand it) the Unjust Steward (Bailey, *Poet*, 86–109). The reader of Luke's Gospel may well ask, If grace is free, is it not also cheap? The arrangement of material gives the reader the answer. In between two great banquet parables, each declaring pure grace (the Great Banquet and the Prodigal Son), is set a collection of sayings that speaks of the high cost of discipleship in clear and demanding terms (Luke 14:25–35). Matthew deals with the same problem in a different way. There, in a sequel to the Great Banquet, the guests (also freely invited) are held accountable to appear in proper garments. The banquet is free but acceptance carries with it responsibilities (Matt. 22:11–14).

Thus the Great Banquet sets forth weighty theological themes in a brief but unforgettable parable that continues to speak with power in every age.

Chapter 7

THE OBEDIENT SERVANT
(Luke 17:7-10)

This little parable's significance far outweighs the attention it usually receives. In the Lucan account the reader has already been told that the master who returns from the wedding banquet will serve his servants (12:35-38). In a few verses the reader will discover that Jesus is among his disciples; not as one who sits at a table, but "as one who serves" (22:27). For the insensitive these texts are invitations to presumption. If Jesus came and is coming to serve us, fine; here we are, expecting to reap the benefits of his service! While in no way denying the thrust of the above parables, here Jesus clearly asserts his authority over his disciples. He is the master! They are his servants, and let there be no misunderstanding! Because this parable uses some of the precise imagery of the parable of the Waiting Servants in 12:35-38, that parable will need to be examined briefly prior to our study of 17:7-10.

In the overall outline of the central section of Luke (Bailey, *Poet*, 79-85), 17:1-10 appears as a miscellaneous collection of sayings on offenses (vv. 1-2), forgiveness (vv. 3-4), faith (vv. 5-6), and duty (vv. 7-10). Thus we see no need to find a relationship between this parable and the dialogue with the apostles that precedes it, or the healing of the ten lepers that follows it. We would rather examine it in the light of the two other major discussions of the master-servant theme mentioned above. If, then, this parable is a part of a miscellaneous collection, to whom is it addressed?

The three previous paragraphs are addressed to the disciples (v. 1) and to the apostles (v. 5). In this parable the text of Luke assumes the same audience. The phrase, "which one of you," is used to introduce sayings to disciples, crowds, and opponents (Bailey, *Poet*, 139f.; against Jeremias, *Parables*, 103, 145, 193). It would appear that Luke is right and the disciples are the audience. The major argument against this view is the assumption that the disciples would not have had servants. Such is not the case. In the West, having a servant puts a

114

person in (at least) the upper middle class, but not so in the East. The poorest of the poor let their children out as servants so that they can be fed, and the people of very little means have such servants in their homes. James, John, and their father, Zebedee, own a boat and have hired servants (Mark 1:20). Other disciples may have been people of similar means. Furthermore, only *one* servant is involved. The plowman/herdsman is also the cook. Thus the master is a man of modest income. Applebaum writes, "Talmudic traditions assume, as a matter of course, that the ordinary man has at least one slave" (*JPFC*, II, 627). Also, the parable does not assume that the master is a landowner. The servant may be plowing a rented field. There is no specific hint in the Gospels that the disciples were from among the poorest of the poor. Finally, the parable appeals to the audience on the basis of commonly known cultural assumptions. It does not necessarily peg the listener in a particular economic class. That is, the parable does not say, "Listen, you masters of servants." Rather it says, "Does not the servant-master relationship, as you know it, presuppose these things?" The same is true in the parable of the Lost Sheep, where Jesus addresses Pharisees with the identical introductory phrase used here ("Which one of you, having . . ."). Shepherds were among the proscribed trades for the Pharisees (Bailey, *Poet*, 147). Thus they were *certainly not* shepherds. In the same way Jesus is appealing here to the common Middle Eastern understanding of how servants and masters act and is not necessarily affirming that they owned slaves or engaged servants. Thus there seems to be no remaining reason for questioning Luke's judgment that the parable was originally addressed to the disciples/apostles.

The parable is a simple three-stanza ballad such as that which we have already observed in 11:9-13; 11:29-32; 15:3-7; and 16:9-13 (Bailey, *Poet*, 69f., 112, 135, 144). It is as follows:

(1)   "Can you imagine having a servant,   SERVANT
              plowing or keeping sheep,   FULFILLING ORDERS
           who on coming in from the field   ORDERS FULFILLED
           you say to him, 'Come at once and recline to   REWARD?
           eat'?

(2)   Will he not rather say to him,
               '*Prepare for me* something and I shall dine,
                 and gird yourself and *serve me*,   SERVE THE MASTER
               till *I eat* and *drink*;   THEN YOURSELF
                 and afterward *you shall eat* and *drink*'?

(3)   Does the servant have special merit   SERVANT
              because he did what was commanded?   ORDERS FULFILLED
         So you, also, when you have done what was commanded
                                                    ORDERS FULFILLED
              say, 'Nothing is owing us servants, we have only done our
              duty.' "   REWARD?

As in the case of Luke 15:3-7, the third stanza is application, yet it deals with a series of themes introduced in the first stanza. These themes (noted on the right) are presented in stanza one and repeated in stanza three. In two cases we have diverged from the traditional translation of the passage. These will be examined in detail below. In the central section we have two couplets of parallelism. *Prepare for me* matches *serve me*, and *I eat and drink* parallels *you shall eat and drink*. Some of the words in the central stanza seems at first glance redundant. Thus the RSV has the first line read simply, "Prepare supper for me," condensing two verbs into one. With the extra verb each line in this central stanza has two major verbs. The three-stanza literary form reinforces Marshall's view that there is no need to identify the central stanza as redactional (Marshall, 646). In most of the parabolic stanzas under study, direct speech occurs at the beginning of the stanza. By contrast here the first and last stanzas end with direct speech. Thus the literary form is again complete, artistically satisfying, and provides an important key to interpretation.

Before proceeding to the interpretation of the parable we must examine the Waiting Servants in Luke 12:35-38, because some of the identical images occur there and function in reverse of what appears here. It is not our intention to make a full study of the parable of the Waiting Servants but to observe its literary form and the use of its images. The form is as follows:

A	1	Let your waist be girded,	SERVANTS PREPARE
	1'	and your lamp burning.	SERVANTS PREPARE
B	2	And be like men who are waiting	SERVANTS WAIT TO SERVE
	3	for their master to return from the wedding,	MASTER COMES
	3'	so that when he comes and knocks,	MASTER COMES
	2'	immediately they may open to him.	SERVANTS SERVE
C	4	Blessed are those servants	SERVANTS BLESSED
	5	whom coming the master finds awake.	MASTER COMES
	6	Truly I say to you, he will gird himself,	MASTER PREPARES
	7	and have them recline at table,	SERVANTS HONORED
	6'	and come and serve them.	MASTER SERVES
	5'	If (in the second or third watch) he comes and finds thus,	
			MASTER COMES
	4'	blessed are those servants.	SERVANTS BLESSED

In this case the literary form is built on a very sophisticated use of the phenomenon of the split parallelism. If all the repetitions are ignored the seven movements of the parable can easily be identified. They are as follows:

1. Servants prepare to serve the master.
2. Servants wait to serve the master.
3. The master's return is anticipated.
4. The servants are blessed in their vigilance.
5. The master comes.
6. The master prepares and serves the servants.
7. The servants recline to be served.

By following the numbers this flow of ideas can be easily traced. Each line/idea, except line 7, is repeated. A prosaic telling of these same seven ideas without the parallel repetitions would read as follows: "Prepare yourselves (1) and wait to serve (2) your returning master (3). You are blessed (4) if the master comes and finds you awake (5). For then he will gird himself to serve you (6) while *you* recline" (7). However, the extra words are not redundant but a part of the literary form. The split parallelism is an artistic device observable in the Old Testament. Freedman writes, "It is as though the poet deliberately split a bicolon or couplet, and inserted a variety of materials between the opening and closing halves of the unit to form a stanza" (Freedman, xxxvi). A clear case of this in the New Testament is in the Lucan Beatitudes (Luke 6:20–26; cf. Bailey, *Poet,* 64). There a very precise series of four couplets is formed with the key words "blessed" and "for." That is,

> *Blessed* are the poor,
> *for* yours is the kingdom of God.

The text has three couplets structured in this fashion. But the fourth of this series has some extra material inserted in between the first and second lines of the couplet. This is as follows:

> *Blessed* are you when men hate you,
> (and when they exclude you and revile you, and cast out your name as evil, on account of the Son of man. Rejoice in that day, and leap for joy, for your reward is great in heaven;)
> *for* so their fathers did to the prophets.

The couplet is intact. Yet extra material is added in the middle. At the same time this extra material in the center is ordered according to a precise pattern. There are three negatives matched by three positives and a reference to the Son of man in the center. This can be seen as follows:

> *Blessed* are you when men hate you,
>   and when they exclude you   −
>   and revile you,   −
>   and cast out your name as evil,   −
>   on account of the *Son of man.*
>   Rejoice in that day,   +
>   and leap for joy,   +
>   for your reward is great in heaven;   +
> *for* so their fathers did to the prophets.

Thus this text is clearly a New Testament example of the phenomenon Freedman has identified in the Old Testament. A two-line parallelism has been split and, in this case, seven lines added in the center. These seven lines have a literary form of their own with a climax in the middle. Thus the larger text has four couplets and the fourth is split to make up a stanza.

Here in Luke 12:35–38 we have the remarkable case of this phenomenon happening twice in a row. The first couplet is a simple synonymous parallelism.

Let your waist be girded,	SERVANTS PREPARE
and your lamp burning.	SERVANTS PREPARE

The first of these two images has to do with being prepared to undertake any strenuous task. The servant must put on a belt and tuck his long, loose-fitting outer garment into that belt to get the edge of the garment up out of the way. The second has to do with preparing to guide the master out of the dark. Only if one has lived in a world without electricity is it possible to appreciate how important it is to prepare and light the lamps before dark. When we compare stanza A and stanza B it is clear that the reference to the *servants* (with their preparation and wait) is repeated on the outside (2), and new material referring to the master is inserted into the center. This can be seen as follows:

Stanza A

1   Let your *waist be girded,*

1'   and your *lamp burning.*

Stanza B

2   And be like men who are *waiting*
    (a couplet on the master's return)

2'   immediately they may *open* to him.

The servant *girds* his waist in preparation (1) and *waits* for his orders from the master on his return (2). The lighting of the *lamps* (1') is for the purpose of opening the door for him with lamp in hand (2'). Thus two lines have been expanded into four by repeating the basic ideas (which have to do with the servants) and inserting between them two new lines (which have to do with the master). Then, remarkably, this process is repeated. Now the four lines are restated (in slightly different form) and again new material is inserted into the center. The matching nature of stanza B and the four outside lines of stanza C can be seen as follows:

Stanza B

2   Be like *men waiting*
    3   for the *master* to return,
    3'   so that when *he comes*
2'   *they may open* to him.

Stanza C

4   Blessed are *those servants*
    5   *coming the master* finds awake.
    5'   If *he comes* and finds thus
4'   blessed are *those servants.*

The outside lines tell of the servants who *wait* (2) to *open* (2') and who are thereby blessed (4,4'). All four inner lines talk of the *coming* of the *master*. The repetitions are needed to complete the parallelisms.

If the parable/poem had ended with these lines it would have made complete sense. The theology would have been in harmony with other things Jesus had taught and the missing three lines would not have been detected. Yet, the perceptive original listener/reader has already seen the first stanza split and new material added to its center to form the second stanza, and thus he may have expected the same stanza-splitting phenomena to take place in the third stanza. If so, he was not disappointed. The third stanza is also split and three new lines are added in the center. Thus the third stanza has seven lines and they are inverted. When parallel lines are inverted in biblical literature, the center is usually the climax (Bailey, *Poet*, 50f.). This is dramatically the case in this parable. The master takes the position of a *servant* and serves his own servant *as if he were the master*. This climax to the parable is such a shock that it is introduced by the phrase, "Amen, I say to you," which is a striking formula. It occurs only six times in Luke and in each case introduces something that comes as a shock, or is a hard saying, or a saying on which there is special emphasis. It also may indicate Luke's use of material he has not redacted (Marshall, 536). Here it introduces a shocking reversal of roles.

In the Middle East the traditional roles of master and servant are well-defined. For a master to serve his own servants is unheard of! This dramatic reversal is enacted by Jesus himself in the footwashing scene in John 13:3–5, and is described theologically and poetically in Philippians 2:6–7. In this parable the message is dramatic and powerful. The one who is prepared and willing to serve, and waits patiently for the final culmination of God's rule, will find himself *served* by the one for whom he is waiting. This scene is set in the *parousia*, but Luke 22:27 and John 13:3–5 make it clear that Jesus is *already* among them as a master who serves. Yet all of this rich imagery when taken alone can lead to a gross misrepresentation of a crucial aspect of Jesus' relationship to his disciples. He *is* among them as one who serves, indeed as *their* servant. At the same time he is still the *master,* and they need to remember who they are as servants. Thus this parable in Luke 17:7–10 is crucial in its presentation of Jesus as a master to whom his servants owe loyalty and obedience.

With this background in mind, we turn to the parable itself.

STANZA ONE

"Can you imagine having a servant,   SERVANT
  plowing or keeping sheep,   FULFILLING ORDERS
    who on coming in from the field   ORDERS FULFILLED
     you say to him, 'Come at once and recline to eat'?"   REWARDS?

In a technological age with the forty-hour week, powerful labor unions, and time and a half for overtime, the world of this parable seems not only distant but unfair. After a long, hard day in the field, such a servant surely has earned the right to a little appreciation, some comforts, and a few rewards. But Jesus is building on well-known and widely accepted patterns of behavior in the Middle East. The master-servant relationship, in its ancient and modern expressions, implies acceptance of authority and obedience to that authority. Yet the outsider needs to be sensitive to the security that this classical relationship provides for the servant and the sense of worth and meaning that is deeply felt on the part of a servant who serves a great man. These qualities of meaning, worth, security, and relationship are often tragically missing from the life of the modern industrial worker with his forty-hour week. The servant offers loyalty, obedience, and a great deal of hard work, but with an authentic Middle Eastern nobleman the benefits mentioned above are enormous. Because of these things, this master-servant image is profoundly appropriate for illustrating the believer's relationship to God and to His unique agent/Son.

Jeremias has convincingly demonstrated that the introductory phrase (17:7) *tis ex humōn* ("which of you") is a phrase unique to Jesus that always expects an emphatically negative answer (Jeremias, *Parables,* 103; Bailey, *Poet,* 121f.). Certainly no one in any Middle Eastern audience could imagine any servant expecting special honors after fulfilling his duty in the field. The master is not *indebted* to him for having plowed the field or guarded the sheep. Then too, the afternoon meal (here specifically referred to in v. 8 by the verb *deipnēsō,* "I shall eat supper/dine"), is not at eight in the evening but rather in the late afternoon around three o'clock (Jeremias, *Eucharistic,* 44f.). Thus we are not dealing with harsh hours imposed by an unfeeling master but rather the normal expectations of a relatively short day's chores. The point is not, "Does the master allow the servant food and rest?" but rather, "Does he extend privilege to the servant who fulfills the daily assignment?" The clear answer is—no!

STANZA TWO

"Will he not rather say to him,
'*Prepare for me* something and I shall dine,
   and gird yourself and *serve me,*   SERVE THE MASTER
till *I eat and drink,*   THEN YOURSELF
   and afterward *you shall eat and drink*'?"

The master is the master and is *not* the equal of his servant. Here the master does not eat with the servant. Again, there is a great deal of imagery on the other side of the coin in the New Testament taken from the language of common meals. Jesus eats with his disciples *and* even with sinners. The disciples are called friends, not servants (John 15:15), even though the servant is not greater than his master (John 15:20). Jesus stands at the door eager to enter and eat with anyone who will open (Rev. 3:20). Whatever these images mean, they do not mean an easy equality between the master (Jesus) and his servant disciples. The easy equality reflected in the popular chorus, "My God and I go through the fields together," is unknown in the New Testament. Again this little parable is a crucial corrective to a disastrous misunderstanding of the above texts. As in Luke 15:3–7 (cf. Bailey, *Poet,* 144f.), the third stanza is commentary and thematically matches the first stanza.

STANZA THREE

"Does the servant have special merit   SERVANTS
  because he did what was commanded?   ORDERS FULFILLED
    So you, also, when you have done what was commanded   ORDERS FULFILLED
      say, 'Nothing is owing us servants, we
        have only done our duty.'"   REWARDS?

The first stanza began with a question expecting an emphatically negative answer. This matching stanza begins in the same way. The four major themes set out in the first stanza are carefully repeated here, as we have observed. In this case the disciples/apostles are called on to identify with the servant of the parable and to see their position illustrated by his. This position is properly understood only when the text is examined carefully in the light of the language and the cultural assumptions of the story. Two key words that we have translated "special merit" and "nothing owing" need special scrutiny.

The traditional understanding of the first line of this stanza is reflected in the RSV, which translates, "Does he thank the servant . . . ?" The common Greek verb "thank" (*eucharisteō*) occurs twice in Matthew, twice in Mark, and four times in Luke. It is used in the account of the healing of the ten lepers in Luke 17:16. Thus Luke knows the word and uses it more than the other evangelists. Yet in this parable the actual words in the text are *mē echei charin tō doulō*. Literally this reads, "Does he have any grace/favor for the servant?" The word *charin* is the common New Testament word for grace. The theological weight of this great word must not be overlooked, as we will note below. But here we need ask only what is meant by the phrase, "have grace/favor for. . . ." In the Epistles there are clear cases where "to have grace for" means "to be grateful to" (cf. I Tim. 1:12; II Tim. 1:3; Rom. 7:25; II Cor. 9:15; Bauer, 886). Yet in Luke the word *grace* has to do primarily with credit (6:32–34) and favor (1:30). Bauer lists a series of passages, most of them in Luke-Acts, where the word *grace* appears in the phrase "to have grace," and says of them, "in these passages the mng. comes close to reward" (Bauer, 885; cf. Luke 2:52; 6:32; Acts 2:47; 7:10, 46). The relational situation implied by the use of this word (in a Middle Eastern context) can be seen clearly in Luke 1:30. There Mary is told, "You have found favor with God." Immediately after this comes the announcement, "You will conceive in your womb and bear a son. . . ." This mirrors the Old Testament refrain, "If I have found favor . . . then . . ." (cf. Gen. 18:3; Num. 11:15; I Sam. 20:29; Est. 5:8). If the servant or inferior has favor from his superior, then the superior is indebted to the petitioner and is expected to grant some special request or offer some special gift. It is true that these texts talk of "*finding* favor" while Luke 17:8 speaks of "*having* favor." But in the first case the petitioner has been granted favor as a gift; it is too great to be earned. Thus he has only *found* favor as a gift. This parable is clearly talking of work accomplished and its results. After all of this work does the servant *have favor*? Is the master indebted to him? Is there any *credit* due him (Luke 6:32–34)? Has he earned any merit? Is there anything owing him? The question is much deeper than a verbal expression of thanks. The master may well express appreciation to a servant at the end of a day's work with a friendly word of thanks. The issue is much more serious than this. Is the master *indebted* to his servant when orders are carried out? This is the question that expects a resoundingly negative answer in the parable.

The above understanding of the text is reflected in the great thirteenth-century Arabic version of Hibat Allah Ibn al-'Assāl, who translates, "Is there to this servant merit because he did what was commanded him?" Montefiore quotes one Merx (?) who writes,

> "Has he (the servant) any favor (i.e., in the sight of his master) because he did what he was told?" Does he acquire any special favor or merit? The sense is improved by this reading (Montefiore, *Gospels*, II, 1009).

Trench translates "doth he count himself especially beholden to that servant?" (Trench, 476). These two scholars differ only on the question of the subject of the verb *to have*. For Montefiore the servant is the subject, and for Trench the master is the subject. In the matching line in the first stanza we also find the verb *to have* and there the master is the subject and the servant the object. This seems to be the best understanding of the present line. This comes across somewhat awkwardly in English and reads literally, "Does he have special merit for the servant? . . ." Semitic languages have no verb *to have* and this further complicates any attempt to understand the language precisely, yet the sense is clear. The point is, does the master *owe* the servant anything because he has carried out his orders? Clearly not.

So, finally, the application is made to the audience. The passive "when you have done *what was commanded*" has been identified by Jeremias as "a periphrasis for the divine name" (Jeremias, *Parables*, 193). The final line, like its counterpart in the first stanza, ends with direct speech. Here again we are faced with a long-standing translation problem. The traditional understanding of this concluding statement is "we are miserable/useless servants, we have only done what was our duty." The key word is *achreios*, which has two shades of meaning. The first is *useless* (which would refer to their unprofitable functions as servants). The other is *miserable*, which is somewhat stronger and refers not to their work but to themselves. B. T. D. Smith summarizes the problem and notes a widely held solution:

> Clearly a slave who does all that is required of him is not useless to his master, and many would therefore omit the adjective as a gloss (B. T. D. Smith, 184).

Yet Smith accepts the adjective and translates it "good-for-nothing." Jeremias rejects *useless* in favor of *miserable* and decides that it is ". . . an expression of modesty" (Jeremias, *Parables*, 193). In summary, the meaning "useless/

worthless'' (in reference to their work) cannot be correct because the servant does his duty and is not worthless. The meaning "miserable/good-for-nothing" (in reference to themselves) seems harsh and unnecessarily self-critical for a hard-working servant. Thus a long list of scholars have decided that the word must be a gloss (Bauer, 128), though *only* the Sinai Old Syriac supports this decision textually. However, there is another way to understand the problematic word *achreios*. The Greek word is actually *chreios* with what the grammarians call an alpha privative prefix. We have this same construction in English with the words moral and amoral. The prefixing of the *a* negates the word. In this case, *chreios* by itself means "need" and thus the word *achreios* very literally means "without need." It is easy to see how such a word could evolve in meaning. The person for whom you are "without need" is the one who is useless. Then the one who is useless usually has some undesirable character traits and so is miserable/good-for-nothing. But in this case, we need to return to the very literal translation of the word that gives us "without need." This understanding of *achreios* was suggested by Bengel:

> akhreios is one *hou ouk esti okreia* or *khreos,* of whom there is no need, a person we can dispense with, dispensable, one to whom God the Master owes no thanks or favor (Bengel, II, 160).

The difficulty here is that Bengel leaves a basic ambiguity unresolved. When we opt for "without need," does it mean the master is "without need" of the servant, or does it mean the servant is "without need" (of reward)? Bengel stated the first and hinted at the second and thus left the question unresolved. T. W. Manson defined unprofitable as "not claiming merit" (*Sayings*, 303). Yet he does not indicate how he reaches this conclusion linguistically. It is our view that he is right and that this understanding *is* linguistically defensible.

We begin with the Syriac and Arabic versions. A number of the major Arabic translations from the eleventh century onward agree with Hibat Allah Ibn al-'Assāl, who translates, "We are servants to whom nothing is owing" (*naḥnu khuddām la ḥāja lana*). Literally this reads, "We are servants and we have no need." Clearly Hibat Allah has read *achreios* as meaning "without need." The question then becomes, Does this translation make any sense in the context? The answer is yes, if the phrase is placed in a Middle Eastern cultural setting. This phrase is unambiguous idiomatic speech among Palestinian and Lebanese village people. One village workman renders some small service to a house owner and the following conversation takes place:

House owner:	*fī ḥāja?*	(Literally: "Is there any need?" Meaning: "Do I owe you anything?")
Workman:	*ma fī ḥāja*	(Literally: "There is no need." Meaning: "You owe me nothing.")

This idiomatic speech form is widespread and, to our knowledge, universal in our Middle Eastern world. With vocabulary variants we have traced it from Syria to the Sudan. Obviously Hibat Allah is translating in a fashion that will make sense to his readers. His thirteenth-century translation gives the reader the above meaning. Furthermore, this translation of "without need" for *achreios* occurs in the Harclean Syriac, which reads *la ḥoshḥo* (Vat. Syr. 268, folio 110ʳ; cf. Bailey, *Hibat Allah*, 22–24). It is well-known that this seventh-century Syriac version is an extremely literal translation of the Greek. Thus the Harclean reading may be merely an attempt at literalism. Yet, at the same time, the translator must have expected his readers to understand *something* by the above phrase. He clearly rejected "unprofitable" for "without need." Is it not possible to affirm that he also recognized the latter as the intent of the text and for that reason chose it over the Peshitta with its traditional reading of "unprofitable"? Following Hibat Allah's lead we can suggest that the original editor/author/compiler of the Travel Narrative has used *achreios* as the equivalent of *ouden chreian*. That is, he has taken the negative and attached it to the word. Thus the original parable instructs the disciples to say, "We are servants to whom nothing is owing, we have only done our duty." This translation is etymologically possible. It makes profound sense in the context of the overall parable. Important early Arabic and Syriac translations give this reading, and we would submit that it is the best understanding of the text. With this meaning the problem of hard-working, "useless" servants is solved without any need to eliminate the word as a supposed gloss.

This is not the only case in the parables where a Greek word with an alpha privative is perhaps better understood as a root word with a negative. In Luke 11:8 the problematic *anaideia* as a Greek composite word means "shamelessness." But when one begins with the root of the word and adds a negative the meaning becomes "avoidance of shame," which we have argued is the original intent of *anaideia* in that parable (Bailey, *Poet*, 125–133).

The word "servant" is *doulos* and means "slave" also. Because the word "slave" in our society has totally negative connotations it is problematic to use it as a translation for *doulos* in this parable. Paul calls himself a "slave of Jesus Christ" (Rom. 1:1) and obviously means it in a positive sense. Here also a positive sense is meant. The disciple is not an employee who can work and expect payment. He is a slave for whom the master accepts total responsibility, and who enjoys total security, and who, at the same time, labors out of a sense of duty and loyalty, not in the hope of gaining rewards. Indeed, after he has fulfilled *all* commands he says, "Nothing is owing me, I have only done my duty."

The theological application of this carefully written parable is weighty indeed. Clearly we are again talking about salvation and good works. The Jewish commentary on the Psalms (*Midrash Tehillim*), in explaining Psalm 46:1, reads,

> Not for their works were the children Israelites redeemed from Egypt, but so that God might make himself an eternal name, and because of his favor . . . (Montefiore, *Rabbinic*, 361).

In commenting on this parable Montefiore mentions the rabbinic doctrine of "tit-for-tat":

In no other point is Jesus' antagonism to, and reaction against, certain ten-
dencies in that teaching more justified and more wholesome than here
(Montefiore, *Gospels*, II, 1009).

For Jesus salvation was a gift.

In addition to works and salvation there is the related topic of motivation
for service and its results. Do we serve in order to gain? Having served do we
have claims on God? This parable says no to both questions.

Some contemporary voices supported Jesus' view here set forth. In the
Sayings of the Fathers (*Pirke Aboth*) one Simeon the Just (*ca.* 300 B.C.) is
reported to have said, "be like slaves who serve the master not with a view to
receiving a present: and let the fear of Heaven be upon you" (Mishna *Pirke
Aboth*, 1:3, Charles, II, 691; cf. also 2:9). Hunter observes,

> The parable of the Farmer and his Man therefore warns us against importing
> into religion that book-keeping mentality which imagines we can run up
> credit with God by our works. Jesus says it can't be done. So does the Apostle
> Paul (Hunter, *Then*, 84).

The Egyptian commentator Sa'īd sees the parable as relating specifically
to the doctrine of justification and affirming that God's grace cannot be earned
(Sa'īd, 424). This becomes abundantly clear when the original language is
allowed to surface from under the traditional translation. The parable asks the
question, "Does he (God) have grace/merit for the servant because he did what
was commanded?" The answer is clearly, No! Jeremias is correct in identifying
the parable as "a demand for renunciation of all Pharisaic self-righteousness"
(Jeremias, *Parables*, 193).

A final question is, Who is the master? The first and foremost answer is
clearly God. Are there then any Christological implications for the parable?
Again these are perhaps more overheard than heard. Yet they are unavoidably
present. Jesus is addressed as "Master" all through the tradition. The disciple in
the Oriental world has always been and remains in traditional society a servant of
the master. The student/disciple literally waits hand and foot on the teacher. He
often sleeps in his quarters and provides the services of a house servant. Foerster
describes the first-century disciple:

> The pupil took his turn in preparing the common meal and catering for the
> general needs of the group. He performed personal services for his teacher,
> observed his conduct and was his respectful, loving, humble companion
> (*JPFC*, II, 964).

Jesus is God's unique agent/Son, and as such he is the master of the disciples and
they are his servants. Certainly these Christological implications develop in the
understanding of the post-Easter Church, but we would suggest that they are
already present in the parable in its original setting.

Finally, we need to ask what was the response that the parable intended to evoke from the disciples and what is the theological cluster used to elicit that response?

The listening disciples were perhaps pressed to perceive, "We are servants whose finest efforts earn us no merit with our master. As servant/slaves we do our duty and expect no pay." This hoped-for response is evoked by the use of a number of theological motifs. We would cautiously suggest the following:

1. The believer is a servant/slave. He is expected to obey and know his place as a servant.

2. Grace/salvation is a gift, not a reward for services rendered.

3. The servant of God labors to fulfill a duty. He does not develop a claim on God nor serve to receive rewards.

4. God is the master of the believer. Yet, at the same time, the believer's servanthood is appropriately fulfilled in obedience to God's unique agent/Son Jesus, who should be served with diligence and loyalty.

In passing, we note that the entire question of rewards is given a great deal of attention in the synoptic material. Bultmann succinctly summarizes the subject: "Jesus promises rewards to those who are obedient without thought of reward" (Bultmann, *Theology*, I, 14).

Thus the mighty theme of the nature of God's grace is set forth. Here it is stated negatively. The most hardworking servant/slave knows that nothing is owing him because of who he is. He does his duty and earns no merit. Obviously the master's gifts come unmerited and unearned, and so it is with God.

Chapter 8

THE JUDGE AND THE WIDOW
(Luke 18:1-8)

As in many of the parables, here also a deceptively simple story hides a complex series of theological themes and interpretive problems. Yet hopefully a close look at the literary background, the rhetorical form, and the culture will help unlock for us at least some of the theological secrets of this treasured story.

Here in the parable of the Judge and the Widow there is a clearly identifiable literary background. As we observed in the parable of the Barren Fig Tree, a careful comparison between the parable in the mouth of Jesus and its prototype is crucial. By doing so we are able to see what he has borrowed, what he has transformed, and, of equal importance, what he has left out. In this case, our prototype is in Ben Sirach. The text in question is as follows:

> He will not ignore the supplication of the fatherless,
>   nor the widow when she pours out her story.
>
> Do not the tears of the widow run down her cheek
>   as she cries out against him who has caused them to fall?
>
> He whose service is pleasing to the Lord will be accepted,
>   and his prayer will reach to the clouds.
>
> The prayer of the humble pierces the clouds,
>   and he will not be consoled until it reaches the Lord.
>
> He will not desist until the Most High visits him
>   and does justice for the righteous and executes judgment.
>
> The Lord will not delay,
>   neither will he be patient with them,
> till he crushes the loins of the unmerciful,
>   and repays vengeance on the gentiles (Ben Sirach 35:15-19).

Points of similarity and dissimilarity are many and significant. These need to be examined in three categories: points of complete similarity, points of similarity (but with a difference), and points of complete dissimilarity.

POINTS OF COMPLETE SIMILARITY

1. In each, the text begins with the topic of prayer in general. Then, after an illustration, each moves on to discuss the specific topic of justice for the righteous in the face of oppression.

2. Both use the rabbinic principle of "from the light to the heavy" (from a "light" illustration from daily life to a "heavy" application).

POINTS OF SIMILARITY (BUT WITH A DIFFERENCE)

1. The basic figure of a widow crying out for help is similar in both stories. (Yet the repeated nature of the widow's actions in Jesus' parable is more prominent. Unlike Jesus, Ben Sirach shifts to the persistent humble *man* who will not be consoled until he has an answer. That is, Jesus makes more of persistence *and* Ben Sirach shifts to a male figure.)

2. The patience of God is mentioned in both texts. (Yet Ben Sirach says God *is not* patient with the *ungodly*. As we will see, Jesus affirms that God *is* patient with the *godly*.)

3. Both texts discuss the vindication of the righteous. (Yet in Sirach God acts in two ways. He executes justice for the righteous and vengeance on the unrighteous. In Jesus' parable the second is omitted.)

4. Each has a concrete illustration, a widow. (Yet Jesus' use of the illustration is expanded into a full parable.)

POINTS OF COMPLETE DISSIMILARITY

1. In Sirach the way to get your prayers heard is to render service that is "pleasing to the Lord." Such a one is accepted and his prayers reach the clouds. None of this God-hears-you-if-you-serve-Him theology is reflected in Jesus' parable.

2. The figure of the unjust judge is a dramatic new thrust in Jesus' parable. It is bold and risky. A negative character symbolically represents God. This then gives a sharper cutting edge to the "from the light to the heavy" principle of interpretation.

Thus it is obvious that some material from Sirach has been used, some transformed, and some omitted. The similarities are so numerous that we assume with Montefiore that there is conscious borrowing. These points of similarity and dissimilarity will be examined in detail as we proceed.

The topic of the parable of the Judge and the Widow and that of the parable which follows it obviously relate to prayer. The close parallels with Luke 11:5-8 have often been noted. Elsewhere I have argued that the central section of Luke has an outline that brings Luke 11:1-13 into a parallel position with 18:1-14 (Bailey, *Poet,* 79-82). In the first case there are three units of tradition on the subject of prayer; in the second there are two. At the same time the passages relates to the question of the coming of the Son of man and thus to the previous passage in 17:22-37. This latter relationship is reinforced by the Lucan introduction in 18:1 and by the conclusion in 8b. Thus two themes are woven into the passage: the topic of prayer and that of the paradoxical suddenness/delay of the parousia. Indeed, as we will observe, each of these two passages (18:1-8, 9-14) has a unique thrust in relation to prayer.

The question of authenticity for the present passage is too crucial to be ignored. The passage breaks down into three sections. First is the evangelist's introduction (v. 1), second, the parable proper (vv. 2-5), and finally, the Dominical application of the parable (vv. 6-8). The introduction is clearly the work of Luke or his source and is not a part of the parable. Significantly, the following parable (18:9-14) also begins with the evangelist's introduction which, as we will see, is also his commentary on what the parable is all about. It is our view that these introductions must be taken seriously as important indications of the original meaning of the parable. Bultmann has placed this parable in a list of parables for which the original meaning is irrecoverably lost (Bultmann, *History,* 199). Yet if we take the literary background in Sirach and the evangelist's introduction seriously, we have evidence for the original intent of the parable.

In regard to the parable and, in particular, the Dominical application at the end, opinion is sharply divided. Linnemann argues that both are secondary (Linnemann, 187f.). Jeremias presents weighty linguistic arguments for the authenticity of both (Jeremias, *Parables,* 154-56; cf. Marshall, 669-671). Kümmel finds specific features that mark the Dominical application as original and argues that it is "in no way a re-interpretation, since the parable, as a metaphor, can bear a particular as well as a general application" (Kümmel, 59). Kümmel's main point is that the text talks of God's salvation coming quickly and that this particular emphasis was strong in Jesus' own teaching (*ibid.,* 54).

In the prototype of the parable (found in Sirach), we noted an application of the figure of the weeping widow to prayer in general, which then turned at the end of the passage to a specific discussion of God's intervention for the community of the faithful. The same move occurs here. Marshall observes an historically closer parallel:

> In fact, we have a structure similar to that in the parable of the prodigal son, where a story, whose central character appears to be the father and whose central concern is to depict the character of God, turns out to have a "sting in the tail" as it presents the picture of the elder brother and asks the audience whether they behave like him. So here, after depicting the character of God,

the parable turns in application to the disciples and asks whether they will
show a faith as persistent as the nagging of the widow (Marshall, 670f.).

Thus from linguistic, theological, and literary points of view there are important
reasons for affirming both the parable and the Dominical application as authentic
to Jesus.

THE INTRODUCTION

And he was saying a parable to them to the effect that they ought always to pray
and not lose heart/be afraid.

The audience is assumed by the text to be the disciples (17:22). The following
parable (18:9–14) is addressed to those with a self-righteous spirit like some
Pharisees. In the parallel teaching material on prayer (Luke 11:1–13) we can
observe the identical shift. There the initial material is spoken to the disciples
(11:1–8) and the parable/poem on the Father's Gifts (vv. 9–13) is most likely
spoken to the Pharisees (Bailey, *Poet,* 139–142).

The introduction reinforces the general theme of persistence in prayer. At
the same time, the specific application at the conclusion of the parable is hinted at
in this introduction. Not only in regard to God's decisive intervention in history
are the faithful to be persistent in prayer, but they are to seek Him whenever He
seems far away and the confidence of the believer wavers. The solution to fear is
prayer. In Shakespeare's famous play Macbeth is fearful lest their plans fail. His
wife tries to steel his nerves with the command, "But screw your courage to the
sticking place, and we'll not fail!" (act 1, scene 7). Macbeth does so and yet his
grand plans disintegrate into tragedy for himself and all around him. Here a
simple piety expressed in trusting prayer is commanded as a solution to the fear
that robs the believer of his tranquility and the will to endure. Jesus and his little
band were faced with intensified rejection and hostility on all sides. Surely this
generalized introduction/interpretation of the parable can be seen as authentic
to the specific situation Jesus faced, as well as an appropriate introduction to the
parable at a later stage in the life of the early Church.

THE PARABLE

The first stanza tells of the judge and the second of the widow. The third
returns to the judge (with the same motifs), and the fourth then returns to the
widow. The three themes of JUDGE–GOD–MAN of stanza one are repeated in
the identical order in the third stanza. Stanzas two and four on the widow have
the same themes, but in the last stanza the order is reversed. It is pointless to
commit one more rash act *metri causa* and suggest that the last stanza may have

Luke 18:1–5

1 A certain judge there was in a certain city.	JUDGE	
God he did not fear	GOD	
and man he did not respect.	MAN	

2   And a widow there was in that city,   WIDOW
      and she was coming to him   COMING
          saying, "Vindicate me from my adversary."   VINDICATE

3   He did not want to for a (certain) time.   JUDGE
      Then he said to himself, "Although I do not fear God   GOD
      and do not respect man,   MAN

4   yet because she causes me trouble, this widow,   WIDOW
      I will vindicate her,   VINDICATE
          lest in continual coming she wear me out."   COMING

had the theme of vindication at the end (like stanza three). Such may be the case, or the language originally may not have been that precisely aligned (as in many cases of parallelism in the Psalms). Yet the stanzas are intact, without any extra interpretive details. Each theme has a balancing line and the overall effect is symmetrical and artistically satisfying.

STANZA ONE—THE PAGAN JUDGE

A certain judge there was in a certain city.   JUDGE
God he did not fear   GOD
    and man he did not respect.   MAN

In II Chronicles 19:4–6 Jehoshaphat chooses judges for the land and tells them,

> . . . consider what you do, for you judge not for man but for the Lord; . . . now then, let the fear of the Lord be upon you, take heed what you do, for there is no perversion of justice with the Lord our God, or partiality, or taking bribes.

Such admonitions are always needed in every society, and the Old Testament keeps trying to establish justice in the gate. Amos in particular was upset over the corruption of the judges (Amos 2:6–7; 5:10–13). In New Testament times the same problem surfaced. Edersheim (*Life*, II, 287) describes judges in the city of Jerusalem who were traditionally so corrupt that they were called *Dayyaney Gezeloth* (Robber-Judges) rather than *Dayyaney Gezeroth* (Judges of Prohibitions), which was their real title. The Talmud speaks of village judges who are willing to pervert justice for a dish of meat (B.T. *Baba Kamma* 114a). In perversion of Jehoshaphat's directive the judge in our parable cares neither for man nor for God. Plummer points out that the word often translated "respect" (*entripō*) can also mean "being abashed, having a feeling of awe" (Plummer,

412). The active of the verb is to "make ashamed" and the passive is either "be put to shame" or "have respect for" (Bauer, 269). But starting with the Old Syriac, down through all the other Syriac and all the Arabic versions for another thousand years, the only translation we have had here in the Middle East is, "He is not ashamed before people." A very important aspect of the description of the judge is thereby overlooked when we read with our Western translation tradition, "have respect for." The point is that Middle Eastern traditional culture is a shame–pride culture to a significant degree. That is, a particular pattern of social behavior is encouraged by appeals to shame. The parent does not tell the child, "That is wrong, Johnny" (with an appeal to an abstract standard of right and wrong) but "That is shameful, Johnny" (an appeal to that which stimulates feelings of shame or feelings of pride). In such a society the vocabulary that surrounds the concept of shame is very important (Bailey, *Poet*, 132). One of the sharpest criticisms possible of an adult in the Middle Eastern village today is *mā jikhtashī* ("he does not feel shame"). The point is that such a person does a shameful thing; you cry "Shame" to him but he does not feel ashamed. His inner sense of what constitutes a good act and what is a shameful act is missing. He cannot be shamed.

In this regard we are dealing with another case where very ancient attitudes are reflected. Jeremiah had the same problem. We are told, "the wise men shall be put to shame" (Jer. 8:9), but in regard to the prophets and priests he writes,

> Were they ashamed when they committed abomination?
> No, they were not at all ashamed;
> they did not know how to blush (8:12).

The Hebrew text uses two strong words for shame (*bwsh, klm*) and speaks precisely to the problem faced with the judge. *Nothing* shames him. There is no spark of honor left in his soul to which anyone can appeal.

The problem with this judge is not a failure to "respect" other people in the sense of respecting someone of learning or high position. Rather it is a case of his inability to sense the evil of his actions in the presence of one who should make him ashamed. In this case he is hurting a destitute widow. He should feel shame. But the whole world can cry "Shame!" and it will make no impression on him. He does not *feel shame* before men. We have precisely the same concept and the same word in the parable of the Rebellious Tenants in Luke 20:13. The tenants refuse to give some of the fruits of the vineyard to the owner. They treat the servants of the owner shamefully. Finally the master says, "I will send my beloved son; it may be they will feel shame before (*entrapēsontai*) him (so translated in all Syriac and Arabic versions). The hope is not that they might treat him kindly, but rather that in his presence they might feel ashamed of what they have done and give up their rebellious acts. But there also the tenants involved *could not be shamed*. In both texts the Greek word carries this meaning. Middle Eastern culture requires it and Middle Eastern fathers give us this meaning in their translations. Thus we have in Luke 18 a clear picture of a *very* difficult man. He has no fear of God; the cry of "for God's sake" will do no good. He also has no inner sense of what is right and what is shameful to which one can appeal. Thus the cry, "For the sake of this destitute widow!" will likewise be useless. Obviously the only way to influence such a man is through bribery. To such a man comes the widow.

STANZA TWO—THE HELPLESS WIDOW

And a widow there was in that city,	WIDOW
and she was coming to him	COMING
saying, "Vindicate me from my adversary."	VINDICATE

The widow in the Old Testament is a typical symbol of the innocent, powerless oppressed (cf. Ex. 22:22–23; Deut. 10:18, 24:17, 27:19; Job 22:9, 24:3, 21; Ps. 68:5; Isa. 10:2; also Jth. 9:4). Isaiah 1:17 calls on the rulers and the people to "plead for the widow." Then, in verse 23, we are told, "everyone loves a bribe . . . and the widow's cause does not come to them." The Jewish legal tradition required that on the basis of Isaiah 1:17 "the suit of an orphan must always be heard first; next, that of a widow . . ." (Dembitz, 204). Thus this woman had legal rights that were being violated. Bruce writes of her, "too weak to compel, too poor to buy justice" (Bruce, *Parabolic*, 159). Plummer observes, "she had neither a protector to coerce, nor money to bribe" (Plummer, 412; cf. Marshall, 669). Ibn al-Ṭayyib comments on the plight of the widow in Middle Eastern society:

> In every time and place the greedy have found the widow vulnerable to oppression and injustice for she has no one to protect her. Thus God commands the judges to give her special consideration, Jer. 22:3 (Ibn al-Ṭayyib, Manqariyūs edition, II, 312).

Jeremias suggests that "a debt, a pledge, or a portion of an inheritance is being withheld from her" (Jeremias, *Parables*, 153); and, as Bruce observes, "A widow was one who was pretty sure to have plenty of adversaries if she had anything to devour" (Bruce, *Parabolic*, 159). The issue is clearly money because, according to the Talmud, a qualified scholar could decide money cases sitting alone (B.T. *Sanhedrin* 4b, Sonc., 15).

Her cry is a call for justice and protection, not vengeance. Smith translates it, "Do me justice with regard to my opponent" (C. W. F. Smith, 186).

By way of summary, the parable thus far makes three assumptions.

1. The widow is in the right (and is being denied justice).
2. For some reason, the judge does not want to serve her (she has paid no bribes?).

3. The judge prefers to favor her adversary. (Either the adversary is influential or he *has* paid bribes.)

Smith comments,

> She may be presumed to have been incapable of rewarding him, and we may assume further that it would probably be to his advantage to let her oppressor have his way (C. W. F. Smith, 186f.).

In the last century a Western traveler witnessed a scene in Iraq that gives us the wider picture behind the parable. He writes,

> It was in the ancient city of Nisibis, in Mesopotamia. Immediately on entering the gate of the city on one side stood the prison, with its barred windows, through which the prisoners thrust their arms and begged for alms. Opposite was a large open hall, the court of Justice of the place. On a slightly raised dais at the further end sat the *Kadi*, or judge, half buried in cushions. Round him squatted various secretaries and other notables. The populace crowded into the rest of the hall, a dozen voices clamouring at once, each claiming that his cause should be the first heard. The more prudent litigants joined not in the fray, but held whispered communications with the secretaries, passing bribes, euphemistically called fees, into the hands of one or another. When the greed of the underlings was satisfied, one of them would whisper to the *Kadi*, who would promptly call such and such a case. It seemed to be ordinarily taken for granted that judgment would go for the litigant who had bribed highest. But meantime a poor woman on the skirts of the crowd perpetually interrupted the proceedings with loud cries for justice. She was sternly bidden to be silent, and reproachfully told that she came there every day. "And so I will," she cried out, "till the *Kadi* hears me." At length, at the end of a suit, the judge impatiently demanded, "What does that woman want?" Her story was soon told. Her only son had been taken for a soldier, and she was alone, and could not till her piece of ground; yet the tax-gatherer had forced her to pay the impost, from which as a lone widow she could be exempt. The judge asked a few questions, and said, "Let her be exempt." Thus her perseverance was rewarded. Had she had money to fee a clerk, she might have been excused long before (Tristram, 228f.).

A long list of commentators from Plummer to Jeremias has noted this account as helpful in filling out the cultural details that are the background of the parable. Yet there is a crucial element both in the parable and in Tristram's account that has gone unnoticed. Ordinarily women in the Middle East do not go to court. The Middle East was and is a man's world and women are not expected to participate with men in the pushing, shouting world described above. There is, furthermore, Jewish evidence for this from talmudic times. Tractate *Shebuoth* reads,

> Do, then, men come to court, and do not women ever come to court? . . . —You might say, it is not usual for a woman, because "all glorious is the King's daughter within," (note: Ps. XLV, 14; the King's daughter [i.e. the

Jewish woman] is modest, and stays within her home as much as possible)
(B.T. *Shebuoth* 30a, Sonc., 167).

In the light of this reticence to have women appear in court one could understand
her presence there as meaning that she is entirely alone with no men in an
extended family to speak for her. This may be the assumption of the story. In
such a case her total helplessness would be emphasized.

Yet there is another even more important element. During the Lebanese
civil war of 1975–76 a Palestinian peasant woman of my acquaintance was
caught in a tragedy. Her cousin disappeared. He was assumed to be kidnapped by
one of the many armed groups fighting in the city of Beirut. The entire extended
family searched in vain for him or his body. He was the only son of his widowed
mother and was not a member of any paramilitary group. In desperation the
family sent a delegation of three peasant *women* to the political/military leader of
the leftist forces in the area where he had disappeared. The man they went to see
was an internationally known, powerful military and political figure. These three
women shouted their way into an audience with him and, once there, flung a
torrent of hard words in his face. The entire scene was vividly described to me
by my peasant friend the following day. I specifically asked, "What would have
happened if the men of your family had said such things to this man?" With
raised eyebrows and a shake of the head she answered, "O, they would have
been killed at once." Tristram heard ". . . a dozen voices clamouring at once,
each claiming that his cause should be the first heard." Thus *many* people were
shouting. How did the *widow* get attention? Obviously her shouting was different
from the others. In traditional society in the Middle East women are generally
powerless in our man's world. But at the same time, they are respected and
honored. Men can be mistreated in public, but not women. Women can scream at
a public figure and nothing will happen to them. In the case of my Palestinian
friend, the family had *deliberately* sent the women because they could express
openly their sense of hurt and betrayal in language guaranteed to evoke a response. The men could not say the same things and stay alive. This same
background is reflected in the rest of the parable.

STANZA THREE—THE RELUCTANT JUDGE

He did not want to for a (certain) time.	JUDGE
Then he said to himself, "Although I do not fear God	MAN
and do not respect man,"	GOD

STANZA FOUR—THE VINDICATED WIDOW

"yet because she causes me trouble, this widow,	WIDOW
I will vindicate her,	VINDICATE
lest in continual coming she wear me out."	COMING

The word "certain" we have cautiously accepted in the text. It occurs in Codex Bezae and some of the Syriac, Latin, and Coptic versions. It reinforces the parallelism between stanzas one and three, but may not be original. In any case, the judge confesses the accuracy of the judgment passed on his character. He knows that he does not fear God and that no one can call him into account and make him feel ashamed. If anyone flings even such accusations at him it will have no effect.

In the phrase "he said to himself," we have what Black has called "a well-known Semitism . . . 'to speak the mind', 'to think'" (Black, 302). This kind of soliloquizing is common in the parables (cf. the Rich Fool; the Prodigal Son; the Unjust Steward; the Master of the Vineyard), and with the Semitic idiom noted above marks the parable's genuineness.

The word here translated "wear me out" is a prizefighting term for a blow under the eye (cf. I Cor. 9:27) and has led many commentators to suggest that the judge is fearful lest the woman get violent (Linnemann, 185). But the language does not require this interpretation and the cultural milieu of the Middle East excludes it. The widow can shout all kinds of insults at him, but if she tries to get violent she will be forcibly removed and not allowed to return. Enough is enough! Derrett argues that the word means "to blacken the face" (Derrett, *Judge,* 189–191). He correctly observes that the phrase is common throughout the East. However, it means "to destroy the reputation of" and describes a man with a sense of personal honor, which he is anxious to preserve. Our judge has no such personal honor. Derrett observes this objection and tries to defend his interpretation by suggesting that the phrase "have no respect for man" is really a compliment offered to an impartial judge. Against Derrett we would argue that "God he did not fear and man he did not respect" is clearly meant to be a double-edged negative statement, not part compliment and part insult. Thus the judge is indeed shameless and as a result you cannot "blacken his face." Again we prefer the long, rich Arabic translation tradition that gives variations of "lest she give me a headache!" Ibn al-Ṭayyib is particularly helpful. He notes that the language can refer to a blow on the head and comments, "This exaggeration on the part of the judge is to indicate the extent to which her persistence has irritated him" (Ibn al-Ṭayyib, Manqariyūs edition, II, 312).

The Greek *eis telos* we have translated "continual." Ibn al-'Assāl gives this an added emphasis with the wording, "lest she forever continue coming and wearing me out." The Greek phrase is strong and implies a will to go on forever. The judge is convinced that the woman will never give up. T. W. Manson calls it a "war of attrition" between the two of them (*Sayings,* 306).

As we have observed, the parable is a clear case of the rabbinic principle of "from the light to the heavy" (*qal waḥomer*). The woman is in an apparently hopeless situation. She is a woman in a man's world, a widow without money or powerful friends. The judge cannot be appealed to out of duty to God, and no human being can make him ashamed of any evil act he may perpetrate on the innocent. *Yet* this woman not only gets a hearing but has the case settled in her favor. Taken with its introduction the main thrust is clearly persistence in prayer. If this woman's needs are met, *how much more* the needs of the pious who pray not to a harsh judge but to a loving Father. However discouraged and hopeless their situation may seem to be, it is not as bad as that of this widow. They can rest assured that their petitions are heard and acted upon. When fear grips the heart the believer is challenged to pray, and to pray continually in the face of all discouragements with full confidence that God will act in his best interests.

Verses 6–8 have long been called a *crux interpretum*. It is not our intent to review all the traditional solutions and debate each in turn (Marshall, 674–77); rather we shall set forth our own understanding with the hope that it may help contribute to a solution of the problems involved. A literal translation of the text with its parallelisms displayed is as follows:

1   *Shall* not *God make vindication for his elect*   (future)

2   the ones crying to him day and night?   (present)

3   Also he is slow to anger over them.   (present)

4   I say to you that *he shall make vindication for them* speedily. (future)

5   Yet when the Son of man comes will he find faith on the earth?

The third line is traditionally read as a question and the key word *makrothumeō* translated as "patience" or "delay" (cf. RSV "will he delay long over them?"). The fifth line is problematic and is thought by many to be a concluding reflection of the evangelist or the Church, or a separate saying of Jesus attached here by the evangelist or his source. Granting any of these as possibilities, this final phrase clearly indicates an uneasiness about the quality of faith in the believing community. *Someone* (either Jesus, or the Church, or Luke's source, or Luke) is nervous because of the less than perfect specimens of faith around him who do not exhibit the will to endure that the woman in the parable exhibited (on *pistis* with the article cf. Marshall, 676). The author of this line is apparently afraid that the believers will fail to pray and will then indeed lose heart and, in the process, lose faith. Why then is this nervousness expressed here? We would suggest that the answer to this question is in the four lines immediately preceding. Line three contains the focus of the discussion.

In considering line three, we are faced with two problems. What is the meaning of the word that the RSV translates "delay"? And is it a statement or a question? First then, the translation of this key word. The word itself (*makrothumeō*) is one of the great New Testament words for patience. But the above translation of "delay" does not do justice to it. The New Testament has three words for patience and they are all applied to God. The first is *anochē* and appears in Romans 2:4 and again in 3:26. God has a divine *forbearance* in passing over former sins. The second type of patience is *hupomonē*, which is the patience of the sufferer and is most clearly illustrated by Christ on the cross. Then in Romans 2:4 *anochē* is linked with our word (*makrothumia*) and is used in the context of judgment and mercy. Literally *makrothumia* applies to the one who can and does "put his anger far away." It is the patience of the victor who refuses to take vengeance. T. W. Manson translates it as "removes his wrath to a distance" (*Sayings*, 307). A classical example of this virtue can be seen in David as he stands over the sleeping body of Saul with spear in hand. Saul has come to kill David. David has penetrated Saul's camp and can easily kill him. David's bodyguard wants to take vengeance and David shows great *makrothumia*; he puts his anger far away and refuses the request (I Sam. 26:6–25). Obviously this is a quality God must exercise if He is to deal with sinners. In Exodus 34:14 God tells Moses that He is both "slow to anger" and at the same time "gracious." Horst, in his article on *makrothumia*, describes this quality of God as it appears in His dealings with His people. Horst writes that He is the God "who will restrain this wrath and cause His grace and loving-kindness to rule. The wrath and the grace of God are the two poles which constitute the span of His longsuffering" (Horst, *TDNT*, IV, 376). This same willingness of God to restrain His wrath and thus be merciful appears in the Book of Wisdom (*ca.* 50 B.C.). This text describes God as "slow to anger" and at the same time "merciful" (15:1). The author in this connection writes, "We are yours even though we have sinned, since we acknowledge your power." Thus God puts aside His wrath and shows mercy to the believer even though the believer has sinned. Again Horst is helpful where he describes this understanding and writes, "alongside this wrath there is a divine restraint which postpones its operation until something takes place in man which justifies the postponement" (Horst, *TDNT*, IV, 376). A marvelous illustration of this (observed by T. W. Manson) is provided by the rabbis. They tell of a king who wondered where to station his troops. He decided to quarter them at some distance from the capital so that on the occasion of civil disobedience it would take some time to bring them. In that interim the rebels would have an opportunity to come to their senses and "So, it is argued, God keeps His wrath at a distance in order to give Israel time to repent" (T. W. Manson, *Sayings*, 308; cf. P.T. *Taanith*, 11.65b). At the same time, according to Ben Sirach (35:19–20), God has no *makrothumia* toward the gentiles. As we noted above he writes,

> And the Lord will not delay,
>> neither will he be slow to anger (*makrothumia*) with them,
>
> till he crushes the loins of the unmerciful,
>> and repays vengeance on the nations.

Here again *makrothumia*, which is a part of the language of salvation, is used to describe God's actions toward His people, *not* toward the nations. Toward the gentiles/nations He has *no makrothumia*.

In the New Testament we see this same background reflected in the parable of the Unforgiving Servant (Matt. 18:23–35). The servant owes his master ten thousand talents and he is not able to pay (v. 25). The master (obviously in anger) orders the entire family sold into slavery. The servant falls on his knees imploring him, "Lord, have patience with me (*makrothumēson ep' emoi*), and I will pay you everything." That is, he calls for the master to set aside his anger, to have patience. This the lord does.

Turning to the rest of the New Testament, the same meaning of "setting aside wrath" is evidenced in each case where the word is applied to God. In Romans 2:4 it is an attribute of God and is attached to repentance. In Romans 9:22 it is connected to wrath. In I Timothy 1:16 Jesus puts aside his anger for Paul. In I Peter 3:20 God exercised His *makrothumia* with the disobedient, and in II Peter 3:9 God exercised *makrothumia* "not wishing that any should perish, but that all should reach repentance." Finally in 3:15, which is parallel to verse 9, the reader is told to "count the *makrothumia* of our Lord as salvation" (obviously this setting aside of wrath is a necessary part of salvation). This unchanging understanding of *makrothumia* must now be applied to the present text.

In his article on *makrothumia* Horst discusses our parable. He links the question of longsuffering in line three with the vindication theme in line four. He affirms that *ekdikasis* ("vindication") in our passage means

> not only final judgment for adversaries but also serious self-examination for the elect. When the Son of Man comes, will He find faith on the earth? (v. 8b). Only in faith can they go into the *ekdikasis* (vindication) of the last judgment and pray for its coming. Thus God's *makrothumein* (slowness to anger) is for them a necessary interval of grace which should kindle the faith and prayer that moves mountains (17:6 par.). In the *makrothumein* of God there now lies the possibility of the existence of believers before God . . . in confidence that they may beseech His righteousness and grace (Horst, *TDNT*, IV, 381).

Furthermore, Horst argues that the phrase under question is a statement, not a question, that it applies to the elect, and that it cannot mean "delay" (*ibid.*; cf. also Bruce, *Parables*, 164). We would submit that Horst's understanding is correct and that it is essential to a proper interpretation of the parable. The phrase in question should be read as a statement, and *makrothumia* does not mean "delay" but has to do with God's willingness to put His anger far away because of the sins of the elect. God will *indeed* vindicate His elect, who cry to Him day and night. But these same elect are also sinners, not sinless saints. If He is not willing to put aside His anger, they cannot approach Him in prayer and dare not call out for vindication lest, with Amos, the Day of the Lord be a day of darkness and not light (Amos 5:18-20). The act of seeking vindication *does not* make them righteous. As in the case of the political enthusiasts encountered in Luke 13:1-5, a righteous cause does not produce righteous people. So here, a sincere cry for God's intervention to vindicate the elect does not in itself make them holy in His presence. Only as God is willing to "put His anger aside" is it possible for them to invoke Him day and night and to "pray and not be afraid." Only with a liberal exercise of His *makrothumia* toward *them* can God vindicate them at all.

The inverted parallelism of the four lines helps to reinforce the above understanding of the text. The first two lines pose the question and the second two provide the answer. The tenses of the verbs reinforce the parallelism with an ABBA sequence. The first line asks, "*Shall* God (future) vindicate his elect?" This is answered in the matching fourth line, "He *shall* vindicate them (future) speedily!" In the second line we find out that they cry (present) to Him day and night. This cry is answered in the third line where God is (present) slow to anger with them.

The theological divergence from Ben Sirach is crucial. As we observed, Ben Sirach also uses the parable of the widow. His parable also shifts from general prayer to a discussion of the vindication of God's people. He also mentions God's slowness to anger. But in Sirach this recollection calls forth an almost vindictive attack on the gentiles. God will *not* be slow to anger with the gentiles but will crush their genitals. In sharp contrast the Lucan text offers *no* words of judgment against the adversaries of the faithful. Rather, the account concludes with a challenging question, a wistful hope that the Son of man will find faith on the earth, and a clear statement that only in the willingness of God to set aside His wrath can they even cry to Him at all. So this text is not a simple question of God delaying salvation, but of God's willingness to put off judgment.

Finally, the question of the nature of God's vindication requires brief reflection. For Ben Sirach the form of this vindication is spelled out. The wicked will be crushed, eliminated, broken, and repaid for their deeds. His people will rejoice in His mercy (35:23). In our parabolic application there are no details. The vengeance on the gentiles is (as we noted) significantly absent. But, in regard to the faithful, how does God vindicate them? Is it only a promise for the end times (near though these times may be), or does the text hint at a dynamic for the present? The tenses of the verbs referring to vindication are future. But must it necessarily mean the distant future? This passage is in Luke 18. The beginning of the passion story is only a few verses away. Jesus' enemies are gathering strength for the final act of their opposition. Will God vindicate *him*? The reader is given a clear answer, but what an answer! Yes, God will vindicate His Son who also prays to Him day and night, but that vindication *will be seen in resurrection and will come by way of a cross.* For centuries the house of Islam has stumbled at the offense of the cross. For them Jesus is a great prophet. In the Psalms God says, "Touch not my anointed ones, do my prophets no harm" (Ps. 105:15). If these things are true, asks Islam, where is God's vindication for His prophet in the passion narratives? How could the story of the cross be true? In an attempt to assure vindication by God for Jesus, the story of the cross is reshaped in Islamic tradition to allow for a divine rescue operation before Good Friday and the crucifixion of a substitute. But is not the Islamic question the right question? Where is God's vindication? And surely the right answer is that God's vindication of *this* prophet far exceeded his followers' wildest dreams. He was vindicated at an empty tomb, and the path to that empty tomb led across Golgotha. If such was the vindication of Jesus, what of his disciples?

The concluding verses of the passage (18:6–8) have been read for centuries in the context of the expectation of the *parousia*. It may well be that this is the context in which Luke himself understood them and perhaps appropriately so. But is it not possible to see an initial application of these texts in the ministry of Jesus himself? Is God going to vindicate him and the little band of fearful followers that have cast their lot with him? T. W. Manson points out that election was to service and not to privilege.

> They are not the pampered darlings of Providence, but the *corps d'élite* in the army of the living God. Because they are what they are, they are foredoomed to suffering at the hands of the wicked; and in many cases the seal of election is martyrdom (*Sayings,* 307).

As fear intensifies during the final approach to Jerusalem, it is addressed in this parable. The clear promise is made that God will indeed vindicate them and will do so quickly!

Finally, to what precise understanding were the disciples pressed to come, and what cluster of theological motifs compose the fabric of the meaning of the parable? For the disciples the hoped-for response was surely something like this:

> In the gathering gloom of intensified opposition we need not fear. God has put His anger far away and He hears us. We must trust and be steadfast in prayer. We do not appeal to a disgruntled judge but to a loving Father who will vindicate His elect and will do so quickly.

The cluster of theological motifs include the following:

1. Prayer conquers fear.
2. Persistence in prayer is appropriate to piety.
3. In prayer the believer addresses a loving Father (not a capricious judge).
4. God must, and indeed does, put His anger aside to hear the prayers of the faithful, for their cry for vindication does not make them holy.
5. God is at work in history and *will* accomplish His purposes and vindicate His elect.
6. A woman is used as an example for the faithful to emulate. Ben Sirach starts with a woman and then shifts to a male figure. Jesus starts with a woman and then makes application to the elect in general. The sexist bias of Ben Sirach is missing. Thus the status of women in the believing community is enhanced by the way the parable is told.
7. The cry for vindication requires self-examination lest the faithful themselves fail to keep faith.

Again a series of weighty theological themes speaks to us out of a deceptively simple story.

Chapter 9

THE PHARISEE AND THE TAX COLLECTOR
(Luke 18:9-14)

The Text:

And he said to certain people who considered themselves
righteous and despised others, this parable.   (INTRODUCTION)

1	"Two men went up into the temple to pray,	TWO GO UP
	one a Pharisee, and the other a tax collector.	PHARISEE, TAX COLLECTOR
2	The Pharisee stood by himself thus praying,	HIS MANNER
	'God, I thank thee because I am not like other men,	HIS PRAYER
3	extortioners, unjust, adulterers,	TAX COLLECTOR
	even like this tax collector.	(THE IMAGE)
4	I fast twice a week.	HIS SELF-
	I give tithes of all that I possess.'	RIGHTEOUSNESS
5	But the tax collector, standing afar off,	TAX COLLECTOR
	would not even lift up his eyes to heaven,	(THE REALITY)
6	but he beat upon his chest saying,	HIS MANNER
	'God! Make an atonement for me, a sinner.'	HIS PRAYER
7	I tell you, he went down to his house	TWO GO DOWN
	made righteous, rather than that one."	TAX COLLECTOR, PHARISEE

For every one who exalts himself will be humbled,
and he who humbles himself will be exalted.   (CONCLUSION)

This famous parable has long been considered a simple story about pride, humility, and the proper attitude for prayer. These themes are certainly present. Yet, as in the case of many of the parables we have examined, a closer look uncovers a weighty theological presentation that is traditionally overlooked. Here also a key word can be translated in a fashion significantly different from the translation tradition common among us. Again a closer look at culture and style unlocks otherwise obscured theological content. The parabolic ballad form noted in many of the previous parables is also evidenced here. In this case the stanzas are inverted in their relationship to one another. This parabolic ballad form will be examined first, then the cultural and religious background of the parable. Our interpretation will attempt to keep these factors in focus. First, then, is an examination of the literary form set forth above.

A series of parallel themes marks out this parable as another of the seven-stanza parabolic ballads (cf. Luke 10:30-35; 14:16-23; 16:1-8). After the introduction (which is supplied by Luke or his source), the parable opens with two men going up to the temple (1). The parable concludes with the same two men going down, but now their order is reversed. The tax collector is now mentioned first (7). Stanzas 2 and 6 clearly form a pair also. The exterior manner of each man is listed first (in each case), then his direct address to God. The second line in each stanza is an explanation of each worshiper's self-understanding. Stanzas 3 and 5 concentrate on the tax collector. He is specifically named in each. Yet there is a sharp contrast between the two pictures. Stanza 3 is the tax collector as seen through the eyes of the Pharisee, while stanza 5 is the reality of the man as portrayed by the storyteller. The center in stanza 4 is a presentation of the Pharisee's case for his self-righteousness. This theme of righteousness is then repeated at the end of the seven stanzas (a feature common to this literary form). Another literary device common to this form of inverted parallelism is the point of turning which occurs just past the center of the structure (cf. Bailey, *Poet*, 48, 51, 53, 62). This feature appears here in stanza 5 where the story turns around with the startling phrase, "But the tax collector. . . ." Only one parallelism is not in precise balance. We are told how each of the participants was standing. But the first appears in stanza 2 and the second in 5. It is possible to see the movement of the parable in a simplified manner that would bring these two ideas in balance. This would be as follows:

> Two went up
>> The Pharisee stood
>>> and prayed
>> The tax collector stood
>>> and prayed
> Two went down

The difficulty with this structure is that the prayer of the Pharisee is five lines while the tax collector's prayer is only one. Also, the ground for the Pharisee's self-righteousness (stanza 4) loses its prominence in the center. Other close parallelisms in the ballad are blurred when this element of how they stand is brought into juxtaposition. Thus we prefer to see the first structure suggested above as that intended by the author. This parable, like that of the Good Samaritan, is seen as deliberately structured with seven stanzas that invert with a climax in the center. The introduction has been added by the editor, and the structure would reinforce the opinion that the conclusion may also be exterior to the parable, which ends with stanza 7. Each double line will need to be examined in turn.

INTRODUCTION

And he said to certain people who considered themselves righteous and despised others, this parable.

This introduction is clearly added by the evangelist or his source. As such it is an interpretation of the parable. The interpreter tells the reader that the subject is *righteousness* and, in particular, self-righteousness. T. W. Manson comments that the parable is addressed to those who

had the kind of faith in themselves and their own powers that weaker vessels are content to have in God, and that the ground of this confidence was their own achievements in piety and morality (*Sayings,* 309).

Centuries earlier Ibn al-Ṭayyib came to the same conclusion. In his comment on this verse he remarks, "Christ saw that some of those who gathered around him relied on their own righteousness for their salvation rather than on the mercy of God" (Ibn al-Ṭayyib, Manqariyūs edition, II, 313). As we have observed, the question of humility in prayer is indeed dealt with. Yet the theme of righteousness and how it is achieved is pointed up by verse 9 as a central thrust of the parable.

We have argued elsewhere that the material in the Lucan central section was compiled by a pre-Lucan editor (Bailey, *Poet,* 79–85). That editor/theologian placed this parable into his outline along with other material on the subject of prayer. Thus *he* identified it as a parable about prayer, and indeed it is. It is not too likely that this editor/theologian, having placed the parable in a collection of material on prayer, then wrote an introduction that highlighted a different aspect of the theology of the parable. Therefore this interpretative introduction is either traceable to a very early Christian commentator who wrote prior to the compilation of the Travel Narrative or to Luke himself. Yet whether this introduction is traceable to a very early evangelist, the editor of the Travel Narrative, or to Luke, it must be taken seriously. As we will observe, the parable is virtually studded with vocabulary pointing to the topic of righteousness and how it is achieved. Thus this introduction is clearly appropriate to the internal message of the parable. This brings us to the parable itself.

1 "Two men went up into the temple to pray, one a Pharisee, and the other a tax collector."	TWO GO UP PHARISEE, TAX COLLECTOR

The Pharisee is mentioned first, then the tax collector. They both *go up.* But when it comes time to *go down,* the tax collector will be in the lead.

We have traditionally assumed that the setting of the parable is that of private devotions. This assumption has deeply colored the way we in the Western tradition have translated and interpreted the text. Middle Easterners read the same text and assume a parable about public worship. Ibn al-Ṭayyib's remark is typical where he comments on the publican standing "afar off" and says, "that is, apart from the Pharisee and *from the rest of the worshipers in the temple*" (Ibn al-Ṭayyib, Manqariyūs edition, II, 315; emphasis mine). Here Ibn al-Ṭayyib affirms the presence of a worshiping congregation almost in passing. This assumption has a basis in the text, as we will see.

A part of our problem in the West is that the English verb "pray" is almost exclusively applied to private devotions, and the verb "worship" is used for corporate worship. However, in biblical literature, the verb "pray" can mean either. In Luke 1:10 Zechariah is participating in the daily atonement sacrifice in the temple and takes his turn at burning the incense in the Holy Place. In the meantime, "The whole multitude of the people were praying outside. . . ." Jesus quotes from Isaiah 56:7 where the temple is called "a house of prayer" (Luke 19:46). The famous listing of early Christian concerns in Acts 2:42 includes the apostles' teaching and fellowship, the breaking of bread, and *the prayers*. In this list the word "prayers" is a synonym for community worship. Acts 16:13, 16 speak of a place of public worship as "a place of prayer." These and many other texts make clear that the context of a given passage must determine whether the verb "pray" means corporate worship or private devotions. When Jesus goes up on a mountain alone to pray, obviously the context is private devotions. But in this parable there is a series of clear indicators that we are here dealing with corporate worship, not private devotions. First, specifically, *two* people go up to a place of public worship at the same time. Second, they go down at the same time (presumably after the service is over). Third, the temple (a place of public worship) is specifically mentioned. The contemporary Middle Easterner has the same double meaning attached to the verb "pray." But when he, as a Christian, says, "I am going to *church* to pray," or, as a Muslim, remarks, "I am on my way to the *mosque* to pray," everyone knows that they mean corporate worship, not private devotions. Even so with the parable, the mention of the temple adds considerable weight to the assumption that corporate worship is intended. Fourth, as we will note below, the text tells us that the Pharisee "stood by himself." The obvious assumption is that he stood apart from the other worshipers. Fifth, we also are told that the tax collector "stood afar off." Afar off from whom? It can mean afar off from the Pharisee, but can also mean afar off from the rest of the worshipers. This is especially the case if it can be substantiated that there *are* worshipers present, apart from whom the Pharisee has also chosen to stand. Finally, the tax collector specifically mentions the *atonement* in his prayer. The temple ritual provided for a morning and evening atoning sacrifice to be offered each day and a congregation was normally present. Indeed, it is always assumed in the discussions of the service (cf. Mishna *Tamid*, Danby, 582–89; Sir. 50:1–21). In summary, the verb "pray" gives us two interpretive options. It can mean private devotions or corporate worship. The weight of evidence in the parable suggests the latter. It is with this assumption that we will proceed through the parable. Yet one can ask, does not each man in the parable offer a private prayer?

Quite likely the traditional assumption that the parable is talking only about private devotions is related to the fact that each of the principal figures in the parable offers a private prayer. Does this not lead the reader to conclude that no service of public worship is involved? Not so. Safrai describes the worship of the temple in the first century.

> Many Jews would go up daily to the Temple in order to be present at the worship, to receive the priestly benediction bestowed upon the people at the end, (and) *to pray during the burning of the incense* (Safrai, *JPFC*, II, 877; emphasis mine).

He also states that they are there to "worship and pray during the liturgy" (*ibid.*, 876). Ben Sirach has an elaborate description of the atonement ritual in the temple (Sir. 50:1–21). He mentions hymns of praise sung by the cantors

> as the people pleaded with the Lord Most High,
>   and prayed in the presence of the Merciful,
> until the service of the Lord was completed
>   and the ceremony at an end (Sir. 50:19).

Clearly, the people are praying *during* the service. The time of the offering of the incense was the often mentioned time of personal prayer (as in Luke 1:10 noted above). Safrai writes, "During the incense-offering, the people gathered for prayer in the court" (Safrai, *JPFC*, II, 888). This was so commonly accepted as the right time for private prayers that people not in the temple were known to offer their own special petitions at that time, particularly during the afternoon sacrifice (cf. Jth. 9:1). Thus there is conclusive evidence that private prayers are offered as a part of the corporate worship during the atonement sacrifice ritual held twice daily.

If then the two men are on their way to participate in corporate worship, can we be sure that the service was the morning or evening atonement sacrifice? Indeed yes, since this was the only *daily* service of public worship in the temple. Thus anyone on any unspecified day on his way to corporate prayers in the temple would naturally be assumed to be on his way to the atonement sacrifice. This service was the sacrifice of a lamb (for the sins of the people) at dawn. A second similar sacrifice was held at three in the afternoon. The elaborate rituals connected with these sacrifices have been fully described (Dalman, *Sacred*, 302f.; Edersheim, *Temple*, 152–173; Safrai, *JPFC*, II, 887–890). The time of incense was especially appropriate as a time of personal prayer because by this time in the service the sacrifice of the lamb had covered the sins of Israel and thus the way to God was open. The faithful could *now* approach Him (Edersheim, *Temple*, 157). The incense arose before God's face and the faithful offered their separate petitions to Him. This background appropriately combines for us the idea of private prayers (which the two actors in this drama do indeed offer) in the context of corporate worship (in that the atonement sacrifice is mentioned in the parable) in a place of public worship like the temple (which is specified as the scene of the action).

If, however, one concludes that the evidence for corporate worship is yet unconvincing as a specific setting for the parable, we are still obliged to assume this same background in general. At dawn each day the atonement sacrifice took place. The smoke from the sacrifice arose over the altar and the temple area. Any believer offering private prayers in the temple any time between the two services stood in the presence of this altar with its burning sacrifice. He knew that it was possible for him to address God with his private needs *only* because the atonement sacrifice had taken place. Any private prayers were, as it were, sandwiched in between the two daily atonement sacrifices. Thus any kind of prayer in the temple area (private devotions or prayer in connection with corporate worship) necessarily presupposes the context of the twice daily atonement sacrifice that is specifically mentioned in the parable itself.

First-century attitudes toward Pharisees and tax collectors are sufficiently well-known as to need no explanation. The one is the precise observer of the law, and the other is a breaker of the law and a traitor to the nation. With the actors on stage, the play proceeds.

> 2 "The Pharisee stood by himself thus praying,   HIS MANNER
> 'God, I thank thee because I am not like other men,' "   HIS PRAYER

The first line of this couplet has within it both a textual and a translational problem. We have opted for the text selected by Kurt Aland *et al.* in the United Bible Societies Text (Jeremias accepts the same reading and identifies it as a Semitic style of speech; *Parables*, 140). The deeper problem (which has most likely created the textual variants) is the question, did he *stand by himself* or *pray to himself*? The phrase *pros heauton* can be read "by himself" and attached to the previous word "stood," which gives us the above translation. Or it can be read "to himself" and attached to the word "praying" which follows. In this latter case it then reads, "The Pharisee stood praying thus to himself." It has been argued for some time that the prepositional phrase *pros heauton* must refer to his manner of praying because to modify the verb *standing* it should read *kath heauton* in accord with the classical Greek usage (Plummer, 416).

However, a number of things can be said against Plummer. First, in the Lucan parables a soliloquy is introduced with the phrase *en heautō*, not *pros heauton* (cf. 7:39; 12:17; 16:3; 18:4). Second, we are told how the tax collector stood in relation to others and it is only natural to have a similar description of the Pharisee. Third, the traditional understanding of the text may be an additional example of the spilling phenomenon. This phenomenon occurs where texts have been read together for so long that, like two rivers flowing together, one text "spills" into the next. That is, meaning is carried over inadvertently from one text to another. An important example of this phenomenon can be seen in Luke

11:5–13, where the idea of persistence has spilled from verses 9–13 back into the parable in verses 5–8 (cf. Bailey, *Poet,* 128f.). So here, in the previous parable the judge talks *to himself (en heautō)*; thus perhaps inadvertently the Pharisee has gradually been seen as also offering a soliloquy. Fourth, Codex Bezae (D), along with a few other minor manuscripts, has *kath heauton,* which indicates that its editors clearly understood the Pharisee to be standing alone, not praying alone. Fifth, the very important Old Syriac from the second century translates this text in an unambiguous fashion and has the Pharisee *standing by himself.* Delitzsch, in his famous Hebrew version of the New Testament, also translates the phrase "standing by himself," as do a number of our Arabic versions. Sixth, when we read the text as a soliloquy this detail adds nothing to the parable. But when the Pharisee is seen as standing apart from the other worshipers, the detail is in precise harmony with everything else that is said and done in the parable and adds considerably to the entire dramatic effect (with Manson, *Sayings,* 310). Seventh, classical Greek usage can hardly be determinative in the Lucan Travel Narrative with its many parables and Semitisms and obvious translation Greek. Thus, with these considerations in mind, we prefer to see the Pharisee standing apart from the remainder of the worshipers about him.

The Pharisee's reasons for standing apart can be easily understood. He considers himself righteous and indeed "despises others," as we see from his description of them. Those who kept the law in a strict fashion were known as "associates" (*haberim*). Those who did not were called "people of the land" (*am-haaretz*). These latter Danby defines as

> those Jews who were ignorant of the Law and who failed to observe the rules of cleanness and uncleanness and were not scrupulous in setting apart Tithes from the produce (namely, Heave-Offering, First Tithe, Second Tithe, and Poorman's Tithe) (Danby, 793).

In our parable, paying the tithe is specifically mentioned. In the eyes of a strict Pharisee the most obvious candidate for the classification of *am-haaretz* would be a tax collector. Furthermore, there was a particular type of uncleanness that was contracted by sitting, riding, or *even leaning against* something unclean (*ibid.,* 795). This uncleanness was called *midras*-uncleanness. The Mishna specifically states, "For Pharisees the clothes of an *am-haaretz* count as suffering *midras*-uncleanness" (Mishna *Hagigah* 2:7, Danby, 214). With this background in mind it is little wonder that the Pharisee wanted to stand aside from the rest of the worshipers. If he accidentally brushes against the tax collector (or any other *am-haaretz* who might be among the worshipers), he would sustain *midras*-uncleanness. His state of cleanliness is too important. It must not be compromised for any reason. Physical isolation, from his point of view, would be a statement and an important one at that. Thus the Pharisee carefully stands aloof from the others gathered around the altar.

Furthermore, the problem of the proud man standing aloof in worship was a contemporary problem. One of the intertestamental books called The

Assumption of Moses gives us an illuminating illustration. This book, written most likely during the lifetime of Jesus (Charles, II, 411), has some very sharp things to say about the leadership of the nation during the time of the unknown author. These "impious rulers" are described as follows:

> And though their hands and their minds touch unclean things, yet their mouth shall speak great things, and they shall say furthermore: "Do not touch me lest thou shouldst pollute me in the place (where I stand) . . ." (7:9-10, Charles, II, 420).

This remarkable text has striking parallels with our parable. In each case the leaders are under attack. In each they "speak great things." The Pharisee in the parable goes down to his house not justified in God's sight, and here the impious rulers are described as defiled with unclean things. Improper attitudes are criticized in each account. We know from John 11:48 that "the place" can mean the temple area, and it is possible that the above text carries this same meaning and is therefore also set in the temple. Thus Jesus' criticism is in harmony with others of his time. Finally, and most important for our discussion, each talks of someone who wants to stand in physical isolation from the others.

Jesus' criticism of the Pharisee is also in harmony with advice offered earlier by the great Hillel, who said, "Keep not aloof from the congregation and trust not in thyself until the day of thy death, and judge not thy fellow until thou art thyself come to his place" (Mishna *Pirke Aboth* 2:5, Danby, 448). Hillel's remark is further evidence that some religious leaders had a tendency to "keep aloof from the congregation."

In summary, the Pharisee in the parable goes up to attend the morning or afternoon atonement sacrifice. In a gesture of religious superiority he stands apart from the other worshipers.

When the problematic phrase *pros heauton* is attached to his mode of standing, it is then possible to understand his prayer as offered out loud. The Sinaiticus original, along with some important early Latin and Coptic versions, leaves out the "to/by himself" entirely and thereby deliberately affirms that he is praying out loud. Marshall observes that "Jewish practice was to pray aloud" (Marshall, 679). This possibility adds further color. The Pharisee is thus preaching to the "less fortunate unwashed" around him. They have little chance to get a good look at a truly "righteous" man like himself, and he is "graciously" offering them a few words of judgment along with some instruction in righteousness. (Most of us, at some point in our worship experience, have been obliged to listen to some misguided soul insult his neighbors in a public prayer.) The officiating priest (as we have observed) is most likely in the Holy Place offering up the incense. At this particular point in the service the delegation of Israel was responsible for making the unclean stand at the eastern gate (Mishna *Tamid* 5:6, Danby, 587). The Pharisee may be wondering why this publican was not ushered out. In any case, during this pause in the liturgy, the Pharisee probably takes advantage of the opportunity to instruct the "unrighteous" around him.

The opening volley of the Pharisee's attack on his fellow worshipers reveals more of himself than he perhaps intended. Prayer in Jewish piety involved primarily the offering of thanks/praise to God for all of His gifts, and petitions for the worshiper's needs. This Pharisee does neither. He does not thank God for His gifts but rather boasts of his own self-achieved righteousness. He has no requests. Thus his words do not fall under the category of prayer at all but degenerate to mere self-advertisement. Jeremias translates a striking illustration of a similar prayer from the period (Jeremias, *Parables*, 142; B.T. *Berakhoth* 28b, Sonc., 172; cf. Edersheim, *Life,* II, 291). Thus Jesus is not portraying a caricature but a reality most likely known to his audience. We have taken the option of translating the *hoti* as "because" rather than "that," since the former strengthens the self-congratulatory thrust of his opening sentence. As he proceeds the prayer goes "from bad to worse."

| 3 | "'extortioners, unjust, adulterers, even like this tax collector.'" | TAX COLLECTOR (THE IMAGE) |

These first two words can also be translated *rogues* and *swindlers* (Jeremias, *Parables,* 140). Obviously the words are selected because they specifically apply to the tax collector, who is already spotted standing at some distance. The tax farmers of the Roman empire were traditionally known as extortioners and swindlers. The third word, "adulterers," is thrown in by the Pharisee for good measure (like the older son in Luke 15:30). It tells us nothing about the tax collector but does inform us regarding the mindset of the speaker. Ibn al-Ṣalībī makes the thoughtful comment,

> We know that the one who is not a thief and adulterer is not necessarily a good man. Furthermore experience demonstrates that the search for the faults and failures of others does the greatest harm of all to the critic himself and thus such action must be avoided at all costs (Ibn al-Ṣalībī, II, 181).

Thus we see a man tearing up the fabric of his own spirituality.

The point at issue in this stanza is the translation of the beginning of the second line (*ē kai hōs*). We need to examine the first word *ē* and the third, *hōs*. The question is, Are we presented with two lists or one? Is the Pharisee saying, I am not like type A (extortioners, unjust, adulterers), nor am I like type B (tax collectors)? Or do we have one list, of which the tax collector is a part and an illustration? We will attempt to demonstrate the second.

A clear translation of the traditional view of this stanza is found in the Good News Bible of the United Bible Societies, which reads, "I thank you, God, that I am not greedy, dishonest, or an adulterer, like everybody else. I thank you that I am not like that tax collector over there." The particle *ē* is the key word in making our choice between the two alternatives suggested above. This particle is relatively rare in Matthew and Mark but common in Luke. In Luke it occurs only eight times in the opening chapters and six times in the passion narrative, but in the central section (9:51–19:49) it is found twenty-three times. Thus it is especially important to observe its use here in the central section. As a word this particle is often translated "or." Yet, as an English word, the particle "or" exclusively joins contrasting elements in a sentence. Someone is asked, "Do you want this or that?" The weight of usage and thus meaning is that of joining contrasting items. However, the Greek particle $\bar{e}$ can join either contrasting or similar elements in a sentence. Bauer observes that this particle can separate "opposites, which are mutually exclusive," or it can separate "related and similar terms, where one can take the place of the other or one supplements the other" (Bauer, 342). He then lists Matthew 5:17 as a clear case of the latter. For this verse the RSV reads, "Think not that I have come to abolish the law and ($\bar{e}$) the prophets." Here the continuity and similarity of the two terms ("law" and "prophets") are so close that $\bar{e}$ is translated "and." In the Travel Narrative in Luke, nineteen of the twenty-three occurrences of $\bar{e}$ separate *similar* terms. In only five cases does it separate *contrasting* elements. In four texts the $\bar{e}$ could just as easily be translated "and," as in Matthew 5:17 (cf. Luke 11:12; 13:4; 14:31; 15:8). An interesting case of the use of $\bar{e}$ as a particle connecting similar terms is in Luke 17:23. In this verse we have three textual alternatives. These are:

        'Lo, there,' or 'Lo, here,'
        'Lo, there,' and 'Lo, here,'
        'Lo, there,'   'Lo, here,'

That is, the particle $\bar{e}$ so often connects similar terms that in the textual tradition it is at times replaced by *kai* ("and") or omitted and in translation replaced with a comma. In summary, we can see that $\bar{e}$ in the Travel Narrative connects similar (not contrasting) terms in three out of four cases. In some texts it can be translated with an English "and" and perhaps even replaced with a comma. The English word "or," which inevitably implies contrasting terms, is thus inadequate. In our text here in 18:11, with adjectives especially selected to apply to tax collectors, we clearly have a case of similar and not contrasting terms. Thus our translation should communicate this linkage of similar terms. The precise combination of $\bar{e}$ *kai* that we have in this text also occurs in 11:11, 12 (?). There also it connects similar and not contrasting terms. To this must be added an examination of *hōs*.

The Greek word *hōs* ("like") is a comparative particle common throughout the New Testament. However, one of its "noteworthy uses" (Bauer, 906) is to introduce an example. The longer text of Luke 9:54 reads, "Lord, do you want us to bid fire come down from heaven and consume them as (*hōs*) Elijah did?" The general statement occurs first, then the specific illustration introduced by *hōs*. The same usage occurs in I Peter 3:6, where a general statement about submissive wives is made and then Sarah (introduced with the word *hōs*) is mentioned as a specific illustration. The well-known phrase "as (*hōs*) it is written" is another common example of this use of *hōs* (cf. Luke 3:4). We would submit that our text here is a further case of this special use of *hōs*.

In summary, the Pharisee gives a list of characteristics selected to apply to the tax collector standing nearby. He concludes his list with an illustration, the tax collector himself. The *ē* connects the similar/identical terms. We opt for joining the adjectives with the illustration and translating "even like this tax collector." Thus the prayer comes through as a ruthless attack on a stereotype, a public accusation of a fellow worshiper at the great altar, that is based on preconceived notions formulated by the Pharisee's own self-righteousness, which he then proudly displays.

4	" 'I fast twice a week.	HIS SELF-
	I give tithes of all that I possess.' "	RIGHTEOUSNESS

The basis of the Pharisee's assumption of righteousness is here verbalized. Moses stipulated a fast for the day of atonement (Lev. 25:29; Num. 39:7). This man goes far beyond that admonition and fasts twice *each* week, a practice that "was confined to certain circles among the Pharisees and their disciples" (Safrai, *JPFC*, II, 816). Regarding the tithe, the Old Testament regulation was clear and limited. Tithes were levied on grain, wine, and oil (Lev. 27:30; Num. 18:27; Deut. 12:17; 14:13). But as Safrai observes, "in tannaitic times the law was extended to take in anything used as food" (Safrai, *JPFC*, II, 825; cf. Mishna *Maaseroth* 1:1, Danby, 66). But even this ruling had exceptions because rue, purslane, celery, and other agricultural products were exempt (Mishna *Shebiith* 9:1, Danby, 49). The practice of tithing nonagricultural products was just beginning to appear, and "the custom was never really widespread, and was confined to those who were particularly strict" (Safrai, *JPFC*, II, 825). Even tax collectors paid *some* tithe (*ibid.*, 819). But this Pharisee—well, he tithed *everything*. Ibn al-Ṣalibī observes, "He is comparing himself with the great examples of righteousness like Moses and the Prophets" (Ibn al-Ṣalibī, II, 181). His acts are works of supererogation (Jeremias, *Parables,* 140). Amos had some sharp words for this type of religion (cf. Amos 4:4). Indeed, we have a picture of a man who prides himself on his more than perfect observance of his religion.

This stanza is the climactic center. We can see the move to this climax in the flow of the action in the previous lines. Standing aloof lest he be defiled by the "unrighteous" around him, he congratulates himself (2) and offers scathing criticism of a tax collector nearby (3). He then brags of having not only kept the law but exceeded its demands (4). The dramatic point of turning is then introduced as the major themes begin to repeat, but with a difference.

5	"But the tax collector, standing afar off,	TAX COLLECTOR
	would not even lift up his eyes to heaven,"	(THE REALITY)

The point of turning in the literary form is intense and dramatic. The image of the tax collector in the mind of the Pharisee (3) is in sharp contrast to the reality of the broken, humble man standing some distance away from the assembled worshipers (5). This same contrast between image (seen through self-righteous eyes) and reality was observed above in our study of Simon and the woman in Luke 7:36–50. There also a self-righteous man looked on a dramatic expression of genuine piety and saw only a defiling sinner to be scrupulously avoided.

This repentant tax collector does not stand aloof but "afar off," for he feels he is not worthy to stand with God's people before the altar. As he comes to voice his petition, he (like the woman in 7:38) breaks into an unexpected dramatic action.

6	"but beat upon his chest saying,	HIS MANNER
	'God! Make an atonement for me, a sinner.'"	HIS PRAYER

The accepted posture for prayer was to cross the hands over the chest and keep the eyes cast down (Edersheim, *Temple*, 156). But this man's crossed arms do not remain immobile. Rather he beats on his chest. This dramatic gesture is still used in villages all across the Middle East from Iraq to Egypt. The hands are closed into fists that are then struck on the chest in rapid succession. The gesture is used in times of extreme anguish or intense anger. It never occurs in the Old Testament, and appears only twice in the Gospels, both times in Luke. The remarkable feature of this particular gesture is the fact that it is characteristic of women, *not men*. After twenty years of observation I have found only one occasion in which Middle Eastern *men* are accustomed to beat on their chests. This is at the *'Ashūra* ritual of Shiite Islam. This ritual is an enactment of the murder of Hussein, the son of Ali (the son-in-law of the prophet of Islam). The murder scene is dramatically presented and the devotees lacerate their shaved heads with knives and razors in a demonstration of intense anguish as they recollect this community-forming event. At this ritual the *men* beat on their chests. Women customarily beat on their chests at funerals, but men do not. For men it is a gesture of *extreme* sorrow and anguish and it is almost never used. It is little wonder that in all of biblical literature we find this particular gesture mentioned only here and at the cross (Luke 23:48). There we are told that "*all* the multitude" went home beating on their chests. The crowd naturally included men and women. Indeed, it takes something of the magnitude of Golgotha to evoke this gesture from Middle Eastern men.

Furthermore, we are told that he beats on his *chest*. Why the chest? The reason for this is given in an early Jewish commentary on Ecclesiastes 7:2:

> R. Mana said: *And the Living will lay it to his heart*: these are the righteous who set their death over against their heart; and why do they beat upon their heart? as though to say, "All is there," (note: . . . the righteous beat their heart as the source of evil longing.) (*Midrash Rabbah*, Eccl. VII,2,5, Sonc., 177).

The same underlying rationale is affirmed by Ibn al-Ṣalībī in his eleventh-century commentary where he writes regarding the tax collector,

> his heart in his chest was the source of all his evil thoughts so he was beating it as evidence of his pain as some people do in their remorse, for they beat upon their chests (Ibn al-Ṣalībī, II, 182).

Thus this classical Middle Eastern gesture is a profound recognition of the truth of the fact that "out of the heart come evil thoughts, murder . . . theft, false witness, slander" (Matt. 15:19). This kind of background gives us a picture of the depth of the tax collector's remorse. What then is his specific prayer?

For centuries the Church, East and West, has translated *hilasthēti moi* in this text as "have mercy on me." However, later in the same chapter the blind man cries out, *eleēson me* (18:38), which clearly means "have mercy on me." But this common Greek phrase is not used in 18:13. Our word *hilaskomai* occurs as a verb only here and in Hebrews 2:17. As a noun it appears four times (Rom. 3:25; Heb. 9:5; I John 2:2; 4:10), and it clearly refers to the atonement sacrifice. Expiation and propitiation as English words must be combined with cleansing and reconciliation to give the meaning of the Hebrew *kaffar*, which lies behind the Greek *hilaskomai*. The tax collector is not offering a generalized prayer for God's mercy. He specifically yearns for the benefits of an atonement. Both the classical Armenian and the Harclean Syriac versions of the early centuries of the life of the Church translate our text literally as "make an atonement for me." Dalman's brief account helps set the total scene. He describes the temple area:

> One coming here in order to pray at the time of the evening sacrifice i.e. at the ninth hour (three o'clock in the afternoon) . . . would see first of all the slaughtering and cutting up of the sacrificial lamb, and would then notice that a priest went to the Holy Place to burn incense (Lk. i.9). Both these were acts at which the Israelite was not merely an onlooker, for they were performed in the name of the people, of whom the priest was a representative, in order to affirm daily Israel's relationship to God, according to His command; and when, after the censing from the steps to the ante-hall was accomplished, the priests pronounced the blessing with outstretched hands . . . and put God's Name upon the children of Israel . . . it was for the reception of the blessing that the people "bowed themselves" (Ecclus. 1.21) to the ground on hearing the ineffable Name. . . . This was followed, in the consciousness that God would graciously accept the gift, by the bringing of the sacrifice to the altar (Dalman, *Sacred*, 303).

Dalman goes on to explain the other elements of the liturgy, the clash of cymbal, the blasts on the trumpets, the reading of the Psalms, the singing of the choir of the Levites, and the final prostration of the people. On reading Dalman and Edersheim (*Temple*, 156f.) one can almost smell the pungent incense, hear the loud clash of cymbals, and see the great cloud of dense smoke rising from the burnt offering. The tax collector is there. He stands afar off, anxious not to be seen, sensing his unworthiness to stand with the participants. In brokenness he longs to be a part of it all. He yearns that he might stand with "the righteous." In deep remorse he strikes his chest and cries out in repentance and hope, "O God! Let it be for me! Make an atonement for me, a sinner!" There in the temple this humble man, aware of his own sin and unworthiness, with no merit of his own to commend him, longs that the great dramatic atonement sacrifice might apply to him. The last stanza tells us that indeed it does.

7   "I tell you, he went down to his house   GO DOWN
       made righteous, rather than that one."   TAX COLLECTOR, PHARISEE

In stanza 1 two went up to the temple at the same hour with the Pharisee in the lead. Now the same two go down (again at the same time). The service is over. The tax collector is now mentioned first. *He* is the one justified in God's presence. For centuries the Church debated whether the sacraments have an automatic effect on the believer irrespective of his spiritual state. Here in this simple parable we already have an answer, and the answer is no! The Pharisee was wasting his time. The self-righteous returns home unjustified. Indeed as Ibn al-Ṣalībī notes, "The false pride of the Pharisee has intensified his guilty condition and increased his sin" (Ibn al-Ṣalībī, II, 182). The sacrifice of the lamb for the sins of the people is made—but the broken of heart, who come in unworthiness trusting in God's atonement, they alone are made right with God. With this the parable ends. A general statement is then attached as a summarizing conclusion.

CONCLUSION

> For every one who exalts himself will be humbled,
> and he who humbles himself will be exalted.

This statement, in various forms, occurs in a number of places in the New Testament (cf. Matt. 18:4; 23:12; Luke 14:11; I Pet. 5:6). It is an antithetical parallelism and is quite likely a proverb of Jesus that Luke or his source may have attached to the end of the parable, which comes to its own conclusion. At the same time, a significant number of the major parables have wisdom sayings attached to their conclusions (cf. Luke 8:8; 12:21, 48; 16:8b; 18:8b; 19:26). There is no reason to deny that Jesus could have attached wisdom sayings to his own parables. This may be the case here. In any event, the saying is profoundly appropriate to the parable and focuses on its major topic of righteousness. As we observed above, either Luke or his source attached an introduction to the parable that highlighted the theme of righteousness and how it is achieved. That introduction is here balanced by this concluding wisdom saying, which discusses the same theme.

This final verse affirms that only the humble will be exalted. The great word "exaltation" has an important place in New Testament theology in relation to the person of Christ. Here, however, we see it used in its Old Testament sense. In regard to this Old Testament usage, Bertram writes, "As God's name alone is exalted . . . so He alone can elevate and exalt men" (Bertram, *TDNT*, VIII, 606). Thus "exalt" approaches the meaning "deliver, redeem" (*ibid.*, 607). Bertram explains, "Exaltation means drawing close to God; the righteous man who is meek and humble may hope for this and claim it" (*ibid.*). In regard to the use of this word in the synoptic Gospels Bertram observes, "Along the lines of the Old Testament revelation of God all exaltation on man's part is repudiated. . . . Exaltation is the act of God alone" (*ibid.*, 608). Thus it is clear that verse 14 in our text is not talking about social rank or man's humility or elevation among his fellow men. Again Bertram observes that exaltation "always has an eschatological reference for the Christian hearer and reader" (*ibid.*). Clearly the verse has to do with man being elevated in relation to God. As in the Old Testament it is almost synonymous with "to deliver" and "to redeem." The introduction to the parable speaks of those who elevate themselves (that is, consider themselves righteous) and humiliate others (that is, despise others). At the end, the self-exalted is humbled and the humble one is exalted.

Finally, then, what is the original listener pressed to understand or do, and what motifs comprise the theological cluster of the parable?

The original self-righteous audience is pressed to reconsider how righteousness is achieved. Jesus proclaims that righteousness is a gift of God made possible by means of the atonement sacrifice, which is received by those who, in humility, approach as sinners trusting in God's grace and not their own righteousness. As Jeremias has succinctly observed, "Our passage shows . . . that the Pauline doctrine of justification has its roots in the teaching of Jesus" (Jeremias, *Parables,* 114).

The theological motifs present in the parable include the following:

1. Righteousness is a gift of God granted by means of the atonement sacrifice to sinners who come to Him in confession of their sin and in a full awareness of their own inability to achieve righteousness.

2. The atonement sacrifice is worthless to anyone who assumes self-righteousness.

3. There is a pattern for prayer set forth. Self-congratulation, boasting of pious achievements, and criticism of others are not appropriate subjects for prayer. A humble confession of sin and need, offered in hope that through the atonement sacrifice this sin might be covered and those needs met, is an appropriate subject for prayer. Along with the subjects for prayer appropriate attitudes for prayer are also presented. Pride has no place. Humility is required.

4. The keeping of the law, and even the achieving of a standard beyond the requirements of the law, does not secure righteousness.

5. Self-righteousness distorts the vision. A profoundly moving demonstration of remorse was enacted by a sincerely repentant man before the eyes of the self-righteous Pharisee. He saw only a sinner to be avoided.

The parable has no evident Christology. The atonement service highlighted is that of the Old Testament. The person of Jesus and his role in salvation history is nowhere mentioned or suggested. Yet a rich theological understanding of righteousness through atonement is set forth in clear and unforgettable terms. This understanding (we would suggest) then becomes the foundation of the early Church's theology. In short, the starting point for the New Testament understanding of righteousness through atonement is traceable to no less than Jesus of Nazareth.

Chapter 10

THE CAMEL AND THE NEEDLE
"What must I do to inherit eternal life?"
(Luke 18:18–30)

The major themes of this remarkable dialogue are inverted. If we reduce the passage to these themes, this inversion can be seen as follows:

1 Inherit eternal life

    2 Five old requirements set forth with special emphasis on:
    —loyalty to family
    —attitude towards property

        3 The demands of the new obedience:
        —sell everything you have
        —come and follow me

            4 The new obedience seen as:
            —too hard

                5 The PARABLE OF THE CAMEL AND THE NEEDLE
                  (Enter the kingdom)

            4' The new obedience seen as:
            —too hard
            —possible only with God

        3' The demands of the new obedience are fulfilled:
        —we have left everything
        —we have followed you

    2' Five new requirements set forth with special emphasis on:
    —attitude toward property
    —loyalty to family

1' Receive eternal life

The entire text with its structure is as follows:

1   A certain ruler asked him,   ETERNAL LIFE
    "Good Teacher, what having done I shall inherit *eternal life*?"

2   And Jesus said to him,
        "Why do you call me good?   THE OLD REQUIREMENTS
        No one is good but one, even God.   —fulfilled
    You know the commandments.
        Do not commit adultery.   7 (loyalty to family)
        Do not kill.   6
        Do not steal.   8 (property)
        Do not bear false witness.   9
        Honor your father and mother."   5 (loyalty to family)
    And he said, "All these I have observed from my youth."

3   And hearing, Jesus said to him,
            "One thing you still lack.   THE NEW OBEDIENCE
            Sell everything you have   —explained (the ruler)
            and distribute to the poor.
            And you will have treasure in heaven.
            And come and follow me."

4   And hearing this
        he became deeply grieved,   NEW OBEDIENCE
        for he was very rich.   —too hard

5   And seeing him Jesus said,
            "How *hard* it is
            for those who have possessions   ENTER THE
                to *enter the kingdom of God.*   KINGDOM

5'   It is *easier* for a camel to go through a needle's eye
                than for a *rich man*
                    to *enter the kingdom of God.*"

4'   And those who heard said,
            "And who is able to be saved?"   NEW OBEDIENCE
        But he said, "What is impossible with men   —too hard
        is possible with God."   —possible with God

3' And Peter said,
        "Lo, we have *left what is ours*   THE NEW OBEDIENCE
        and *followed you.*"   —fulfilled (disciples)

2' And he said to them,
        "Truly, I say to you,
        there is no one who has left   THE NEW REQUIREMENTS
            house   (property)   —fulfilled (all believers)
            or wife   (loyalty to family)
            or brothers   "
            or parents   "
            or children   "
        for the sake of the kingdom,

1' who will not receive much more in this time,
    and in the age to come—*eternal life.*"   ETERNAL LIFE

In Luke 10:25–37 we studied the same question set forth here. In the overall outline of the Lucan Travel Narrative that passage parallels this text (cf. Bailey, *Poet,* 80–82). In each passage there is first a discussion about the law. In each there follows a dialogue with a parable in its center. Yet, at the same time, the two passages are structured differently. The first passage (10:25–37) has two rounds of debate with two questions and two answers in each round. This passage, however, has five inverted topics with a parable in the center. We turn then to the details of this structure.

The passage begins with the topic of eternal life and comes full circle back to the same topic at the end. But yet there is a difference. In the opening stanza the rich young ruler wants to *do* something to gain eternal life as an inheritance. At the end of the discussion eternal life is received as a gift, not awarded as an earned right. In the second stanza five commands are selected from the Decalogue. These five are then placed out of their original order (note the numbers to the right of the laws above). We are almost obliged to assume that the rearrangement is intentional and serves some purpose. Those responsible for the text in its present form obviously knew the original order and would not leave Jesus to repeat such a rearrangement to no purpose. Granted, the commandment on adultery is often placed before the commandment on murder (Deut. 5:17; Rom. 13:9; James 2:11; Nash Papyrus). Yet Hosea has it at the end of his list and Jeremiah has it in the middle (Hos. 4:2; Jer. 7:8–9). To our knowledge the placing of the commandment on honor to parents at the end of a selection of the Decalogue is without precedent. Marshall affirms that no reason for the present arrangement has been found (Marshall, 685). We would cautiously suggest such a reason. It is our view that the selection and arrangement is deliberate.

What purpose then does the rearrangement serve? We suggest that the present text is edited to give special emphasis to the subjects of loyalty to family and attitudes toward property. The question of adultery (i.e., loyalty to family) heads the list. The command to honor one's parents concludes it. "Do not steal" is placed in the middle. It is possible that a full inversion is intended. This would give us:

    Do not commit adultery   (loyalty to family)

     Do not kill   (physical destruction of another)

      Do not steal   (respect for property)

     Do not bear false witness   (verbal destruction of another)

    Honor your father and mother   (loyalty to family)

The list in Luke 14:26 is somewhat similarly arranged (see following page). There is an introduction and a conclusion with seven specifics in the center. Clearly the high points of the list are the beginning (the father) and the end (the self). These two are the highest demands for loyalty that any person in the Middle East could or can imagine. These two loyalties are given special prominence by their position at the beginning and the end of the list of seven. In a similar

Luke 14:26

If anyone comes to me and does not hate

his own father
and mother
and wife
and children
and brothers
and sisters,
yes, even his own life,

he cannot be my disciple.

fashion, here in Luke 18:20 the rearrangement of laws gives special emphasis to the topic of loyalty to family by placing it at the beginning and at the end of the list. The question of respect for property is given prominence by placement in the center. Then, in stanza 2', there is a second list of demands. There we again see five specifics and, significantly, the two topics of loyalty to property and family make up the entire list. Thus the selection and rearrangement of material from the Decalogue can be seen as a deliberate effort to make stanzas 2 and 2' balance thematically.

In stanza 3 two demands are made of the ruler. In the matching stanza (3') the disciples specifically state that they have met these demands. In stanza 4 the ruler finds the new demands too difficult. In the matching stanza 4', the bystanders agree. Stanza 4' is also the point of turning for the entire passage. In many of these literary structures we have observed a crucial change of direction just past the center. Here also an important new element is introduced as the inversion begins. This theme is the affirmation that only with God is salvation possible.

A further shift at center can be seen in the move from singular to plural. The first half is addressed to a particular case, the ruler, and all the verbs are in the singular. In the center the parable makes a generalizing application, and from then on the text deals with plurals and collectives. This particular observation is crucial for an understanding of the passage. The discussion with the rich ruler sets the stage for a discussion of the significance of the same question for *all disciples*.

The center of the structure has a short parable that informs the entire drama. Then finally, as is often the case, a major theme that occurs at the beginning and at the end of the structure is repeated in the center. This feature is also present here. The theme of eternal life, which appears at the beginning and at the end of the passage, relates thematically to the theme of ''enter the kingdom of God,'' which is twice repeated in the parable in the center. Thus the overall passage has all of the major features of inverted parallelism. The themes are presented and then repeated in an inverted fashion. The center repeats the theme with which the structure opens and closes. There is a point of turning just past the center. With such a carefully constructed structure it is obvious that the passage must be examined as a whole and the parable studied in the light of the entire theological mosaic in which it is placed.

This literary structure is strikingly similar to the form we studied in Luke 7:35–50. There also we observed a brief parable that forms the climax of a much longer discussion. In both texts the inversion principle is used throughout. In both, dialogue forms a crucial part of the passage with its inversions. Thus we have two clear examples of a brief parable functioning as the center of a much larger discussion of which it is a part and in the light of which it must be understood. With this structure in mind, the separate stanzas must be examined.

STANZA 1

A certain ruler asked him,
"Good Teacher, what having done I shall inherit *eternal life?*"

There is a significant cluster of parallel terms used throughout the passage. These are:

inherit/receive eternal life = follow me = enter the kingdom = be saved.

The parallel nature of this set of terms will become evident as we proceed.

Our literal translation is awkward English but perhaps highlights the thrust of what the ruler is saying. He clearly wants to achieve eternal life by his own efforts. His focus is on the future. He assumes that a certain standard of performance now will secure eternal life for him in the future. The topic of eternal life has significance for him only for that future. This emphasis is shifted by Jesus in his reply at the end of the passage, as we have noted. The question of rewards in the kingdom is also raised (although indirectly). It is also dealt with at the end of the discussion but in an entirely new context. The act of God that is "impossible with men" must take place first, and only then can rewards be brought into focus. The question as stated here is identical to the lawyer's question in Luke 10:25 with the one addition of the word "good." Jesus' response begins with a focus on this unusual address.

STANZA 2

And Jesus said to him,
"Why do you call me good?
    No one is good but one, even God.
You know the commandments.
    Do not commit adultery.   7   (loyalty to family)
    Do not kill.   6
    Do not steal.   8   (property)
    Do not bear false witness.   9
    Honor your father and mother."   5   (loyalty to family)
And he said,
    "All these I have observed from my youth."

Jesus' initial response has been problematic for centuries. The phrase, "No one is good but one, even God," has often been quoted to deny any form of high Christology in the self-understanding of Jesus. A return to the sterile polemics of the past would be meaningless, yet in fairness to the passage the intent of this phrase must be examined.

One possible approach to the text is to understand Jesus to be asking, "Why do you call me good? Do you mean what you are saying? 'Good' is only appropriate for God. Are you serious in applying this title to me?" However, the ruler does not answer. Would we not expect an answer if this kind of high Christology was the intent of the text? Yet it could be argued that the question is left unanswered deliberately so that the reader must answer the question for himself. Many parables end unfinished, and the reader is left with the tension of responding to the dialogue. A clear example of this is in Luke 9:57–62, where the reader has no hint regarding the final response of any of the three potential disciples. We do not know how the older brother responds to the plea to come in to the banquet hall (Luke 15:32), nor do we know what happens at the end of the great banquet (14:24). The final fate of the unjust steward is likewise unknown (16:8). In this same vein, here in 18:19 we may have a case of a bold question that means, "Are you serious in attributing to me a title that is appropriate only for God? Are you ready to accept the implications of such an affirmation?" Leaving this possible option as an alternative we would examine another possibility.

The title "Good Teacher" is found only once in the rabbinic tradition where a rabbi is asked to report a dream and says,

> To me in my dream the following was said: Good greetings to the good teacher from the good Lord who from His bounty dispenseth good to His people (B.T. *Taanith* 24b, Sonc., 126).

In this text we are dealing with a dream, not a normal salutation. Furthermore there is clearly a dramatic repetition of the word "good." In any case the greeting is extremely rare. Thus Jesus is best understood as responding to a tendency on the part of the ruler to "overdo it." The ruler is trying too hard. He tries to impress with a compliment and perhaps hopes to be greeted with some lofty title in return. In the Oriental world, one compliment requires a second. The ruler starts with "Good Teacher" and may expect "Noble Ruler" in response from Jesus. This seems to be the tension of the text because Jesus answers with *no* title at all, and this response can indicate irritation in the Gospels (cf. Luke 15:29; John 4:17). This abrupt, almost harsh response of Jesus is a technique we observe on his lips on a number of occasions. The purpose is apparently to test the seriousness of the inquirer's intentions (cf. Matt. 15:25; John 3:3). The same type of an introduction and response can be seen in Luke 12:13–14 where the inquirer begins with a title and is spoken to in a somewhat harsh manner. This forthright challenge to the seriousness of the questioner's intentions thus seems to be the best understanding of Jesus' answer.

But going beyond the mood of Jesus' response, we still must ask if the text is affirming the insignificance of his person, particularly in relation to God. When the full passage is examined, this is clearly not the case. In stanza 1 the ruler wants to know what he must *do* to inherit eternal life. Jesus tells him (3) to sell everything and "come and follow *me.*" If the passage intended to affirm the insignificance of Jesus in contradistinction to God, it would have Jesus tell the ruler to "follow the way of God (even as I follow the same way)," or some such affirmation. Rather the ruler is told that to *follow Jesus* is the climax of what is required of him. Thus Jesus appears again as God's unique agent through whom obedience to God is appropriately expressed.

We have noted the special emphasis on family and property in the selection and arrangement of the laws listed. The ruler's reply that he has observed all of these since his youth can be paralleled and is yet somewhat presumptuous. In the Talmud, Abraham, Moses, and Aaron are reported to have kept the whole law (Plummer, 423). The rich ruler seems to calmly put himself in rather exalted company. Thus Jesus' response comes almost as a judgmental challenge flung in the face of a comparatively self-righteous ruler.

STANZA 3

And hearing, Jesus said to him,
  "One thing you still lack.
Sell everything you have
  and distribute to the poor.
  And you will have treasure in heaven.
And come and follow me."

The theme of "one thing lacking" also follows the question of eternal life in Luke 10:42 in the story of Mary and Martha. The one thing that Mary has and Martha lacks is an appropriate expression of loyalty to the person of Jesus. This lawyer lacks the same thing. As happens again and again in Luke, a theme is dealt with twice, and in one case it is illustrated by a woman and in the other, by a man (cf. 4:25-27; 15:3-10; etc.).

There is the possibility that the two lines, "and distribute to the poor" and "you will have treasure in heaven," may be an editorial expansion of the original text. The matching lines in stanza 3' omit any reference to treasure in heaven. This particular concern has clearly been edited into the text in Luke 6:23 (as we observed in chapter six). The literary structure of 14:12-14 suggests that 14:14b, on the same topic, is also a brief comment added by way of explanation (the treasure in heaven is the eternal life he seeks). The case for two literary layers (an original composition, then an addition to that composition) can be made with ease in the case of Luke 6:23. It can be affirmed with less confidence in 14:14b and 18:22. Such pious expansions (when they can be demonstrated) are evidence of an old piece of literature, revered in the life of the early Church, being reused with some expansion. They oblige us to place a pre-Lucan date to the composition of the material itself.

The demands themselves (sell everything and follow me) touch at the heart of the same two primary values suggested by the rearrangement of the commandments, namely property and family. The family estate is of supreme value in Middle Eastern society because it is a symbol of the cohesiveness of the extended family. One must observe at close range the lengths to which a Middle Eastern family will go to keep a part of the extended family in the ancestral home (even in today's mobile society) to sense the thrust of what is demanded of the ruler. He is asked to place loyalty to the person of Jesus higher than loyalty to his family and his family estate, for in a very deep sense the latter two are one. Abraham was faced with a similar type of demand on two occasions. He left his estate in Ur in a response of obedience. Then on Mount Moriah God required of him a willingness to put his obedience to God on a higher level than his loyalty to his own family. Abraham passed that great test of obedience/faith. The ruler failed even on the first type of test. Had he measured up to the demand he might have received his estate back as a gift of God to be used in His service. Regarding these things we can only speculate. What is clear is that the focus of the language on the question of possessions clearly implies a discussion of family (as stanzas 3' and 2' make eloquently clear). Thus, in this stanza, a self-assured man is faced with the radical demands of obedience. His response is recorded in stanza 4.

STANZA 4

And hearing this
he became deeply grieved,
for he was very rich.

The new obedience does not contradict the old law but rather goes beyond it. The new standard set for the ruler is beyond his ability to fulfill. Yet surely the ruler's deep grief is not just a result of his love for his wealth. More than this, he comes to the painful awareness that he cannot *earn* his way into God's graces. People of wealth are often proud of their own achievements. They accept no favors, ask for no special consideration, and with exceptional effort achieve wealth. But status in God's presence cannot be earned. It can only be received with gratitude. When a self-made person senses a need for acceptance in God's presence, his entire understanding of merit and worth must be painfully reevaluated. With God there is no pulling up of one's self by the bootstraps. The self-confidence of the self-made person crashes and dissolves like a mighty wave on a sandy shore when eternal life is at issue. The ruler *hears* (4) as do the bystanders (4'), who put a tongue to their (and perhaps his) thoughts. No doubt he grieves because of his love of wealth. But, as we have indicated, a significant portion of that wealth is his family estate, which is a visible symbol of the extended family itself, of which he, as a ruler, is a leader. Jesus is demanding that loyalty to him must be higher than loyalty to even such a treasured symbol. The ruler grieves in silence. His brash self-confidence is destroyed. Observing this, Jesus responds with a six-line parable set in step parallelism.

STANZA 5

And seeing him Jesus said,
"How *hard* it is
   for those who have *possessions*
      to *enter the kingdom of God*.
It is *easier* for a camel to go through a needle's eye
   than for a *rich man*
      to *enter the kingdom of God*."

Standing alone, the second three lines have a four-line structure as follows:

It is easier for a camel
   to go through a needle's eye
than for a rich man
   to enter the kingdom of God.

But, as we observed in Luke 7:44–48, line length is not crucial for a semantic parallelism that has no need to fit poetical molds. Here a brief proverb of four lines may be reworked, with the addition of three extra lines, to make the six-line stanza. The three ideas that bring the six lines together are "how hard," "wealth," and "entering the kingdom." The two sets of three lines are parallel, yet there is progression. Entering the kingdom through reliance on possessions and wealth is hard (1); indeed, it is impossible (2). Anyone with possessions has a natural tendency to want to earn his way into God's good graces. It is hard, indeed impossible, both to set aside this drive to "make it on one's own" and to accept grace.

In the history of interpretation there are two attempts to soften the blow of the text. One attempt is linguistic and very ancient. It involves a change of a Greek vowel. Rather than *kamēlon*, if we read *kamilon* (as some ancient manuscripts give us) we are not talking about a large, four-footed animal but rather a rope. Thus, if you imagine a thin rope (string?) and a large enough needle, it becomes difficult, but not impossible, for the rope to be pulled through the needle. It would appear that some copyists in the early centuries tried to soften the text and make salvation somehow possible for a rich man if he tried hard enough. Yet the textual evidence for "rope" is slight and unconvincing. This option was already discarded by Ibn al-Ṭayyib in the eleventh century:

Some say that the word "camel" in the text means a thick rope. Others think that it is the large beam that provides support for the foundation of the roof, and others say that it simply means the well-known animal; and this is the correct opinion (Ibn al-Ṭayyib, Manqariyūs edition, I, 323).

A second alternative comes from the Middle Eastern village scene. Here peasant homes sometimes have a large set of double doors that open from the street into the courtyard of the family home. In the village these doors must be large enough to allow the passage of a fully loaded camel. Thus the doors must be at least ten feet high and together some twelve feet wide. Such doors are constructed of massive timbers. So much manpower is required to move them that they are opened only when loaded camels are transporting something through them. The ordinary movement of people in and out of such doors is facilitated by a small door cut in the large door. This small door is easily opened. In the past some commentaries explained that this is the "needle's eye" of the text. F. W. Farrar quotes private correspondence recollecting travels in the Middle East in 1835 in which the correspondent did find such a door called the needle's eye (Farrar, 375f.). Yet a few years later Scherer, a longtime resident in the Middle East, wrote bluntly, "There is not the slightest shred of evidence for this identification. This door has not in any language been called the needle's eye, and is not so called today" (Scherer, 37). Our experience substantiates Scherer. In any case, Farrar himself opts against his correspondent's suggestion in favor of evidence from the Talmud.

In the Talmud Rabbi Nahmani suggests that a man's dreams are a reflection of his thoughts. We are then told,

This is proven by the fact that a man is never shown in a dream a date palm of gold, or an elephant going through the eye of a needle (B.T. *Berakhoth* 55b, Sonc., 342).

That is, a man is never shown something that is clearly impossible. The elephant was the largest animal in Mesopotamia and the camel the largest in Palestine. In each case we are illustrating something that is quite impossible, as the text itself affirms (v. 27). We would see both of the above attempts to explain away the thrust of the text as misunderstandings of it. The parable deliberately presents a concrete picture of something *quite impossible*. As Ellis succinctly states, "The camel-needle proverb (25) is to be taken very literally. Anyone's salvation is a miracle" (Ellis, 219). A rich man (through his own efforts) *cannot* enter the kingdom. The decision to dethrone his wealth he cannot make unaided. The profounder levels of the theological content of the parable miss the bystanders. What they do understand is that rich men cannot themselves enter the kingdom. These sentiments are expressed in the following stanza.

STANZA 4'

And those who heard said,
"And who is able to be saved?"
But he said, "What is impossible with men
   is possible with God."

The bystanders' question emerges out of a special mentality. This mentality says,

> Rich men are able to build synagogues, endow orphanages, offer alms to the poor, refurbish temples, and fund many other worthwhile efforts. If anyone is saved, surely it is they. Jesus says that such people cannot enter the kingdom by such noble efforts. We commoners do not have the wealth to carry out such noble deeds. Who then can be saved?

The ruler found the demands of Jesus too hard (4). The bystanders echo this feeling and shape it as a question (4').

We have noted the fact that just past the center of an inverted literary structure there is usually a point of turning. Something crucial is usually introduced just past the center that informs the entire passage. True to form, a key statement of this kind appears at precisely this point in this structure. Salvation is affirmed as an action of God. No one unaided *enters* the kingdom. No one achieves great things and *inherits* eternal life. An inheritance is a gift, not an earned right. No one has rights in the kingdom, not even rich men with all their potential for good works. Indeed, if Jesus had given the rich man a list of expensive good works to be funded or carried out, the ruler would likely have begun on them with great enthusiasm. Rather, he is told that his best efforts are worthless in the achievement of his goal of *entering* the kingdom. Salvation is impossible with men and possible only with God. As Marshall succinctly states, "God can work the miracle of conversion in the hearts even of the rich" (Marshall, 686). The flow of the inverted dialogue naturally returns to the demands the ruler found too hard (3). The question becomes, Has anyone met them? Stanza 3' gives the answer.

STANZA 3'

> And Peter said,
> "Lo, we have *left what is ours*
> and *followed you.*"

The parallelism between the requirements laid before the ruler and the speech of Peter is noticed already by Ibn al-Ṣalībī (I, 387). This can be seen as follows:

The Ruler (3)	*The Disciples* (3')
Jesus said to him,	Peter said,
"Sell everything you have . . .	"We have left what is ours
Come and follow me."	and have followed you."

We have argued that the demands laid on the ruler are not only dealing with wealth, but also with the dethronement of the demands of the extended family. This same background is significant here also. It becomes all the more evident in the stanza that follows. Peter says, "We have left *ta idia* and have followed you." We grant that this is a neuter plural that ordinarily refers to things. In John

1:11 we have, "He came into his own home (*ta idia*) and his own people (*hoi idioi*) did not receive him." Thus a distinction is made between the home (*ta idia*) and the people (*hoi idioi*). The first is neuter and the second masculine. Yet here in Luke it is clear from Jesus' response that Peter is talking about far more than buildings and furniture. This broader understanding of *ta idia* in Peter's speech is caught in many of the early Arabic versions, which read, "We have left what is ours." The phrase can imply both people and property. Thus Peter and the disciples, for whom he is a spokesman, are living examples of the miracle of which Jesus speaks. They also had families and possessions. They too were Middle Easterners, and the cultural pressures to make these things absolutes were felt by them as well. But with them the miracle happened. What was impossible with men was demonstrated as possible by God in their own concrete disciple-ship. Indeed, men and women of faith in every age discover that the impossible demands of obedience are made possible through the miracle of God's grace. Peter affirms the reality of this miracle having happened in their lives. Ibn al-Ṣalībī comments, "Indeed their following of Jesus was the only reason they were able to leave everything" (Ibn al-Ṣalībī, I, 387f.). Jesus' response to Peter forms stanza 2' and stanza 1'.

STANZA 2'

And he said to them,
"Truly, I say to you,
there is no one who has left

house	(loyalty to property)
or wife	(loyalty to family)
or brothers	"
or parents	"
or children	"

for the sake of the kingdom,

STANZA 1'

who will not receive much more in this time,
and in the age to come—*eternal life.*"

In the case of the ruler we observed that his relationship to his wealth was such that he could not submit to a higher loyalty. So here, Ibn al-Ṣalībī observes,

> He does not mean by these words that we should dissolve marriages or break the ties to families but rather he teaches us to give honor and priority to our fear of God over marriage, brothers, race, and relatives (Ibn al-Ṣalībī, I, 389).

It is no mistake that "house" occurs first on this list of specifics. Members of the family then make up the other four items in the list of five. We have already observed that in stanza 2 five commandments are selected and rearranged in order to give special prominence to the question of property and family. Here these two themes are the only items on the list. A comparison between the old and the new requirements of obedience is revealing.

In the old obedience the faithful were told not to steal another's property. In the new obedience, one's own property may have to be left behind. In the old obedience one was told to leave the neighbor's wife alone. In the new obedience the disciple *may* be required to leave his *own* wife alone. In the old obedience the faithful were to honor father and mother, which of course, popularly understood, meant (and still means) to stay home and take care of them until they die and are respectfully buried. In the new obedience the disciple may have to *leave* them in response to a higher loyalty. It is nearly impossible to communicate what all of this means in our Middle Eastern context. The two unassailable loyalties that any Middle Easterner is almost required to consider more important than life itself are *family* and the *village home*. When Jesus puts both of these in *one* list, and then demands a loyalty that supersedes them both, he is requiring that which is truly impossible to the Middle Easterner, given the pressures of his culture. The ten commandments he can manage, but this is too much. Only with God are such things possible. Surely the shock of the passage cuts deeply into the presuppositions of any culture. Our point is that this shock is felt all the more intensely in a traditional culture where these particular values are supreme. Jesus is fully aware of the radical rupture of the fabric of cultural loyalties that his words create. Thus he introduces these incredible statements with "Amen, I say to you." In Luke this phrase occurs only six times and in each case it introduces a saying of awesome proportions that shocks the listener. Its use here is no exception.

The final stanza returns again to the question of rewards. Here we see this important topic presented in two aspects. The ruler already had his reward in mind. He wants eternal life. He asks about what he must do to inherit this reward. The standard is presented and he fails to meet it, for indeed it is impossible to achieve. Salvation is demonstrated to be a work of God, not an achievement of people. The disciples were given the grace to respond to the new pattern of obedience. They did so in the past (we have left what is ours). They broke the pattern of their cultural demands and placed obedience to Jesus higher than loyalty to family and property. Jesus responds and confirms that the kingdom has boundless rewards for those who respond in obedience with no thought of rewards. Marshall affirms that Peter's speech is not a "claim for a selfish reward." Rather it is "an opportunity to give a promise that self-denial for the sake of the kingdom will be vindicated" (Marshall, 688). In addition, these rewards are for this time *and* the age to come. Furthermore, they will *receive* eternal life, they cannot *earn* it. There also is an emphasis in the text on the theme of assurance. *No one* who has responded to the call to obedience will be left out. Thus this final stanza, with its return to the opening theme of eternal life, is rich in theological affirmations.

In conclusion, then, what is the response expected from the ruler and what cluster of theological motifs comprise the theological content of the passage? The ruler is pressed to understand that eternal life is not inherited through good works but *received* by those who allow God to work the impossible within them. The ruler's ability to do good works (through his wealth) proves only a stumbling block to his humble acceptance of a miracle of grace that could enable him to respond with the radical obedience demanded of him.

The theological motifs that appear in the passage are as follows:

1. Salvation is beyond human reach; it is possible only with God.

2. There is a new obedience that does not cancel the old, but rather builds on it and surpasses it.

3. Salvation, entering the kingdom, receiving eternal life, are all integrally related to following Jesus. Thus the passage affirms a high Christology. Jesus is God's unique agent through whom obedience to God is to be expressed.

4. The life of faith is defined in terms of loyalty to the person of Jesus. This loyalty must surpass loyalty to family and property.

5. Those who seek to earn rewards, like the ruler, find insurmountable obstacles in their path.

6. Disciples like Peter, who accept the miracle of God's work of salvation and respond in radical obedience, are assured the rewards of the kingdom. These are offered freely to all disciples and are for this life as well as the life to come.

7. Possessions and what they represent can be a major obstacle to an obedient response to the call, "Follow me."

Our study closes as it began. Not only is the literary form of this passage parallel to the scene in the house of Simon, but each passage proclaims salvation as a free gift of grace. In each we see some who accept and some who reject. It is our earnest hope that this modest effort may have made a little clearer the winsomeness of the person of Jesus, the clarity of his mind, and the attractiveness of his costly discipleship.

CONCLUSION

At the end of our brief study it is perhaps appropriate to tie together a few threads. We are anxious to summarize general observations and major themes. Can any general observations be made and are there any theological themes that appear especially prominent?

Our first general observation is that the parables do fall into a series of short dramatic scenes, and that these scenes relate to one another in a variety of recognizable patterns. Four are in a straightforward sequence. The ABAB pattern was noted twice. In six cases there was some form of inverted parallelism. A recognition of these scenes and patterns became an important aid to interpretation.

A second observation is the fact that the person of Jesus in the flesh takes on more clarity. At a banquet he is sharply critical of his host, and yet he is careful not to suggest that the host should have washed his feet. He subtly attacks racial prejudices by making a hero out of the hated Samaritan. He elevates the place of women by pairing them with men as examples of faith. He emerges as courteous and compassionate, and yet willing to use words like naked steel. Keen perception and penetrating intelligence are woven together, and these two elements are so fused that to touch one is to touch the other. The Middle Eastern details of the encounter in the house of Simon are culturally so precise as to have the ring of authenticity. Remarkable personal courage surfaces on numerous occasions. Indeed, we are able to sense the emergence of a more distinct personality that maintains its integrity through the theologies of the evangelists.

Our third observation is the emerging picture of Jesus as a theologian. The range of his mind is in itself remarkable. We have long been conditioned to think only of Paul, John, Luke, Mark, and the other New Testament authors as theologians. Jesus has been seen as the one through whom God acts to bring in the kingdom, but about whom little is known due to the heavy editing of the early

Church theologians. The preacher turns to him for ethical examples, not theological content. If the findings of this study can be sustained, this view will need some revision. We are convinced that it is indeed possible to speak of Jesus the theologian, and that, in the parables we have studied, four themes are especially prominent. These are as follows:

1. The love of God is offered freely and cannot be earned. Righteousness through human effort cannot be achieved. The Pharisee, proud of his works of supererogation, is unjustified. The servant labors but earns no merit. The ruler has kept the law but has not earned eternal life. The guests at the great banquet are totally unworthy to be present. The lawyer's attempt to justify himself fails.

2. The theme of the costly demonstration of unexpected love surfaces again and again. The Samaritan risks his very life to complete his acts of mercy. The woman before Simon knows Jesus will be despised for what he accepts from her and for what he says in her defense. The unexpected love offered to the outsiders at the banquet will infuriate the original guests and everyone knows it. This theme is more fully presented in the parable of the Prodigal Son but is yet deeply embedded in a significant number of parables here studied. It relates to the passion.

3. The acceptance of the freely offered love of God triggers a response in the form of costly acts of love. The woman in the house of Simon shows great love. The disciples have left houses and families. The servant labors, knowing that nothing is owing him. The eager volunteers are challenged with the cost of discipleship.

4. The person of Jesus functions as God's unique agent whose call of "Follow me" is seen again and again as equivalent to "Follow the way of God." He mediates forgiveness and personally accepts the gratefully offered response of love. He is the host of the great banquet, and unwavering service to him is equated with participation in the kingdom of God.

Thus, an examination of the Middle Eastern culture and literary forms of these sayings of Jesus can bring us, if ever so slightly, to a clearer perception of the person of Jesus and a more precise understanding of him as a theologian.

SELECTED BIBLIOGRAPHY

Aland, K., "Evangelium Thomae Copticum," *Synopsis Quattuor Evangeliorum.* Stuttgart: Württembergische Bibelanstalt, 1964.

Aland, K., M. Black *et al.,* .editors. *The Greek New Testament.* Second Edition. New York: The United Bible Societies, 1968.

Arberry, A. J. *The Koran Interpreted.* London: George Allen Ltd., 1955.

Arndt, W. F. *The Gospel According to St. Luke.* St. Louis: Concordia, 1956.

Bailey, Kenneth E. *The Cross and The Prodigal.* St. Louis: Concordia, 1973. (Cited as: *Cross*)

_____, "Hibat Allah Ibn al-'Assal and His Arabic Thirteenth Century Critical Edition of the Gospels (with special attention to Luke 16:16 and 17:10)," *Theological Review* (Near East School of Theology, Beirut, Lebanon), 1 (April 1978), 11–26. (Cited as: *Hibat Allah*)

_____. *Poet and Peasant: A Literary-Cultural Approach to the Parables in Luke.* Grand Rapids: Eerdmans, 1976. (Cited as: *Poet*)

_____, "The Manger and the Inn: The Cultural Background of Luke 2:7," *Theological Review* (Near East School of Theology, Beirut, Lebanon), 2 (November 1979), 33–44. (Cited as: *Manger*)

_____, "Women in Ben Sirach and in the New Testament," *For Me To Live. Essays in Honor of James L. Kelso.* Cleveland: Dillon/Leiderbach, 1972, 56–73. (Cited as: *Women*)

_____, "Recovering the Poetic Structure of I Cor. i 17–ii 2: A study in Text and Commentary," *Novum Testamentum,* 17 (1976), 265–296.

Barth, K. *The Doctrine of the Word of God.* Vol. I, Part II in *Church Dogmatics.* Edinburgh: T. and T. Clark, 1956.

Bauer, W. *A Greek-English Lexicon of the New Testament.* Translated and adapted by W. F. Arndt and F. W. Gingrich. Chicago: University Press, 1957. (Cited as: Bauer)

Bengel, J. A. *Gnomon of the New Testament.* 2 vols. New York: Sheldon, 1963 (1742).

Bertram, G., "Symmetrical Design in the Book of Ruth," *Journal of Biblical Literature,* 84 (1965), 165–68.

Bishop, E. F. F. *Jesus of Palestine.* London: Lutterworth Press, 1955.

Black, M. *An Aramaic Approach to the Gospels and Acts.* Third Edition. Oxford: Clarendon Press, 1967.

Blass, F. W. and A. Debrunner. Translated and revised from the 9th and 10th German ed. by R. W. Funk. *A Greek Grammar of the New Testament and Other Early Christian Literature.* Chicago: University of Chicago Press, 1961.

Blauw, Johannes. *The Missionary Nature of the Church.* London: McGraw-Hill, 1962.

Bornkamm, G. *Jesus of Nazareth.* New York: Harper, 1960.

Bruce, A. B. *The Parabolic Teaching of Christ.* New York: A. C. Armstrong and Sons, 1896. (Cited as: *Parabolic*)

———. *The Synoptic Gospels.* Vol. I of *The Expositor's Greek Testament.* New York: Doran, n.d. (Cited as: *Synoptic*)

Brueggemann, W., "The Bible and The Consciousness of the West," *Interpretation,* 29 (1975), 431–35.

Buckingham, J. S. *Travels in Palestine.* London: Longman, Hurst, Rees, Orme, and Brown, 1821.

Bullinger, E. W. *The Companion Bible.* Oxford: University Press, 1948 (1913).

Bultmann, R. *The History of the Synoptic Tradition.* Oxford: Basil Blackwell, 1963. (Cited as: *History*)

———. *Jesus and the Word.* New York: Charles Scribner's Sons, 1958 (1934). (Cited as: *Jesus*)

———. *Theology of the New Testament.* 2 vols. New York: Harper, 1951. (Cited as: *Theology*)

Burton, Richard F. *Personal Narrative of a Pilgrimage to al-Madinah and Meccah.* London: G. Bell and Sons, 1924 (1855).

Cadoux, A. T. *The Parables of Jesus.* London: James Clarke, n.d.

Carlston, C. E. *The Parables of the Triple Tradition.* Philadelphia: Fortress Press, 1975.

Charles, R. H., editor. *The Apocrypha and Pseudepigrapha of the Old Testament.* 2 vols. Oxford: The Clarendon Press, 1963 (1913).

Cohen, A., translator. *Midrash Rabbah Lamentations.* London: The Soncino Press, 1939. (Cited with reference and Sonc.)

Creed, J. M. *The Gospel According to St. Luke.* London: St. Martin, 1930.

Crossan, J. *In Parables.* New York: Harper, 1973.

Dalman, G. *Sacred Sites and Ways.* London: SPCK, 1935. (Cited as: *Sacred*)

_____. *The Words of Jesus*. Edinburgh: T. and T. Clark, 1902. (Cited as: *Words*)

Danby, H., editor and translator. *The Mishnah*. Oxford: The Clarendon Press, 1933.

Daube, David, "Inheritance in Two Lukan Pericopes," *Zeitschrift der Savigny-Stiftung für Rechtsgeschichte, Romanistische Abteilung*, 72 (1955), 326–334. (Cited as: *Inheritance*)

Dembitz, L. N., "Procedure in Civil Causes," *The Jewish Encyclopedia*, X. New York: Funk and Wagner, 1905, 102–106.

Derrett, J. D. M. *Law in the New Testament*. London: Darton, Longman and Todd, 1970.

_____, "Law in the New Testament: The Parable of the Unjust Judge," *New Testament Studies*, 18 (1971–72), 178–191. (Cited as: *Judge*)

Dodd, C. H. *More New Testament Studies*. Grand Rapids: Eerdmans, 1968. (Cited as: *More*)

_____. *The Parables of the Kingdom*. Revised edition. New York: Charles Scribner's Sons, 1961. (Cited as: *Parables*)

Edersheim, A. *The Life and Times of Jesus the Messiah*. 2 vols. New York: Longmans, Green and Co., 1896. (Cited as: *Life*, I or II)

_____. *Sketches of Jewish Social Life in the Days of Christ*. Grand Rapids: Eerdmans, 1974 (1876). (Cited as: *Social*)

_____. *The Temple: Its Ministry and Services as they were at the Time of Jesus Christ*. London: The Religious Tract Society, n.d. (Cited as: *Temple*)

Ehlen, A. J., "The Poetic Structure of a Hodayat from Qumran." Unpublished Ph.D. Thesis, Harvard Divinity School, Harvard University, Cambridge, Mass., 1970.

Ellis, E. Earle, editor. *The Gospel of Luke* in *The Century Bible*. London: Nelson and Sons, 1966.

Epstein, I., editor. *The Babylonian Talmud*. 35 vols. London: Soncino, 1935–1960. (Cited with tractate and verse and Sonc. with page number)

Farrar, F. W., "Brief Notes on Passages of the Gospels. II. The Camel and the Needle's Eye," *The Expositor (First Series)*, Vol. 3 (1876), 369–380.

Freedman, D. N., "Prolegomenon," in *The Forms of Hebrew Poetry* by G. B. Gray. New York: Ktav Publishing House, 1972. Pp. vii–lvi.

Freedman, H., and M. Simon, editors. *Lamentations* in *Midrash Rabbah*. London: Soncino Press, 1939.

Glueck, N. *The River Jordan*. Philadelphia: The Westminster Press, 1946.

Gray, G. B. *The Book of Isaiah (ICC)*, Vol. I. New York: Scribner's Sons, 1912.

Hunter, A. M. *Interpreting the Parables*. London: SCM Press, 1960. (Cited as: *Interpreting*)

_____. *The Parables Then and Now*. Philadelphia: Westminster Press, 1971. (Cited as: *Then*)

Ibn al-Ṣalībī, Diyūnīsiyūs Ja'qūb. *Kitāb al-Durr al-Farīd fī Tafsīr al-'Ahd al-Jadīd*. 2 vols. (The Book of Unique Pearls of Interpretation of the New Testament.) Written in

Syriac *ca.* 1050. Translated into Arabic by Abd al-Masīḥ al-Dawlayānī in 1728. Published in Arabic in Cairo: n.p., 1914.

Ibn al-Ṭayyib. *Tafsīr al-Mishriqī* (The Commentary of al-Mishriqī). 2 vols. Edited by Jūsif Manqariyūs. Cairo: al-Tawfīq, 1908.

————. Commentary on the Four Gospels, Paris Arabic Manuscript 86. National Library of Paris.

Jeremias, J. *The Eucharistic Words of Jesus.* New York: Charles Scribner's Sons, 1966. (Cited as: *Eucharistic*)

————. *New Testament Theology.* New York: Scribner, 1971. (Cited as: *Theology*)

————. *The Parables of Jesus.* London: SCM Press, 1963. (Cited as: *Parables*)

————. *The Promise of the Nations.* London: SCM Press, 1958. (Cited as: *Promise*)

Jones, G. V. *The Art and Truth of the Parables.* London: SPCK, 1964.

Josephus. *Jewish Antiquities* (Loeb Classical Library). Cambridge: William Heinemann, 1961 (1926).

Jowett, William. *Christian Researches in Syria and the Holy Land.* Second Edition. London: L. B. Steeley, 1826.

Jülicher, A. *Die Gleichnisreden.* 2 vols. Tübingen: J. C. B. Mohr, 1910.

Kitāb al-Injīl al-Sharīf al-Ṭāhir (The Holy, Noble, Pure Gospel). Al-Shawayr (Lebanon): Monastery of St. John, 1818 (1776).

Kittel, G., and G. Friedrich, editors. *Theological Dictionary of the New Testament.* 9 vols. Translated and edited by G. W. Bromiley. Grand Rapids: Eerdmans, 1964–1974. (Cited as: *TDNT*) Articles cited:
    Bertram, G., "Hupsos," Vol. VIII, 602–620.
    ————, "Phrēn," Vol. IX, 220–235.
    Bultmann, R., "Euphrainō," Vol. II, 772–75.
    Foerster, W., "Klēros," Vol. III, 758–769.
    Horst, J., "Makrothumia," Vol. IV, 374–387.
    Windisch, H., "Aspazomai," Vol. I, 496–502.

Kümmel, W. G. *Promise and Fulfillment.* No. 23 in *Studies in Biblical Theology.* Naperville: Alec R. Allenson, 1957.

Lamartine, Alphonse. *A Pilgrimage to the Holy Land; comprising Recollections, Sketches, and Reflections, Made During a Tour in the East in 1823–1833.* Philadelphia: Carey, Lea, and Blanchard, 1838.

Lees, G. Robinson, "Village Life in the Holy Land," *Pictorial Palestine Ancient and Modern.* Compiled and edited by C. Lang Neil. London: Miles and Miles, n.d. Pp. 163–247.

Levison, L. *The Parables: Their Background and Local Setting.* Edinburgh: T. and T. Clark, 1926.

Lightfoot, John. *Horae Hebraicae et Talmudicae: Hebrew and Talmudical Exercitations upon the Gospels and the Acts.* 4 vols. Oxford: University Press, 1859.

Linnemann, E. *Parables of Jesus.* London: SPCK, 1966.

Louw, J. P., "Discourse Analysis and the Greek New Testament," *Technical Papers for the Bible Translator,* 24 (1973), 101–118.

Lund, N. W. *Chiasmus in the New Testament.* Chapel Hill: U. of North Carolina Press, 1942.

Manson, T. W. *The Sayings of Jesus.* London: SCM, 1937. (Cited as: *Sayings*)

_____. *The Servant Messiah.* Cambridge: University Press, 1966 (1953). (Cited as: *Messiah*)

_____. *The Teaching of Jesus.* Cambridge: University Press, 1935. (Cited as: *Teaching*)

Marshall, I. Howard, *The Gospel of Luke.* Exeter: Paternoster Press, 1978.

Martin, R. P., "Salvation and Discipleship in Luke's Gospel," *Interpretation,* 30 (1976), 366–380.

Meyer, H. A. W. *Critical and Exegetical Handbook to the Gospels of Mark and Luke.* New York: Funk and Wagnalls, 1884.

Miller, D. G. *Saint Luke.* London: SCM Press, 1959.

Montefiore, C. G. *Rabbinic Literature and Gospel Teaching.* London: Macmillan, 1930. (Cited as: *Rabbinic*)

_____. *The Synoptic Gospels.* 2 vols. London: Macmillan and Co., 1909. (Cited as: *Gospels*)

Moule, C. F. D., "Mark 4:1–20 Yet Once More," in *Neotestamentica et Semitica: Studies in Honour of Matthew Black.* Ed. by E. E. Ellis and M. Wilcox. Edinburgh: T. & T. Clark, 1969, pp. 95–113.

Muir, William. *The Caliphate: Its Rise, Decline, and Fall.* Second Edition. London: The Religious Tract Society, 1892.

Neusner, J., "Pharisaic Law in New Testament Times," *Union Seminary Quarterly Review,* 26 (1971), 331–340.

Newbigin, Lesslie. *The Open Secret.* Grand Rapids: Eerdmans, 1978.

Oesterley, W. O. E. *The Gospel Parables in the Light of their Jewish Background.* London: SPCK, 1936.

Plummer, A. *The Gospel According to S. Luke.* Edinburgh: T. and T. Clark, 1975 (1896).

Rice, E. W. *Orientalisms in Bible Lands.* Philadelphia: The American Sunday-School Union, 1912.

Rihbany, A. M. *The Syrian Christ.* Boston: Houghton Mifflin, 1916.

Robertson, A. T. *A Grammar of the Greek NT in the Light of Historical Research.* Nashville: Broadman, 1934.

Sa'īd, Ibrāhīm. *Sharḥ Bishārit Lūqā* (Commentary on the Gospel of Luke). Cairo: The Middle East Council of Churches, 1970 (1935).

Safrai, S., and M. Stern, editors. *The Jewish People in the First Century: Historical Geography, Political History, Social, Cultural and Religious Life and Institutions.*

Section One of Two Volumes in *Compendia Rerum Iudaicarum ad Novum Testamentum*. Philadelphia: Fortress Press, 1976. (Cited as: *JPFC*) Articles cited:
Flusser, D., "Paganism in Palestine," Vol. II, 1065–1100.
Foerster, G., "Art and Architecture in Palestine," Vol. II, 971–1006.
Rabin, Ch., "Hebrew and Aramaic in the First Century," Vol. II, 1007–1039.
Safrai, S., "Education and the Study of the Torah," Vol. II, 945–970.
———, "Home and Family," Vol. II, 728–792.
———, "Religion in Every Day Life," Vol. II, 793–833.
———, "The Temple," Vol. II, 865–907.
Stern, M., "Aspects of Jewish Society. The Priesthood and Other Classes," Vol. II, 561–630.
———, "The Reign of Herod and the Herodian Dynasty," Vol. I, 216–307.

Scharlemann, M. H. *Proclaiming the Parables*. St. Louis: Concordia, 1963.

Schegloff, E. A., "Notes on Conversational Practice: Formulating Place" in *Studies in Social Interaction*. David Sudnow, ed. New York: The Free Press, 1972. Pp. 78–89.

Scherer, G. N. *The Eastern Colour of the Bible*. London: The National Sunday-School Union, n.d.

Sim, K. *Desert Traveller: The Life of Jean Louis Burckhardt*. London: Victor Gollancz Ltd., 1969.

Smith, B. T. D., *The Parables of the Synoptic Gospels*. Cambridge: University Press, 1937.

Smith, C. W. F. *The Jesus of the Parables*. Revised edition. Philadelphia: United Church Press, 1975.

Strack, H. L. and Paul Billerbeck. *Kommentar zum Neuen Testament erläutert aus Talmud und Midrasch*. 6 vols. München: C. H. Beck'sche, 1924–61.

Summers, R. *Commentary on Luke*. Waco: Word Books, 1973.

Thomson, W. M. *The Land and the Book*. 2 vols. New York: Harper and Brothers, 1871.

Trench, R. C. *Notes on the Parables of Our Lord*. New York: D. Appleton and Company, 1881.

Tristram, H. B. *Eastern Customs in Bible Lands*. London: Hodder and Stoughton, 1894.

Vermes, G. *The Dead Sea Scrolls in English*. Baltimore: Penguin Books, 1962.

Via, D. O. *The Parables*. Philadelphia: Fortress Press, 1967.

ORIENTAL VERSIONS USED IN THIS STUDY

Century	Version
2 (?)	The Old Syriac
4 (?)	The Peshitta
7	The Harclean Syriac (Vat. Syr. 268)
9	Vatican Arabic 13
9 (?)	Vatican Borgianus Arabic 71

10 (?)   Vatican Borgianus Arabic 95

11   The Arabic Diatessaron

11   The Four Gospels of 'Abd Allah Ibn al-Ṭayyib (Vat. Syr. 269)

13   Vatican Coptic 9

13   The Four Gospels of Hibat Allah Ibn al-'Assāl (British Mus. Or. Mss. 3382)

17   The London Polyglot Version

17   The Propagandist Version

18   The Shawayr Version

19   The Shidiyāq Version

19   The Van Dyke-Bustānī Version

19   The Jesuit Version

(For a full description of these versions cf. Bailey, *Poet,* 208–212; the Shawayr Version is a Lectionary first published in Lebanon at the Monastery of St. John in Shawayr in 1776. The text was brought from Aleppo in the seventeenth century. Our copy was printed in 1818.)

INDEX OF AUTHORS

INDEX OF REFERENCES

OLD TESTAMENT